MAINSTREAM GROWTH ECONOMISTS AND CAPITAL THEORISTS

Mainstream Growth Economists and Capital Theorists

A Survey

MARIN MUZHANI

McGill-Queen's University Press
Montreal & Kingston · London · Ithaca

ISBN 978-0-7735-4365-2 (cloth)
ISBN 978-0-7735-4366-9 (paper)
ISBN 978-0-7735-9210-0 (ePDF)
ISBN 978-0-7735-9211-7 (ePUB)

Legal deposit fourth quarter 2014
Bibliothèque nationale du Québec

Printed in Canada on acid-free paper that is 100% ancient forest free (100% post-consumer recycled), processed chlorine free

This book has been published with the help of a grant from the Canadian Federation for the Humanities and Social Sciences, through the Awards to Scholarly Publications Program, using funds provided by the Social Sciences and Humanities Research Council of Canada.

McGill-Queen's University Press acknowledges the support of the Canada Council for the Arts for our publishing program. We also acknowledge the financial support of the Government of Canada through the Canada Book Fund for our publishing activities.

Library and Archives Canada Cataloguing in Publication

Muzhani, Marin, 1973–, author
Mainstream growth economists and capital theorists: a survey / Marin Muzhani.

Includes bibliographical references and index.
Issued in print and electronic formats.
ISBN 978-0-7735-4365-2 (bound). – ISBN 978-0-7735-4366-9 (pbk.). – ISBN 978-0-7735-9210-0 (ePDF). – ISBN 978-0-7735-9211-7 (ePUB)

1. Economics – History – 20th century. I. Title.

HB75.M89 201 330.09'04 C2014-904349-X
C2014-904350-3

Typeset by Jay Tee Graphics Ltd. in 10.5/13.5 Sabon

Professor de Vries ... once described economic theory as a storeroom of thoughts. I suppose it is also a storeroom of errors. I am under no illusion that I have avoided adding a few errors to the contents of the storeroom. But part of the job of economics is weeding out errors. That is much harder than making them, but also more fun.

Robert Solow (1963), Nobel Prize winner 1987

Contents

Figures and Tables

FIGURES

TABLES

MAINSTREAM GROWTH ECONOMISTS AND CAPITAL THEORISTS

Introduction

In the wake of the Second World War, and for a number of reasons, the problematic aspects of economic change – that is, economic growth and economic development – attracted increased attention. This research consumed enough space in the economic literature to form two distinguished families of theories and models: one concerned with growth and one with development. The distinction between these two streams of literature is uncertain and often widely empirical. *Growth* is the term applied to those countries where the gross domestic product (GDP) per capita is greater than a determined level of income reached by a pool of countries called "industrialized countries."[1] The term *development* refers to those countries or areas where the GDP per capita is below the level considered necessary for the satisfaction of basic needs. Broadly speaking, growth is a general increase in economic activity, with a permanent rise in the flow of goods and services. This increase allows for higher consumption and welfare, and also permits high returns on capital that stimulate additional investments. As a result, growth is a self-generating process. Although the topic of growth has always been present in the debates between various schools of economic thought, the issues of growth and income distribution have been treated separately in the literature.

The theory of income distribution is the oldest and most controversial component of neoclassical theory; it is an integral part of the "marginalist revolution"[2] of the nineteenth century. Many fundamental elements of the theory of growth were established by classical economists like Adam Smith, Thomas Malthus, David Ricardo, and Karl Marx. They understood the process of growth to be connected to the accumulation of capital by those who controlled the means of production. These owners obtain a profit that is in part consumed and in part saved and is then converted into new capital, which accumulates along with the existing capital stock. Therefore, the source of economic growth lies in profits and in the process of capital accumulation. Following this formulation, the interests of economists shifted to the determination of profit and, consequently, to the elaboration of a theory of value that is able to explain the process of price formation and the distribution of income, rather than the dynamic aspects of a pure theory of growth. With the advent of the marginalist school, the attention of economists then moved to the mechanism of the market as an allocative system, omitting the problems of growth, distribution, and accumulation. The market mechanism considers the economy as a temporal trend carried out in a succession of periods. The system of prices operates efficiently in every period, ensuring equilibrium between agents and available resources (temporary equilibrium). The succession of temporary equilibriums brings about the dynamic path of the economy. However, there is no theory of growth that can explain the precise causes and mechanisms of income distribution and economic cycles.

A decisive push to reconsider the problem of economic development and unemployment came with the Great Depression of the 1930s, which not only revealed the social costs of severe economic crisis, but threatened political stability. The Great Depression prompted the desire for a new economic theory able to prove that market forces alone could move the economy toward full employment. A profound elaboration of economic growth came with the ideas of John Maynard Keynes and the emergence of the Keynesian school, beginning in the late 1930s and early 1940s. The big challenge for both the Keynesian school and mainstream economists was to understand how to generate stable growth, in order to control the crisis of the Depression and prevent future crises. Consideration of this challenge raised the following three questions, which have been the subject of debate among economists ever since:

- What are the reasons for and factors that affect economic growth?
- Is it possible for an economy to have stable growth, such that (a) all markets are constantly adjusting toward equilibrium and (b) development happens in a way to create no sectoral disequilibrium and inflationary pressures?
- Why do real economies develop unsteadily, such that development is contingent on fluctuations correlated with accelerated growth alternated with stagnation and recession?

Even in different contexts, the discussion has always centred on these three questions, and within the fierce debate between those who believe that government intervention is necessary to promote growth and those who believe in the efficiency of free market mechanisms.

The primary objective of this book is to introduce, in the form of a survey of the economic literature, a straightforward account of modern growth theory and capital theory from the 1930s to the present, along with a critical examination of each. This volume outlines the main issues, insights, and controversies from the field of economic growth and capital theory. The chapters reveal the shifts in focus that have occurred since the first formal growth models in the 1940s. Interest in the development of macroeconomics and growth theory among mainstream economists was revived in the 1950s and 1960s. The initial concern for ensuring the stability of economic expansion, motivated by the Keynesian paradigm, was replaced by research focused on optimizing the long-run growth path, once the neoclassical view on equilibrating economic forces became a more acceptable approach. The new theory also addressed the long-term growth experience of developing countries as they modernized. This experience was recapitulated into a stylized view of the economic facts, and, by developing theories based on these facts, was shaped into tendencies to indicate a steady path of economic growth (Kaldor 1961, 177–220). The modern theory of growth has proceeded along purely theoretical lines by taking into consideration sometimes convenient assumptions, to simply express the possibility of steady growth equilibrium rather than the real causes of growth.

The book's secondary objective is to re-establish what really determines the rate of growth. Is the warranted path of growth, determined jointly by the propensity to save and the quantity of capital as demonstrated by Roy Harrod, more important than the accumulation of capital and technological progress? Are savings, technological progress, population expansion, and consumers' spending patterns the causes of growth, or is the attitude toward investing by society and, in particular, by entrepreneurs the main cause? Is the share in profits between wage earners and capital investors more important than the rate of technological progress? Is the influence of "learning by doing" central to the rate of economic growth?

The purpose here is not simply to survey the developments in economic growth theory but also to identify some topics that have been important in the past and yet are neglected in recent contributions, even though they still have the potential for interesting elaboration – in particular, the effects on growth of demand, unemployment, biased technological change, international trade, history, and institutions. The intention of this second objective is to identify the variables and problems that growth economists have found most relevant rather than to present a simple exposition of their theories. This study will explore how growth theorists chose to deal with a number of variables, models, and problems posed by the dynamics of economic growth in determining the causes of growth, and will provide an extended analysis of the continuity between neoclassical models and a new theory of growth, developed by Romer and Lucas in the 1980s.

Put simply, this survey is like a string pulled out from a jungle of papers, articles, and books on growth economics, macroeconomics, and capital theory. It will help the reader to grasp the major ideas of mainstream growth economists and their models without getting lost in the vast economic literature.

ECONOMIC MODELS AND GROWTH THEORIES

In economics, a model is a theoretical construct that represents economic processes by a set of variables and a set of logical and quantitative relationships. As in other fields, models are simplified frameworks designed to shed light on complex processes. Broadly speaking, modern economic models are simplifications and abstractions from observed data. Simplification results from abstraction. Abstraction is a process of focusing on particular aspects of some real phenomenon, with such a focus leading to the marginalization of other aspects (Nell and Errouaki 2013, xxii–xxiii). This does not mean that the less important aspects of the phenomenon are completely neglected; rather, they are put to the periphery of our attention as they can eventually be used in other abstractions to form models complementary to the main theory.

Simplification and generalization are particularly important for economics as a science, given the enormous complexity of economic processes. This complexity is the result of the diversity of factors that determine economic activity. These include individual and cooperative decision-making processes, resource limitations, environmental and geographical constraints, institutional and legal requirements, and purely random fluctuations. Economists, in order to create their models, are required to make reasonable choices regarding which variables and relationships are relevant and which ways of analyzing and presenting this information are most useful. Sometimes it is not clear whether any distinction should be drawn between an economic theory and an economic model. In many contexts, the terms are used interchangeably. Some authors argue that the term *theory* is used in the complex interrelationships of the real-world economy and the term *model* is reserved for the abstract and logical construct of postulates or theoretical statements. Koopmans emphasized that

> We look upon economic theory as a sequence of conceptional models that seek to express in simplified form different aspects of an always more complicated reality. At first these aspects are formalized as much as feasible in isolation, then in combinations of increasing realism. Each model is defined by a set of postulates, of which the implications are developed to the extent deemed worthwhile in relation to the aspects of reality expressed by the postulates. (Koopmans 1957, 142)

Thus, an economic model is valid if the assumptions explaining the relationship are valid as well. Assumptions may take different forms. They may be expressed as predicates on model parameters or they may assume qualitative and asymptotic forms. This basic concept is sometimes not considered properly. The most common example used in most macroeconomic textbooks is the application of the Keynesian economy to government fiscal policy. The simple Keynesian model postulates that output is a function of aggregate demand. Government spending is one component of aggregate demand, so Keynes's model is often applied to conclude that increasing government spending will have the same positive effect on output as private investment. This application is correct in the short run, but the model does not take into account the results of this policy change (fiscal policy), which may affect business cycles, interest rates, tax rates, private investments, and other factors that may, over the long term, either reduce or increase output. This simple example highlights one of the difficulties of applying economic models: that is, correctly inferring the short- and long-term effects of economic policy.

The term "modern" theories of economic growth indicates that these theories have been developed in the second half of the twentieth century, following the Keynesian revolution. The principal characteristic of modern growth theories is their use of a relatively small number of precisely defined economic variables in the construction of formal models. A modern economic theory is supposed to illuminate a particular problem or specific phenomenon in a society using complex real-world facts (H.G. Jones 1975, 5). Sometimes economists use multifarious models implementing a large number of facts that are transformed into tens of equations; these models are often not easily comprehensible, nor do they always have relevant economic meaning. Despite this, some assumptions or postulates of modern growth theories are often criticized as being unrealistic. Sometimes a good portion of economic theory is attained in a less empirical way and is often based in abstract concepts. According to Harrod,

> The great fruitfulness of the analytical map in yielding valid prescriptions has obscured the extreme paucity of our knowledge with regard to causal sequences. Two circumstances militate against the more deductive method. One is the impossibility of crucial experiment. In the mature sciences which rely mainly on this method, such as physics, or, to name a more recent comer, genetics, the crucial experiment is of central importance. Secondly, it is extremely difficult to test hypotheses by the collected date of observation. The operation of plurality of causes is too widely pervasive. Thus numerous hypotheses are framed, and never submitted to decisive test, so that each man retains his own opinion still. (Harrod 1938, 407)

According to Koopmans, if the scope of an economic theory is the representation of the real world and the prediction of economic phenomena, the practicality of its underlying assumptions is irrelevant to the main purpose of whether the model's predictions are accurate (Koopmans 1957, 87). Theories of economic development are closely related to the mainstream of modern growth theories but differ in the sense that they are intended to apply to particular topics and specific trends in developing countries. The subject of these theories is very broad and includes topics outside economics – for example, sociological theories, political and historical topics, and so forth. Koopmans, among others, argued that as a scientific enterprise, economics requires a clear separation between logical and factual sources of our knowledge (Koopmans 1957, 94). He affirmed that the process of reasoning from principles to conclusions within a given postulational system does not depend on any factual knowledge. As soon as the terms of a postulational system with a descriptive interpretation are provided, the system assumes relevance and economic meaning that can explain the facts of the real world.

According to Nell and Errouaki (2013, xxii), in economics as in any other field dealing with the real world, it appears that there are two different worlds: the real world as we observe it and the world of theories and mathematical models created by theorists. The world of mathematical models is populated by idealized individuals who behave in a certain way that may or may not correspond to reality. Technically speaking, the correspondence between real world and model world is not accurate; errors of measurement, irrational human behaviour, habit changes, and new trends that affect human conduct make perfect correspondence impossible.[3] This is the reason that present-day economists create stochastic models that have the capability to put together the stochastic nature of the correspondence. The measurement errors in the world model, for example, leave the observations in a normal random distribution about the true values of the model. Therefore, putting it in a simple way, the correspondence itself is nothing more than the stochastic element of the model world. Economists in general can choose to consider the world stochastic only if they assume that economic models are true and that, as a consequence, any variability of the correspondence is due to unexplainable alterations and sometimes sudden transformations and changes in the real world (Nell and Errouaki 2013, xxii).

An important aspect of the models used in economic theories is their methodology, which is often referred to as the relationship between the theories and methods of reaching conclusions about the nature of the real world. Bolland (2003) distinguishes between two kinds of methodologies: "small-m" methodology and "big-M" methodology. Small methodology, "small-m," refers to applied methodology and is concerned with the issues surrounding the practical decisions made when building economic models. By contrast, "big-M" methodology concerns the big philosophical questions and dilemmas that have troubled philosophers of science for centuries. In modern economics it has been observed that mainstream economists are not interested in "big-M" methodology, but are only interested in"small-m" methodology, concentrating their efforts on helpful methodological ideas that they use on many assumptions and postulations in order to build their models and theories (Bolland 2003, 2–6). In fact, "Mainstream economists do not feel any need to consult philosopher-kings or philosopher-priests.

Instead, mainstream economic model builders need "methodological plumbers" (Bolland 2003, 4). The practice of "small-m" methodology is different for each case regarding economic models and theories. This is the case because modern economics is dominated by classical and neo-classical economics, both of which are based on the idea or view that the economy is the result of people making decisions independently in the pursuit of their own interests.

It is important to emphasize that this study is intended to discuss modern growth theories by taking into consideration a certain method of analysis, a method which takes into account the original contribution of those economists who have worked to resolve the problems of development and economic growth. Modern economic growth theory has been swamped for decades with hundreds of different models, offering different suggestions and solutions about a steady and balanced growth. This has presented a challenge to young scholars who are attempting to identify, follow, and understand the main theories of growth. This work aims to treat mainstream growth theory in an infinite world of economic models. It is a synthesis that treats an extensive and difficult tradition of scholarship, and that ultimately offers readers a clear path through the dense forest of models about growth.

ECONOMIC GROWTH IN HISTORICAL PERSPECTIVE

Modern growth models developed after the Second World War[4] held out the promise of understanding macroeconomic stability. In the 1950s and 1960s several macroeconomists directed their efforts to the examination of the Harrod-Domar model (1939–46), in which growth does not necessarily lead to full employment. The assumption of dependability on both the savings rate and the capital/output ratio produced a constant rate of growth of the capital stock, which is only by coincidence equal to the rate of growth required to create enough employment opportunities for a growing labour force. New theories were developed in which the warranted rate of growth and the natural rate of growth adjust to the long-run equilibrium. The role of effective demand in the process of growth was essential from the Keynesian perspective. Many authors have seen growing investments as a successful policy for increasing demand in output and promoting stability. It has been realized that significant investment in infrastructure, research, and leading industries provides an important path for economic stability.

The question raised by economists is whether investment and capital accumulation that are only by coincidence equal to the rate of growth needed to create sufficient employment are able to expand output to absorb a growing labour force. It has been recognized that changes in income distribution, as well as changes in substitution between labour and capital and in demand for real money balance, make the warranted rate of growth flexible and allow technological change to be adjusted to the natural rate of growth.

After Roy Harrod and Evsey Domar's contribution regarding the warranted rate of growth theory, Nicholas Kaldor focused his attention on income distribution between two broad categories: profit earners and wage earners. By assuming that capitalists save more than workers, Kaldor demonstrated that the redistribution of income increases the rate of savings and may even raise capital accumulation to absorb unemployment.

Later, Robert Solow (1956) and Trevor Swan (1956) tried to resolve the Harrod-Domar instability by introducing factor substitution between capital and labour. The key aspect of the Solow-Swan model is the neoclassical production function, a condition that assumes constant returns to scale, diminishing returns, and elasticity of substitution between inputs. Solow's perception of the production function not only became the cornerstone in growth theory, but in neoclassical economics in general. Solow's contribution opened the path to the modern neoclassical theory of growth. Solow and Swan tried to prove that, in the absence of continuing improvements in technology, per capita growth must eventually cease. This supposition is most likely derived from Malthus and Ricardo's assumption of the diminishing return process as a stage of a non-growing economy. The neoclassical growth theorists of the late 1950s and mid-1960s, however, recognized that the diminishing return process is insufficient to explain the rate of economic growth and tried to fix it by assuming technological progress as exogenous. This tool was introduced to reconcile the positive constant per capita growth in the long run with the prediction of conditional convergence.

Few attempts to endogenize technological change were made in the early 1950s. Normally entrepreneurs prefer the introduction of technical improvements when labour is scarce. The shortage of labour pushes several sectors toward more advanced technological improvements and not just simple upgrades. The effect on the natural growth rate ensures that balanced growth may arise even with a fixed savings rate and capital-output ratio. An economy could often be subject to short-run market imperfections and in the long run to the tendency toward equilibrium. Unemployment, however, as in all post-Keynesian models, is considered a structural phenomenon. In particular, unemployment does not arise because of lack of effective demand but rather from the inability of the market to create sufficient jobs. The question of unemployment is related to economic growth and capital accumulation through the Harrod-Domar type of instability. In the neoclassical production function framework, unemployment would not arise because low wages would ensure full employment as a result of the immediate substitution (of labour with capital and vice versa). In the vintage framework,[5] capital and labour requirements are fixed, and there is no substitution of labour and capital per vintage. Technological change is represented as labour saving, as newer vintages of capital equipment require less labour per unit of output. Since the replacement of old machines with newer vintages may create unemployment, full employment will be reached only if the new vintage of equipment is sufficiently larger in value than the old one. In neoclassical models, however, full employment is maintained if there is a large range of previously installed vintages. The effective abundance of labour is not only determined by the rate of capital accumulation but also by the rate and bias of technological change. A labour-saving bias in innovation makes labour effectively more abundant, to be diverted to or applied to the sectors where labour is more urgently needed. The substitution process between labour and capital in the vintage approach seems to work less smoothly. A higher savings rate makes labour relatively less abundant and results in a shorter lifetime of capital. This situation modernizes the total capital stock by raising the percentage of more productive new machines. Full employment is maintained if a lower labour income induces firms to increase the lifespan of capital. Therefore, in general, if technological change is exogenous, both the neoclassical model and the vintage approach foresee that labour is positively related to the rate of investment and technological change.

In neoclassical theory, if firms maximize profits in a perfectly competitive market, the labour share is solely determined by the production function. For instance, in the case of the Cobb-Douglas production function, the labour share is constant. In the more general constant elasticity substitution (CES) production function, with an elasticity of substitution between labour and capital below one (CES<1), the labour share is higher and less abundant.

The income distribution is determined along Kaldorian lines. Both spending and investment depend on the distribution of income, because the propensity to consume is higher than capital income. In the theory of income distribution, investment spending is stimulated by high profits. The equality of spending and income is assured by adjustments in the distribution of income over labour and capital, which gives rise to interdependency between growth and income distribution. A positive demand shock increases profits and stimulates technological progress at the cost of a lower quantity of labour.

Many growth theorists subsequently proved that the diffusion of technology is more important for the growth of output per capita than for the accumulation of physical capital. Since Solow (1957) assumed that technological progress is an exogenous factor, for a long time the neoclassical models accepted technological progress as being exogenous. In fact, some models were based on the assumption of exogenous, disembodied, and neutral technological progress. Several empirical studies based on exogenous technological progress considered Solow's residual factor as a consequence of technological progress. Later, however, attempts were made by several theorists to set up macroeconomics models with the assumption of endogenous technological progress. Broadly speaking, endogenous technological progress was related mostly to aggregate variables such as investment, market structure, and the allocation of research expenditure. Most of the models developed during the neoclassical era in the early 1960s were not able to explain the stability of income distribution, despite efforts to describe the course of technological progress influenced by economic variables. The theory of induced bias in innovation introduced by Weizsäcker, Kennedy, and Fellner proved best able to explain constancy in distributive shares.

In 1965, Cass and Koopmans again considered Ramsey's analysis of consumer optimization and provided an endogenous determination of the savings rate. Their conclusion was that the endogeneity of savings rates does not eliminate the dependence of the long-run per capita growth rate on exogenous technological progress. The equilibrium state of Cass-Koopmans is supported by a competitive structure in which labour and capital are paid their marginal products. Cass and Koopmans accepted the "Golden Rule" introduced by Phelps (1961, 1965), but disagreed that it was optimal. They argued that, in the theory of optimal growth, one should look for maximal utility and not for maximal consumption. In fact, the Golden Rule in Phelps is maximal consumption along a balanced growth path when the rate of interest is equal to the rate of growth, but in the Cass-Koopmans model, it is the consumers' maximum utility that guarantees the optimal path. Thus, the optimal growth path is determined independently of consumers' utility functions. The concepts of the Golden Rule and optimal growth reached a peak in the development of growth theory in the 1960s. On the other side, development economists were called on to suggest empirical solutions to the progress of underdeveloped countries. They tended to use theories that were more technically simple than growth theories but that were more empirically useful when confronting real-world problems. The fields of economic growth and economic development split.

The history of economic growth offers fertile ground for discussion of divergences about the concepts of applied economics. Rostow (1990) argued that the applied economics of growth theories have often meant different things to different theorists; indeed, he pointed out that some theorists have not considered measurement and testing as applied economics in the history of economic growth. Likewise, Sen, after closely scrutinizing the early stages of growth theorists (such as Harrod, Domar, Kaldor, Swan, and Solow), concluded that these theorists were more interested in doctrinal debates and in solving measurement problems than they were in defining the field of application of their theories.[6]

Later, the task of applying growth theories was developed through the field of econometrics and through complicated mathematical equations, which resulted in the isolation of theory from the practical aspects of growth. Solow (1997) has suggested that the applied side of growth theories has consistently exerted much more influence on the development of these theories. After a long period of intense development in the late 1970s and early 1980s, interest in theories of long-term growth resurfaced again in the late 1980s and early 1990s, this time by giving way to more concern with short-term macroeconomic problems in underdeveloped economies.

Once it was realized that neoclassical models of growth relied strongly on exogenous technological progress as the ultimate source of growth, theories of endogenous technological progress became significant and were the central focus of growth theory in the 1990s.

Developments in the past two to three decades, in combination with insights from earlier developments, have called for a new approach to growth theory – one that is comprehensive enough to explain growth over long periods in a large range of countries (both developed and developing). In the mid-1980s, economic growth theory experienced new progress, beginning with the pioneering work of P.M. Romer (1986, 1990) and Lucas (1988). This new wave is often called the first generation of endogenous research and development (R&D) growth models. The research of new models was based primarily on the idea that the rate of long-run economic growth is more important than the mechanisms of short-run and business cycles. The new research theorists, represented by P.M. Romer (1986, 1990), Lucas (1988), and Rebelo (1991), based their models on Arrow's (1962) seminal paper on "learning by doing," and on Uzawa (1965). No technological change is involved in their models. For them, growth is considered endogenous, which means that the output may increase not only because of population growth but also as a result of focused research efforts due to the increasing returns to scale in the output sector. Growth may continue for an indefinite period as the returns to investment in capital goods do not necessarily diminish as economies expand.

A second generation of endogenous R&D growth models, represented by those of Aghion and Howitt (1992), Grossman and Helpman (1991a and 1991b), Howitt (1999), Peretto (1998), and Young (1998), incorporated R&D theories into the growth structure. The scale effect in these models was eliminated. The simultaneous expansion of variety and quality of intermediate goods occurred under conditions that made the steady-state productivity growth dependent on the ratio between intensive R&D and total employment.

A typical feature of the models of the 1990s was that the production function for new knowledge became the core of the model, surpassing the relevance of the goods production function. Knowledge production functions were used in the 1960s as well, but the new object in endogenous growth theory was the consistent modeling of R&D in a general equilibrium structure with optimizing firms and consumers. The fixed cost of R&D expenditures requires some monopoly power for the first-comer firms to recuperate their costs. Monopolistic firms maximize profits by setting their prices and choosing R&D expenditures. Moreover, new firms enter the new markets by expanding the range of products available to consumers. In this way, the new endogenous models combine productivity improvements and variety expansion, which were kept separate in most exogenous growth models of the late 1960s. In 1977, Dixit and Stiglitz (1977, 297–308) resolved the difficulties of modeling monopolistic competition in general equilibrium and explained the discontinuity in modeling endogenous technological change.

The major distinction between the growth theories of the 1960s, the 1980s, and the 1990s is that the recent research pays more attention to empirical implications, and to the relation between theory and data, than to the pure economic growth models. Some analyses of empirical implications are based on the older theories; a noteworthy example is the neoclassical growth model's prediction of conditional convergence (Barro and Sala-i-Martin 1995). Other analyses are applied more directly to the recent theories of endogenous growth, including the roles of increasing returns, R&D activity, human capital, and the diffusion of technology. A formal classification of R&D growth models is used in recent literature to explain the fact that not only R&D employment but also the R&D employment share have risen dramatically, contributing to high stages of development in advanced countries over the last sixty years.

THE STRUCTURE OF THE BOOK

Part One of this book deals with the origins of modern growth theory, Part Two is about the rise and decline of neoclassical growth theory, and Part Three takes into consideration endogenous growth models. Chapter 1 describes the roles of growth, technological progress, and occupation in the thought of classical economists like Smith, Ricardo, and Marx. Chapter 2 discusses the emergence of the modern theory of growth, beginning with the first neo-Keynesian growth theorists, Harrod and Domar. This chapter takes into account the path of warranted rate of growth in Harrod's model and the process of increasing productivity in Domar's model. Chapter 3 deals with the old Keynesians (Kaldor and Pasinetti) and the theory of income distribution. In part two, chapter 4 covers the neoclassical theory of growth, including the neoclassical factor substitution models ranging from Solow-Swan in the 1950s to Cass-Koopmans in the 1960s. The chapter also investigates the Golden Rule accumulation in Phelps and the optimal economic growth, as well as the two-sector growth models in Uzawa and Solow. Chapter 5 introduces the relationship between technological progress and growth. It describes the neutrality of technological progress in Hicks and Harrod, the technological progress function in Kaldor, the residual technical change in Solow, the transmission of technological progress, and the measurement of technological change. Further, this chapter explains the economic improvement of "learning by doing" and induced bias in innovation. Chapter 6 explores the views of the two Cambridge schools (in the United Kingdom and the United States) and the debate over capital controversy. Chapter 7 explores early modern development theories after the Second World War, dealing broadly with development theorists such as Kuznets, Lewis, Myrdal, Rostow, Chenery, Harris, and Todaro. The "Intermezzo" offers some conclusions about modern neoclassical growth theory.

In part three, chapter 8 investigates the new theories of growth that emerged in the late 1980s and provides extensive detail on the models of Lucas, P.M. Romer, and Rebelo. Chapter 9 focuses on the new endogenous growth models regarding innovation and new consumer goods applications. Chapter 10 discusses the new Schumpeterian approach of Creative Destruction rediscovered by Aghion and Howitt. Finally, in the closing chapter, I outline some final conclusions, lessons, and suggestions that emerge from this survey of modern growth theory.

PART ONE

Origins of Modern Growth Theory

1

Growth, Technological Progress, and Unemployment in the Thought of the Classical Economists

The theory of growth is central in the thought of great classical economists like Smith, Ricardo, and Marx. The study of economic growth concentrates mainly on a dynamic economy able to reproduce and develop itself. The common idea of classical economists is that, in an economic system, there is surplus value, which, if accumulated or transformed into capital, nourishes the growth of the system. The surplus value is what remains of the social product once incorporated into the consumption goods necessary for subsistence and reproduction of labour. For Smith, Ricardo, and Marx, the role of technological progress in the society is central. It helps to enhance the productivity of labour, using the same number of workers employed (for example, on a farm), but it increases the productivity and supports the process of accumulation. Regarding technological progress, what distinguishes the contribution of Ricardo and Marx from that of Smith is the effect that technological progress generates employment. For Smith, thanks to technological progress and an increase in productivity, a greater level of prosperity is achieved; this in turn constitutes a stimulus for a further process of accumulation and a greater level of subsistence assigned to productive workers. The notion that this pattern can create unemployment in the short run is not part of Smith's optimistic approach. In fact, he believes that an increase in productivity is always associated with an expansion of the market, so the occupation grows as the economy grows.

Ricardo, in contrast, plants the doubt that economic growth could happen in the presence of labour-saving innovations. Such innovations are translated into unemployment when compensation mechanisms stimulated from the market are not sufficient to absorb the unemployed workers.

If for Ricardo, technical progress constitutes a possibility, then for Marx it constitutes a historical necessity for the development of the capitalist system and determines the increase of unemployment and the creation of the "reserve industrial army" (Marx 1867, Vol. I, Ch. 25). The Smithian vision is overturned; there is no invisible hand that harmonizes the individual interests and leads the system toward higher prosperity. According to Marx, economic evolution leads to the unavoidable consequence of impoverishment of many in the working class. With the advent of marginalism, the problem of development is, in fact, set aside, and the analysis of the economists is directed instead to the conditions that allow for an optimal allocation of resources. It is the static economy that is the object of study for neoclassical economists. "The phenomenon of development – if about development in marginalist context we can speak of – was not studied for itself but in an incident way, analyzed, with the methods of comparable statics which modifications would be taken into consideration to determine the position of equilibrium in an economic system as a result of variations taken part in some data or exogenous variables" (Cozzi 1972, 126).

For a long time (at least until Schumpeter), the problem of economic development and its occupational effects remained at the margin of economic theory. Beginning with Harrod and especially after the Second World War, the relationship between growth and unemployment returned, to a great extent to the attention of economists. This chapter examines briefly the early classical concerns about growth in Smith, Ricardo, and Marx.

GROWTH, INCREASE OF PRODUCTIVITY, AND OCCUPATION IN *WEALTH OF NATIONS* OF ADAM SMITH

According to Adam Smith,[1] the ability of an economy to produce wealth depends on the division of labour – a continuous process of productive activity that is subdivided and entrusted to different workers. Smith, at the beginning of Book One of *Wealth of Nations,* "Of the Division of Labour," asserted that, "The greatest improvement in the productive powers of labour, and the greater part of the skill, dexterity, and judgment with which it is any where directed, or applied, seem to have been the effects of the division of labour" (Smith 1970, 45). In a more specific way, the increase of productivity is based on different factors.

> First, the improvement of the dexterity of the workman necessarily increases the quantity of the work he can perform; and the division of labour, by reducing every man's business to some one simple operation, and by making this operation the sole employment of his life, necessarily increased very much the dexterity of the workman. Secondly, the advantage which is gained by saving the time commonly lost in passing from one sort of work to another, is much greater than we should at first view be apt to imagine it. Thirdly, and lastly, every body must be sensible how much labour is facilitated and abridged by the application of proper machinery. (Smith 1970, 69)

The technological progress, or "the invention of a great number of machines," is one of these factors. It is endogenous regarding the mechanism of division of labour, as Smith emphasized when he asserted,

> I shall only observe, therefore, that the invention of all those machines by which labour is so much facilitated and abridged seems to have been originally owing to the division of labour. Men are much more likely to discover easier and readier methods of attaining any object, when the whole attention of their minds is directed towards that single object, than when it is dissipated among a great variety of things. But in consequence of the division of labour, the whole of every man's attention comes naturally to be directed towards some one very simple object. It is naturally to be expected, therefore, that some one or other of those who are employed in each particular branch of labour should soon find out easier and readier methods of performing their own particular work, wherever the nature of it admits of such improvement. (Smith 1970, 72)

The introduction of machines provokes a diminishing ratio between workers and the means of production. Smith never put into consideration, however, the argument that the new machines are adopted to work using a quantity of work superior than the quantity of work used by men in the same type of production; in short, this change does not imply an absolute decrease of work because the introduction of machines is motivated by the need to increase the volume of production through the augmentation of labour productivity.

Smith's theory of investment is closely linked to his distinction between productive and unproductive labour. The productive sector is mainly the agricultural one, in which workers produce and "add to the value of the subject upon which is bestowed" (Smith 1970, 314–15). Workers and manufacturers are part of the productive sector and create the annual production in the agriculture or in manufacturing sector by adding value to goods. Conversely, the unproductive sector consumes but leaves nothing in return for further consumption; hence, there is no value added to goods. As Smith stated, "The portion of the revenue which a rich man annually spends is in most cases consumed by idle guests, and menial servants, who leave nothing behind them in return for their consumption" (Smith 1970, 315).

Of the rest, the economies in which Smith is interested are those of the main European nations, where an extraordinary stage of development took place at the end of the sixteenth century, assisted by a systematic growth of the national product – an increase that is not accidental or tied to favorable hypothetical circumstances but rather occurred by a mechanism of self-feeding or internal growth. The object of Smithian analysis is represented by the explanation of growth in production volumes, the cause of which is identified in capital saving.

In fact, like the division of labour, the same technological progress is regulated by the process of accumulation, through which capitalists assign part of their profits to the anticipation of primary goods, to the subsistence for productive workers (circulating capital), and to machineries and other means of production (fixed capital). There is a combination of fixed and circulating capital in the process of production. According to Smith the scope of fixed capital is to increase the productivity of labour by employing the same number of workers to produce a large quantity of useful labour. Useful labour or real labour (different from abstract labour, which creates only a new value) reproduces the previously existing value in the new form of a useful product. Its role is complementary, as the useful labour is carried out by the labour force.

In Smith's view, the fixed capital derives from circulating capital and is supported continuously by it. No fixed capital is able to offer any kind of revenue or surplus without the support of circulating capital. The useful machines will not be able to produce without circulating capital, which both provides materials utilized during the process of manufacturing and pays workers (Smith 1970, 265). Smith described a virtuous circle, in which the process of accumulation begets greater division of labour and the introduction of new machinery because the two lead to increased production that ultimately results in increased accumulation. It is important to underscore that, in Smith's view the rate of productivity growth is governed by the rate of aggregate demand growth. Technological change helps to raise the output per man when there is a growing demand. The accumulation of capital and investment in technological change is seen as part of a growing economy. In reality, "the issue of reabsorbing displaced workers never came up because he took it for granted that output expansion and cost reductions due to the introduction of new machinery were inseparably linked. Essentially, Smith looked upon capital as a complement of rather than a substitute for labour. The growing market makes possible the introduction of new technologies which in turn, by attracting labour, help the market to grow" (Hagemann 1995, 37).

The productivity increase helps to augment the consumption of goods, allowing the continuation of productive activity by stimulating capitalists to accumulate. Smith was interested in economies in which the intensity of accumulation determines the level of development, meaning not only raising the number of productive workers with respect to unproductive workers but also introducing greater numbers of perfect machines that are able to raise production levels without increasing the number of employees. The process of accumulation generates the conditions by which technological progress and increase of labour productivity are realized. This provides new opportunities for profits, thus stimulating savings while at the same time supporting the process of accumulation. This process does not lead to a decrease in employment but rather to an increase.

It's hard to believe but the Smithian theory has often been criticized that the distinction between "productive" and "unproductive" labour is unclear, and there is no difference between the share of output dedicated to "productive" labour and the share of output devoted to "unproductive" labour. Many decades later, Marx, while praising Smith for noticing that labour creates a surplus, heavily criticized him on the ground that he was not able to see the difference between the two types of labour (productive and unproductive) as well as for excluding services from the definition of productive labour (Chaudhuri 1989, 24–5).

The growth of population and employment in the Smithian view is one of the signs that distinguished the early European capitalist economies – those that dismissed the feudal system and were involved in a deep and irreversible growth process by increasing the number of productive workers, wealth, and revenue of their inhabitants – from the underdeveloped economies that were not caught up in the process of capitalist development. According to Smith economic development is beneficial to workers because it increases the demand for labour, population, and wages. Population, occupation, and salary are, in fact, connected by a positive relation. On one hand, the process of accumulation increases the demand for labour and, consequently, its price. On the other hand, there is a demographic mechanism by which the "demand" for workers as well as for goods is regulated by the "productivity" of workers, stimulating demand if it goes too slowly and stopping it when it goes too fast. As a result, it is almost improbable that the phenomenon of a growing population and employment could occur either in a stationary economy or in a recession. Therefore, a situation of high salaries positively influences the wealth of nations and causes the population to grow. In fact, a good remuneration of labour is crucial to increasing the productivity and the wealth of common workers.

Thus, the essence of Smith's theory is that a robust and steady process of economic development requires productivity-increasing investment in agriculture as well as in manufacturing and commerce. On the contrary, the mercantilist doctrine before Smith was inclined to regard agriculture as an "infertile" (i.e., unproductive) sector.

In summary, for Smith, the accumulation of funds is what facilitates economic growth and improves labour productivity; it increases wages, employment, population, and the demand for labour.

DYNAMICS, EMPLOYMENT, AND GROWTH IN RICARDO

The theory of growth was developed later in Ricardo's economic theory,[2] which, considering how comprehensively he explored the development of economics as a science, has rightly been hailed as "magnificent dynamics." His masterpiece, *On the Principles of Political Economy and Taxation* (1821), has been a corner stone for several generations of economists who started studying economics reading pure classics.

Ricardo has often been praised by adding two key contributions to the traditional analysis of growth. First, the process of economic growth does not continue forever, in the sense that it has an end. Second, the economy approaches a particular level of output (or growth), at which point further growth is halted. This is nothing more than the classical "stationary state." Ricardo, among others, was looking to demonstrate how the distribution of income is affected by the process of growth

(Chaudhuri 1989, 31). The portion of rents, profits, and wages, received respectively by landlords, capitalists, and workers, were related to particular stages of growth. Each share of rent, profit or wage depends on three factors: the supply of land or the fertility of soil, the accumulation of capital, and the instruments and skills (agricultural technology) employed in agriculture (Ricardo 1951, 5).

The core of the Ricardian model is the agricultural sector. The two main factors of production are land and labour. Land, being the "original and indestructible property of the soil" (Marshall 1920, 19N), is considered as fixed in supply, but its quality varies from place to place. At a given point of time, there is also a fixed supply of labour. The workforce is always fully employed and hired by capitalists at a certain wage level. Competition among capitalists ensures that under the influence of the law of diminishing returns, the marginal product of labour will rise in one farm and fall in another until the two are equal. This means that if the marginal product of labour is lower in one farm, it will be profitable for capitalists to shift labour from that farm to another more productive one. Consequently, the more "fertile" (i.e., productive) farms will be cultivated more intensively. The margin of cultivation will be extended to the farm that is worth cultivating, in the sense that its average product of labour is equal to the common level of the marginal product of labour on all cultivated farms. Farms that are less fertile than marginal farms, with an average product of labour less than the marginal product, will be left uncultivated.

There is a two-way relationship between labour, capital, and food production. The ability of labour to produce something more that it was used in production or a "surplus" encourages capitalists to reinvest part of the surplus for profit by employing more labour. The employment of more labour in agriculture enables this sector to produce more food and, in return, allows a larger population to subsist.

The distribution of income among workers, capitalists, and landlords plays an important role in the economic cycle. At any point, according to Ricardo there is a fixed stock of corn known as the wage fund, which is owned by capitalists and is used to hire labour during the growing season. The wage rate per worker is then determined by the size of the wage fund in relation to the labour force (i.e., the wage fund divided by the labour force). The wage rate is, therefore, independent of the marginal productivity of labour. In fact, the marginal product of labour is higher than the wage rate; the difference between these two quantities is the profit that the capitalist earns per worker employed. The marginal productivity of labour is, itself, less than the average product on all intramarginal farms. The difference between the average and the marginal productivity of labour multiplied by the number of workers employed on the farm goes to landlords as a rent for the land. A more fertile land earns a higher rent because the average of labour productivity is higher and because more workers are employed. The marginal farm does not earn any rent.

There are two dynamic forces pushing the economy upward, namely, population growth and increase of the wage fund. Landlords, as a class, spend the bulk of their rental incomes on "unproductive consumption" (Ricardo 1821, 168). Capitalists, however, save a high proportion of their profits, which is added to the wage fund. The other dynamic force, the growth of population, follows the Malthusian theory of demographic behaviour. According to this theory, population growth is an endogenous variable. If the wage rate, determined by the relation between the wage fund and the size of the labour force, leads the standard of living for workers to rise above the subsistence level, then the population will increase in size. On the contrary, if the wage rate is such that the standard of living is below the subsistence level, there will be a decline in population size. A steady expansion of the wage fund thus leads to a steady growth in population. During this process, the wage rate fluctuates around the subsistence level and, as a result, the marginal productivity of labour will fall steadily, both through the more intensive cultivation of intramarginal farms and the outward movement of the extensive margin of cultivation to less fertile farms. The rate of profit per worker employed will fall; the profit incomes of capitalists may rise for a time, but they will eventually decline while, at the same time, the rental incomes of landlords will rise continuously. Thus, the rate of profit will fall to zero, the wage fund will stop expanding, and the economy will reach the classical stationary state. Therefore, according to Ricardo, the threat to growth arises not from the fact that a wealthier economy may support a larger population but rather that population grows with respect to the supply of land, constantly worsening the ratio of population to land.

Ricardo favors the use of machines in chapter 31 of his book, which was added in the third edition of 1821. He takes into consideration the case of an industrialist (entrepreneur) who produces both food and manufactured goods and assumes that the entrepreneur uses half of his working force to manufacture a new machine. And what happened is that,

> once the machine is in operation, his fixed capital expands, but he (entrepreneur) now operates regularly with half of the circulating capital formerly used and in Ricardo's system, therefore, half the level of employment. Thus, the machine throws some workers out of their jobs. They would then have less to spend on manufactured "necessaries." Output would decline because of reduced workers' incomes, but profits would be maintained because the entrepreneur would have fewer workers to pay (Rostow 1990, 82).

In the long term, there is a possibility of unemployment because of technology which, according to Ricardo, is the result of the lack of coordination in the introduction of new technologies. The accumulation of capital may, through the mechanisms of compensation, reduce or eliminate unemployment. Reconsidering the possibility of an increase in net income, Ricardo abandons the idea of given capital and reconsiders the potentialities of reabsorption of the displaced workforce that derives from the transformation of profit to fresh capital that can be made available for new investments, thus increasing the employment of the workforce. In this way, he considers the possibility of an increase in capital accumulation. In other words, his analysis moves from long to short term. Moreover, in his *Principles*, Ricardo did not give the impression that he was against the use of machines and tried to emphasize, albeit in a contradictory way, that

> all I wish to prove, is that the discovery and the use of machinery may be attended with a diminution of gross produce; and whenever that is the case, it will be injurious to the labouring class, as some of their number will be thrown out of employment, and population will become redundant, compared with the funds which are to employ it ... if the improved means of production, in consequence of the use of machinery, should increase the net produce of a country in a degree so great as not to diminish the gross produce ... then the situation of all classes will be improved. (Ricardo 1821, 472–6; see also Ricardo 1951 and Blaug 1985)

Later, he expressed the hope that his statements would not lead to the conclusion that machinery should not be encouraged. In effect, Ricardo argued that machines and more capital-intensive production processes were the result of a long-term rise in food prices because of diminishing returns. High food prices are a reflection of higher wages, which are a motivation for owners of capital to use or increase their use of machines. Accumulation and technological progress appear, therefore, to be closely related. Ricardo was also quite conscious that profits enlarged by labour-saving inventions could, in time, result in an expansion of savings, investment, and employment.

GROWTH, TECHNOLOGICAL PROGRESS, AND OCCUPATION IN MARX

Marx's economic theory is a part of a much wider explanation of how and to what extent a society evolves and progresses.[3] The topic of technological progress and of occupation in a capitalist system assumed a central role in Marx's analysis. As mentioned earlier, the classical economists placed great importance on the role of labour as a primary input that uses technology to attain a productivity level capable of producing a surplus that is well above the cost of subsistence. In a capitalist society, the economy operates through the appropriation of this surplus by others. The subsequent behaviour of the society is then determined by the process of surplus reinvestment. Marx differs profoundly from Smith and Ricardo in his explanation for social and economic phenomena as well as the conclusions he draws from the theory. The Marxian economy, like the Ricardian one, does not grow forever; its end is found not in an approach to a "stationary state" but rather in crisis. For Marx, capital has a strong influence on the working class. The most important factor of his analysis is the composition of capital and its variation during the process of accumulation.

Marx, for the convenience of his analysis, divides capital into two kinds: constant and variable. Constant capital consists of raw materials and machinery, and its value remains unchanged during the whole production process. Variable capital consists of wage goods that are used to employ labour and has the capability to produces an output that has normally a higher value than the cost. It is true that the Marxian concept of constant and variable capital approaches the fixed and circulating capital of Smith, but only if the material side (the productive process) alone is considered. The value side is absolutely different. In effect, the adjectives *constant* and *variable* have another meaning. According to Marx, what should be considered is only that part of capital which acquires labour and generates profits to capitalists. This part is called "variable" because it possesses the quality of being able to change its value in the production process and is different from constant capital, in which value is transmitted immutably during the whole productive process.

It is from "variable capital" that capitalists extract "surplus" – that is, the difference between the value of exchange of labour (subsistence level) and the value of labour able to be produced. The relationship between fixed and variable capital is called the organic composition of capital.

If, however, the value side is considered, the relationship expresses, respectively, the "technical composition" and the "value composition" of capital. The total value of output is given as,

$$y = c + v + s \tag{1.1}$$

where y is the total output, c is the constant capital, v is the variable capital, and s is the surplus value that is created by labour above its cost of production. The production condition is that the higher the c/v, the cheaper the output. The diminishing returns in Ricardo are merely substituted by increasing returns (because the land factor was important in Marx as it was in Ricardo).

Capitalism causes progressive changes in the technological composition of capital and increases the means of production. This transformation is reflected in the composition of capital. On one hand, there is an increase of the constant part of capital at the expense of its variable part, and on the other hand, there is a necessity manifested during the process of accumulation to increase labour productivity.

For Marx, the inequality of distribution in means of production and the spread of technological progress have brought about a situation in which society consists of two classes: workers and capitalists. Workers offer as a form of exchange the only commodity they possess: the capacity to work to generate surplus value. The real wage they receive is the subsistence wage, or the cost of reproduction of labour power. It is the same rate that enables workers to subsist and make available a supply of labour through reproduction. The wage rate is maintained at a subsistence level through a chronic excess supply of labour at the wage that, in turn, is due to the nature of technological progress.

The increase in labour productivity that is part of the organic composition of capital is naturally associated with an increase of surplus value rate, defined as the ratio between "surplus value" and variable capital. The profit rate (the relationship between surplus value and total capital) depends positively on the rate of surplus value and negatively on the organic composition of capital. There is an incentive for capitalists to use capital more intensively because it is more efficient. Marx assumes that new techniques are always becoming available and that technology is continuously evolving in a labour-saving direction. Therefore, the organic composition of capital, the ratio c/v, is continuously rising. Technological progress constantly creates an excess supply of labour, which means less labour is required per unit of capital. The excess supply of labour constitutes the "reserve army of labour," (Marx 1867) which in turn prevents any increase of real wages above the level of subsistence.

The creation of an unemployed mass or a "reserve army" is not, as in Ricardo, only a possibility; instead, it is what effectively happens in a further advancement of capitalistic process, thus pushing down the real wage rate. Unemployment and overpopulation are not due to an abstract law of population of the Malthusian kind, but rather to the operation of the capitalistic system. It is not the population that increases but rather the accumulation process that creates overpopulation and unemployment. The capital wants "free hands" (Marx 1997, 406) because the labour force available for production, which also helps the natural population growth, is not enough. Therefore, it is necessary to have a "reserve army of labour" available in expansion moments. In other words, a part of the population that is able to work at the subsistence wage rate is essential.

The capitalist system is efficient only in one aspect: the constant capitalization of productive process and the reinvestment of the surplus lead to high levels of productivity and output. Marx's prediction, however, is that the system is inherently unstable and leads to continuous "crises," and implies that there is growing instability. The main form of instability in capitalism (capitalist crisis) according to Marxian theory is the tendency of the rate of profit to fall in the long run. By denoting "r," the rate of profit, it implies

$$r = s/(c + v) = s/v\ [1 - c/(c + v)] \qquad (1.2)$$

By assumption, the rate of exploitation is constant. The organic composition of capital $[c/(c + v)]$ is, of course, always rising because of technological progress. Therefore, the rate of profit must fall. When the rate of profit begins to fall, capitalists react in a destabilizing manner by attempting to accumulate and reinvest additional surplus to make the production process more productive and more competitive. This process accelerates the rise of the organic composition of capital and the fall of profit which is at the base of the problem (Chaudhuri 1989, 49).

The volume of output keeps rising as a result of the accumulation of capital and a market has to be found for goods produced but not sold. The consumption goods, which are all wage goods, must be purchased by the working class. But the purchasing power of workers cannot be expanded continuously to absorb a growing volume of output. It tends to decrease as a result of the growing unemployment which is mostly reflected in the reserve army of labour. The consequence is growing stocks, falling prices, and falling profits, all of which lead to the general crisis and the collapse of the capitalistic system.

CONCLUSIONS

In concluding this chapter it is essential to highlight that Ricardian and Marxian economies, although for different reasons, lead to the common perception that there is a tendency for the rate of profit to decline with the accumulation of capital. In Ricardo, the rate of profit falls as a result of the increasing cost of producing wage goods and the growing rate of rent in total output, the combination of which leads to a stationary state. According to the Marxian theory, the causes are the changing organic composition of capital and the destabilizing reaction of the capitalist system to these changes. The consequence is a general crisis of the capitalist system that stops the continuation of growth. The capitalist crisis will give rise to revolutionary movements led by the working class and "reserve army of labour," which ultimately will transform the society into a socialist economy where everyone is equal and does not possess more than is required for a normal living under a socialist rule. Government controls and runs all the enterprises, owns the infrastructure and all natural resources, which are distributed equally to the population (unfortunately in an inefficient way).

Much has been said about the failure of Marxian predictions regarding the impoverishment of the work force. Given the considerable number of contributions in the theory of growth, it is believed that some of the neoclassical predictions, such as full employment or the economic instability of saving rates to influence long-run growth, have likewise not proven to be correct.

Another classical economist, J.S. Mill, assumed that a capitalist economy cannot grow without interacting with other economies. In fact, the rate of growth of capitalist countries has the tendency to fall toward minimum as a result of the increased costs of producing wage goods. But, according to Mill, the export of capital to the poorest countries – where capital is scarce while land is plentiful, making it possible to produce wage goods for trade more cheaply – would prevent the rate of profit from falling. The accumulation of capital and the amount of output would keep rising as a result of high returns on investments in underdeveloped countries. The more capital is sent to poor countries, the higher the rate of profit retained in capitalist countries. The phenomenon of capital exportation could, at least, defer crises, which would be favorable for capitalist economies.

2

The Beginning of the Modern Theory of Growth: The Neo-Keynesians

Harrod (1939, 1948) and Domar (1946) were the first Keynesians to develop macroeconomic models capable of formalizing the problems of growth. They emphasized in particular the relationship between the consumption-saving behaviour by households and the investment decision by entrepreneurs, although theories about these behaviours were not fully developed. In fact, the consumption-saving decision is defined, following the Keynesian approach, by an exogenously given propensity to consume, while the investment decision is defined by the multiplier coefficient.[1]

Harrod and Domar, following Keynes, believed that the market mechanisms would not be able to create full employment, so they chose to develop a theory of output rather than a theory of employment. Their view is focused mainly on the equilibrium of the goods market (which holds stable when savings are equal to the desired investment) rather than on the general equilibrium of goods and labour markets. An economy growing along a path of equilibrium in the goods market is said to be on its warranted growth path. The behaviour of investors and producers, however, can cause the warranted growth path to be unstable. If the warranted path also helps reach the full employment of labour, then the economy can achieve what is normally called the *golden age* of the growth path.

Another economist, who did not use models and formalizations but nonetheless made an important contribution to growth theory, was Joseph Schumpeter. Schumpeter attempted to introduce the role of entrepreneurship in the economics of investment decisions and business cycles. He worked mainly with neoclassical concepts and used them to analyze problems ignored by neoclassical theory. This chapter considers the beginning of the modern growth theory and the pioneering models of Harrod and Domar. A brief overview of Schumpeter's business cycles and economic development theory is also provided to help lay the groundwork for the later discussion of growth theories by Harrod and Domar.

It might be interesting to say two words about the neo-Keynesians. The term *neo-Keynesians* is often used to refer to those economists who belong to the school of macroeconomic thought that was developed right after the Second World War, inspired by the economic theories of John Maynard Keynes. In this neo-Keynesian context, Harrod and Domar developed their growth theories. In the late 1970s and early1980s, the Keynesian macroeconomics was hit by a series of developments, such as the slow economic growth and high inflation, which contributed to the decline of the neo-Keynesian theory. The combination of macroeconomic studies with microeconomic research such as consumer's behaviour and game theory gave to the Keynesian school a new development, which is often called the *New-Keynesian* economics. But some of the neo-Keynesians kept working on the macroeconomic Keynesian themes, despite the new developments, and were later labeled as *Old-Keynesians*. Kaldor and Pasinetti, in an "old" Keynesian perspective, developed their distribution and growth theories which will be discussed in the next chapter.

BEFORE THE STEADY GROWTH: ECONOMIC DEVELOPMENT AND BUSINESS CYCLES IN SCHUMPETER

The marginalist school developed late in the second half of the nineteenth century, bringing a change of perspectives in economic theory. The year 1848, in which the *Communist Manifesto* and the first edition of Mill's *Principles* were published, could be considered the conclusive moment of the classical period of growth analysis, which had lasted about a century. It would take another twenty years to see a new shift in economic theory – the advent of marginalist theory and the works of Jevons (1871), Menger (1871), and Walras (1874). The attention of economists shifted from the problems of growth to those of optimum resource allocation and welfare. Whereas the classical economists were interested in growth because they thought it was desirable to propose economic policies for the development of nations and countries around the world, the success of these policies and also the manifestation of new problems made economists lose interest in growth, and they "felt it increasingly necessary to direct their attention to the evils, or at least the blemish, of the existing system – inequality in the distribution of income and wealth, the growth of monopolies and combines, the trade cycle and unemployment" (Arndt 1978, 14).

Therefore, the classical theory of economic development, after delivering several theories in capital accumulation, was replaced by the concept of general equilibrium within an essentially static environment and from political economy to an economic science (Blaug 1968, 299–300). At that time, the neoclassical economists believed that the market forces, operating through variations in relative prices and substitution of production factors, were able to move to a new equilibrium toward full employment.

Rostow (1990, 153–64) recognized in the works of a few great prewar and wartime economists the precursors of growth models of the postwar period: Marshall (in particular, with the fourth book of his *Principles*, "The Agents of Production," set up an explicit and complex model of growth), J.B. Clark (*Essentials of Economic Theory*, 1907), and Gustav Cassel (*The Theory of Social Economy*, 1918).

From 1914, new problems of unemployment, imbalances in the interaction between payments and deflation, and the Great Depression forced economic research toward new elaborations. The result was a significant concentration on the problems of exchange rates, balance of payments, and unemployment as well as the approach of applying fast solutions to the most urgent problems, mainly following the Marshallian assumptions of short-term analysis. This did not, however, prevent mainstream economists from emerging with new works dedicated to growth theory. Colin Clark (*National Income and Outlay*, 1937) set up a new model of national income analysis under the influence of Keynes's *The General Theory of Employment, Interest and Money* (1936). Clark proposed that the accumulation of capital was not the only key to growth; he stated that "the very rapid expansion in productivity at the present time is taking place at a time of heavily diminishing capital accumulation," (Clark 1937, 43) so the growth should be found elsewhere, in the effects of technological progress and the growth of a generation of trained and experienced workers.

Simon Kuznets had already published the *Secular Movements in Production and Prices* in 1930. It was one of the few books published between 1870 and 1939 that was dedicated almost entirely to the process of growth. He recognized four determinant factors in the growth cycle: the growth of population, changes in demand, technological changes (including both mechanical and engineering progress), and improvements in business organization. Kuznets understood that innovation and a high degree of sector disaggregation was necessary for technological progress and growth.

Schumpeter's book *The Theory of Economic Development*[2] (1934 MIT edition, 1911 first German edition) was an enormous contribution to the theory of growth at the beginning of the twentieth century. In Schumpeter's view, all capitalist economies had two main characteristics: they were unstable and they experienced rapid growth. As a result, the development process is not easy and straightforward. In fact, he noted the following: "Development in our sense is a distinct phenomenon, entirely foreign to what may be observed in the circular flow or in the tendency toward equilibrium. It is spontaneous and discontinuous change in the channels of the flow, disturbance of equilibrium, which forever alters and displaces the equilibrium state previously existing" (Schumpeter 1934, 63–4).

The inventions are discontinuous revolutionary phenomena: what is the passage from an invention to an innovation? Schumpeter made explicit reference to five cases: introduction of new products, introduction of new methods of production, the opening of new markets, the discovery of a new source, and new types of organization within the industrial sector. In particular, these economic changes happen in an irreversible and revolutionary way – a creative destruction[3] where innovations overtake the obsolete and eliminate processes that are no longer effective and/or profitable.

Schumpeter was one of the earliest economists to study business cycles and the regular fluctuations experienced by developed economies. He emphasized the role of big capitalist concentrations (a term used in the 1930s for large-sized enterprises and industrial concentrations) and monopolies in the industrial growth and innovation process (Schumpeter 1942). This development has a cyclical and sectorial nature. The cycle is the "shape" assumed from economic downturns and upturns during the capitalist era. The innovations are not distributed regularly in time but rather appear in a discontinuous way or in clusters. In general, the first attempt of innovation by an entrepreneur is followed by others, and the innovation is then spread to the rest of the economy. The main effect of this process is the increase in investments, employment, real wages, and interest rates.

The transformation into entrepreneurial innovations, however, occurs in distinct waves because the economic, social, and institutional environment is resistant to change. A step forward occurs only after a considerable reservoir of new ideas is accumulated. Once a few entrepreneurs have broken through, success is then easier for others, at which point the reservoir is quickly emptied in a wave of innovation. The environment again resists further change until the innovative pressure in the reservoir has risen to the critical point. It is basically the Marxian mechanism of social dynamics but in the context of business cycles rather than class struggles.

Schumpeter identified three different types of concurrent cycles: First, there are short-run fluctuations of three to four years (Kitchen cycles). For one to two years, businesses would expand production and inventories to meet the demand for rising sales (Schumpeter 1939, 220). But when the growth of sales slows, inventories begin to remain in the warehouses, and as a result, the production is reduced for a year or two in order to decrease the inventory stock. When inventories return to more desirable levels and sales again rises, businesses would try to expand their stocks (Pressman 1999, 106–7). The second cycle is when there are changes in business investment in new plants and equipment, and it lasts around eight to eleven years (Juglar cycles). The productive expansion lasts from four to five years because businesses want to modernize and expand their capital equipment. However, after most businesses expand their production, they have no need for new investments. Accordingly, the new equipment and plants last at least four to five years and then they get obsolete. Consequently, another wave of investment boom starts, lasting four to five years. Third, Schumpeter considered long-run cycles that last forty-five to sixty years (Kondratieff waves). Invention and innovation are at the base of long-run cycles. During the period of slow growth, businesses struggling to keep up with slow or steady sales and market segments, would not be able to introduce new innovations, and thus new inventions and discoveries would be placed on hold for several years. Then after few decades when rapid growth finally begins, the stocked innovations are employed in the production process, and the economy grows quickly. Schumpeter considered the industrial revolution as the starting point of modern innovations in industry. For example, the inventories and discoveries of James Watt and Samuel Crompton Colt, such as the steam engine and spinning mule, in 1779–80 aided long-term economic expansion. The introduction of steel and railroad construction in the mid-nineteenth century then began a second Kondratieff wave. The third Kondratieff wave started in the early twentieth century where electricity, automobiles, and chemicals were introduced. Thus, innovations, in Schumpeter's view, are the main catalyst for investment.

In his early work, Schumpeter (1934 [1911]), assumed that invention was not an economic factor or at least was determined by non-economic forces. With this affirmation, he traced a demarcation between the concept of economic growth and that of economic development. The latter is assumed to have completed a fracture in the organization of the productive process. The reason for this fracture was the figure of the entrepreneur. Schumpeter introduced a new conceptual category not directly quantifiable, in this way innovating knowledge normally employed in the analysis of economic phenomena. The traditional stream of economic thought had, instead, constrained the theory of economic development to mere aspects of quantitative growth.

In his later work, Schumpeter (1942) supposed that innovation was created and driven by economic forces inside a large corporation. He believed that innovation was not a rational activity but a creative one that could hardly be explained as the result of a rational thinking process, and the mediator of innovation and invention was the entrepreneur. The entrepreneurs were willing to take risks by investing and introducing innovations in the production process. They were the dynamic force causing the capitalist economies to advance and grow. A large number of talented entrepreneurs would make the capitalist system prosper as a result of increasing number of innovations and new applications introduced by them. But, for different reasons if the entrepreneurial spirit was annihilated or hindered, capitalism would lose this dynamic force and transform itself into a system where government is the only driving force of the economy, which is socialism. Success, for Schumpeter, was satisfying the consumer's taste. Consumer preferences do not lead to production and innovation. They lead to the improvement in the quality of products. Innovation, however, leads to product development and new goods and services that consumers either reject or develop a taste for. Invention and innovation are the essential forces that push the economy in long-run cycles.

The vision proposed by Schumpeter for economic cycles and the relations among technological progress, innovations, and growth would become a fundamental point of reference for further research in this field.[4] The Kuznets and Schumpeter evidence, like the sectorial nature of economic development, the discontinuous and increasing process of technological progress, would mostly be taken into consideration in the new theory of growth in the postwar period. Then, nearly at the same time as the English translation of Schumpeter's work in 1934, another article was published in German that greatly influenced modern growth theory and was an attempt to provide some answers to the questions left unresolved. The creative destruction of the Schumpeterian vision followed the elegant equilibrium model of an abstract economy written by John von Neumann 1945 [1937]) a distinguished scholar of the twentieth century.

THE NEO-KEYNESIANS: HARROD AND THE PATH OF "WARRANTED RATE OF GROWTH"

Whereas Schumpeter had constructed a theory in which growth, technological progress, and unemployment were considered in the same context, a decisive push to reconsider the problems of economic growth and unemployment came from the Great Depression in the 1930s, when, in some ways, the political stability was threatened as well. There was an urgent need for a new economic theory capable of explaining if the market forces alone were able to lead the economy toward full employment.

The prewar and immediate postwar concern with the recurrence of deep depression strongly influenced both Harrod and Domar. The main problem Harrod faced was whether an economic system was able to have a stable growth with full employment of its workforce.

In the same year in which Schumpeter published *Business Cycles* (1939), Roy Harrod,[5] an economist at Oxford, developed the modern theory of growth. The basic concepts he used, however, were not new. Gustav Cassel, who was part of the group of "neoclassical" economists, had articulated the concept of an economy in balanced growth with unchanging structure, in which all components grow at the same time as the population (Cassel 1921). Despite the well-known fact that growth accelerates by technological progress, Cassel was convinced that it can proceed even with unchanged technology. He assumed that as more and more increasingly populous generations have to be equipped with capital goods, balanced growth requires saving, and capital accumulation may continue evermore without going into recession. In the early 1930s, business cycle research underwent a further development with the elaborate, dynamic models of Ragnar Frisch and Michael Kalecki. In 1937, another economist, Erik Lundberg, published an important work in the theory of growth called *Studies in the Theory of Economic Expansion*. Lundberg focused mainly on short-term fluctuations, but he also made a vast contribution to the problems of balanced growth. In particular, he assumed that all components of an economic system must grow at a constant exponential rate. This common growth rate must equal the ratio between the savings rate and the capital-output ratio. This is the core of the first modern theory of growth, or what later was called the Harrod-Domar model.

The publication of John Maynard Keynes's *The General Theory of Employment, Interest and Money* in 1936 influenced many economists. As a result, in the late 1930s the attention of economic theorists moved from the dynamics of growth to the statics of unemployment. Harrod did a great job of putting together Keynesian macroeconomics with the classical tradition of growth economics and providing the starting point for a modern theory of economic growth.

Harrod was in close contact with Keynes when Keynes was working on *The General Theory*. The two books Harrod published in the 1930s – *International Economics* (1933) and *The Trade Cycle* (1936) – brought his principal economic interest to the attention of professional readers. Trade cycles had previously been taken into consideration by several theorists, along Keynesian lines, as the interaction of the acceleration principle[6] with the multiplier[7] but they had never arrived at an explicit model. Here is where Harrod got involved by trying to resolve the interaction or the "marriage of the 'acceleration principle' and the 'multiplier' theory" (Sen 1970, 43). In effect, this is where Harrod made his first contribution to the theory of growth in 1939 with "An Essay in Dynamic Theory" and then later elaborated in *Towards a Dynamic Economics* (1948). Harrod's important papers of this period were later collected in a volume of essays published in 1952.

Harrod started from the observation, already prefigured in *The Trade Cycle* (1936), that a state with positive saving cannot be stationary. Positive saving involves investment, which in turn expands the productive capacity of the economy. He suggested that it may be possible to analyze a growing economy using essentially static techniques by simply pressing all magnitudes. In his 1939 article, in which Harrod described policy conclusions, he virtually assumed that an economic system was vulnerable to lapsing into a recession before reaching full unemployment because of a decline in the rate of growth of population, a rise in the savings rate, or a tendency of technological change and capital saving. In his 1948 work, *Towards a Dynamic Economics*, Harrod discusses some positive postwar developments, but both his short-run and long-run recommendations are still affected by the interwar pessimism that formed his dynamic system. Based on the concepts and methods of Keynesian short-run macroeconomics, Harrod concentrated his theory of growth on the necessary conditions required for equilibrium between aggregate saving and investment in a dynamic economy.

Therefore, the objective of the Harrod model of economic growth is to emphasize the necessary conditions for full-employment steady growth in a developed economy. This model considers three main issues: (1) the possibility of reaching steady-state growth at full employment, (2) the improbability of steady-state growth at full employment, and (3) the instability of the warranted rate of growth. Probably the best way to introduce Harrod's model is to start off with the fundamental dynamic propositions. The dynamic theory is assumed in two propositions: First, a unique warranted path of growth is determined jointly by the propensity to save and the quantity of capital required by technological progress ($g_w = s/w$).

Second, from both sides of this path, there is a "field" in which centrifugal forces operate, the magnitude of which varies directly at the distance of any point in it from the warranted path. Any kind of departure from the warranted path sets up an incentive to depart farther from it. "The moving equilibrium of advance is thus a highly unstable process" (Sen 1970, 54–5). In effect, here the main ideas of Harrod are expressed: the existence of a growth rate that permits the system to grow in equilibrium, and this rate is unstable. Simplifying, the type of the economy studied by Harrod is based mainly on six assumptions:

1. The relative prices are fixed but not necessarily constant, although, according to Hicks (1949, 106–21), they are constant. Harrod does not say anything about the changes in prices, implying to the reader that modifications in prices are probably not that important. Such an assumption is clearly unsatisfactory in the context of a general theory of economic growth, but it does give more precise meaning to different aggregates.
2. The interest rates are exogenous and constant. Harrod is rather skeptical about the "ability" of interest rates to determine the intensity of capital (the capital-output ratio) and saving. Harrod's analysis is

often concerned with the effects of modification of the interest rates, but given the ambiguity of the results he reached, he accepted the assumption of a constant interest rate.

3 The rate of marginal saving, s, is given.
4 C is the value of capital goods required for the production of a unit increment of output. C depends on the state of technology and the nature of goods constituting the increment of output.
5 The labour force, L, is assumed to grow at a constant exogenous rate, n. The assumption of exogeneity implies that the rate of growth of the labour force is completely uninfluenced by other components of the economic system.
6 Capital stock does not depreciate, and the technological progress is neutral.

Here it is considered a linear neoclassical production function with no technology, $Y = F(K,L)$, where Y is defined as output, K as capital, and L as labour. The question raised by Harrod is this: what are the conditions under which an economy can progress with a constant rate of growth in such a way that, in every moment, there is equilibrium between demand and supply and every agent in the market is satisfied with the decisions made? Formally, the model is made up of a few equations that represent the conditions of equilibrium, in which is contained what Harrod calls the axiomatic base of his theory. This theory consists of three propositions:

1 The level of a community's income is the most important determinant of its supply of savings.
2 The rate of increase of its income is an important determinant of its demand for saving.
3 The demand is equal to supply (Sen 1970, 43).

The equations that give the conditions of equilibrium are given as

$$I = \Delta K^d = C\Delta Y \tag{2.1}$$

or $(I = v\Delta Y)$

$$\text{and } I = S \tag{2.2}$$

where the symbol C[8] characterizes the ratio of capital stock to the flow of output. Equation (2.1) represents the increment in the capital stock associated with an increment in output required by entrepreneurs. Equation (2.2) delivers the general equilibrium condition of macroeconomics. It simply says that the aggregate planned investment must equal the aggregate planned saving. Saving is equal to the proportional savings function, calculated as a fraction of output, and is given as

$$S = sY \tag{2.3}$$

As for investments, using the "acceleration principle," we have

$$I_t = C\,(Y_{t1} - Y_{t0}) \tag{2.4}$$

where Y_{t1} is output at the period 1 and Y_{t0} is the output at the period 0. Combining (2.1) and (2.2), we get

$$sY_t = C\,(Y_{t1} - Y_{t0}) \tag{2.5}$$

from which we obtain

$$(Y_{t1} - Y_{t0})/Y_{t0} = s/C = g_w \tag{2.6}$$

where g_w is the rate of growth of output and satisfies entrepreneurs who are investing the correct amount. Using the symbol G_a for the actual rate of growth on national income over any period of time, the equation (2.6) can be rewritten as

$$G_a - \frac{s}{Cp} \tag{2.7}$$

where Cp is the value of the increment of capital per unit of output actually produced. Equations (2.6) and (2.7) imply that

$$G_a C_p = s = G_w C \tag{2.8}$$

If the actual rate of growth, G_a, equals the necessary rate of growth, G_w, then it is obvious that C_p must equal C, which is the required marginal capital-output ratio. In other words, if national output grows at the rate G_w, then the actual increase in capital stock will equal (associated with the growth of income) the increase entrepreneurs require for the production of the current level of national output. Harrod called the rate of growth, G_w, the "warranted" rate. If the output actually grows at the warranted rate, then the actual capital stock will also conform to the desired capital accumulation. Thus, there is no reason for entrepreneurs to increase or decrease the rate of growth of output. Harrod's conception of "warranted rate" is a particular notion of equilibrium growth, and the economy happens to follow this path. The model of Harrod here has been described through his original analysis completed in 1939, although a strong limitation of Harrod's work is the formalization of his theory. In his first article on growth theory, Harrod lacked a rigorous definition of investment function, probably because of his reluctance to use the expectations in the rate of growth explicitly. For example, Costa (1970) proposed another version of Harrod's model in which the future is connected to the present by entrepreneurs' expectations relative to the level of output.

A Simplification of Harrod's Model

It is assumed that C expresses the relationship between capital, K^d, required by the entrepreneurs and Y, the expected output, so it implies that

$$K^d = C(1+g_e)Y \qquad (2.1.1)$$

where g_e is the expected rate of growth. The equation that gives the rate of "warranted" capital accumulation is given as

$$\frac{I}{K} = g_e + h(C(1+g_e)\frac{Y}{K} \quad \text{where } 0 < h \leq 1 \qquad (2.1.2)$$

The entrepreneurs plan to invest in capital stock until the capital grows up at a warranted rate determined from the expected rate of growth and from the fraction of a proportional distance that separates the effective capital from the warranted rate of capital. Therefore, the equation that gives the savings rate relationship, S, takes the form as

$$\frac{S}{K} = \frac{sY(1+g_e)}{K} \qquad (2.1.3$$

The dynamics of a generic Keynesian model say that, in the short run, if investments exceed the savings the production should increase to meet the demand. In the long run, entrepreneurs will increase not the output but the rate of growth. Calling, g, the effective rate of growth, we get the following:

$$\frac{dg}{dt} = \phi\left[\frac{I-S}{K}\right] \text{ where } (0) = 0 \text{ and } \Phi\text{'} > 0. \tag{2.1.4}$$

It is assumed that the inverse of the relationship between capital and production, or the inverse of C, is x. If saving plans are always realized, the two fundamental equations representing the model are given as the following (where g is the derivative with respect to time):

$$\dot{g} = \phi\{(g_e - h) + [(1+g_e)C(h-g_e)]x\} \tag{2.1.5}$$

$$\dot{x} = x\left(g - \frac{\dot{K}}{K}\right) = x(g - s(1+g_e)x) \tag{2.1.6}$$

Finally, we make the assumption that the expected rate of growth is equal to the warranted rate of growth:

$$g_e = s/C = g_w \tag{2.1.7}$$

Studying this equation, it is observed that

$$\dot{g} \geq 0 \quad \text{if} \quad x \geq \frac{1}{C+s} \tag{2.1.8}$$

$$\dot{x} \geq 0 \quad \text{if} \quad g \geq \frac{s}{C}(C+s)x \tag{2.1.9}$$

(Costa 1970, 401–9).

HARROD'S INSTABILITY PRINCIPLE AND THE QUESTION OF UNEMPLOYMENT

Harrod suggested that the warranted rate of growth was basically unstable because the divergences of the actual rate of growth, *Ga*, would produce larger deviations from the warranted rate, *Gw*. He states,

> Suppose that there is a departure from the warranted rate of growth. Suppose an excessive output, so that G exceeds Gw. The consequence will be that Cp, the actual increase of capital goods per unit increment of output, falls below C, that which is desired. There will be, in fact, an undue depletion of stock or expansion. G, instead of returning to Gw will move further from it in an upward direction, and further it diverges the greater the stimulus to expansion will be. Similarly, if G falls below Gw, there will a redundance of capital goods, and a depressing influence will be exerted; this will cause a further divergence and a still stronger depressing influence; and so on. (Sen 1970, 52–3)

From equation (2.8), we see that the actual rate of growth, Ga, will be equal to the warranted rate, Gw, if the actual marginal capital-output ratio, Cp, equals the required capital-output ratio, C. So if Ga exceeds Gw, then C will exceed Cp . Conversely, if Gw exceeds Ga, then Cp will exceed C. This is the core of Harrod's instability problem. If the actual rate of growth exceeds the warranted rate, entrepreneurs will find that the increase in capital is actually less than required. Thus, there is a persistent discrepancy between the actual and desired capital stock.

The warranted rate of growth, Gw, that ensures the entrepreneurs' satisfaction also contemplates the possibility of an increase in involuntary unemployment. So, to avoid involuntary unemployment, the economy has to grow at the natural rate of growth, which is defined by assuming neutral technological progress.[9]

At full employment, the economy can only grow at the rate at which its labour force grows. Therefore, at full employment, $g = n + p$, where p is the rate of growth of labour productivity and n is the natural rate of population growth. The natural rate of growth represents the production path in which workers are satisfied because they realize a correct balance between work and time off. Harrod comments,

> In dynamics I have used the expression "natural rate of growth" for something that may be regarded as corresponding to an optimal static pattern (My "warranted" rate of growth corresponds to the equilibrium pattern of statistics) ... I conceive the natural rate of growth as being adapted to absorb any increase of population and any adjustments required by technological progress. I confess that there is some ambiguity in my concept in relation to the optimal

> distribution of effort between the provision of present and future needs; I have intended to imply that we could regard as optimal that distribution which was determined by the savings that individuals prefer to make when comfortably fully employed at each point on the line; but I am ready to admit that this subject requires further clarification. (Harrod 1953, 554. Based on Pilvin 1953)

According to Harrod, if the economy proceeded along the line of natural growth, people would be comfortably and fully employed at each point on the line. They would feel that the balance between work (reward) and leisure would correspond to their preferences (Harrod 1953).

The rate of productivity growth is the sum of entrepreneurial expectations with respect to their market prospects. The natural rate of growth, instead, is the product of demographic developments and, partly, of technological progress. Full employment is maintained if entrepreneurial expectations are influenced in a way to bring the warranted rate in line with full employment. The longer the economy has been at full employment, the easier it is to stay there. Conversely, the longer it stays away from full employment, the more difficult it is to restore it. The problem is that there is no direct relation between G and Gw. Because the mechanism that determines the value of these two rates does not have any relation, the equality (between G and Gw) can take place only by chance.

If $G \neq Gn$ enters into action, "the instability principle" brings the system into disequilibrium. Harrod wants to demonstrate that the same forces determining growth render the economic system unstable. He assumed that high productivity and population growth are not explained by endogenous variables but by exogenous ones. Technological progress affects the labour supply, conditioning the demographic rate in a positive way through the reduction of mortality. Conversely, during the classical economists' era, the increase in "natural rate of growth" was caused not by the rise of wages but by the decline of mortality (Harrod 1973, 25). Moreover, in the first place, the rate of technological progress is given exogenously and conditioned from the rapidity and ability with which entrepreneurs are able to use the new inventions for productive scopes, and therefore, Harrod notes,

> It is to be observed that the increase of capitalization required to secure this steady advance must *not* be supposed to be due to technological innovation requiring increased capitalism. Technological

> change is already catered by my theory of the steady rate of growth, and, I should suppose, by Mr. Hamberg's. To enable us to focus our minds upon the essential point it may be useful, merely for the sake of argument, to suppose that no technological change is occurring or at least no technological change that involves a net increase in the round-aboutness of productive methods. As the steady state of growth that we are considering corresponds to the equilibrium of statics, we have regard to the motives that actuate individuals in proceeding upon this path. Given the state of technology, the choice of productive methods is determined by the supply of prices of the factors. (Harrod 1953, 555)

Thus, the amount of technological progress and the rate of growth depend on the intelligence, imagination, and competence of the entrepreneurs (Harrod 1973, 27). The rate of natural growth, *Gn*, constitutes a limitation to the development of an economic system because it is not possible to maintain for an indefinite period the growth of the population and the prolongation of technological progress. Beyond the natural rate, Harrod thinks there are other corrective mechanisms that will enter into action once the system has accumulated enough instability. These will create the conditions for a possible reverse (1948, 144).

At any point at which $g \neq gw$, the entrepreneurs will be able to adjust the warranted rate of growth to the actual rate of growth based on past experience. For some reason it is believed that the warranted rate of growth is a pattern of expectations, not easily determined. Entrepreneurs will not be able collectively to learn to form a set of expectations in equilibrium. This implies, in some cases, the presence of analytical planning. In a "passive" labour market, like that imagined by Harrod and following the Keynesian theory, the dynamics of (involuntary) unemployment are regulated by the difference between the natural and the effective rates of growth. There are two distinguishing cases, accordingly, if the rate of growth is greater or smaller than the natural rate of development.

If $Gw>Gn$ is the case, the labour force grows less than is necessary. Considering a situation of full occupation, to assure a growth rate corresponding to *Gw*, the effective rate of growth must be inferior to the warranted one. The overall investment by entrepreneurs will be lower than required, and this state will lead to a recession. The inflationary and depressive trend, not finding stability, assumes the shape of an accumulative process.

Instead, if $Gw<Gn$, the labour force grows less than is demanded to maintain the warranted rate of growth, which is lower than the effective rate of growth. The entrepreneurs invest more than is required, and by the principle of acceleration, the increase of demand will be higher than their expectations, while the productive capacity will remain lower than desired to satisfy the increasing demand. Consequently, increasing inflationary tendencies will take place.

Harrod suggests that the solution to the instability principle requires a powerful tool to combat the tendency to oscillate. There are two remarkable points: first, the nature of measures suitable to combat the propensity to oscillate may depend on whether the natural rate is above or below the proper warranted rate; second, when the tendency to oscillate occurs, it may be advantageous to have a long-range policy designed to influence the relation between the warranted and the natural rate of growth (Sen 1970, 63).

In Harrod's model (1939), the condition that determines the equilibrium is more rigid than the uncertainty that characterizes the investors' decisions. The equilibrium of the warranted rate of growth is not stable. Instead, it is like a two-edged knife: once outside the equilibrium, the tendency is to move farther from it, and there is no return if not "by case" or accidentally. The normal state of the economy is thus instability. Moreover, the only form of technological progress capable of maintaining the equilibrium is the neutral state because every variation would provoke instability. In practice, the system grows in dimensions, but there is no development.

A full explanation of Harrod's model is found in *Towards a Dynamic Economics* (1948), although his first version was published in 1939. In 1960, he published the "Second Essay in Dynamic Theory," which basically includes the same idea of steady growth and the same Keynesian origin as his earlier publications. In this version, however, he reconsiders the equation for the warranted growth, $Cw= s/Cr$ (or $gw= s/w$), by emphasizing this time the idea that saving is taken as an independent variable, where its value depends on the convenience of individuals and companies to save or accumulate to finance themselves from their own profits. If individuals and firms, for personal motives, are unwilling to use the amount of saving for the needs of economy, then the warranted rate of growth is not equal to the natural rate. In addition, Harrod (1960) assumes the natural growth (Gn) as a welfare optimum, in which resources are fully employed and the best available technology is used.

He supposes that the "natural" rate itself is indeterminate unless the rate of interest is specified. Harrod sets out a second equation, which derives from a lecture by Ramsey (1928) on optimum saving,

$$rn = pcGn/e \tag{2.9}$$

where rn is the rate of interest appropriate to a natural rate of growth, $pcGn$ is the natural rate of growth per capital, and $e = (C1 - Co)/C1$ is the difference in consumption from year 0 to year 1 (e is considered normally as a weighted average); e can be expressed in terms of marginal utility of consumption as follows:[10]

$$e = u(C_1) - \frac{u(C_0)}{u(C_1)} \tag{2.10}$$

No redistribution of consumption from year 0 to 1 would increase utility. Gn is determined by the rate of interest and is given as $pcGn = f(rn)$. For Gn, there are two different propositions: first, if the rate of interest is low, more capital-intensive methods of production will be chosen by manufacturers or preferred by consumers, so a higher capital-output ratio will bring a higher output per person; second, if there is no full employment, then a drop in the rate of interest will increase the rate of unemployment (Harrod 1960, 280–3).

From equation (2.9), we see that the fraction of income actually saved, s, would tend to approximate the social requirement of savings, s_r. If the actual savings, s, exceeds the required rate of savings, s_r, the warranted rate of growth will be above the natural rate of growth.

Following Keynesian tradition, Harrod believed that market mechanisms were not able to attain full employment, so he focused his attention on the equilibrium of market goods, where saving is equal to the desired investment.

BACK IN TIME, BEFORE THE THEORY OF GROWTH THE PRINCIPLE OF INSTABILITY IN HARROD'S THEORY OF TRADE CYCLE

Harrod became famous with his model of growth in 1939, although in 1936, the year of Keynes's *General Theory*, he published the trade-cycle theory, which criticized the existing theories of cycles, especially the lagged relationship between income and saving. In this section, before concluding with Harrod's theory of growth, it will be interesting to give a short treatment of some questions he raised in trade-cycle theory, such as the principle of instability and steady advance that were incorporated later in his model of growth.

According to Besomi – who did profound research on the Harrodian trade cycle – Harrod was not in favor of Pigou's theory of cycles because it was based on the psychological approach of entrepreneurs in terms of waves of optimism and pessimism. The explanation of economic fluctuations, in Pigou's view, was mainly focused on the persistence of an error of judgment on the part of entrepreneurs rather than on dynamic forces leading to instability (Besomi in Rampa, G., L. Stella, and A. P. Thirlwall, eds., 1998, 110). The starting point was the position of stability. If equilibrium is stable, any deviation from it would set up forces to bring the system back into the initial position (the stable equilibrium), and the fluctuation would endure until these destabilizing forces are in operation. Harrod instead argued that the starting point is not the equilibrium position but the instability position itself; in fact, if equilibrium becomes unstable, any accidental force would depart from it and start a mechanism that could increase or reduce the original deviation. The accidental forces that depart from inside the system have no exogenous causes (Besomi 1998, 111–16). Harrod's view was that when a departure from equilibrium occurs the system increases its instability and tends to move farther from and not back to the equilibrium position. This was the "instability principle," which was taken into consideration later in his model of growth published in 1939. The necessity of introducing a destabilizing factor preceded the development of a trade cycle theory in logical and chronological terms (Besomi 1995). In Harrod's trade cycle the principle of instability, according to Besomi (1997, see also Young 1989), was applied twice.

First, it was applied to the static system of forces determining the level of output of individual producers. Analyzing the independent static determinants like decreasing returns, flexibility of prime costs, and the diminishing elasticity of demand, he deduced that these factors operate in a stabilizing sense. There is a fourth factor, the general price level, which then must act with a destabilizing power to neutralize the stabilizing effect of the first three static determinants. In Harrod's analysis, the equilibrium level of output is neutral, so any displacement between positions is possible.

Second, the instability principle was applied to dynamic forces determining the variations in the level of output. Harrod considered the starting point a condition in which a steady advance – when the ratio of output between two stages is constant – is in progress. For example, investments and consumption in a given period will increase in a proportionate rate over the preceding period. In addition, this depends on three dynamic determinants: the propensity to save, the shift to profit connected with a given advance of output, and the relation of capital per unit of output used in production. These determinants are dynamic because they characterize the rate of growth of output differently from the statistic determinants that are related to the level of output at a particular stage (Besomi 1998, 111–12). The dynamic determinants change their value according to the state of the economy, making it sometimes difficult to maintain the equilibrium. For example, the first determinant may be restrictive because individuals might choose to save a major proportion of income by diminishing the rate of investment, putting output close to the level of replacement. The second determinant, the shift to profit, depends on the behaviour of costs and on the behaviour of the elasticity of demand (Harrod 1936, 102). The third determinant, the proportion of capital goods to the output flow, would tend to rise at a constant rate of interest. If the rate of interest were to fall, this would produce an expansive force. The third determinant is the most likely (relative to other determinants) to work in an expansive sense if the first two are working in a restrictive sense. These forces operate in opposite directions until the steady advance is reached. Harrod's argument is that the determinants cannot maintain the equilibrium. If they do so, they do it by coincidence. For instance, a decline in the rate of steady advance involves a cut in investments and, in accordance with the multiplier, a consumption decrease. When the net investment begins its decline, the recession might reach the bottom, and the rise will start from there. The joint operation of the relation of capital per unit of output used in production (the third determinant) and multiplier should be broken out to avoid the recurrence of other slumps. The principle of instability is required to make the cycle work and is an essential component of Harrod's trade cycle mechanism. The "warranted rate of growth," described later in his work (1948), seems to be the state of moving to equilibrium. If the actual rate of growth diverges from the warranted rate there are forces (determinants) that via multiplier will bring the system to a further divergence until the bottom is reached. From this point, there is an upturn via accelerator by which multiplying coefficients change, bringing the system to reach the peak (ceiling). At this point, the warranted rate would surpass the actual rate, bringing up new forces to diverge from it, and the inverse process of recession will start over again.

The principle of instability, as a necessary condition for a dynamic motion, was applied to a system moving toward the state of equilibrium. The concept of equilibrium is explained by two ideas: first, as a balance of forces; second, as a principle where forces affecting the level of output are considered independently from the forces determining the variations of output. The concept of trade cycle in Harrod's view is about fluctuations in economic activities and output; the causes of fluctuations are found in the unstable forces leading the system.

INCREASING PRODUCTIVE CAPACITY AND GROWTH IN DOMAR: THE DOMAR MODEL

Domar's[11] theory of growth is frequently connected with that of Harrod because of the similarity between Domar's fundamental results and Harrod's essential equation. The conclusions assumed in Harrod's model are similar to those attained from Domar's model. For this reason, in recent economic literature, the two theories are often studied together. The main author of the neoclassical school, Solow, combined the contributions of two authors into one model, named the "Harrod-Domar model." Even Solow, however, who is considered the major person accountable for the neoclassical diffusion of the two models, had recognized that, "although their names are often mentioned together, the two versions have important differences. Harrod is more interested in the entrepreneurial expectations in an economic system able to reach the warranted growth. The analysis of Domar, instead, is connected more naturally to the recent ideas in the theory of growth" (Solow 1999b, 640).

Indeed, there are meaningful differences. In the first place, as emphasized by Solow, Domar's model does not contemplate an explicit theory of investments but is limited to considering the dynamics of the investment in the case of full employment in every period (Casarosa 1998, 780–1). Moreover, Domar, differently from Harrod, admitted that his model referred to the case of fixed coefficients of production only (Jossa 1993, 636). Finally, the principle of instability that constitutes the crucial result for Harrod is only briefly mentioned in Domar.

Harrod discussed some positive postwar developments in his 1948 work, but his short-run and long-run recommendations are rooted in the interwar Keynesian pessimism, especially for developing countries. In the same way, Domar, in his theory of growth published in 1946, reflected the current consensus among most economists that the postwar world economy would soon fall into depression unless rather vast countermeasures were undertaken by public authorities. This is because spontaneous investment is insufficient to maintain full employment. Domar proposed, essentially, that the growth of income should be guaranteed by public authorities on a scale such that the volume of total investment required for full employment must be generated via the accelerator; hence, a boost in investments would generate an increase in income. Domar examined the effects of investment on growth, passing from the analysis of the short run to that of the long run (Domar 1946). He introduced the idea of investment and saving by considering the dual nature of investment in a capitalist economy.

Therefore, Domar's objective is to focus visibly on the dual nature of the rate of investment:

1 Investment determines the actual level of income, *Y*, through the Keynesian multiplier process.
2 Investment, through capital stock accumulation, increases the maximum potential level of income (ignoring capital depreciation).

Given the constant average and marginal propensity to save, *s*, the output in terms of investment is written as

$$\frac{dY}{dt} = \frac{dI}{dt} \cdot \frac{1}{s} \tag{2.11}$$

where the investment, dI/dt, affects the productive capacity, *P*, which expresses the potentialities of the system in terms of output to generate an increase in the stock of capital. Investing in major sectors increases the productive capacity of the economy, and this process is given by the equation

$$P/K = \rho \tag{2.12}$$

where ρ has the following characteristics:

- It is concerned with the increase in productive capacity of the system
- It depends on production factors and the type of technology used, which will not remain constant
- It is a technical coefficient that relates investment and the maximum potential level of income able to produce capital.

The equation that gives the increase in the productive potential capacity takes the form

$$\frac{dP}{dt} = \rho\frac{dK}{dt} = \rho I \tag{2.13}$$

The equilibrium condition requires the potential productive capacity, P, to be completely used. The income, Y, must therefore be equal to the potential capacity of the production obtainable from the capital entrepreneurs have at hand ready to invest:

$$P = Y \tag{2.14}$$

Because we are interested in dynamics, to the previous static definition must be added another equation:

$$\frac{dP}{dt} = \frac{dY}{dt} \tag{2.15}$$

This equation expresses the necessity of equality between variations in the productive capacity and aggregate demand. The rate of investment must equal ρs. Defining with Io the starting investment, we have that

$$I_t = I_0 e^{\rho st} \tag{2.16}$$

where ρs is the equilibrium rate of growth (Domar 1946, 142). Both s and ρ are assumed constant. The rate of growth of investment that maintains the actual income is a constant proportional rate of ρs. If ρs is constant, the preservation of full employment requires investment to grow at a constant compound interest rate (Domar 1946). The only way to avoid excesses or deficits in productive capacity is to make sure that the flow of investments grows at a constant rate, ρs. This is the rate of growth that leaves the entrepreneurs satisfied because they are using the maximum productive capacity acquired through investments. This process is similar to Harrod's warranted rate of growth, *Gw*.

In Harrod, we have seen that there is no certainty that the warranted rate of growth equals the natural rate of growth, which would assure full employment. Alternatively, in Domar, the guaranteed growth of income, σ, in a state of full employment is maintained if investment and income grow at an annual rate, ρs, without any reference to the rate of growth of the labour force (Jones 1975, 64). The economy starts from an equilibrium position of full employment, where the rate of growth of investments is equal to ρs and to the warranted rate of growth:

$$\sigma = s \tag{2.17}$$

In this case, σ is reasonably close to *s*. The amount of investment will equal the volume of savings, and the system will be in equilibrium.

If $\sigma < s$, the guaranteed rate of growth is smaller than the natural rate, so the investment will probably fall short of savings and the equilibrium will be destroyed. Domar (1946) does not speak about instability but instead focuses on the unemployed capital (idle capital). He asserted, in a phrase that contains a nascent idea of the Harrodian principle of instability, that "*the unemployed capital is extremely important, because its presence inhibits new investment*," (Domar 1946, 145) encumbering, in this way, the full employment equilibrium.

THE PROBLEM OF CAPITAL ACCUMULATION IN DOMAR

After the Second World War, the majority of economists, especially those who believed in the Keynesian revolution, were concerned about the problem of capital accumulation. They were convinced that the amount of capital the economy could absorb at a given level of income and over a period of time was limited. The higher capital accumulation was exhausted in investment opportunities, and depression often was ensured. Domar's view, along with other scholars of the postwar period, was that there exists a stable relationship between a given amount of annual output (income) and the stock of capital needed to reproduce it. The ratio of these magnitudes, *k* (annual output/capital stock), is supposed to be stable. Despite this, the distribution of income between labour and capital is not taken into consideration. The stability of *k* is a necessary but insufficient condition for the capital stock accumulation to be reproduced. There is also a need for a stable propensity to save, *s* (in the original paper 1948, Domar indicates it by α).

A stable *k* implies that at any given level of income, there exists a determinable stock of capital able to reproduce itself (Domar 1948, 779). If there is a faster capital accumulation, the saturation point will be reached quickly, and then investment will be undertaken only in response to dynamic changes, such as the emergence of new methods of production, population growth, or changes in tastes and habits. These changes may alter the value of *k*, probably lowering it, thus causing a relative shortage in capital stock. A lack of capital stock means a drop in investment and a recession. Domar supposes an increase in the rate of investment via the multiplier, but only for a while because afterwards it will fall, quickly impeding prosperity. Domar, like Harrod, had no doubt that the rate of growth is a function of two factors: the propensity to save, *s*, and the ratio of output to capital, *k*.[12] A higher *s* means that a large amount of income is invested to maintain full employment and to assure a further rise in income. Likewise, a large *k* means that more output can be produced, which helps to increase income. Regularly, in a capitalist economy, capital and the existing facilities are replaced by new investment and by new plants. If the junking (futile) capital is processed on a large scale, it inhibits new investment. However, to abandon this process completely is impossible. The total output would grow at the rate of growth, given as *sk* (the propensity to save times the ratio of output to capital). The question raised by Domar was whether the income would be able to grow at the relative annual rate of *sk*. In fact, he stated, "We should make a clear distinction between *can* and *will*. If income cannot grow at the required rate, it clearly will not. But if it can, there is no assurance that it will. The failure to distinguish between these two aspects of the problem has been a source of considerable confusion" [italics in original (Domar 1948, 782).

The economy would like to enhance the national income at the required rate, but actually it does not happen in this way. In a capitalist society, investment is influenced by a number of rational factors and depends significantly on various dynamic changes not easily predicted. The presence of frequent and sharp dynamic changes makes excessive accumulation of capital less important because some industries expand at the expense of others. On the contrary, less investment will ensure a decrease in output. Domar, in a different way from Harrod, considers dynamic changes, rather than the instability process, in the system. The best way to assure a guaranteed growth of income in a capitalist economy is to encourage investment by different plans, such as incentive taxation, liberal loss offsets, accelerated depreciation, or scientific and industrial research. If the government decides that the economy is going to grow at a required rate for some time to come (encouraging investment), this objective will be also taken seriously by the business community. The government guarantee may call on businesses for sufficient investment to reach the required rate of growth and assure full employment. Normally, when the government decides the rate of growth in the coming years, it takes as a base the growth of the population (for some industries). Therefore, industries planning along the lines of the rates of growth proposed by the government would probably invest more and could expect a growing economy. Domar indirectly assumes that the economy approaches the natural rate of growth, although the problem of stabilization of capital accumulation remains.

THE IMPORTANCE OF CAPITAL DEPRECIATION AND REPLACEMENT IN A GROWING ECONOMY

At the beginning of the 1950s, capital depreciation was another topic developed devotedly by Domar. The concept of capital depreciation is important because a large part of current investment is needed to keep the capital stock intact. It became more important in industrialized countries if investment was not seen as an employment-creating device but instead as the core of the capitalist system and as a solid base for a growing economy and capital regeneration. Domar argued that the investment net of depreciation is not the same as investment net of replacement (1953). He suggested that existing growth models, which had taken this identity for granted, should be revised. Except for the propensity to save and the capital coefficient, a major role in capital replacement is played by the life span or the duration of capital.

By assuming that investment equals \$1 *m* years ago, we see that its growth over the last *m* years can be expressed as a geometric expression: $1, (1 + r), (1 + r)^2, \ldots (1 + r)^{m-2}, (1 + r)^{m-1}$. Its sum over a period of *m* years – that is, the present gross stock of capital – equals

$$\frac{(1+r)^m - 1}{r}$$

with D being 1/mth of the present stock of capital, is equal to

$$\frac{(1+r)^m - 1}{r}$$

Dividing this function by $G = (1 + r)^{m1}$, we get the expression (Domar 1953, 4)

$$\frac{D}{G} = \frac{1 - \frac{1}{(1+r)^m}}{rm} \qquad (2.18)$$

which indicates the relation among annual depreciation, D, gross investment, G, and the annual rate of growth, r. Using t to indicate the length of time that passes from the initial period and $t<m$, we have the following:

$$\frac{D}{G} = \frac{1 - \frac{1}{(1+r)^t}}{rm} \qquad (2.19)$$

The final value of D/G in a continuous form implies

$$\frac{1 - e^{-rm}}{rm} \qquad (2.20)$$

where m indicates the average life span of all assets (Domar 1953, 4–6). The role of m explains that longer-lived capital reduces the charge of depreciation. Higher r reduces the D/G ratio. In effect, the value of r is not so clear. Domar is conscious of this fact. A higher r means that the magnitude of investments in the past has been great; thus, the existing stock of capital should be reduced.[13] With stable prices, it is proven that an average American firm should be able to finance nearly two-thirds of its fixed capital requirements from depreciation. Capital depreciation was important for the American economy to keep intact the stock of capital without diminishing the rate of growth, especially after the Second World War. The relationship between replacement and gross investment and the relationship between replacement and depreciation are given as

$$\frac{R}{G} = \frac{1}{(1+r)^m} \tag{2.21}$$

and
$$\frac{R}{D} = \frac{rm}{(1+r)^m - 1} \tag{2.22}$$

where R is the rate of replacement (in the case of constant prices; Domar 1953, 7). The excess of D over R is caused by the growth of G over the period of m years. The disparity between D and R will be greater when r and m are larger. R/D varies inversely with r and m. In the same way, D/G varies inversely with their products. In the case of changing prices, the equations (2.21) and (2.22)[14] assume the following forms:

$$\frac{R}{G} = \frac{(1+i)^m}{(1+r)^m} = \frac{1}{(1+u)^m} \tag{2.23}$$

and
$$\frac{R}{D} = \frac{rm(1+i)^m}{(1+r)^m - 1} = \frac{m(u-i)(1+i)^m}{[1+(u+i)]^m - 1} \tag{2.24}$$

where u is the rate of price increase given by $i = r - u$. From the equation (2.24), we have that an increase in m intensifies the effect of price changes on R/D (Domar 1953, 9–10). If prices fall, then R/D falls. If prices rise, an increase in m may move R/D up or down, depending on the relative magnitudes of the variables involved. An increase in the R/D ratio means (when prices are up) that a larger part of depreciation is needed for replacement. This effect is inflationary. Similarly, in the case of a decrease in the R/D ratio, we have the phenomenon of deflation. In this case, there is not much need for replacement. This practice of charging depreciation on the basis of original cost of capital, according to Domar, brings instability into the system. He demonstrated that, in an economy such as that of as the United States, apparently there is no equality between R and D because of the rise in prices (Domar 1953, 12–13). Normally, the concentration of depreciation charges in the first few years of the life of an asset increases the disparity between D and R. If the productive capacity of the asset declines gradually over time, its replacement by other assets is a gradual process, so it is more probable that R and D would become identical. In the case of the United States and other Western countries, assets usually are well maintained and retired more in response to technological obsolescence rather than physical deterioration. But if an asset's capacity should decline particularly fast in the early years, replacement will precede depreciation. Some models in the theory of economic growth, such as those of Harrod or Fellner, have been built assuming that depreciation and replacement expenditures are equal. Domar argued, however, that as the divergence between *D* and *R* caused by growth and price changes is recognized by empirical studies, the revision of these models is necessary. In fact, he proposed that the capital coefficient, *C*, of Harrod's growth model can be expressed in terms of depreciation and replacement. Hence, an increase in capacity in terms of gross national product, *P*, should be proportional to net investment. He called this the factor of proportionality, where the capital coefficient *C* is expressed as $C = (G - R)/\Delta P$ (*G* indicates gross investment); while including the depreciation, *D*, it is expressed in the following form: $G - D/\Delta(P - D)$ (Domar 1953, 14). As a result, the productive capacity of an asset is always proportional to its net depreciated value.

Domar argued that the subject of depreciation and replacement is very important and must be part of growth models. Many economists, for the purpose of building up perfect models, often fail to take into consideration the problem of replacement, which is significant for industrialized countries. In the United States, for example, 50 per cent of investment expenditures are made for replacement purposes, and in the postwar period (1947–51), depreciation charges exceeded personal savings by a ratio of almost three to one.

Domar uses the case of accelerated depreciation in firms with high fixed investment as a possible method for helping their growth. Normally, an accelerated depreciation has a higher rate of amortization in machinery and fixed assets than the normal one and stimulates investment for both expansion and replacement. It is an alternative method – different from tax reduction or capital cost allowance – to stimulate growth and new investment. Accelerated depreciation, like tax relief, must encourage companies in difficulty during the first years of their existence.

Domar is convinced that accelerated depreciation is better than a lower tax rate. Accelerated depreciation, for some reasons, may intensify economic fluctuations; it will encourage investment when profits are high and have tax relief effects in the absence of profits. The accelerated amortization during a boom is helpful because it will leave little-depreciation to charge during a recession. Furthermore, it will minimize tax benefits during the boom period and maximize them during the recession. Domar was one of the first authors in the postwar period to treat the problem of depreciation and replacement as an important factor for growing economies. Despite his attempts, however, these variables were neglected in most growth models.

HARROD AND DOMAR: SIMILARITIES AND DIFFERENCES

The models of Harrod and Domar are often dealt with jointly as the "Harrod-Domar model" because of the similarities in the central results. The remarkable achievement of the Harrod-Domar model is that it studies long-run problems with usual short-run tools (Solow 1956, 66). The common assumption is that production takes place under conditions of fixed proportions, and the possibility of substituting labour for capital is not taken into consideration.

For Harrod, steady-state growth at full employment requires the warranted rate, s/C, to equal the natural rate, n. For Domar, ks is the equilibrium rate of growth that will ensure the maintenance of full employment without any explicit reference to the rate of growth of the labour force. Domar's model does not consider an investment function. His equilibrium growth rate is the rate that would optimize the productive capacity, thus ensuring the equality of actual and potential income.

It is important to note the following: In both the Harrod and Domar models the equilibrium condition is based on a proportional rate of growth of the economy. They both assume the equivalent of a constant capital-output and they both imply long-run difficulties in reaching equilibrium growth at full employment. The long-run difficulties in Harrod come mostly because of the market mechanism failure to ensure the equality of the warranted and natural rates of growth. In Domar, instead there is a persistent tendency to underinvest so that the growth equilibrium cannot be attained. Both models have also an element of instability, although it is expressed in different ways. The core of Harrod's instability problem is that the actual rate of growth exceeds the warranted rate, and the entrepreneurs discover that the increase in capital stock is less than the required increase. Thus, there is a persistent discrepancy between the actual and desired capital stock. In Harrod, instability is seen as an interaction of the investment function and the fundamental equation (which is the entrepreneurial expectations) (Jones 1975, 65).

Conversely, in Domar investment incentives are continually in decline, and the presence of frequent and sharp dynamic changes make a steady capital accumulation difficult. Both models assume a constant capital-output ratio; both models imply a constant proportional rate of growth of the economy; and both models involve long-run growth, and the equilibrium is attained at full employment. However, the mechanisms of reaching the equilibrium are the short-run tools, such as the accelerator or the coefficient of the capital-output ratio. In Harrod's model, there is no mechanism to ensure the equality between the warranted and the natural rate of growth. The system, in general, is unstable. Conversely, in Domar, the unemployed capital inhibits new investment, and there is a chronic tendency to low investment. Both models are Keynesian because they move from a short-run to a long-run growth period and use the capital coefficient as a derivation of the multiplier principle, which is a short-run mechanism.

HARROD AND DOMAR: SOME CONCLUSIONS

Harrod and Domar were the most important references in the pioneering period of the modern growth theories. At this early stage, the notion of applying growth theory seems to have been closely related to the provision of rough guidelines for economic policy, but the matter of application did not receive special attention from theorists and, consequently, from policy-makers. In Harrod, the applied side of his model exclusively involves manipulation of the "warranted rate of growth" through the use of anticyclical policies that would firmly influence the expectations of entrepreneurs and new investments. In the same way, Domar (1946), by discussing the application of his model, limited himself to brief comments on policy consequences, which consist basically of supporting compensatory measures of public policy to increase investment. Domar (1957) acknowledged, however, that for the attainment of a "practicable theory of growth," a middle way between general treatises and simplified symbolic models exists. He advocated the inclusion of less formal variables and emphasized the creation of consistency as a precondition for the successful use of growth models. Despite their apparent relevance, caution was involved in the use of different models. The difficulty of growth models remains in linking the increasing demand for goods and services with other variables and their expression in terms of mathematical equations. Generally speaking, the mainframe of a model or a theory consists of taking from reality the right variables and assembling them together in an "astute" way for the purpose of presenting reality. Domar writes,

> However difficult it was to express the rate of growth of the demand for goods and services in terms of a few relatively simple variables, our task on the capacity side is even more complex – and the result much less reliable. Everything is involved here: the growth of the labor force and the change in its composition, hours worked, training and skills of the workers, amount of effort, institutional conditions, geographical movements, accumulation of capital, and the most important and also most elusive of all variables, technological progress in the broad sense, which changes the character of labor and of capital and of everything else. The nature of these factors and of changes in them are still very imperfectly understood; nor can most of them be analysed in isolation from demand side, because whatever may be said about population change, investment and technological progress are undoubtedly responsive to movements in demand ... The construction of a model or of any theory, for that matter ... consists of snatching from enormous and complex mass of facts called reality, a few simple easily manageable key points which, when put together in some cunning way, become for certain purposes a substitute for reality itself. (Domar 1952, 484)

Domar provides a good illustration to support the idea that different uses of growth theories are related to different styles of argument. He discusses the view that continuous government borrowing might result in ever-rising public debt, which in turn would require increasing taxes. He builds up some numerical examples to examine the behaviour of the tax rate over time under alternative assumptions (Domar 1957, 45–78). He also calculates the evolution of the tax rate and the ratio of debt to national income for given original values of debt and income. Domar's applied economics lies in a descriptive and numerical style of argument concerning theoretical outcomes that could provide a basis for successful growth policies.

Harrod's view of the theory of growth was that it was pure theory, which could in same cases be applied in a real economy. He seems to have maintained throughout his life the vision that"we shall continue in consequence, to formulate well based principles in applied economics that policy makers can understand and act upon" (Harrod 1973, 101). Growth theory, in Harrod's "specter," is a "political economy" dimension embracing a greater range of factors typically specified by statistical measurement. Both Harrod and Domar were, in some sense, partisans of the Keynesian revolution and, naturally, incorporated many special Keynesian features in their models (Jones 1975, 66). Harrod and Domar, following Keynes, believed that market mechanisms are not able to attain full employment, so they focused on the equilibrium of market goods – which holds when savings are equal to the desired investment – rather than the general equilibrium of goods and the labour market.

Harrod is skeptical of the influence of interest rates on the method of production. He does not take into consideration the assumption, presumed by many Keynesians, that the fall in the interest rate will increase the capital per unit capacity when technological conditions allow the variation.[15]

The influence of the Harrod-Domar approach has been so widespread that today it is one of the most popular and common models of the theory of growth; in fact, it can be found in every textbook on growth theory. An important contribution of Harrod's theory was his emphasis on the role of entrepreneurial expectations as a central source of difficulty for the attainment of full employment in a warranted path of growth.

The Harrod-Domar approach is based mainly on the rigidity of its assumptions and the simplicity of its construction. The variables are assumed to be exogenously determined, but both Harrod and Domar were explicitly searching for simple relationships relevant to the dynamics of the macroeconomy, although, substantially, they were not very realistic. Even though their purpose was to isolate and develop some of the problems concerning growing economies, their assumptions and tools were not appropriate. Solow states: "The characteristic and powerful conclusion of the Harrod-Domar line of thought is that even for the long run the economic system is at best balanced on a knife-edge of equilibrium growth ... But this fundamental opposition of warranted and natural rates turns out in the end to flow from the crucial assumption that production takes place under conditions of fixed proportions" (Solow 1956, 65). Once the assumption of non-substitution between labour and capital is abandoned, the "knife-edge" notion of unstable balance goes with it. Because of this, the "vision" associated with their theories was not so credible in the view of other theorists. The relative prosperity of Western economies after the war, however, and the boom that characterized most industrialized countries in the late 1950s and the beginning of the 1960s have led many economists to suggest that the most convincing reason for doubting the Harrod-Domar model is that it simply does not fit the reality in different countries. Sometimes it seems that the line of thought in the Harrod-Domar view would imply that the economy is in a state of depression rather than in steady-state growth. But, fortunately, the world economy did not plunge into a great postwar depression as happened in 1929. By the mid-1950s, the US economy had emerged with vivacity from the Korean War, the western European countries had experienced an exceptional rate of growth after the Marshall Plan, and the Japanese economy passed from a surprising recovery to an astonishing surge of sustained growth. In this context, there were a number of economists who began to think that the fragility of growth in the advanced world may have been overcome, and several among them explored forces endogenous to the economy that might react to movements away from dynamic equilibrium in ways that were able to bring it back in to track or to a steady growth path (Rostow 1990, 333–5). These economists developed a new approach to the analysis of the growing economy – the so-called neoclassical theory of growth. The pioneering economists of these new theories were Tobin, Solow, Swan, and, without a doubt, Meade, who published the first textbook of neoclassical growth theory in 1961.

3

Theory of Distribution and Growth: The Old Keynesians

Harrod and Domar did not take into consideration the relation between growth and distribution, as they were more concerned with the determination of the growth rate in a depressed economy rather than the distribution of income among different groups in the society. For many post-Keynesian economists, the relation between distribution and growth has been too close, and one such approach was investigated by a number of scholars from Cambridge in the United Kingdom, particularly Kaldor, Pasinetti, Mirrlees, and Robinson. The view of the Cambridge school is that the theory of growth is indivisible from the theory of distribution.

The contribution of these economists has been to advocate a different concept of applied economics, in a certain sense evoking Alfred Marshall. For Marshall, the application of economics implies the isolation of a particular situation and the conjunction of all the different aspects related to that situation (Marshall 1923). Within this perspective, the role of statistical analysis is limited to some inputs into the general framework of the application of the theory, where the main objective is to provide concrete guidelines for historically determined situations. The "old Keynesians," such as Kaldor, Pasinetti, and Robinson, attempted to call attention to the issue of income distribution as an important determinant of saving and growth. Kaldor in particular argued that the basic difficulty with the neoclassical approach to growth and distribution lies in the definition of capital as a factor of production. He proposed a new referential unit for an empirical assessment of his theory that was meant to give new light to the definition of capital in neoclassical applied economics.

In this chapter, the theories of income distribution developed by two well-known economists, Nicholas Kaldor (1956) and Luigi Pasinetti

(1962), are introduced briefly. But first let us have a quick look on how cyclical fluctuations and economic growth are connected.

THE RELATIONSHIP BETWEEN ECONOMIC GROWTH AND CYCLICAL FLUCTUATIONS

Kaldor[1] was skeptical about the ability of a capitalist economy to grow with full employment. Therefore, he made greater efforts than Robinson to account for the proper conditions of steady-state growth.[2] Kaldor's view, inspired by Schumpeter's trade cycle theory and Keynes's *General Theory*, was that there is a connection between cycles and historical boom periods. He proposed the idea that cycle and dynamic growth are intrinsically connected: the cycle cannot occur if there is lack of progress. He emphasized that the Keynesian investment demand is not an independent variable but rather a function of the existing stock of capital and the current rate of output. The current rate of output, however, depends (via the Keynesian multiplier) on current investment, whereas the current change in capital stock depends on the past investment.

He proposed a kind of "static" trade cycle, with constant forces or movements and an absence of dynamic changes such as technical innovation, population growth, or institutional framework (Kaldor 1954, 56). The whole movement and its duration are determined by the parameters of the system. The cycle has four phases: an upward phase, a boom phase, a downward phase, and a depression phase. The first and third phases are believed to be relatively short in duration in relation to the second and fourth phases (Kaldor 1954, 56–7). According to Kaldor, the duration of the boom phase and the depression phase is a matter of relationship between the investment-goods industries and the regular annual depreciation of capital stock. If the output capacity was twice as large as normal depreciation, the duration of the boom and depression phase would be identical; if it was more than twice as large, the depression phase would last longer than the boom phase, but if it was less than twice as large, the depression phase would be shorter than the boom phase. The length of the boom depends on the annual output capacity of the equipment-goods industries in relation to the capital stock, the innovating phase of entrepreneurs, and the Keynesian multiplier, which determines the extent of utilized capacity during the boom and depression period. The duration of the depression depends on the rate at which existing capacity is reduced by scrapping the old equipment and replacing it with new (Kaldor 1954, 57–8).

The length of the boom in relation to the length of the cycle depends on the relationship between the average annual depreciation of capital stock and the annual output of capital goods. The capacity of capital-goods industries is an important factor in the whole mechanism of the boom phase, because it determines the rate of capital accumulation. The greater this factor is, the shorter the duration of the boom and the greater the amplitude of cyclical movement. If the capacity of capital-goods industries with respect to consumer-goods industries is assumed to be dependent on the proportion of income saved at full employment, then the cycle mechanism is determined by the short-run savings function. Typically, if the marginal propensity to save is assumed to be constant, then the average propensity to save is a rising function of income in the short run (Kaldor 1954, 60–1). If the maximum rate of investment during a boom period – determined by the actual capacity of the capital-goods industries – is less than the investment needed for full employment output, the amplitude and character of cyclical movement is determined simply by the character of the short-run savings function. Kaldor emphasizes that capital stock and output determine the phase of the cycle. The trend is a linear percentage growth in population over time. This means that the amount of capital in each successive boom is higher than in the previous boom, while the capital used in the depression phase is consistently smaller than the capital created in the previous boom phase. For Kaldor, two factors are important in a trend: technological progress and the growth of population. These two factors are additive, and the trend is the result of the two, because the rate of growth of full employment output is the sum of increase in productivity and population.

The accumulation of new investment opportunities over time is another factor that leads to a periodic boom. Kaldor argued that the fundamental motive of the boom phase is that (Kaldor 1954, 63),

1 the output capacity of the investment-goods industries is greater than the current rate of new investment opportunities;[3] and
2 the economic system possesses no short-run stability at levels of investment that are below a certain maximum or above a certain minimum.

An economy that shows high rates of growth over long periods is a system that is almost approaching the full employment ceiling and does not expand until it comes up against the physical limitations of capacity or the scarcity of labour. Scarcity of labour may stimulate two growth variables:

1 Population growth through immigration and through a higher effective rate of natural growth;
2 Technological progress through the innovation of labour-saving machines.[4]

However, it is not only the rate of growth that determines the duration of booms, but also the strength and duration of booms that outline the trend and amount of the rate of growth. The process of over-expanding during the boom makes recession inevitable. The same cyclical forces that cause booms to end after a time and convert them into slumps also cause slumps to end and convert them into new booms (Kaldor 1954). In other words, the boom eventually must end and the recession must turn to a new boom. The Kaldorian cycle is like a "vicious cycle," in which all internal and external factors help the economy to take the same course. There are no deviations, or if there are, they are inside the cycle. The long-term growth instead depends on the degree of irresponsibility of entrepreneurs. Kaldor had a Schumpeterian view of long-term "conditioning factors" such as the attainable rate of saving, the maximum attainable rate of population growth, and the maximum attainable flow of new ideas. He asserted, "The *actual* values of these variables in any given society and at any given age, are not determined by their theoretical maximum values, but are capable of being slowed down or accelerated in accordance with the push or pull exerted by entrepreneurial behaviour" (Kaldor 1954, 69).

The trade cycle and economic growth are the result of particular attitudes of entrepreneurs, and both depend on entrepreneurial expectations. Trade cycle depends on long-term investment decisions, current profits, and positive long-term expectations. It is the higher volatility of entrepreneurial expectations that makes the expansionary period of the cycle likely to be vigorous and sustained. The cessation of investments after the boom, however, does not mean a return to the bottom of the previous slump. Instead, the slump now has a higher "floor" than before, and the "full-employment-ceiling" between successive booms is itself conditioned by the wave of optimism in booms (Kaldor 1954, 67).

Kaldor – differently from Hicks, who considered the trend rate of growth as the only important factor of cyclical mechanism, and from Harrod and Domar, who stated that warranted growth rate (*g*) and natural rate of population are the only factors for a sustained growth trend – pointed out that the growth and cyclical fluctuations depend on all these factors and added another factor that is the most important feature for a cycle: Schumpeter's hero, which is the "innovating entrepreneur" and entrepreneurial expectations.

THE THEORY OF DISTRIBUTION AND GROWTH IN KALDOR

Kaldor's theory of economic growth was proposed in a series of papers (six altogether, but the most important were four printed in 1954, 1956, 1961, and 1962) published between the mid-1950s and 1960s.

Kaldor was one of the first economists after the Second World War to suggest a Keynesian theory of macrodistribution, to which he then added a technological progress function and a particular investment function. He believed that, in a process of growth with full employment and full utilization of capacity, it is impossible to separate the problem of income distribution from that of growth. The economy cannot grow, in real terms, more rapidly than the natural rate of growth.

Kaldor suggested that it is not saving, investment, technological progress, and population growth (being just features of growth) that cause growth but rather the attitude of investing by society and, in particular, by entrepreneurs. He criticized the Harrod-Domar model on the ground that it explains only the growth of a non-cyclical economy with full employment rather than the actual rate of growth that does not maintain a stable equilibrium. His view was that, in a system characterized by successive booms and slumps, the actual trend is determined by the "natural rate" of growth (Kaldor 1954). Kaldor's main role in economic growth was the income distribution theory, and his major contribution was in solving in an original way the stability problem of the Harrod-Domar model. This is achieved by allowing the system to grow along the natural path of growth through adjustments in the rate of savings as a result of changes in distributive shares between wages and profits (or between the owners of profits, workers, and capitalists) and by assuming that the rate of population growth is constant.

A special feature of the post-Keynesian growth models, which Kaldor as well as Pasinetti share with Harrod and Domar, concerns the capital-output ratio, which is constant. This is not a simplified hypothesis but rather an essential property of these models. Kaldor made the greatest effort to legitimize the assumption of a constant capital-output ratio and tried to give an empirical justification as well as a theoretical explanation. From historical observation, he came to the conclusion that in the course of its evolution, capitalist accumulation had been governed by a series of empirical regularities, which he defined as "stylised facts"(Kaldor 1961, 177–8). Particularly important are those relating the constancy of wage share and profit rate to the properties of steady-state growth models.

Kaldor published his first model on growth and distribution in 1956. A simple presentation of this model is the following:

The objective of Kaldor's theory of growth and distribution is to find out that the rate of return on capital depends on the rate of growth and on the distribution of capitalists' income between consumption and saving. The primary assumption here consists on dividing the income between two broad categories: profit earners or wage earners, where wages (*W*) are comprised of manual labour and salaries, and property owners, where profit (*P*) includes income from property as well as profit for entrepreneurs. The basic mechanism of Kaldor model is based on three important equations that express the relationship between wage, profit, and saving (Sen 1970, 83):

$$Y = W + P \tag{3.1}$$

$$I = S \tag{3.2}$$

$$\text{and } S = Sw + Sp \tag{3.3}$$

where Sw and Sp are the propensities to save out of wages and profits. Substituting the saving functions $Sw = SwW$ and $Sp = SpP$ to (3.3), we get

$$\begin{aligned} S &= SwW + SpP = Sw\ (Y - P) + SpP = (Sw - Sp)\ P + SpP \\ &= (Sw - Sp)\ P + SpY \end{aligned} \tag{3.4}$$

From the equilibrium equation (3.2) we obtain

$$I = S = (Sw - Sp)\,P + SpY \tag{3.5}$$

Dividing equation (3.5) by Y and rearranging to obtain the share of profits in national income, P/Y, we attain

$$\frac{I}{Y} = (s_p - s_w)\frac{P}{Y} + s_w \tag{3.6}$$

and

$$\frac{P}{Y} = \frac{1}{\left(s_p - s_w\right)}\frac{I}{Y} - \frac{Ss_w}{s_p - s_w} = \frac{\frac{I}{Y} - S_w}{s_p - s_w} \tag{3.7}$$

Given the propensities to save out of wages and profits, the share of profits in income depends simply on the ratio of investment to output. The ratio of investment to output depends on the "Keynesian" hypothesis that investment is an independent variable, invariable with respect to changes in the two savings propensities, *Sw* and *Sp* (Kaldor 1956, 96). The condition for positive profits and a positive profit share is given as

$$Sw < I/Y < Sp \tag{3.8}$$

If the propensity to save out of wage income is zero, the equation (3.7) is reduced to

$$\frac{P}{Y} = \frac{I/Y}{s_p} \tag{3.9}$$

Kaldor showed that the share of profits varies directly with the growth rate of income (or capital-output ratio) and the saving rate out of wages, but it varies indirectly with the saving rate out of profits. With the assumption of "full employment," demand determines prices in relation to wages; a rise in investment will raise prices and profit margins, while a drop in investment will cause a fall in prices and in the level of consumption. Another assumption made by Kaldor is that prices and profit margins are flexible, so the system is in equilibrium and stable at the level of full employment. By distinguishing two saving propensities out of wages and profits, Kaldor assumed that his model is valid if the two savings propensities differ: *Sp*> *Sw* (marginal propensity to save exceeds marginal propensity to wage) (Sen 1970, 84–5). It follows that distribution of income between workers and capitalists is the only thing that makes steady growth possible.

Later, in 1960, Kaldor published a collection of essays on economic stability and growth. Among these papers, there was a further development of the theory of growth from his first article published in 1956, but the most known work is his second contribution in the theory of growth published in 1957. His model is based on Keynesian techniques and follows the Harrodian approach. Kaldor takes into account six properties called facts or "stylized" view of facts, with appropriate assumptions about production function, technological progress, population growth, and saving propensities (Kaldor 1957, 593–602).

The first one is based on the assumption that the general level of output at any time is limited by available resources and not by effective demand. His model assumes the state of "full employment," in which the short period supply of goods and services is inelastic and independent of further increases in monetary demand. Another assumption is the Keynesian hypothesis that equilibrium between savings and investment is secured through an adjustment of prices and incomes rather than through changes in the rate of interest.

The second property is based on the relationship between capital growth and productivity growth. So, any distinction between changes in techniques (in productivity) and those induced by technological invention or innovation is missing. The link between the proportionate growth in capital and productivity shows the ineffective adjustment in capital-output ratio. According to Kaldor, the capital-output ratio depends not on the technical nature of inventions but simply on the relationship between the flow of new ideas and the rate of capital accumulation.

The third fact states that the measurement of real capital stock must be in terms of amount of mechanical power that the outstanding capital goods represent. Another kind of measurement would be the total physical weight of all capital goods produced.[5]

The fourth fact assumes a continued state of growth where the output increases as a result of capital investment and investment takes place in response to the increase in output. Kaldor assumes an investment function that makes the investment of any period partly a function of the change in output in the previous period and partly of the change in profit on capital in that period.[6]

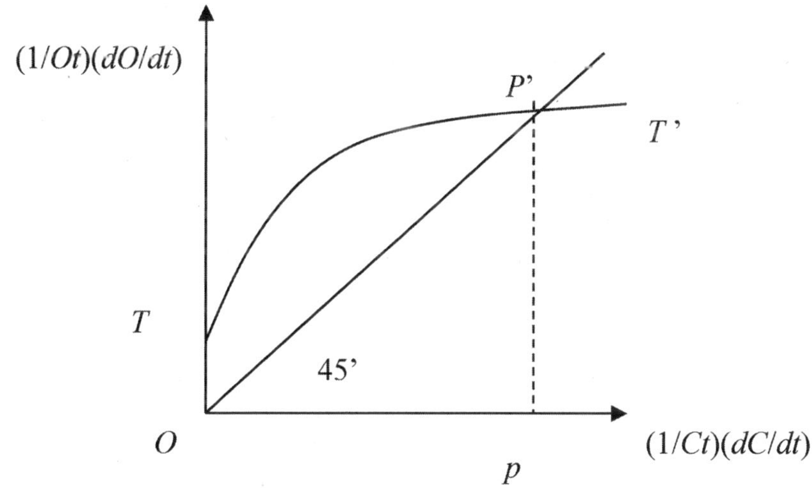

Figure 3.1 Technical progress function

The fifth property is that monetary policy is neutral or plays a passive role in economic growth.

The sixth fact is that the share of wages and profits and the rate of profit on capital are determined quite independently from the principle of marginal productivity. The choice of alternative methods of production loses its central importance in this theoretical model. Practically, according to Kaldor (1957, 602), the choice of techniques is regarded as a matter of relative prices of different types of capital goods and is supposed to change with the accumulation of capital and the progress of techniques.

Kaldor, in a way different from Harrod and Domar, considers technological progress a necessary element of his theoretical model. The main feature of his model is to establish a relationship between capital investment and the technological progress function. Technological progress is not a separate factor (endogenous and exogenous) influencing the rate of growth but rather is combined with capital investment into one single relationship. The form of this "technical progress function" is given by the *TT'* curve[7] as it appears in figure 3.1.

Ct and *Ot* represent, respectively, the capital per worker and the annual output per worker at time *t*, while $[(1/Ct)(dC/dt)]$ (measured by the abscissa) represents the annual percentage growth in capital per worker, and the ordinate $[(1/Ot)(dO/dt)]$ represents the annual percentage growth in output per man (J.E. King 1994, 163). The shape and the position of the curve reflect both the magnitude and the character of technological progress. The *TT'* curve represents the main relationship between capital growth and income growth (with technological progress) during the investment process. *P* represents a specific point on the *TT'* curve crossed by a line drawn from the origin at an angle of 45 degrees, where the percentage of capital growth and output are equal (J.E. King 1994, 164). A certain amount of technological progress is assumed to take place independently of new capital investment. This is the reason why the *TT'* curve lies above the origin and the line drawn from the origin. The height of the curve depends on the knowledge and creativity of the community, although according to Kaldor, certain constancy in the stream of new ideas is required. The capital-output ratio rises or falls depending on the relationship between the flow of new ideas and the rate of capital accumulation. If capital accumulation is less than required to develop the current stream of inventions, then the capital-output ratio will fall and the character of inventions will be "capital saving" rather than labour saving. On the right of the *P* point, the character of inventions is labour saving. The system normally tends toward the point (*P* point in figure 3.1), where the growth of capital and productivity are equal.

Kałdor (1957) assumes full employment, so the adjustment mechanism via employment is not admitted. His theory of distribution appropriates the Keynesian division of society into two categories: capitalists or profit earners and workers or wage earners. Wage earners include not only those performing manual labour but also those earning salaries, and profit earners include the income of entrepreneurs and property owners. The profit depends on the expense of entrepreneurs and, more exactly, on their plans of investment. Employment is given as a combination of two factors: variations in income distribution and the average saving propensities out of wages and profits. Kaldor's saving function (1957, 604) takes the form

$$St = \alpha\, Pt + \beta\, (Yt - Pt) \qquad 1 > \alpha > \beta \geq 0 \tag{3.10}$$

where α is the propensity of aggregate profit *Pt* and β is the saving propensity of wages earners ($Yt - Pt$). Because α is assumed to be greater than β, any shifts in shares from wages to profits will increase savings and vice versa. In a different way from his predecessors, Kaldor separates the propensities to save into two parts, which allows us to understand better the effects of change in the distribution of incomes. The investment function takes the form (Kaldor 1957, 604)

$$K_t = \alpha' Y_{t-1} + \beta' \left(\frac{P_{t-1}}{K_{t-1}} \right) Y_{t-1} \tag{3.11}$$

$$I_t = K_{t+1} - K_t = (Y_t - Y_{t-1})(\alpha' + \beta' [\frac{P_{t-1}}{K_{t-1}}]) + \beta' \left(\frac{P_t}{K_t} - \frac{P_{t-1}}{K_{t-1}} \right) Y_t \tag{3.12}$$

$\alpha' > 0, \beta' > 0$

$$\frac{Y_{t+1}}{Y_t} - 1 = \alpha'' + \beta'' \left(\frac{I_t}{K_t} \right) \tag{3.13}$$

where $\alpha'' > 0$ and $I > \beta'' > 0$.

Equation (3.11) shows that the stock of capital at time t (which is assumed to be equal to the desired stock of capital at time (t - 1) is given by a coefficient α' of the previous output period and a coefficient β' of the rate of the previous profit capital period. Equation (3.12) derives from equation (3.11) by using a differential equation and shows that investment in period t corresponds to the difference between the desired and actual investment at t. Investment is equal to the increment in output over the previous period ($Y_t - Y_{t-1}$) times the relationship between capital and output in the previous period (K_t/Y_{t-1}) plus a coefficient β' of the change in the rate of profit over the period, multiplied by the output of the current period. Equation (3.12) implies that the investment, It, is equal to the expected rate of growth of turnover and is assumed to be equal to the actual rate of growth in turnover of the previous period if the profit on capital is constant. However, it is greater (or smaller) than this if the rate of profit on capital is rising (or falling) (Kaldor 1957, 605). The equation (3.13) gives the technological progress function. Assuming that capital stock $K1$ satisfies the condition

$$\frac{K1}{Yo} = \alpha' + \beta' (\frac{Po}{Ko}) \tag{3.14}$$

where $K1$, Y0, and Y0 are given. Now equation (3.12) can be written in the following form:

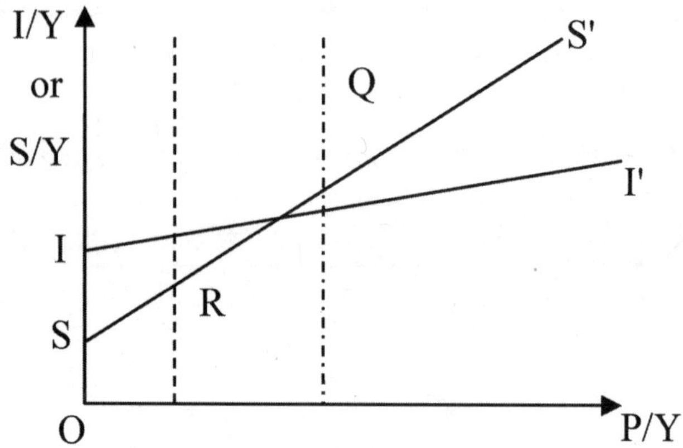

Figure 3.2 Saving-investment equilibrium

$$\frac{I_1}{Y_1} = \left[\left(\frac{Y_1}{Y_0} - 1\right)\left(\frac{K_1}{Y_1}\right)\right] + \beta'\left(\frac{P_1}{K_1} - \frac{P_0}{K_0}\right) \tag{3.15}$$

This function gives the equality between the rate of investment in period 1 and the rate of growth of the previous period times the capital-output ratio. Equation (3.10) can be written as

$$\frac{S_1}{Y_1} = \alpha\frac{P_1}{Y_1} + \beta\left(1 - \frac{P_1}{Y_1}\right) = \beta + (\alpha - \beta)\frac{P_1}{Y_1} \tag{3.16}$$

Equations (3.14) and (3.15) determine the distribution of income between profits and wages and the proportion of income invested at $t = 1$ (Kaldor 1957, 605–6). In Kaldor's system, α and β are constants that have decisive influence on the division of income between profits and wages. This makes the distribution of income the unique, certain result of independent factors. The savings depends on income, and both yield the saving-investment equilibrium of income distribution as seen in figure 3.2.

The vertical dotted line in figure 3.2 represents the maximum permissible level of *P/Y* obtained by the difference between full employment income and the subsistence salary. If the dotted line falls to the left of *Q*, the short-period equilibrium will be represented not by *Q* but by *R*. The position of the dotted line in relation to *Q* depends on the productivity of labour, which in turn depends on the capital stock.

In the short run, there are several historical and sociological factors (trade unions, negotiating power, government intervention, etc.) that influence the saving propensities and the distribution of income. In Kaldor's system, there is not a unique *St*/*Yt* related to a given *Pt*/*Yt*. So in figure 3.2, there will be not just one but several *SS'* curves. The equilibrium point between saving and investment will depend on the path by which this point is reached.

The long-run rate of growth in income and capital is independent of savings and investment functions but dependent on the coefficients of technological progress function. It is given by

$$G = \frac{\alpha''}{I - \beta''} \tag{3.17}$$

This is the rate of growth of productivity that makes the rate of growth of capital and income equal (with assumed constant rate of population). Putting together the ratio of investment to income, the share of profits to income, the rate of profit on capital, and the function of technological progress, investment, and savings, Kaldor obtains (given full employment and constant working population)

$$\frac{P}{Y} = \frac{\varepsilon \frac{\dot{K}}{Y} - \beta}{\alpha - \beta} \tag{3.18}$$

where the variable ε represents the technological progress function, *K*/*Y* is the investment function, and α and β are the two propensities to save (J.E. King 1994, 173). The set of equations in Kaldor's model has some similarities but, at the same time, important differences from Harrod's model and especially Harrod's rate of growth.

HARROD AND KALDOR: SOME SIMILARITIES AND DISSIMILARITIES

By putting in relationship the coefficients of technological progress function (G) and the technological function ε, we get

$$\frac{\alpha''}{I - \beta''} = \varepsilon \tag{3.a}$$

and deriving equations (3.11) and (3.16) implies

$$\frac{I}{Y} = \varepsilon \frac{K}{Y} \tag{3.b}$$

Given that from (3.17) we have

$$\frac{s}{Y} = \alpha \frac{P}{Y} + \beta (I - \frac{P}{Y}) \tag{3.c}$$

therefore, we get

$$\frac{P}{Y} = \frac{\varepsilon \frac{\dot{K}}{Y} - \beta}{\alpha - \beta} \tag{3.d}$$

and $$\frac{P}{Y} = \frac{\varepsilon - \beta \frac{Y}{K}}{\alpha - \beta} \tag{3.e}$$

Equation (3.b) and equation (3.17) are variants of Harrod's "warranted rate of growth," with two important differences: first, the assumption of given savings propensities is consistent with any number of warranted rates depending on the distribution of income, which determines the average propensity to save for the entire category taken in consideration; second, the rate of growth is not determined by the savings function but by equation (3.19), which, is nothing else than a variant of Harrod's "natural rate." The implications of Kaldor's model in terms of Harrod's terminology could be summarized as the trend of the system toward an equilibrium rate of growth at which the "natural" and the "warranted" rates are equal. If there is any divergence between these two rates the system will set up forces to eliminate the divergence and adjust both rates (Kaldor 1957, 611–12).

The relationship between the rate of return on capital, technological progress, and propensity to save is given as (Kaldor 1957, 613)

$$\frac{P}{K} = \frac{\varepsilon}{\alpha} \tag{3.19}$$

As we can see from (3.19), the rate of profit on capital depends on the rate of growth, ε, and on the coefficient of profit, α. Therefore, the rate of return on capital depends on the rate of growth and on the distribution of capitalists' income between consumption and saving and is independent from the factors determining the share of profits between income and capital-output ratio.

THE RESTRICTING CONDITIONS AND THE STAGES OF CAPITALISM IN KALDOR

Kaldor's model (1956, 1957) is subject to two restrictions: first, profits should not be greater than the surplus available after the labour force has been paid a subsistence salary, and second, profits are higher than the minimum required securing a margin of profit below which entrepreneurs would not reduce prices (J.E. King 1994, 174).

The subsistence salary and the minimum profit largely depend on what level the profit earners and wage earners have been able to obtain for themselves in the past. If the profit earners will accept a fall in profit margins the full employment adjustment of redistribution of incomes will soon come to an end because of the resistance of wage earners to reduce their salaries (as the result of reduced profit margin by profit earners). This means that the steady full employment growth is limited and unlikely to be fulfilled in an unregulated capitalist economy without exogenous factors or interventions, such as government involvement. Kaldor assumes that the long-term investment requirements and saving properties are the underlying factors responsible for the gradual change in the standard of living in any particular economy (J.E. King 1994, 175). In fact, the share of profits on income depends entirely on the ratio of investment to output as well as on the propensity to save on profits and wages. Furthermore, the share of profits on income is acceptable only if it is taken into consideration in the long run because changes in these factors have limited influence in the short run.

Kaldor considered two stages of capitalist evolution. The first stage consists of the rising of productivity being not large enough to allow a surplus over the subsistence wage, which permits the rate of investment to attain the level required by equation (3.12) in the previous section. This stage will come to an end when capital stock reaches the level of "desired capital" indicated by equation (3.11). From that point, the share of wages becomes residual, equaling the difference between production and the share of profits, as determined by the propensities to invest and save.

When the accumulation of capital has absorbed the entire workforce available, there is a second phase. This stage occurs when production and employment continue to grow and real wages steadily rise with the expansion of output. The rate of growth is no longer determined by the quota of income destined to be saved but instead by the increasing working force and the technological progress. The consequence of this is the increase of salaries.

As mentioned above, Kaldor considered two categories of saving: profit earners and wage earners. The simpler case on the propensity for saving is the classic one, in which workers do not save; all the saving in the economic system is done by capitalists. Only the entrepreneurs accumulate, so they invest all the profits. In these conditions, there is a curious result. At the normal rate of propensity to save, capitalists will invest their entire quota of profits, so they will benefit from the distribution. On the contrary, at the regular rate of investment, if capitalists increase their rate of saving, they will invest less than required, and their quota of profits will go down. Therefore, for capitalists, it is convenient to invest more and save less. The Kaldorian theory of distribution confirms the classic idea of the asymmetry between the factors of production and the distribution of income.

The profit (made by the category of profit earners) is determined first because it is required to support the capital accumulation, the rise in labour force, and the increase of productivity. The category of salaries (wage earners) then absorbs all the rest. Once the requirements of capital accumulation are satisfied, all of the growth in productivity (resulting from technological progress) is translated into the increase in salaries. The expansion ability of the economy and the distribution of income depend mostly on what capitalists do. This distributive mechanism assures also the stability of the system because the increase in prices induced by the expansive demand for investments provokes a real diminution of salaries because the propensity to consumption of wage earners has a greater value than that (the propensity to consumption) of profit earners.

The contribution of Kaldor has been subsequently taken into consideration by Pasinetti, who evidenced that it was valid not only in the case of capitalist savings but also in the case where workers save, their saving is remunerated, and the profits are distributed between capitalists and workers. In Pasinetti's model, the rate of growth depends on the rate of profit and on the propensity of capitalists to save.

GROWTH THEORY WITH INDUCED TECHNOLOGICAL PROGRESS IN KALDOR AND MIRRLEES

Kaldor and Mirrlees presented a new model of growth in 1962 in which, differently from the earliest ones (Kaldor 1956, 1957, 1961), technological progress is brought to the economic system through the creation of new equipment, which depends on gross investment expenditure (and not on net investment as in the 1957 model) (Kaldor and Mirrless 1962). Both authors suggest that the basic functional relationship (in the long period) is not a production function, expressing output per head as an increasing function of capital per head, but rather a technological progress function, expressing the rate of increase per head on the latest machine as an increasing function of the rate of investment per head. Here, as in the prior Kaldor model (1957), the level of investment is based on the volume of investment decisions made by entrepreneurs and is independent of the propensities to save. Kaldor and Mirrlees transform the Keynesian apparatus into a full employment analysis, which is more relevant than the unemployment theory. As a result, in a situation of continuing full employment, the volume of investment decisions for the economy as a whole is governed by the number of workers available (per unit period) and by the amount of investment per worker (Kaldor and Mirrless 1962, 175). Each entrepreneur aims for the maximum attainable growth of his business. The technological progress is integrated into the production function. The authors speak of the "technical progress function" as a single relationship between the growth of capital and growth of productivity, and they emphasize that any distinction between the movement along the production function or any shift in the production function caused by a change in the state of knowledge is arbitrary and artificial.

The objective of Kaldor and Mirrlees model consists on how an economy can grow as a result of growth productivity due to technological progress brought to the economic system through the creation of new equipment based on gross investment expenditure.

The main assumption made by Kaldor and Mirrlees consists of the growth of productivity that is entirely due to the introduction of new machines through investment. So the technological progress is a function of the rate of investment per worker (Kaldor and Mirrless 1962, 176)

$$\frac{\dot{p}_t}{p_t} = f\left(\frac{\dot{i}_t}{i_t}\right) \tag{3.20}$$

The rate of growth of productivity is an increasing function of the rate of growth of investment per worker, though at a diminishing return. The entrepreneurs face the risk on new investments in two ways (Kaldor and Mirrless 1962, 177).

First, the new investment in capital is consistent with maintaining the earning power of the fixed assets above a certain minimum, which represents the earning power of fixed assets; the expected profits after full amortization would be at least equal to the assumed rate of profit on new investment, and the equation for an investor is written as

$$i_t \leq \int_{t}^{t+T} e^{-(p+\delta)(\tau-t)}\left(p_t - w_{\tau*}\right)d\tau \tag{3.21}$$

where p is the general rate of profit for the entrepreneurs, $w_{\tau}{}^{*}$ is the expected rate of wages given as a rising function of the future time, and δ is the rate of decay of machines.

Second, the cost of fixed assets must be recovered within a certain period of time, and the gross profit earned in the first years (denominated as h) of operation must be sufficient to repay the cost of investment, written as

$$i_t = \int_{t}^{t+h} (p_t - w_{\tau}^{*})d\tau \tag{3.22}$$

The relationship of the labour force distribution is given as

$$N_t = \int_{t-T}^{t} n_t e^{-\delta(t-\tau)}d\tau \tag{3.23}$$

where δ is the depreciation rate and $T(t)$ is the age of equipment. The function of total output is written as

$$Y_t = \int_{t-T}^{t} p_\tau n_\tau e^{-\delta(t-\tau)} d\tau \tag{3.24}$$

where p_τ is the profit at time *t*. According to Kaldor and Mirrlees model (1962) Yt is divided into categories of income, wages and profits and the rest of output left after profits is equal to the total wage bill. In fact the output is given as

$$Y_t(1-\pi_t) = N_t w_t \tag{3.25}$$

where w_t is the rate of wages at t, π_t is the profit and $N_t$is the population who receives wage bills. The system is in the steady growth when the rate of growth of output per head is equal to the rate of growth of productivity on new equipment and both are equal to the rate of growth of fixed investment per worker and to the rate of wage growth. The equilibrium condition yields (Kaldor and Mirrless 1962, 180)

$$p^{\cdot}/p = y^{\cdot}/y = i^{\cdot}/i = w^{\cdot}/w \tag{3.26}$$

where the share of investment of output, *I*/*Y*, the share of profits of income, π, and the period of machine depreciation, *T*, remain constant. According to the assumption given by equation (3.5.1), it implies that there is some value (called γ) that equals

$$p^{\cdot}/p = i^{\cdot}/i = \gamma \tag{3.27}$$

at which the equilibrium is possible. From equation (3.26), it can be seen that, as long as $w^{\cdot}/w$ does not diverge too far from $p^{\cdot}/p$, $i^{\cdot}/i$ would increase if it is less than $p^{\cdot}/p$ and decrease if it is greater than $p^{\cdot}/p$. If $p^{\cdot}/p$ is less than γ, the rate of growth of investment, $i^{\cdot}/i$, would require a higher $p^{\cdot}/p$ until the equilibrium position is reached – and vice versa when $p^{\cdot}/p$ is greater than $i^{\cdot}/i$.

For Kaldor and Mirrlees, the equilibrium would be, in general, stable, although instability cannot be excluded. A downward shift in the technological progress function might allow the rate of growth of profits, *p*, to fall and remain below the rate of growth of wages, *w*, long enough that, with falling investment, unemployment and stagnation set in (and vice versa when there is an upward shift in the technological function).

Practically, there is no production function or a single-valued relationship between the magnitude of capital, *Kt*, the labour force, *Nt*, and output, *Yt*. Everything depends on investment done in the past or on how the equipment goods are built up. Output, *Yt*, could be greater for a given capital, *Kt*, if a greater part of the existing capital stock is of more recent creation. So it is not possible to derive a production function from a technological progress function because productivity over time depends not only on the stock of capital but also on the rate at which it is installed.

The technological progress function is consistent with a technological "investment function," which is given as a relationship between investment per worker and output per worker. Technological progress has two elements: an exogenous element consisting of new ideas or innovations and another element that is the exploitation of these ideas by learning (Sen 1970, 392–3).[8] There are some restraints in the nature of technological process: every change in capital per worker implies a change in technology and innovations. Capital-saving innovations (affecting the output-capital ratio) are much more profitable to entrepreneurs than labour-saving innovations (affecting the output-labour ratio), so the increase in investment per man would be greater. The authors of this model, among others, assume that technological progress is neutral, so the rate of increase in investment per head remains unchanged over time and, what is more important, capital-saving and capital-using innovations remain unchanged in the total flow of innovations. Later, Hahn and Matthews (1964) assumed that Kaldor's technological progress function can be regarded as an extension of the Cobb-Douglas technological progress function. In fact, Cobb and Douglas have argued that the technological progress function $[\delta(\dot{Y}/Y)/\delta(\dot{K}/K)]$ is constant in all circumstances (Sen 1970, 394). Kaldor argued a similar result with $\dot{K}/K$. Both have in common the assumption that this slope ($\dot{K}/K$) is independent of K/Y. Without this assumption, a technological progress function relating $\dot{Y}/Y$ and $\dot{K}/K$ might not be formed.

SOME NOTES ON KALDOR'S APPLIED ECONOMICS AND LAWS OF GROWTH

Kaldor was one of the first Keynesians to criticize the quantitative approach of the applied dimension of neoclassical economics, arguing that capital could not be measured either in terms of value or in physical units. He emphasized that,

> Hence the theorist, in choosing a particular theoretical approach, ought to start off with a summary of facts which he regards as relevant to his problem. Since facts, as recorded by statisticians, are always subject to numerous snags and qualifications, and for that reason are incapable of being accurately summarised, the theorists, in my view, should be free to start with a "stylised" view of the facts – i.e. concentrate on broad tendencies, ignoring individual detail, and processed on the "as if" method, i.e. construct a hypothesis committing himself to the historical accuracy, or sufficiency, of the facts or tendencies thus summarized. (Kaldor 1961, 177–80)[9]

From this point of view, the capital-output ratio in Britain caused the slow rate of economic growth. It declined, more or less, steadily in the last half of the nineteenth century; then it rose and fell back in the period before the First World War and continued in a downward course after the Second World War until the midst of the 1950s, when it was in the boom phase. In "The Case for Regional Policies," Kaldor shows examples of applied economics (1989). He starts by establishing the basic stylized facts from empirical evidence taken from a pool of countries, and then develops the theoretical backdrop that explains the facts, and concludes with suggestions for some economic policies. He illustrates a number of stylized facts based on the historical evidence through the use of regression equations. In "The Case of Regional Policies," Kaldor argues that the principle of cumulative causation privileges a theoretical mechanism that explains stylized facts better than the neoclassical argument based on exogenous differences in the allocation of resources. Kaldor's applied economics was created in a way to allow him the use of economics in real historical contexts, in which the quantification strategy regarding historical facts and events could not be converted into economic models. Applied economics was then strongly related to the historical events that were presented in some growth models, which allowed discussing only simple arguments. He also examined the consequences of full employment policies on the revenue and expenditures of public authorities. For example, his statistical analysis (Kaldor 1964) was contextualized to the historical circumstances present in Great Britain in 1938 and was divided into two periods, pre- and postwar. Moreover, he seemed to be concerned with practicable methods available in order to achieve effective and practicable policies. Kaldor thought that economists must use theories that embody significant features of the world economy as a first step to applying economics. The concept of applied economics is one that minimizes the inconsistencies involved in the application of closed-system results to open systems, events, or situations.

Kaldor placed great emphasis on increasing returns to scale as a factor contributing to economic growth.[10] The meaning of increasing returns is referred to firms that produce an increasing volume of some goods with the result that each worker becomes more productive. He was convinced that increasing returns were present in the manufacturing sector, especially after the Second World War.

His belief was based on three empirical correlations or laws found when he studied the growth experiences of several developed countries (J.E. King 1994, 57–59).

First, there is a positive correlation in all industrialized countries between the growth rate of manufacturing output (gm) and the growth rate of GDP (g_{GDP}). Taking a cross-section of twelve industrial countries during the 1950s and 1960s, Kaldor found that the high correlation between two variables (g_m and g_{GDP}) is not simply the result of the fact that manufacturing output constitutes a large proportion of GDP, but is the result of a significant positive association between the general rate of growth of GDP and the excess of growth of manufacturing over non-manufacturing output. He found no correlation between the growth of GDP and the growth rate of agriculture or the mining sector, but he did find a significant correlation between GDP growth and the growth in the service sector. Therefore, he assumed that the growth rate of services should be attributed to the growth of GDP rather than the other way around. He, among others, presumed that aggregate growth rates depend mostly on manufacturing growth rates, which in return, could explain the increasing returns to scale in industrial activities. The economies of scale reduce the unit costs as output grows over time and bring both the "induced" technological progress embodied in new capital and learning-by-doing as a function of cumulative output in the past. Another reason for growth in the manufacturing sector is that this sector is able to attract labour from other sectors – like agriculture – that have hidden unemployment or have not reached full employment in the sense that there is no relationship between the growth of output and an increase in employment; therefore, the transfer of the workforce to the manufacturing industry causes no decline in the output of these other sectors.

Second, there is a high correlation between productivity growth in the manufacturing sector and the growth of manufacturing output. Here Kaldor believes that productivity growth in manufacturing depends on the growth of manufacturing output. The faster the rate of growth of manufacturing output, the faster the rate of growth of GDP (Kaldor's first law). If the demand for manufacturing products rises, the firms producing these goods will expand production and because of economies of scale, productivity growth accelerates and costs fall.

Third, the growth of a country's manufacturing output is correlated with the growth of productivity in other economic sectors. As the manufacturing sector grows, it absorbs surplus agricultural labour. As a consequence, productivity and living standards rise in the agricultural sector (Pressman 1999, 151). Kaldor assumes that employment increase is determined by output growth in other economic sectors; hence, the growth of output in manufacturing is not constrained by a shortage of labour. He found that the faster the growth of manufacturing output, the faster the rate of labour transfer from non-manufacturing to manufacturing. The third law states, among other points, that the growth of GDP is positively related to the growth of output and employment in manufacturing and negatively correlated with the growth of employment outside manufacturing (J.E. King 1994, 64–5). The process of industrialization tends to accelerate the rate of change of technology not just in one sector but also in the economy as a whole. Productivity rises in all sectors, and living standards improve for the entire nation.

From these empirical regularities, Kaldor concluded that economic growth depends largely on the growth of the industrial sector. As a matter of fact, an energetic and flourishing manufacturing sector means rapid economic growth, increasing consumption, and rising standards of living. The deep analysis of the growth experiences of a variety of developed countries in the 1950s and early 1960s brought him to the conclusion that governments must support domestic manufacturing industries. This support can be achieved by direct purchase of manufacturing goods or by supporting manufacturing industries with tax relief, industry incentives, and other forms of assistance.

INCOME DISTRIBUTION AND ECONOMIC GROWTH IN PASINETTI

Kaldor's approach has been developed further by Pasinetti[11] and by a fairly vast body of literature that has, however, by emphasizing the study of equilibrium paths, shifted the attention from the original efforts to construct a growth theory out of the business cycle to a more traditional view of constructing a theory of economic growth based on the natural rate. Pasinetti developed the post-Keynesian theory of growth by assuming that market forces operate along lines that are different from those envisaged by neoclassical authors and similar to those described by classical economists (Pasinetti 1962).

The objective of Pasinetti's model is to create a simplified post-Keynesian theory of income distribution where the main focus is based on two main groups, the workers' and capitalists', propensity to save.

His analysis is carried out with constant reference to the assumption of full employment, because full employment is the situation considered mainly by all post-Keynesians. Pasinetti reformulated the equations given by Kaldor and gave a new form to income distribution's identity (Sen 1970, 96–7),

$$P = Pc + Pw \tag{3.28}$$

where Pc stands for profits that accrue to capitalists and Pw stands for profits that accrue to workers, so the saving functions now become

$$Sw = sw(W + Pw) \tag{3.29a}$$

$$\text{and } Sc = scPc \tag{3.29b}$$

where sw and sc represent the propensities to save of the workers and capitalists, respectively, while Sw and Sc are two broad categories, the workers' savings and capitalists' savings. The equilibrium condition is given as

$$I = sw\ (W + Pw) + scPc = swY + (sw - sc)\ Pc \tag{3.30}$$

and the equation of distribution of income between wages and profits is written as

$$\frac{P_c}{Y} = \frac{1}{(s_c - s_w)} \cdot \frac{I}{Y} - \frac{s_w}{(s_c - s_w)} \tag{3.31}$$

whereas the identity for the corresponding rate of profit is

$$\frac{P_c}{K} = \frac{1}{(s_c - s_w)} \cdot \frac{I}{K} - \frac{s_w}{(s_c - s_w)} \cdot \frac{Y}{K} \tag{3.32}$$

These identities are different from those assumed by Kaldor because they refer to the part of profits that accrue to capitalists. Equation (3.31) expresses the distribution between capitalists and workers, whereas the distribution of income between profits and wages is something different. Equations (3.31) and (3.32) represent the ratio of profit (*Pc*) to total income (*Y*) and to total capital (*K*). What we really need is the ratio of total profits to total income (both capitalists' and workers' income) and the ratio of total profits to total capital (total rate of profit). By adding to both sides of equations (3.31) and (3.32), *Pw*/*Y* and *Pw*/*K*, respectively, we have the appropriate expressions for the distribution of income between wages and profits given as:

$$\frac{P}{Y} = \frac{P_c}{Y} + \frac{P_w}{Y} \tag{3.33}$$

and $$\frac{P}{K} = \frac{P_c}{K} + \frac{P_w}{K} \tag{3.34}$$

Starting from equation (3.32), we can write *Yw* as the amount of income owned by workers indirectly through credits or lending (*r* is the rate of interest on these credits), so we get

$$\frac{P}{K} = \frac{1}{s_c - s_w}\frac{I}{Y} - \frac{s_w}{s_c - s_w}\frac{Y}{K} + \frac{rY_w}{K} \tag{3.35}$$

In a dynamic equilibrium, the equation for *Yw*/*K* is given as

$$\frac{Y_w}{K} = \frac{S_w}{S} = \frac{s_w(Y - P_{c)}}{I} = \frac{s_w s_c}{s_c - s_w}\frac{Y}{I} - \frac{s_w}{s_c - s_w} \tag{3.36}$$

After substituting (3.36) in equation (3.35), the general function for the distribution of income between workers and capitalists from expression (3.33) takes the following form (Sen 1970, 98):

$$\frac{P}{Y} = \frac{1}{(s_c - s_w)}\frac{I}{Y} - \frac{s_w}{(s_c - s_w)} + r\left(\frac{s_w s_c}{s_c - s_w}\frac{K}{I} - \frac{s_w}{s_c - s_w}\frac{K}{Y}\right) \tag{3.37}$$

Following the same procedure, from the equation (3.34), we have the new general equation of income distribution between wages and profits given as:

$$\frac{P}{K}=\frac{1}{s_c-s_w}\frac{I}{K}-\frac{s_w}{s_c-s_w}\frac{Y}{K}+r\left(\frac{s_w s_c}{s_c-s_w}\frac{Y}{I}-\frac{s_w}{s_c-s_w}\right) \tag{3.38}$$

This equation[12] tells us the amount of capital workers own indirectly through loans to capitalists, where r is the rate of interest on these loans. In Pasinetti's view, the rate of interest is equal to the rate of profit in the long-run equilibrium, so he simplifies equations (3.30), (3.31), and (3.37), (3.38) by transforming them into

$$\frac{P}{K}=\frac{1}{s_c}.\frac{I}{K} \tag{3.39}$$

and $$\frac{P}{Y}=\frac{1}{s_c}.\frac{I}{Y} \tag{3.40}$$

These identities show, in the long run, the propensity of workers to save, although (eq. 3.30) influencing the distribution of income between capitalists and workers, does not influence the income distribution between profit earners and wages earners (eq. 3.40) (Sen 1970, 99). The main difference between Kaldor and Pasinetti is that the former considers the distribution of income in the short run while the latter considers it in the long run. In fact, Pasinetti (1962) argued that, in a long-run exponential growth, the ratio of profits that each category of individuals receives to savings will always be the same for all categories, and the fundamental relationship between profits and savings is now written as

$$\frac{P_W}{S_W}=\frac{P_C}{S_C} \tag{3.41}$$

The meaning of the above identity is that, for each category of individuals, profits are, in the long run, proportional to savings. This follows the principle that profits are distributed in proportion to the ownership of capital. Substituting the saving functions (3.29a) and (3.29b) in equation (3.41), we get

$$sw\,(W+Pw)=scPw \tag{3.42}$$

According to Pasinetti, whatever is the propensity of workers to save (sw), there is always a distribution of income and a distribution of profits that makes valid the identities (3.41) and (3.42) or makes the ratio $Pw/sw\,(W + Pw)$ equal to Pw/Sw where sw indicates the propensity of savings while Sw indicates the category of workers' savings. So, there are infinite proportions between profits and savings that could be derived from identity (3.41). The rate of profit of workers is indeterminate, and in the long run, the amount of profits is proportional to their savings and does not depend on the rate of profit.

Workers save a constant proportion of their income, sw,[13] and live on both wages and profits they receive. The long-run profit is equal to the natural rate of growth divided by capitalists' propensity to save. The propensity of saving (sw) is independent from any assumptions about how technological progress may influence the change in the profit rate.

In Pasinetti's view, the model of income distribution has two important implications: first, the workers' propensity to save is irrelevant because the rate of profit and the income distribution between profits and wages are determined independently of sw (workers' propensity to save); second, the capitalists' propensity to save is relevant for the entire system to save. Just one group of individuals, the capitalists, decides for the whole system to save, and the other group, the workers, has no influence in the system, although the amount of saving depends on the workers' savings behaviour.

KALDOR AND PASINETTI: SOME CONCLUSIONS ON THE THEORY OF INCOME DISTRIBUTION

The post-Keynesian theorists introduced new equations in the theory of growth to prove that, in steady state, the rate of profit is equal to the ratio between the rate of growth and the capitalists' propensity to save and does not depend on technology and on the workers' propensity to save. Two scholars of the British Cambridge School, Kaldor and Pasinetti, assumed the propensities to save of different income earners (or classes) are not equal and argued that variations in income distribution bring about variations in total saving and aggregate demand, thus leading the economy to steady growth. By focusing on the role of income distribution in the growth process and underlining the links with classical economists and the differences with neoclassical authors, the theory proposed by these scholars failed to emphasize the idea that the tendency to full employment does not necessarily happen.

Kaldor's major contribution was to solve the stability problem of the Harrod-Domar model. This is achieved by allowing the economy to grow along the natural growth path through adjustments in the rate of savings due to changes in the distributive shares between wages and profits and assuming that the population growth is constant.

Pasinetti's contribution was based mainly on the correction of Kaldor's theory of distribution. He suggested that, in any type of society, when individuals save a part of their income, they must be allowed to own part of the profits in order to save. By dividing the society into capitalists and workers, some part of total profits must accumulate to workers as a result of their past savings. For Pasinetti, the convergence of the economy on a growth path will depend mainly on the capitalists' propensity to save (if the rate of return is the same for wage and profit earners). Pasinetti reformulated Kaldor's model to reflect better his assumptions. In fact, as seen above, his systems of equations are rather similar to those of Kaldor despite the conclusions that, because of the nature of his model, are different.

Kaldor developed policy proposals to improve the market system by using economic incentives. If saving is good for the economy and spending is bad for the economy, then spending should be penalized through higher taxes. Similarly, if manufacturing production is good and a large service sector would lead to slower growth, the government should tax the latter sector and provide tax relief for the former sector. This focus on new policies to improve economic outcomes in developed and less developed countries makes Kaldor one of the founders of the post-Keynesian school of economics.

During the development of income distribution theory, the role of demand coming from the government sector was also examined. Kaldor, for example, considered government policies necessary to pursue stability and growth. For him, monetary policy is the appropriate tool against the fluctuations, whereas fiscal policy is proper to pursue the long-range objective of sustained growth. Kaldor's view was that governments must support domestic industries through tax breaks and incentives, especially in slump phases.

During the late 1960s and the beginning of the 1970s, when inflation became the main economic problem in developed countries, Kaldor changed the focus of his attention. His proposal was that monetary policy had to stabilize short-term interest rates in order to avoid some undesirable consequences (Pressman 1999, 152–3). The instability of interest rates develops financial speculations and reduces the ability of the markets to transmit financial resources toward productive enterprises. Moreover, higher long-term interest rates can cause trouble in the management of government debt and increase the prospect that firms may not be able to pay back their loans, thereby making lending institutions and financial markets more fragile. Finally, they tend to cause economic stagnation. To justify the tendency to stagnation, Kaldor made explicit reference to his theory of growth and distribution. In a steadily growing economy, the average rate of profit on investment can be taken as being equal to the rate of growth in the money value of the gross national product divided by the proportion of profit saved. To keep the process of investment going, the rate of profit must exceed (long-term) interest rates by a considerable margin (Kaldor 1961). However, a monetary policy causing unstable interest rates can raise the long-term rates to a level considered by investors too high to keep accumulation going. Under these situations, stagnation prevails unless the rate of profit is raised as well. According to Kaldor, this can be done through fiscal policy. If the rate of interest is higher than the level sustaining investment, the process of accumulation would be interrupted, and the economy would definitely plunge into recession. To get the economy out of the recession, it would be necessary to stimulate the propensity to consume (by tax cuts or incentives), which would in turn raise the rate of profit and restore the incentive to invest. Kaldor had in mind to use the equilibrium condition of the commodity market and the equation of income distribution to determine the intensity of fiscal policy that would be compatible with a desired rate of growth and with the rate of interest determined by the monetary authority. The argument on the role of the government sector in the post-Keynesian theory of growth has acknowledged the existence of some common ground between the classical and Keynesian traditions, considering in this way the reconciliation of two approaches to the theory of income distribution. These approaches proposed by Kaldor and Pasinetti implied the need to take into account the rate of profit rather than the wage rate as an independent variable.

PART TWO

The Rise and Decline of the Neoclassical Theory of Growth

4

Neoclassical Theory of Growth: Factor Substitution, Optimal Growth, and Money Growth

A few years later, it seemed that the conclusion from the Harrod-Domar model might appear overly pessimistic. Growth theory was given a new dimension. A different attempt to resolve the stability of full employment is the steady state, developed by Solow (1956) and Swan (1956), and this theory is often called the Solow-Swan model, although the two economists contributed independently from one another. The work of both economists consists in the introduction of a neoclassical production function able to analyze the process of growth. The assumption of substitution between productive factors gives the growth process an adjustability that is extensively explored in these models. Solow has in mind a different approach, which allows him to change completely the object of his analysis from that of Keynesian growth theory. In his view, the most important concern is to ensure the convergence of the economy toward the natural growth path. Therefore, growth theory has to explain the potential growth of economies without paying too much attention to cyclical trends and their effects on the long-run trend. Solow assumes only capital and labour as factors of production. Technology is represented by means of the neoclassical production function, with constant returns to scale and decreasing productivity with respect to physical capital and labour-increasing technological progress. Production is distributed between savings and consumption on the basis of a Keynesian saving function. Thus, if savings are equal to the level of investment that ensures the constancy of per capita capital with full employment, then the economy is in a steady state. Otherwise, price adjustment on the capital market yields equalization between savings and investments until the steady state is attained. The convergence progress toward the steady state is ensured by the assumption of decreasing productivity of capital.

The period of neoclassical growth theory of the 1950s and 1960s initially meant a move from the vague notion of applied economics to a more quantitative and empirical approach toward the application of growth theories. Before treating the neoclassical theory of growth, however, it might be interesting to say something about the meaning of neoclassical. The original neoclassical economists were those who, in the second half of the nineteenth century, introduced for the first time the concept of the marginalist revolution (marginal utility and marginal production). They also concentrated their attention mainly on the analysis of the pricing of individual goods and factors of production in competitive markets, as well as on the possible existence of a set of prices that would ensure the equality of supply and demand in all markets (called Walrassian equilibrium).[1] The modern description of neoclassical refers to that part of economic theory that incorporates some of the central ideas of the nineteenth century through the use of specific theories and concepts, such as a marginal productivity explanation of wages or the idea of perfect competition and perfect flexibility of all prices. Another interpretation of the term neoclassical is that it highlights the subordination of short-run developments to long-run trends in modern neoclassical economic theory. More generally, neoclassical models are those in which capital and labour are continuously substitutable.

Another explanation of this term derives from the Keynesian revolution, in which many economists, particularly Samuelson, argued that "a neoclassical synthesis" was possible because of the recognition of the validity of Keynes's theory and that governments could take action via fiscal and monetary policies to maintain full employment income (Samuelson 1947). Therefore, another meaning of neoclassical is the description of theories that assume that governments could and should use policy instruments at their disposal to maintain the full-employment level of aggregate demand.

Another topic related to the neoclassical theory of growth is the problem of optimal allocation of resources, which has been a fundamental concern of economic analysis. The theory of optimization has been viewed as an aspect of economic growth that emphasizes, in general, the issues arising in the allocation of resources over an infinite time horizon and, in particular, the consumption-investment decision process in models in which there is no "end date." The main scope of optimal growth theory in the 1960s was to discover the optimum per capita output in a normal state of growth. Solow showed that an economy can follow a balanced growth path if its capital intensity is appropriately adjusted to its savings rate. In other words, the more that is saved, the higher the capital intensity in balanced growth and the higher the per capita output. The question that may arise is this: what is the preferable per capita output for an economy in a steady path of growth? Edmund Phelps, then a young associate professor at Yale, was the first economist to publish the answer in 1961. He seems to have been among the first to discover the "Golden Rule" (Phelps 1961). The golden rule path, however, seems to be a reference path in the study of optimal capital accumulation and of intertemporal (between generations) efficiency in general. Phelps suggested that each generation should invest on behalf of future generations the share of income that it would have wished past generations to invest on its behalf (1961, 642). Even before Phelps's golden rule was published, however, essentially the same rule had occurred to other economists. Specifically, Jacques Desrousseaux and Maurice Allais used the golden rule in papers published respectively in 1961 and 1962; Trevor Swan presented it in 1960 at a conference of the International Economic Association; James Meade added a variant to the second edition of *A Neoclassical Theory of Economic Growth* (1962a); Weizsäcker introduced a variant of the golden rule in his dissertation in the summer of 1961 (published in 1962). Then, shortly after Phelps's paper, Maurice Allais made the golden rule a part of his Bowley-Walras Lecture of 1961 (published in 1962). In the following year, the golden rule also appeared in the contributions of Joan Robinson (1962b), David Champernowne (1962), and James Meade (1962b) to a symposium in the *Review of Economic Studies*. In this chapter, it is assumed that the path of consumption and the savings rate are determined by optimizing households and firms. The households maximize consumption and savings and are subject to intertemporal budget constraints.

Another well-known aspect of the neoclassical theory of growth that will be considered in this chapter is the money growth. Tobin and Johnson were the first neoclassical authors to include a monetary theory on neoclassical growth. Tobin's first paper in neoclassical monetary growth was published in 1955 in the *Journal of Political Economy* and represents a predecessor of the Solow-Swan theory. This model is an amalgamation of Keynesian and neoclassical models. The cyclical behaviour included in Tobin's model has many similarities with non-linear cyclical models of Kaldor (1940), Goodwin (1951a and 1951b), and Hicks (1950). Tobin extended his contribution in his later work published in 1965 by considering government monetary debt as an alternative store of value. He, among others, was interested to discover how much saving should be directed to government debt in order to bring the warranted rate of growth down to the natural rate. Here, the capital intensity and interest rates are determined by pure monetary factors and saving behaviour. In the state of equilibrium, the real monetary debt grows at the natural rate by deficit spending or by inflation. Based on Tobin's works, Johnson subsequently discussed the problem of money growth in a neoclassical growth model. His model relates saving behaviour to other variables rather than to the traditional rate of return on investment. Later, Sidrauski, Levhari, and Patinkin objected to the Tobin theory arguing that, to better explain the monetary theory of growth, money should be part of the utility function.

Part Two, which includes chapters 4, 5, 6, and 7, deals with the great and unprecedented rise of the neoclassical growth theory. The Intermezzo section will give the reasons of the decline of the neoclassical growth theory and the birth of the new endogenous growth theory.

THE NEOCLASSICAL ONE-SECTOR THEORY OF GROWTH: THE SOLOW MODEL

The model of Solow[2] was created as a reaction to the models developed by Harrod and Domar, which show instability during the stable path of growth with full employment. Solow used a different attempt to solve the stability problem. By adopting a neoclassical framework, Solow changes the object of analysis with respect to the Keynesian growth theory; in his view, the major problem was to construct a theory of general full employment growth and, most importantly, to ensure the convergence of the economy with the natural growth path. Solow's 1956 article starts with a critique of the earlier theories of growth:

> All theory depends on assumptions which are not quite true. That is what makes it theory. The art of successful theorizing is to make inevitable simplifying assumptions in such a way that the final results are not so sensitive. A "crucial" assumption is one on which the conclusions do depend sensitively, and it is important that crucial assumptions be reasonably realistic. When the results of a theory

> seem to flow specifically from a special crucial assumption, then if the assumption is dubious, the results are suspect. I wish to argue that something like this is true of the Harrod-Domar model of economic growth. The characteristic and powerful conclusion of the Harrod-Domar line of thought is that even for the long run the economic system is at best balanced on a knife-edge of equilibrium growth. (Solow 1956, 65)

The "crucial" assumption of the Harrod-Domar model is the fixed proportions in a production function, but this assumption is inadequate to analyze the problems of economic growth. Solow writes,

> A remarkable characteristic of the Harrod-Domar model is that it consistently studies long-run problems with the usual short-term tools. One usually thinks of the long run as the domain of the neo-classical analysis, the land of margin. Instead the Harrod and Domar talk of the long run in terms of the multiplier, the accelerator, "the" capital coefficient. The bulk of this paper is devoted to a model of long-run growth which accepts all the Harrod-Domar assumptions except that of fixed proportions. Instead I suppose that the single composite commodity is produced by labor and capital under the standard neo-classical conditions. (Solow 1956, 66)

Solow observed that the propensity to alternate between unemployment and overemployment in the Harrod-Domar model may be due to the assumed rigidity of the capital-output ratio rather than to inherent flaws of the economic system. If factors cannot be used except in fixed proportions, it is hardly surprising that some cannot be sufficiently employed. Until the divergence between the natural rate of growth and steady rate of growth disappears, it is sufficient, according to Solow, to assume that prices are flexible and to introduce a production function that allows the substitution between two factors: capital and labour. Solow's growth model establishes the stability of neoclassical growth equilibrium in terms of an extremely simple adjustment mechanism.

The inevitability of growth equilibrium is demonstrated with the aid of an adjustment process that has been used earlier for the neoclassical analysis of non-growth problems (Sen 1970, 21).

The main objective of the neoclassical model of Solow was to prove that the economy consistently tends toward a balanced growth path whatever the initial capital-labour ratio. In the long run, output per worker, capital per worker, consumption per worker and saving per worker are all constant. Before starting with the one-sector model, it is necessary to observe some assumptions:

- The model is conducted in the context of an economy in which only one good (called also "jelly") is produced. There is no distinction between saving and investment, and no separate investment function is included in the model.
- In Solow's model, as in Harrod's, a simple proportional savings function is assumed. So we have $S = sY$, where $0 < s < 1$ (s is the propensity to save).
- Here, as in the Harrod-Domar model, the capital stock is not depreciated. Investment is simply the rate of increase of capital stock. Thus, we have $I = \dot{K}$, and given that investment is identically equal to saving we can write $\dot{K} = S$ and $\dot{K} = sY$.
- The labour force grows at an exogenous constant rate n given by $\dot{L}/L = n$.
- The technological possibilities of the economy are presented by constant returns to scale. The fixed capital-output ratio is replaced by a linear homogeneous production function, $Y = F(K, L)$, allowing substitution between capital and labour. The assumption of constant returns implies that the aggregate production function $Y = F(K, L)$ can be written in the intensive form, $y = f(k)$, where $y = Y/L$ and $k = K/L$, which means that output per labour is a function of capital per labour.

Now aggregate supply (output), with the help of two factors, capital and labour, is given by a production function of a linear form,[3]

$$Y = F(K, L)$$

which is assumed to vary continuously with K and L. The marginal product of capital (or labour) is positive (denoted by $f'(k)$, F_k or $\delta F/\delta L$) and diminishes as capital per labour increases. In fact, we have

$$\frac{\partial F}{\partial L} > 0 \text{ e } \frac{\partial^2 F}{\partial L^2} < 0 \tag{4.1}$$

$$\frac{\partial F}{\partial K} > 0 \text{ e } \frac{\partial^2 F}{\partial K^2} < 0 \tag{4.2}$$

Moreover, according to Inada conditions,[4] the marginal product of capital (or labour) tends toward infinity when capital (or labour) tends toward zero; it tends toward zero when capital (or labour) tends toward infinity:

$$\lim_{K \to 0} F_K = \lim_{L \to 0} = \infty \tag{4.3}$$

$$\lim_{K \to \infty} F_K = \lim_{L \to \infty} = 0 \tag{4.4}$$

The production function is homogenous of first order and shows constant returns to scale of the type

$$F(\upsilon K, \upsilon L) = \upsilon F(K, L) \quad \forall\ \upsilon > 0 \tag{4.5}$$

The production function may, therefore, be written as

$$Y = F(K, L) = LF(K/L, 1) = Lf(k) \tag{4.6}$$

where, by the assumptions shown above, we have $y = Y/L$ and $k = K/L$. The production function can now be written in the intensive form

$$y = f(k) \tag{4.7}$$

where f(·) is the "intensive" or "per capita" form of the production function F(·). As a result, the macroeconomic equilibrium condition is rewritten as

$$i = sf\ (k) \tag{4.7a}$$

This might be thought of as representing equilibrium investment per person. By assumption, macroeconomic equilibrium holds always if $I = S$; then $i = sf\ (k)$ is also referred to as the actual investment per person. Figure 4.1 depicts the intensive production function $y = f\ (k)$ and the actual investment function in equilibrium, given by equation (4.7a).[5] The

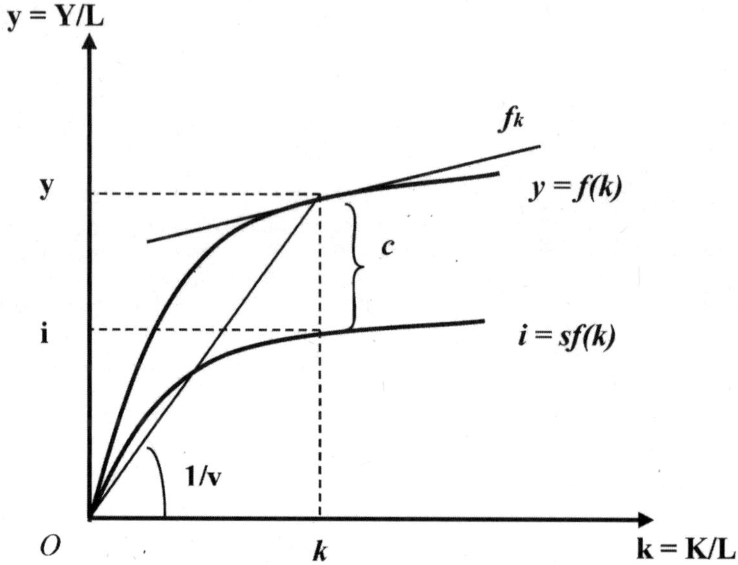

Figure 4.1 Intensive production function and investment function

slope of the intensive production function is $f_k = \partial f\,(k)/fk$ and happens to be the marginal product of capital, that is, $fk = FK$. Finally, notice that the capital-output ratio, $v = K/Y = k/y$, is captured as the slope of a ray from origin to the production function. Hence, changing k will change the ray and, thus, v. So, unlike the Harrod-Domar model, v is not exogenously fixed.

By taking into consideration equation (4.7), the marginal product of capital and labour is given by the following equations:

$$\frac{\partial Y}{\partial K} = f'(k) \tag{4.8}$$

$$\frac{\partial Y}{\partial L} = f(k) - kf'(k) \tag{4.9}$$

In a dynamic economy, the amount of capital with respect to labour is determined by the process of capital accumulation and by the exogenous rate of growth of population. Investment (see assumptions above) is identically equal to savings; given the propensity rate of saving s, and considering S as proportional to income I, we have this identity:

$$\dot{K} = sF(K, L) = S = I \quad \text{with } 0 \leq s \leq 1 \tag{4.10}$$

By considering the assumption that the workforce grows at an exogenous proportional rate n (Harrod's natural rate of growth) and in the absence of technological change, it implies (Solow 1956, 67–9)

$$L = L_0 e^{nt} \tag{4.11}$$

when L is the labour force. Introducing the variable k, we have

$$K = kL = kL_0 e^{nt} \tag{4.12}$$

where k is a capital-labour ratio. Differentiating (4.12) with respect to time, we get

$$\dot{K} = L_0 e^{nt}\dot{k} + nkL_0 e^{nt} \tag{4.13}$$

Substituting the above equation in (4.10), we have

$$(\dot{k} + nk)L_0 e^{nt} = sF(K, L_0 e^{nt}) \tag{4.14}$$

Substituting $L = L_0 e^{nt}$, we get

$$(\dot{k} + nk)L = sF(K, L) \tag{4.14.a}$$

But because of constant returns to scale, we can divide both variables (K and L) by L and multiply by F. As a result, we get the following identity:

$$(\dot{k} + nk)L = sLF(\frac{K}{L}, 1) \tag{4.15}$$

After dividing the common factor, we then obtain the fundamental equation of neoclassical economic growth in terms of capital-labour ratio (Solow 1956, 69):

$$\dot{k} = sf(k) - nk \tag{4.16}$$

This is the fundamental equation of neoclassical economic growth. On the right side of equation (4.16), $sf(k)$ is simply the saving per worker.

According to the assumption that saving automatically becomes investment, $sf(k)$ is interpreted as the flow of investment per worker. The second term on the right side, nk, is the amount of investment required to keep the capital-labour ratio constant given the labour force growing at a constant rate, n. The rate of change in capital-labour ratio, $\dot{k}$, is given by the difference between the amount of saving per worker and the amount required to keep the capital-labour ratio constant as the labour force grows. Dividing both sides by the capital-labour ratio, we obtain

$$\frac{\dot{k}}{k} = \frac{sf(k)}{k} - n \tag{4.17}$$

The first term on the right side of the equation represents, in the terms of Harrod, the warranted rate of growth. The second term, then, represents the natural rate of growth. Having assumed capital and labour as a rigid offer curve, if the warranted rate of growth exceeds the natural rate of growth, the capital intensity of production will grow. Similarly, if the warranted rate of growth is less than the natural rate of growth, the process of production will be characterized by less capital intensity. The marginal productivity of capital and labour for the property of constant returns to output production depend on the capital-labour ratio, and the prices will be adjusted to satisfy the equation:

$$\omega = \frac{w}{r} = \frac{f(k) - kf'(k)}{f'(k)} \tag{4.18}$$

Knowing the amount of capital and labour, it is then possible to determine the equilibrium prices. The adjustment process will continue until it reaches the steady-state growth. Therefore, until it is satisfied, we have the following condition:

$$sf(k^*) = nk^* \tag{4.19}$$

The steady-state k is illustrated in Figure 4.2 by imposing the required investment function, $ir = nk$, to the line through origin with slope n. The curve $sf(k)$ gives the level of savings per worker associated with any level of the capital-labour ratio. The curve $f(k)$ is the production function, and each point on the curve is associated with the quantity per worker with any given level of capital per worker. Notice that only at k^* does the

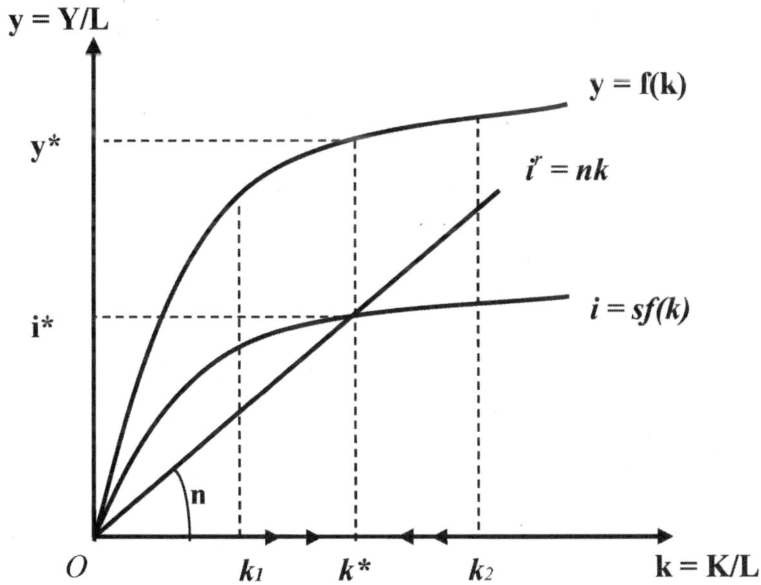

Figure 4.2 The steady state and the required investment function

actual investment (*i*) equal the required investment, $i = ir$. At any other k, $i \neq ir$.

From figure 4.2, we can see that the economy will spontaneously try to reach a steady-state path where the warranted rate of growth and the natural rate of growth converge. If the economy is originally at $k1$, the change is positive; the economy then moves to the right toward higher k. If the economy is initially at a point such as $k2$, the change is negative, and the economy then moves to the left. From both sides, the economy will converge toward k^*, which denotes the balanced growth path. Thus, the steady-state capital-labour ratio, k^*, is stable in the sense that any other k will have the tendency to approach it over time. The equilibrium point is given from the intersection of the straight line nk with $sf(k)$. This growth path is stable, and there is generally no knife-edge.

The first important proposition of the neoclassical economic growth theory is based on the existence of a balanced growth (steady-state) solution; the steady-state solution is stable in the sense that, whatever the initial values of all variables in the model, the economy moves steadily toward the balanced growth path (Jones 1975, 78–82). Moreover, we have that

$$\frac{\dot{K}}{K} = \frac{\dot{C}}{C} = \frac{\dot{Y}}{Y} = n \tag{4.20}$$

In this situation, the balanced rate of growth is determined exogenously; in the long run and in absence of technological progress, the economy grows at the rate of growth of population. The model of Solow shows that there are market forces that equalize the natural rate of growth and warranted rate of growth, thus allowing the economy to grow in a steady state. Assuming in the base of equation (4.10) that all of the savings of full employment are invested – which represents a proportion *s* of output generated with all the capital and labour available – the problem of instability seems to disappear. Furthermore, in the steady-state path of growth, there will be full occupation of capital and labour forces.

The second important proposition of neoclassical growth theory is that the balanced rate of growth is the constant exogenous rate of growth of the labour force. In the long run, the economy converges to the balanced growth path. The long-run rate of growth in neoclassical economics, *n*, is completely independent of the proportion of income saved (Jones 1975, 82–3). In a perfect labour market, it is possible that the rate of growth might coincide with a constant and positive rate of voluntary unemployment. So an elastic labour supply function of the type

$$L = L_0 e^{nt} (w)^{\eta} \tag{4.21}$$

can be introduced, where *L* indicates the labour supply; it increases at a rate, *n*, with respect to time and presents a constant elasticity with respect to salary equal to η. The labour supply curve, however, has a defect: high salaries must be modified in a way to make the curve asymptotically tend to reach the entire workforce. In our case, it is assumed that the labour force available, which is also assumed constant with respect to salary, is represented by population, *P*, which grows always at a rate, *n*. In the light of what was said above, the fundamental equation of neoclassical economic growth (4.16) becomes

$$\dot{k} = sf(k) - nk - \eta k(\frac{\dot{w}}{w}) \tag{4.22}$$

Because the rate of salary in equilibrium is adjusted until it equals the marginal productivity of labour, and because the marginal productivity of labour is constant, the rate of growth of salary is zero. Therefore, in this case, the growth of steady-state rate will also be equal to the rate of growth of population. The unemployment, $u(t)$, however, is constant, positive, and equal at every time t to the difference between the labour force available $P(t)$ and labour supply $L(t)$:

$$u(t) = P(t) - L(t) \tag{4.23}$$

Nonetheless, this equation does not influence the evolution of the system. In Solow's model, the rate of balanced growth is entirely independent of savings. The propensity to save determines the capital intensity of production and, thus, the real income, but the growth rate depends only on population and technology. All of the policy prescriptions based on Harrod-Domar models, which were meant to accelerate long-term growth, were now revealed to provide temporary impulses or pushes. Whether these impulses would last for only a few or many years, however, remains in doubt.

FIXED PROPORTIONS PRODUCTION FUNCTION AND UNEMPLOYMENT: THE HARROD-DOMAR MODEL IN THE LIGHT OF SOLOW

The common interpretation of the Harrod-Domar model as a model of fixed coefficients has its origin in an article by Solow in 1956.[6] Here, the Harrod-Domar model will be analyzed assuming the substitution between productive factors.[7] A fixed proportion production function is given as

$$Y = \min\left(\frac{K}{a}, \frac{L}{b}\right) \tag{4.24}$$

Now we have that the fundamental accumulation equation in Solow is written as

$$\dot{k} = s\min\left(\frac{k}{a}, \frac{1}{b}\right) - nk \tag{4.25}$$

where k is the ratio of capital to labour, and n is the natural rate of growth of population. When the capital-output ratio is smaller than a/b, there is a larger workforce than it is possible to employ, and the previous equation becomes

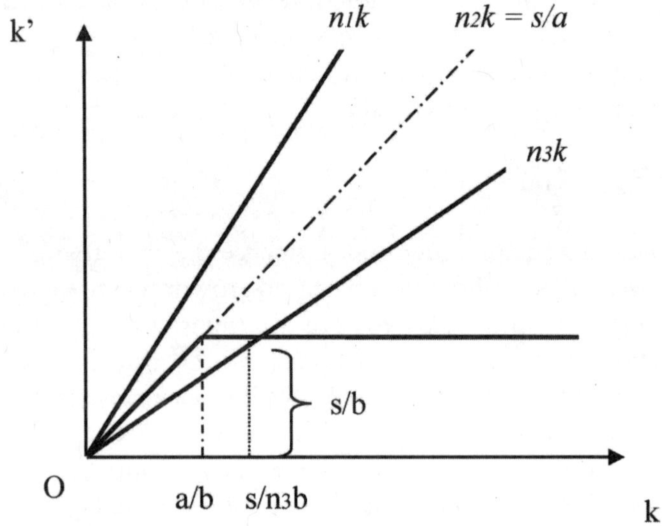

Figure 4.3 Fixed proportions production function and unemployment

$$\dot{k} = s\frac{k}{a} - nk \tag{4.26}$$

If k is greater than a/b, the capital is redundant, and the marginal productivity of capital falls to zero, so the equation becomes

$$\dot{k} = \frac{s}{b} - nk \tag{4.27}$$

This explains the presence of involuntary unemployment in the model. Graphically, in figure 4.3, the first term of the right-hand side in equation (4.25) is represented by a broken line; there is a ray from the origin with slope s/a until k reaches the value a/b and, after that, a straight line parallel to k at height s/b. The second term of equation (4.25) (in the right side), nk, is a straight line passing through the origin, with a positive slope, n.

According to the slope of this line, there are three different cases. The first case is when the population grows with a rate equal to n_1 and the natural rate of growth exceeds the warranted rate of growth, as illustrated in figure 4.3 by the line n_1k. The value of the capital-labour ratio decreases continuously; therefore, labour becomes redundant, causing unemployment to grow. Moreover, the economy is then destined to become stationary, characterized by zero growth. In the second case, the rate of population is equal to $n2$, so $n2 = s/a$, and the economic system is in equilibrium. Using the Harrodian terms, we could say that the natural rate, in absence of technological progress, is equal to the rate of population and to the stock of capital. Or, stating it differently, capital stock and labour supply grow at a common rate, $n2$. What happens to the rate of unemployment in this case? If $k>a/b$, then the capital-labour ratio will decrease, reaching a/b; from that moment forward, growth will be warranted with full employment. Conversely, if $k<a/b$, then there will be a stationary state in the presence of a constant rate of unemployment. Finally, in the third case, if the population grows with a rate equal to $n3$, the warranted rate of growth will be greater than the natural one. In this case, the economy will reach a situation of balanced growth exactly at the point where the capital-labour ratio is equal to $s/(n3b)$. Here capital is redundant (the marginal productivity of capital in this case falls to zero), and the capital stock employed in equilibrium growth is $s/(n3b)$. But because the capital stock is growing, the absolute amount of excess capacity grows as well.

GROWTH, TECHNOLOGICAL PROGRESS, AND UNEMPLOYMENT IN SOLOW'S MODEL

Until now, we have seen that, without technological progress, the model of Solow cannot explain some of the empirical results that have characterized the evolution of modern economic systems. For a better understanding of Solow's model, it is important to list some stylized facts of economic growth, such as:

1. a relationship exists between capital and constant output;
2. a relationship exists both between capital and labour as well as production and the rate of employment;
3. there is a constancy of interest rate; and
4. there is an increase of the real wage rate.

The introduction of technological progress in Solow's model is important in order to match the "stylised facts" b and d. The neoclassical theory of growth considers technological progress as an increase in the efficiency of productive factors, the rate of growth of which is constant. By considering technological progress, the production function $Y = F(K, L)$ now becomes

$$Y = F(K, L, t) \tag{4.28}$$

where t indicates the influence of technological progress on other productive factors that increase over time. In neoclassical growth theory, then, only a Harrod-neutral technological progress[8] – that is, only if the relative input quota, defined as KF_K/LF_L, remains invariable for a given relationship between capital and output – is compatible with the existence of the stable rate of growth.[9] This type of technological progress is defined as labour augmenting. In fact, it can be proved that the production function assumes, in this case, the form $Y = F(K, p(t)L)$, where $p(t) \geq 0$ is an index of the technology.[10] Assuming that p grows with a constant and exogenous rate equal to g, we have

$$p(t) = p_0 e^g \tag{4.29}$$

Defining the capital-labour ratio as an efficiency unit of the type $k^p = K/pL$, the law of capital accumulation then becomes

$$\dot{k}^p = sf(k^p) - (n+g)k^p \tag{4.30}$$

and the fundamental equilibrium of steady-state growth is given by the identity

$$sf(k^p) = (n+g)k^p \tag{4.31}$$

This solution is not qualitatively different from others if we do not consider technological progress. The aggregate variables in equation (4.31) now grow at a rate that is the sum of the population growth rate and the technological improvement rate. From equation (4.31), we derive that

$$\frac{\dot{K}}{K} = \frac{\dot{C}}{C} = \frac{\dot{Y}}{Y} = n + g \tag{4.32}$$

As in the case where technological progress is not present, we introduce now the labour supply, which is positively elastic with respect to the real wage, and we observe the consequences that this modification will have on the neoclassical model of growth. Based on equation (4.21), the labour supply grows at the same rate as population and is positively correlated with the rate of growth of the real wage as follows:

$$\frac{\dot{L}}{L} = n + \eta \frac{\dot{w}}{w} \quad \text{with } 0 \leq \eta \leq \infty \tag{4.33}$$

The steady-state growth is equal to

$$\frac{\dot{Y}}{Y} = \frac{\dot{L}}{L} + g \tag{4.34}$$

whereas the real wage grows at a rate equal to the rate of labour productivity as follows:

$$\frac{\dot{w}}{w} = g \tag{4.35}$$

The steady-state growth can also be expressed through the equation of the type

$$\frac{\dot{Y}}{Y} = n + g(1 + \eta) \tag{4.36}$$

If $g > 0$, then, along the path of balanced growth, the real wage increases, thus provoking the reduction of unemployment at a rate

$$\frac{\dot{u}}{u} = n - \frac{\dot{L}}{L} = -\eta g \tag{4.37}$$

where u is the rate of unemployment. The solution to the equation (4.37) is negative; consequently, the growth does not take place at a constant rate of unemployment.

HARROD'S INSTABILITY PROBLEM AND SOLOW'S SOLUTION

In the third section of chapter 2 it was demonstrated that Harrod's approach to the analysis of economic growth involves two problems.

First, the natural rate of growth *s/v* cannot equal the natural rate of growth *n* in the long run because there is no mechanism to achieve this equality. Therefore, in the long run, the instability problem is given as

$$Gw \neq Gn \tag{4.38}$$

Second, the warranted rate of growth is fundamentally unstable because the divergences of the actual rate of growth *Ga* would produce larger deviations from the warranted rate *Gw*. Hence, the system in general is unstable (*two* knife-edges).[11]

In this case, the short-run instability problem shows the paradox of Harrod's model and is given as

$$Ga > Ge > Gn \tag{4.39b}$$

$$\text{or } Ga < Ge < Gn \tag{4.39c}$$

where *Ga* is the actual rate of growth, *Ge*, the expected rate of growth, and *Gn*,the natural rate of growth. If investors anticipate more than the warranted rate of growth, then the actual rate of growth demanded will exceed the expected rate of growth (equation 4.39b). Similarly, if they anticipate a growth rate lower than the warranted growth rate, then the actual growth rate will fall short of even the expected growth rate, as in equation (4.39c) (Sen 1970, 12).

The issue of macroeconomic stability is overlooked by Solow because he assumes that, at all times, planned investment equals planned savings. The principal view of neoclassical economic growth was that there is smooth convergence to a path of balanced growth at the natural rate, *n*. Frank Hahn noted the following: "It will be noted straightaway that [Solow's] argument has no bearing on Harrod's knife-edge claim. Harrod had not proposed that warranted paths diverge from the steady state but that actual paths did. The latter are neither characterized by a continual equality of ex ante investment and savings nor by continual equilibrium in the market for labour. Thus although Solow thought he was controverting the knife-edge argument he had only succeeded in establishing the convergence of warranted paths to the steady-state" (Hahn 1987a, 4–5).

The particulars of macroeconomic adjustment and explicit theories of interest and expectations, which were the main concerns of Harrod and Domar, are almost missing in Solow. As Hahn (1960) demonstrated, when even the slightest attention is paid to the underlying macroeconomic adjustment of the Solow model in a proper manner, the stability of its steady state can be put into serious doubt. Still, let us turn to the first Harrodian instability problem. We can translate the Solow model into Harrod-Domar terms as follows. Previously, we have shown that the balanced growth in the neoclassical model implies

$$sf(k)/k = n \tag{4.40}$$

Substituting Y/L and K/L for k, the above identity can be written as

$$s(Y/L)\,(L/K) = n \text{ or } s(Y/K) = n \tag{4.41}$$

But from the definition of the capital-output ratio $(Y/K) = 1/v$, we have

$$s/v = n \tag{4.42}$$

In Harrod's terms, then, the warranted rate of growth equals the natural rate. We have already seen, however, that the economy converges steadily to the balanced growth path. Comparing Harrod's approach with the Solow model, we have that, in the former, s, v, and n were all fixed constants. In the latter, the assumption of a continuous aggregate production function implies that there exists a large range of values of capital-output ratio, and the economy adjusts to a particular value that ensures that the warranted rate equals the natural rate (Jones 1975, 84–5). Balanced growth in Solow implies that $sf(k) = nk$, or, dividing both sides of the identity by s, we get

$$f(k) = n/s\,(k) \tag{4.43}$$

In figure 4.4, the steady-state growth is obtained when the capital-labour ratio k^* is associated with the intersection of the line nk with $sf(k)$. We know k^* is stable, however, so k_1 approaches k^*, implying that the ratio s/v_1 declines to meet n. Hence, it is through adjustments in the capital-output ratio, v, that the neoclassical model "solves" Harrod and Domar's first instability problem.

The second Harrod problem regarding the divergences between the actual rate of growth, Ga, and the warranted rate, Gw, was not considered by Solow. Harrod's instability dilemma arises from the

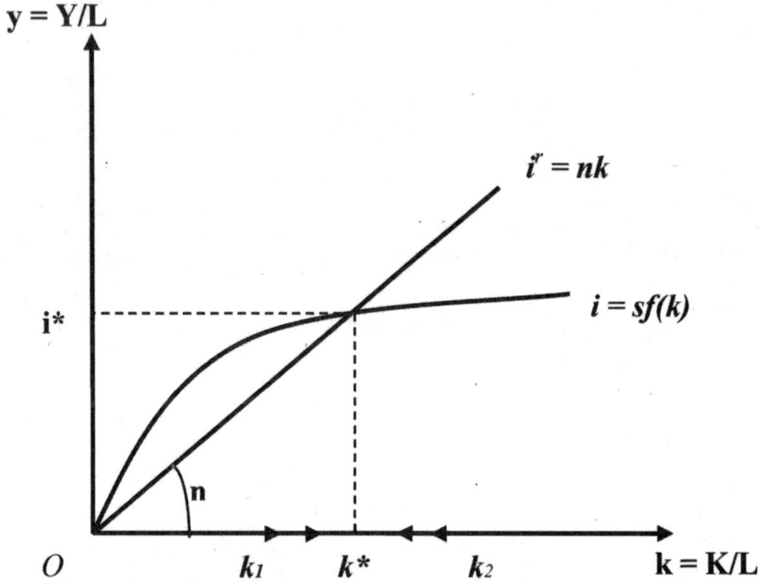

Figure 4.4 Steady-state growth

interaction between his investment function and entrepreneurs' expectations by generating a mechanism that tolerates cumulative divergences between saving and investment plans or between saving and entrepreneurs' expectations. In fact, Solow noted: "This fundamental opposition of warranted and natural rates turns out in the end to flow from the crucial assumption that the production takes place under conditions of *fixed proportions*. There is no possibility of substituting labor for capital in production. If this assumption is abandoned, the knife-edge notion of unstable balance seems to go with it. Indeed it is hardly surprising that such a gross rigidity in one part of the system should entail lack of flexibility in another [italics in original]" (Solow 1956, 65–6).

As a result of the absence of an independent investment function, the second instability problem in Harrod is not reflected in Solow's model. Therefore, the expectations of entrepreneurs have no influence on the economy in general and on the aggregate production function in particular. In effect, Sen commented on the following:

> Since, however, no independent investment function is introduced and since expectations are not given an independent existence

(e.g. basing them on past experience), the problem of being away from warranted growth to start with is not allowed to trigger off a dis-equilibrium in the Harrod-Domar fashion. Thus what Solow and Swan do consists not merely of relaxing the assumption of fixed coefficients, but also of changing the expectational assumption. This robs Harrod's warranted growth path of its unstable equilibrium property, even before its reconciliation with natural growth rate is started.[12] (Sen 1970, 230)

CAPITAL DEPRECIATION IN SOLOW'S MODEL: AN EXTENSION OF A SIMPLE NEOCLASSICAL MODEL

The basic neoclassical model of a growing economy can be extended also in the case of a depreciating capital stock. Accordingly, the macroeconomic equilibrium condition can be rewritten as $i=sf(k)$ from equation (4.7a). In order for k to remain constant, capital must grow not only as a result of population growth but also to cover the depreciation of old capital. Specifically, we now have

$$ir = (n + \delta)k \qquad (4.44)$$

as our required investment rate, where δ is the capital depreciation rate. The fundamental Solowian differential equation now needs to be rewritten as

$$k^{\cdot} = sf(k) - (n + \delta)k \qquad (4.45)$$

In terms of figure 4.2, all that will happen when we insert capital depreciation is that the required investment line irwill become steeper (with slope $n + \delta$) and the steady-state ratio k_2^* will be lower, as seen in figure 4.5, than k_1^*. Now the growth rates of the variable-capital stock, output, and consumption, however, all rise to $n + \delta$ as illustrated in figure 4.5.

Solow has extended and modified his basic model by considering alternative production functions that include technological change, endogenous labour supply, variable savings rate, and taxation. For example, he took into consideration the case of the Cobb-Douglas production function. In fact, all the analyses outlined previously could be duplicated using the Cobb-Douglas form of the aggregate production function rather than the general form on which our exposition has been based.[13]

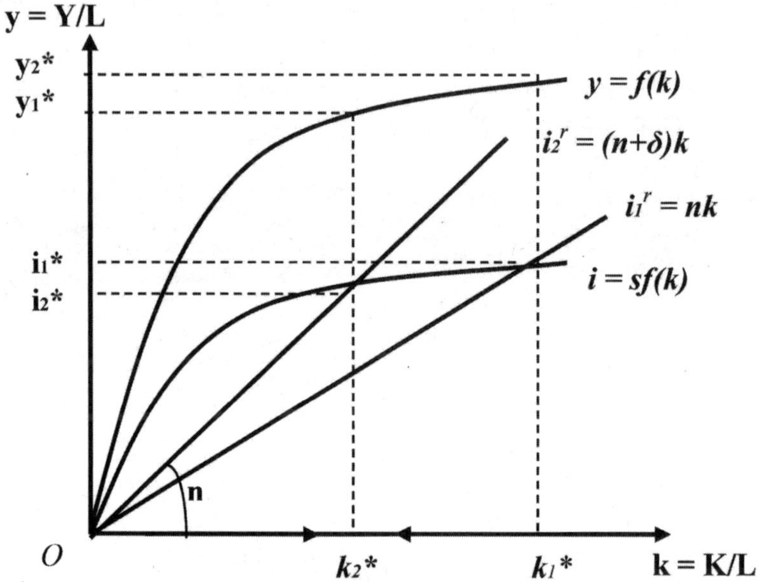

Figure 4.5 Steady-state growth with depreciation

SUBSTITUTION VS. FIXED PRODUCTION COEFFICIENTS: THE JOHANSEN[14] MODEL

Most growth models in the 1950s and 1960s were based either on the assumption of fixed production coefficients for labour and capital or on the assumption of substitutability between factors. Johansen classified the models of neoclassical growth into three groups (Johansen 1959, 157). In the first group were models with a given capital coefficient, where the labour input (or the growth of population) is not considered directly in the analysis but rather is treated vaguely and not much specified. This group includes the pioneering growth models generated by Harrod (1939), Domar (1946), Hans Brems (1957), and Robert Eisner (1952). In the second group, we have models with fixed production coefficients for labour input as well as for the capital stock. Here we have a number of economists who have done a great deal of work in the field of input-output analysis, such as Wassily Leontief (1953), Oskar Lange (1957), and others. The third group consists of models with expressed possibilities of substitution between labour input and capital stock in a production function. The most representative studies of this group are the works of Solow (1956) and Swan (1956), but of the same importance are also the works of Jan Tinbergen (1950), Trygve Haavelmo (1954), and Stefan Valavanis-Val (1955). Johansen (1959), diverging from other authors, recommended a new model of growth based not on fixed or substitution production coefficients but instead on a middle ground between the two positions called "substitution possibilities *at the margin*" (Johansen 1959, 158). He proposed a model of compromise between two extremes (fixed and substitution coefficients) using an increase in labour and capital inputs, where a proportion of capital that is already installed will continue to operate by using a constant amount of labour.

The object of Johansen's model is to prove that there is always an alternative in choosing the substitution of production factors based on the purpose of the research such as, the possibility of adopting new techniques, the new rate of investment, the relationship between population growth and unemployment, etc. Johansen assumed that the substitution possibilities between capital and labour are ex-ante, or *at the margin*, and not ex-post as suggested by the greater part of neoclassical substitution models. As such, once a portion of capital is produced and has been put into operation, it will continue to operate through all its life with a constant amount of labour input. So the gross increment in the rate of production is obtained by different increments in capital and labour input ex-ante. Johansen finds the hypothesis of ex-ante substitution possibilities more realistic and applicable than the widely accepted ex-post substitution possibilities. He stated, "In fact, I have the feeling that the hypothesis applied in this paper is closer to the experience of many students of economic growth who approach these questions from a 'practical' point of view, and it may possibly be helpful in removing some of the 'guilty conscience' of some theorists in the field who rely either on fixed coefficients or on full substitutability in a 'classical' sense" (Johansen 1959, 174).

His model of growth later became known as the putty-clay model of production, where factor proportions are variable ex-ante and fixed ex-post. The paradoxical result in Johansen's putty-clay model – that savings and investment do not seem to affect growth – is examined by using a growth-accounting framework in which investment efforts generally influence output growth. However, this influence is not revealed in a proper way when the investment ratio is fixed. Interpreted in a one-country case, the existence of a positive relationship between the propensity to invest and the growth rate of output is demonstrated.

The Johansen (1959) model is characterized by two factors of production, labour and capital, thus producing an output that is used either for consumption or for accumulation. It assumes full employment of labour and capital, and the new production techniques are introduced only by means of new capital equipment. Johansen assumes the declining value (shrinkage) of capital over time, which means that an amount of capital produced will shrink (proportionately to the original capital) according to a given function of its age. In fact, if an amount of capital $k(t)$ is produced in the time interval $t - 1$, then an amount $f(\varepsilon)k(t)$ of this capital will still be active at time $t + \varepsilon$. The total rate of production at time t is obtained simply by the integration of output from all ages of capital (Johansen 1959, 162)

$$x(t) = \int_{-\infty}^{t} f(t-\varepsilon)y(\varepsilon)d\varepsilon \tag{4.46}$$

where $y(\varepsilon)$ is the gross investment, which is given as

$$y(t) = \delta[n(t), k(t), x(t), t] \tag{4.47}$$

where $x(t)$ is the rate of production at time t, $n(t)$ is the labour force, and $k(t)$ is the rate of gross investment. The function δ is assumed to be homogeneous of degree one in n and k. An increase $\dot{x}(t)$ affects a gross increase $y(t)$ because of $n(t)$ and $k(t)$, and a deduction $y(t) - \dot{x}(t)$ is the result of the decrease of the existing capital. The total labour force $N(t)$ is exogenously given and is distributed over capital of different ages. The total labour force obtained as a result of integration is given as

$$N(t) = \int_{-\infty}^{t} f(t-\varepsilon)n(\varepsilon)d\varepsilon \tag{4.48}$$

where at time t the labour input $n(t)$ is reduced by $f(t - \varepsilon)n(\varepsilon)$. By a similar integration, we obtain the total amount of capital as

$$K(t) = \int_{\infty}^{t} f(t-\varepsilon)k(\varepsilon)d\varepsilon \tag{4.49}$$

The rate of production $x(t)$ is related to $N(t)$ and $K(t)$. The necessary and sufficient condition for the production structure to hold is that the function δ (from [4.47]) must be linear in n and k. Moreover, the Johansen model is built with no substitution possibilities. So once the capital equipment has been constructed, there is no possibility of changing the factors. To maintain this rigidity, the capital equipment designed must use a definite amount of labour. Johansen uses a simple rule for the revaluation of capital. A new unit of capital will last as follows (Johansen 1959, 163):

$$T(0) = \int_{0}^{\infty} f(\varepsilon) d\varepsilon \tag{4.50}$$

A unit of capital η periods old on average will have

$$T(\eta) = \frac{1}{f(\eta)} \int_{0}^{\infty} f(\varepsilon) d\varepsilon \tag{4.51}$$

periods left. Using an integration form, the value of total capital is given as

$$V(t) = \frac{1}{T(0)} \int_{-\infty}^{t} f(t-\varepsilon) T(t-\varepsilon) k(\varepsilon) d\varepsilon \tag{4.52}$$

which is written as

$$V(t) = \frac{1}{T(0)} \int_{r=-\infty}^{t} k(\varepsilon) \int_{\xi=t-\varepsilon}^{\infty} f(\xi) d\xi d\varepsilon \tag{4.53}$$

By differentiation of equation (4.53), we obtain a simple form of the rate of net investment:

$$I(t) = V(t) = k(t) - \frac{1}{T(0)} K(t) \tag{4.54}$$

If a constant fraction β of savings is applied, then the rate of net investment can be written as

$$I(t) = \beta x(t) - \frac{1}{T(0)} K(t) \tag{4.55}$$

which implies

$$k(t) = \beta x(t) + \frac{1}{T(0)} (1-\beta) K(t) \tag{4.56}$$

The above fundamental function means that the rate of gross investment $k(t)$ depends on the rate of production at time t, which is proportional to the rate of saving β and on the total stock of capital $K(t)$, which is inversely proportional to the unit of capital $1/T(0)$ at time 0.

Johansen wants to focus his model on the behaviour of the producers, and to accomplish this, he works out the solutions for special cases with different forms of production functions. In the case of a fixed lifetime for every unit of capital used in production, we have

$$T(0) = \theta \tag{4.57}$$

where θ is the time limit of each unit of capital. In this case, a linear and homogeneous production function is assumed:

$$\mu\ (n, k, x, t) = an + bk \tag{4.58}$$

with a and b constants. By combining the equations (4.46), (4.48), and (4.49), we now have a production function relating the rate of production $x(t)$ with labour force, N, and capital stock, K:

$$x(t) = \int_{t-\theta}^{t} y(\varepsilon)d\varepsilon = aN(t) + bK(t) \tag{4.59}$$

Considering the savings function (4.56), we get

$$k(t) = \beta x(t) + \frac{1}{\theta}(1-\beta)K(t) \tag{4.60}$$

Taking into account the exponential growth of the labour force N, we have

$$N(t) = N_0 e^{\upsilon t} \tag{4.61}$$

From equation (4.48), we obtain

$$N(t) = \int_{-\infty}^{t} n(\varepsilon)d\varepsilon \tag{4.62}$$

By differentiating (4.62) and then combining it with equation (4.61), we get

$$n(t) = N(t) = n_0 e^{\upsilon t} \qquad (4.63)$$

where $n_0 = \dfrac{\nu N_0}{1 - e^{-\upsilon\theta}}$

Combining equations (4.59) and (4.60) using a mixed difference–differential equation,[15] we obtain

$$\dot{k}(t) = \gamma\left[k(t) - k(t-\theta)\right] + a\beta\upsilon N_0{}^{\upsilon t} \qquad (4.64)$$

where $y = \dfrac{1}{\theta}[1 - \beta(\theta b - 1)]$

From (4.64), it is implied that the solution of a homogeneous equation can be expressed as a sum of exponential expressions (Johansen 1959, 172). By using an exponential expression $Ce^{\sigma t}$ for $k(t)$ in equation (4.64), we get a simplified growth equation,

$$\omega = \gamma(1 - e^{\sigma\theta}) \qquad (4.65)$$

where $\omega = 0$ is the first solution and $\gamma\theta = [1 + a(\theta b - 1)] \neq 1$ is the second solution. For $\theta b > 1$, there is a profitability of production through the employment of capital, b, where θ is the productive lifetime of capital. Reconsidering equation (4.58) and introducing a changing marginal productivity of labour by using a given exponential function of time, we obtain

$$\mu(n,k,x,t) = a_0 e^{\lambda t} n + bk \qquad (4.66)$$

where a_0 is the marginal productivity of labour (at $t = 0$) and λ is the constant rate of increase in this productivity. If $n = 0$ and $k = 0$, then it satisfies $\mu(0,0, x, t) = 0$.

Thus, in Johansen's study, the shift in the form of production function from the regular assumption of substitutability to the assumption of "substitutability at the margin" is more sensitive. Before the equipment is built ex-ante, there is a wide choice of factor proportions. However, after the machine is constructed and installed, ex-post, there are no opportunities for substitution, and a fixed amount of labour per machine is required. The industry normally does not have fixed coefficients because can be a deviation in the capacity employed; therefore, a rise in demand may create a rise in the employment of old labour-intensive machinery.

According to Johansen, the choice of the type of substitutability between production factors depends more on the objects of study – such as the rate of investment, the possibility of adopting new techniques, the importance of obsolescence, the relation between population growth and unemployment, and so forth – rather than on the general case of substitutability between two factors as used by neoclassical economists.

FIXED PRODUCTION COEFFICIENTS AND INPUT-OUTPUT ANALYSIS IN LEONTIEF[16]

An interesting point in this section will be to have a further development of the fixed production coefficients for labour input and stock capital, but this time, in terms of input-output analysis. Broadly speaking, the input-output analysis is the study of inter-industry relationships in a national economy. An understanding of inter-related sectors goes back to the work of French economist François Quesnay (1968[1758]),[17] who developed an earlier version of input-output technique called Tableau économique, which was further developed by Léon Walras in 1874 in his well-known work *Elements of Pure Economics* on general equilibrium theory. Leontief's main contribution was to put the relationships between sectors into mathematical terms and simplify Walras's study so that it could be implemented empirically in real world input-output tables. His model describes a system of production and demand processes, and how changes in demand in one economic sector would influence production in another. The system representing inter-industry relations demonstrates how the output of one industry is an input to each other industry, and all the information contained in this system is put in a form of a matrix. Leontief published his first input-output tables of the United States economy in 1936. The structure of the first table was a matrix listing of 42 sectors drawn from the 1919 US Census of Manufactures, which were put in same sequence both vertically and horizontally. Leontief is indebted for his analysis of input-output tables to the physiocrat François Quesnay (1758) who divided the French economy into three sectors – farmers, manufacturers, and landowners – and proved how these three sectors were interrelated with each other. Léon Walras, a nineteenth-century economist, by using the sophisticated equations of an economy in general equilibrium in which the balance is created to the intersection of demand and supply, motivated Leontief in his study. Leontief reformulated the Walrasian general equilibrium system, in which intermediate goods were expressed as a set of equations of the sales and purchases of intermediate sectors, creating a self-contained system of economic interrelationships called also a "closed system." It is a closed system because the final demand and value added components are taken as endogenous. In 1941 Leontief published a more complete exposition of input-output tables including 44 industrial sectors and more than 2,000 production coefficients with a full empirical structure containing the US Census of Manufactures for the 1919–29 period. In 1951 Leontief decided to modernize the economic system to an "open model" where the final demand and value added components are considered exogenous. The production relationships for major industries were presented in a large set of mathematical equations, one for each commodity produced in the economy, which were solved with the aid of a computer. The solution of these linear equations had a great value for an economy, as it tells how much of all other goods had to be produced in order to get one more durable good like a refrigerator, washing machine, oven, or car. If the other components were not produced as required by production needs, there would be shortages of parts and whole production lines could be in difficulties, and therefore the new refrigerator, stove or car could not be made. But if all inputs were produced, then there would be no problem to get extra final outputs and commodities. In Leontief's input-output analysis it is possible to compute the direct and indirect effects of a given change in the final demand for one particular commodity on the total of outputs of all sectors of the economy. The input-output tables of an open system can determine the relationship between three sets of parameters: 1) the set of all prices, 2) the set of all wage rates, and 3) the set of all unit profit rates. If two sets are known the third one can be computed indirectly (Leontief 1949a, 215). From Walras' description of general equilibrium, Leontief recreates the relationship between the total output of a given industry and the total input of commodities and services from other industries. This relationship is given in terms of production function and fixed coefficients of production, each coefficient describing an input necessary to produce a final output. Referring to the final demand or consumption of the *i*th good as *Ti* we can write a system of equations representing the equilibrium conditions of production and consumption of each commodity in different industries (Leontief 1949b, 275).

$$\begin{aligned} &X_1 - x_{21} - x_{31} - \dots - x_{m1} = T_{n1} \\ &-x_{12} + X_2 - x_{32} - \dots - x_{m2} = T_{n2} \\ &-x_{13} - x_{23} + X_3 - \dots - x_{m3} = T_{n3} \\ &\dots\dots\dots\dots\dots\dots\dots\dots\dots\dots \\ &-x_{1m} - x_{2m} - x_{3m} - \dots + X_m = T_{nm} \\ &-x_{1n} - x_{2n} - x_{3n} X_2 - \dots - x_{mn} + X_n = 0 \end{aligned} \tag{4.67}$$

The X_1 shows the total output of the industry 1 in the first equation of the system (4.67) where each of the x_{i1} represents the amount of the commodity of industry 1 used in other industries (i = 2,3…). The last equation, instead, represents the labour inputs x_{in} absorbed by different sectors/industries and the total labour input X_n. By using constants a_{ik} as coefficients of production, where each constant represents input per unit of output (the ratio of input/output for each industry), we can get to a simple system of equations written as

$$x_{ik} = a_{ik} X_i, \ i = 1,2,3\dots, m; \ k = 1,2,3,\dots m,n; \ i{\neq}k \tag{4.68}$$

The next step is to substitute all equations created in (4.68) into (4.67), eliminating in this way the x_{ik} from all equations of the system (4.67). Each input in one industry can be represented as a function of the total output X_i of the same industry. Thus, the system is written as:

$$\begin{aligned} &X_1 - a_{21} X_2 - a_{31} X_3 - \dots - a_{m1} X_m = T_{n1} \\ &- a_{12} X_1 + X_2 - a_{32} X_3 - \dots - a_{m2} X_m = T_{n2} \\ &- a_{13} X_1 - a_{23} X_2 + X_3 - \dots - a_{m3} X_m = a_{n3} \\ &\dots\dots\dots\dots\dots\dots\dots\dots\dots\dots \\ &-a_{1m} X_1 - a_{2m} X_2 - a_{3m} X_3 - \dots + X_m = T_{nm} \\ &-a_{1n} X_1 - a_{2n} X_2 - a_{3n} X_3 - \dots - a_{mn} + X_m + X_n = 0 \end{aligned} \tag{4.69}$$

Every X_i which represents total outputs can be expressed as functions of the final demands given by T_n. If the magnitude of all coefficients a_i is known, under certain assumptions, the output of individual industries can be computed as a function of final demand T_n (Leontief 1949b, 278). Therefore, the solution of the system (4.69) takes the general form of equations:

$$X_i = A_{i1}\, T_{01'} + A_{i2}\, T_{n2} + \ldots + A_{im}\, T_{nm} \quad i = 1,2,3\ldots, m,n \tag{4.70}$$

where A is a fixed coefficient calculated from the determinant of the matrix coefficients of all production coefficients a_{ik}. A is given is given in a relationship with the determinant M as :

$$A_{ik} = | M_{ik} | / | M | \tag{4.71}$$

where the determinant $| M |$ has its base on the matrix $| a_{ik} |$ and $| M_{ik} |$ is a complement element of the matrix a_{ik}. By calculating the inverse of the structural matrix (even of large sizes) we can compute the dependence of each output on the each kind of final demand.

Another problem considered by Leontief is the price relationships in the input-output matrices. The final demand on outputs is made of primary inputs, which receive returns/profits. A primary input is normally a non-produced factor of production such as land or labour, and the magnitude of these inputs is measured in monetary amounts. For example, workers sell their labour skills to firms for a salary and in return use their salary to buy consumption goods, which are produced by different industries. Using the industry system in (4.69) and having *n* prices, *P1*, *P2*, …, *Pn* one for each particular kind of output and having the wage rate defined as w_n and profit rate as π for each industry, we have a new industry system given as,

$$\begin{aligned}
&P_1 - a_{21}\, P_2 - a_{31}\, P_3 - \ldots - a_{1m}\, P_n - a_{1n}\, w_n - \pi_1 = 0 \\
&- a_{21}\, P_1 + P_2 - a_{23}\, P_3 - \ldots - a_{2m}\, P_n - a_{2n}\, w_n - \pi_2 = 0 \\
&- a_{31}\, P_1 - a_{32}\, P_2 + P_3 - \ldots - a_{3m}\, P_n - a_{3n}\, w_n - \pi_3 - 0 \\
&\ldots\ldots\ldots\ldots\ldots\ldots\ldots\ldots\ldots\ldots\ldots\ldots \\
&- a_{n1}\, P_1 - a_{n2}\, P_2 - a_{n3}\, P_3 - \ldots + P_n - a_{nn}\, w_n - \pi_n = 0
\end{aligned} \tag{4.72}$$

The (4.72) system lies in certain limits (Leontief 1949b, 279). For example, if all the prices were fixed and wages were forced to remain to certain levels then there would be only one profit system composed of one column of profit rates which could be earned in different sectors and be mostly consistent with certain prices and wages.

The markup sale price must cover the cost of input or raw materials from other firms and wages for the labour used to produce output. In the absence of surplus, equality can be assumed between sectors.

$$\begin{aligned} P_1 &= P_1 a_{11} + P_2 a_{21} + ... + P_n a_{n1} + wa_{01} \\ P_2 &= P_1 a_{12} + P_2 a_{22} + ... + P_n a_{n2} + wa_{02} \\ &\cdots\cdots\cdots\cdots\cdots\cdots\cdots\cdots \\ P_m &= P_1 a_{1n} + P_2 a_{2n} + ... + P_n a_{nn} + wa_{0n} \end{aligned} \tag{4.73}$$

where a_{n1} is the amount of labour necessary to produce a unit of good *m* and *w* is the wage received by workers to produced the finished goods. The systems of equations (4.73) can be translated into a matrix form,

$$\begin{aligned} &P_1 \; a_{11} \; a_{21} \; \cdots \; a_{n1} \; P_1 \; a_{01} \\ &P_2 = a_{12} \; a_{22} \; .... \; a_{n2} \; P_2 \; a_{02} \\ &\cdots\cdots \; \cdots\cdots \; \cdots \; \cdots\cdots\cdots \; \cdots\cdots + \cdots\cdots \\ &P_m \; a_{1n} \; a_{2n} \; .... \; a_{nn} \; P_m \; a_{0n} \end{aligned} \tag{4.74}$$

where a unit of labour can be written as a column vector $a_0 = [a_{01}, ..., a_{0n}]$, then the coefficients a_{nn} are represented by A (*nx n* matrix) so the matrix (4.74) assumes the simple form as

$$P = AP + wa_0 \tag{4.75}$$

Using the identity matrix *I* (AA-1 = A-1A = I_n), expression (4.75) is transformed in,

$$(I - A)P = wa_0 \tag{4.76}$$

Given that (4.76) is not a homogeneous system the inversion matrix can help find a solution, and therefore is *P* given as,

$$P = (I - A)\text{-}1wa_0 \tag{4.77}$$

where (I – A)-1 is the inverse matrix which exists and is non-singular. This can be proved by calling up the Hawkins-Simon condition (1949), which requires that when the principal leading minors are positive, then an inverse matrix $(I - A)^{-1}$ exists and is non-negative.[18] Therefore, for any given non-negative set of unit wage bills, wa_0, there is a set of non-negative prices that solve the system (4.75). This has an interesting application to explain the relation between prices, wages, and profits. For example, if there is a wage increase by 5 per cent the matrix system on calculation will tell the price increase in all different industries. This

Table 4.1 Example of a simple input-output table (in dollars)

Sectors	*Into*				
	Agriculture	*Manufacturing*	*Households*	*Exports*	*Total output*
From					
Agriculture	40	50	70	40	200
Manufacturing	60	30	90	60	240
Households	70	100	50	90	310
Imports	30	60	100	70	260
Total input	200	240	310	260	

analysis is much more significant than some index of an average price increase for the whole system. Leontief's extensions of input-output analysis demonstrated that the estimated coefficients were sufficiently stable to be used in comparative static analyses. Table 4.1 is an example of an intersectorial input-output table.

Despite Leontief's efforts on input-output analysis, input-output tables encountered two major problems: first, only part of the information used for production coefficients was technically available in statistical standard format (through the US Census of Manufactures); the rest had to be found from other, unconventional statistical sources like business journals, trade magazines, and other sources. Second, Leontief's analysis is largely based on the assumption that production coefficients remain constant for extended periods. Realistically, this proposition was not possible with the neoclassical theory of production, where the factors of production such as different quantities of labour and capital expressed in isoquants were substituted for one another affected by price changes.

Leontief was a master of new economics findings that sometimes would contradict even consolidated theories and models. In fact, Leontief's findings based on empirical studies undermined the validity of the Heckscher-Ohlin (H-O) model, which was based on the supposition that each country exports the commodity which uses its abundant factor intensively and that trade was based on countries' comparative advantage in the main factors of production such as capital and labour. This is commonly known Leontief's paradox. According to theory, therefore, a capital-rich country like the United States, Germany, France, or the United Kingdom should export capital intensive-goods and import labour-intensive goods. The H-O theory was generally accepted based on some casual empirical data, as there was no tested technique available until the input-output analysis was introduced. Leontief (1986, Ch.5, 6), after aggregating the American economy in 50 sectors (38 industries producing commodities for the international market and 12 sectors counting for non-traded goods) and combining factors in two categories, labour and capital, found that American exports used less capital and more labour in their production than did American imports.

During the 1970s interest in input-output analysis declined for a few reasons. One is that the economic studies were shifting away from inter-sector planning and back toward allowing the market to determine growth. Another reason is that input-output analysis had limitations: it was extremely difficult and expensive to estimate all the current input-output relationships for a large and complex economy or region. On average the analysis takes 3–5 years or more. In addition, some countries do not collect all the required data, and data quality varies even though there is a set of standards for data collection set out by the United Nations though the System of National Accounts (SNA). As a result, many input-output data were out of date and useless for effective policy analysis. Technological improvements in the 1980s meant also that production coefficients were continuously changing, which resulted in changes in input-output relationships. But input-output analysis takes these relationships as fixed, and therefore the input-output tables were not very reliable on an environment of continuous economic change.

The methodology of economics was a field that did not go unnoticed for Leontief. He felt that many economists were ignoring empirical estimates in favour of building abstract models and formal theories that did not have much practical evidence to support them. He went also further to address this issue of how his colleagues were doing economics in his presidential address to the eighty-third meeting of the American Economic Association in 1970. Leontief (1971) criticized the mathematical models built with assumptions that were not realistic and not based on statistical testing techniques. By simply analyzing the articles published in the *American Economic Review* journal in one year, he found that over half of articles fell into the category of mathematical/formal models without any data, and and therefore unrelated to actual economic relationships,

Despite the loss of interest by many economists in input-output tables, for the reasons mentioned above, input-output analysis remains today an active branch of economics with numerous functions. Some of its most popular applications are those related to national accounts and trade, environmental studies, and forecasts of technological change.

ECONOMIC GROWTH AND THE GOLDEN RULE ACCUMULATION IN PHELPS

To derive the golden rule, Phelps[19] assumed that the economy is constrained to follow a path of balanced growth, with a growth rate determined by population (and perhaps technology). Suppose for a moment an economy with capital stock sufficiently large that desires to reach a certain capital-labour ratio that, once achieved, must be maintained forever out of the economy's own savings. If the capital stock is large, per capita output will be high, but most of it will have to be saved, therefore leaving little for consumption. If the capital stock is low, almost the whole income is available for consumption, but income itself will also be low. So between large and low capital stock, there must be a certain level of capital stock for which per capita consumption is at its maximum. According to Phelps, a golden-age path is a growth path in which every variable changes at a constant relative rate. He commented that, "In a golden age, if investment is positive, then investment, consumption and output must all grow at the same constant relative rate, denoted g ... If investment (hence output and consumption) is growing at some constant rate, g, and capital is growing exponentially then capital must also be growing at rate g" (Phelps 1965, 797 and 801).

Phelps derives the golden rule path from two different aggregate models: one with a neoclassical production function and the other with simple, fixed coefficients (the Harrod-Domar production function). Both models assume that technological progress is not embodied in capital goods and is purely labour augmenting. Phelps proves that a necessary condition for the existence of the golden rule path is that technological progress must be labour augmenting. He assumes that the labour force grows exponentially at the rate γ, given as[20]

$$L(t) = L_0 e^{\gamma t}, \gamma \geq 0 \tag{4.78}$$

and output $Q(t)$ is a continuous function of capital $K(t)$, labour $L(t)$, and time

$$Q(t) = F\left[K(t), e^{t\lambda} L(t)\right] \lambda \geq 0 \tag{4.79}$$

where λ is a constant exponential rate (referred to as labour augmentations). Capital is subject to exponential decay at rate δ. Denoting $I(t)$, the rate of gross investment, we get

$$I(t) = \dot{K}(t) + \delta(t) \quad \delta \geq 0 \tag{4.80}$$

The consumption $C(t)$ is the difference between output and gross investment, written as

$$C(t) = Q(t) - I(t) \quad C(t) \geq 0 \tag{4.81}$$

Considering the neoclassical production function,[21] the output in virtue of constant returns to scale is given as (from equation [4.78])

$$Q(t) = L_0 E^{(\gamma+\lambda)} F\left[\frac{K(t)}{L_0 e^{(\gamma+\lambda)t}}, 1\right] \tag{4.82}$$

If we denote $k(t)$ as capital per unit of effective labour, we have

$$k(t) = \frac{K(t)}{L_0 e^{(\gamma+\lambda)t}} \tag{4.83}$$

Defining $f(k(t)) = F[k(t),1]$, the production function can be expressed for all t as

$$Q(t) = L_0 e^{(\gamma+\lambda)t} f(k(t)), \text{ where } f'(k(t) > 0, f''(k(t) < 0 \tag{4.84}$$

Hence, the economy will grow in the manner of the golden age if output grows exponentially at rate $g = \gamma + \lambda$. Thus, for $Q(t)$, we have the following identity (Phelps 1965, 796):

$$Q(t) = L_0 e^{(\gamma+\lambda)t} f(k) = Q(0) e^{gt} \tag{4.85}$$

And for capital stock, it implies

$$K(t) = L_0 e^{(\gamma+\lambda)t} k = K(0) e^{gt} \tag{4.86}$$

From equation (4.80) and the relation $K^{\cdot}(t) = g\, K(t)$, gross investment will grow at the rate g. So we have

$$I(t) = (g+\delta)K(0)e^{gt} = (g+\delta)L_0 k e^{gt} \tag{4.87}$$

If investment and output grow at the same rate, g, then consumption also will grow at the same rate. Substituting equations (4.85) and (4.87) in (4.81), we get

$$C(t) = \left[Q(0) - (g+\delta)K(0)\right]e^{gt} = \left[f(k) - (g+\delta)k\right]L_0 e^{gt} \tag{4.88}$$

The marginal productivity of capital is given as

$$(\delta F/\delta K) = f'(k) \tag{4.89}$$

Maximizing the term $C(t)$ to obtain the neoclassical optimal growth, we then get the first-order condition for maximum optimization. Differentiating equation (4.88) with respect to k, we have the final product as follows:

$$\frac{dC(t)}{dk} = f'(k) - (g+\delta) = 0 \tag{4.90}$$

Therefore, the consumption-maximizing golden age is reached when $K(0)$ is increased to the point where $(\delta F/\delta K) - (g + \delta) = 0$. In other words, the marginal product of capital will equal $g + \delta$ on the golden rule path; hence, we have

$$(\delta F/\delta K) - \delta = g \tag{4.91}$$

The left-hand side of the above equation – where $(\delta F/\delta K)$ is assumed as the gross rental rate of capital and $[(\delta F/\delta K) - \delta]$ is the equilibrium rate of interest – is the social net rate of return to investment (Phelps 1965, 798). Equation (4.91) states that a golden age consumption maximum exists if the social net rate of return to investment equals the golden-age growth rate. Equation (4.91) also implies that, on the golden path, the interest rate is equal to the golden age growth rate.

Figure 4.6 depicts the relation between $K(0)$ and $C(0)$ in a golden-age phase as given by equation (4.88). It represents a golden-age consumption maximum at $K(0) = K'(0)$, where $(\delta F/\delta K) = g + \delta$. What is to be maximized is the vertical distance between the $I(0)$ curve (necessary investment) and the $Q(0)$ curve (the required capital accumulation)

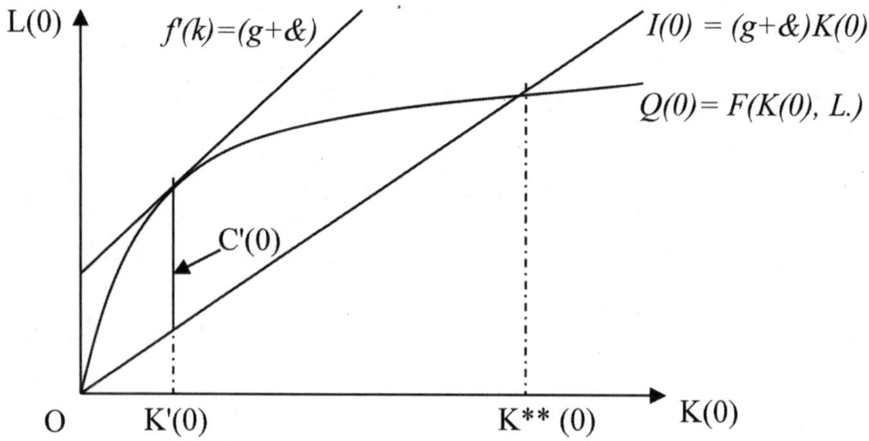

Figure 4.6 Golden-age consumption maximum

given by the rate of consumption $C'(0)$, which is maximized at $K'(0)$. The highest point of difference is simply found by placing a line parallel to $I(0)$ at its tangency with the $Q(0)$ curve. This is shown in figure 4.6, where $f'(k) = (g + \delta)$. Therefore, $C'(0)$ is determined by subtracting the ordinate of the straight line, given by $(g + \delta)K(0)$, from the ordinate of the curve, given by $F(K(0), L)$. It can be immediately confirmed that $0 < C'(0) < Q(0)$, so the constraints on the control variable are satisfied. For reference, in figure 4.6 $K^{**}(0)$ is drawn, which is the value at which $Q(0) = (g + \delta)K(0)$. Thus, the golden rule growth is the condition for optimal growth. The solution $K'(0)$, $C'(0)$ is called the balanced growth path because, in it, both capital and consumption per head are constant, which means that capital stock and consumption grow at the same rate as population.

In economic terms, the golden rule result is interpreted as the outcome where the same amount of consumption is provided to members of current as well as future generations' ability to have a steady-state growth. Moreover, a savings rate also exists that maximizes the steady-state consumption per person, which is called the golden rule saving rate.

OVERSAVINGS AND DYNAMIC INEFFICIENCY

The other side of the golden rule is the dynamic efficiency. An economy is said to be oversaving if the per capita consumption is lower than the

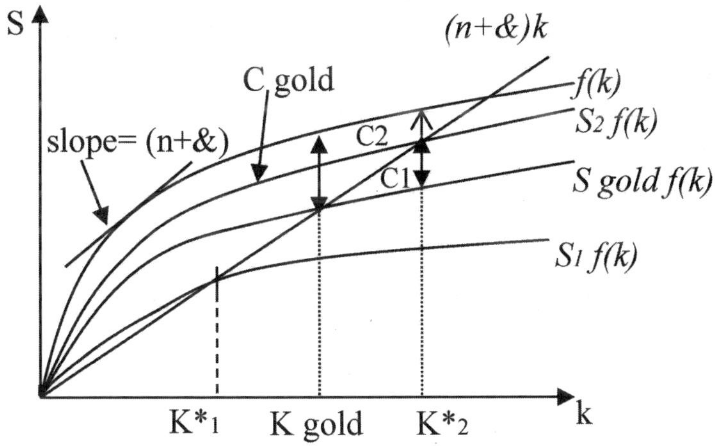

Figure 4.7 Dynamic inefficiency

steady-state level of consumption. This means that the economy is saving more than required. A savings rate above the golden rule is supposed to be dynamically inefficient. To better understand dynamic inefficiency, we consider the following illustration:

Figure 4.7 considers three possible savings rates: the golden savings rate and other two rates of saving that are positioned on either side of the golden saving rate, $s_1 < s_{gold} < s_2$. As seen in the figure, consumption per person, *c*, in each case equals the vertical distance between the production function $f(k)$and the appropriate $sf(k)$ curve. For each savings rate, *s*, the steady-state value k^* corresponds to the intersection between the $sf(k)$ curve and the $(n + \delta)k$ line (Barro and Sala-i-Martin 1995, 19–22). The steady-state per capita consumption, c^*, is maximized when $k^* = k_{gold}$ because the tangent to the production function at this point parallels the $(n + \delta)k$ line. The savings rate, s, that gives $k^* = k_{gold}$ is the one that makes the $sf(k)$ curve cross the $(n + \delta)k$ line at the value k_{gold}. Because $s_1 < s_{gold} < s_2$, we also have that $k^*_1 < k_{gold} < k^*_2$. A savings rate that exceeds s_{gold} forever is inefficient because higher quantities of per capita consumption could be obtained at all points in time by reducing the savings rate. To make things easier we can take into consideration an economy having a savings rate s_2, for which $s_2 > s_{gold}$, so $k_{gold} > k^*_2$ and $c_2 < c_{gold}$, and supposing (starting from the steady state) that the savings rate is reduced permanently to s_{gold}. The figure above shows that per capita consumption, *c* (given by vertical distance between $f(k)$ and

$s_{gold}f(k)$ curves) initially is increased by a discrete amount. So the level of c drops during transition toward its new steady-state level, c_{gold} and because $c_2 < c_{gold}$, we have that c exceeds its previous value, c_2, at all transitional states as well as in the new steady state, c_{gold}. The most typical economy that happens to be in the oversaving state is when $s > s_{gold}$. This distinctive position means that per capita consumption at all points in time could be raised by simply lowering the saving rate. Therefore, an economy that oversaves is technically dynamically inefficient because the path of per capita consumption at all points in time or most of the time lies below possible alternative paths.[22]

The golden rule offered to economists a simple criterion for the evaluation of economic performance. This, however, was accomplished at the price of simplifying growth models, the nature of which can best be appreciated by posing the problem of optimal capital accumulation in a more general form. The ingenious mathematician Frank Ramsey was the first to use the calculus of variations to determine an optimal savings path (Ramsey 1928). The key of Ramsey's model was the proper evaluation of future consumption against present consumption; it was limited to a constant population with an unchanging satisfaction level of consumption.

The optimal path normally involves a variation of savings over time as it starts with an arbitrary level of initial stock. As a matter of fact, the combination of initial capital goods with the restriction of balanced growth by preventing the need to evaluate present against future consumption, led some economists to make efforts to derive growth without comparing present and future satisfactions.[23] Unfortunately, well known as it is, the golden rule has not provided much practical help in reality. In fact, if the inherited capital stock is below the golden rule capital stock, it will first have to be increased by savings in order to reach the golden rule savings; in a second possible case, the economy can first afford extra consumption. If both cases are taken in consideration, optimization would require a weighing of present against future consumption. The golden rule was a significant contribution to the neoclassical theory of growth because it describes the relationship between interest rates and growth, despite its lack of practical applicability to the real economy.

It is interesting here to mention that in Von Neumann's general equilibrium model (1937[1945]),[24] the growth rate and the interest rate result from the dual problem of maximizing the former and minimizing the latter without any optimization of consumption. Conversely, in the Solow model, the same equality turned out to be a condition for maximal permanent consumption for a given growth rate. Thus, in whatever way they are examined, the interest rate and the rate of growth are taken in consideration jointly and seem to live together.

NOTES ON OPTIMAL SAVINGS IN RAMSEY

Before considering the neoclassical optimal growth models of the 1960s, it might be interesting to say a few words about the optimum savings model of Ramsey (1928).[25] It is worth noting that the rate of households' savings is taken as endogenous. In fact, the early models following this approach are characterized by a new interpretation of the accumulation process, in that economic decisions concerning production and saving are made by an agent or planner considering unlimited prospects. The production side and income deriving from employment are not separated, as in modern economic growth models, and the single agent has control over both production and saving decisions. Furthermore, the economy in Ramsey's model is decentralized, thus opening the way for the construction of growth models in which the equilibrium path is independent of the optimal centralized path. Ramsey stated at the beginning of his analysis that the proportion of income to be saved for a nation must follow the rule that "the rate of saving multiplied by the marginal utility of money should always be equal to the amount by which the total net rate of enjoyment of utility falls short of the maximum possible rate of enjoyment" (Ramsey 1928, 543).

Ramsey refers to an economy at time *t*, which is endowed with a technology set, *Mt*, a given amount of capital, *Kt*, and labour, *Lt*. The agent chooses the best method of production, *M*t*, and the amount of labour and capital to produce output, *Yt*. The agent also decides how to allocate the amount of *Yt* between consumption and savings, which is then transformed into investment, *It*. The level of consumption, *Ct*, is chosen in such a way as to maximize the sum $\sum p^t u(C_t)$ where p^t is a discount factor (the present value) of an enjoyment at any future date, subject to the constraint $X_{t+1} = Y_t-(1-\delta)K_t-C_t$ where δ is the capital depreciation rate. Investment at time *t* and the initial stock of capital, *Kt*, determine the stock of capital available at the new period, *Kt*+1. The amount of labour available at time $t + 1$,*Lt*+1, is determined by a demographic rule given exogenously.

Ramsey (1928) stated that the rate of savings multiplied by the marginal utility should always equal bliss (happiness) minus actual rate of utility enjoyed and is given by the fundamental equation (Sen 1970, 481–2),

$$dc/dt = f(a,c) - x = [B - (U(x) - V(a)]/u(x) \tag{4.92}$$

where $U(x)$ is the total rate of utility (of the consumption) and $V(a)$ is the total rate of disutility of the labour denoted by a. The maximum value of the income earned, w, in an infinite time is given by

$$\int_b^y w^{\frac{r}{r-\rho}}(y)dy \tag{4.93}$$

The $w(y)$ increases until bliss is reached (point B in equation [4.92]) in a manner in which consumption dc/dt cannot be negative. The marginal utility is given by the power $r/(r - \rho)$. This has the effect of accelerating the decrease of marginal utility and reducing the relative importance of high incomes. In this way, the discounted utility of future consumption can be translated into the discounted utility of high incomes, and this is reached when rate ρ is 0 (independent of the rate r). If the rate of interest, r, is less than the rate of discounted utility, the marginal utility of consumption will rise at a rate $\rho - r$, and consumption will fall toward the subsistence level at which the marginal utility may be taken as infinite. During this process, all capital will be exhausted and will be available only in small quantities for the future periods. It will be possible to borrow an amount such that should be possible to keep alive at a subsistence level after paying the interest on it.

The accumulation process in Ramsey's model is similar to that of Solow's described previously, but differs on the consumer's side as it technically makes efforts to endogenize saving. Along the optimal path, the rate of savings changes over time and converges toward the long-run level associated with the steady state. Ramsey's attempt was concentrated on finding an optimal path of savings rate in a very innovative model of growth for his time. Four decades later, in the modern growth models (Koopmans 1965, Cass 1965), the assumptions concerning the production function are neoclassical, and the agent is endowed with a separable and stationary utility function $u(\cdot)$ and a constant discount rate ρ. The optimal path, which usually has the structure of a saddle point, is unique and converges toward the steady-state path.

OPTIMAL ECONOMIC GROWTH IN CASS AND KOOPMANS

The work of Koopmans (1965) and Cass (1965) was very similar in purpose to Ramsey's classical paper (1928) and to Tinbergen's exploration in 1960. Tjalling Koopmans[26] (1960, 1965, 1967) and David Cass[27] (1965) agreed on the existence of the golden rule as introduced by Phelps, but disagreed that it was optimal. They argued that it is maximized utility that they should seek, not maximal consumption.

In the Cass-Koopmans version, the objective of the representative agent is to maximize utility over an infinite horizon, and therefore the main purpose of this model is to find the maximized utility between generations.

This model avoids all market imperfections and all issues raised by heterogeneous households and relations among generations (i.e., two-period relations between two generations – young and old).

Considering an aggregate model of capital accumulation of Solowian type and given an aggregate production function $y = f(k)$ we have that a simple economy is given as (Cass 1966, 834),

$$c(t) + i(t) = y(t) \tag{4.94}$$

where $y(t)$ is the allocation of output per capita between instantaneous consumption given by $c(t)$ and gross investment per capita given by $i(t)$. The capital growth per head is given

$$\dot{k}(t) = i(t) - \theta k(t), \text{ with } \theta = n + \delta \tag{4.95}$$

where the labour force is expanding exogenously at the positive rate n and the capital stock is depreciating at the positive rate δ.[28] It is assumed that the utility function at any time t is defined as a positive function of consumption per capita at time t, $U(c_t)$. Given an infinite horizon and continuous time, consumption will thus be infinite and continuous. The present value of future utility gains from individual consumption at any time t implies

$$U(c_t)e - p_t \tag{4.96}$$

where p is the subjective rate of time preference, $0 < p < 1$. For a continuous stream of utility-adding consumption from now (time 0) until infinity, the present value of the stream is

$$U = \int_0^\infty U(c_t)e^{-pt}dt \tag{4.97}$$

where $U'(c) > 0$, $U''(c) < 0$ for $c > 0$, and p is the social discount rate. The utility flow or the instantaneous utility function in (4.97) is a strictly concave, increasing, and twice differentiable function $U(c_t)$ of the consumption flow c_t. The objective of the representative agent (or household) is to maximize this intertemporal stream of utility subject to economy-wide constraints. The constraint is obvious enough; the more is consumed now the less is saved; thus, less growth and consumption are left for tomorrow. Conversely, consuming less now means consuming more tomorrow, and time-preference says that we have less utility today than tomorrow. There must be an equilibrium somewhere between all the periods such that the total stream of utility is maximized. In this model it is required to determine the optimum growth path {c(t), i(t), k(t)} by maximizing the utility function criterion (4.97) subject to (4.94) and (4.95). For a discount social rate p and any feasible growth path generating consumption per capita c, we have the following:

$$\int_0^\infty U(c)e^{pt}dt \leq \frac{U[f(k)]}{p}(1 - e^{pT)} \tag{4.98}$$

where $0<T<\infty$ and p takes a positive value. It is assumed that the labour force $L(t)$ and the current population $P(t)$ grow at the same positive rate n and this expression is given as

$$U = \int_0^\infty P(t)u[c(t)]dt = \int_0^\infty U[c(t)]e^{-pt}dt \tag{4.99}$$

where $U[c(t)] = \frac{L(0)}{\gamma}u[c(t)]$ and $p = -n < 0$

The labour force $L(t)$ is a fixed proportion γ of the total population $P(t)$. To illustrate the optimum growth path it is useful to define the gross investment ratio s such as $0 \leq s = i/f(k) \leq 1$ and the price of a unit of gross investment per capita, $q = q(t)$. The value of gross national product per capita is given as

$$\varepsilon = U(c)+qi \tag{4.100}$$

Subsequently applying the present-value Hamiltonian function to the value of net national product per capita we have

$$(\varepsilon - q\lambda k)e^{-pt} \tag{4.101}$$

Therefore, there are two necessary conditions for an optimum growth path when there is an imputed price of a unit of gross investment per capita $q = q(t)$. So the first optimal condition is (Cass 1966, 837):

$$\dot{q} = (p-\lambda)q - U'(c)f'(k) = \frac{d\left(\int_t^{\infty} \frac{\delta(\varepsilon - q\lambda k)}{\delta k} e^{p(\tau - t)} d\tau\right)}{dt} \tag{4.102}$$

where $c + i = f(k)$ and $c \geq 0$, $i \geq 0$. And the second optimal condition is expressed as

$$\left(\frac{\delta \varepsilon}{\delta i}\right)_{c=f(k)-i} = -U'(c) + q \leq 0 \tag{4.103}$$

with equality for $z>0$. In Cass's model the relationship between current consumption and gross investment per capita is feasible and maximizes the gross national product at each point of time.

$$k = i - \lambda k \text{ with } k(0) = k^0 \tag{4.104}$$

Two distinct feasible paths are considered; (c_1, i_1, k_1) and (c_2, i_2, k_2) where $k_1(\tau) \neq k_2(\tau)$ for $0 < \tau < \infty$ and $k_1(t) \neq k_2(t)$ for $t\ \varepsilon I(\tau)$, where $I(\tau)$ is an open interval around τ. The utility stream between two paths is given as

$$\int_0^{\infty} [U(c_1) - U(c_2)]e^{-pt} dt \tag{4.105}$$

From equation (4.95) we add and subtract $U'(c_1)(c_1 - c_2)$ and using a zero expression $q_1(i_j - \lambda k_j - k_j)$, $j = 1,2..$, which is derived from equation (4.94) we get the new integral form (Cass 1966, 838–41),

$$\int_0^\infty [U(c_1)-U(c_2)-U'(c_1)(c_1-c_2)+U'(c_1)(c_1-c_2)+$$
$$q_1(i_1-\lambda k_1-k_1)-q_1(i_1-\lambda k_2-k_2)]e^{-pt}dt \qquad (4.106)$$

Again adding and subtracting $U'(c_1)f'(k_1)(k_1\text{-}k_2)$, and substituting for c_j, j=1,2.., which is derived from $c + I = f(k)$ and rearranging all terms we obtain a new integral form.

$$\int_0^\infty [U(c_1)-U(c_2)-U'(c_1)(c_1-c_2)+(q_1-U'(c_1))(i_1-i_2)+$$
$$(U'(c_1)f'(k_1)-\lambda q_1)(k_1-k_2)+$$
$$U'(c_1)(f(k_1)-f(k_2)-f'(k_1)(k_1-k_2)-q_1(k_1-k_2)]e^{-pt}dt \qquad (4.107)$$

Now to further simplify the above integral expression we use the strict concavity of $f(\cdot)$ in combination with $k_1(t) \neq k_2(t)$ for $t\ \varepsilon I(\tau)$, and the concavity of $U(\cdot)$ and integrating this time by parts we attain the new integral expression

$$\int_0^\infty q_1(k_1-k_2)e^{-pt}dt \text{ and}$$

$$\int_0^\infty [(q_1-U'(c_1))(i_1-i_2)+(q_1+U'(c_1)f'(c_1)f'(k_1)-(\delta+\lambda)q_1)(k_1-k_2)]e^{-pt}dt \qquad (4.108)$$

The solutions to the pair of autonomous differential equations (4.102), (4.103), and (4.104) are depicted in figure 4.8. [29] The figure divides the quadrant k>0, q>0 according to the signs of k_t and q_t and it draws the trajectories of point (k_t, q_t) starting from arbitrary initial values (k_0, q_0). The singular curve of each differential equation divides the plan into four regions and each region shows the behaviour of the system reaching the optimal path. The point (k^*, q^*), which is the intersection of four curves represents the unique balanced growth path defined by a singular solution of the equations (4.102), (4.103), and (4.104), $f'(k^*) = p + \lambda$, $i^* = \lambda k^*$ and $c^* = f(k^*) - i^*$ and $q^* = U'(c^*)$, where c^* is the level of consumption, k^* is the capital-labour ratio and i^* is the investment per capita. The singular point (k^*, q^*) is a saddle point that is a joint of two type of arms or branches, the stable path (k^*, q^*)– (the stable arm)

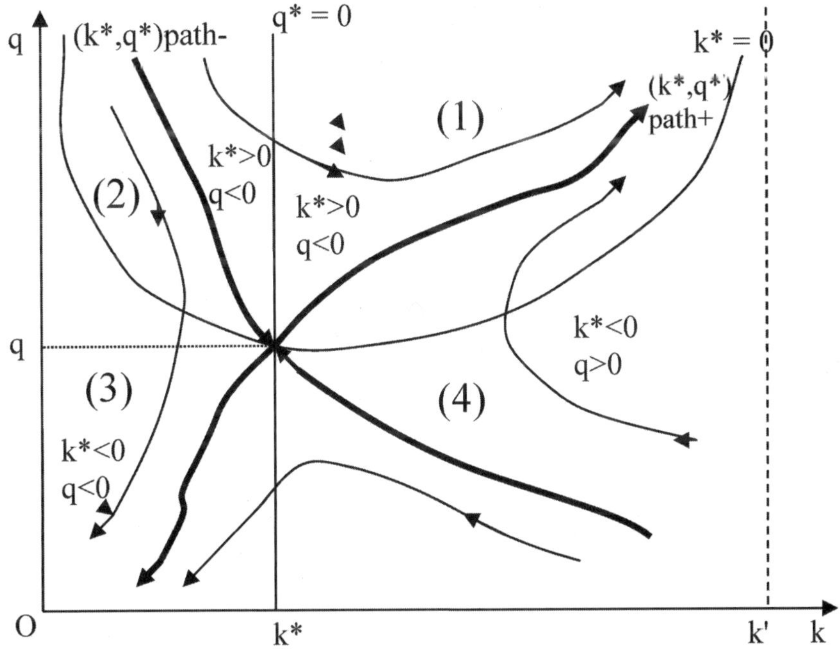

Figure 4.8 The solution to optimal growth path

and the unstable path $(k^*, q^*)+$ (the unstable arm). For $p>0$, part of the $(k^*, q^*)-$ path is the unique optimum growth path. Figure 4.8 shows that the arrows are such that the system approaches the steady state from regions 2 and 4.

To explain in a simple way, given some initial k, we choose consumption such that we jump on the saddle path and make our way to the balanced growth point at (k^*, c^*). In this type of optimal growth model, all of the paths yield a steady state. The saddle path, in a simple form, is visualized in figure 4.9.

For any positive value in the initial level k, there is a unique initial level of c that is consistent with the optimization program of intertemporal utility. The function $c^* = f(k^*) - i^*$, which gives the initial c as a function of k, is known as the saddle path. By and large, as shown in figure 4.9, for any starting value of k, the initial c must be the value on the saddle path. The economy, intended to reach the optimum growth path, moves along the saddle path to point E.

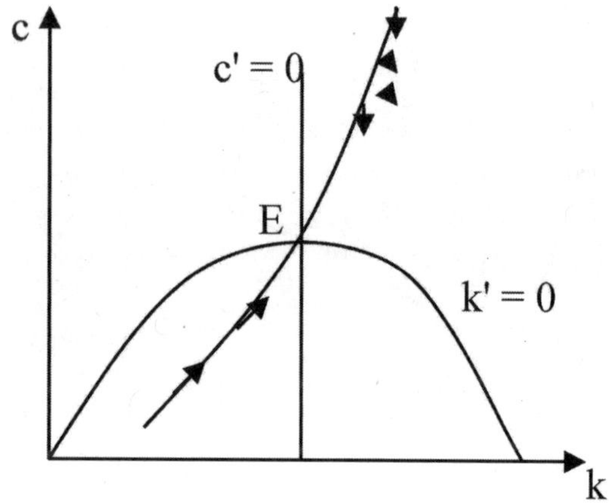

Figure 4.9 The saddle path

KOOPMANS' SIMILARITIES WITH CASS'S MODEL IN THE OPTIMAL GROWTH PATH

In a similar way, Koopmans (1965) reaches the same conclusions as Cass regarding the optimality path. According to his model, there is a unique optimal path (x_t, z_t) characterized by two conditions:

1 $\lim_{t\to\infty} z_t = z(\delta)$ for all z_0

2 the inputted prices p_t and q_t (the price of consumption good and price of capital good) defined as

$$p_t = e^{-\delta t} u'(x_t) \text{ and } q_t = p_t g'(z_t)$$

satisfy the differential equation

$$q_t + \dot{p}_t = 0 \text{ for all } t \geq 0.$$

These two conditions are sufficient for the optimality of the path (x_t, z_t). Calling the Euler condition, the second condition of optimal path takes the form

$$\dot{p}_t + q_t = u'(x_t)(g'(z_t) - \delta) + u''(x_t)\dot{x}_t = 0 \quad (4.a)$$

Given that $x_t + \dot{z}_t = f(z_t) - \lambda z_t = g(z_t)$ the condition in (4.a) is transformed into the system of differential equations.

$$\dot{z}_t = g(z_t) - x_t \text{ for } t \geq 0 \tag{4.b}$$

and $$\dot{x}_t = -\frac{u'(x_t)}{u''(x_t)}(g'(z_t) - \delta) \tag{4.c}$$

As in figure 4.9 the trajectories of the point (x_t, z_t) start from the initial values (x_0, z_0). Each curve in figure 4.9, as referred to Koopman's model which is similar to Cass's model, is defined as the solution x(z) with x(z_0) = x_0 or z(x) with z(x_0) = z_0, related to differential equations, respectively obtained from (4.b) and (4.c):

$$\frac{dz}{dx} = -\frac{u''(x)}{u'(x)}\left(\frac{g(z) - x}{g'(z) - \delta}\right) \tag{4.d}$$

and $$\frac{dx}{dz} = -\frac{u'(x)}{u''(x)}\left(\frac{g'(z) - \delta}{g(z) - x}\right) \tag{4.e}$$

The two differential equations above describe the trajectory that defines the optimal path in figure 4.9 (Koopmans 1965, 276–9).

Although the golden rule in Phelps is the maximum consumption along a balanced growth path when the rate of interest is equal to the rate of growth, in the Cass-Koopmans theory it is the consumers' maximum utility which guarantees an optimum path, and the rate of interest is determined independently of consumers' utility functions. On the optimum path, the rate of interest must equal the natural rate of growth, which, in the particular case of a stationary economic system, is equal to zero. This means that individuals' preferences (without imposing any restrictions) are not a determinant of the optimum rate of interest-(Pasinetti 1965). It may be concluded that the whole idea of maximizing the utility function is not flexible enough to fit the inequality of opportunity between generations.[30] The only remarkable difference between the balanced growth paths of Solow and Cass-Koopmans[31] is that a balanced growth path with a capital stock above the golden rule level is not possible in the Cass-Koopmans model. In Solow, a sufficiently high savings rate causes the economy to reach a balanced growth path with the property of feasible alternatives involving higher consumption at every moment. In contrast, in the Cass-Koopmans model, saving is derived from the behaviour of households whose utility depends on their consumption, and there are no externalities. Therefore, the economy will not be able to follow a path where higher consumptions are attained in every period. If the economy were on such a path, households would then reduce their saving and take advantage of this opportunity.

The golden rule and optimal growth marked a culmination of the development of growth theory in the 1960s. Schumpeter's entrepreneurial innovation, Harrod's knife-edge, Solow's self-regarding device of growth, Phelps's golden rule, and Cass-Koopmans's optimal growth all seemed to communicate significant insights about real economics. The same had been true of the Von Neumann path and Samuelson's turnpike.

NEOCLASSICAL TWO-SECTOR GROWTH MODELS: THE UZAWA MODEL

The two-sector growth model is seen as a natural extension of the simple one-sector model. The two-sector extension of the Solow-Swan model (1956) was introduced by Hirofumi Uzawa[32] (1961a, 1963a, and 1964) and James E. Meade (1961). The neoclassical model of economic growth, as it has been developed by Solow and Swan, is formulated in terms of the aggregate production function. The aggregate production function gives the relationship between output and input. There are two types of productive inputs: investment goods and consumption goods, which are produced by two factors of production: capital and labour. These two inputs are substitutable (with each other) in the production of consumer goods as well as in a separate sector that produces machines. Labour and machines are freely transferable from one sector to another. Capital is assumed to depreciate at a fixed rate, and the labour rate of growth is constant and is determined exogenously (Sen 1970, 275–6).

The objective of Uzawa model is to show that, in a more complex economy where two sectors are considered, the state of growth exists and the growth process approaches some steady growth in the long run. He discovers that his model economy is always stable if the consumption goods sector is more capital intensive than the investment goods sector. Let K_t and L_t be the quantities of capital and labour, respectively, allocated in each sector; P_1 and P_2 be the price of investment goods and of consumption goods; and r and w the return rates to capital and labour, respectively. By presenting this model, it is useful to set up the following definitions and assumptions (Uzawa 1961a):

Y_i = the produced amount in i-sector
L_i = the amount of labour allocated to i-sector
K_i = the amount of capital allocated to i-sector
P_i = price of i-sector
k_i = the capital-labour ratio in i-sector ($k_i = K_i / L_i$)
k = the aggregate capital-labour ratio ($k = K/L$)
r = the returns to capital total
w = the wage rate
ω = the wage-rental ratio ($\omega = w/r$).
μ = the rate of depreciation in capital
λ = the rate of growth in labour.

The production functions for the investment goods sector and consumption goods sector are given, respectively, as follows:

$$F_1(K_1, L_1) \tag{4.109}$$

$$F_2(K_2, L_2) \tag{4.110}$$

Both the consumption good and the capital good sectors are assumed to maximize profits in conditions of perfect competition. The wage rate, w, and the profit rate (or rental rate) of capital, r, must be the same in both sectors, and capital and labour employed in each sector are paid their marginal productivity in value terms, given as

$$P_i(\delta F_i/\delta K_i) = r \tag{4.111}$$

$$P_i(\delta F_i/\delta L_i) = w \tag{4.112}$$

where $\delta F_i/\delta K_i$ and $\delta F_i/\delta L_i$ are the marginal products of capital and labour in consumption and capital sectors, respectively. The total amounts of capital and labour are simply specified as (Uzawa 1961a, 41),

$$K1 + K2 = K \tag{4.113}$$

$$L1 + L2 = L \tag{4.114}$$

Then we have

$$P1Y1 = rK \tag{4.115}$$

and

$$P2Y2 = wL \tag{4.116}$$

where the value of output of capital sector $P1Y1$ is equal to the profits (rK), and the value of output of consumption sector $P2Y2$ is equal to total wage payments (wL). Combining conditions (4.109) and (4.116) implies the following:

$$y_i = f_i(k_i),\ i = 1, 2, 3.... \tag{4.117}$$

Labour market and capital market equilibrium are given, respectively, as

$$p_1 + p_2 = 1 \text{ where } p_i = L_i/L,\ i = 1, 2, 3,... \tag{4.118}$$

$$p_1k_1 + p_2k_2 = k \tag{4.119}$$

The production functions above fulfill the famous Inada conditions.[33] In the investment goods sector, the labour allocation $p1$ can also be written as follows:

$$p1f1(k1) = f'1(k1)k \tag{4.120}$$

Labor market and capital market prices are given by the following identities:[34]

$$w = f1 - k1f1' = p(f_2 - k_2f_2') \tag{4.121}$$

$$r = f_1' = pf_2' \tag{4.122}$$

Defining ω as the wage-profit ratio – that is, $\omega = w/r$ – and by combining equations (4.120) and (4.121), we get

$$\omega = \frac{w}{r} = \left[\frac{f_1(k_1) - k_1 f_1'}{f_1'}\right] = \left[\frac{f_2(k_2) - k_2 f_2'}{f_2'}\right] = \left(\frac{f_i(k_i)}{f_i'}\right) - k_i$$
$$i = 1, 2, 3, \ldots \qquad (4.123)$$

The optimum capital-labour ratio k_i, corresponding to the wage-rentals ratio, ω, determined by equation (4.123), will also be denoted as $k_i = k_i(\omega)$, i = 1, 2, 3,.... Differentiating (4.122) with respect to k_i, we have the following:

$$\frac{d\omega}{dk_i} = -\frac{f_i(k_i) f_i''(k_i)}{[f_i'(k_i)]^2} > 0 \qquad (4.124)$$

Combining equations (4.123) and (4.120), we get the following identity:

$$p_1 = \frac{k}{[(\omega + k_1(\omega)]} \qquad (4.125)$$

Substituting (4.123) and (4.120) into (4.119), we obtain the fundamental capital (and labour) market equilibrium as follows:

$$k = \left[\frac{\omega + k_1(\omega)}{\omega + k_2(\omega)}\right] k_2(\omega) \qquad (4.126)$$

Uzawa (1961a) proves that, if both production functions in both sectors are well behaved and capital and the capital-labour ratio in the consumption goods sector are higher than the capital-labour ratio in the capital goods sector, then the momentary equilibrium of balanced growth exists.

Uzawa, for simplicity, assumes the classical savings assumption that the whole value of the output of the consumption goods sector (P_2Y_2) is equal to total wage payments (wL), or all wages are consumed and the whole value of the output of capital goods sector (P_1Y_1) is equal to total profits (rK), or all profits are saved as seen in equations (4.115) and (4.116). Equation (4.115) implies that savings equals investments. The rate of capital stock change is given as follows (Uzawa 1961a, 43):

$$\frac{\dot{K}}{K} = Y_1 - \mu \qquad (4.127)$$

From equation (4.115), we have that $Y1 = rK/P1$, so equation (4.127) can be written as follows:

$$\frac{\dot{K}}{K} = \frac{r}{P_1} - \mu \tag{4.128}$$

We already know that $\dot{L}/L = \lambda$. We also know (see Solow's model) that the growth of the capital-labour ratio $\dot{k}/k$ is equal to the rate of growth of the capital stock minus the rate of growth of the labour force:

$$\frac{\dot{k}}{k} = \frac{\dot{K}}{K} - \frac{\dot{L}}{L} \tag{4.129}$$

Combining (4.128) and (4.129), we get the fundamental equation of the two-sector model[35] as follows:

$$\left(\frac{\dot{k}}{k}\right) = f'_1(k_1) - \lambda - \mu \tag{4.130}$$

Uzawa considers the capital-labour ratio, k^*, if

$$f'1(k^*1) = \lambda + \mu \tag{4.131}$$

where $k^*1 = k1(\omega^*)$ and ω^* is an equilibrium wage-rentals ratio corresponding to the aggregate capital-ratio k^*. In Uzawa's model, if we employ the capital classical savings function, the marginal product of capital in the capital goods sector equals the total of the depreciation rate and the growth labour force.

If the consumption goods sector is more capital intensive than the investment goods sector, then the optimum capital-labour ratios, given by $k1 = k1(\omega)$ and by $k2 = k2(\omega)$ in both sectors, and the optimum outputs for investment goods, $y1 = y1(\omega)$, and consumption goods, $y2 = y2(\omega)$, are all uniquely determined by the capital-labour ratio, k, if the following condition is satisfied:

$$\lim_{k_1 \to 0} = f_1'(k_1) > \lambda + \mu > \lim_{k_1 \to \infty} f'_1(k_1) \tag{4.132}$$

If the balanced capital-labour ratio k^* exists, then the growth process starting at an arbitrary initial capital-labour position approaches the balanced capital-labour ratio k^* as t tends to infinity. According to Uzawa (1961a) the economy gravitates to the balanced growth path independently of the initial conditions if the capital-labour ratio in the consumption goods sector is greater than or equal to the capital-labour ratio in the capital goods sector, regardless of the value of the wage/rate of profit ratio $\omega = w/r$. Considering the fundamental equation (4.130), we have two cases.

First, if $f'1(k1) > \lambda + \mu$, the capital-labour ratio is rising, so $(\dot{k}/k) > 0$. Then the marginal product of capital $[f'1(k1)]$ in the capital goods sector must be falling. It will eventually equal $\lambda + \mu$, achieving the balanced growth path.

Second, if $f'1(k1) < \lambda + \mu$, the capital-labour ratio is decreasing, so $(\dot{k}/k) < 0$. Then the marginal product of capital in the capital goods sector must be rising. It will probably equal $\lambda + \mu$, and the balanced growth path will be achieved. Uzawa (1963b) had demonstrated the stability of the two-sector model when both the general capital-labour ratio and the capital-labour ratio in the capital (machine) sector move in the same direction. He, in fact, found that the economy is always stable if the consumption goods sector is more capital intensive than the investment goods sector. Solow observed that "It seems paradoxical to me that such an important characteristic of the equilibrium path should depend on such a casual property of the technology. And since this stability property is the one respect in which Uzawa's results seem qualitatively different from those of my 1956 paper on a one-sector model, I am anxious to track down the source of the difference" (Solow 1961, 48).

The two-sector model represents a further advance in complexity over the single model. Most of its principal conclusions are similar to those derived from the single-sector model, although the smooth convergence to balanced growth cannot be proved for all combinations of assumptions.

Many authors had a common opinion that it is easy to accept the assumption that the capital goods sector is less capital intensive than the consumption goods sector. Furthermore, there are other modifications to the standard Uzawa two-sector model. For example, Drandakis (1963) demonstrated that stability is ensured if the sum of the elasticities of substitution in both industries is greater than one, which also endogenizes the labour supply by making it responsive to wages (thus actually getting closer to the classical way of thinking). Michio Morishima tried to do the same, but he found that the Uzawa capital-intensity condition was no longer sufficient for stability (Morishima 1969).

Joseph Stiglitz (1967) has allowed capital to be owned by explicitly different capitalist-worker classes and then analyzed the consequent implications. Adopting the savings assumptions from Pasinetti (1962) – specifically, that the savings propensity of capitalists exceeds that of workers – he found that the Uzawa capital-intensity assumption is sufficient for the uniqueness of factor market equilibrium and also for the uniqueness and the stability of a steady-state growth path. For the existence of a steady-state path, however, the necessary and sufficient condition is that the savings rate of workers is less than the ratio of investment to output pro capita. Two-sector models with fixed proportions of technological rate have also been considered by Y. Shinkai (1960) and John Hicks (1965). Inada (1963), for instance, has allowed for the savings rate itself to be a function of income, $s = s(y)$.

Frank Hahn (1965), by examining the Uzawa capital-intensity condition, carefully concluded that savings hypotheses probably never or rarely hold in the real world because the real world is more complicated than one-sector and two-sector models. He, among others, noted,

> It is evident that in all these constructions the condition that the equilibrium at a moment of time be unique is crucial. The rest of the story is really concerned with ensuring that there is a steady state with positive factor prices. But the assumptions required to establish uniqueness of momentary equilibrium are all terrible assumptions. People differ in the assets they hold in their age and, alas, in their tastes. Simple proportional savings assumptions no doubt have their place in political arithmetic but seem rather desperate at this level. Morever assuming all these uniqueness problems away prevents us from facing the interesting, although admittedly philosophical, question of what is supposed to happen when the assumptions do not hold. After all, some decisions are taken at any moment of time. (Hahn 1965, 345)

Rather than the smooth convergence to a single steady-state path that we found in the Solow-Swan one-sector model, the Uzawa two-sector model indicates that we might expect a good amount of indeterminacy, instability, and cyclical behaviour in growth paths. And this comes closer to the real world.

GOVERNMENT DEBT AND MONETARY GROWTH IN TOBIN

Tobin's "A Dynamic Aggregate Model," published in 1955, deals with the variables of real magnitudes and the world of money and prices. Tobin's model was considered a precursor of the Solow-Swan model, regarding monetary problems (Sen 1970, 233). The main finding of Tobin[36] was that the price level as capital grows depends on the increasing rate of the labour force, the rate at which supply of currency is augmented by government deficits and the rate of technological progress.

Tobin later constructed a model of monetary growth in order to address a particular problem originally contained in the Harrod-Domar model (Tobin 1965, 674–6). If the warranted rate of growth is greater than the natural rate of growth, then capital accumulation will occur and the marginal product of capital will keep falling continuously. But if we consider the case when the marginal product of capital falls below the rate of interest, this will imply that investment will always lie below savings. Hence, the economy goes into a slump. But by placing a floor, continual stagnation might be prevented. Tobin introduced a government sector that spends a fixed proportion of national income, financing this expenditure either by levying money or simply by issuing paper money, which is injected into the economy by means of transfer payments. These payments are independent of individuals' holding of money. Money affects the workings of the economy through its effect on the real disposable income, which determines the consumption and savings behaviour of individuals. The general equation of disposable income is given as follows (Levhari and Patinkin 1968, 714–15):

$$Y_D = Y + \frac{d\left(\frac{M}{P}\right)}{dt} = Y + \frac{M}{P}(\psi - \pi) = n + d \qquad (4.133)$$

where M/p is the real quantity of money supplied in the economy, $\psi = M'/M$ is the rate of change of the money supply, and $\pi = p'/p$ is the rate of change of the price level. The real disposable income is the total of net national income given by Y and the real value of nominal quantity of money $(\psi(M/p))$ minus the decrease in the real value of existing cash balances caused by a price increase $((\pi(M/p))$. The government deficit is equal to $M/p(\psi - \pi)$, and Y is the natural rate of growth or the exact amount of investment relative to capital stock. The deficit is supposed to absorb a certain proportion of income and is given as

$$\frac{d}{Y} = \frac{M}{P}(\psi - \pi) - \frac{n}{Y} + 1 \tag{4.134}$$

Despite the wealth of owners who hold money and capital in different proportions, the size of the cumulated deficit is irrelevant. In Tobin's model there are two physical assets: physical capital and real money balances. The rate of return of physical capital is given by the real rate of interest, $r = \delta F(K,L)/\delta K = f'(k)$ and the rate of return of real money balance is $-\pi$.[37] It is also assumed that individuals save a certain proportion, s, of their disposable incomes and hold a proportion, λ, of the national income, Y. In the equilibrium situation, we have a positive money rate of interest given as $-\pi < r$ and the same anticipated and actual rates of return $r - (-\pi) = r + \pi$ (Fisher's equation). Therefore the rate of capital accumulation is given as

$$K' = F(K,L) - (1-s)\left[F(K,L) + \frac{M}{P}(\psi - \pi)\right] \tag{4.135}$$

The total consumption is represented by $(1-s)[F(K,L)+(M/p)(\psi+r)]$ and deducting it from total commodity output the consumption the equation (4.135) takes the following form (Levhari and Patinkin 1968, 719):

$$\dot{K} = F(K,L) - \left\{(1-s)\left[F(K,L) + \frac{M}{p}(\psi + r)\right] - \frac{M}{p}(r + \pi)\right\} \tag{4.136}$$

where M/p represents the real quantity of money in the system, under the assumption that the demand for real money balances equals the supply (M/p), which is given as

$$\frac{M^d}{p} = \lambda F(K,L) = \frac{M}{p} \tag{4.137}$$

From (4.136) we have that the desired level of physical consumption is the amount of liquidity services which individuals desire to consume (deducted from total consumption) and is given as

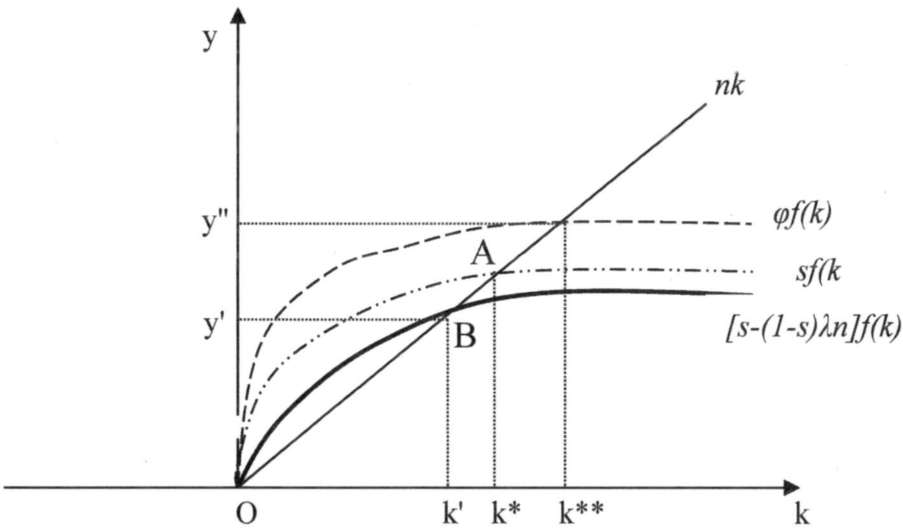

Figure 4.10 The steady-state capital-labour ratio

$$C = (1-s)\left[F(K,L) + \frac{M}{p}(\psi + r)\right] - \frac{M}{p}(r+\pi) \tag{4.138}$$

where the volume of transfer payments received by individuals $(\psi M/p)$ and the income from the real balances held (rM/p) is considered convertible into physical capital by individuals yielding at rate of return r.

We already know that the demand for real money balances is equal to thc supply, $M/p = \lambda F(K,L)$, and the basic equation of the steady-state value of the capital-labour ratio, k, is simply given as[38]

$$[s-(1-s)\lambda n]\, f(k) = nk \tag{4.139}$$

which is similar to our Solowian differential equation, except that instead of $dk/dt = sf(k) - nk$, we now have the term $[s-(1-s)\lambda n]$. In the Solowian steady-state, we had $dk/dt = 0$, so $sf(k) = nk$ at point A of the diagram in figure 4.10, where there is the intersection between the nk line and the $sf(k)$ curve at A. Having a look at figure 4.10, we have that the equilibrium value is determined by the intersection of the solid curve with the ray nk at k'. This is less than the equilibrium ratio k^* (because s is less than unity) that would be determined by the intersection of

$sf(k)$, with nk as in the neoclassical Solowian model. Hence, in comparison with $sf(k)$, the savings function is smaller; some savings are being drained off into money holdings instead of being invested. Thus, as shown in figure 4.10, we get a smaller savings function with equilibrium at B as compared with the regular Solow equilibrium at A. The steady-state capital-labour ratio under the Tobin model (k^*) is lower than the steady-state capital-labour ratio under Solow (k^{**}). Similarly, there is lower per capita output under Tobin's (y') than under Solow's (y''). Thus, the equilibrium settles at a lower capital-labour ratio and lower output-labour ratio with the presence of money, although the rates of growth of the aggregate variables are the same (both at n).

With the introduction of money, output per capita collapses. Therefore, the greater the money demand the smaller the savings available for investment and the lower the rate of growth. Tobin recommended moderate levels of inflation in order to increase the rate of return and attract capital as a store of value. In this case, people would prefer to invest their money in capital, and in doing so, they could help to increase the rate of growth of the whole economy. However, if the rate of return on money falls to zero, which means that no money is held at all, the new equilibrium will be at point A or at the steady-state equilibrium. Afterward, we will have a higher rate of growth starting from A (as k rises) and reaching k^{**} and a higher rate of inflation as a consequence of a higher rate of growth. The phenomenon of a higher rate of inflation on a higher rate of growth is called the Tobin effect. It follows that money is not neutral. Any changes in the money supply will have an effect on the rate of return (on money), which will then change the steady-state capital-labour ratio. Consequently, in Tobin's view, money has real effects on the economy.

MONEY GROWTH AND THE UTILITY FUNCTION: THE SIDRAUSKI MODEL

H.G. Johnson (1967),[39] Sidrauski (1969), and D. Levhari and D. Patinkin (1968) all objected to Tobin's model on the basis that it treats money solely as a store of value, thus ignoring the services it performs in overcoming transaction costs. They simply argued that, at some point, Tobin's suggestion should have developed the idea of placing money in the utility function. H.G. Johnson (1967) stated that the long-run capital intensity is independent of the steady-state rate of inflation, and this is drawn from the peculiar treatment of the government transfers to the private sector. The demand for real cash balances is a function of the expected rate of inflation and of the holding of real capital. The steady-state expected rate of inflation is equal to the rate of monetary expansion less the steady-state rate of growth. An increase in the rate of monetary expansion has two opposite effects on the long-run demand for real money: i) a higher rate of money supply lowers the demand for real money as it raises the cost of holding cash; and ii) it increases the demand for cash balances as it raises the steady-state holdings of the alternative asset.

Because the rate of return on real capital is fixed to the capital-labour ratio, the desired ratio of real balances to output will vary inversely with the rate of price increases maintained by the monetary authority. Thus, an expansionary monetary policy will influence the rate of growth and have a higher level of capital per head at which the economy reaches its long-run equilibrium growth path. Sidrauski[40] takes into consideration the long-run neutrality but allows short-run non-neutrality as the system moves toward its steady-state values. His view is based on the analysis of individuals' saving behaviour, which is viewed as a process of wealth accumulation intended to maximize some intertemporal utility function. Sidrauski (1969), in line with Patinkin's work (1956), places money into an instantaneous utility function, which is given as

$$U_t = U(c_t, m_t) \tag{4.140}$$

strictly concave with continuous first and second derivates. The total welfare, W, associated with (c_t, m_t), is represented by the utility function (Sidrauski 1969, 576),

$$W = \int_0^\infty \left[U\left(c_t m_t\right)\right] e^{-\partial t} dt \tag{4.141}$$

where δ is the subjective rate of time preference. Wealth restraint requires that total assets can be held in the form either of money or capital:

$$a_t = k_t + m_t \tag{4.142}$$

The family's gross disposable income includes the net transfers from the government (v_t) and is given as

$$y(k_t) + v_t = c_t + s_t \tag{4.143}$$

where c_t and s_t are, respectively, the consumption and the real savings, and the real savings are the sum of gross capital accumulation (i_t) and real cash balances (x_t). So, the equation for real savings is the following:

$$s_t = i_t + x_t \tag{4.144}$$

The gross capital is the total amount of the net capital stock for existing members and the replacement of depreciated capital, including the new members of economic unit, given as

$$i_t = k_t + (u + n)k_t \tag{4.145}$$

where k_t is the existing stock of capital, u is the instantaneous rate of depreciation of capital, and n is the rate of growth of the new number of individuals. In the same way, the gross accumulation of real cash balances is given by

$$f_t = m_t + (z_t + n)m_t \tag{4.146}$$

where z_t is the expected rate of change in prices, m_t is the net money accumulation for existing members of society, and $(z_t + n)m_t$ is the money accumulation necessary to endow new members, thereby keeping the existing assets unchanged in real terms. Putting together equations (4.18.4), (4.144), (4.145), and (4.146), we have

$$y(k_t) + v_t = (z_t + n)m_t + (u + n)k_t + m_t + k_t + c_t \tag{4.147}$$

Differentiating the wealth restraint equation (4.142) with respect to time and substituting to the above equation, we get (Sidrauski 1969, 577).

$$a\dot{}_t = y(k_t) + v_t - (z_t + n)m_t - (u + n)k_t - c_t \tag{4.148}$$

which states that accumulation of both assets (capital and money) is equal to the difference between income (from $y(k_t)$), transfer payments (v_t), consumption (c_t) with accumulation accounted for to provide new members $(u + n)k_t$, and money expansion to keep up with inflation (unchanged).

Following the Sidrauski model, we maximize the utility function of consumption and real money per capita; hence, we have a new function,

$$I =$$
$$\int_0^{\infty}(U(c_t m_t) + \lambda_t\left[y(k_t) + v_t - (z_t + n)m_t - (u+n)k_t - c_t - \dot{a}\right] +$$
$$q_t\left[a_t - k_t - m_t\right])$$
$$e^{\delta t}dt \tag{4.149}$$

where λt and qt are the respective Lagrangian multipliers attached to the flow constraint and the stock constraint. The conditions for a maximum function using the Euler equations are given by the following five equations (Sidrauski 1969, 578):

1 $U_c(ct, mt) = \lambda t$ (4.150)

2 $U_m(ct, mt) = \lambda t(zt + rt + n)$ (4.151)

3 $y'(kt) = (\mathrm{u} + \mathrm{n}) + rt$ (4.152)

4 $\frac{\dot{\lambda}}{\lambda} = \delta - r_t$ (4.153)

5 $\lim_{t \to \infty} a_t \lambda_t e^{-\delta t} = 0$, (4.154)

where $U_c(ct,mt)$ is the utility function of consumption and real money accumulation, while rt is equal to the ratio of two Langrangian multipliers, $qt/\gamma t$. The intention of the rational consumer is to maximize the intertemporal money holdings or find a balance between savings and consumption. Hence, using the current-value Hamiltonian function, we have

$$H = U\,(ct, mt) + p[Y(kt) + vt - (zt + n)mt - (u + n)kt - ct] \tag{4.155}$$

where p is the present value. The necessary conditions to maximize the intertemporal holding are the first order conditions with respect to consumption and money holdings:

1 $dH/dc = dU/dm - p = 0$ (4.156)

2 $dH/dm = dU/dm - p(zt + n) = 0$ (4.157)

$$3 \ -dH/dK = dp/dt - pkt = -p\ (Y(kt) - n) \tag{4.158}$$

$$4 \ dH/dp = dk/dt = Y(kt) + vt\text{-}\ zt + n)mt - (u + n)kt - ct \tag{4.159}$$

From the four equations of the first order conditions above, we have that $dU/dc = Uc = p$ and $dU/dm = Um = p(n + zt)$; thus, the utility function of real money accumulation and consumption gets the following simplified ratio form,

$$Um/Uc = n + zt \tag{4.160}$$

where zt is the inflation (or the money expansion) and n is the real interest rate. Equation (4.159) states that the marginal rate of substitution between money and consumption is equal to the nominal rate of interest. For our purpose and for the present/future consumption relation, the rate of interest is equal to the marginal rate of time preference. Equation (4.158) states that, in the steady state, it implies

$$dp/dt = -p(Y(kt) - n - zt) \tag{4.161}$$

From above equation, we have that, at the steady state, $g(v) = (dp/dt)p$, so $Yk = n + zt$, which means that the rate of return on capital is equal to the neutral rate of growth, n, plus the rate of time preference, zt. This is the maximum utility condition. Therefore, the rate of interest has no monetary variables. The real rate of interest determines the optimal rate of capital, and the inflation does not affect income, Yk. In a different way from the Tobin effect, the rate of inflation in Sidrauski's model does not affect capital accumulation. The necessary condition for the stability of the growth path equilibrium is given by (k, z) as follows:

$$y'(k) - (u+n) - \frac{dc}{dk} < 0 \tag{4.162}$$

$$\left(1 + \frac{dm}{dz}\frac{1}{m}b\right) > 0 \tag{4.163}$$

where k is the capital stock and z is the price change or inflation. The condition (4.162) reflects the fact that an increase in the capital stock has two opposite effects: on one side it increases real consumption, and on the other side it raises the net output, which stimulates capital accumulation in the long run. Equation (4.163) indicates the expected rate of inflation on demand for money. A rise in the rate of inflation reduces the demand for money, thus causing a new rise in prices. The stability of the system depends on the existence of the lag between the adjustments of the actual stock and the desired stock of money. In conclusion, we have that, in the long run, the capital stock of the economy is independent of the rate of monetary expansion and does not affect the steady-state consumption. In the short run, a change in the rate of monetary expansion lowers the rate of capital accumulation, which results in consumption increase.

MONEY AND CAPITAL AS PERFECT SUBSTITUTABLE GOODS

Following Tobin's monetary growth theory (Tobin 1968), there is the case where money and capital are perfect substitutes in the savers' or investors' portfolios, which means that owners of wealth are not concerned about the proportions in which they hold the two assets as long as their yields are equal. Considering the quantity of government debt expanding at the natural rate of growth, we get

$$\frac{\dot{M}}{M}-\frac{\dot{p}}{p}=g \tag{4.164}$$

where M is the nominal quantity and the real interest on money is given by

$$R_M=r-\frac{\dot{p}}{p}=r-\frac{\dot{M}}{M}+g \tag{4.165}$$

Consequently, the issue of optimal value of nominal quantity is converted to the question of optimal value of real rate of return on money, R_M. As assumed above, money and capital are perfect substitutes, so the real rate of return on both money and capital are equal to (Tobin 1968, 837).

$$R_K=R_M=r-\frac{\dot{M}}{M}+g \tag{4.166}$$

From equation (4.166), it is easily understandable that government, which controls r and $\dot{M}/M$, can determine the real rate of interest on capital, R_k, and, as a consequence, the equilibrium capital-labour ratio.

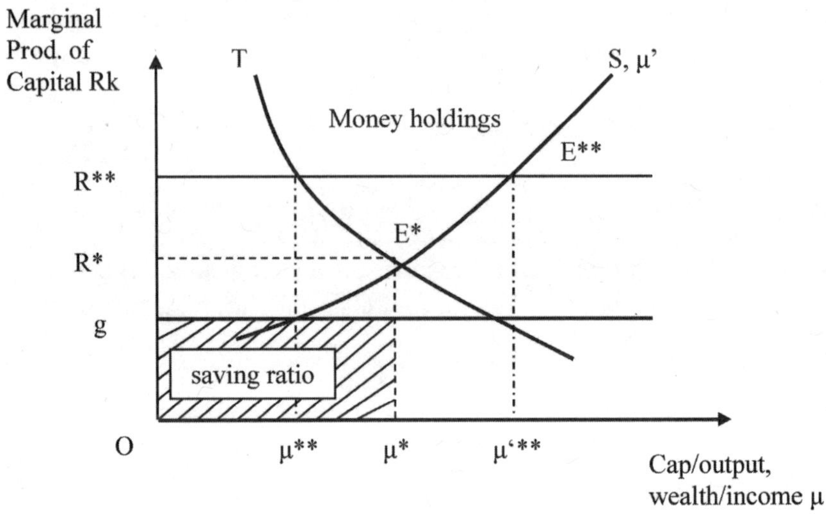

Figure 4.11 Money and capital as perfect substitutes

Figure 4.11 helps to better understand the relation of money and capital as perfect substitutes.

The figure simply represents the relation of the capital-output ratio, μ, to the net marginal productivity of capital, R_k. The curve S stands for the amount of wealth savers' desire relative to national income; in a balanced growth equilibrium, it represents the desired wealth-income ratio, μ'. The ratio of wealth to disposable income, μ', is given by

$$\mu' = \frac{K(1+m)}{(Y+gmK)} = \frac{\mu(1+m)}{(1+gm\mu)} \tag{4.167}$$

$$\mu = \frac{\mu'}{1+m(1-g\mu')} \tag{4.168}$$

where gμ' is considered as the ratio of total saving, including the accumulation of money (in real terms) as well as capital, and $m = M/pK$ is the ratio of money to capital holdings, which is supposed to be constant in equilibrium. As this ratio is smaller than one, the capital-output ratio is smaller, equal to, or larger than μ' according to whether m is positive, zero, or negative (Tobin 1968, 838). If the real rate of interest (R_M or R_K) is set at R^{**}, the government guides the economy to a capital-ratio μ**, and the desired wealth-income ratio is given by curve S at μ'**.

This then exceeds the capital-output ratio μ^{**}. So, the two ratios must be reconciled by a positive value of m that is necessary to satisfy equation (4.168). Because any value of the ratio of money to capital holdings m is acceptable to wealth owners, the situation is in equilibrium. As money and capital are perfect substitutes, m can adjust to any horizontal difference between curves T and S that exists at the established real interest rate. Any substitution of money for capital (any positive m) will move the capital-output ratio in the wrong direction unless the marginal productivity is below g. If the government can set a real rate of interest, it should not be below the natural rate of growth, g, because a balanced growth path with a marginal productivity of capital below the growth rate is inefficient, having higher consumption, less savings, and a lower capital-output ratio. In this case, the economy could be trapped in an inefficient equilibrium path.

The authorities could improve the situation by issuing money and/or government debt with a real rate of interest equal to g, thereby absorbing the excessive saving of the population and raising the marginal productivity of capital to g. In the case of an absence of government debt, if the equilibrium marginal productivity of capital exceeds g, it is not optimal to absorb any saving in government debt. Hence, the government should not try to make government debt competitive by offering a higher rate g. Authorities would lend at the interest rate g, which is also the rate of increase of the private economy's debt. If the accumulation of capital offers a higher remuneration in future consumption for current saving, then government debt is the best solution for making such trades. The issue will then be if the government should push the economy to the golden rule state of capital intensity by increasing the private saving with public saving.[41] If the economy is not in the golden rule stage regarding the capital stock, however, any additional capital will reduce the spending of consumers during the transition period, and taxpayers will be forced to save involuntarily in order to build public saving, which can be used instead of private saving.

SOME CONCLUSIONS ABOUT THE NEOCLASSICAL THEORY OF GROWTH

The modern neoclassical theory of growth was developed by two neoclassical growth economists, Solow (1956) and Swan (1956). The model of the Australian economist Swan (1956) is not analyzed here because of its similarities with the neoclassical model of Solow. Solow's paper, however, initiated a rapid expansion of growth theory in various directions, to which Solow himself was one of the principal contributors. From the beginning of his analysis, we had a very neoclassical factor market equilibrium adjustment process. However, and perhaps more prominently, the macroeconomics in Solow's model is very different. A complete Keynesian growth model would have investment as a function of financial conditions and savings derived from investment via the multiplier. Conversely, in the Solow model, the Keynesian financial factors causing the multiplier are omitted, and the direction of causality between savings and investment is reversed. This is equivalent to reimposing Say's law. As a result, the Solow growth model in all respects is neoclassical and not Keynesian.

Solow's model is more flexible concerning technological changes, whereas the Harrod-Domar model is not. It is not the technology that is critically different but rather the adjustment process. It should be useful to compare the predictions of neoclassical theory with those of the Harrod model. According to the Harrod equation ($g = s/v$), a rise in the savings propensity with given technology will make the economy grow with a faster rate than usual, which is not the case and will hardly happen in the neoclassical model. An increase in the savings propensity will raise both the actual and the warranted rate of growth by the same amounts, causing no trouble to the stability of the economy (Chaudhuri 1989, 74). The Harrodian economy, different from the neoclassical economy, needs to grow most of the times at a full employment rate and, although it reaches the realized natural rate, it will also create instability in the form of inflation by causing the actual rate to rise above the warranted rate. But the neo-classical growth rate, once adjusted (after a population growth rate increase), will then hold or continue ceaselessly. The assumption of equivalence of saving and investment as well as the existence of an independent investment function that is subject to uncertainty about the future rate of growth is one of the main sources of the Harrod instability. The constant capital-output ratio that is a major assumption of the Harrod model is barely mentioned in the neoclassical theory (a residual) (Jones 1975, 83–4).

Harrod and Domar make less restrictive assumptions because they do not consider a very stable macroeconomic equilibrium or any specific factor price adjustment mechanism. The model of Solow has its key to success in the introduction of a production function that is less rigid and not very complex compared to earlier models. In fact, Domar noted the following:

> I thought that the mere introduction of labor as another factor in a simple production function would be a rather minor improvement, and that any serious attempt to make these models more realistic should require a very complex production function with a great degree of disaggregation. On the whole this is true, and yet a recent article by Robert M. Solow, which appeared in print just as I was writing these lines, has shown how a growth model can be enriched by the use of a not very complex but less rigid production function. (Domar 1957, 8)

The question of generality, then, can only be resolved by an empirical race between the two models. If, for example, the Harrod-Domar model can explain certain things better than Solow's model, then Harrod-Domar is evidently superior because it does so with fewer assumptions; otherwise, Solow's model can be declared better. According to some authors (e.g., Abramovitz 1956), however, Solow's model does not seem to perform so well when confronted with empirical evidence. Substantial modifications need to be added to make it comply with the data. Interestingly, the kind of modifications to the Solow growth model that "endogenous growth theory" has proposed in recent years turns out to generate a reduced-form dynamic system that is practically identical with the Harrod-Domar model.

The introduction of technological change raised further questions regarding the extent to which the historical increase in per capita income is due to capital accumulation and technological progress, respectively. Abramovitz (1962) and Solow (1957) from their empirical analyses concluded that the majority of growth can be attributed to technological progress, whereas the contribution of capital accumulation is small. The principal conclusion of the Solow model is that accumulation of physical capital cannot account for either the massive growth over time in output per person or the immense geographic difference in output per person. This emphasizes Schumpeter's idea that technological change, innovation, and entrepreneurial skills play a crucial role and give powerful support to the growth of an economy.

Technological progress was stressed earlier by Kaldor and others and, according to Kaldor, it was embodied in capital equipment. Its utilization requires new equipment, while existing equipment continues to apply old technologies. To allow this factor, Solow (1962a) has developed models in which capital goods of different periods embodied different technologies. Solow's early empirical work on economic growth was based on Cobb-Douglas production functions. It naturally led Solow and other economists to experimentation with other classes of functions that would be less restrictive, thereby allowing changes in factor substitution. Some results regarding neoclassical factor substitution published by Arrow, Chenery, Minhas, and Solow in 1961 were about the constant elasticity of substitution of production function.

It is remarkable to note that the development of neoclassical growth theory has been largely a logical curiosity, in particular regarding the position of steady growth equilibrium, rather than explaining observed growth experiences in different countries (Sen 1970, 33). By restricting the analysis to the case of linear homogenous production functions, neoclassical growth theory disregards the case of increasing returns, which has played an important role in economic growth. To the extent that it refers to actual data, efforts with the theory attempt to explain how "the broad facts about the growth of advanced economies were thought to have experienced some steady rates of growth" and to suggest that "the steady state is at least not a bad place for the theory of growth to start" (Solow 1970b, 7). In particular, the theory has little to offer to the explanation of the inclination for some deceleration of growth that was observed even in advanced industrial economies in the 1960s and 1970s.

The neoclassical achievement of growth theory is undeniable, and its influence has pervaded the way economists think about economic growth. Although there has been a lot of elaboration of growth theory, the basic models are still those developed in the 1950s and 1960s. The assumption of substitution between productive factors was the key to success for growth theory. Solow, differently from Keynesian analysis, was concerned with ensuring the convergence of the economy toward the natural growth path. In fact, he assumed that factors of production, such as capital and labour, are substitutable with each other, which was the biggest news in the modern neoclassical theory of growth. The original papers of Solow (1956, 1957) and Swan (1956) (with distant predecessors in Ramsey [1928] and Meade [1936]) gave rise to a theoretical framework in which the stability of growth equilibrium (in one-sector models) was guaranteed through the adjustment mechanism of factor substitution, which made possible the use of statistical techniques. It was in this context that the concept of applying a theory became very closely associated first with measurement and then with using econometrics in order to report empirical regularities and provide predictions for policy-making. Solow justified the applied dimension of his theory by "the introduction of some technological flexibility that had opened up growth theory to a wider variety of real-world facts and to a closer connection with general economic theory" (Solow 1997). Solow's model has shown that, independently of economic conditions, in every system the tendency of the long period toward equilibrium is inevitable. The initial conditions of growth could be better or worse regarding the state of equilibrium, but, unavoidably, the rate of growth would increase or decrease until the attainment of equilibrium. Poor countries might grow faster than rich countries because they have a lower ratio *K/L*, and in the long run, all countries must have identical production per capita, *Y/L*. So, underdeveloped countries must catch up with industrialized countries, or in other words, the gap must be shortened between rich and poor countries. According to the assumption of the Solow-Swan model, countries will have the same rate of growth. It is clear that, in many underdeveloped countries, this implication of Solow's model has not taken place. Nonetheless, this remains a fundamental work in the theory of neoclassical growth and has not been entirely abandoned but instead integrated. It is worth emphasizing that the Solow-Swan neoclassical model has influenced not only theorists' ideas about the determinants of economic growth but also their conception of applied economics.

Neoclassical theory is used also to study changes in the distribution of income between capital and labour and their relative contribution to growth of output over time. These two uses are related because they both arise from the application of theory to the measurement of relative contribution of two factors to production. Regarding the distribution of income, neoclassical theory places the burden of the explanation on savings propensities and technology. In the new neoclassical models, there are more behavioural and technological factors than social and institutional arrangements within the economy. Ricardo also sought to explain changes in the distribution of income, except that the law of diminishing returns provides a much solid basis for theory than a neoclassical production function.

Despite the contribution of neoclassical theory to growth theory, it was not able to explain the real economic growth in the 1960s and 1970s for at least three reasons. First, the relationship between investment and growth of output in practice is not as strong and obvious as it seems to be. Instead, a much more important influence on economic growth is technological progress and expansion in the variety of products. Second, the assumption that savings determines investments is contrary to the entire Keynesian theory. Third, in neoclassical theory, it is assumed that savings are determined by the level of income, but it actually is more likely that savings are determined by investment opportunities. For instance, an important reason for the low rate of savings in some of the poor countries is the lack of profitable opportunities to invest. If, for example, such opportunities existed, the required savings would slowly approach the optimal savings. This is because the rate of savings depends not so much on the average level of income as on its distribution and on targeted profitable assets that give a quick and good return on investment.

Much attention was paid to the analysis of economic growth by means of two-sector models. The examination of conditions for the stability of balanced growth with both capital and labour fully employed were presented by Uzawa (1961a, 1963b, 1964) and Srinivasan (1964). Uzawa proved that in the long run, under certain conditions, balanced growth will occur in the sense that capital stock and labour supply will grow at nearly the same rate as time increases without limit. His analysis was carried out in terms of dynamics, and the proof was based in two main conditions: first, that the capital goods industry is less capital intensive than the consumption goods industry; and second, that capitalists save all their income and workers consume all their income. These conditions are derived from the assumption that the allocation of factors between the two sectors (capital goods and consumption goods) determines the rate of capital accumulation. This assumption, however, does not consider the possible production lag in the investment goods sector, which may affect (by delaying) the allocation of factors in capital accumulation by compromising the stability of balanced growth (Yoichi 1965). The conventional Uzawa two-sector model requires the use of capital-intensive investment for stability. But by adding the optimality criterion of consumption path and the social planner, it will drive the economy right to the balanced growth path without the difficulties and conditions required in a simple two-sector growth model.

We have seen also that, in the Cass-Koopmans model, saving is derived from the behaviour of households whose utility depends on their consumption. The primary concern of economists, according to optimal growth theorists, is the behaviour of households and their propensity for consumption and not so much the distribution of their income. In fact, today, from the growth point of view, optimal growth theory and consumer optimization in the Ramsey and Cass-Koopmans models are considered as actual and genuine representations of how the economy works.

On input-output empirical front pioneered by Leontief, a study directed by him and published in 1977 on the growth of the world economy using a multiregional input-output model covering 15 regions consisting of 45 sectors each, found that little progress would be possible to close the gap between rich and poor regions unless there is a change in trade policies and international finance. Increased aid for poor regions and a significant increase in the flow of imports from the developing economies to industrial economies was needed to assure a global balanced growth and a closing gap between rich and poor regions.

The Keynesian difficulties, associated with divergence between warranted and natural rates of growth, arise when capital intensity is limited to the reluctance of investors to acquire capital at low rates of return. It seems that the community wishes to save when rates of return are not attractive, which could happen if there are stores of value instead of capital whose rates of return of the marginal productivity of capital are more attractive. In this chapter we have also seen that Tobin studied this problem by demonstrating that the monetary debt of the government should be taken as an alternative store of value and showed how much saving must be converted into this form in order to bring the warranted rate of capital growth down to the natural rate. Equilibrium capital intensity and interest rates are determined by portfolio behaviour and monetary factors as well as by saving behaviours and technology. In Tobin's view, the real monetary debt grows at the natural rate, either by deficit spending or by deflation. The motivation of the community to hold a stock of capital depends on the rate of return of capital and the value of the monetary wealth. Tobin's research is focused on the link between the world of real variables and the world of monetary magnitudes, which is ignored in other growth models. He proved that, as capital grows, the course of price level depends on the rate of expansion of the labour force, the rate at which the monetary supply is increased by government deficit, and the rate of technological progress. Tobin, following the Keynesian tradition, showed that, both in the short and long run, monetary factors and portfolio decisions modify the determination of the interest rate and the process of capital accumulation. Money supply and portfolio behaviour influence the interest rate and the degree of capital intensity, which means that money is not neutral (the Tobin effect). Many of Tobin's contributions are included in Johnson's work by introducing money in a standard neoclassical growth model. H.G. Johnson (1966) attempted to integrate the monetary structure of an economy into the aggregative Solow-Swan model and to analyze the problems related to the stability of growth path equilibrium. The assumed influence of monetary policy on real magnitudes (e.g., on the growth rate) is confined mostly to the influence of the target rate of inflation on the utility yield of real balances. This supposition leads to the observation that, for non-neutral monetary models, money is non-interest bearing, which is a result of the convenience to the classical tradition of monetary analysis (outside the money concept) of representing the neutrality of money. The neoclassical monetary models (Tobin 1965; H.G. Johnson 1966) focus mainly on the steady-state solutions, and there is no analysis of how changing people's expectations can influence their behaviour through time. A few years later, Tobin's model was disputed by Sidrauski (1969) and Levhari and Patinkin (1968) as treating money exclusively as a store of value of the Keynesian type, thus ignoring any effects it may have in performing transactions costs. Their study was focused on the possibility of placing money into a utility function. Their work is based on the analysis of the individual's saving behaviour (and expectations), observed as a process of wealth accumulation aimed at maximizing some intertemporal utility function. Here, some configuration hypotheses are introduced regarding expectations in which the demand function for assets and consumption is derived from the analysis of the maximizing behaviour of individual economic units. The utility maximization in Sidrauski, as seen above, guarantees two main conditions: the rate of capital accumulation is a decreasing function of the capital stock, and the existence of a lag in the formation of expectations is fulfilled in order to maintain the path of steady state. In fact, the rate of return on capital is the sum of the natural rate of growth and the rate of time preference (the utility condition). Therefore, time preference or people's expectations influence economic growth through time, and the rate of interest is independent of the monetary variables, which implies that money is neutral (in the long run but not during the short-run adjustments).

5

Technological Progress and Growth in Neoclassical Perception

In the modern theory of growth, it is common to assert that most of the output increase is due to technological change. Growth of input alone, of course, cannot explain the growth of output. Most of the classical economists put the accumulation of capital in the centre of their attention rather than technological revolution of their time. Smith, Marx, and Mill discussed the contribution of knowledge and skills of a nation's labour force to its aggregate output and often assigned to discoveries and inventions a vital role in development. Similarly, the protection of domestic infant industry was based on the time needed for investments (or the accumulation of capital) to take place. Decades later, economists in the orthodox tradition such as Alfred Marshall, Frank Taussig, and Irving Fisher did appreciate the matter of technological progress, although it was not the main object of their attention. Heterodox economists like Veblen, Schumpeter, and Kuznets usually put technological progress as technical change at the centre of their analysis. However, although technology has been recognized by these economists as an important part of the economic scene, invention has not been fully incorporated into economic analysis. The Schumpeter tradition, for example, had treated invention as an exogenous force affecting the economic system, which led to widespread neglect of fundamental relations between inventions and economic activity.

Many economists, especially after the Second World War, have shown that the diffusion of technology is more important for the growth of output per head than the accumulation of physical capital. They have proved that there is a close connection between accumulation and technological progress if the latter is endogenized. Furthermore, technological progress has been given a wide range of meanings and interpretations. For instance, A.P. Thirlwall and Charles Kennedy (1972) give two meanings of technological process. The first refers to the effects of changes in technology or, more specifically, to the role of technological progress in the process of growth. In this sense, technological progress has been quantified as a determinant for the growth of output. The second meaning is related to changes in technology and in the process of production. It is used more to explain the process of technological change, usually in firms and industries. Within the industry, technological progress may take several different forms, including new processes of production, new commodities, and methods of industrial organization. Technological progress also implies advances in knowledge, which improve the living standard quantitatively through increases in real income per head and qualitatively through increasing people's choices in goods and welfare.

Some authors think that the scientific breakthroughs leading to inventions in a first phase may be a random process. If technological progress consists only of these random processes, it may be considered as an exogenous process. But this is only one phase of the whole process. The later phase usually consists of the application of inventions to actual production activities. Hence, at least in the later phase, the rate of technological progress will be subject to economic influences, so it can be endogenous to some extent.

Technological progress itself can be analyzed in terms of supply and demand factors. It depends on the application of modern science and on supply factors such as the stock of scientific and technical manpower and the state of the scientific organization. On the demand side, it depends on the profitability of applying new inventions that may be available and on the demand for products that can be produced using new technologies. In this chapter, some of the main theories in technological progress following a historical line will be examined.

THE NEUTRALITY OF TECHNICAL PROGRESS IN HICKS AND HARROD

Classifying technological progress either as neutral or as capital saving and labour saving is important in order to indicate the characteristics of technological progress and its effects on the distribution of income. Technological progress is defined as neutral when it leaves unchanged the balance between labour and capital – for example, when the ratio of marginal product of labour to the marginal product of capital (K/L) is unchanged – and, as a result, will permit the steady state. The definition usually is taken in a stricter sense to require that the ratios of marginal products be unaffected by technological progress at any value of K/L. John Hicks (1932) was one of the first economists to introduce the classification of technical progress (1932, 121–2). In fact, he defines inventions as "labour-saving," "neutral," and "capital-saving" as their respective initial effects are to increase, remain unchanged, or diminish the ratio of the marginal product of capital to that of labour. The general form of Hicks-neutral technical progress with two factors of production is given by Uzawa (1961b) as,

$$Y = A(t)\, F(K, L) \tag{5.1}$$

where $A(t)$ is an increasing function of t. Hicks neutrality tries to prove what would happen if the K/L ratio remains constant. Denoting the marginal products of capital and labour (before the technical progress) in time 0 as $F_K(0)$ and $F_L(0)$, respectively, and the marginal products of capital and labour (after the technical progress) in time t as $F_k(t)$ and $F_L(t)$, the Hicks-neutral condition can be defined as follows (Jones 1975, 163):

1 If $F_K(t)/F_L(t) > F_K(0)/F_L(0)$, the technical progress is labour saving in Hicks's definition.
2 If $F_K(t)/F_L(t) = F_K(0)/F_L(0)$, the technical progress is Hicks neutral.
3 If $F_K(t)/F_L(t) < F_K(0)/F_L(0)$, the technical progress is capital saving in Hicks's definition.

A labour-saving invention decreases the wage-rental ratio, given by w/r, and increases the ratio r/w. So, an invention that saves labour implies that the wage rate will decline with respect to the rental rate of capital. In the same way, a capital-saving invention increases the wage-rental ratio w/r and decreases the r/w. Thus, technical progress that saves capital implies that the rental rate of capital will decline relative to the wage rate and that capital will be less scarce relative to labour following the invention. Supposing that the ratio of relative shares, indicated as π, is equal to rK/wL, for all changes in which the capital-labour ratio K/L remains constant, the technological progress, which affects r/w, will also affect the ratio of relative shares. In terms of the effect of technical

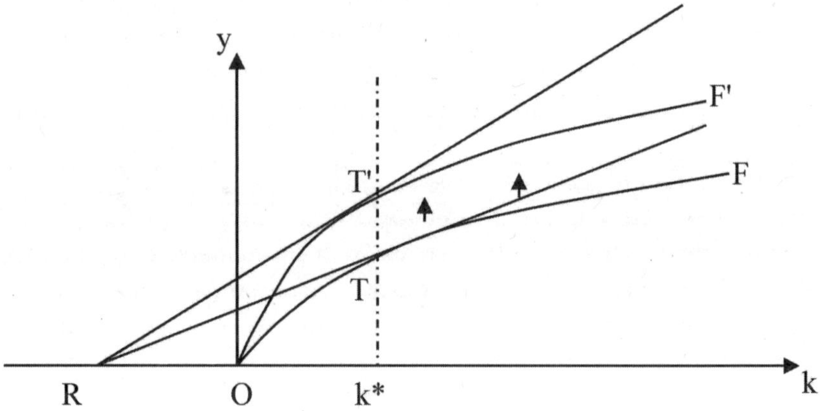

Figure 5.1 Hicks technical change

progress on the ratio of relative shares, Hicks's definition can be stated in the following paragraph.

Technical progress is labour saving in Hicks's sense if, at any constant value of the capital-labour ratio, the ratio of relative shares, $\pi = rK/wL$, is increasing ($\pi > 0$). In the same way, technical progress is capital saving in Hicks's sense if, at any constant value of the capital-labour ratio, the ratio of relative shares, $\pi = rK/wL$, is decreasing ($\pi < 0$). And, last, the technical progress is Hicks neutral if, at any constant value of the capital-labour ratio, the ratio of relative shares, $\pi = rK/wL$, remains constant ($\pi = 0$) (Jones 1975, 164–5). In figure 5.1, the production function is shown before and after Hicks-neutral technical change.

Suppose that the economy has a capital per labour ratio, k^*. The marginal product of capital is then measured by the tangent slope *RT*, and the wage-rental ratio *w/r* is measured by the distance *OR*. If technical progress causes the production function to shift upward to *F'*, then Hicks neutrality requires the ratio of the rate of capital to the wage rate, *r/w*, to remain constant. The Hicks-neutral shift from *F* to the new production function *F'* requires that the tangent to the new production function at the capital-labour ratio *k* remain the same after the shift. Hence, the shift of the production function from *T* to *T'* represents Hicks-neutral technical progress.

In 1938 Joan Robinson, considering the Hicks classification of inventions, analyzed the effects of invention on the relative shares of the factors in the total product (when the amount of capital is adjusted to the new technique so that the new technique is attained with zero investment). Robinson found that, if the relative shares are unchanged in equilibrium by an invention, the elasticity of substitution is equal to unity,[1] whereas, if an invention is labour-saving or capital-saving, the relative shares are changed and the elasticity of substitution is less or greater than unity (J. Robinson 1938, 139). Harrod (1948) criticized this position and suggested that it would be more convenient to use a classification in which an invention is neutral when it leaves the relative shares of factors unchanged after the stock of capital has been adjusted to the new situation. However, according to Robinson, "Neutral progress in Mr. Harrod's conception results from an equal rate of increase in output per head at all the stages of production" (J. Robinson 1949, 70).

Harrod (1937b) analyzed technical progress with a constant population and divided inventions and improvements into neutral, capital using, and capital saving, according to the tendency of the ratio of capital to output (assuming a constant rate of interest) to remain unchanged, to increase, or to diminish (J. Robinson 1938, 139–40).

Uzawa (1961b), years later, demonstrated that Harrod-neutral technical progress is the only type of technical progress consistent with a stable steady-state ratio k^*. This is because the Harrod-neutral technical progress keeps the capital-output ratio, v, constant over time. The Harrod definition is based on the comparison of points on the production function at different times where the marginal product of capital is constant (Hahn and Matthews 1964). The general form of Harrod-neutral technical progress with two factors of production, as given by Uzawa (1961b), takes the form[2]

$$Y = F(K, A(t)L) \tag{5.2}$$

where the term t is prefixed to L instead of to $f(K,L)$, as in the Hicks-neutral case. The above production function, assuming constant returns to scale, shows clearly that an equal rise in K and $A(t)L$ leads, usually, to an equal rise in Y.

Technical progress is labour saving in Harrod's sense if, at any constant value of capital-output ratio, the ratio of relative shares, $\pi = rK/wL$, is increasing. In the same way, technical progress is capital saving in Harrod's sense if, at any constant value of capital-output ratio, the ratio of relatives shares, $\pi = rK/wL$, is decreasing.[3] Technical progress is said to be Harrod neutral if, at any constant value of the capital-output ratio,

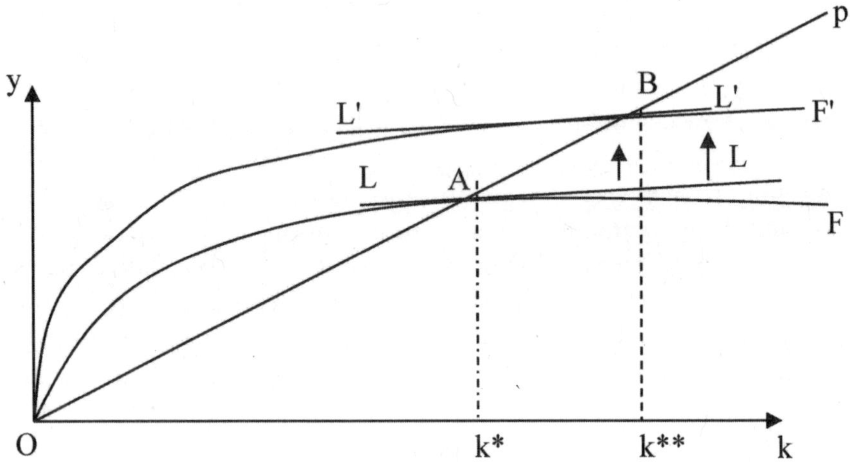

Figure 5.2 Harrod-neutral technical progress

the ratio of relative shares, $\pi = rK/wL$, remains constant. The Harrod and Hicks methods of classifying technical progress differ where the old and the new production functions are compared. Harrod's method is based on comparing all of the points with equal capital-output ratios, whereas Hicks's method is applicable to the comparison of points with equal capital-labour ratios. Figure 5.2, shows the per-worker production function in the Harrod-neutral sense.

In figure 5.2, *OF* is a conventional per-worker production function. The economy is initially operating at a capital-labour ratio equal to k^*, and the marginal product of capital is equal to the tangent *LL* at the point *A* on *OF*. Technical progress shifts the per-worker production function to the new position *OF'*. The shift is Harrod neutral when the marginal product of capital is the same as that given by the slope of the tangent *LL*, when the capital-output ratio is the same as that determined by the slope of the line *OP*. The technical progress is such that, if this ratio is constant, so is the rate of profit (the slope of the tangent). At point *B*, the capital-output ratio is the same as the capital-output ratio at point *A* and the economy is operating at a capital-labour ratio equal to k^{**}. The marginal product of capital at point *B* is equal to the slope of the tangent *L'L'*, and because this tangent is parallel to the tangent *LL* at point *A*, it is also equal to the marginal product of capital at point *A*. Therefore, the shift from *A* to *B* represents Harrod-neutral technical progress. Different from Hicks-neutral technical progress, the shift of the whole curve generated by Harrod-neutral technical progress is possible only when the marginal product of capital remains constant, regardless of what the constant value of the capital-output ratio may be. In J. Robinson's view, the invention is Harrod-neutral when it leaves the ratio of capital product unchanged and raises the elasticity of the average productivity curve (J. Robinson 1938, 140). A capital-saving invention, which reduces the ratio of capital to product, lowers the elasticity of the average productivity curve, whereas a labour-saving invention, which increases the ratio of capital to product, raises the elasticity of the average productivity curve. Robinson demonstrated geometrically that Harrod-neutral technical progress is equivalent to labour-augmenting technical progress. She wrote,

> It thus appears that an invention which is neutral in the sense required by Mr. Harrod, that is, an invention that leaves the ratio of capital to product unchanged if the rate of interest is constant, raises the average productivity curve iso-elastically. A capital-saving invention, which reduces the ratio of capital to product, lowers the elasticity of the average productivity curve (at a given value of *y*) while a labour-saving, or more properly capital-using, invention, which increases the ratio of capital to product, raises the elasticity of the average productivity curve. (J. Robinson 1938, 140)

According to Kennedy (1961), there is a distinction between neutral technical progress and neutral inventions. Neutral technical progress refers more to the economy as a whole, whereas a neutral invention refers to a particular line of production. This means that a number of neutral inventions do not together constitute neutral technical progress. A neutral invention does not necessarily require a net investment for its implementation. Neutral progress may require some net investment, but this is due to the capital-using character of inventions that constitute neutral technical progress.

The tendency of capital to accumulate relative to labour over time is accompanied by a tendency for the price of capital goods to fall relative to the price of labour, normally as a result of technical progress taking place in the capital-goods sector itself. In fact, Salter reaches the broad conclusion that neutrality regarding invention and neutral technical change are reasonable hypotheses (1966, Chs. 4–7). Salter uses a classification closely related but not identical to the Hicks classification.

Instead of looking at the effects of technical progress on relative marginal products with given factor proportions, he considers the effect on factor proportions with given relative marginal products. Both classifications imply the same definition of neutrality, but Salter gives some convincing reasons why his classification is more suitable for analysis at the industry level. Salter's argument in support of his main conclusion is, in part, theoretical. In effect, he rejects Hicks's approach of bias in invention induced to relative price changes on the grounds that the aim of the entrepreneur is to minimize total costs.

It is worth noting that Salter made an important contribution to research at the industry level by analyzing prices, costs, and output for twenty-eight British (during a range-period of 26 years ending in 1950) and twenty-three American industries. He found two tendencies: first, the industries that experienced average rates of productivity gains tended to pass the results along to consumers in the form of lower relative prices rather than to labour in the form of higher relative wages; second, those industries in which the rate of productivity gain was sufficiently rapid to permit declining relative prices were also industries that experienced the greatest gains in output. He suggested that differences in the rate of growth of labour productivity between industries were best explained by a combination of pure factor substitution and an unequal rate of neutral technical advance rather than a pure neutral technical progress as in the Hicks or Harrod classification of inventions.

TECHNICAL PROGRESS FUNCTION IN KALDOR AND BLACK

Kaldor was one of the first economists to introduce the notion that technical progress needed to be explained by the process of investment itself (Kaldor 1957). He assumed that the proportionate growth rate of output per worker is an increasing function of the proportionate growth rate of capital per worker. Kaldor supposed that, in a model of economic growth, the effect of accumulation in the maximum attainable level of production can be better analyzed in terms of a technical progress function than in terms of a production function. In fact, a technical progress function relates the rate of growth of possible production to the rate of investment at any time.[4] The technical production function, which is assumed to replace the neoclassical production function, is given as

$$y^{\cdot} = F(k) \; F'>0; \; F''<0; \; F(0) > 0 \qquad (5.3)$$

where y˙ and *k* are output and capital per worker, respectively. Their derivatives with respect to time are given as

$$y^{\cdot} = (dy/dt)/y, \text{ and } k^{\cdot} = (dk/dt)/k \tag{5.4}$$

The technical progress function can easily be specified in a linear form,

$$y^{\cdot} = A + Bk^{\cdot} \tag{5.5}$$

or can be given in a more technical relationship between rate of growth in productivity and capital per worker (Kaldor 1957, 604–5),

$$\dot{y}_t = \alpha' + \beta'\frac{I_t}{K_t} \quad \text{where } \alpha'>0 \text{ and } 1>\beta'>0 \tag{5.6}$$

where I_t and K_t are investment and capital at the time *t*, and α' and β' are proportion terms of the growth of the stock of capital . The rate of growth of labour productivity and income in expression (5.6) is given as an increasing function of the rate of net investment expressed in coefficients (proportion terms) α' and β' of the rate of growth of capital stock.

The long-run equilibrium is given by G as

$$G = n\frac{\alpha'}{1-\beta'} \tag{5.7}$$

where the rates of growth of income and capital are equal and *n* is the exponential growth rate of the labour force. From equation (5.7) can be seen that the long-run equilibrium rates of growth of income and capital are equal and depend only on the coefficients α' and β' (Kaldor 1957, 611). The rate of technical progress, as represented by the proportionate growth rate of labour productivity, is constant and, therefore, independent of the rate of investment. In Kaldor's view, in most of the developed economies, the technical progress function is given as a relationship between the rate of growth of output per worker and the rate of growth of capital per worker (J.E. King 1994, 52–3). The technical progresses function, as depicted in Figure 5.3 illustrates on the vertical axis the rate of growth of labour productivity and on the horizontal axis the rate of growth of capital per worker. The technical progress function *F* intersects the vertical axis presenting positive rate of growth of labour productivity and is concave from below. The 45° line drawn through the origin determines the equilibrium growth and

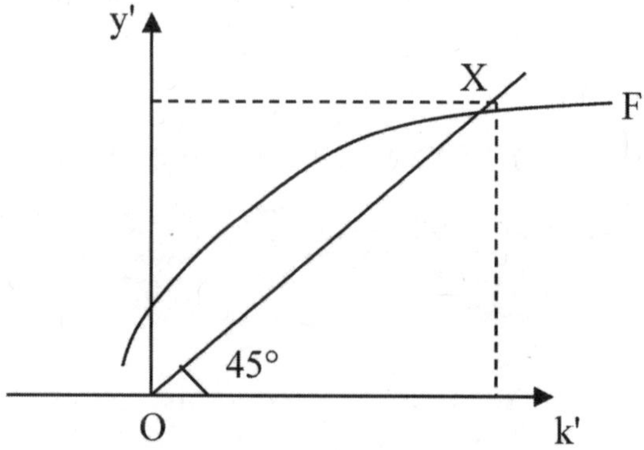

Figure 5.3 Kaldorian technical progress function (Kaldor 1957)

shows all the points where output and investment per worker grow at the same rate.

Therefore, the economy can be in the steady-state if growth is somewhere on the 45° line and somewhere on the technical progress function F. The intersection of the 45° line and function *F* at *X* gives the only point where the steady-state equilibrium is sustainable.

Kaldor's technical progress function was later revised by Kaldor and Mirrlees (1962). In the revised version the technical progress is related to gross investment instead of net investment (which, in the case of Kaldor's earlier version [1957], is neutral to capital-labour ratio). Technical progress is also contained in the replacement of investment (depreciation).

Practically, after a deep review of the Kaldor and Mirrlees model (1962), we are aware that there is no production function or a single-valued relationship between the magnitudes of capital, *Kt*, labour force, *Nt*, and output, *Yt*. Everything depends on investment done in the past – on how the equipment goods have been built up. Output *Yt* would be greater for a given *Kt* if a greater part of the existing capital stock is of more recent creation. So, it is not possible to derive a production function from the technical progress function because productivity over time depends not only on the stock of capital but also on the rate at which it is installed. The technical progress function is then consistent with a technical "investment function" that has a relationship between investment per worker and output per worker. Thus, technical progress has two elements: an exogenous element in new ideas and the exploitation of these ideas by learning (Hahn and Matthews 1964, 825–32).

For Kaldor and Mirrlees (1962), it is convenient to assume technical progress as neutral, so the rate of increase in investment per head remains unchanged over time, and, what is more important, capital-saving and capital-using innovations remain unchanged in the total flow of innovations. Later Hahn and Matthews (1964) assumed that Kaldor's technical progress function can be regarded as an extension of the Cobb-Douglas technical progress function. In fact, however, Cobb and Douglas have argued that the technical progress function, given as $[\delta(Y^{\cdot}/Y)/\delta(K^{\cdot}/K)]$, is constant in all circumstances. Kaldor argued in the same way with $K^{\cdot}/K$. All have in common the assumption that this slope is independent of K/Y. Without this assumption, a technical progress function relating $Y^{\cdot}/Y$ and $K^{\cdot}/K$ cannot be drawn.

Black, in a short article (just one month before Kaldor and Mirrlees's article), proved that there is a technical progress function but not a production function (Black 1962). In other words, it is not possible to integrate the technical progress and, what is more important, to derive from it a production function. In fact, he assumed a production function of the form

$$Q = AK^b \tag{5.8}$$

And, taking the derivate with respect to time in (5.8), we have (Black 1962, 166)

$$\frac{dQ}{dt} = AbK^{b-1}\frac{dK}{dt} \text{ and } Q^* = \frac{1}{Q}\frac{dQ}{dt} - b\frac{1}{K}\frac{dK}{dt} = bK^* \tag{5.9}$$

where Q^* and K^* are the proportional rates of growth of output and capital, and b is the elasticity of output with respect to capital. Assuming technical progress as independent of accumulation, we have

$$A_t = A_0 e^{et} \tag{5.10}$$

where e is the rate of technical progress and the production function at time t is given as

$$Q_t = A_0 e^{et} K^b \tag{5.11}$$

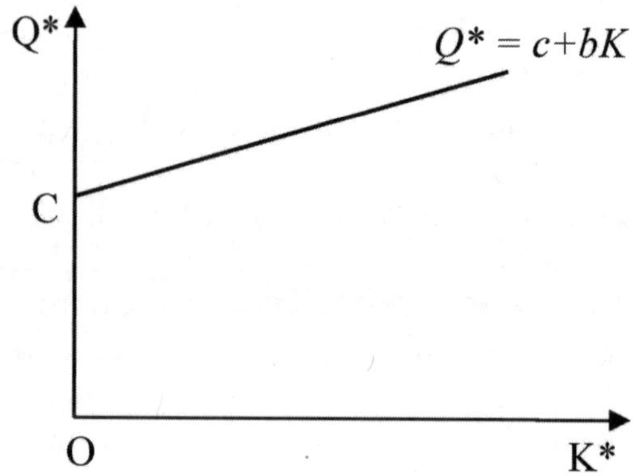

Figure 5.4 Linear technical progress function

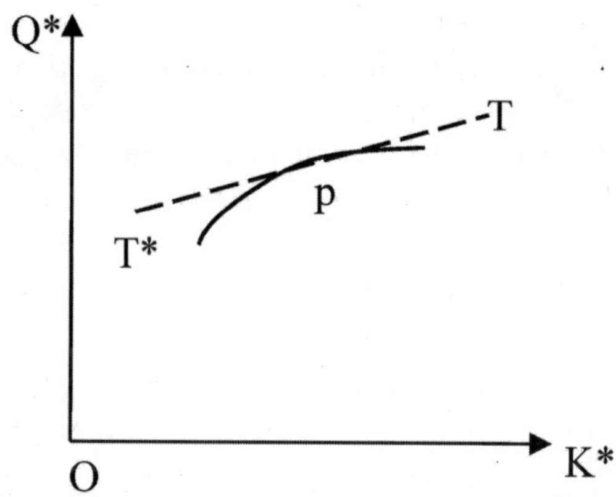

Figure 5.5 Concave dynamic technical progress function

If the technical function is found to be of the form $Q^* = c + bK^*$, it can be integrated to give a production function of the general form

$$Q = A_0 e^{c} K^{b} \qquad (5.12)$$

This function is linear (of Kaldorian type), cutting the vertical axis at $Q^* = c$ and having a constant slope equal to b, as seen in figure 5.4.

Figure 5.5 illustrates a dynamic technical progress function with a decreasing return, concave downward in the short run. The slope of

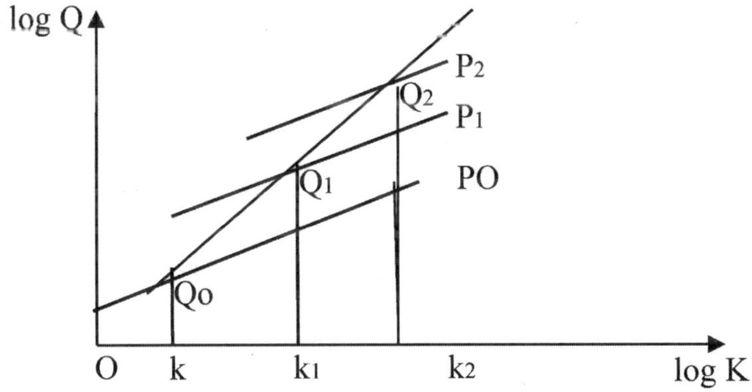

Figure 5.6 Production functions (Black 1962)

the curve in figure 5.5 gets steeper from left to right when the elasticity of response of marginal productivity of capital *dQ/dK* is positive to changes in *dK/dt*. Conversely, if the elasticity of response is negative, the curve gets flatter for movements from left to right (Black 1962, 169; Kaldor 1960, 267).

Black (1962), among others, argued that the amount of technical progress should not be independent of the rate of accumulation. Technical progress and accumulation are connected. In fact, they are both related by the rate of accumulation on research and innovation, which has been incorporated in new equipments. He also assumed that there is only one dynamic technical progress function, which is no longer linear in form.

A production function can be depicted as it exists at successive times (P_0, P_1, and P_2), as shown in figure 5.6, with capital stock showing at each time (k_0, k_1, and k_2). The axes *x* and *y* are exposed by *log K* and *log Q* for convenience when comparing the proportional changes.

According to Black, an approximated technical progress can be drawn, as represented in figure 5.7, with K_0 and Q_0 predetermined. This represents a curve of possibilities T_1T_1 for time t_1, which is attained on the basis of the rate of investment at time t_0. Once the T_1T_1 is chosen, K_1 and Q_1 are determined, and a set of possibilities for time t_2 becomes available. The second position T_2T_2 depends on what position the T_1T_1 adopts, and so on. The rate of capital accumulation will be spread over several periods of time, making possible different final outputs, Q_n, if

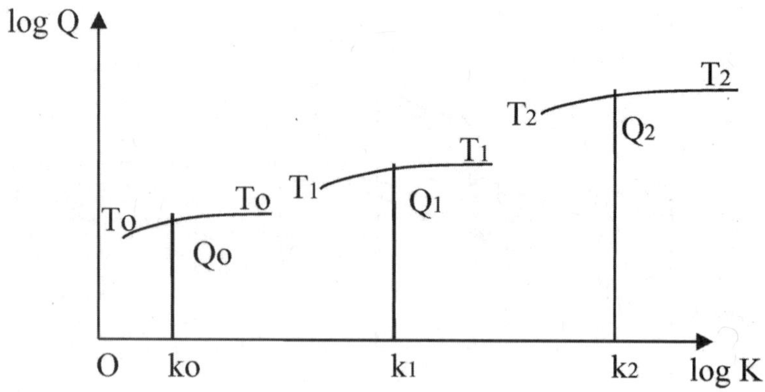

Figure 5.7 The curve of possibilities (Black 1962)

the technical progress is stable from period to period. Q_n will be maximized if capital is accumulated at a steady proportional rate during the n periods. Consequently, as the rate of investment able to increase output depends on the time at which investment is carried out, it implies that it is not possible to integrate the technical progress function and derive from it a production function (Black 1962, 169). Wording it differently, the technical progress function is not linear and cannot be integrated to yield a production function.

TECHNICAL PROGRESS AND PRODUCTIVITY CHANGE IN SOLOW

Solow uses the idea of technical progress as a shorthand expression for any kind of shift in the production function (Solow 1957). He considers technical change as part of slowdowns, speedups, improvements in the education of labour force, or any other types of changes related to production. By assuming that all factors are paid their marginal productivity, we have a generalized aggregate production function of the form

$$Q = F(K, L, t) \qquad (5.13)$$

where Q represents output, K and L represent capital and labour, and t represents the time incurred during the production. Solow explicitly assumes that technical progress is Hicks neutral, and the aggregate production function can, therefore, be written in a labour-augmenting form,

$$Y = A(t)\, F(K, L) \tag{5.14}$$

where the multiplicative factor $A(t)$ measures the cumulated effect of shift over time. Differentiating equation (5.14) totally with respect to time and dividing by Q, we obtain the following identity (Solow 1957, 312):

$$\frac{\dot{Q}}{Q} = \frac{\dot{A}}{A} + A\frac{\delta f}{\delta K}\frac{\dot{K}}{Q} + A\frac{\delta f}{\delta L}\frac{\dot{L}}{Q} \tag{5.15}$$

Denoting by $w_k = (\delta Q/\delta K)(K/Q)$ and $w_L = (\delta Q/\delta L)(L/Q)$ the relative shares of capital and labour, respectively, and substituting them in equation (5.15), we get

$$\frac{\dot{Q}}{Q} = \frac{\dot{A}}{A} + w_K\frac{\dot{K}}{K} + w_L\frac{\dot{L}}{L} \tag{5.16}$$

The fundamental equation of Solow's research in technical change can be expressed in terms of intensive magnitudes. If we define $Q/L = y$, $K/L = k$, and $w_k = 1 - w_L$, noting that $\dot{y}/y = \dot{Q}/Q - \dot{L}/L$, we obtain the following central equation:

$$\frac{\dot{y}}{y} = \frac{\dot{A}}{A} + w_K\frac{\dot{k}}{k} \tag{5.17}$$

So, the rate of growth of output per head, $\dot{y}/y$, is equal to the rate of growth of capital per worker, $\dot{k}/k$, multiplied by the relative share of capital, w_k, plus the rate of technical progress, $\dot{A}/A$. From the fundamental equation (5.17) of Solow, an estimate of the rate of technical progress, $\dot{A}/A$, can be easily obtained using estimates of the rate of growth of output per worker, $\dot{y}/y$, of the rate of growth of capital per worker, $\dot{k}/k$, and the relative share of capital.

Solow was one of the first growth economists to be interested directly in the effects of technical progress on the growth of the economy. Before Solow's contribution, capital accumulation was almost uncontrovertibly taken as the most important factor of economic growth. Hicks, for example, saw the relevance of induced prejudice to macro models, but he did not give any detailed account of an adjustment mechanism. He simply supposed that factor-saving characteristics of inventions tend to play a part in the adjustment of factor share stability. The need for an adjustment mechanism became apparent when it was found that, in the one-sector neoclassical growth model, steady growth exists only if Harrod-neutral technical progress is assumed. Since Solow's 1957 paper, technical progress has been accepted as the major driver of growth, while the role of factor inputs has been pushed to the background. For a long time (at least until the 1980s), however, technical progress was treated largely as an exogenous factor, something like manna from heaven, and Solow's model was, without doubt, part of this doctrine.

Solow's method involves treating statistics of capital share, the rate of growth of output per worker, and capital derived from a real world of heterogeneous outputs (and items of capital equipment) as if they were equivalent to the aggregate concept of the simple neoclassical model. He applied his technical change to US data for the period 1909–49 using three time series: output per unit of labour, capital per unit of labour, and share of capital. Solow (1957) showed that, over the period 1909–49, shifts in the aggregate production function netted out to be approximately neutral. In fact, he defined neutrality as if the shifts were pure scale changes in production function, leaving marginal rates of substitution unchanged at the given capital-labour ratio. According to Solow (1957, 320), the conclusions emerging from a crude application of American data (period 1909–49) imply that

- technical change during that period was neutral on average;
- the upward shift in the production function was, apart from fluctuations, at a rate of about 1 per cent per year for the first half of the period and 2 per cent per year for the last half;
- gross output per man hour doubled over the interval, with 87.5 per cent of the increase attributed to technical progress and the remaining 12.5 per cent to the increased use of capital; and
- the aggregate production function, corrected for technical change, gives a distinct impression of diminishing returns.

Moreover, Solow (1957), in his empirical work, concluded that almost 90 per cent of the growth of output per worker in the United States during the period 1909–49 was due to the effect of the residual factor A, which was supposed to measure the effect of technical progress. Other research employing more sophisticated cyonceptions of technical change have tried to resolve most of the difficulties related to the aggregation production difficulties with the available crude data, thereby weakening somehow Solow's conclusion about the effects of technical progress. For instance, the work of Jorgenson and Griliches (1967) has suggested that almost all of the observed economic growth in the United States between 1945 and 1965 has been accounted for in terms of growth of the conventional inputs of capital and labour rather than in terms of change in technical progress.

Most of the empirical work in the 1950s and 1960s was inspired by a simple type of approach to technical progress in which the effects of technical progress and capital accumulation are separated conceptually. The basic procedure used by many authors in the 1960s was to calculate the contributions made to growth in terms of output by increases in inputs of labour and capital over a period of time and by multiplying the observed input increases by observed factor prices and deducting the result from the overall growth in output. In this way, the residual is attributed to technical progress. The result almost always shows that technical progress contributes much more to growth than capital accumulation does. This approach has been deeply criticized in two different positions (Hahn and Matthews 1964): first, it attributes the residual mostly to technical progress, thus excluding other influences, such as improvement in the quality of labour, knowledge, and the level of education; second, the method of technical progress depends on the assumption that each production factor receives the value of its marginal products and, therefore, lead to misleading consequences unless there is perfect competition in the market. This generally has serious effects on the empirical conclusions drawn from the method in practice.

CAPITAL FORMATION AND THE TRANSMISSION OF TECHNICAL PROGRESS

Productivity movements are regarded as the net result of a complicated interaction between technical advance and changing factor prices. Technical change is measured by the relative change in total unit costs when the techniques in each period minimize unit costs and when factor prices are constant (Salter 1960, Jorgenson and Griliches 1967). Particular attention is given to the problem of separating the effects of technical factors (primarily arising out of non-neutral technological change) and price factors (primarily changes in factor prices relative to each other), which tend to influence the total productivity (output per unit of total input) measured as an indicator of technological change. For instance, Salter considered some important aspects of factor productivity in his theory of technical change (Salter 1960, Chs. 2–3). His model of technical progress is based on two basic key points: first, technical change is introduced into the production process through capital investment; second, capital equipment currently in use will remain in use until its earnings in the form of quasi-rent fall to zero. In many aspects, this model is very similar to the Johnson-Edwards model (G.L. Johnson 1960 and Edwards 1959). The discussion of the impact of technological change on the substitution of capital equipment for labour remains available. Salter (1960) proved that technical change occurring generally throughout the economy will be accompanied by the substitution of capital goods for labour. In fact, he stated, "The continuous cheapening of capital goods resulting from technical advances in their manufacture ... automatically generates powerful pressures for the substitution of capital equipment for labour" (Salter 1960, 30).

New investment in the neoclassical theory of growth is often considered to be the transmission mechanism of the new ideas. Innovations are embodied in new kinds of durable equipment before they are made effective. It is said that capital accumulation and technical progress influence each other in such a way that the separation of the two becomes impossible. Kaldor, considering the effect of capital accumulation on technological progress, stated that "The use of more capital per worker (whether measured in terms of the value of capital at constant prices, in terms of tons of weight of the equipment, mechanical power, etc) inevitably entails the introduction of superior techniques which require "inventiveness" of some kind, though these need not necessarily represent the application of basically new principles or ideas" (Kaldor 1957, 595).

With embodied technical progress, however, there is no presumption that a fall in quasi-rents on existing machines will be matched by a fall in the general rate of profit. Entrepreneurs' expectations by and large determine the choice of technique at a given wage and the valuation of capital stock. They also determine the path followed by the economy from any starting point. In some models (Salter 1965, Svennilson 1963) entrepreneurs are presented with constant wage rates rather than rising rates to be compatible with steady growth. This makes them deal with erroneous expectations regarding production and the choice of techniques. According to Solow (1962a and 1962b), shifts in technology can be divided into two kinds: disembodied and embodied. A new technology is embodied in capital equipment when it allows an increase in output from the same quantity of input but requires the construction of new capital goods before the knowledge (of the new technology) can be made effective and available in the industry. Disembodied improvements in techniques are usually organizational and permit more output to be produced from unchanged inputs, with no investment required. The representation of technology as purely disembodied is a way of improving the organization and operation of inputs without reference to the nature of the inputs themselves. The striking assumption is that old and new capital equipment participate equally in technical progress. So, the level of disembodied technology advances in the economy without any need to invest in new vintages of capital goods.

The logic of Solow's model about capital formation and technology transmission is relatively straightforward, although the manipulations required to produce his central results are moderately complex (Solow 1962a). Solow, in his 1962 model, assumes that new technology is introduced into the production process only through investment in new plants and equipment. He assumes that capital goods produced in any year are more productive than those produced the year before. If a gross investment of $I(v)$ is made in year v, the amount in the later year t will be $B(t - v)$. The labour and machines of various vintages are arranged to yield maximum output, so that the stock of surviving capital goods of different vintage and productivity can be given by an "equivalent stock of capital" in the year t of the form (Solow 1962a, 72),

$$J(t) = \sum_{v=-\infty}^{t} (1+\lambda)^{v} B(t-v) I(v) \qquad (5.18)$$

where $B(t - v)$ is the gross investment ($(t - v)$ years old) made in the later year t and v is the former year. Solow introduces a kind of "index of technology," $B(t)$, that is neutral and advances at rate λ. The nature of technology is that, at every point of time it affects the efficiency of only new capital goods. Every capital good embodies the latest technology at the moment of its creation, but it does not participate in subsequent technical progress. Hence, equation (5.18) defines the equivalent stock of capital for any constant rate of increase in the productivity of capital goods. The total output in Solow's model is a function of the stock of capital denoted by $J(t)$ and of the input of labour, $N(t)$. The general form of the production function is (Solow 1962a, 77),

$$P(t) = F(J(t), N(t)) \tag{5.19}$$

In this function, there is no explicit mention of technical progress. It is supposed to be included in the stock of capital $J(t)$. Solow permitted the substitution of labour and capital before capital goods take concrete form. He, among others, assumed that the ratio of actual output to potential output is a function of the unemployment rate. The actual production function takes the form

$$A(t) = f(u(t))P(t) = f(u)\,F(J, N) \tag{5.20}$$

where $f(u)$ stands for the unemployment rate. Using a Cobb-Douglas function with constant returns to scale for $F(J, N)$, Solow gives the actual production function a general Cobb-Douglas form:[5]

$$A = a10^{b+cu+du^2}\, J^{\alpha} N^{1-\alpha} \tag{5.21}$$

$$\text{or } A(t) = a10^{b+cu+du^2}\, J(t)^{\alpha} N(t)^{1-\alpha} \tag{5.21'}$$

where a and $10^{b+cu+du^2}$ are constant terms belonging, respectively, to production function F and index $J(t)$. These terms can be separated once they have been given the definition of full employment. Equations (5.21) and (5.21)' are quite similar to the conventional Cobb-Douglas function except for the index $J(t)$, which adds up all the machines of different vintages, giving a smaller weight to old machines with small vs, which are part of the stock capital, $J(t)$, in equation (5.18) than to new machines in the year t.[6] Dividing both sides by N and taking the log of each side of the above equation, we obtain the simple linear form

$$\log(A/N) = \log a + b + cu + du^2 + \alpha \log(J/N) \tag{5.22}$$

The measure of unemployment and employment, considered by Solow (1962a), is assumed to coincide with the usual labour force. Equation (5.21) gives the actual output produced as a function of capital stock J with a degree of technical progress embodied in it. The multiplicative term $a10^{b+cu+du^2}$ in equation (5.21) is plugged into the aggregate production function of the Cobb-Douglas form and represents the technical progress growing at a constant rate, a. Solow admitted that the economy is not free to move back and forth along the production function presented by equation (5.21). In fact, it could happen that an accelerated movement out of the function may have the effect of shifting the function itself (Solow 1962a, 86.). For example, a sharply higher rate of investment may bring premature scrapping of old equipment, or a change in the composition of investment quota may bring large changes in the composition of output. In effect, he suggested a new analysis of the productivity investment, sector by sector, by giving the best sectorial composition of investment.

Solow estimated the production function during the period 1929–61 and found that it depends on the improvement factor for equipment rather than for plants (Solow 1962a, 80). The ordinary stock of plants increased by about 50 per cent, whereas the stock of equipment grew by almost 170 per cent. So the estimated elasticity of output declined as the improvement factor (especially in equipment) increased. His estimation suggested that the maintenance of capital intensity and the achievement of low rates of growth of output can be obtained with a much smaller amount of investment than the consideration of the ordinary stock of capital. In order to obtain a high rate of output, the equivalent stock of capital must grow faster than the input of labour. Solow (1962a, 86) concluded that capital formation is not the only source of growth in productivity; investment is also a necessary albeit insufficient condition for growth. There are also other factors, such as research, education, welfare, and public health that can make a significant contribution to the process of economic growth.

VINTAGE GROWTH MODELS: THE PHELPS MODEL

Phelps (1962) adopted Solow's idea and constructed a growth model incorporating both embodied and disembodied technical progress in the long run. Vintage models provided what Phelps used to call a "new view of investment."[7] In these models, new investments are added to the existing stock of productive capital, thus lowering the average age of the "old" capital stock and increasing the proportion of capital stock able to embody recent technologies.

As in Solow (1962b), and by adopting a Cobb-Douglas production function to the machines of each vintage, we have that the sum of homogeneous outputs of the various vintages is given by

$$Q_t = B_0 J_t^{\alpha} N_t^{1-\alpha} \tag{5.23}$$

where Jt is the effective capital, including capital goods of older vintages. The effective capital Jt is given as (Phelps 1962, 552)

$$J_t = \int_{-\infty}^{t} e^{\alpha v} K_v(t) dv \qquad (5.24)$$

where J above represents the weighted sum of machines of different vintages (from the past periods to t), $e^{\alpha v}$ characterizes the contemporary machines, and Kv is the (vintage) capital of age v. Current investment increases output per man, which comes, to some extent, through affecting the average of capital stock.

The objective of Phelps's model is to compare a pure new-view model and a new view of investment with a pure old-view model. The easiest approach to do this was by taking a general production function of the type

$$Q_t = B_0 e^{\mu t} J_t^{\alpha} N_t^{1-\alpha} \qquad (5.25)$$

The new and old views of estimation are given, respectively, by λ and μ, whereas J, again, is in the function of investment I of age v as follows:

$$J_t = e^{\delta t} \int_{-\infty}^{t} e^{(\frac{\lambda}{\alpha}+\delta)v} I(v) dv \qquad (5.26)$$

The long-run rate of growth, g, using γ and μ as parameters, is given by

$$g = \frac{\lambda + \mu}{1-\alpha} + n \qquad (5.27)$$

where n is the rate of growth of the labour force. From equation (5.27), we have that the balanced rate of growth, g, is independent of the investment ratio. Capital that is $(t - v)$ years old will grow at the rate g like almost everything else.

THE FUNDAMENTAL GROWTH RATE FUNCTION IN PHELPS

Assuming that the labour force grows at a constant relative rate n, and that most of the capital goods depreciate exponentially at the annual rate ψ we have the equations for labour force and capital goods respectively as

$$N_t = N_0 e^{nt} \tag{5.a}$$

$$\text{and } K_v(t) = I(v)e^{-\psi(t-v)} \tag{5.b}$$

Differentiating Qt in (5.25) with respect to time we get a new form of equation

$$\dot{Q} = \mu Q + \alpha Be^{\mu t} J^{\alpha-1} N^{1-\alpha} \left[e^{\frac{\lambda t}{\alpha}} - \psi J \right] (1-\alpha) Be^{\mu t} N^{-\alpha} J^{1-\alpha} \dot{N} \tag{5.c}$$

where the relation $\dot{J}_t = e^{\frac{\lambda}{\alpha}t} - \psi J$

comes as the result of the function (5.b). Using (5.a) and (5.b) we obtain a differential equation with four parameters, d_1, d_2, d_3, and d_4 which gives us the growth path of output

$$\dot{Q} = d_1 Q + d_2 Q^{d_3} e^{d_4 t} \tag{5.d}$$

where $d_1 = \mu - \alpha\psi + (1 - \alpha)n$, $d_2 = \alpha s B^{\alpha} N_0^{\frac{1-\alpha}{\alpha}}$, $d_3 = \frac{2\alpha - 1}{\alpha}$ and $d_4 = \frac{\lambda + \mu + (1-\alpha)n}{\alpha}$

The path growth is asymptotic to a balanced-growth equilibrium path where all variables like production, consumption, investment and the capital stock grow exponentially at the same rate. By indicating with Q^(t) the balanced growth equilibrium path we have an asymptotic function of the type

$$Q\hat{}(t) = Q_0^{\wedge} e^{\frac{d_4}{1-d_3}t} \tag{5.e}$$

where the growth rate denoted as, g, tends in the long run to the constant parameter $\frac{d_4}{1-d_3}$

From here we get the fundamental growth rate function using the original variables λ, μ and n, as described in equation (5.27), (Phelps 1962, 554–6).

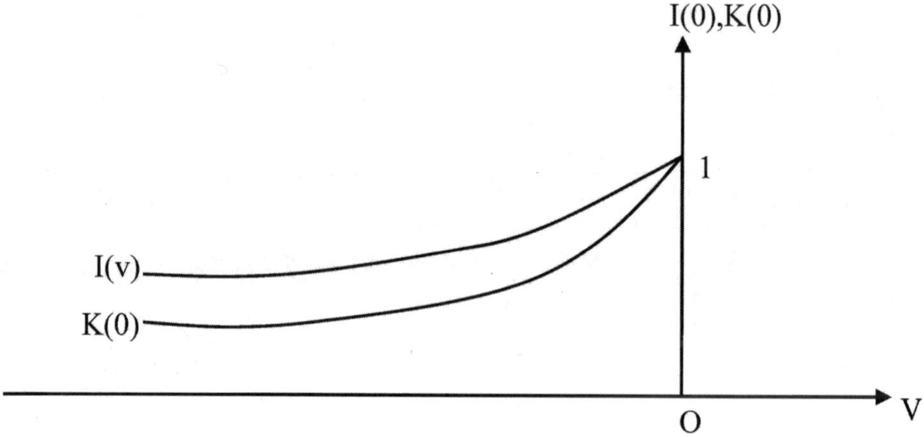

Figure 5.8 The curves of capital vintages

That capitals of different vintages get different technical weights is irrelevant in the determination of the exponential equilibrium growth rate. The long-run growth rate depends mainly on the total rate of technical change, given by $\lambda + \mu$, and not on the nature of technical progress. In the equilibrium of the exponential rate of growth, the distribution of capital depends on two variables: the rate of growth and the rate of depreciation. Because both rates are independent of the investment ratio, a change in these ratios can have no permanent influence on the proportion of national output saved, the age of distribution of capital, and the long-run growth. For example, supposing that the economy is growing at a rate, g, along the growth path corresponding to the chosen fixed investment ratio, we have the amount of capital of vintage v still in use at time $t = 0$, $Kv(0)$, given as

$$K_V(0) = I(0)e^{(g+\delta)_v} \tag{5.28}$$

where $I(0)$ is the investment at time zero. The relation between $I(v)$ and $I(0)$ is written as

$$I(v) = I(0)e^{gv} \tag{5.29}$$

The curve of $Kv(0)$ and $I(v)$ is shown in Figure 5.8.

To obtain the average age and the age distribution of capital, it is necessary to normalize the curve $K_v(0)$ so that its area is equal to 1. Dividing $K_v(0)$ by $I(0)/(g + \delta)$ for all v, we get the fundamental equation for the proportion of equipment of age v:

$$f(v) = (g + \delta)e^{(g+\delta)v} \quad (5.30)$$

From equation (5.30), we see that the age of capital (given as $1/(g + \delta)$) depends on the rate of depreciation (δ) and the rate of growth (g). Furthermore, both of these rates are, in the long run, independent from the investment ratio.[8] In fact, according to Phelps,

> A little reflection will indicate that the new view estimate λ will exceed the old view estimate of μ if the mean age of capital has been steadily increasing and will fall short of the old-view estimate if the mean age has been steadily falling. A fluctuating mean age complicates the picture. In any event, the estimates could not be presumed to be equal unless the economy had happened to be in long-run equilibrium. Therefore if the mean age of capital had been falling sharply, the estimate of λ might be smaller than the estimate of μ by a factor of α or more. In this event, the old-view model would paint a more dynamic and adaptable economy than would the new-view model. Further, a wide discrepancy between the λ and μ estimates could be only temporary. As the economy approached long-run equilibrium, they would have to come together. (Phelps 1962, 562–3)

An increase in the proportion of income saved can have no permanent effect on the age distribution of the capital stock or the long-run rate of growth. Phelps (1962) concluded that the size of increase in steady-state output following an increase in the propensity to save will be the same regardless of whether technical progress is embodied or disembodied. Hence, the long-run growth rate will depend on the rate of technical progress but not on the type of progress.

Matthews (1964) argued that Phelps's assumptions are valid in an economically significant sense only if the elasticity of substitution (implied by the Cobb-Douglass function) between labour and capital is equal to unity. In fact, Matthews adopted a general form of a Cobb-Douglas constant-elasticity-substitution production function,

$$Q_v = (a_v K_v^{-\beta} + b_v N_v^{-\beta})^{-\frac{1}{\beta}} \tag{5.31}$$

where Qv is the output from capital and labour, Kv is the number of machines of vintage v, Nv is the amount of labour used in machines, and β is the function of the elasticity factor substitution given by $\beta = (1 - \sigma)/\sigma$, where σ is the elasticity of substitution between labour and capital. Supposing that technical progress is exponential (wholly embodied), the production function for any vintage v is

$$Q_v = (a_v K_v^{-\beta} + e^{-\beta g v} b_v N_v^{-\beta})^{-\frac{1}{\beta}} \tag{5.32}$$

where g is the rate of technical progress. What we need to prove is that the weighted average age will vary with s if the relative number of workers on machines of different vintages varies with propensity to save, s. According to Matthews (1964, 166), we should compare the steady growth path of two economies that differ only in s. From this comparison, it will be seen that the economy with the bigger s will have a higher wage at any point in time. Differentiating equation (5.32) with respect to Nv and equating the result to wage w, we have

$$\frac{N_v}{K_v} = \alpha^{\frac{\sigma}{1-\sigma}} b^{\sigma} e^{-gv} \left[w^{\sigma-1} g^{-gv(\sigma-1)} - b^{\sigma} \right]^{\frac{\sigma}{1-\sigma}} \tag{5.33}$$

Equation (5.33) shows that the labour-capital ratio on machines of vintage v falls over time as w rises exponentially. The ratio of two labour-capital ratios, the latest vintage, t, and the earlier vintage still in use, v, is written as

$$\frac{N_t / K_t}{N_t / K_t} = \left[\frac{w^{\sigma-1} e^{-gt(\sigma-1)} - b^{\sigma}}{w^{\sigma-1} e^{-gv(\sigma-1)} - b^{\sigma}} \right]^{\frac{\sigma}{1-\sigma}} e^{-(t-v)g} \tag{5.34}$$

From equation (5.34), we have that, for $t > v$, the ratio of two vintages varies directly with w if $\sigma < 1$, where a higher s is associated with a lower average age of capital in steady growth, and it varies inversely with w if $\sigma > 1$, where a higher s is actually associated with a higher average age of capital (Matthews 1964, 166). For $\sigma = 1$, the ratio Nt/Kt to Nv/Kv is independent of the wage, w, and of the propensity to save, s. Hence, the average age of machines, as long as the economy is on the steady growth path and is independent of the propensity to save, *s*, and of the wage, *w*, is equal to unity.

Matthews's model is slightly different from Phelps's because it takes into account the responsiveness of steady-growth output to changes of the savings ratio, whether technical progress is embodied or disembodied. Furthermore, the result of his study depends on the elasticity of output from the existing installed capital with respect to current investment.

THE MEASUREMENT OF TECHNICAL CHANGE: THE JORGENSON-GRILICHES MODEL

Most of the procedures used to handle the various measurement problems are inevitably conventional, but in order to result in meaningful measures, they have to be basically reasonable. Kuznets noted that "All concepts in the field of national income are, in one way or another, non-operational ... They are goals that forever elude measurement and for which measurable approximations are substituted ... All these operational measures assume meaning only because they are approximations to the 'purer' non-operational concepts behind them" (Kuznets 1957b, 272).

Frequently, when technical change is introduced, the measurement of physical capital diverges and becomes more complex. The physical capital stock rises more rapidly than the volume of labour. Empirical studies based on a disembodied conception of technical progress suggest that the greater rate of observed economic growth cannot explain the increases in inputs and capital accumulation, but rather the explanation must lie in the "residual" or technical changes. Technical progress consists – as pointed out by Domar (1961) – of "a whole group of actors," the so-called residuals, such as economies of scale, external economies, improved health, education, innovation, a skilled labour force, better management, change in product mix, and so forth.

In addition, there are four methods expressing the residual or capital change: the first is defined as the difference between the value of outputs and inputs in constant prices in the work of Hiram Davis (1955, 51–65); the second is the ratio between arithmetical indexes of output and input in the work of Schmookler (1966), Abramovitz (1956), and Kendrick (1961); the third is the ratio between an aggregate arithmetical index of output and inputs embodied in a linear homogenous production function in the work of Solow; the last is the weighted arithmetical average of relative changes in input coefficients between two points of time, originated by Leontief (1953, 27–35) and studied more in details in input-output matrices (Domar 1961, 709–29).

Two brilliant American economists, Zvi Griliches and Dale Jorgenson, made some estimations regarding the residual factor in the US economy (Jorgenson and Griliches 1966 and 1967). The objective of their study was to prove that during the measurement of real product and real factor inputs, significant errors were regularly made, which may introduce serious biases in the measurement of total factor productivity. Therefore, they proposed the correction for bias because of errors of measurement in the allocation of changes in real product and real factor input between movements along a given production function. The starting point of the price-based measurement of embodied technical change is the observation by Jorgenson and Griliches (1966) that nominal investment is invariant to the units in which the goods are measured. To measure the total factor productivity, it is useful to indicate Y_i as the quantity of the *i*th input, $X_j$as the quantity of the *j*th input, q_i as the price of the *i*th output, and p_j as the price of the *j*th input. The fundamental equation of each accounting period is that the value of output is equal to the value of input (in the case of *m* outputs and *n* inputs):

$$q_1Y_1 + q_2Y_2 + \ldots q_mY_m = p_1X_1 + p_2X_2 + \ldots p_nX_n \tag{5.35}$$

Denoting w_i as the weights of relative shares of the value of the *i*th output in the value of the total output and v_i as the weights of the relative shares of the value of the *j*th input in the value of total input, we have

$$w_i = q_iY_i/\Sigma\, q_iY_i, \text{and } v_j = p_jX_j/\Sigma\, p_jX_j \tag{5.36}$$

Another index of total quantity of output may be defined in terms of the weighted average of the rate of growth of the individual outputs. In fact, denoting the index of output by *Y* and the index of total input by *X*, the rate of growth of both indexes implies

$$\Delta Y/Y = \Sigma\, w_i(\Delta Y_i/Y_i) \text{ and } \Delta X/X = \Sigma\, v_j(\Delta X_j/X_j) \tag{5.37}$$

In the same way, the price indexes for total output and total input, say *p* and *q*, have the rates of growth given as

$$\Delta q/q = \sum w_i(\Delta q_i/q_i), \text{ and } \Delta p/p = \sum v_j(\Delta p_j/p_j) \tag{5.38}$$

By using the quantity indexes in (5.37), the rate of growth of total factor productivity is now expressed as

$$\Delta P/P = \Delta Y/Y - \Delta X/X = \sum w_i(\Delta Y_i/Y_i) - \sum v_j(\Delta X_j/X_j) \tag{5.39}$$

The rate of growth of factor productivity in equation (5.39) is defined as the difference between the rate of growth of the total output index and the rate of growth of the total input index. Jorgenson and Griliches (1967, 253) expressed the rate of growth of total productivity as

$$G\Delta F = \Delta P/P^{\cdot} \tag{5.40}$$

where $G\Delta F$ is the weighted average rates of growth of both outputs and inputs. The rate of growth of total factor productivity is zero if and only if the shift in the production function is zero. This theory of production implies the existence of a factor price frontier relating the price of output to that of input.

A simple system of capital accounts that provides the basis for measuring capital input can be presented by denoting I_k as the quantity of output of the kth investment good, K_k as the quantity of input of the kth capital service, q_k as the price of the kth investment good, and p_k as the quantity of the kth capital service. Thus, the cumulated stock of capital is given by the relationship (Jorgenson and Griliches 1966, 51)

$$I_k - K_k + \delta_k K_k \tag{5.41}$$

where δ_k is the instantaneous rate of replacement of the kth investment good. The price of the kth capital service[9] will be given as

$$p_k = q_k(r + \delta_k - \frac{\Delta q_k}{q_k}) \tag{5.42}$$

where r is the rate of return on all capital, δ_k, as before, is the rate of replacement of the kth investment good, and $\Delta q_k/q_k$ is the rate of capital gain on investment good. The rate of return on capital is estimated by subtracting from the value of output (plus capital gains) the value of labour input and replacement, whereas the value of the kth capital good is given as

$$p_k K_k = q_k \left(r + \delta_k - \frac{\Delta q_k}{q_k} \right) K_k \tag{5.43}$$

The most common error in the measurement of capital input – as pointed out by Kendrick (1961) – is to confuse the aggregation of capital stock with the aggregation of capital service. If, for instance, the rate of growth of the price of a particular type of labour service is measured with an error and all relative shares remain the same, the resulting error in the price of total labour input has a rate of growth equal to the rate of growth of error multiplied by the relative share of the labour services. Denoting by C the quantity of consumption goods and by L the quantity of labour input, the rate of growth of total factor productivity is presented as

$$\frac{\Delta P}{P} = w_I \frac{\Delta I}{I} + w_C \frac{\Delta C}{C} - v_K \frac{\Delta K}{K} - v_L \frac{\Delta L}{L} \tag{5.44}$$

where w_I is the relative share of the value of investment goods in terms of total output, w_C is the relative share of consumption goods, v_k is the relative share of capital input in terms of total input, and, lastly, v_L is the relative share of labour. Denoting, P^*, the measured index of total factor productivity by using the erroneous "price" of investment goods and I^* the quantity of investment goods output using the erroneous "price" of investment goods, we have

$$\frac{\Delta P^*}{P^*} = w_I \frac{\Delta I^*}{I^*} + w_C \frac{\Delta C^*}{C^*} - v_K \frac{\Delta K^*}{K^*} - v_L \frac{\Delta L^*}{L^*} \tag{5.45}$$

Subtracting equation (5.45) from equation (5.44), we obtain the bias in the rate of growth of total factor productivity (Jorgenson and Griliches 1966, 54),

$$\frac{\Delta P^*}{P^*} - \frac{\Delta P}{P} = w_I \left(\frac{\Delta I^*}{I^*} - \frac{\Delta I}{I} \right) - v_K \left(\frac{\Delta K^*}{K^*} - \frac{\Delta K}{K} \right) \tag{5.46}$$

If Q^* is the relative error in the measurement of the price of investment goods, we have that the bias in the rate of growth of investment goods output is given as,

$$\frac{\Delta I^*}{I^*} - \frac{\Delta I}{I} = -\frac{\Delta Q^*}{Q^*} \tag{5.47}$$

Denoting K^*, the quantity of capital calculated using the erroneous price of investment goods we get the exponential form,

$$K^* = \int_{-\infty}^{t} e^{-\delta(t-s)} \frac{I(s)}{Q^*(s)} ds \tag{5.48}$$

The bias in the rate of growth of the quantity of capital is given as the difference between the quantity of capital using the erroneous price K^* and the actual quantity of capital K, expressed in the exponential form,

$$\frac{\Delta K^*}{K^*} - \frac{\Delta K}{K} = \frac{I}{Q^* K^*} - \frac{I}{K} = \frac{I}{\int_{-\infty}^{t} e^{-\delta(t-s)} \frac{Q^*(t)}{Q^*(s)} I(s)ds} - \frac{I}{e^{-\delta(t-s)} I(s)ds} \tag{5.49}$$

Substituting equation (5.49) to (5.46), using the relative error Q^* and substituting (5.47) to (5.46), we get the constant rates of growth of the relative error in the investment goods price index expressed in the short form,[10]

$$\frac{\Delta P^*}{P^*} - \frac{\Delta P}{P} = (v_K - w_I)\frac{\Delta Q^*}{Q^*} \tag{5.50}$$

Technically speaking, if the investment and error in measurement are growing at a constant rate, the biases in the rate of growth of the quantity of investment goods produced and quantity of investment services offered are equal. The net effect is equal to the rate of growth of error measurement of the price of investment goods multiplied by the difference between capital share in total input and investment share in total output. Jorgenson and Griliches (1966), in their empirical studies, suggested that if inputs were accurately measured, almost all observed economic growth in the United States between 1945 and 1965 could had been accounted for by input growth rather than technical progress, and the effects of increases in total factor productivity based on technical progress and innovation were not so significant as was thought.

To calculate the constant quality measurement of investment goods, Jorgenson and Griliches (1966) generalized Solow's (1962a) concept of embodied technical change. The "embodied hypothesis" of these authors states that economic growth could be interpreted, equivalently, as "embodied" in investment or "disembodied" in productivity growth. Later Jorgenson and Griliches (1967) removed the indeterminacy by introducing constant quality indexes for investment goods.

RATE OF RETURN AND TECHNICAL PROGRESS: THE LEVHARI-SHESHINSKI MODEL

Levhari[11] and Sheshinski[12] (1969) have studied the general nature of the relation between the rate of return and the rate of technical progress. They have, however, demonstrated that, in the presence of embodied technical progress, the rate of return cannot be considered as a monotonic function of the rate of technical progress. Therefore, embodied technical progress has no relevance for the level of steady-state output, even in the case of a vintage model.

The result found by Levhari and Sheshinski (1969) is related to the fact that, with no capital-labour substitution, the effective lifetime of capital equipment is always lengthened as the rate of embodied technical progress accelerates.

Hence, the conclusion of their study is that the rate of return on savings is constantly an increasing function of the rate of disembodied technical progress. The main assumption of this model consists on the output-capital ratio g and the labour intensity measured in efficiency units h to be equal to a constant given as,

$$g(h) = g'(0)h = h = a \tag{5.51}$$

For each age, x, the labour intensity, h, is determined by the marginal productivity condition of output-capital ratio,

$$g'(h) = we^{\alpha x} \tag{5.52}$$

or, in terms of labour intensity h,

$$h = h\left[we^{\alpha x}\right] \tag{5.53}$$

where $h = g^{r-1}$. The workers are allocated to the oldest equipment in use, and the marginal productivity will be

$$g'(0) = we^{\alpha m} \tag{5.54}$$

where m stands for the economic lifetime of capital equipment. Given that $g'(0) = 1$, we have

$$w = e^{-\alpha m} \tag{5.55}$$

The quasi-rent of a unit of capital of age x is a decreasing function of x, reaching zero at $x = m$.

$$\rho(x) = g(h) - we^{\alpha x}h = g(h) - g'(h)h \tag{5.56}$$

The relationship between the rate of return to investment and the lifetime of capital gives us more clarification about the rate of embodied technical progress. The rate of return on investment is defined by equating the price of new equipment (equal to 1) to the discounted stream of quasi-rents over the lifetime of equipment.

$$1 = \int_0^m \rho(x)e^{-rx}dx \tag{5.57}$$

This is the integral function for the unknown rate of return in the function of lifetime, m. The expression to determine m with fixed savings rate will be (Levhari and Sheshinski 1969, 366)

$$1 = s\int_0^m g(h\left[e^{\alpha(x-m)}\right])^{-(\alpha+\beta+n)x}dx \tag{5.58}$$

where α stands for the rate of embodied technical progress, β for the rate of disembodied technical progress, and n for the rate of growth of labour. From equation (5.58), we have a relationship between the rate of return, the rate of savings, and the parameters of the system (s, α, β, and n). Using functions ψ and Φ, we have

$$\psi(m,\alpha,\beta,n,s) = s\alpha\int_0^m e^{-(\alpha+\beta+n)x}dx \tag{5.59}$$

$$\varphi(m,\alpha,r) = a\int_0^m \left[1-e^{\alpha(x-m)}\right]e^{-rx}dx \tag{5.60}$$

The derivative of ψ with respect to α and m is given by the following two expressions:

$$\psi_\alpha = -sa\int_0^m xe^{-(\alpha+\beta+n)x}dx < 0 \text{ and } \psi_m = sae^{-(\alpha+\beta+n)m} > 0 \tag{5.61}$$

Hence, combining both functions of ψ in (5.61), it implies

$$\frac{dm}{d\alpha} = -\frac{\psi_\alpha}{\psi_m} > 0 \tag{5.62}$$

We can see that a higher parameter, α, of technical progress means an increase in the effective labour force; thus, faster embodied technical progress extends the economic lifetime of capital. In the same way, the derivative of r with respect to α is given by

$$\frac{dr}{d\alpha} = -\frac{\varphi_m}{\varphi_r}.\frac{d_m}{d_\alpha} - \frac{\varphi_\alpha}{\varphi r} = \frac{\varphi_m}{\varphi_r}.\frac{\psi_\alpha}{\psi_m} - \frac{\varphi_\alpha}{\varphi_r} \tag{5.63}$$

For $\Phi m > 0$, $\Phi r < 0$,and $\Phi > 0$, we have that $\frac{dr}{d\alpha} > 0$, so a higher rate of technical progress, α, means a higher rate of return. A faster rate of embodied technical progress shortens the economic lifetime of capital. By considering a simple Cobb-Douglas function of the form $g(h) = h^{1-y}$, where $0 < \gamma < 1$, we have a critical rate of embodied technical progress, α, which makes $r = 0$.

$$\alpha = \frac{\gamma(1-\gamma)(\beta+n)}{s\gamma-(1-\gamma)} \tag{5.64}$$

In this case, the negative relationship between rate of return, r, and technical progress, α, at the critical value of saving, s, implies (increasing rate of savings) that the economy is operating inefficiently; therefore, the rate of return is not necessarily a monotonic function of the rate of technical progress. If less is saved, it is probably easier to increase both consumption per capita and the rate of return. Levhari and Sheshinski's conclusions are that the transmission mechanism of the new investments in vintage models is not more important than the rate of return.

The embodied technological progress does not guarantee a steady-state level of output.

INDUCED BIAS IN INNOVATION

Endogenous technical progress is generally assumed when the bias of invention and innovation is determined by forces within the economic system. The discussion of the factors determining most inventions in the first part of the twentieth century emphasized the economic pressure to innovate on a large scale in all industrial fields (as happened during the industrial revolution in Great Britain in the eighteenth century) and to develop particular inventions in response to particular economic changes. J.R. Hicks, in the *Theory of Wages*, argued that the fall in the price of capital relative to labour would induce inventions of a labour-saving type (Hicks 1932). In fact, "A change in the relative prices of factors of production is itself a spur to invention, and to invention of a particular kind – directed to economizing the use of a factor which has become relatively expensive"(1932, 112–13). Therefore, he suggested that it was necessary to distinguish between "induced" and "autonomous" invention. Salter (1960) argued Hicks's view regarding changes in prices of production factors and induced invention. He stated that

> The entrepreneur is interested in reducing costs in total, not particular costs such as labour costs or capital costs. When labour costs rise any advance that reduces total cost is welcome, and whether this is achieved by saving labour or capital is irrelevant. There is no reason to assume that attention should be concentrated on labour-saving techniques, unless, because of some inherent characteristic of technology, labour-saving knowledge is easier to acquire than capital-saving knowledge ... the above argument makes it difficult to accept any priori reason for labour-saving biases sufficiently strong to explain the much greater increases in aggregate labour productivity compared to aggregate capital productivity. It therefore appears reasonable to place primary emphasis on the substitution induced by cheaper capital goods. (Salter 1960, 43–4)

To Salter, the cheaper substitution as a result of cheaper capital goods might be adequate for any kind of greater rise in aggregate labour productivity compared to aggregate capital productivity, but it cannot explain the constancy in distributive shares in advanced economies. The theory that better explains the constancy in distributive shares is the theory of induced bias in innovation. Salter (1960) firmly sustains that one of the reasons Hicks's theory of induced invention has not been developed is that changes in relative factor prices are not essential for the theory of induced bias in innovation. This theory was developed by Weizsäcker (1962)[13] and Kennedy (1964). What the theories of Weizsäcker and Kennedy have in common is the transformation tradeoff relating technical improvements and input requirements of the respective factors of production. A similar idea, but not so explicitly stated, can be found in the writings of some authors such as Fellner (1961). This author assumed that steady accumulation of capital relative to labour is expected to continue in the future as in the past. It is reasonable for companies to extrapolate a rising trend of wage rates, a historical trend of the profit rate, and the associated downward trend in rental rates for equipment of the same technical type. The dynamic expectational effect of relatively high wages should promote inventions designed to lower labour-input requirements.

In light of the Kennedy-Weizsäcker model, there is a neoclassical production function of two factors, $V1$ and $V2$, subject to technical changes, $F(V1, V2; t)$,[14] and a special "factor augmenting" form, $F(V1/p(t), V2/q(t))$, where a decrease in the proportion p means a saving of the Vi factor needed to produce any given output (the same thing, we may say, for the factor proportion, q). A technical improvement will reduce the amount of labour required to produce a unit of product in a certain proportion (p) and the amount of capital required in a proportion (q). An improvement will be labour saving, neutral, or capital saving according to whether p is greater than, equal to, or less than q. It is fair to suppose that entrepreneurs will choose the type of improvement to reduce the total unit cost, r, in the greatest proportion, given by the following identity (Kennedy 1964, 543):

$$r = \lambda p + \gamma q \tag{5.65}$$

This recommends that the choice of innovation by an entrepreneur is influenced by the economic weights λ and γ. If labour costs are high relative to capital costs ($\lambda > \gamma$), it is convenient to introduce a labour-saving innovation. In the same way, if capital costs are high relative to labour

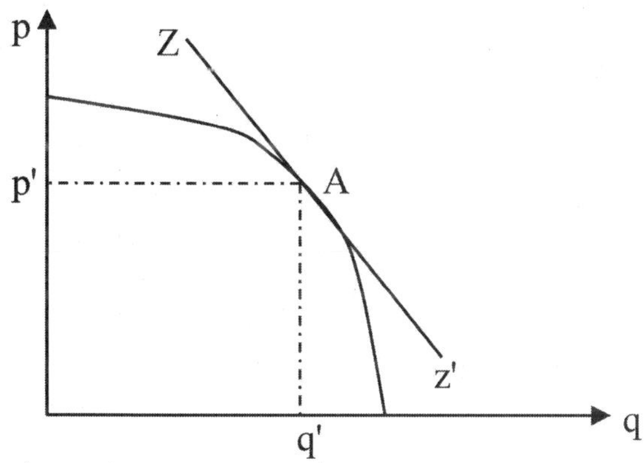

Figure 5.9 The invention possibility function

costs, it is more profitable to introduce a capital-saving innovation. Kennedy (1964) assumed that entrepreneurs are concerned with maximizing the instantaneous rate of unit cost reduction at given factor prices, which is equivalent to maximizing the current rate of technical progress. And so, by maximizing r, subject to constraint $p = f(q)$, we obtain the following identity:

$$dp/dq < -\gamma/\lambda \qquad (5.66)$$

The rates of improvement are related by a "transformation" function with the usual convexity properties of a production function possibility frontier. Primarily, to set up the invention possibility frontier, the first derivative must be smaller than zero:

$$dp/dq < 0 \qquad (5.67)$$

This identity means that the greater the reduction in the labour required to produce a unit of output, the smaller the possible reduction in capital. An increase in capital requirements will be necessary to make possible a further reduction in labour requirements. Second, the second derivative must also be smaller than zero:

$$d^2p/dq^2 < 0 \qquad (5.68)$$

From (5.67), it derives that, for p to approach its upper limit of 1, a large increase in the amount of capital is required, and in the same way, for q to approach 1, a large increase in labour is needed. The general shape of the innovation possibility function is shown in figure 5.9.

The invention possibility frontier slopes downward, reflecting the tradeoff between capital and labour augmentation. It is also concave to the origin, which means that increasing amounts of p have to be sacrificed to obtain an increase in q. The invention possibility frontier represents the constraint placed on entrepreneurs in deciding which inventions to take into consideration. Entrepreneurs generally want to maximize the instantaneous rate of unit cost reduction at given factor prices, which is equivalent to maximizing the current rate of technical progress. The rate of cost unit reduction will depend on the rates of labour and capital augmentation (p and q) and on the proportion of total costs attributable to the employment of capital and labour. Therefore, the rate of unit cost reduction is given as

$$M = \alpha 1p + \alpha 2q \tag{5.69}$$

where $\alpha 1$ and $\alpha 2$ represent the relative shares in total cost of capital and labour, respectively. The concave technical frontier, $p = f(q)$, is tangential to the equi-unit-cost contours of $M = \alpha 1p + \alpha 2q$ given by ZZ' at A (as shown in Figure 5.9), whose tangency gives $-f'(q) = \alpha 1/\alpha 2$. If we consider each set of factor prices ($W1$, $W2$) at any stage, there will be a minimum unit cost of production, written as

$$M[W1\lambda(t),\ W2\gamma(t)] \tag{5.70}$$

where

$$M(W1,\ W2) = min\ {}^{2}\Sigma 1\ W_j,\ V_J, \text{ which is subject to } F(V1, V2) \tag{5.71}$$

The relative derivatives of $M_i(W1, W2)$ are proportional to $V1$ and $V2$. Function (5.71) is completely "dual" to $F(V1, V2)$, having the same homogeneous concavity. $M(W1,\ W2) = 1$ defines the important factor price frontier, giving the tradeoff between a real factor price in terms of another.[15] From identities (5.66), (5.67), and (5.68), we have the result that the greater the share of labour cost, the greater the labour-saving will be if a type of innovation is chosen by entrepreneurs.

Kennedy's possibility function is sometimes seen as a camouflaged Kaldorian (1957) technical progress function. In view of estimating the relationship between the rate of technical progress and the rate of capital accumulation, Kaldor (1957, 1961) suggested that the whole production function must be abandoned; instead, the relationship between the rate of growth of per capita output and the rate of growth of capital per worker must be considered. Kaldor related the proportional change in output per man-year to the proportional change in capital per man. In effect, from these variables, it is possible to derive the proportional changes in output per unit of capital, and, given the technical progress function, it is also likely that it is possible to derive Kennedy's innovation function and the invention possibility frontier. Samuelson (1965b), based on the Kennedy-Weizsäcker idea of the tradeoff between labour augmentation and capital augmentation, proved with a theorem that a long-run equilibrium of constant relative shares will exist if the elasticity of substitution is less than unity; it will be unstable if the elasticity of substitution is greater than 1. Any initial tendency for the share of labour to float upward will make it profitable to introduce relatively labour-augmenting innovations. But if factor supplies remain in balance, Kennedy-Weizsäcker (K-W)–induced innovation deduces the equilibrium of Harrod-neutral technical change. This means that it leaves unchanged the balance between labour and capital, or it takes place when the ratio of marginal product of labour to the marginal product of capital (*K*/*L*) is unchanged. The induced-invention assumption provides an escape from the Harrod neutrality technical change. One of the most important and ingenious formulations of the K-W model was the invention possibility frontier, reflecting the tradeoff between capital and labour augmentation and representing the limitation placed on entrepreneurs in deciding which inventions to take into account. Kennedy's idea of induced invention is focused on the entrepreneur's choice in technical progress rather than on technological change in general. The K-W-induced innovation proved that the steady growth of the capital-labour ratio will lead to a long-run equilibrium in which there is induced labour-augmenting invention to adjust the degree needed to keep the ratio of capital to labour constant. The induced-invention model provides a much more satisfactory picture of an important aspect of the process of technical progress in the long run than any of the models that merely incorporate an exogenous representation, as does, for instance, Solow's model (1957). Going back in time, we might recall

Schumpeter, who was one of the first economists to perceive innovation formed by economic forces inside the large firm (Schumpeter 1942). In fact, he believed that innovation was not a rational activity but rather a creative activity and he supposed that the agent of innovation and invention in the company was the entrepreneur or the modern businessman who makes his decisions based on rationality, intuition, and experience. The entrepreneur is the protagonist of innovation, technical progress, development, and growth. But in the K-W model and, for most part, in neoclassical models, the entrepreneur is a very rational person who makes the decisions on the choice of technology and the model of organization. Simply put, he is an executive-manager rather than a hero industrialist.

CHOICE OF TECHNIQUES AND ECONOMIC DEVELOPMENT IN SEN

The choice of techniques – according to Sen[16] (1960) – is by no means solely a question of technical efficiency; "it is ultimately a human problem, not an engineering one." (Hicks 1962, 380).[17] An appropriate criterion for choice among techniques of production is the maximum "reinvestable surplus" yielded by investments rather than the rate of capital turnover, the marginal social product, or the import-export desiderata. This argument, in the age of neoclassical economists after the war, was developed by Sen, Galenson, and Leibenstein (1955), Polak (1943), Buchanan (1945), A. E. Kahn (1951), and Chenery (1953). Planning economic development is seen as the choice among alternative growth paths attained with given initial resources and anticipated future growth rates. This choice, as in the case of microeconomics, depends crucially on the preferences of the society, usually summarized by a more or less precisely defined social welfare function. The time path that maximizes a given social welfare function, subject to the constraints of resource availability, will have a bearing on the choice among the alternative techniques of production available to each industry.

The investment which takes place in planned economic development is often believed to occur at three main levels: (1) determination of the total volume of investment out of the national product; (2) the distribution of investment among industries; and (3) the choice of specific techniques of production within each industry. Some neoclassical economists, such as Sen, Chenery, and A.E. Kahn, were concerned more about the choice of specific techniques of production within the industry. The basic model of Sen (1960) divides the economy in two sectors: a backward private enterprise sector, which is most of the time outside of government control and administration rules and consists primarily of agriculture; and a new public sector under central administration, having both a consumer-goods subsector and a capital-goods subsector that produces equipment for use in making consumer goods. The type of the economy analyzed is characterized by underdevelopment, overpopulation, and hidden unemployment, which results in an infinitely elastic supply of labour to the modern public sector at a low wage rate. The capital-goods subsector uses few investments, often coming from central government (with the help of private sector) or foreign investors, to produce capital goods. There is constant return to scale and no technological change; the wage bill is entirely consumed, and the surpluses generated in the public consumer-goods subsector are entirely reinvested.

The choice of techniques associated with the maximization of a particular social welfare function in Sen's model is more important than the choice of the function itself. In fact, according to this model, a two-sector, two-commodity, closed economy consisting of an advanced sector (A), like an industrial sector, and a backward sector (B) like an agricultural sector, a consumer good (for example, corn), and a capital good (machines) is considered. Sector A consists of two divisions, the first of which produces machines using only labour but not machines, and the second of which produces corn using machines and labour. The role of Sector B is to yield an initial surplus of corn to launch Sector A and then to supply unlimited amounts of labour to sector B. The corn productivity of labour in Sector A depends on the labour intensity of the technique used in division 2 (which uses both machines and labour). The wage rate in Sector A is assumed as given, and the wage bill in any given period satisfies the production of corn in that period in Sector A. The objective of the planners is to maximize the undiscounted sum of corn production in Sector A over a number of periods (denominated as U periods). The rate of growth of output, for the planners, turns out to be a special case with $U = 1$ and $U \rightarrow \infty$, respectively. With an unlimited supply of labour at a given wage rate, and assuming that the surplus over the wage bill is entirely reinvested, it follows that the rate of growth of the output of corn at Sector A is simply equal to the rate of interest on the initial surplus of corn invested – that is, the rate of surplus over wages per unit of investment. The labour intensity of the technique that maximizes this rate of return will be higher, the lower the given wage rate. In most of the models in planning economic development, however, the assumption that Sector B (the backward sector) provides unlimited supplies of labour without causing a drop in its output is maintained. This is generally a restrictive case, especially when the horizon of planning, over *U* periods, is large and the optimal labour intensity will reduce the marginal product of labour to zero. In general, the concern with the total output over *U* periods disregards the time path of output within the *U* periods. In many cases, the models of development, such as that of Sen (1960) and others, are of interest not because they give satisfactory solutions to the problems of choice of techniques but most likely in their exposition of difficulties and troubles encountered in the formulation of the social welfare function on which such choices are based.

THE ECONOMIC IMPROVEMENTS OF "LEARNING-BY-DOING"

A different method of technical progress that was conceived of as endogenous to the economic system was introduced for the first time by Arrow[18] (1962) in the famous model of "learning-by-doing." He assumed that knowledge of creation was a byproduct of investment. A firm that increases its physical capital learns simultaneously how to produce more efficiently. So this positive effect of experience on productivity is called learning-by-doing. According to Arrow (1962), the acquisition of knowledge is a product of experience. He stated, "Learning is the product of experience. Learning can only take place through the attempt to solve a problem and therefore only takes place during activity" (Arrow 1962, 155).

Another generalization coming typically from the classic learning experiments is that learning related to recurrence of essentially the same problem is subject to sharply diminishing returns. Arrow writes,

> The role of experience in increasing productivity has not gone unobserved, though the relation has yet to be absorbed into the main corpus of economic theory. It was early observed by aeronautical engineers, particularly T.P. Wright, that the number of labour-hours expended in the production of an airframe (airplane body without engines) is a decreasing function of the total number of airframes of the same type previously produced. Lundberg (1961) has given the name "Horndal effect" to a very similar phenomenon. The Horndal

iron works in Sweden had no new investment (and therefore presumably no significant change in its method of production) for a period of 15 years, yet productivity (output per manhour) rose on the average close to 2% per annum. We find again steadily increasing performance which can only be imputed to learning from experience. (Arrow 1962, 156)

Arrow refers to the study of Lundberg that supports this idea by analyzing the Horndal iron works in Sweden, where the average increase of about 2 per cent per year was explained only by the increase in the cumulative outputs – thus, learning by doing. He also describes the empirical regularity with which, after a new design, the time required to build the frame of a marginal aircraft is inversely proportional to the cube root of the number of aircraft of that model that have already been produced; this improvement in productivity occurs without any evident innovations in the production process. The accumulation of knowledge occurs, in part, not as a result of hard work and efforts in the production process but as a side-effect of conventional economic activity. Arrow's view is that technical change can be attributed to experience – that is, the very activity of production. In effect, if during the production process problems occur, these are diligently considered and given favourable responses based mostly on experience.

The objective of the learning-by-doing model in Arrow is to prove that the acquisition of knowledge through learning-by-doing is a product of experience, which helps the industries increase their efficiency and, as a result, the economy as whole to grow. Arrow constructed a complete theory of growth based on the assumptions of fixed coefficient production embodying labour-augmenting technical progress, full employment, constant exponential growth of the labour force, and a constant saving ratio.[19] The neoclassical production function with labour-augmenting technology for a firm *i* is of the type

$$Y_i = F\,(K_i,\, A_iL_i) \qquad (5.72)$$

where K_i and L_i are input factors and A_i is the index of knowledge available to the firm. The technical augmentation factor, A_i, might appear specific to the firm, but it is, in fact, related to the total "knowledge" of the economy. For Arrow, this knowledge is common to all firms: a free and public good. It arises from the past cumulative investment of all firms and is related to the stock of total capital. In brief, Arrow made two assumptions that better explain his theory.

First, learning by doing works through each firm's investment, so an increase in a firm's capital stock leads to a particular increase in its stock of knowledge. Knowledge and productivity come from investment and production. Output depends on both capital and stock of knowledge. The stock of knowledge is a function of time and a consequence of investment and the educational effect of each act of investment, and it decreases exponentially in time. The total output and the total labour force are written as (Arrow 1962, 157–8).

$$Y = \int_{G'}^{G} \gamma G dG \tag{5.73}$$

$$\text{and } L = \int_{G'}^{G} \lambda G' dG \tag{5.74}$$

where Y is the total output, G stands for the cumulative gross investments through time, L is the labour force, $\lambda(G)$ is the amount of labour used in production with a cumulative capital stock G, and $\gamma(G)$ stands for the output capacity of a cumulative capital stock G. The magnitudes Y, L, G, and G' are all functions of time. It is assumed that $\lambda(G)$ and $\gamma(G)$ are, respectively, a non-increasing and a non-decreasing function. From equations (5.73) and (5.74), we see that total output and labour force depend on cumulative gross investment over time and the knowledge level at each step of investment from G' to G.

The second assumption is that each firm's knowledge is a public good that any other firm can access without cost. Arrow stated that "the presence of learning means that an act of investment benefits future investors, but this benefit is not paid for by the market" (Arrow 1962, 168). This assumption implies that the change in each firm's technology term, Ai, in equation (5.73) corresponds to the economy's overall learning and is, therefore, proportional to the change in the aggregate capital stock, K. The direct benefits of investments are appropriated by investors, and the indirect benefits of increasing experience and knowledge are appropriated by the whole society.

The experience of a particular firm is related to the accumulated stock of total capital, G, by the function

$$Ai = Gz \tag{5.75}$$

As the physical capital stock G accumulates, knowledge used by a particular firm also accumulates by a proportion, z. Experience and knowledge raise labour productivity over time through learning by doing. It is assumed that productivity is determined by an endogenous element, q(K/K), and by an exogenous element, g, so we get

$$A^{\cdot}/A = q(K/K) + g, 0 < q < 1 \tag{5.76}$$

where $A^{\cdot}/A$ is the increase of productivity over time as a result of knowledge and experience (through learning by doing), q is the learning coefficient, and g stands for the exogenous rate of labour-augmenting technical change. Taking a Cobb-Douglas production function, we have the Arrow equation of the intensive form

$$y = k\alpha \tag{5.77}$$

And the growth rate of the capital stock takes the form

$$k_g = \frac{sk\alpha}{k} - \delta \tag{5.78}$$

where s is the saving rate, a is a parameter of intensive form, and δ is a differential variable. The growth rate of the effective labour is given as

$$L_g = \theta\left(\frac{K}{K}\right) + \lambda + n \tag{5.79}$$

where n is the labour force growth rate. Growth of the capital-labour ratio is written as

$$kg = s(1 - q)ka - [g + n + d(1 - q)]k \tag{5.80}$$

and is a non-linear, first order differential equation in k. The capital effective labour ratio reaches the exponential form

$$k' = \left[\frac{s(1-\theta)}{y + n + \delta(1-\theta)}\right]^{\frac{1}{1-\alpha}} \tag{5.81}$$

For $\partial k/\partial q < 0$, the rate of the effective labour q increases, output ALk given by (5.72) increases, and the capital-labour ratio k decreases. There is a steady growth rate in Arrow ($\dot{k} = 0$) when capital stock is given as $gK = (g + n)/(1 - q)$, output as $ALka$: $gY = (g + n)/(1 - q)$, and income per worker as Y/L: $(g + nq)/(1 - q)$. One of the Arrow implications is that the learning coefficient, q, raises the level of effective labour, thus reducing steady-state capital to the effective labour ratio and increasing steady-state growth rate of output per worker. There is, as well, a positive relationship between population growth rate, n, and the growth rate of output pro capita.

The non-compensation of learning effect in the market leads Arrow to conclude that the private marginal productivity of capital of new investment is less than the social marginal productivity. In other words, competitive markets will generate less investment than would be socially optimal. If learning by doing is the source of technological progress, the rate of accumulation would depend not on the fraction of the economy's resources engaged in research and development but instead on how much new knowledge is generated by conventional economic activity.

Levhari (1966) extended Arrow's model from fixed factor proportions to a homogenous production function of the first degree and technological change. Levhari, using a labour augmenting technological change as in Arrow and assuming that labour is allocated in order to maximize production, describes the output Y_t as the sum of production with capital of all vintages given by expression (5.82) as

$$Y_t = \int_{t-k(t)}^{t} F(I_v, G_v^n, L_{v,t})dv \tag{5.82}$$

where $I_v = G_v$ is the investment in new machines at time v, and $k(t)$ is the age of the oldest capital in use at time t. The total labour force L_t is equal to labour used in machines of all vintages born at v and satisfies

$$L_t = \int_{t-k(t)}^{t} L_{v,t}dv \tag{5.83}$$

The marginal productivity of labour utilized with all vintages in order to take full advantage of production should be the same. It is given as,

$$\frac{dF(I_v, G_v^n L_{v,t})}{dL_{v,t}} = w_t \tag{5.84}$$

where w_t is the marginal product of labour. Levhari (1966, 118) uses the properties of a monotonic decreasing function $dF(x,y)/dy$ as a function of $m(y/x)$, which has an inverse M, to show the decreasing function of marginal product of labour.

$$G_v^n \frac{dF(I_v, G_v^n L_{v,t})}{d(G_{v,t}^n)} = G_v^n m\left(\frac{G_v^n L_{v,t}}{I_v}\right) = w_t \tag{5.85}$$

And the condition for maximum output is given as

$$\frac{G_v^n L_{v,t}}{I_v} = M(G_v^{-n} w_t) \Rightarrow L_{v,t} = G_v^{-n} M(G_v^{-n} w_t) I_v \tag{5.86}$$

where M is a typical monotonic decreasing function in its form, but an increasing function of G_v. The marginal product of labour at $L(v,t) = 0$ is equal to investment in new machines G_v at time v and for $t - k(t)$ we get

$$\frac{dF(I_v, G_{v,t}^n)}{dL_{v,t}} = G_v^n m(0) \Rightarrow G_{t-m(t)}^n m(0) = w_t \tag{5.87}$$

Consequently, labour allocated at time t, to machines made at v satisfies

$$L_{v,t} = G_v^{-n} M[G_v^{-n} G_{t-k(t)} m(0)] I_v \tag{5.88}$$

Substituting (5.87) to (5.82) and (5.83) we get the new equation for total output and labour force at time t (Levhari 1966, 119).

$$Y_t = \int_{t-k(t)}^{t} F(1, M[m(0) G_v^{-n} G_{t-k(t)}^n] I_v dv) \tag{5.89}$$

$$L_t \int_{t-k(t)}^{t} G_v^{-n} M[m(0) G_v^{-n} G_{t-k(t)}^n] I_v dv \tag{5.90}$$

The right side of equation (5.90) is an monotonic increasing function of $k(t)$, which represents the age of the oldest machine used at t. As $k(t)$ increases, $w_t = G_{t-k(t)}^n m(0)$ decreases and this helps increases the labour allocated to each of the vintages.

By differentiating (5.82) with respect to time, we have a better chance to see the properties of output $Y(G, L)$. In fact, we have

$$Y_t = F(I_t, G_t^n L_{t,t}) + \int_{t-k(t)}^{t} \frac{dF(I_v, G_v^n L_{v,t})}{dL_{v,t}} \frac{dL_{v,t}}{dt} dv - F(I_t, G_{t-k(t)}^n L_{t-k(t)})[1 - k'(t)]... \tag{5.91}$$

The third term of the right side of equation (5.91) vanishes and taking into consideration condition for maximum product for all v given in equation (5.87), we can write a new expression

$$\dot{Y}_t = F(I_t, G_t^n L_{t,t} + w_t \int_{t-k(t)}^{t} \frac{dL_{v,t}}{dt} dv \tag{5.92}$$

The second term of equation (5.92) is negative, if $w\dot{}t>o$ and differentiating (5.87) with respect to t, we get

$$\frac{dL_{v.t}}{dt} = G_v^{-n} \frac{dM(w_t G_v^{-n})}{dw_t} I_v \dot{w}_t \tag{5.93}$$

where M is a monotonic decreasing function and

$$\frac{dL_{v,t}}{dt} < 0 \text{ as } w\dot{}t>0$$

Taking into consideration equation (5.83) and differentiating it with respect to time, we have

$$\dot{L}_t = L_{t,t} + \int_{t-k(t)}^{t} \frac{dL_{v,t}}{dt} dv + L_{t-k(t)}[1 - k'(t)] \tag{5.94}$$

By substituting $\int_{t-k(t)}^{t} \frac{dL_{v,t}}{dt}$

in (5.92) and rearranging (5.94), the total output Y_t at time t is given in the following form

$$\dot{Y}_t = [F(I_t, G_t^n L_{t,t}) - w_t L_{t,t}] + w_t \dot{L}_t \tag{5.95}$$

In order to know the growth of output *Yt*, it is worth representing the rental of capital at time *t* created at vintage *v* by $b_{v,t}$.

$$b_{v,t} = \frac{F(_v, G_v^n L_v) - w_t L_{v,t}}{I_v} \tag{5.96}$$

And the growth of output, using the rental of capital *b* is given as

$$\dot{Y} = b_{v,t}\,\dot{G}_t + w_t\,\dot{L}_t \tag{5.97}$$

where the tendency of output *Y* to grow by the quasi-rent $b_{v,t}$, and by w_t comes as a result of having an extra unit of capital and an extra employee. Differentiating output, $Y = Y(G.L)$, the rental of capital *b* and wage rate, w_t, with respect to time we get

$$\dot{Y}_t = \frac{dY}{dG}\dot{G} + \frac{dY}{dL}\dot{L} \tag{5.98}$$

$$\text{and } b_{r,t} = \frac{dY}{dG} \quad w_t = \frac{dY}{dL} \tag{5.99}$$

The quasi-rent of capital $b_{v,t}$, in (5.97) can be extended further by using the optimum allocation of labour (Levhari 1966, 121) which assumes the following form,

$$b_{v,t} = F(1, M[m(0)G_v^{-n}G_{t-k(t)}^n]) - m(0)G_v^{-n}G_{t-k(t)}^n M[m(0)G_v^{-n}G_{t-k(t)}^n]$$
$$\text{for } v<t \tag{5.100}$$

Equation (5.97) gives us the growth of production where by having an extra unit of capital, output is increased by the quasi-rent of the new capital, $b_{v,t}$, and in the same way by adding an extra worker to the linear production function, output is increased by w_t.

It is interesting to see the Arrow's model in terms of exponential growth. By assuming $G_t = G_0 e^{gt}$, $I_t = I_0 e^{gt}$, and $Y_t = Y_0 e^{gt}$, where g is the rate of exponential growth we have the exponential solution for output and labour given by equations (5.89) and (5.90).

$$Y_0 e^{gt} = sY_0 \int_{t-k(t)}^{t} F[1, M(m(0)e^{-ng[v-t+k(t)]})]e^{gv}\,dv \tag{5.101}$$

$$L_0 e^{\sigma t} = \int_{t-k(t)}^{t} G_0^{-n} e^{-ngv} M[m(0)e^{-ng[v-tk(t)]}] g G_0 e^{gv} dv \tag{5.102}$$

where σ is the constant rate used at the equation of labour and *s* is a constant saving rate used in the growth of production. By denoting *g(1-n)* = σ and *g* = σ/*(1-n)* and after cancellation of *Y*0 at (5.101) we have total output and labour force expressed as

$$1 = se^{-gk} \int_0^k F(1, M[m(0)e^{-ng[v-t+k(t)]}] e^{gv} dv \tag{5.103}$$

$$L_0 = gG_0^{1-n} e^{-\sigma k} \int_0^k M[m(0)e^{-ng[v-t+k(t)]}] e^{\sigma v} dv \tag{5.104}$$

Equation (5.103) shows that the length of life of machinery and level of output depends on the rate of saving. Given that the exponential path is denoted as $G_0 = \frac{s}{g} Y_0$, we have that the total labour is represented in term of output as

$$L_0 = g^n s^{1-s} Y_0^{1-n} e^{-\sigma k} \int_0^k M[m(0)e^{-ng[v-t+k(t)}] e^{\sigma v} dv \tag{5.105}$$

According to Levhari (1966, 122) the necessary condition for the existence of an exponential path is the existence of a solution *k* and *Y*0 to equations (5.103) and (5.104), which require the equation

$$1 = se^{-gt} \int_{t-k}^{t} F(1, M[m(0)e^{-ng[v-t+k(t)]}]) e^{gv} dv \tag{5.106}$$

to have at least a solution *k*, which denotes the constant economic life of machinery. The right side of equation (5.106) is a monotonic increasing function of *k*, and the existence of a solution requires that for a large *k*, the monotonic increasing function of the right side of the above equation reaches values greater than 1. Hence, we have that for k→∞ the right side of (5.106) tends to

$$se^{-gt} \int_{-\infty}^{t} F[1, M(0)] e^{gv} dv = \frac{s}{g} F(1, \infty) > 1 \tag{5.107}$$

where (s/g)F(1, ∞) is the condition for the existence of exponential path given by equations (5.103) and (5.104).

The work of Levhari (1966) demonstrated that most of Arrow's results can, with some modifications, be expanded to a homogenous production function of the first degree that shows regular convexity and includes technological change.

The greatness of Arrow in a full neoclassical era was to prove that the main reason for technical progress is not the assumption of technical change, which occurs spontaneously and costlessly like manna from heaven; not the labour augmenting and capital augmenting; not Kennedy's theory of induced invention; but rather it is the improvement of the productive process by using a whole range of knowledge accumulation, known simply as learning by doing.

Sheshinski (1967) tested the learning-by-doing hypothesis against the experience of several manufacturing industries. Contrary to Arrow, he assumed that variations in the labour-capital ratio are possible all the time. Sheshinski also examined two assumptions: first, cumulative experience depends on accumulated gross investment, so investment is seen as being capable of changing the environment in which production takes place by providing the continual stimulation required for learning to take place; second, accumulated experience depends on accumulated output, so even in the absence of investment, the production process itself generates additional learning.

Many innovations, ranging from the introduction of entirely new products to small improvements in existing goods, receive little or no external support and are motivated almost entirely by the desire for private gain. The modeling of these private research and development activities and of their implications for economic growth, years later, has been subject to considerable research by authors such as P.M. Romer (1990), Grossman and Helpman (1991a and 1991b), Barro and Sala-i-Martin (1995), and Aghion and Howitt (1998), who obtained major inspiration from Arrow's learning-by-doing concept.

SOME CONCLUSIONS ABOUT TECHNICAL PROGRESS IN NEOCLASSICAL PERCEPTION

The literature on technical progress has grown very rapidly since the late 1950s and the beginning of the 1960s. Many empirical studies during this period agreed in suggesting that technical progress was an important factor in determining the rate of growth. The earlier models of technical progress, such as those of Hicks, Harrod, and Kaldor, had been confined to the assumption of labour-augmenting technical progress and the use of a single input in the research sector. These solutions obviously provide the existence of steady-state solutions. Relaxing these rather restrictive assumptions is essential for economists to build models with useful implications for the real world. For many economists, capital accumulation was an important factor in economic growth. Hicks considered the factor-saving characteristics of inventions as part of the adjustment factor stability. In fact, the adjustment mechanism in one-sector neoclassical steady growth was assumed to be Harrod-neutral technical progress. Technical progress is defined as neutral when it leaves unchanged the balance between labour and capital, in this way, permitting the steady state. Later Solow (1957) assumed technical progress as an exogenous factor, or something like manna from heaven. For a long time, the neoclassical growth models accepted technical progress as exogenous, but later attempts were made to build up macroeconomic theories assuming technical progress as endogenous. Some of them described how the direction of technical progress is affected by economic variables, and others were primarily concerned with the rate of technical progress. Some models using factor substitution were not able to explain the steadiness of distributive shares in advanced economies. The theory that explained better the constancy in distributive shares was that of induced bias in innovation, which was developed by Weizsäcker, Kennedy, and Fellner.

In the macro-studies of technical progress, endogenous technical progress was related mainly to aggregate variables such as investment and relative factor prices. In the micro-studies, the rate of technical progress is related to the form of market structure, the allocation of research expenditure, and government policy. In the most recent decades a good number of economists and theorists with their contributions in economic science have helped to narrow the gap between the micro- and macro-studies of technical progress. A good part of the empirical studies during this period was based on the assumption of exogenous, disembodied, and neutral technical progress, in contrast with the very few empirical studies on growth with endogenous technical progress. Some studies based on exogenous technical progress considered Solow's residual factor as attributed mostly to technical progress. In fact, empirical studies using such an approach have typically found the contribution of capital accumulation to growth to be small, on the order of 15 per cent, whereas the residual has come out to be on the order of 37 per cent to

43 per cent (Solow 1957, 81–9 and Denison 1979, 122–7). There are at least two reasons for feeling disappointed by the way the effects of technical change are explained.

First, it is not possible conceptually to separate technical change from an increase in the capital stock. In many cases, technical progress is introduced into the production process through new investments, improved capital equipment, and adoption of new knowledge within firms. Solow supposed that, to resolve the problem of separation between technical change and increase in capital stock, it is necessary to disaggregate the total capital stock into different vintages, where the most recent part of capital already incorporates some of the benefits of technical progress through its higher productivity (Solow 1970b).

Second, the neoclassical production function assumes constant returns to scale. If technical progress is embodied in new capital, a constant return production function will minimize the contribution of capital and overemphasize the residual of learning by doing. In empirical studies, at least, some efforts have been made by Denison (1979) and Matthews (1982) to estimate independently the effect of increasing returns to scale without the residual factor. These two reasons suggest that it is not easy to dissociate technical progress from the process of capital accumulation. Neither one can continue for long without the other.

It might be interesting to mention that some theories of technological progress have emphasized the demand side exclusively, leaving the supply side less explored. Schmookler (1966) conducted an empirical study of the industrial sector regarding the number of patents taken out by investors in the United States. He concluded that technological change was largely induced by the rate at which the demand for various products grew over time; "the amount of invention is governed by the size of the market" (Schmookler 1966, 172). If demand plays a dominant role in the market, it implies that the supply of inventions is infinitely elastic. In contrast to the studies on the demand side, there have been others that pressure the supply side, especially in relation to the diffusion of technological progress. According to these theories, countries can borrow new technology from more advanced countries, and the rate at which innovations actually occur in a country depends on the technology gap between that country and the most advanced country from which it is borrowing. The rate of absorption of technology depends on the stage of development of the country. Underdeveloped countries absorb a low rate of technological progress, whereas more developed countries have the capacity to absorb a high rate of technical change. Gomulka (1971) proposed that maximum benefits from borrowing technologies occur when per capita incomes in the imitating country vary from one-tenth to one-half of those of the industrial country. For example, the most successful case of technology borrowing after the war was Japan, whose per capita income in the early 1950s was approximately 12 per cent of that of the United States. The borrowing country must also have the skills and institutions needed to acquire and adapt the new technology successfully; Japan was one of those countries. These conditions are called "social capability"[20] and refer to all the factors that determine a country's ability to utilize an international backlog of technological progress, such as political and social structure, institutions, education, and labour force skills. Abramovitz (1986) later suggested that the "social capability factor" which is supposed to allow countries to absorb new technology is not sufficient to take full advantage of technology accumulation. It depends also on the rapid expansion of demand for consumer goods produced with new technology and capital goods to embody the new technology.

6

Some Accounts of Capital Controversy and Growth

The neoclassical "vision" of economic growth, together with many specific concepts and methods employed in its elaboration, has been subjected to a series of attacks from a group of distinguished economists collectively known as the "Cambridge School" because of their association with the faculty of economics at the University of Cambridge in the United Kingdom. The school rotates around the works of D.G. Champernowne, R.F. Kahn, Nicholas Kaldor, Luigi Pasinetti, Pierangelo Garegnani, and Joan Robinson. On the other side of Atlantic Ocean, there is the neoclassical school of Cambridge, Massachusetts in the United States, represented by the work of Robert Solow, Paul Samuelson, and Frank Hahn, along with Christopher Bliss (not in the United States). The controversies regard the work of both sides from the mid-1950s to the early 1970s and the work of these scholars appears mainly on first-rank journals like the *Quarterly Journal of Economics*, the *Review of Economic Studies*, and the *Economic Journal*. Both Cambridge schools have different thoughts and cannot properly be considered homogeneous in their visions. The individuals in each group differ in how they treat the various problems in the theory of growth and capital, and often they criticize one another as well as their common adversary.

The Cambridge School theorists are interested in different questions and, partly, in making their respective points from the dissimilar techniques they apply. In fact, in some of the controversies, the Cambridge School seems more interested in the study of the properties of different balanced growth paths, where neoclassical growth theorists would not necessarily accept that these studies are either particularly interesting or valuable.

Considering methodological and theoretical differences between the two groups as to what constitutes a good model led them to the endless debate about constructing a general theory of capital. For example, the Cambridge authors are skeptical about the validity of incorporating a marginal productivity theory of factor shares in a model. Similarly, the neoclassical school is not likely to acknowledge that the methodology of constructing a model is seen as a justification to create a theory in economic growth and capital studies rather than to analyze the results and solutions. Hence, the question raised by the two groups was what a "scientific" method is. For some of the economists of the two schools the use of economic models in growth theory was object of passion and obsession. There remained the danger emphasized by Cambridge writers: that the "mere models" do not remain the property of those who construct them but, combined with other theories, are altered, simplified, and eventually put to uses for which they were not invented (Jones 1975, 127).

One of the most important debates in which both groups were involved was the so-called capital controversy and their approach to saving. Why have theories of capital been so controversial? Solow suggested that controversy in this area arises from two sources: the difficulty of the subject matter and the ideological insinuations. There is no doubt that the theory of capital, due to its nature, is more complicated than other theories. The mathematical techniques and the different types of applications required for the analysis of a careful model in capital theory, using different kinds of capital goods, have become increasingly difficult and challenging for many economists and theorists involved in this class of studies. For more than two centuries since Adam Smith (1776) the principal historical controversy has been ideological rather than a simple matter of comprehension of the various theories. The idea that capital is a "factor of production," whose marginal productivity determines the profit, has been interpreted as an institutional arrangement known as capitalism, in the foundation of which stands the reward for the owners of capital.

The neoclassical conception of capital employed in a one- or two-sector model has two functions. First, capital, together with the labour stock, is included into an aggregate function to explain the flow of output forthcoming. Second, capital's marginal productivity "explains" the rate of profits per unit of labour (Jones 1975, 128). In this chapter the controversies between some Cambridge economists and neoclassical theorists regarding, typically, the theory of capital accumulation are reviewed briefly.

JOAN ROBINSON AND THE ACCUMULATION OF CAPITAL

A specific attempt to discredit neoclassical economists was developed by the British economist Joan Robinson[1] and some of her colleagues at Cambridge University in the late 1950s and mid-1960s. The so-called two Cambridges capital controversy was apparently about the implications and limitations that two major neoclassical economists, Paul Samuelson and Robert Solow, had regarding capital accumulation and treating the aggregate as an input in a production function. This controversy was deeply rooted, however, in a clash of ideas about what would constitute a satisfactory theory of capital and income distribution. What became the post-Keynesian position was that the distribution of income was best explained by power differences between workers and capitalists, whereas the neoclassical explanation, which later became mainstream economics, was developed from a market theory of factor prices. Economic growth is primarily interpreted as capital accumulation, but an accumulation that is largely related to technological change. Robinson started the so-called Cambridge controversy by heavily criticizing the marginalist theory of distribution. This theory, among others, suggests that the rate of profit is determined by the marginal productivity of capital. The problem raised by Robinson was how to measure capital in order to find its marginal productivity when the rate of profit is unknown. This question ignited an intense debate between Cambridge economists in the United Kingdom and neoclassical authors on Massa chusetts in the United States. Robinson pointed out that capital is not homogenous in its nature. It consists of machines, computers, assembly lines, plants, industrial patents, hardware programs, and computer software. All these items have nothing in common that can be added up to find a value or quantity of capital. Therefore, the demand for capital (the demand curve) to measure marginal productivity, which is used in the marginal productivity theory of distribution, cannot be known. The value of capital or the (future) profitability of capital is not easily determined because the theory does not explain the rate of profit of capital. Robinson emphasizes that the rate of profit cannot be simply assumed to measure the quantity of capital and determine the profitability of capital, and hence the marginal productivity theory of distribution must be neglected because it has no sound ground to explain the nature of capital.

Afterward, she worked together with Kaldor regarding the theory of growth. Later on in her life, Robinson focused her research on more methodological problems in economics and tried to reintroduce the original message of Keynes's *General Theory* in the community of international economists.

Robinson, following the Keynesian line, in the early 1950s tried to define a general theory of steady accumulation, including different factors and several tools, and to explain various aspects of capital accumulation. Influenced by Harrod and Cassel, she employed as an analytical tool a concept of "steady capital" accumulation (J. Robinson 1952). This concept is realized under some conditions: (1) a steady rate in technical progress; (2) a normal rate of capital investment; (3) a neutral technical progress; (4) competition sufficient to keep the normal profit rate quite constant; and, finally, (5) the proportion of net income remaining constant. Despite these conditions, Robinson tried to emphasize that the steady path of development in an imaginary golden age does not represent an equilibrium position because the system cannot restore itself in the face of a chance shock. The golden age, in Robinson's vision, is a desired rate of accumulation equal to the possible rate of growth of population and of output per head where the state of near full employment is maintained. Generally speaking, the condition that makes the golden age possible is that total output increases at the same proportional rate as the stock of capital, measured in terms of product. But the golden age is disturbed by limiting factors – vicissitudes – and the rate of growth. Robinson stated that,

> If for any reason investment were to rise above the steady rate, demand would expand relatively to capacity (in accordance with the multiplier based on the short-period marginal propensity to consume; both capital-goods and consumption-goods entrepreneurs would find themselves in a seller's market, prices would tend to rise relatively to costs, profits would rise above normal; in the short; the system would be in a boom. Contrariwise, any fall off the rate of investment would plunge the economy into a slump, that is, into a position where demand is insufficient to keep the existing stock of capital working at capacity. (J. Robinson 1952, 97)

Thriftiness (the first vicissitude) is one of the influences that drive the economy into slump conditions. An increase of thriftiness or underconsumption may slow down the rate of capital accumulation. In her argument, Robinson followed the underconsumption theory and implied that, as the economy grows richer, there is some level of optimum propensity to consume. She believes that there are forces that may counteract, sometimes quite effectively, the tendency toward a declining propensity to consume. Such forces, like trade unions and labour organizations, have the complicated task of persuading monopolists to pass part of their profits to workers in the form of wages in order to keep a sustained level of consumption. Also, thriftiness must rise as a consequence of growing income inequalities, and inequality tends to grow as capitalism develops new ways of substituting technical progress for labour skills, thereby reducing the share in the manufacturing industry received by labour. Robinson is much predisposed to accept the traditional emphasis on the negative impact of technological change on employment and the conditions governing the quantity of labour applied. In this context, she develops a second category of vicissitudes: "the supply of labour." In modern society, labour has become "human capital" to the extent that the society and the private firms invest more and more in training and education. Labour is engaged more in administrative activities, idea creation, projection, and planning and less in manual activities. The third sector – services – in most of the developed countries is the dominant sector, compared to the supremacy of the manufacturing sector in the nineteenth century. The conditions of work, technological progress, investment, and saving are improved and are more visible in industrialized countries. Regardless of this, Robinson sometimes considers technology as the main generator of the labour redundancy. If the productivity per man-hour rises faster than the total output, there is a continually growing amount of "technological unemployment" as a consequence of a continual fall in hours worked per year. In the steady state, the economy is growing because the population is growing, so the economy does not suffer a rate of "underconsumption." When the growth of population slows down, the community suffers from underconsumption, and it falls into a slump. Contrarily, when the population grows faster than the demand for labour, the existing employment per unit of output tends to stay high.[2] This creates the "reserve army" of technological unemployment. Robinson suggested that some of the redundant workers may get themselves into employment through the demand for housing, which has the same effect as an innovation favourable to capital that tends to promote investment.

The third vicissitude is the "supply of land." Her analysis of capital and property refers to the classical theory of land pricing and the effects of pricing on income and investment. She came up with the idea that the "closing" of frontier, or the scarcity of free land, has contributed much to increasing unemployment and the growing "reserve army," which are characteristics of modern capitalist society. Her position is that the redundant labour created by technological changes has been absorbed by the process of taking of what she calls "free land." Therefore an economy that has discovered new territories in the past but then finds itself with no more worlds to discover (or conquer) may suffer a profound shock, which could influence the formation of the "reserve army." This is one of the differences between nineteenth- and twentieth-century capitalism.

The "supply of finance" is one of the vicissitudes that imposes institutional decline. Robinson emphasized that this condition is severely limiting on economic growth. The supply of finance may fall short of the actual outflow as a consequence of the money supply failing to increase correspondingly to the increment in the stock of real capital. In this case, there is a tendency for the rate of interest to rise and for the new borrowing to become more difficult. The rate of interest, which is related to the supply of finance, is a much more important vicissitude than others. Expectations about changes in interest rates are especially examined and are viewed as being fairly difficult to handle. Robinson's argument of the Keynesian interest theory constitutes an important contribution to her general theoretical framework. She disagrees with the Keynesian suggestion that full employment might be maintained by sufficient variations in money-wage rates. According to the Keynesian proposal, if the quantity of money is not reduced equally, the existence of cash redundant to the needs of active circulation causes the rate of interest to fall, and this process continues until the fall in the interest rate stimulates investment adequately to restore full employment. She argued that the rate of investment, in the Keynesian view, is presented as a function of the rate of interest. But nothing can be said about the appropriate rate of investment with a given rate of interest without knowing for how long the rate of interest will prevail and how long the investment will go on (J. Robinson 1952). A rise in national income would drive up the rate of interest, whereas a fall in national income would not lower it. So, if for any reason the system is found in the position where the full employment value of the rate of interest lies below its actual value, there are no forces to bring it to the initial position. The automatic correction of interest rate because of its "very nature" tends to be too little or too late with respect to its future expectations. Her theory of interest rates takes its main frame from the Keynesian "liquidity preference," but does not depend on uncertainty. As Robinson writes,

> If the economy has had no such experience but has lived through prosperous times when the rate of interest had no occasion to fall, the tendency of the rate of interest to respond to changes in the demand for money must have atrophied. Owners of wealth in such a case must be supposed to have been endowed by past experience with confident belief in a normal value of the rate of interest ... and then, if a short-period situation should arise which (according to the theory) required a fall in the rate of interest, the rate of interest would refuse to fall. (J. Robinson 1952, 75)

The several vicissitudes lead to significant variability in economic growth. They may act as disturbances leading to deviations from the trend. These deviations are similar to trade cycles, and Robinson defined the boom of a trade cycle as "part of the trend." The cycle itself is tied up with packing the accumulation into a short period of time, and this packing is broken up as accumulation exceeds demand. The boom then turns into depression and, therefore, is characterized by an excess of accumulation.

Robinson's theory of economic growth is based mainly on what may be called the physical factors of growth. Moreover, she seems to believe that there are auxiliary elements, especially the effect of these vicissitudes on expectations. In fact, she found that it is not fully determinable if a cessation of population growth will affect the private enterprise sector because of the operations of expectations.

SRAFFA AND THE AGGREGATION OF CAPITAL

The Cambridge controversy, initiated by J. Robinson and followed by Sraffa, involved the argument that the orthodox theory of value was circular and not going anywhere useful for the economic science, so a new approach to interpret this theory was needed. Sraffa,[3] in his masterwork, *Production of Commodities by Means of Commodities,* published in 1960, went back to the economics of Ricardo and the classical notion of a surplus to find this approach. According to Sraffa, a logically consistent theory of value and distribution had to return to the classical conception of the circular nature of production: goods used to produce goods and a surplus created if, as output, more goods are produced than in the initial phase of production. Sraffa, in order to show the consistency of his theory, argued that his model could be used to explain the value of the relative prices as well as the principles that determine the distribution of income between wages and profits (Pressman 1999, 110). His model is an uncontaminated reconstruction of the Ricardo's corn model that validates in many aspects the classical alternative to the conception of price as a scarcity index-price based on the shortage and complexity of production (Cohen 2010, 13). Sraffa's view, among others, was that there was an intrinsic measurement problem in applying the theory of income distribution to capital. In fact, if the capitalist income is the rate of profit multiplied by the amount of capital, the measurement of the amount of capital would involve the summing up of incompatible physical objects, like trucks and computers. This is because technically it is not possible to add heterogeneous objects to measure the amount of capital.

Neoclassical economists agreed with the idea of adding up the money value of different capital items to get an aggregate amount of capital. But Sraffa (and Joan Robinson of the Cambridge school before him) did not concur the neoclassical idea of simple adding up the incompatible capital objects to get an aggregate value of capital. Sraffa strongly defends his vision that the financial measurement of the amount of capital depends on the rate of profit, which brings this argument to the circular nature of production.

The aggregate amount of capital is usually obtained by multiplying the amount of each type of capital goods by its price and then adding up all the multiples, corrected by the effects of inflation.[4] The problem with this technique is when there are taken into consideration different sectors of an economy producing consumption and capital goods. As a matter of fact, if the distribution of demand for products between sectors changes, it will change the price of the products and the price of each capital good. This will cause the total amount of capital goods to change with the distribution of income. If we consider, by taking a simple example, a rise in property income at the expense of wages and salaries, the demand will shift from basic consumer goods to capital goods like vehicles, boats, or building new houses and apartments. As a result, the price of capital goods used in building new houses would rise, and the price of capital goods used in producing basic consumption goods would fall. This observable fact will cause a change in the price amount of the two types of capital goods in two different sectors.

In general, this brings the idea that physical capital is heterogeneous in all its components and cannot be added in the same way as financial capital, where wealth is based on liquidity and other mechanisms representing cash money.[5] Sraffa suggested a simple technique (based in part on the Marxian theory) by which a measure of the amount of capital could be produced by reducing all machines to *dated labour* or the year when they are produced. For example, a machine produced in the year 1960 can be treated as the labour and commodity inputs used to produce it in 1959 (multiplied by the rate of profit), and the commodity inputs in 1959 can further be reduced to the labour and commodity inputs used to make them in 1958, and so on, until the non-labour components are reduced to a insignificant amount. By using this method it is much easier to add up the dated labour value of a vehicle to the dated labour value of a radio.

Sraffa suggested, however, that this accurate measuring technique still involves the rate of profit; the amount of capital depends on the rate of profit. But according to the neoclassical theorists there is a relationship between the rate of profit and the amount of capital, such that an increase in the amount of capital employed should cause a fall in the rate of profit. Sraffa instead advocates his theory that a change in the rate of profit would cause a change in the measured amount of capital in those sectors where consumption and capital goods are produced (in non-linear ways). For example, an increase in the rate of profit might initially cause an increase in the perceived value of the car more than that of a radio or television, but then reverse the effect at a still higher rate of profit.

It is also worth mentioning that in an earlier publication, Sraffa (1926) attacked the assumption of diminishing returns in production. He argued that most production, especially of manufactured consumer goods, occurs under conditions of increasing returns. Sraffa proved that the diminishing returns cannot apply to a particular industry, because changes in the cost of production in a particular industry will affect the cost of production in all other industries. He suggested that the economic model of perfect competition had to be abandoned and be replaced by a model of recognizing interdependence of firms and the existence of monopoly and oligopoly. This critique in the early 1930s led to the development of models of monopolistic competition by Joan Robinson and others.[6]

The aggregate value of capital was a serious test to the neoclassical theories of income distribution and production, which led to a long debate – the capital controversy involving the finest economists of both Cambridge schools.

THE GOLDEN AGE AND CONCEPT OF EQUILIBRIUM IN ROBINSON

In 1962 Robinson published a new collection of essays mainly focused on economic growth, the most important of which was "A Model of Capital Accumulation" (J. Robinson 1962a, 43–101) The purpose of this theory was to accentuate a generalization of Keynes's *General Theory* in relation to long-run growth problems, in the hope of clarifying what was said in her earlier work (J. Robinson 1952, 90–8). The model of capital accumulation is a typical closed two-sector model, composed of consumption and investment, with constant returns to scale. Robinson takes into consideration six principal determinants: (1) technical conditions such as the size and growth of the labour force; (2) thriftiness conditions – saving done only by business firms and rentiers (but not by wage earners); (3) investment policy – investment presented as an increasing (non-linear) function of the expected profit rate; (4) the state and possibility of improvement of the industrial production, which are of great importance in influencing the process of production; (5) the wage bargain that affects the behaviour of money wages in response to changes in prices; and (6) the competitive conditions that influence the propensity to save. The dominant determinant, in Robinson's view, is the "the animal spirit" of entrepreneurs. In effect, within any given context of high or low spirits, profit expectations can exercise a qualifying influence, sufficient to show how high rates of profit will induce high rates of accumulation. For a given rate of capital accumulation, the rate of profit varies inversely with the saving coefficient. Because the rate of accumulation is itself an increasing function of the profit rate, a higher rate of saving will result in a lower rate of capital accumulation. The

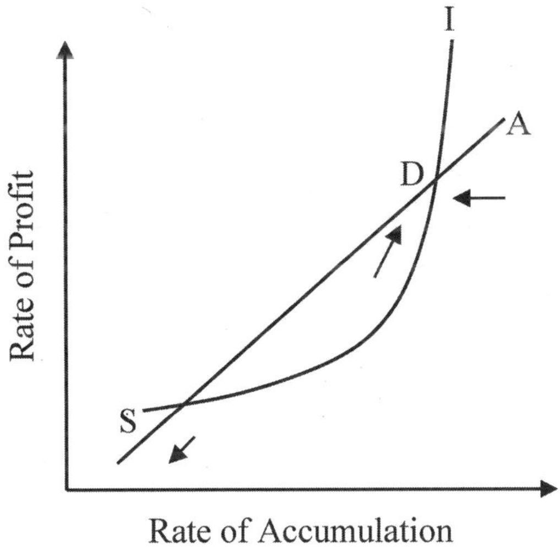

Figure 6.1 The desired rate of accumulation

famous "paradox of thrift" applies in the long run as well as the short run. According to Robinson (1952) when the schedule connecting the rate of capital accumulation to the expected rate of profit intersects the relating rate of profit, we have a "desired" rate of capital accumulation, because, at the point of intersection, the actual rate of profit equals the expected one. The point of intersection is assumed to satisfy the stability conditions, and the economy is supposed to be in a state of general equilibrium, characterized by a steady growth of investment and output.

If the short-run conditions were such as to yield the "desired" rate of growth, and if this happens to equal the possible rate of growth given by the growth of the labour force and the growth of output per head, we have what Joan Robinson (1962a) called a golden age of steady growth with continuous full employment. The desired rate of accumulation is depicted in figure 6.1.

The curve $A = E(\pi)$ represents the expected rate of profit on investment as a function of the rate of accumulation. The curve I, given as $I = d(k)/d(t) = f(r)$, corresponds to the rate of accumulation as a function of the rate of profit. The point D represents the rate of accumulation that generates the profit expectation required by firms, or the desired rate of accumulation. This concept, as pointed out by Robinson, is very similar to Harrod's warranted rate of growth, although the latter was not clear as to whether the firms are supposed to be satisfied with the stocks of productive capital they are operating or with the rate at which they are growing. For Robinson, the desired and the actual rate of accumulation coincide in the short-period situation, but there is no guarantee for the long-run period. The desired rate of accumulation will be established in the long run if there are no disturbing events and if technical conditions permit. Only in this case will the stock of productive capital be adjusted to requirements of the industries.

A "limping golden age" develops when the initial stock of equipment, from the point of view of desired accumulation, is too small to employ the entire labour force. If the desired rate of growth exceeds the possible one, however, the system is heading toward full employment. If output per head grows faster than the total output, so that there is a rising unemployment, the economy descends into a Malthusian "leaden age," in which the rate of unemployment and misery is large enough to keep the population growth rate low compared to the desired rate of capital accumulation. Growing unemployment in this age is normally accompanied by falling living standards. A "golden age" is "restrained" if technical progress is not fast enough for the desired rate of accumulation. A "bastard golden age" arises when the desired rate of accumulation is held in check, even in the presence of widespread unemployment, by the refusal of labour to accept a reduction in real wages that would result from the process induced by a higher rate of accumulation. Any attempt to increase the rate of accumulation (unless there is a reduction of consumption) is restrained by an inflationary rise in money-wage rates. In this case, the rate of accumulation is limited by the "inflation barrier." Both in a limping golden age and in a bastard age, the stock of capital in existence at any moment is less than sufficient to offer employment to all available labour. A "bastard platinum age" arises when there is either too little or too much basic capital stock to begin with and growth is either accelerating or decelerating.

The Keynesian paradox of thrift[7] in Robinson's model reappears in a long-period context. Higher thriftiness involves lower rate of profit, which causes a lower desired rate of accumulation. This seems to be a logical proposition about comparative "golden ages" in the long run, as she stated, "When the actual rate of growth is limited only to the desired rate, therefore, greater thrift is associated with a lower rate of accumulation. This is the central paradox of the *General Theory* projected into long-period analysis" (J. Robinson 1962a, 60).

Her hypothesis is that a real economy, at a point in historical time, is not in an equilibrium position or moving along an equilibrium path. In effect, she outlined possible outcomes, fluctuations, unsteady growth, or stagnation. She is in favor of Kalecki's approach (1962), but she does not elaborate a single articulated model. For Robinson, equilibrium positions used by modern economists are not useful reference points, because they do not represent the regular outcome of an economical process getting into equilibrium. Equilibrium must be considered in historical time using open models for economic processes. Open models, differently from closed equilibrium models, describe trends, sequences of events that are subject to historical contexts, and economical processes over historical time. Meanwhile, closed equilibrium models composed of simultaneous equations and mathematical expressions have no link to historical models because causal relations have to be specified. In fact, in open historical models things are less complicated, as they describe the causal sequence of historical events that happen in the real economy without taking into consideration a "large quantity" of assumptions and logical abstractions. Her notion of equilibrium as a "logically self-contradictory" concept is inconsistent with the phenomenon it is intended to explain, based on the sequence of events occurring in historical time. Equilibrium models are not satisfactory, as they do not describe the outcome of an actual economic process; therefore they are not useful in the explanation of historical events (J. Robinson 1974, 48–51).

The inconsistency in her thoughts between the equilibrium concept and the analysis of historical facts is the real movement that pushed Robinson to switch from closed deterministic equilibrium models to open historical models based on the historical events. Bliss, in his work on *Capital Theory and the Distribution of Income* published in 1975 (27–8), makes a clear distinction between the two concepts of equilibrium. The first concept of equilibrium is based on the realized expectations of an actual outcome when the dynamic forces bring the economy to a state of stability and balance or simply equilibrium. The second meaning of equilibrium is based on an analytical stepping-stone, which is a simplification of dynamic forces in progress in historical time. Robinson rejects the first meaning of equilibrium as an actual outcome of dynamic forces operating in the system, but accepts the second meaning of equilibrium as an analytical stepping-stone where the real dynamic forces are not related to actual outcomes but to the sequence of historical events.

Robinson's growth theory is a pure Keynesian theory and, thus, is easy to associate with the Kaldor and Harrod models. In her model, there is no output growth function comparable to Kaldor's technical progress function. Her desired and possible growth rate would merge in the long-run equilibrium, and the economy would grow at the possible growth rate. Robinson's model would appear to be based on the assumption (originally due to Kalecki) that saving automatically adjusts to the rate of investment through changes in the distribution of income.

Differently from the Cambridge School economists, however, she implicitly suggests that the state of employment is not of great importance, and, at the same time, she does not give a rational explanation why prices must rise in the "bastard golden age" during the presence of prevalent unemployment. Despite differences in assumptions about the determination of the aggregate propensity to save and about the purpose to obtain the long-run equilibrium growth with near full employment, J. Robinson's theory of growth (1962a) arrives pretty much at the same growth rate as neoclassical growth models do.

THE MEASUREMENT OF CAPITAL: THE CHAIN INDEX METHOD IN CHAMPERNOWNE

The degree of capital intensity is easy to measure in nominal terms. It is simply the ratio of the total money value of capital equipment to the total amount of labour hired. This measure is not related, however, to the real economic activity because it can rise as a result of inflation. Then the question that might arise is how we can measure the "real" amount of capital goods? Do we use the historical price or the replacement cost? This controversy emphasizes that the measure of capital intensity is not independent of the distribution of income, so changes in the ratio of profits to wages lead to changes in measured capital intensity. Moreover, it represents a definitive critique of the Solow growth model. Most of the debate is mathematical, but there are some elements that can be explained in relatively simple terms.

J. Robinson supposed that goods can be regarded as quantities of labour units (or "labour time") performed at various dates in the past when the goods were produced (J. Robinson 1953).[8] To sum the cost of expenditures of labour units at various dates, it is necessary to accumulate them from the time when they were produced until the present time at some rate of interest, deducting the yield that must be credited for the value they have produced meanwhile. The relation between the real cost of capital goods depends on how their respective costs in terms of man hours are affected by differences in the interest rate. According to Robinson, differences in interest rates have large effects on the capital goods to be constructed. This also affects the period of useful life of capital goods. A lower interest rate corresponds to a higher product wage; for example, two machines, exactly alike in most of their aspects, have different values because the investment required to create them is different. The difference in value remains if they are deflated by the wage rate in terms of capital per labour unit. In Robinson's view, if two similar machines have different production wage rates, the rate of profit and, therefore, the rate of interest are different. So two exactly similar equipments may represent different quantities of capital accumulation measured in labour time (because they may require different quantities of labour to operate them). The measure of capital in labour units, in Robinson's conception, has thrown light on the manner in which the factor ratio affects the choice of productive technique, the rate of interest, and the real wage. Harcourt observed that "this measure has an intuitive appeal as a measure of capital in its role of productivity agent in capitalist society," but it is clear that, given a production function with capital measured in terms of labour time, the neoclassical marginal productivity could hardly be sustained (Harcourt 1972)[9].

Champernowne (1953, 112), commenting on the measure of capital in labour time, stated that it is not convenient to proceed in this manner because of the following: (1) the same stock of capital equipment and working capital producing consumption goods can appear under two different equilibrium conditions (differing with respect to the rate of interest and to the rate of real wages) as two different amounts of capital; (2) the wage-rate of labour and the remuneration per unit of capital may differ from the partial derivatives of output with respect to the units of labour and capital employed; (3) output per head may be negatively correlated with the quantity of capital per head measured in labour units, and this may lead to the contradictory result that a reduction of capital per head, measured in labour units, is required to increase productivity (Champernowne 1953). Champernowne[10] (1953) made some attempts to use a chain index to measure the value of capital. He proposed a method of using the index quantity of capital in a historical sequence in the form of a chain index, increasing the index at every step by the amount at which the cost of capital at current wage and interest rates at the end of the step exceeds the cost of capital at the beginning of the step, estimated at the same wage and interest rates. So, changes of cost due to changes in the interest rate do not affect the measure of the quantity of capital. Champernowne's method compares the amounts of capital in different effective equipments as the chain index method in analogy with a chain index of quantities. Two equipments, denoted by *E* and *E'*, are both competitive at the rate of interest, $R(V)$. Employer *A* utilizes quantities *Y* of *E* and *Y'* of *E*, but employer *B* employs $Y + y$ of *E* and $Y' - y$ of *E'*. The cost of food-wage-rate *V* (a term introduced by Champernowne) and interest rate $R(V)$ of the total equipment of each employer is the same. It is also assumed that the interest paid by each employer is the same. The difference between two wage-bills must equal the difference between the values of two product flows. Therefore the extra product of the entrepreneur employing more labour is sufficient to pay the wages at the competitive rate. In this way, the competitive wage of labour equals the marginal product of labour.

Arithmetically, Champernowne's chain index method of capital can be expressed as (Champernowne 1953, 117):

$$w_L = \frac{\partial}{\partial_L} f(L, K) \tag{6.1}$$

where w_L is food-wage of labour, *L* is the amount of labour employed, *K* is the quantity of capital, and $f(L, K)$ stands for the flow of product from these quantities of factors. For each technique of production, constant returns prevail, so $f(\lambda L, \lambda K) = \lambda f(L, K)$ for all real λ. Thus, we have

$$L\frac{\partial f}{\partial L} + K\frac{\partial f}{\partial K} = F \tag{6.2}$$

Maximizing the rate of interest the employer can pay without incurring losses, we obtain

$$Lw_L + Kw_K = F \tag{6.3}$$

where w_K is the food-reward under competition of each unit of capital. The remuneration of each unit of capital is equal in value to its marginal social product and is written as

$$Kw_K = F - Lw_L = F - L\frac{\delta f}{\delta L} = K\frac{\delta f}{\delta K} \tag{6.4}$$

$$\text{and } w_K = \frac{\partial f}{\partial K} \tag{6.5}$$

Champernowne's method provides a means of expressing capital as a quantity under the conditions of perfect competition.[11] The two factors, labour and capital, are paid according to their marginal rate of productivity.

He believed that the prospect of constructing an index number of capital using the simple neoclassical conception was attractive, but later he noticed some anomalies in his model. In effect, the function *f*(*L*, *K*) proposed by him, expressing output as a function of labour and capital, must be a single value, but the assumptions do not guarantee this. For example, there is no explanation that a gradual fall in the rate of interest would involve increases both in productivity and in the quantity of capital per head. But it is plausible that a fall in interest rates and a rise in food-wages in a stationary state will generate a fall in output per head and a fall in the quantity of capital per head. If there is a rise in real wages and a fall in the ratio of interests, it would make competitive only equipment with lower productivity employing more workers per unit quantity and, as a consequence, requiring negative net investment. Most probably, the only way that investment could remain positive would be when real wages (or food wages) increase and the rate of interest decreases to levels at which capital equipment becomes competitive. A fall in the rate of interest would cause an increase in the demand for new capital equipment, and conversely, an increase in wages would raise the replacement cost of existing equipment more than its value so that no more of the existing equipment would be put in production.

The output may be regarded as determined by a function of the amounts of labour and capital employed, where capital itself is increasing at a rate equal to the net rate of saving measured in capital units. The remuneration of labour and capital in Champernowne's method is found by the rule of marginal productivity. Specifically, the investment will increase or decrease the relative share of capital according to whether the elasticity of substitution of capital and labour is greater or less than unity.

THE DISCONTINUOUS PRODUCTION FUNCTION AND THE THEORY OF CAPITAL

Joan Robinson, attacking the neoclassical perception about the theory of capital stated, "The ambiguity of the conception of a quantity of capital is connected with a profound methodological error, which makes the major part of neo-classical doctrine spurious" (1953, 84). She also notes, "The real trouble source is the confusion between comparisons of equilibrium positions and the history of a process of accumulation" (1974, 121).

She criticized the neoclassical theory of capital and the general equilibrium as a position to which an economy tends to move as time goes on. According to her, in the long run, neoclassicals confuse the position of equilibrium with a "Wicksell process"[12] of accumulation without technical progress. For an economic system, it is impossible to converge to the position of equilibrium because the system is already there. Important in her analysis is not the distance from one point of equilibrium *A* to a new point *B* but rather the time of moving from *A* to *B*. The meaning of general equilibrium is related more with the significance of time than with the magnitude of geometrical space. The neoclassical approach to the theory of capital examines general equilibrium using comparative statics that reflect mainly differences in initial conditions. Robinson often argued that neoclassical authors were not able to distinguish between a difference in the parameters of an equilibrium model and the effects of a transformation that takes place at a moment in time. As a matter of fact, she stated that "In time the distance from today to tomorrow is twenty-four hours, while the distance from today to yesterday is infinite ... therefore a space metaphor applied to time is a very tricky knife to handle, and the concept of equilibrium often cuts the art that wields it" (J. Robinson 1974, 85).

She emphasized that the state of equilibrium has to be maintained when the stock of equipments is operated by capitalists producing one commodity. This requires the period of composition of the stock of equipment to be replaced continuously from the amortization fund provided by the stock of capital. In equilibrium, it is assumed that the stock of equipment is stable. The amount of capital incorporated in a stock of equipment is equal to the sum of supply prices and to the ratio of capital to the original cost of the plants. The state of equilibrium is reached when the present rate of profit is equal to the expected rate of future profit calculated in the present time. Robinson demonstrated that comparisons between equilibrium positions with different factor ratios (the amount of capital per man) cannot be used to analyze changes in factor ratios taking place through time in neoclassical terms. Changes in factor ratios are not appropriate to study diverse equilibrium situations because they do not reveal anything about the process of accumulation and growth, but rather that differences in factor ratios may be more suitable for the scope of comparison. The factor ratio may increase when the wage rate rises, which causes capital to be absorbed by the "Wicksell effect." The changes in factor ratios also depend on the speed at which the old equipments are replaced by new ones. If capital per head is rising, entrepreneurs will tend to invest in new capital goods. Despite these explanations, the concept of accumulation under the conditions of equilibrium at changing factor ratios is not so satisfactory. To explain the changes in factor ratios in an acceptable way, Robinson took into account the differences in factor ratios. She observed the relation between the factor ratio (the amount of capital per man) and the ratio capital (the amount of capital per man in terms of product) to labour employed in order to set up a production function with discrete techniques. She examined what happens when there is a series of discrete values corresponding to particular techniques of production.

It is assumed that, with fixed technical knowledge, net output per head Y is a function $f(k)$ of the value of capital per person. In figure 6.2, the curve of production function $Y = f(K)$ depicted by Champernowne describes the quantity of capital in terms of output and is discontinuous with discrete techniques (based on Robinson's theory of capital [1953]).[13]

The horizontal sections in figure 6.2 correspond to changes in the capital-output ratio because of changes in real wages and interest rates at the levels $Y\alpha$, $Y\beta$, and $Y\gamma$ associated at the x axis with changes in capital per head $K\alpha$, $K\beta$, and $K\gamma$. At any factor ratio, the amount of capital per head (capital in terms of product) is equal to real capital per person multiplied by the wage rate. Thus, at the straight line segment with slope (denoted) β2, capital per person is $OK\beta OW\gamma\beta$, and the rate of profit is given by $W\gamma\beta Y\beta/OK\beta OW\gamma\beta$. At β2, all men are employed with beta technique, and a rise in factor and capital ratio requires an increase in the wage rate to $OW\beta\alpha$. Capital per man then increases to $OK\alpha$ on the horizontal axis. The slope β2 in the diagram (given by $W\gamma\beta\beta 2OK\beta$) is the rate of profit on capital obtained when gamma and beta techniques are indifferent, and in the same way, the slope of the straight

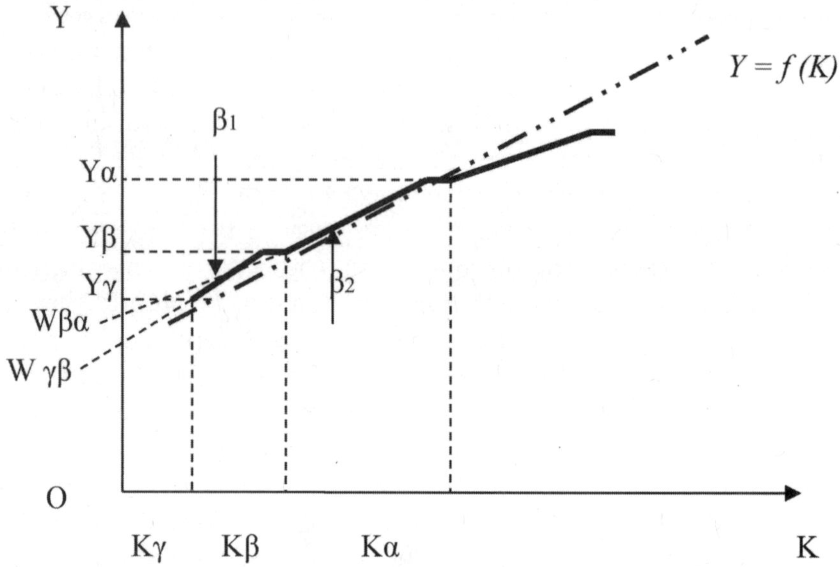

Figure 6.2 The discontinuous production function with discrete technique

line segment β1 is the rate of profit when beta and alpha techniques are indifferent. At a certain range, it may happen that a reduction in the rate of interest produces a larger reduction in capital cost of the equipment for a lower technique than for a higher technique, bringing down the wage rate.

The function $Y = f(K)$ is best conceived as relating to a smoothened version of the stepped curve, as suggested by the dotted curve drawn through the stepped curve. Robinson (1955) showed that, during the phase of transition in the process of production – for example, from *Y*γ to *Y*β – the profit rate and real wage will remain constant, but at *Y*β, they will skip to new levels, at which they stay until *Y*α is reached. The consequence is that, in a discontinuous case, a productivity curve relating productivity to the value of capital per man will have the characteristics of the stepped curve shown above (Champernowne 1958). The fundamental nature of the mechanism of the relationship between the rate of wages and the choice of technique can be better comprehended in terms of discontinuous curves; for this reason, the curve of the production function – differently from that of the neoclassical school, where the curve is straight – is presented as stepped in the above diagram (figure 6.2).

The conclusions drawn by Robinson are that the rate of profit on capital will tend to be higher and the wages lower if: (1) the technical opportunities for mechanizing production are more plentiful; (2) the rate of capital accumulation is slower in relation to the growth of population; and (3) the force competition and the bargaining power of the workers are weaker.

Robinson created the theory of discontinuous production function to better explain the theory of capital accumulation and the changing of techniques. In a neoclassical system, the balanced rate of growth is determined exogenously, and the economy, in the long run, grows at the rate of growth of the population. The balanced rate of growth is also the constant exogenous rate of growth of the labour force. In Robinson's view, the technique is a function of the wage rate. She assumed the neoclassical postulate that the technique of employment, given the quantity of capital and the wage rate, employs the labour force. Robinson, correctly recalling Keynes, stated that it is not the wage bargain that determines the amount of employment but rather the force competition. In a competitive economy, there is a uniform rate of profit at a given technical progress and quantity of capital, which is compatible with the value of wage rate at the full employment of the labour force. She is not interested in the neoclassical preposition of the steady state. She also does not give any significant importance to the convergence of the economy toward the balanced growth path in the long run. She is concerned only about the relationship between technical progress, rate of profit, and rate of accumulation in the long run, which derives from short-period oscillations. The concept of long run, in her view, is made of the sum of short-period fluctuations. This is one of the reasons that the production function is discontinuous and not linear. In the long-run period, given the rate of population, the rate of profit depends on the interaction between technical progress and the rate of accumulation. Technical progress normally tends to increase the rate of profit, whereas accumulation tends to reduce it, and this is what happens in developed capitalist economies.

THE CAPITAL THEORY AND RATE OF RETURN IN SOLOW

Solow (1963, 16–17), following arguments with Robinson over capital and its marginal product, argued that it is better to switch the theory of capital to the rate of return on investment derived from Irving Fisher

(1930) and Knut Wicksell (1934)[14] rather than to former concepts of this theory, which many critics agreed were incoherent. The one-commodity and two-factor production function allowed him to measure the respective contribution of capital and technical growth in output per head over time (Solow 1956). In response to the critics coming from the Cambridge School in the United Kingdom, Solow tried to build a new theory of capital based on the rate of return by avoiding the problems connected to the measurement of capital and its marginal product.

Solow developed the theory of capital in his 1963 work. He was convinced that the central concept in capital theory is the rate of return on investment. As he stated,

> In short, we really want a theory of interest rates, not a theory of capital. I do not believe that this shift of emphasis makes the theory of capital easy. But I do believe that concentrating on the rate of return leads to clarity of thought while concentrating on "time," or "capital," or the "marginal productivity of capital," or the "capital-output ratio" has led to confusion. It seems to me that almost any important planning question we wish to ask about the saving-investment process has an unambiguous if perhaps approximate answer in terms of rates of return, whereas the answers sometimes given in terms of marginal products of capital and capital-output ratios are sometimes right, sometimes wrong, and often misleading. (Solow 1963, 16–17)

Solow suggested that capital theory is best approached by asking technocratic planning questions. Much has been made of the conceptual difficulties of measuring capital. Following the technocratic approach, he is able to define the rate of return on investment in such a way that the problem of measurement of capital simply does not arise.

The one-period rate of return is fundamental for a growing economy because saving-investment decisions are made at every period and can easily be changed. The planning department may compare the consumption stream that comes by planning allocation with alternatives coming out over a period of, say, two years. If, for example (the first example), the planning department decides to save in period *Co* and to consume in *Cn* period, and if *Cn* is the originally planned consumption and *Cn'* is the alternative plan, then the average *n* period rate of return is given by the solution $(Cn' - Cn)/(Co - Co') = (1 + rtn)^n$, when *Co -Co'* is assumed to be small enough. Based on Solow's model (1963) the planning department could choose to sacrifice an extra h units of consumption in order to add a constant amount to each period in perpetuity. Denoting $Co' = Co - h$, $C1' = C1 + p$, $C2' = C2 + p$, where p is considered the perpetual increment to consumption, the average rate of return in perpetuity is given by $(C2' - C2)/(Co' - Co) = p/h = r$. The relation p/h is described as the average rate of return in perpetuity. In one period, the rate of return on investment depends on the actual level of consumption as it appears in the original plan. For longer periods (for example, the tenth period), the flow of returns from a marginal act of saving-investment will depend on what had been planned for the future in the earlier periods. According to Solow (1963), in a modern economy, the one-period return is likely to be important because decisions are generated quickly. In fact, for the numerous problems regarding the measurement of capital, it is enough to calculate the one-year rate of return on investment, the rate of return in perpetuity, and the rate of return of the n period. There is no need to measure the stock of capital goods, inventories, or generalized capital in order to give a value to the capital. It is not certain that the rate of return on investment should be equal to the rate of interest defined as the ratio of the value of a certain flow of goods to the value of capital stock. In Solow's observation, the neoclassical assumption that capital goods are "malleable"[15] is not valid at all. He assumed that neoclassical theory can be built around the rate of return concept, including the efficiency price theory, the perfect capital market, and the interest rate.

Solow made some efforts to prove that the rate of return on investment does not depend on the marginal productivity (or on the proportion between the production factors). For this explanation, he considered (the second example, Solow 1963, 30–4) an economy producing a single consumer good by using two kinds of techniques. The first one is a handicraft method in which a man produces b units of consumable goods per year. The second technique uses machines at which n men are employed and produces nc units of consumables goods per year. By assumption, a fraction d of machines are depreciated at the end of the year, whereas $(1 - d)$ are still in use in the next period. Denoting with V the stock of machines in existence, the annual output of machines must be dV. The programming authorities take into account the sacrifice of the present consumption in order to maintain a stable flow of future consumption. If one man from the handicraft-technique sector is transferred to the machine-producing sector, it will produce $1/v$ machines. So in the next period, the stock of machines will be increased to $V + (1/v)$. But at the same time, the stock of machines will diminish by depreciation to $[(1 - d)(V + (1/v)]$. To replace them at the end of the period during the stationary level P, the production of $dV - (1 - d)$ machines is required and, so, the work of $dpV - (1 - v)$ men. The number of men left to produce consumer goods in the handicraft industry is $L - dpV + (1 - d) - Nv - n/v$, where L is the total number of workers. The total output of consumer goods in the second period exceeds the consumer goods of the old plan by $(nc/v) + b[(1 - d) - n/v]$. As the amount of consumption initially sacrificed is b, the rate of return in the second period is equal to $nc/vb - n/v - d = (n/v)[(c/b) -1] -d$, according to the analysis done before (the first example).[16] In the second example, the rate of interest must equal the rate of return on investment. In effect, the nc units of consumer goods produced by one machine and n men must cover the wages of n men and the rate of depreciation. So we have $nc = wn + wv(d + r)$, where w is the wage of consumer goods and r is the rate of profit. By assuming $b = v$, we have that one worker can produce b units of consumable goods in the handicraft sector. Thus, $nc = bn + bv(d + r)$, which implies that the rate of return is $r = nc/bv - d - n/v$. In this case, without considering the marginal productivities, the interest rate equals the rate of return in investment in a competitive equilibrium. But what happens when there is technical change?

Solow emphasizes that, for many economists, "technical change" is something like a simple artifact that emerges as a residual when you try to explain growth of output in terms of the growth of inputs. Using technological progress to build a growth model normally has the tendency to reduce the residual growth of output per unit of input. He outlines this problem, pointing out that the rate of return will fall short of the net marginal product of capital as ordinarily understood.

Solow (1963) was trying to prove that if the private and social marginal products of capital coincide, then the social rate of return will coincide. Recalling Irvin Fisher's theory, he points out that there are discrepancies between his estimated rates of return on investment in the United States and the indications given as order of magnitude of marginal time preferences by the rate of interest on non-risky assets. The production function used for his model (with embodied technical progress) is of the Cobb-Douglass type, and the possibilities of direct substitution between labour and capital goods are retained throughout the lifetime of capital goods. The distinction between new and old capital is made not by substitution but instead by being more productive. The aggregate production function of Cobb-Douglas type is given as

$$Q_t = AJ_t^{\alpha} L_t^{1-\alpha} \tag{6.6}$$

where Q_t is the potential capacity of output, L_t is the full employment supply of labour, and $J_t = \Sigma(1+\lambda)^v K_v(t)$ is the effective stock of capital, with λ representing the rate of technical progress and $K_v(t)$ the quantity of capital goods built in year v. Solow estimated the elasticities of output with respect to labour and capital for some rates of technical progress, λ, in the United States and found that if λ is taken as 2 per cent, 3 per cent, 4 per cent, or 5 per cent, then the estimated contribution of technical change to the rate of growth of output goes from 1.3 per cent to 1.5 per cent to 1.7 per cent to 1.8 per cent per year, respectively. He suggested that higher rates of technical progress are accepted because of the Cobb-Douglas elasticity with the share of income from capital in total income. He realized that, for every rate of technical progress, the elasticities of the United States are almost the same as the elasticities of Germany (differing only by a rate of technical progress one percentage point higher). For example, if the rate of increase of productivity of new capital, λ, is 0.02 in the United States, the elasticity of output with respect to effective capital, α, is 0.63; whereas for Germany, it is 0.03, and α is 0.67. When λ in the United States is 0.03, α is 0.51; when λ for Germany is 0.04, α is 0.51. From this analysis, he suggested that the capital elasticity should be almost the same as the share of capital in income and output. On the basis of equation (6.6), Solow proposed that the social rate of return on investment is equal to the marginal product of effective capital minus depreciation and is given as

$$r = \alpha(Q/J) - (\lambda + d)(1 + \lambda) \tag{6.7}$$

where Q stands for output and J for capital, d is the rate of depreciation, α is the elasticity of output with respect to capital, and λ is the rate of technical progress. A depreciation rate of 4 per cent is the right order of scale. Using the equation above, Solow calculated the life of effective capital during 1954 in the United States and found out that it was, on average, seventeen to twenty years for equipment and approximately fifty years for plants (buildings). For Germany, it was twenty-five years for equipment and plus infinity for buildings.

The social rate of return on investment from one period to another is considered as the payoff of future savings for the society. Under conditions of perfect competition exists a certain relationship between the social rate of return on investment, the marginal product of capital, and the rate of return of profits.

Solow's theory about the transition path, although compatible with full employment of labour but incompatible with full growth capacity, holds, and this is partially because he studied the case of the rate of returns only at the switch point of two production systems sharing the same production factors and same profits. The case of common general equilibrium position was not considered. As Hagemann states, "Solow did not arrive at the rate of return through comparisons of equilibrium positions but understood it as that interest rate which discounts to zero the stream of consumption differences associated with transition. This surely is not tautology. However, Solow discussed only a very narrow class of transitions, namely those that take place at switch point of two production systems. Hence the two systems share the same rate of profit and a common price system" (Hagemann 1997, 155).

Even the fact that two steady-state equilibriums share the switching price system does not imply that resources can be moved from one point to another without any price adjustments. Solow, as Harcourt stated, "confined himself to models of centrally planned economies," (Harcourt and Kerr 1982, 264) and the switch from a capitalist to a planned economy corresponds to the switch from stationary equilibriums to a class of transitional processes. The next section will explore in more detail the switching of techniques of production.

THE SWITCHING OF TECHNIQUES AND THE INTEREST RATE: PASINETTI VS. SOLOW

The discussion of pure theory of interest and capital in the late 1960s was concentrated on the switching techniques when the rate of interest changes. According to this theory, it is possible that the same technique may be the most profitable of all possible techniques at two or more values of given rate of profits. Capital reversing is the possibility of a positive relationship between the value of capital and the rate of profit when a switch from one technique to another is considered. The switching techniques and the rate of interest in capital theory were considered further by Solow in his 1967 paper in light of Irving Fisher's writings (I. Fisher

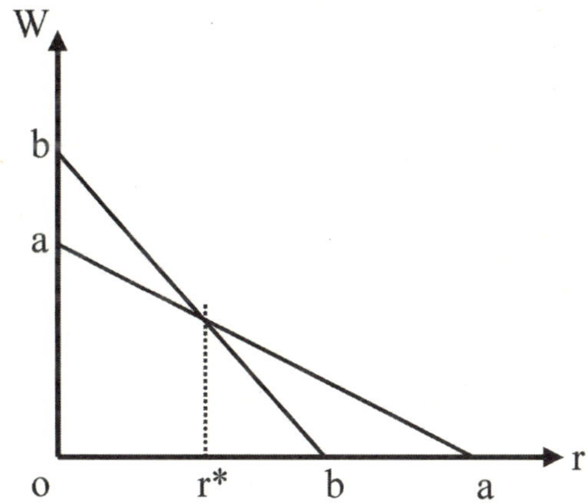

Figure 6.3 The switching techniques and the rate of interest

1930). The switching point of techniques between two situations is used to establish the quality of social rate of return with externally given values of the rate of interest and to indicate the nature of the transition process involved. Solow (1967) considers a simple model, where *a* is a particular technique producing one single consumable good, *r* is the rate of interest, *w* is the wage in any unit of account, and *p* is the commodity price in the same unit of account. The technique, *a*, is feasible at the interest rate *r* and at the price vector given by *p*/*w*. If there is only one technique, this means that it is the only competitive technique at the given rate of interest because it offers the highest real wage and a higher value of capital good per man. If there are two techniques, *a* and *b*, which have exactly the same price *p*/*w*, then they both can coexist; but suppose that, at the interest rate *r*, only *a* technique is competitive and, at a slightly lower interest rate, there is a point r^* at which both *a* and *b* are competitive, whereas for a smaller *r* only *b* is competitive. So, the interest rate r^* is a switching point for techniques *a* and *b*, as drawn in figure 6.3.

Figure 6.3 shows a case in which there are two possible techniques, *a* and *b*. For the rates of profits less than r^*, competition will ensure that only technique *b* is used because, in that range, this technique provides a higher rate of profit for any given wage rate *w* than technique *a*. At the rates of profit greater than r^*, technique *a* is more profitable, whereas at r^*, the two techniques are equally profitable.

If x is the level of activity and c the level of consumption at period one, the linear presentation of using technique a implies

$$x = c + ax \tag{6.8}$$

The economy tries by the next period to get into a new steady state using technique b, with output y and consumption c^*, so we have

$$y = c^* + by \tag{6.9}$$

However, moving from the first period to the second one, the system has to reduce the consumption in order to keep its circulating capital [by] out of its current output, x. Thus, the consumption has to be reduced to a temporary value, c', and the activity level now is given as

$$x = c' + by \tag{6.10}$$

The transition is completed when the economy sacrifices consumption $c - c'$ during one period to achieve a continuous gain in consumption, $c^* - c$, in the next period. With r^* as the interest rate at which a and b are both competitive, p^* as the price vector, and w as the wage rate equal to the unity, the social rate of return to saving, R, is the ratio of the perpetual consumption gain to the initial one-time sacrifice. R is given as

$$R = \frac{p^*(c^* - c)}{p^*(c - c')} \tag{6.11}$$

The interest rate at which a and b can both compete is equal to the social rate of return on saving in passing from a steady state with technique a to a steady state with technique b (Solow 1967, 32). The society earns extra consumption later in return for consumption foregone in the past. In the case of a single consumption good, it seems to be a paradox regarding the rate of return. If, for example, the techniques a and b are competitive at two or more distinct interest rates, it appears that, whenever a shift occurs from a to b, the social rate of return is equal to the competitive interest rate, but the physical act of shifting from a to b is exactly the same whatever the interest rate. So, the paradox of transition between techniques stands on the fact that the rate of return is equal to two or more different interest rates instead of one interest rate as assumed by the neoclassical theory. Again, if both *a* and *b* are competitive at more than one interest rate, the possible consumption path between two techniques has to admit more than one rate of return. Any interest rate at which the two techniques can compete will serve as a rate of return. According to Solow, the switching phenomenon of techniques does not invalidate the neoclassical capital theory in its full generality.

Pasinetti (1969), returning to Fisher's writings in the light of Robinson's and, especially, Sraffa's theory, argued that Solow's approach was as vulnerable to the new results as were the foundations of the aggregate production function. Pasinetti, among others, believed that Fisher, in his theory of interest, had in mind the annual rates of interest, which clear the loan market (this is called the first meaning of Fisher's interest rate). Basically, the interest rate of any year does not have to equal those of other years, and they certainly are not the same concept as the long-run natural rate of profit. It was this view of Fisher, together with Solow's work on the rate of return on investment, that led Pasinetti to investigate the conditions under which the rate of return on investment is calculated independently of the value of the rate of profit. Pasinetti (1969) showed two notions of the rate of return deriving from the concept of Irving Fisher. The first definition is the rate of profit, r^*. This may happen when, in two systems denoted as *a* and *b*, the wage rates are to be fixed at a level at which the rate of profit and the price system are the same. Denoting w^* as a particular wage rate, r^* as the rate of profit, and p^* as the price vector corresponding to w^*, we have that, at wage rate w^*, the two systems are equally profitable, which means that their rates of profit are equal to the value of capital goods at $i = r^*$. This statement also means that, at any of the systems (*a* or *b*), a wage rate w^* may not exist or, if it does, may not be unique. Pasinetti argued that Solow's rate of return position at which two production possibilities are equally profitable cannot explain anything at all. According to Pasinetti,

> There is therefore no unambiguous way of evaluating what society "sacrifices" and what society "gains" in the transition from a to b; for any evaluation, one needs a system of prices. In his calculations, Solow uses the particular system of prices of the switch point. He does not notice that these prices pre-suppose precisely that rate of profit which he wants to "explain." Solow does not seem to realize that a physical rate of return represents a very particular case … while, on the other hand, the equality on which he insists so much

is indeed general, but refers to an accounting expression.(1970, 429–30)

The second meaning of Fisher's theory, according to Pasinetti (1969), regards the rate of return associated with a particular investment project when the overall rate of profit is accepted as given. It is assumed that an economic system has two phases, *a* and *b*, with commodities *Ya* and *Yb* and capital goods *Ka* and *Kb*. The differences between two net products are expressed by vector (*Yb* - *Ya*)[17] and physical differences between the capital goods by vector (*Kb* - *Ka*). The later physical capital, denoted by *K*a*, is assumed not to be reused in any way in the system during phase *b*. The physical quantities (*Ka* - *K*a*) can, as well, become capital goods in the phase *b*. When the passage from phase *a* to phase *b* takes place, the society enjoys a permanent physical increase (*Yb* - *Ya*) in the net product against physical quantities (or once-for-all cost represented by [*Kb* - *Ka* + *K*a*], which is added to the capital goods). Choosing an arbitrary system of prices, $p(r)$, we have Fisher's second notion of rate of return, written as

$$\frac{p(r)[Y_b - Y_a]}{p(r)[K_b - K_a + K_a^*]} = R \qquad (6.12)$$

Given two techniques, *a* and *b*, this ratio differs from the first definition of Fisher's rate of return (r^*) and can always be computed; whereas a rate of profit r^* of the first notion may not exist. The ratio R (equation [6.12]) provides a good criterion for a rational choice between alternatives *a* and *b*. The shift of techniques may or not be profitable, and this depends on whether the ratio R is greater or smaller than the predetermined rate of profit. According to Pasinetti (1969, 526), the marginalists have seen in ratio R something more than a simple tool for the choice of techniques; they have seen the foundation of the theory of the rate of profit and they believe that the theory of capital relies on a very specific principle on the rate of profit. On the other side, Pasinetti was concerned with showing neoclassical economists that the rate of return has been confused by two different concepts having the same idea, which is the marginal product of capital.

Pasinetti strongly believed that Fisher's rate of interest and the rate of profit are not the same thing. This is the main critique addressed to Solow regarding the coincidence in the idea of the rate of return. Although the rate of return appears to have a theoretical content, when attached to the marginal productivity theory, it is reduced to a mere definition and is "dispossessed" of the marginal theory of capital. Effectively, if the rate of interest is changed to the rate of profit, Fisher's context of the rate of profit changes to the specification in Solow's theoretical and empirical work, and the marginal consideration of rate of interest changes to a neoclassical context of the rate of return.

THE NEOCLASSICAL PARABLES IN SAMUELSON

As previously seen, the process of switching techniques occurs when the same technique is preferred at two or more rates of interest. At lower values of interest rates, the cost-minimizing technique "switches" from *a* to *b* and then "reswitches" back to *a*. So the same physical technique is associated with two different interest rates. Hagemann, in an excellent article about the rate-of-return debate and the validity of Solow's theorem, stated,

> Now it is clear that a transition path from technique α to technique β need not exists and, if it does exist, it need not be efficient in the sense that all resources (including labour) are permanently fully employed and that there does not exist any other path with a higher consumption per head in any one of the periods of the transition phase. Yet Solow's theorem rests decisively on the assumption that such an efficient transition path exists. In order to form an opinion on the relevance of Solow's theorem one has to consider the conditions under which such a path exists ... If at least one pure capital good used with technique α cannot be reused with technique β, capital goods wastages are unavoidable. Hence the transition path is inefficient and Solow's theorem does not hold. (Hagemann 1997, 150–1).

The question arising from this phenomenon is why the switching process happens? In the mid-1960s, Samuelson[18] provided the answer using the Austrian conception of capital as a measure of time, so the productivity of capital results as the productivity between two or more periods (Samuelson 1966). However, before that 1966 article, in another article published in 1962 Samuelson tried to argue that, for some reason, the aggregate neoclassical growth models and the aggregate production functions are better explained if abstracted from the marginal product of social capital. He made an effort to introduce the tools of modern linear programming in so-called neoclassical models in order to understand how incomes are distributed among different kinds of workers and different kinds of capital owners, including the changing of technology. Samuelson proposed that it is possible to arrange a theory of capital using the factors of a surrogate production function between the world of jelly and the reality of the heterogeneous capital goods,[19] excluding any kind of substitution between capital goods and labour within a predetermined technique. Samuelson (1962) suggested as a model that a single consumption good (corn) is produced by a combination of labour and capital with constant-returns-to-scale techniques. Each technique in a stationary state contains a consumption goods sector and a capital goods sector and employs a different capital good, but at each value of the rate of profit, only some of the techniques are competitively feasible. So, corresponding to any given value of either w or r, there is one technique that is the most profitable (or pays the highest wage rate). It is assumed that a capital good, called alpha, is totally different from another capital good, called beta. The capital good alpha and the labour used in production can produce a final output and (by assumption) a flow of new alpha machines.[20] The same assumptions are held for capital goods beta, gamma, and so forth. Each of them, using a particular proportion of work, can produce the basket flow of finished goods. This model (Samuelson 1962) does not require any proportion of beta to help in producing alpha. Each capital good is independent of another. Figures 6.4a and 6.4b depict the profitable techniques when real wages and technical input coefficients are given.

In figure 6.4a, (Samuelson 1962) the horizontal intercept $M\alpha$ gives the maximal possible rate of profit if the labour force is a free good. The technical coefficients ensure the faster rate at which the capital good, alpha, makes itself grow at the net of depreciation of 30 per cent (the gross rate per annum is 40%; subtracting 10% for depreciation, we get 30%). The vertical intercept $N\alpha$ ensures the highest productivity of labour, assuming the interest rate is zero. The real wage $w = W/P$ is completely determined by the technical input coefficients. The straight line between two intercepts is the frontier line of physical good alpha. The straight line means that every stationary state produces exactly the same output related to the size of total labour employed, without substitutability between factors. For example, if the relative share of labour

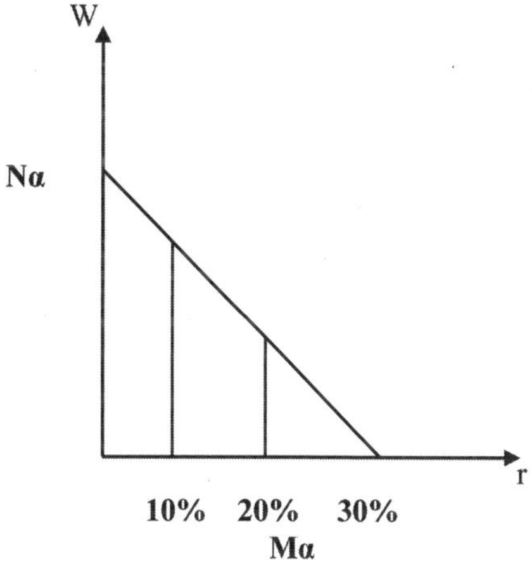

Figure 6.4a The frontier line

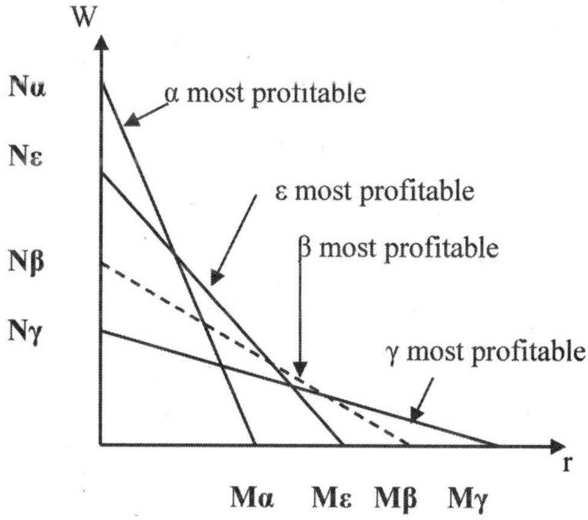

Figure 6.4b The optimal frontier line

productivity falls from one unit to half, its real wage falls exactly to half and the rate of profit (interest rate) rises a half unit. Figure 6.4b shows the various straight-line frontiers that hold for physical capital goods, alpha, epsilon, beta, and gamma. Each of them is distinguished by its technological intercept coefficient of *N* and *M* type and is associated with a straight-line wage frontier. The optimal frontier line means that alpha will be used at very high interest rates in preference to beta, but if for any reason the interest rate is lower, say below 12 per cent, society would let the physical capital good alpha wear out and put the resources into gross capital formation beta that results to be more capital intensive than alpha. Alpha (α) is the most profitable technique at the northeastern frontier for the highest wage levels (lowest rates of interest profits). We can use the same interpretation for epsilon and gamma capital goods. Figure 6.4b shows what is sometimes called the "grand factor-price-frontier." From the factor price frontier, we can see that the slope of each wage frontier is equal to the aggregate capital-labour associated with each technique. The high rates of profit and low levels of the wage-rate are associated with low levels of the capital-labour ratio. It is easy to imagine that the case of a simple two-technique economy, using two different capital goods, gives exactly the same predictions as the neoclassical parable (in Figure 6.4b, four different techniques are used). It is simple to verify that all of the basic conclusions of the main neoclassical parable (or the three neoclassical parables),[21] incorporating "malleable"

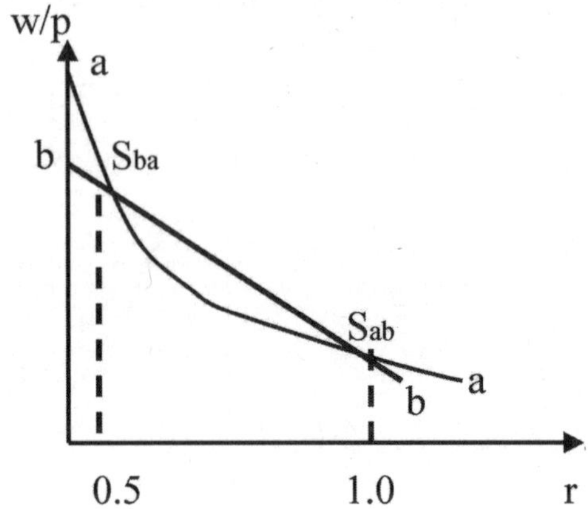

Figure 6.5 The factor-price frontier and switching techniques

capital, are identical to those coming from the grand price frontier of the fixed proportions in a heterogeneous capital model. Thus, Samuelson (1966) proved that, for the core neoclassical parable (or the conventional Austrian model), the real wage always rises as the interest rate falls because, even without any change in technique, normally there is less discounting of the wage product at lower interest rates.

In most cases, as seen in figure 6.5, (Samuelson 1966) the factor-price frontier is downward sloping, with real wage rising as interest rate drops. This figure shows that the factor-price frontier is appropriate to each technique. The switching points are *Sba* and *Sab*, which ensure the switching techniques from *a* to *b* and from *b* to *a*. For example, at *Sab*, when the interest rate is 1 per cent, there is a shift from technique *b* to *a* because technique *a* at high rates of interest is more profitable than technique *b*.

In 1962 (in the "Surrogate Production Function" article) Samuelson extended the one commodity model to the heterogeneous commodity model, including a variety of distinct capital goods. He assumed the ratio of the two factors of production (i.e., the capital-labour ratio) should be equal in all sectors, thus making relative prices independent of any changes in distribution between wage earners and capital earners. Furthermore, in the 1962 article, Samuelson brought up what today is considered by many economists as the three neoclassical parables. Citing Cohen,

> The simple model exhibits what Samuelson (1962) calls three key "parables:"
> Parable 1 The real return on capital (the rate of interest) is determined technically by the diminishing marginal productivity of capital.
> Parable 2 There is an inverse monotonic relation between quantity of capital and the rate of interest.
> Parable 3 The distribution of income is determined by relative factor scarcities and marginal products. (Cohen 2010, 9)

Later, in the 1966 "Summing Up" article Samuelson went back to one commodity model. According to Cohen and Harcourt, "Samuelson's (1966, p.588) judicious 'Summing Up' article admitted that outside of one-commodity models, reswitching and capital-reversing may be usual, rather than anomalous, theoretical results and that the three neoclassical parables 'cannot be universally valid'" (Cohen and Harcourt 2003, 206). In this article Samuelson illustrated that the neoclassical parable remains valid to the extent that, in the factor-price frontier, a trade-off exists between real wage and rate of interest. He also demonstrated that, in the case of switching techniques, the process leads to an incoherent order between pairs of unchanged technologies that are dependent on the interest rates prevailing in the market. In conclusion, a simple neoclassical model, in Samuelson's view, was still appropriate and could be regarded as a stylized version of a modern heterogeneous capital goods model.

SOME CONCLUSIONS ON CAPITAL CONTROVERSY AND GROWTH

To some extent, this chapter has tried to shed light on some of the central subjects in capital controversy and economic growth associated with the Cambridge and MIT writers in the 1960s. Most of this chapter has revolved around controversy and criticism of the Cambridge viewpoint that emerged during the discussion of the various theories and models. Since the end of the nineteenth century, there has been a series of capital controversies within neoclassical economics, but the most important seem to have been in three periods: (1) in the high period of neoclassical economics in the 1890s, when the debate focused on the marginal productivity theory of distribution, with its implications for the policy questions about income distribution between wages and profits; (2) in the 1930s, when the debate concentrated on the homogeneous fund of values versus the heterogeneous collection of capital goods within the policy context of the Great Depression and the concept of average period of production; and (3) in the 1960s (the new neoclassical period), when the debate was mainly about the aggregation and scarcity pricing of capital within the context of growth theory.

Many questions have risen about the meaning of capital and have generated a huge amount of literature, the content of which sometimes has common features but, more often, seems to be very dissimilar and numerous works were concentrated on the measurement of capital rather than the meaning of capital. Sraffa (1960) tried to provide some crucial insights about what kind of society should be analyzed in order to translate it into a theory. He demonstrated that, in the supply-and-demand approach, it is impossible to find a unit that is independent of the distribution process and a price with which to measure capital. Sraffa argued that the approach of the classical economists, in particular Marx – whose crucial organizing concept was the surplus, its creation, its distribution, and its use – was a more fruitful way to view the economic process. He criticized the neoclassical theorists and the traditional economic theory and tried to create a new theory of value, which unfortunately had very few followers. Regardless of the new theory of value (and capital) developed by Sraffa, some years later, David Levhari claimed that Sraffa's results, especially his demonstration of capital-reversing and reswitching, were not true for a model of an economy as a whole but only for a model regarding a single industry (Levhari 1965). The claim of Levhari was soon refuted by Pasinetti (1966), whose theories proved to be true also in the case of the economy as a whole.

It is pretty much known that the Cambridge school of the United Kingdom has followed in many aspects the path traced by Ricardo and Marx, whereas the Cambridge school of Massachusetts has followed the pure marginalists like Jevons, Walras, Clark, and the Austrian school. According to the school of Massachusetts, an increase in the wage relative to the rate of interest helps improve the technique of production, thereby increasing the output per head. J.B. Clark (1891) introduced a set of relations within the theory of capital in order to make the output written as a function of homogeneous capital and labour. He maintained that, if capital increases, supposing that all other factors remain unchanged, interest falls and, as the labour force increases, wages also fall. The inverse relation between factor proportions and relative factor prices, which provides a connection between factors of production, commodity markets, and technical progress has been a key for both theories of capital (those of the former neoclassical school of the 1890s and the later neoclassical school of the 1960s).

Joan Robinson, having initiated the controversies, declared that the neoclassical theory of capital, in the case of heterogeneous capital goods, was not more valid. She criticized the neoclassical concept of one-commodity capital (or homogeneous capital) as a variable of the aggregate production function with continuous factor substitution. She, among others, pointed out that, in the case of heterogeneous capital goods and discrete production techniques, the value of capital varies with factor prices and depends on the distribution of income between wage and profits. Without a doubt, the core of neoclassical economics, the general equilibrium model, has never been under such serious attack in the course of the controversies as it was in the 1960s and the aggregation of capital was the central point in the controversies of Cambridge schools. Cohen and Harcourt, writing on general equilibrium theory involving the Cambridge capital controversies, indicate that:

> The general equilibrium approach revitalized Robinson's concerns about equilibrium. Theoretical work, specifically, the disappointing Sonnenschein-Mentel-Debreu stability results, found no particular reason to believe in the stability of the general equilibrium outcome. In discussing these results, Hahn (1984, 53) wrote: "[T]he Arrow-Debreu construction ... must relinquish the claim of providing necessary descriptions of terminal states of economic processes." (Cohen and Harcourt 2003, 207)

The unstable general equilibrium process raised many issues and put in jeopardy the whole concept of general equilibrium as the end of the economic process following variables shifts, parameter changes, and comparative statics.

The neoclassical school tried to defend itself by using all the knowledge it had regarding the aggregation of capital.

The first line of defence of the neoclassical school was to examine the necessary conditions for writing heterogeneous capital goods as homogenous capital goods in a production function. Samuelson was the first defender of the neoclassical school to demonstrate that a fixed proportion model could be used to obtain a simple neoclassical theory of capital. Unfortunately, his theory of capital did not hold for long. It was soon suggested that Samuelson's results were purely causal, because his assumption of an equal capital-labour ratio reduces the two-sector model to a one-sector model; therefore there is no need to measure the value of capital because capital and output are the same.

The second line of defence of the neoclassical school was that a fixed proportions model of production function introduces the problem of a choice of discrete techniques (Harcourt 1972).

Given that there is no reason to believe that exists only an inverse relation between interest rates and capital intensity in real terms, a technique with low capital intensity may be profitable at more than one rate of interest, and a reswitching process from technique alpha to beta (and vice versa) will take place. Solow (1963), on his social rate of return, tried to prove the necessary conditions for reswitching to occur (although later it was proved that the reswitching process is prevented if there is enough substitutability among production factors and sufficient change in relative commodity prices). Despite all of this, the relative importance of reswitching remained uncertain in both Cambridge schools. Neither of them was able to give good reasons for reswitching techniques to occur unless they decide to set a priori the inverse relation between the rate of interest and capital intensity. Several authors of both schools attempted to answer their critics by rewriting the parable in terms of capital malleability, and the idea of capital vintages was introduced to escape the complexity of technical problems related to the accumulation of capital over time. Solow was the first neoclassical scholar to get liberated from the capital measurement problem by emphasizing the social rate of return on investment in order to avoid the problems (and the critics) connected with the measurement of capital and its marginal product. What the critics were really saying is that neoclassical economists have confused the return on capital as a property with capital as a factor of production on a par with the other factor, labour. Later they argued that the concept of capital and its marginal product are meaningless in the aggregate, and, thus, the neoclassical theory of distribution holds. Therefore, the acceptance of the theory of distribution does not reject the neoclassical paradigm as the Cambridge critics would have done.

Another characteristic that distinguishes the two Cambridge schools is the rationality of individuals. For Cambridge economists in the United Kingdom, individuals conform to a simple rule of savings that implies constant propensities to save for workers and capitalists. In a different way, the neoclassical authors of MIT suggest that investment tends to concentrate on elaborate programs of optimal capital accumulation, which maximize the discounted flow of profits. British Cambridge economists argued for a return to the classical political economy vision and especially to Keynes' observations. In fact, Robinson analyzed investment decisions in terms of what Keynes called "animal spirits," spontaneous urgent actions rather than inactions. Capitalists and the rate of profit that is associated with saving of different classes in a society are the main source of the capitalist system. These resources ensure the reproduction and the growth of the economy as a whole. The Cambridge School distinguishes the rate of profit, which is the rate of return on investment, from the rate of interest, which is the hiring price of capital. The neoclassical authors of MIT do not make this distinction. For them, the rate of interest and profit are considered similar terms to explain the same concept of the rate of return on investment.

Bliss's book in capital theory and distribution of income published in 1975 was for many economists and historian regarded as the ultimate neoclassical treatment of capital theory that ended the Cambridge controversies. In fact, in the late 1970s and early 1980s this argument fell out of favor as the new theories in endogenous growth and real business cycle got the headlines.

In present days, decades after the controversies took place, many things have changed especially with the introduction of endogenous growth theory and for many twenty-first century economists the capital controversies were nothing more than a tempest in a teapot that disrupted for some time the course of economics and delayed the event of endogenous theories. Cohen and Harcourt wrote that:

> The Cambridge controversies, if remembered at all, are usually portrayed today as a tempest in a teapot over anomalies involving the measurement of capital in aggregate production function models, having as little significance for the neoclassical marginal productivity theory of distribution as do Giffen good anomalies for the law of demand. When theories of endogenous growth and real business cycles took off in the 1980s using aggregate production functions, contributors usually wrote as if controversies had never occurred and the Cambridge, England contributors had never existed. (Robinson and Sraffa obliged by dying in 1983). Since neoclassical theory has survived and the challengers have largely disappeared, the usual

> conclusion is that the "English" Cantabrigians were clearly wrong or wrong-headed. (Cohen and Harcourt 2003, 199)

The neoclassical school, with its one-commodity model and two-factors production function (and the general equilibrium analysis), was able to place the basis for empirical work by considering the relative scarcities as a principal feature that is empirically important in order to determine the relative price of production factors. In doing so, they were successful. This is also one of the main reasons that neoclassical models were accepted by the large community of international economists and were dominant in most textbooks in economic growth. In contrast, the British Cambridge School was not able to provide empirical work for their models because of the causes and effects of capital investment. Despite their attempts, most of the Cambridge economists in the United Kingdom lacked empirical work on the causes of capital investment, and what is more important, failed to develop new sets of theoretical instruments in order to avoid the problems associated with general equilibrium and the one-commodity capital-good theory. Hence, they remained largely ignored by modern economists, who started relying on modern tools and new methods to better explain the general equilibrium and the aggregation of capital.

7

Theories of Growth and Convergence between Poor and Rich Countries: The Early Development Theories

Many ideas in economic theory by and large try to filter through gradually from the world of intellectual construct to the world of practical decision. Those who maintained that growth models have contributed very little or nothing to the formulation of economic policy would benefit from reading the policy proclamations and analyses of the late 1950s and early 1960s. Comparing present-day economic policies with those of the first two decades after the Second World War demonstrates clearly the improved standard of reasoning with regard to the problems of economic growth. Formal models of economic growth in the 1950s and 1960s have played their part in changing the intellectual atmosphere.

As seen in previous chapters, the years 1955 and 1956 represented an important interval in the history of growth analysis. This was the period when Solow, Swan, and Tobin launched their neoclassical models, thereby providing a boost to empirical growth analysis. The model of Solow has shown that, independently of economic conditions, in every system, the tendency toward equilibrium in the long period is inevitable. The initial conditions of growth could be better or worse, but unavoidably, the rate of growth would increase or decrease until the attainment of equilibrium. Therefore, poor countries might grow faster than rich ones because they have a lower K/L ratio, and in the long run, all countries must have identical production per capita, Y/L. According to Solow, there must be a catching up, or a shortening gap, between rich and poor countries. Therefore the convergence is the relation of inverse proportionality between the rate of growth of productivity and the starting level of income per capita.

In addition, based on the assumption of the Solow-Swan model, several countries will have the same rate of growth in equilibrium. It is clear that, in many underdeveloped countries, the implication of Solow's model has not taken place.

Solow's model remains, however, a fundamental point in the growth theory of the postwar period, and it has not been entirely abandoned but rather integrated.

The main economic characteristics that have deeply marked the second half of the twentieth century are inequalities in incomes, in all their varied aspects. It is believed that technical progress has been continuously widened and modified. The final impression emerging from the study of growth theory is that the most appropriate economic theories are those that increase the possibilities of surveying the problems of income distribution and do not leave them at the margin.

The theoretical models are often abstractions from concrete conditions of particular countries, including the rich ones. It seems complicated, but theory must necessarily simplify complex realities, trying the elements that are common to many economies.

For example, low growth in England in the postwar period could be explained by similar phenomena that can explain the missing growth in Africa or the slow economic expansion in Latin America.

Different economists after the Second World War, based on the concept of growth, started a common effort to generate a theory of development and to define the appropriate policies of the developed countries toward the problems of the poor nations in Latin America, Africa, the Middle East, and Asia.

In the 1950s many economists were called to study the problems of underdeveloped nations. For example, the CENIS (Center for International Studies) at MIT mobilized a team of distinguished economists in 1952 to study the problems of growth in Asia and Latin America. Some of the members of the team were Max Millikan, W.W. Rostow, Everett Hagen, Benjamin Higgins, Wilfred Malenbaum, and P. N. Rosenstein-Rodan. There was also a group of other researcherss from political science and sociology (Lucian Pye, Dan Lerner, and Ithiel de Sola Pool) who contributed extensively. CENIS's work on development began formally and included intensive studies on South Asia, Latin America, and Africa. The complete synthesis of the collective work was published in a short book entitled *A Proposal: Key to an Effective Foreign Policy* (Millikan and Rostow 1957). This study mainly considered some key proposals for development assistance and political achievements (including full independence) in developing countries around the world. The authors proposed a much-expanded, long-term program of American participation in the international community to provide sufficient external capital to match the capacity of those developing countries to absorb capital. The Millikan-Rostow book recommended to the United States of America an international plan to help underdeveloped countries with technical assistance and support for education in order for them to generate sufficient resources to enlarge their absorptive capacity.

Rostow published a series of articles and several works related to the possible connection between the abstractions of growth theories and the reality of several countries. In the late 1950s he considered the stages of economic growth and the concept of takeoff. He argued that two centuries of growth had yielded five stages in the life of modern economies: the traditional society; the preconditions for takeoff; the takeoff itself; the drive to maturity; and the age of high mass consumption. His genius theory was intended to put into an economic model the growth of nations as a result of historical and political changes. There were many other economists and theorists who, like him, tried to explore this path.

Hence, in this chapter, some of the development theories and the work of early mainstream development theorists such as Kuznets, Lewis, Myrdal, Rostow, Chenery, Hirschman, Harris, and Todaro will be considered.

INEQUALITY, INCOME, AND GROWTH: THE KUZNETS HYPOTHESES

Broadly speaking, for many economists, economic development is the analysis of the progress of nations. The economy of development is not only "real economics" but also a combination of sociology, anthropology, history, politics, and, often, ideology. Early economic development theory was merely an extension of conventional economic theory, which associated development with growth and industrialization. Latin American, Asian, and African countries were seen mostly as "underdeveloped" countries, compared to the well-established institutions and superior standards of living in Europe and North America. After the Second World War, with the increasing number of independent countries in the Third World, the problem of development and economic growth came to the attention of politicians, policy makers, and economists.

Economic historians and policy makers responded to this challenge by taking into consideration the historical experience of industrialized countries like the United Kingdom, the United States, Germany, France, Russia, and Japan. Some economists mostly focusing their research on theory and abstract economic models went back to the Harrod-Domar model (of short-term Keynesian theory), arguing that higher savings rates had to be applied to Third-World countries in order to catch up with industrialized nations. But other economists and social scientists disagreed with this approach, because they assumed that there is an enormous disparity between poor nations scattered around the globe and advanced countries mostly concentrated in Europe and North America (with the exception of Japan).

It was in this scorching debate that, in 1948, Simon Kuznets[1] suggested an idea that he then converted into a proposal to study in a comparative manner the economic growth of several nations. His proposal consisted of taking the quantitative data from the national income accounts and building the groundwork and the analytical structure for comparative studies among nations (Kuznets 1949). This proposal was first presented to the National Bureau of Economic Research (NBER) in the United States as a new program of empirical studies based on the economical realities of different nations and continental areas. It was turned down, perhaps because of skepticism among economists in NBER about the quality of the data likely available. Persisting in the scope of his research, Kuznets finally found support from the Rockefeller Foundation and Social Science Research Council (SSRC), which established a Committee on Economic Growth with Kuznets as chairman. Prior to the Second World War, empirical studies on economic development had been incomplete. Most probably one of the best-known works was the *Conditions of Economic Progress* of Colin Clark (1940), whose conclusions recommended that economic growth in many countries comes with a shift from primary to secondary and to tertiary industrial structure, and there hardly could be a deviation from this linear pattern of growth. Kuznets was more than convinced that a complete different approach had to be taken to study the progress and development of different countries. He in fact suggested that the measurement of national income must be done by type of product, industry, factor share, and size of income rather than by large structural sectors, which give little explanation about progress and growth. He also computed studies on demographers' work on population and labour force, which led to a much more comprehensive understanding of the economy of development.

Kuznets was one of the earliest workers on development economics, in particular collecting and analyzing the empirical characteristics of developing countries (Kuznets 1965, 1966, 1971, 1979). His major thesis was that today's underdeveloped countries possess characteristics different from those that the industrialized countries faced before they developed. This theory helped put to an end to the simplistic view that all countries went through similar "linear stages" in their history, and it created the new field of development economics, which then focused largely on the analysis of modern underdeveloped countries.

Among the most important findings of Kuznets (1966) was the substantial level of consistency in the nature of modern economic growth in countries varying in institutional structure culture and historical background, such as the United Kingdom, the USSR, and Japan (Kuznets 1966, 456–506). Another finding from his empirical studies was that there is evidence of high rates of output growth and similar reallocation of resources common to many countries undergoing economic development (Kuznets 1973). His data demonstrated that the economic systems of all countries undertaking modern economic growth change in a quite similar way. Kuznets (1965), among others, found also certain regularities (about six) in developed countries.[2] First, for thirteen developed countries, the rise in per capita product was attained with no apparently great rise in inputs per capita measured in simple conventional terms. Only one-eighth of the growth in output per capita over the nineteenth century might be explained by the growth in inputs per capita. Second, the high rate of structural change and the high rate of output per unit of inputs are basic characteristics of modern economic growth. Third, the later the ingress into economic modernization, the higher the rate of growth tends to be after several decades of the initial period. Fourth, the high growth rates of the 1950s in Europe and Japan were considered a "catching up" in a double sense of recovering from material losses sustained during the Second World War and of compensating for the failure (during and immediately after the war) to exploit technical changes. Fifth, the rate of growth of product per capita in the United States during the 1950s was low compared to the long-term average, but the growth in product per worker was relatively high. Sixth, the size of a country has a profound effect on the structure of its economy and, particularly, on the level to which a country will be involved in foreign trade (Rostow 1990). Large countries, in terms of population, normally trade less than small countries because most resources are already found in their immense domestic market.

Kuznets emphasized the importance of technological progress and knowledge combined with institutional and social arrangements. High growth rates are achieved when there is a high rate of technical change. The effects of technological progress and the rise of income per capita induce changes in the industrial structure, urbanization, and factor mobility. The process of industrialization provokes increasing income inequality as the labour force shifts from low-income agriculture to the high-income sectors. Kuznets suggested that in the early stages of development, the rate of growth and income inequality both rise. For developed countries, income inequality shows a tendency of narrowing, whereas for less-developed countries, it does not show this trend. The trend comes as a result of a secular shift from the low-income and low-inequality agriculture sector to the high-income and medium-inequality industrial sector. This finding leads to the suggested "inverted U"–shaped relationship between the rate of growth and income inequality. The so-called Kuznets curve (1955) asserts that inequality increases over time until it reaches a certain level of distribution; then, at a critical point, it begins to decrease. In the early stages of development, when investment in physical capital is the main instrument of economic growth, inequality promotes growth by deploying resources toward those who save and invest most. Conversely, in the mature economies, human capital takes the place of physical capital as the main source of growth, and inequality slows down growth. On more advanced levels of development, inequality starts decreasing, and industrialized countries are again characterized by low inequality because of the smaller weight of agriculture in production (and income generation). The diagram in figure 7.1 shows an inverted U curve with income inequality, or the Gini coefficient, on the *Y* axis and economic development, or per capita income (GDP per capita), on the *X* axis.

There is a U shape because inequality tends to increase in the early stages of development and decline slowly afterward. Kuznets[3] gives two reasons for this historical phenomenon: (1) the increasing efficiency of the established urban population decreases inequality within the industrial sector; (2) the growing political power of the poor urban population results in protective and supportive legislation, thereby increasing

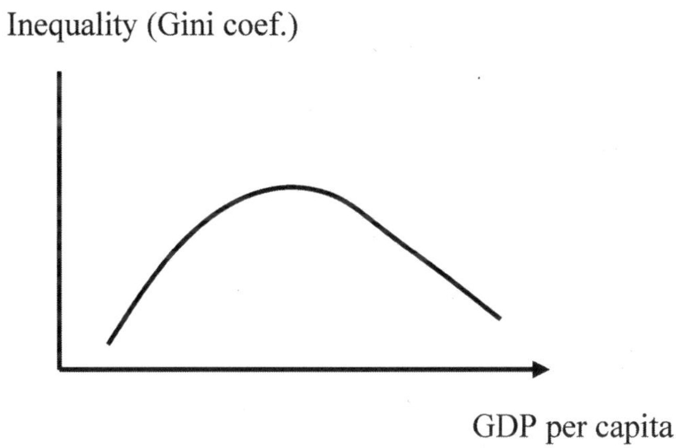

Figure 7.1 The Kuznets curve

the overall standard of living. The Kuznets curve was criticized by many economists on the grounds that he used cross-sectional data from many countries during the same period rather than time series data that show the progression of individual countries' development (Van Zanden 1995). The U shape in the curve comes not from progression in the development of individual countries but rather from historical differences between countries. In his data set, many of the middle-income countries were in Latin America, a region with historically high levels of inequality. The Latin American countries are richer than countries such as India, Sri Lanka, or Bangladesh, but they are poorer than Korea or Taiwan. Both sets of Asian countries have lower inequalities than their Latin American counterparts. It seems that the inverted U is just an artificial consequence of the Latin American countries (the Latin effect). Ahluwalia (1976) checked this in his study using a particular regression function. He analyzed a sample of sixty countries – forty developing, fourteen developed, and six countries part of the socialist camp – with GDP measured in US dollars at the 1970 prices. He then divided the population of each country into a sample of five quintiles, running from the quintile of the population with the lowest income share to the quintile with the highest income share. For each quintile, Ahluwalia used the following regression,

$$Si = A + by + cy^2 + D + error \quad (7.1)$$

where *Si* is the income share of the *i*th quintile, *y* is the logarithm of per capita GNP, and *D* is a dummy variable that takes the value, 1, if the country in question is socialist and, 0, is otherwise; whereas *A*, *b*, and *c* are coefficients to be estimated from regression. By drawing several graphs, it is easy to understand that a U shape can occur if *b* and *c* are of different signs. For example, if $b > 0$ and $c < 0$, the shape that results is precisely an inverted U. Conversely, if $b < 0$ and $c > 0$, then the graph must take the form of an upright U. In the case of the Latin American countries, a dummy variable is placed in the regression (7.1), which is interpreted as the importance of being Latin American per se (as far as inequality is concerned).[4]

Deininger and Squire (1996) used the data set containing an average of more than six observations per country and found that the Kuznets inverted-U hypothesis disappears. This gives the impression that structural differences across countries or regions may create the illusion of an inverted U when, indeed, there is no such correlation in reality. When countries are examined one by one, there is some evidence of a direct inverted-U relationship among countries (for example, it is true for the United States, United Kingdom, Mexico, Trinidad, the Philippines, and India). In 80 per cent of the sample, there is no significant relationship between inequality and income levels (Deininger and Squire 1996). The failure of the inverted-U hypothesis over the cross section led to economists considering other methods to validate that U curve. Even though the U curve was proved to be true only in Latin American countries, the law of Kuznets in the late 1950s opened new horizons to extended studies about the real problems of inequality and poverty in the Third World. It also proved that the underdeveloped world is not characterized by the same phenomena, but rather it differs from country to country, region to region, and continent to continent, and even within a country from area to area. The underdeveloped countries usually tend to exhibit analogous patterns of development, although, in many cases, big differences do persist, and the Kuznets curve was the proof.

A MODEL OF ECONOMIC DEVELOPMENT WITH UNLIMITED SUPPLIES OF LABOR IN LEWIS

The main focus of Arthur Lewis's[5] research was to uncover the fundamental forces determining the rate of economic growth. It was this major topic that was addressed in his 1954 pioneering paper on unlimited supply of labour and then developed further in his 1955 treatise on the theory of economic growth (Lewis 1954; 1955, 226–38). For Lewis, the main problem about development was to understand the process by which a community that was previously saving and investing 4 or 5 per cent of its national income or less converts itself into an economy where saving runs from 12 to 15 per cent of the national income (1954, 225–6). The solution Lewis gave to the problem was based on the idea of nineteenth-century classical economists that was developed in order to provide a dualistic model of the development process. He dropped the assumption made by neoclassical economists that the supply of labour was fixed, and added instead, the assumption that it was infinitely elastic. As Colin Clark in his *Conditions of Economic Progress* (1940) and Kuznets in his *Economic Growth and Income Inequality* (1955) had proposed, Lewis suggested that the effect of economic growth on income distribution is more appropriate to advanced economies that can afford to take the growth of output as given and explore its effect on income distribution. Unfortunately, researching the effect of economic growth of output in underdeveloped countries does not help in investigating income distribution, because these countries have more primary concerns like providing basic needs for the entire population, etc. However, Lewis is concerned with underdeveloped countries, where the most relevant question is: how does a change in income inequality affect capital formation and eventually economic development? To answer this, he set up a model in which the economic system comprises two distinct sectors: the capitalist sector and the subsistence sector. The capitalist sector has higher productivity, higher income, and higher wages per head than the subsistence sector. The subsistence sector is both at a very low level and stagnant, with negligible investments and a low rate of technical progress. In the capitalist sector, the wage rates are set at levels higher than the supply price of labour. The subsistence sector contains a reservoir, which provides an elastic labour supply to the capitalist sector. The rate at which labour is transferred from subsistence to capitalist sector depends on the rate of capital accumulation in the latter. The surplus of output over wages is captured by capitalists as profit. The process of growth occurs as the share of profit in national income rises and profits are directed to new investments. Unlimited supplies of labour ensure that capital accumulation is sustained over time. The growth of the capitalist sector is essentially at the expense of subsistence sector. When the surplus labour in the subsistence sector is exhausted, the wages in the subsistence sector begin to rise, thus pushing up the wages in the capitalist sector and reducing the profit level. The process of capital accumulation slows down, and at some point in the process, the transfer of labour from the subsistence to the capitalist sector comes to reflect sectorial differences in the marginal productivity of labour. During the structural economic transformation, both wages and profits are determined by marginal productivity.

Lewis was aware that the various reformulations derived from his model could be useful, including those produced by Fei and Ranis (1964, 534–5), but he was more than convinced that his specifications were central to his analysis. He observes,

> The divisions of the economy into two sectors had to turn on profits. The two sectors are a capitalist and a non-capitalist sector, where a "capitalist" is defined in the classical sense as a man who hires labor and resells its output for profit. This distinction was vital for my purpose. Other writers, with different purposes, have made different divisions. A now popular division is between industry and agriculture, but capitalist production cannot be identified with manufacturing. The model is intended to work equally well whether the capitalists are agriculturalists or industrialists. Indeed in its first version the model presupposes that the capitalist sector is self-sufficient and contains every kind of economic activity. This explanation may serve to refute the charge that the model identifies economic growth with industrialization. (Lewis 1972, 76)

Agriculture in Lewis's model is assumed to be stagnant, and this gives a static bias to the apparently dynamic model, which at points is misleading. The emergency of production in agriculture – for example, cash crops grown by individual producers – has regularly been a key instrument in economic development; in fact, in this type of agriculture, there is an important capital formation, and this leads to the suggestion that the small-scale agriculture is often far from stagnant. Although many underdeveloped countries have progressed rapidly over the past decades, they are still at low levels. All of the countries that are now relatively developed have, at some time in the past, gone through a period of rapid acceleration, over the course of which their rate of annual net investment has moved from 4 to 5 per cent to over 10 to 12 per cent. That is what is called an industrial revolution. Taking India as a classic example, where the net investment rate in the early 1950s was around 4 to 5 per cent of the national income and real income per capita nearly stagnant, Lewis (1954) suggested that, to achieve a 1.5 or 2 per cent increase in the standard of living, a 12 per cent net investment rate would be necessary (a figure achieved in about the 1960s). Lewis argued that the rapid growth of the British economy during the Industrial Revolution had come as a consequence of capital accumulation, a high level of trade, and significant advances toward a money economy. Despite the huge efforts in industrialization and economic growth, the present underdeveloped world is still far from this favourable scenario.

Lewis, in his research, explores the source of savings (forced saving via inflation, public borrowing, taxation, and foreign borrowing), putting forward that underdeveloped countries save little because their capitalist sector is too small to put in motion a deeper process of transformation capable of leading to a major rate of growth per capita and a major structural development. In fact, he states,

> This means that the fundamental explanation of any "industrial revolution," that is to say, of any sudden acceleration of the rate of capital formation, is a sudden increase in the opportunities for making money; whether the new opportunities are new inventions, or institutional changes which make possible the exploitation of existing possibilities. If the process of converting an economy from a 5 to a 12 per cent saver is essentially dependent upon the rise of profits relatively to national income, it follows that the correct explanation of why poor countries save so little is not because they are poor, but because their capitalistic sectors are so small. (Lewis 1955, 233–5)

Lewis's perspective on the development of the world economy is considered concisely in *The Evolution of the International Economic Order* (1978a). For him, the Industrial Revolution in the nineteenth century challenged the rest of the world in two ways. The first challenge was to imitate developed countries, and the second was to trade with developed countries. Because the underdeveloped countries have followed the model of trading with industrialized nations, the problem that Lewis wished to solve was related to the differential in the relative prices of products of industrialized and underdeveloped countires. The dilemma of the world economy model is the factoral terms of trade of the domestic food-producing sector between the developed and underdeveloped world. In the world economy model, Lewis considered what he describes as overpopulated countries (i.e., India, Pakistan, Bangladesh, etc.) that produce products in sectors in which there is an unlimited supply of labour available. In a national economy model, he is concerned about how surplus labour might lead a particular country toward rapid development. Conversely, in the world economy model, he seeks to show how surplus labour on a world scale can limit the possibilities for development in a particular country. His countervailing discussion in a national (closed) economy was rising agricultural productivity as a condition considered ideal for development. A rise in productivity in the subsistence sector tends to push up wages in the capitalist sector, but this happens only if the subsistence producers were allowed to keep the benefit of the increased production. A capitalist sector, which has a higher productivity than the subsistence sector, develops by drawing labour from a non-capitalist subsistence sector.

With reference to "comparative advantage," Lewis argued that small, densely populated countries like Haiti or Jamaica should specialize in manufacturing and importing food from other countries that have a comparative advantage in agriculture, such as the United States, Mexico, or Canada. Foreign investors should be encouraged to introduce modern technology and invest capital. Broadly speaking, industrialization had to start by addressing the domestic market. Lewis recommended import substitution combined with agricultural development. He suggested the need to increase productivity in the domestic food-producing sector as a precondition for successful economic development. Lewis's discussion of rising agricultural productivity brought him back to one of his basic ideas: "It is not profitable to produce a growing volume of manufactures unless agricultural production is growing simultaneously. This is also why industrial and agrarian revolutions always go together, and why economies in which agriculture is stagnant do not show industrial development" (Lewis 1954, 173).

The process of accumulation that is initially started by an expanding capitalist sector would increasingly be driven by two sources of capital formation: agriculture and industry. By and large, the overpopulated countries lack a productive agriculture and, thus, could not generate the surplus for an initial agricultural revolution followed by a later industrial revolution. However, once the initial process of accumulation in the capitalist sector has started and after a certain time has achieved an acceptable level, it then becomes possible to raise an agricultural surplus and simultaneously initiate agricultural and industrial revolutions, which then support each other. The ability of Britain and other nations that have followed the process of industrial revolution has been dependent on a related agricultural revolution. To the labour-scarce tropical countries, Lewis proposed a path of development that more closely matches the classic British road. The focus of development policy was to be on raising the agricultural surplus.

The Lewis model also has its weaknesses. It was criticized on the validity of its central assumption that the subsistence sector in developing countries contains an abundance of labour, thus ensuring that the low wage in the subsistence sector dominates the entire economy. Another critique addressed to Lewis is that was that he is a backer of industrialization at the expense of neglecting agricultural development. The assumption that labour migrates from the subsistence sector to wage employment in the capitalist sector was also criticized, especially in light of the urban unemployment observed so often in less-developed countries (Todaro 1969, Godfrey 1979). Another critique charged to Lewis's account was that the notion that "labour surplus" implies a zero marginal productivity of agricultural labour that is highly unlikely. But Ted Schultz later (1964a) proved with his empirical studies from India that the withdrawal of a large portion of the agricultural population did not lead to a decline in agricultural output, therefore indicating a zero marginal productivity.

This assertion was rejected by Sen (1967) as well, who assumed that any movement of the labour force from agriculture is likely to come with a reorganization of production by those who are left behind (i.e., organizational and technological change), avoiding a stagnant situation and a low trend on marginal productivity.

The criticism of Lewis's model, as could have been easily predicted, opened the path to a widespread literature focusing on criticisms of the basic (and simple) model of development and exploration of new methods and more complicated techniques to resolve the dilemma of economic progress and development in Third-World countries. Moreover, Minami (1973), Ohkawa (1972), and Fei and Ranis (1964) have pointed out that Lewis in fact contributed significantly to transition growth theory, the notion of development phases, and the modern economics of development.

THE ECONOMICS OF UNDERDEVELOPED REGIONS IN MYRDAL

The main theme of Gunnar Myrdal's[6] work on development was that the gap between rich and poor nations not only exists but is actually getting wider. As the eminent Swedish scholar pointed out, "Though these inequalities and their tendency to grow are flagrant in our present world, they are usually not treated as a central problem in the literature on underdevelopment and development" (Myrdal 1957a, 18).

Myrdal's opinion is that economic theory is too preoccupied with the concept of equilibrium to be able to explain the divergent movements between rich and poor countries.[7] He observed that an examination of the sources of income inequality between regions within a country provides the model for interpretation of the international differences. Whereas some attention goes to political factors, the analysis is concentrated on the role played by free market forces. Myrdal focused his analysis on a theory of circular causation that leads to cumulative movements. For him, economic growth is conceived as a cumulative process, in part because of a circular interaction of rising investment, income, demand, and investment, and in part because of ever-increasing investment and external economies, which include a working and a training population, easy communications, and the spirit of new entrepreneurship (Myrdal 1957a, 27). This is all set forth in a somewhat emotional language of "spread" effects and "backward" effects.[8] The spread effects are the multiplier effects by which development in one region stimulates development elsewhere, and the backward effects refer to the competitive impact by which expansion in one area may impede similar changes somewhere else. An initial change for the better is conceived to produce a cumulative movement upward; on the contrary, an initial change for the worse sets in motion a cumulative process downward. If a cumulative upward movement is initiated in one region, it gives rise via movements of goods and resources to some adverse changes (backward effects) in other regions, which initiate a downward movement. According to Myrdal, if market forces are allowed free play in the economic relationship between rich and poor countries, the backward effects of growth in the developed countries prevail over the spread effects. In these circumstances, market forces tend, cumulatively, to accentuate international inequalities. In fact, "A quite normal result of unhampered trade between two countries, of which one is industrialized and the other underdeveloped, is the initiation of a cumulative process towards the impoverishment and the stagnation of the latter" (Myrdal 1957a, 99).

As a consequence of the cumulative process, the richer countries get richer and the poor countries get poorer and stagnant. There are also, however, some positive repercussions or spread effects on the poor regions, such as new markets of raw materials for the developing industries in the growing region. Furthermore, there are factors that may decelerate the cumulative process in the growing region and have favorable repercussions on the poor regions: external "dis-economies" arising from excessive concentration of industry and population, rising wage costs, outmoded equipment, and unions, which may drive the industry away. Myrdal is preoccupied with the possibility of widening differences in income levels. His analysis of backward effects points to the real problem of international trade. It is possible to find pockets of stagnation even in developed countries, where the people live in bad conditions compared to the rest of the country. There is no doubt that this could happen internationally. He observed that, as a country becomes richer, the spread effects within it automatically gain in strength relative to the backward effects. But this does not happen internationally, or if it does happen, it happens only for developed countries. Some of the spread effects may be obstructed by the fact that, for example, the communication of ideas and the spread of higher levels of education may be more difficult internationally than domestically. When the analysis shifts to the all-important problem of international as opposed to regional income differences, however, it is clear that "the spread effects are much weaker and the cumulative process will more easily go in the direction of inequality if the forces in the market are given their free play " (Myrdal 1957a, 53).

Myrdal is convinced that the backward effects have prevailed internationally. The he raises is why free market forces should worsen international income differences? The answer seems to be found in the great poverty and weak spread effects within the underdeveloped countries. The weak spread effects in are the outcome of market forces. Myrdal argued that there is also a natural trend in the free play of market forces to produce regional inequalities and that this tendency becomes the more dominant the poorer a country is. These are two of the most important laws of economic underdevelopment and development under laissez-faire. International trade has not helped underdeveloped countries get out of their stagnation as might have been expected. The reason appears to lie in various social and economic aspects of their domestic panorama, which has limited the multiplier effects of export expansion.

The progress of underdeveloped countries will not come through the integration of national economies into a world economy. The situation seems much more complicated that it was for European economies in the nineteenth century. As a matter of fact, the national integration that has been achieved by some countries is not complete and has not been able to expand into other countries. According to Myrdal, the sort of integration suggested by free trade (laissez-faire) would most probably leave the underdeveloped countries trapped in their own stagnation. He disputes the conclusions of standard economic theory that accumulation of capital and distribution of income through trade, migration, and capital flows tend to have the opposite effect in underdeveloped countries. At this point, he stated, "The movements of labor, capital goods and services do not by themselves counteract the natural tendency to regional inequality. By themselves, migration, capital movements and trade are rather the media through which the cumulative process evolves – upward in the lucky regions and downward in the unlucky ones" (Myrdal 1957a, 27).

The progress of underdeveloped countries will not come through the integration of national economies into a world economy. Broadly speaking, the diffusion of new techniques, under competitive conditions, *should* proceed rapidly and without problems. In reality, however, such an argument fails to allow for the wide differences among nations in many factors, such as historical heritage, sociopolitical structure, demographic pattern, and so forth. The absorption of new technologies in underdeveloped countries requires extensive internal adaptations not only in economic organization but also in the whole structure of political, individual, and social life. So far as policy is concerned, Myrdal suggests that economic development cannot be left to the free play of market forces but rather needs to be brought about by policy interferences by the world community, governments, or individual underdeveloped countries.

THE STAGES OF ECONOMIC GROWTH IN ROSTOW

Rostow,[9] in his most ambitious work, *The Stages of Economic Growth* (1960), aimed to link social and economic behaviour in a theory of social and historical change. The stages of economic growth constitute merely one component of the general framework he devised. Rostow brings attention to the periodization of historical analysis of developed countries in phases or stages as opposed to the standard classical continuity. His "takeoff" theory arose as an inescapable discontinuity in the story of Britain, France, Germany, Belgium, the United States, Japan, Russia, Canada, Australia, and others. The theoretical explanation for Rostow to use discontinuities came as a result of so-called leading-sector analysis. There is always a sector that leads progress and development no matter what stage a country is in. "In essence it is the fact that sectors tend to have a rapid growth-phase, early in their life, that makes it possible and useful to regard economic history as a sequence of stages rather than merely as a continuum, within which nature never makes a jump" (Rostow 1960, 14).

The discontinuity was inevitable because modern economic growth is a result of the invention and efficient absorption of increasingly technological changes. Rostow, to better explain the social and economical relationship in historical change, uses two related schemata. The first one is the "dynamic production theory," in which the leading industrial sector interacts with income elasticities of demand and with the social welfare function. The second is the description of economic growth in five stages. The economic generalization of modern history takes the form of a set of stages that constitute a theory of economic development. The stages "have an analytic bone structure rooted in a dynamic theory of production," (Rostow 1960, 13) with population, technology, organization, entrepreneurship, and other factors taken as variables rather than as being fixed. Keynesians and neoclassical economists have tended to generate growth models including several variables without in some way catching up to the essence of growth phenomena. Indeed,

> As modern economists have sought to merge classical production theory with Keynesian income analysis, they have introduced the dynamic variables: population, technology, entrepreneurship, etc. But they have tended to do so in forms so rigid and general that their models cannot grip the essential phenomena of growth, as they appear to an economic historian. We require a dynamic theory of production which isolates not only the distribution of income between consumption, saving, and investment … but which focuses directly and in some detail on the composition of investment and on developments within particular sectors of the economy. (Rostow 1960, 13)

Rostow did not see the economic system as leading growth theorists have modeled it. Growth theory in the 1960s consisted of highly abstract models focusing on a limited number of variables such as output, the production function, and technology. Most of the growth models were characterized by steady growth paths (a general and static equilibrium), and very often growth theorists simply assumed that each of these models could be applied to all countries, including the underdeveloped ones. Instead, by focusing on historical and social changes, Rostow proposed that the process of economic development passes through at least five phases: traditional society, preconditions for takeoff, takeoff, drive to maturity, and the age of high mass consumption. It was necessary to look dig deeply into historical facts in order to identify each stage for different countries or groups of countries. Rostow typically assumed that the key lay in identifying elements common to each stage. And these elements are the "leading sectors" that have benifited from technical progress. Rostow then identified how the technical change, management reorganization, and work attitudes have spilled over from the leading sector into other secondary sectors. The leading sector has attracted steady investments in production process by introducing new techniques, which has helped changed attitudes toward the borrowing and lending process, and caused changes in prices in terms of trade between agriculture and industry, radically transforming the economy from an agricultural- to an industrial-oriented one.

The first Rostovian stage is the traditional society, whose structure is developed within limited production functions. The situation is not static, and there is some growth and change, but there is a ceiling for attainable output per head. Food production absorbs 75 per cent or more of the work force, and a high proportion of income is spent in non-productive outlays. The economy is largely agricultural, and the social structure is hierarchical. The second stage is when preconditions for takeoff are developed, frequently as the result of peaceful or other intrusion from outside. It is a time of transition, with elements from the old period mixed with others from the new. There is a gradual evolution of modern science and of modern scientific attitudes. The productivity of agriculture improves greatly, and social overhead capital is developed. The widening of the market brings the development of trade, increased specialization of production, inter-regional and international dependence, and the creation of large finance institutions. The third stage is the takeoff. Old obstacles and resistances to steady growth are finally overcome, and forces making for economic progress expand and come to dominate the society. The takeoff consists of the achievement of fast growth in those sectors where modern industrial techniques are successfully applied. The takeoff is distinguished from other stages by the fact that concurrent developments make the application of modern industrial techniques a self-sustained rather than an abortive process (Rostow 1959, 7). Growth becomes normal. The period is relatively short and involves greatly increased productive investment, the development of manufacturing, and considerable changes in the social and political framework. The fourth stage is the drive to maturity, an interval of sustained progress and heavy investment lasting about forty years, where modern methods and techniques of production are applied largely in many sectors. During the drive to maturity, the industrial process is diversified, with new leading sectors replacing the older leading sectors of the takeoff, where deceleration has slowed down their expansion. The period is also marked by changes in the work force, the leading industry, and leadership. The fifth stage is the age of mass consumption. High mass consumption is the most common result of maturity with a shift toward durable consumer goods and services. According to Rostow the extension of modern technology is seen as a primary factor able to offer increased security, welfare, and leisure to the work force. It provides increased private consumption, including single-family homes and durable consumer goods for the major part of the population. As a number of countries developed and attained maturity, two phenomena happened: first, real income per capita reached the point where a large number of persons were able to reach mass consumption, surpassing the income required for basic food, shelter, and clothing; and second, the increase of the urban proportion of the total population and the boost of the share of the work force working in offices, services, or in qualified factory jobs, who were in a positition to acquire mass consumption goods of a mature economy.

In the advanced economies, during the maturity age and the stage of mass consumption, Western governments have chosen to invest in social welfare, security, pension plans, health care and education, in order to achieve a diffusion of services on a mass basis.

According to Rostow, takeoff normally occurs when a country simultaneously achieves three conditions: (1) a rise in the investment ratio from 5 per cent of the net national product to 10 per cent; (2) the appearance of one or more "substantial manufacturing sectors with a high rate of growth"; and (3) the emergence of a growth-oriented political, social, and judicial framework. Rostow (1960) showed that his stages of growth deal with the same problem that Karl Marx handled by way of feudalism, bourgeois capitalism, socialism, and communism, and he noted several broad similarities between his growth theory and Marx's theory of development. However, he also pointed out many differences and indicated the mistakes in Marx's theory of capitalism. He believed that his scheme is, in some sense, an alternative to Marxism. He stated, "Marx belongs among the whole range of men in the West who, in different ways, reacted against the social and human costs of the drive to maturity and sought a better and more humane balance in society" (Rostow 1960, 158).

Rostow's *The Stages of Economic Growth* became so famous that right after its publication it attracted widespread interest among development economists and economic historians worldwide as never seen before.[10] It is also true that no other conceptual structure emanating from economists of the developed world drew such attention among scholars of all kinds throughout the Third World itself. Moreover, interest in both worlds crossed disciplinary boundaries: political scientists, sociologists, and anthropologists all weighed in as the conversation went forward.

The main criticism of Rostovian stages of growth was launched at the Konstanz Conference in 1960, which Rostow edited in 1963 under the title *The Economics of Take-Off into Sustained Growth*.[11] The main critics of his work were Kuznets and Solow. Kuznets argued that Rostow's model of takeoff was not realistic and had a deep lack of empirical basis. In a similar way, Solow questioned whether Rostow's work had the character of a theory at all, rather than being a collection of historical facts in growth economics.

The empirically pursued controversy hinged on the issue of whether a takeoff stage for individual countries could be verified. The criticisms can be summarized briefly as follows: Rostow's "theory" was not a pure theory of growth; rather it was taxonomy and, therefore, had no predictive usefulness. The stages could not be precisely identified as time intervals. It could be difficult to distinguish, based on empirical studies, the preconditions for takeoff from the takeoff proper. Most importantly, sustained growth did not always follow the stage identified as "takeoff" in some countries.

A few economic historians, like Gerschenkron (1962, 1969) – another advocate of discontinuity – tended to stand on Rostow's side, whereas the majority of growth economists were among the critics. By carefully reading the work of Gerschenkron and Rostow it seems that the most significant difference lies in their view of the growth process over time. According to Rostow, it is possible to fit the diverse national experience into a single set of stages, including takeoff, drive to maturity, and high mass consumption. Instead, according to Gerschenkron's theory of relative backwardness, the industrialization does not reluctantly tolerate diversity but, on the contrary, leads to expected diversity. The process of industrialization gives rise to a new era in the history of a country; it delineates a particular path of economic development that leads to the stage of drive to maturity, and the epoch of high mass consumption.

It was not until 1978, in *The World Economy*, that Rostow tried to provide empirical proof for his stages of growth (*Rostow* 1978, 11–61, 778–9). On these efforts, he himself established the connection to the Historical School of Economics. Basically, later in his life, his enormous research program was nothing other than an attempt to put straight his earlier critics. Rostow summarized his findings in terms of stages of growth rather than introducing variables affecting the periods of growth, which was valuable as a summary description of historical record though less useful as a theory about how this pattern of growth occurred, and this is mainly because of a fundamental implication that the succession of the various stages was an inevitable function of the mere passage of time.

DEVELOPMENT PATTERNS AMONG COUNTRIES IN CHENERY

Kuznets was concerned with treating growth as a process that, once started, had a number of identifiable structural characteristics associated with different levels of real income per capita. Hollis Chenery,[12] instead, based his perceptions on the foundations laid by Kuznets and Colin Clark and, dealing with structural changes in a large number of countries, he developed his own conception of the stages of growth defined in terms of sectorial analysis. As he states, "The bulk of empirical research in this field has been stimulated by the need to devise better methods for making economic projections and allocating investment resources. Efforts are also directed toward explaining historical changes in the economic structure by means of interindustry analysis" (Chenery 1960a, 649).

Chenery's work was principally cross-sectional. He had a strong interest in the structure of developing countries. He also fully acknowledged the importance of new technologies as fundamental to growth and approached the problem of technological change in a different way from Kuznets. Chenery identified some of the problems Kuznets left unresolved, such as the similarities and differences between countries and time series estimates of development patterns, the role of trade and capital flows in development, and the translation of causal sequences into more formal models and testable hypotheses. His cross-sectional method differs notably from Kuznets's comparison of long historical time series. Kuznets's contribution to structural changes is confined only to a consistent set of changes in the composition of demand, production, trade, and employment, reflecting the different aspects of resource allocation that take place when income levels change without considering policy analysis and cross-country analysis. Chenery uses correlation analysis to establish the average patterns (or "stylized facts") and includes several social categories – remarkably, education and demographic transition. His *Patterns of Development* (1975, Ch. 1–3, 5), written with Moses Syrquin, best considers his method of research and his achievement. The book developed research initiated by Chenery in 1960 (1960b, "Patterns of Industrial Growth") and after that, in 1968 with Lance Taylor ("Development Patterns: Among Countries and Over Time"), which represents an elaboration of the revolutionary work of Clark and Kuznets. Chenery and Syrquin's *Patterns of Development* starts with an analysis of accumulation and allocation of factors by adding the accumulation of human capital to the formation of material capital. The interactions between factor labour and other aspects of the growth process – in particular, foreign trade and international capital movements – were studied. The growth of a country traditionally takes place in an environment in which trade and technology are constantly changing. Chenery interprets growth as a cross-sectional analysis, which helps him find out the development patterns at different levels of income in the presence of international trade and technological progress. Chenery commented that,

> historically, the growth of a country takes place in an environment in which trading possibilities and technology are constantly changing. The growth function derived from cross-section analysis, on the other hand, represents the adaptation of countries at different levels

of income to conditions of technology and trade existing at one time. Ideally, they may be thought of as indicating the path that a typical country would follow if its income increased so rapidly that conditions of trade and technology were relatively constant. (Chenery 1960b, 633)

Intercountry and intertemporal comparisons of economic structure are expected to give some regular (development) patterns regarding how economic structure changes as per capita income increases. As both authors stated, "A development pattern may be defined for a given country by the time paths of variables describing production, domestic use, international trade, and resource allocation in each sector. A comparable cross-section pattern may be defined by the variation in the same set of variables among countries at a given moment in time. The two patterns can be compared by expressing both as functions of per capita income and other variables" (Chenery and Taylor 1968, 391).

The assumptions on the basis of which such development patterns are postulated are: (1) similar variation in the composition of consumer demand with rising income; (2) accumulation of capital – both human and physical – at a rate exceeding the growth of the labour force; and (3) access of all countries to similar technology and access to international trade and capital inflows. Chenery and Taylor (1968) observed ten types of structural characteristics and twenty-seven structural variables,[13] which provide the dependent variables of the statistical analysis and are used to describe the economic structure of different types of countries. A remarkable distinction is made between large and small countries. In their study, they found that the structure of so-called advanced countries has been changing very quickly: employment in manufacturing industry going down; the service sector being the most expansive compared to others; the ownership of capital becoming depressed; and new types of relationships being developed between labour and management. There are important implications for the developing countries. In the course of further development, they are not likely to approach the structure of the advanced countries. Chenery and Taylor (1968), and later Chenery and Syrquin (1975), predominantly used two procedures to compare the economic structures. The first is the one used by Kuznets (1957a, 1966), which consists of exploiting the values of some variables as a basis for subdividing the sample into groups of countries that are expected to have more homogeneous growth patterns. The second procedure is that of Chenery (1960b), which utilizes all the explanatory variables in a single multiple regression equation. Three basic regression equations are used to estimate the cross-country data:

$$\ln x_i = \alpha + \beta_1 \ln y + \beta_2 (\ln y)^2 + \gamma \ln N + \delta \ln k + \varepsilon_1 \ln e_p + \varepsilon_2 \ln e_m \quad (7.2)$$

$$\ln x_i = \alpha + \beta_1 \ln y + \beta_2 (\ln y)^2 + \gamma \ln N \quad (7.3)$$

$$\ln x_i = \alpha + \beta_1 \ln y + \gamma \ln N \quad (7.4)$$

where y is per capita GDP, N is the population in millions, k is the share of gross fixed capital formation in GDP (I/Y), e_p is the share of primary exports in GDP (E_p/Y), and e_m is the share of manufactured exports in GDP (E_m/Y). Regression (7.2) provides an explanation of the variation in the shares of industry and primary production. The non-linear income term $(\ln y)^2$ allows for the decline in elasticities with rising income noted in most industrial sectors. Regression (7.3) determines whether the cross-section relations vary appreciably over the period of observation by including non-linear term $(\ln y)^2$. The last regression, (7.4), establishes the same cross-section relations as regression (7.3) but does so without considering the non-linear term $(\ln y)^2$. Chenery and Taylor (1968) considered more than fifty-four countries and observed that large countries' regressions show the industrial share rising at a rapid rate during the early phase of growth, reaching a peak at around $1,200 of per capita income. Conversely, small countries' regressions show lower income elasticity in the early phases but no tendency for decline at higher levels. Small countries were then divided into two equal groups on the basis of trade orientation toward either primary or manufactured exports. From different series of experiments, Chenery and Taylor (1968) found three development patterns. The large-country pattern, the first, shows industry rising rapidly from 16 per cent of GDP at an income of $100 to 32 per cent at $400; afterward, the increase is slower, reaching the peak share of 37 per cent at $1,200. The development pattern of large countries is primarily determined by the growth of domestic demand because trade and resource differences are relatively insignificant. The second development pattern is related to small, industry-oriented countries and is very similar to the large-country pattern. The only difference is that the share of investment (k) has a less significant effect in small countries because capital goods are largely imported. The third pattern is related to small, primary-oriented countries, where the primary production declines much more slowly than in the other two groups and exceeds industry up to an income level of nearly $800. In this group, the variation in trade pattern has a greater effect on the share of industry than in other development pattern groups. The description of development patterns is later improved by splitting the industrial sector into its components (around twelve industry groups).

The differences among the three development patterns are concentrated in sectors particularly affected by international trade and comparative advantage. Chenery and Taylor (1968) classify sectors on the basis of the stage at which they make their main contribution to the rise of industry. There are, in fact, three stages of industries. Early industries are those that (1) supply essential demands of the poorest countries, (2) can be kept going on with simple technology, and (3) increase their share of GDP relatively little above income levels of $200 per capita. These industries consist largely of food, leather goods, and textiles, which exhaust their potentials for import substitution and export growth at low income levels. Middle industries are those that double their share of the GNP in the lower income levels but show relatively little rise above income levels of $400–$500 per capita. They consist of nonmetallic minerals, rubber products, wood products, chemicals, and petroleum refining, and they account for about 40 per cent of the increase in the industrial share in large countries. Late industries are those that double their share of the GDP on the later stages of industrialization (above $300) and include clothing, printing, basic metals, paper, and metal products. This group includes consumer goods with high income elasticities like durables, clothing, printing, investment goods, and the principal intermediate products to produce them. The analysis based on industrial stages, and the combination of time series and cross-sectional analyses, provides a valuable basis for determining the significance of technological change, trade, and income levels over time.

There are some sectors in which technological change strengthens the cross-sectional pattern and establishes rise or fall in the share of the sector over time. According to Chenery and Taylor (1968), there is no doubt that the introduction of time series and cross-sectional analysis should improve the empirical basis of development theory. In effect, they undertake the difficult task of establishing a typology of developing countries. After taking into account different structural variables, resource endowments, and differences in development strategies, four

Table 7.1 The logistic pattern of growth

Country class by income per capita	*Per capita income (1970 US $)*	*Time in years*	*Growth rate of* GDP *(%)*	*Growth rate of population (%)*	*Growth rate of* GDP *per capita (%)*
(0)	100–140	27	3.81	2.55	1.26
(1)	140–280	35	4.8	2.78	2.02
(2)	280–560	22	5.67	2.5	3.17
(3)	560–1,120	17	6.3	2.2	4.1
(4)	1,120–2,100	14	6.58	2.0	4.58
(5)	2,100–3,360	10	6.21	1.5	4.71
(6)	3,360–5,040	9	5.6	1.0	4.6

Source: Chenery 1986, 232.

principal development strategies are isolated: (1) primary specialization, (2) balanced allocation, (3) import substitution, and (4) industrial specialization. Larger developing countries usually fall into the second and third categories; smaller developing countries fall largely into the first and fourth categories (primary specialization and industrial specialization). Furthermore, the uniformity of patterns among larger developing countries at similar income levels is greater than for smaller countries.

On the basis of an econometric analysis of postwar data from a large sample of countries, Chenery (1986) built up a model of growth process as summarized in table 7.1.

The table shows the general pattern: a low rate of growth at low levels of income, a faster rate of growth at intermediate levels of income, and a dropping rate of growth at the highest levels of income. This pattern mostly holds during the first three decades of the postwar period but does so to a less significant extent after the 1980s.

Most of the processes analyzed by Chenery can be described by S-shaped curves: structural changes being slow during the early stages of development, then faster, and later slowing down again. The development process is described as a complex transition from a moderately constant structure to another. There is a relationship flowing from the level of income to the rate of growth, which, in turn, affects the future level of income as a function of time described by the S-shaped curve. The two ways of describing the logistic pattern are drawn in figure 7.2.

The historical record of economic growth, which has been studied by several economists (e.g., Kristensen 1974, Chenery 1986, Rostow 1978 and 1980), has shown that the historical growth experience over a long

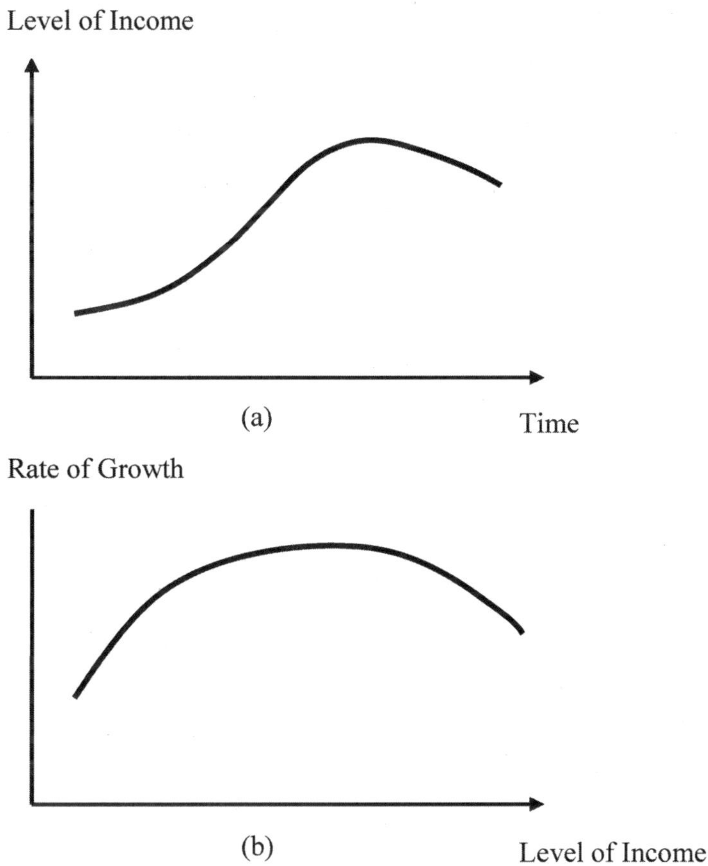

Figure 7.2 The S-shaped curves

period has, in fact, followed the same logistic pattern as depicted by figure 7.2, namely, a tendency for a slow growth in traditional economies with low levels of income, followed by a rapid growth during the period of modernization, and ending with a sluggish economic growth in mature economies.

LABOUR MIGRATION AND URBAN UNEMPLOYMENT IN THE HARRIS-TODARO MODEL

The main focus of Arthur Lewis regarding development, as previously mentioned, was on the organizational dualism and intersectorial labour markets. His study does not provide much insight about intersectorial commodity markets and the intersectorial terms of trade. For the most part, Lewis's research has been qualitative and has not provided any outline with which to analyze the mechanism of labour migration between two sectors (the subsistence and capitalist sectors). Other extensions of the basic Lewis model can be found in the contributions of Todaro (1969), Harris and Todaro (1970), and Fields (1975). Harris and Todaro in a joint contribution introduced the concept that intersectorial labour reallocation is affected not only by the intersectorial wage gap but also by the probability that migrants will obtain a formal job. Michael P. Todaro (1969) built a seminal model to analyze rural-urban migration in less developed countries, extending and formalizing ideas from various authors that followed the work of W. Arthur Lewis (1954). The central assumption of the model is that the decision of the rural worker to migrate depends on the expected wage differential: "The crucial assumption to be made in our model is that rural-urban migration will continue so long as the *expected* urban real income at the margin exceeds real agricultural product – i.e., prospective rural migrants behave as maximizers of *expected* utility" (Harris and Todaro 1970, 127).

In Todaro's analysis, the decision to move is seen as an investment decision tied to expected net returns. The expected returns crucially depend on the probability of getting a job in the modern sector versus a job in the traditional urban sector, the underground economy.

The main objective of the model is to show how the employment rate tends to the state of equilibrium below full employment, even in the long run when there is rural-urban migration. Harris and Todaro (1970) present a general equilibrium analysis in which the wage gap between the rural and urban sectors leads to an inefficient equilibrium. Although the informal sector is now excluded from the model, the concept of expected wage is kept. What establishes the expected wage is employment or unemployment in the urban sector.

The Harris-Todaro model (1970) is described as a two-sector (urban and rural sectors) internal trade model with unemployment. The urban sector is specialized in the production of manufactured goods, a part of which is exported to the rural sector in exchange for agricultural goods. The main deduction from Harris and Todaro's model is that rural-urban migration will continue as long as the expected urban real income at the margin exceeds real agricultural product. Therefore the periodic job selection process exists even when the number of available jobs is exceeded by the number of job seekers. The consequence of this assumption is that the expected urban wage will be defined as equal to the fixed minimum urban wage. The agricultural production function is given as (Harris and Todaro 1970, 128),

$$Xa = q(Na, \tilde{L}, \tilde{K}a) \quad q' > 0,\ q'' < 0 \tag{7.5}$$

where Xa is the output of the agricultural good, Na is the rural labour used to produce this output, $\tilde{L}$ is the fixed availability of land and, $\tilde{K}a$ is a fixed capital stock and q' is a variable factor which calculates the derivative of q with respect to Na. The manufacturing production function is written as

$$Xm = f(Nm, \tilde{K}m) \quad f' > 0,\ f'' < 0 \tag{7.6}$$

where Xm is the output of the manufactured good, Nm is the total labour (urban and rural migrant) used to produce this output, $\tilde{K}m$ is fixed capital stock, and f' is the derivative with respect to Nm. The agricultural real wage determination is given by the following identity:

$$Wa = P\,q' \tag{7.7}$$

where Wa is the agricultural real wage and P[14] is the price of agricultural goods in terms of manufactured goods. The manufactured real wage is given as

$$Wm = f' \geq \tilde{W}m \tag{7.8}$$

The equilibrium condition in the Harris-Todaro model is written as

$$Wa = W'u \tag{7.9}$$

This condition is derived from the assumption that migration to the urban area is a positive function of the urban-rural expected wage differential and is given as

$$N_u = \psi\left(\frac{\overline{W_m} N_m}{N_u} - Pq'\right) \quad \psi' > 0,\ \psi(0) = 0 \tag{7.10}$$

The urban migration, denoted as N_u, is supposed to cease when the expected income differential is zero. The real wage in manufacturing, expressed in terms of manufacturing goods, is equal to the marginal product of labour in manufacturing (as a consequence of profit maximization on the part of perfectly competitive producers) and is supposed to be greater than or equal to the fixed minimum urban wage. The equation for the urban expected wage is written as

$$W_u^{\varepsilon} = \frac{\overline{W_m} N_m}{N_u}, \quad \frac{N_m}{N_u} \leq 1 \tag{7.11}$$

The expected real wage in the urban sector is equal to the real minimum wage $\bar{W}_m$ adjusted to the proportion of total urban labour force employed, N_m/N_u. The Harris-Todaro model describes urban to rural migration in terms of migrants in period t, which is given as a function of the difference between the urban expected wage and the rural (current) wage,

$$M_t = h(p W_u^{\varepsilon} - W_a) \tag{7.12}$$

where M_t is the number of rural to urban migrants in period t and p is the probability of finding an urban job. When considering whether to migrate or not, the labourer will compare what he can expect to earn in the city with what he earns in the rural sector. The urban expected wage is the weighted average of the wages that the labourer can expect to earn if he emigrates (the urban expected wage is the probability of finding a job in the urban sector multiplied by the urban wage plus the probability of not finding a job in the urban sector multiplied by the wage without a job):

$$\textit{expected urban wage} = p W_m - (1-p)0 = p W_m \tag{7.13}$$

where p, again, is the probability of finding an urban job, W_m is the urban wage, $1 - p$ is the probability of not finding an urban job, and o is the wage if the labourer does not find an urban job.[15] The probability of finding a job in the urban sector (p) is

$$p = \frac{E_u}{E_u + U_u} \tag{7.14}$$

where p stands for the probability of finding a job in the urban sector, E_u is the number of urban labourers employed, and U_u is the number of urban labourers unemployed. Equation (7.14) is based on the simplifying assumption that the urban sector is open to everybody and that all workers have the same chance of landing a job; E_u is the total number of workers who will get a job (which is equal to the number of jobs available), and $E_u + U_u$ is the total number of people looking for jobs.

For example, if there are 100,000 people employed in the urban sector and 100,000 looking for a job, then the chance of getting a job in the urban sector is

$$p = \frac{100{,}000}{100{,}000 + 100{,}000} = \tfrac{1}{2}$$

If the probability of finding a job is 0.5 ($p = 0.5$) then, as long as the urban wage is greater than twice the rural wage ($W_u > 2W_r$), migration will continue ($M_t > 0$).

Todaro (1969) along with Harris and Todaro (1970), attained their main conclusions from the assumption that the time horizon of workers is only one period, as they (the workers) take into account more the present value of the expected real income flow rather than the flow of expected real income. As a result, to adjust the mechanism associated with the aggregate supply of workers to the urban sector, the differential in real income for time t substitutes the differential of the present value of flow of expected real income along two or more periods. Todaro gives the reason for this by saying that an "assumption is made necessary by mathematical convenience but is in fact probably a more realistic formulation in terms of actual decision making in less developed nations. In any case, the general conclusions are not sensitive to the assumption" (Todaro 1969, 143).

Harris and Todaro suggest the competitive wage determination as performing two functions. First, it determines the level of employment in the industrial sector, and second, it gives the allocation of labour between rural and urban areas. As long as the wage received by workers exceeds agricultural earnings, there will be migration and urban unemployment. If the authorities will try to put restrictions on migration from rural to urban areas, it will prevent the minimum wage having its effect on unemployment, whereas it will not help increase the level of industrial employment. An optimum condition in the labour market is achieved when a wage subsidy is introduced such that industrial employment will be able to reach the level of full employment where the marginal product of labour is equal in manufacturing and agriculture. According to the Harris-Todaro model, the subsidy will be positive and equal to the difference between the minimum wage and marginal productivity. The original Harris-Todaro model was designed to demonstrate how the urban unemployment rate, in the case of sticky wages, would act as an equilibrating factor in regulating urban migration and, eventually, to show the increasing migration, even in the face of a high rate of urban unemployment. A number of well-known modifications to the original model were published over the years, including outstanding articles by Gary Fields (1975), Joseph Stiglitz (1974b and 1976), Jagdish Bhagwati and T.N. Srinivasan (1974), W. Max Corden and Ronald Findlay (1975), George Johnson (1971), Peter Neary (1981), M. Ali Khan (1980), and Thomas McCool (1982), who have introduced new conditions, hypotheses, variables, factors, assumptions, and methodological contributions to this model. One of the authors of the original model, more than fifteen years after its first publication, declared, "By these standards, the basic Todaro and Harris-Todaro models as modified and refined by successive writers over the past fifteen years seem to have withstood the test of time reasonably well" (Todaro 1986, 568).

IMPORT-SUBSTITUTING INDUSTRIALIZATION AND THE STRATEGY OF DEVELOPMENT IN HIRSCHMAN

The focal point of Albert Hirschman's[16] research activity in the 1950s and 1960s was the explanation of the relationship between the evolution of the social system and the economic process. According to Hirschman (1958, 5–12), economic growth is not an easy process, and an attempt to make it smooth and balanced may reduce the possibilities of growth. Normally, people act in response to disequilibria. The strategies for economic development are chosen to lead, through the creation of disequilibria, to further economic actions to stabilize economic growth. Hirschman is against the plan of overall development programs and the use of investment productivity as a basis for priorities.

The rate of growth is limited not by the availability of savings but rather by the ability to invest. Hirschman admitted that the savings capacity will replace the ability to invest as the factor limiting growth. The main problem of less developed countries is to make investment decisions

(Hirschman 1958, 39). The key to development policy is the best use of resources and the ability to invest. The development of inter-related industrial sectors must be the priority for government. Hirschman argued that unfortunately countries caught in low-level equilibrium traps do not have the resources or efficient institutions to achieve "balanced growth" through planned and coordinated investments that may create positive externalities, which will help develop an infant industrial sector.

The basic development strategy is the discovery of the key investment that will create a high pressure for further investments. In fact, Hirschman suggested that it may be more effective to deliberately create a shortage of investments in a power-generating sector and transportation infrastructure, within limits, and invest in private sectors rather than anticipating them.

As outlined in his 1958 *Strategy of Economic Development*, Hirschman revolted against the importation and application of conventional economic doctrinal prescriptions for economic development. Rather, he insisted that economic development should be analyzed on a case-by-case basis, exploiting original resources and structures to achieve the desired results.

Import substitution industrialization is a process of industrial development driven by the substitution of imported products with domestically produced manufactures. Hirschman (1958 and 1968) and Chenery (1960) were the first authors to develop the theory of import substitution industrialization (ISI). According to Hirschman (1968), there are four motives for ISI: balance-of-payments difficulties, wars, gradual growth of income, and deliberate development policy. For many underdeveloped countries, balance of payments difficulties are fought out regularly by the imposition of quantitative import controls. These controls allow the supply of more essential goods traditionally imported at the cost of non-essential ones, which will be produced domestically. The second motive, wars, causes interruption of international trade and commodity flows and, consequently, provides an incentive to domestic production of imported goods. The third motive, the gradual growth of incomes and savings, stimulates the domestic production of both essential and non-essential goods. The fourth motive, deliberate development policy, is likely to plan the production of essential goods that have previously been imported.

There are two particular stages of import-substitution industrialization. The first stage usually starts with the manufacture of finished consumer goods that before were imported. The second stage involves the domestic production of imported intermediate goods, machinery, and consumer durables (through backward linkage effects). During the first phase, the bulk of new industries are in the consumer goods sector. Industrialization in less developed countries or "late latecomers"[17] in Latin America and Asia – as different from early industrialization in Europe, North America, and Japan – is less learning-intensive and is based on imitation and importation of tried and tested processes and production cycles. According to Gerschenkron, the late industrialized countries of the nineteenth century have at least six main characteristics: (1) a backward country starts its industrialization discontinuously by proceeding relatively at a high rate of growth of the manufacturing sector; (2) the more backward a country's economy the greater is the emphasis on its industrialization and on the creation of leadership entrepreneurs; (3) capital and producers of goods are given priority over consumers goods; (4) the backward countries must press on high mass consumption to reach a faster industrialization; (5) government, policymakers, and institutions must have a greater role to increase the supply of capital and entrepreneurial leadership to the emerging industries; and (6) agriculture plays a less active role in expanding the market for the growing industries (Gerschenkron 1962, 343–4).

Of the six characteristics, only the fifth has played an important role for the "late latecomers" in the mid-twentieth century. In reality, according to Hirschman, the special institutions intended to provide capital and entrepreneurial assistance became important in Latin American countries only after the industrialization process had started.

Another characteristic of import-substitution industrialization is the state of protection for newly established industries through the use of import duties, quotas, or prohibition. These restrictions limit competition and give rise to high production costs, which limit the rate of return and, hence, the overall output. The newly established industries also have to overcome sales resistance because of the preference for the imported goods. According to Hirschman (1968), demand during this phase is easily overestimated for at least two reasons: first, with domestic protection, the price of local products is going to be higher than that of the imported goods; second, market studies based on import statistics often overestimate the domestic market for the infant domestic industry because the statistics include a volume of specialty products that domestic industry is unable to supply. As a result, the new industry is likely to find itself encumbered with excess capacity in the first stage of import-substitution industrialization.

Moving from the first to the second phase, import-substitution industrialization encounters considerable difficulties arising from the characteristics of intermediate and capital goods. The capital goods produced in the second stage are highly capital intensive and are subject to significant economies of scale. Efficient production is possible when domestic markets are sufficiently large, as costs normally rise quickly at lower levels of output.

Going further on this topic, it might be interesting to illustrate that there are three motivations for exhaustion of import-substitution industrialization as it has appeared in Latin America (Hirschman 1968, 13).

First, import-substitution industrialization tends to get stuck or to go into a halt after its first successes as a result of the exhaustion of import-substitution opportunities. It leaves the economy with high-cost plants and limited demand for domestic products because imports now consist of semi-finished materials, spare materials, and machinery equipment essential for maintaining and increasing production of existing facilities. The creation of an industry based on imported inputs sets up resistances against backward linkage investments. In fact, industrialists who have been working with imported materials in the past will think that domestic products are not of as high a standard and as good as the imported ones. They also feel that they might become dependent on a single domestic supplier when they could have suppliers from all around the world. The domestically produced inputs may have to be purchased at a higher price than was paid for the imported goods, which were probably obtained duty free or at a preferential exchange rate. Despite this, the balance-of-payments development and the vertical industrial integration will help the industrialists reach their target of profits. If the decrease of profits in one operation of an integrated industrial process – as a consequence of higher price for inputs – is compensated for by the emergence of profits in another new operation, then industrialists may have good prospects of developing an import-substituting industry with positive results.

The second motivation against the industrialization process is that new industries are affected by the inability to move into export markets. The main reason for this is that new industries have been set up exclusively to substitute for imports, without any export perspective on the part of either the industrialists or the government. The new industries operate under tariff protection plans and suffer high production costs in countries subject to inflationary pressures, which makes it impossible for them to compete in international markets. Domestic industrial investment became attractive, especially in Latin American countries, during the 1960s and 1970s because of the combination of internal inflation, overvaluation of currency, and exchange controls. The overvalued exchange rate permitted the acquisition at favourable prices of machinery and essential industrial materials to create new industries, thus transferring part of the income from the traditional raw material export sector to the new import-substituting industries. At the same time, the exchange overvaluation impeded the new domestic industries from being able to export their products. There are many difficulties for new industries to attempt exporting. To start an export drive, the industrialists must make huge investments in research, design, packaging, and marketing. So, they periodically incur risks and new overhead costs, which will be recoverable only over a long period of successful exporting. The industrialists also must have a certain control over the monetary and fiscal policies of the government in order to create stable foreign operations and minimize possible risks (Hirschman 1968, 28). Policy makers must ensure that domestic industrialists and all investors feel secure about fiscal, monetary, and foreign exchange policies. Any changes in these policies will be communicated to all affected interest groups. In other words, exporting "late latecomers" are faced with political and institutional, rather than purely economic, obstacles.

The third motive against the industrialization process is that new industries are making inadequate contributions to the solution of the unemployment problem. The creation of new industries has not softened, as many policy makers have hoped, the problem of unemployment. The location of industrial facilities near urban areas has attracted a great number of labourers from rural areas in the hopes of finding a stable job. The decision of rural workers to migrate depends on expected wage differential. The rural-urban migration will continue so long as the expected urban real income at the margin exceeds real agricultural productivity. This kind of migration has often created high rates of unemployment and slums in large cities, a problem that remains unresolved today.

Numerous empirical studies of import-substitution industrialization have suggested that less developed countries undergoing this pattern of development in the second half of the twentieth century fall into three major categories: first, we have export-oriented countries or those involved in the aggressive promotion of export production of manufactures after the completion of the first-stage import-substitution industrialization (the so-called four Asian tigers: Hong Kong, Korea, Singapore, and Taiwan); second, we have those countries that moved into second-stage import-substitution industrialization after completing the first stage but later adopted export-oriented policies that were not as successful as those of the four Asian tigers (Brazil, Argentina, Colombia, and Mexico); and third, we have those countries that limited production practically to the extension of the domestic market (India, China, Chile, and Uruguay). Balassa's (1981, 1–26, 108–17) study of these groups of countries shows that the rate of capacity utilization was higher in the first category of countries and increased considerably in the second category after the countries adopted export-oriented policies, but it remained low in the third category. This study showed that export-oriented policies adopted by import-substitution industries in several countries in Asia and Latin America offered a good solution to the problems often occurring after the first stage of import-substitution industries.

SOME NOTES ON STRUCTURALISM

The structuralist approach to development macroeconomics tries to identify specific features of the structure of developing economies that influence economic adjustment and the choice of development policy. This approach has particular significance as it takes into account the structural characteristics when undertaking economic analysis. Early structural development economics were associated with the work of Raúl Prebisch and Brazilian economist Celso Furtado. Raúl Prebisch as the director of ECLA, the Economic Commission for Latin America, from May 1950 to July 1963 elaborated a different development approach called the Latin American Structuralist approach. The industrialization of the Third World started to slow in the immediate postwar period as a result of some factors that were dominating in the developing economies. Some of these factors were: first, the developing countries were not able to compete directly with the industrialized countries, because the terms of trade of underdeveloped countries relative to developed countries had deteriorated and trade barriers had been erected in advanced countries to protect the jobs of the middle class. Second, the availability of low and very competitive wages in the developing economies did not help them, as their output to compete with the industrialized world depended largely on imported capital equipment. This led to what is called the Singer-Prebisch thesis, developed independently by Hans Singer and Raúl Prebisch in the 1950s, which postulates that the terms of trade between primary products and manufactured goods get worse over time, as developing countries that export commodities have the tendency to import less and less manufactured and capital goods for a certain volume of exports.[18] The reason for this trend was that the income elasticity of demand for manufactured and capital-intensive goods is much greater than for primary goods (raw materials). Hence, a steady increase in income will make the demand for manufactured goods rise faster than the demand for primary goods. This simple thesis leads to a conclusion that the structure of the market is to blame for the existence of the inequality among nations, as a result of the division of the world into central and peripheral countries.

The purpose of structuralist economists was to identify specific rigidities, barriers and other structural problems of the developing countries that could, within timeframes and available resources, be adjusted using adequate development policies. One of the barriers and specific rigidities emphasized by this approach is the price mechanism failure of primary goods to act as an equilibrating mechanism in underdeveloped countries to produce a preferred income distribution and a fair distribution of resources able to deliver a balanced growth.

There are at least three main fields or aspects of structuralism, summarized as wholeness, transformation, and self-regulation (Piaget 1971). Wholeness is related to the scope of investigation, which, differently from the neoclassical approach, is paramount for structuralists. Wholeness takes the analysis of economic phenomena as whole, not isolated to one region or country but rather analyzing the world system, centre and periphery together. The most representative models of this wholeness were the North-South models initiated by some prominent structuralists in the 1980s such as Taylor (1983), Dutt (1990), and Chichilnisky and Heal (1986), where a structuralist analysis of the economic relations between the rich North and the poor South came to life. The second aspect of structuralism, transformation, emphasizes changes. Therefore, the structuralist models are dynamic, created mostly for the medium run, 3 to 5 years, where structural and institutional parameters undergo substantial changes and, differently from neoclassical models, do not always converge to a steady state. The third characteristic, the self-regulating aspect of the structuralist models, refers to the internal forces that cause the system to regulate itself and not to external forces. For example, capacity utilization is a key parameter of self-regulation that covers the effects of supply and demand and the labour market in the economy.

The criterion of validity of the theory is important to structuralists. Structuralists – differently from econometrists who base their regressions and results on historic or actual data – must validate their theories first by testing the structure itself. A regression based on real data that has a rational meaning for an econometrist has no meaning for structuralists if the context in which it is run is not valid. The structuralists' models are tested by how well they represent the complex economic reality they seek to model and have to pass what is called the inductive reasoning or "duck test." The "duck test" in economics means that the economists have to create rational models by observing and identifying the habitual characteristics of the reality they model. Based on this, the structuralists have to validate the structure of the model. The structuralists' models provide a comprehensive and realistic approach to the economic system by tracking the data well, based on unambiguous mechanisms they use, regressions and algebraic formulations referred to specific countries. These models, in recent years, have grown and became particularly complex, counting more attributes of the economies under study and, in a different way from econometric models, all parts of the model function independently in order to accomplish simultaneous verification of the historical data. Each component of the model is tested to validate the reality, the historical records, and the model's scope.[19]

As in the other social sciences, structuralists are using more and more simulation models as they become more realistic. Lance Taylor (1990, 1991), in the early 1990s was one of the more prominent late structuralists who completed several studies of simulation models. He pioneered in what is called the *structuralist* approach to development macroeconomics and led numerous projects on economic policy in a number of developing countries where computable models were developed. Recently, Taylor (2004) focused his efforts on reconstructing macroeconomic theory from a general one to a more applied macroeconomic theory of developed and developing countries. His main critique of mainstream economics is that the economists must construct their theories in a way that they can be applied directly to development issues for the developing countries rather than fitting economic theories of industrialized countries to Third World countries. Taylor's analysis of specific structures and institutions of individual countries brought him to the conclusion that the optimization technique has no reason for being the basis of modern economic theorizing. However, his departure from mainstream economics was because he was convinced that the structuralist macroeconomic alternative is more convincing because it has appropriate equations representing the behaviour of significant groups and historical records pertaining to the specific attributes of particular economies and realities.

SUMMARY AND CONCLUSIONS ABOUT THE EARLY DEVELOPMENT THEORIES

For common people the term growth may have the same significance as the term development, but for economists they are two different things. Growth theory focuses on how a nation's output-labour ratio grows over time, while development theory tries to explain why nations possess different standards of living, different income per capita, and different level of infrastructures, and what less-developed countries can do to catch up with advanced countries. The essential difference between a developed and an underdeveloped nation is that one has a high income per capita whereas the other has a lower one. Increasing the national income per capita is not very significant if it is very unequally distributed and does nothing to ease mass poverty and does not focuses on structural problems.

The pioneers of modern development theory emphasized that long-run economic growth is a highly non-linear process. This process is characterized by the existence of multiple stable equilibriums, one of which is a low-income-level trap (Leibeinstein 1954 and 1957, Rosenstein-Rodan 1961, and Nurske 1953). Most of the developing countries are caught in the low-income-level trap, which occurs when there is a low level of capital accumulation reflected in low levels of productive and infrastructural capital, but high rates of population growth. Industrial production is a complicated process and is subject to technical and continuous challenges, which give rise to technological and positive externalities (Rosenstein-Rodan 1961). Several times coordination failures from investments based mostly on individual profit maximization have led to realization of lower rates of return. In contrast, coordinated and synchronized investment programs by entrepreneurs and governments have led to high profits and sustained capital accumulation. It was broadly accepted among development authors that it is necessary to call for government action to drive the economy from an uncoordinated, low-income, non-steady-growth, static equilibrium to a coordinated, high-income, dynamic equilibrium, and golden-growth path.

In the 1950s the discussion of economic development was dominated by a "stage theory" mentality. In fact, stage theorists like Alexander Gerschenkron (1953 and 1962) and Walt W. Rostow (1960), suggested that, given that the advanced countries passed through the same historical stages of economic development, current underdeveloped countries must follow the same path because they were at an earlier stage in the linear historical process. Hollis Chenery and Simon Kuznets argued that the theories of "linear stages" have no basis, because the countries did not exhibit similar patterns of development but rather showed different patterns, based on many factors and not simply on historical facts. Ragnar Nurske (1953) opted for a different approach. By equating development with output growth, he identified capital formation as the essential component to speed up development. Arthur Lewis (1954 and 1955) instead introduced the concept of the "dual economy" and emphasized the role of savings in development. Meanwhile, neo-Keynesians and growth theorists, such as Kaldor, Pasinetti, and Joan Robinson, focused their attention to the issue of income distribution as an important determinant of savings and growth. The modern and convinced Marxian Maurice Dobb (1951 and 1960), who saw insavings formation an important key in the process of growth and structural development, was of the same view.

The process of development, in broad terms of growth models, was acknowledged as the effort of nations to raise their capital-labour ratio (i.e., to accumulate capital at a faster rate than the rate of population growth, in this way increasing income per capita).

In the late 1960s this view gradually disappeared. The idea that underdeveloped nations were merely outmoded versions of industrialized nations was seen as unsustainable. Underdeveloped nations in the modern world face many challenges and problems that industrialized nations never had to contend with when they were "growing up" during the end of the nineteenth century and the beginning of the twentieth century. For instance, a country that is trying to develop and at the same time is trying to integrate itself into an advanced international economic order is something quite particular and not easily theorized. As a result, development economists in the late 1970s and early 1980s began focusing on the particular experiences of underdeveloped nations, with all their peculiar features and structural problems, which brought the materialization of new structuralist models.

The structuralist macroeconomic models have recently become known for their theoretical alternatives used by the economists of developing countries. The work of Lance Taylor in this field represents a milestone, and his research characterizes a new generation of structuralist models that integrate the relationships between the main institutions and social groups, finance and complex macroeconomic realities, historical data, and tests of their inductive reasonableness.

Intermezzo: Overall Conclusions about the Evolution of Growth Theories in the First Four Decades of the Postwar Period

Here we should be able to draw some conclusions regarding the evolution of growth theories in the first three or four decades after the Second World War as things stood in about the 1970s and early 1980s. The primary objective posted at the beginning of this work was to show in a historical context the development of the modern theory of growth, and the second objective was to re-establish what really determines growth in the economy. In other words, what are the variables, determinants, and factors that most affect (directly or indirectly) the rate of growth?

The classical economists, who developed the first systematic theory of growth in the context of an agricultural economy, were so impressed with the force of diminishing returns that they predicted a steady decline of the rate of growth resulting from the steady rise of the pressure of a growing population on a limited area of land. More than a century and a half later, in the early postwar years, neoclassical economists produced an alternative theory, referring mainly to an industrial economy in which the main factor of production was fixed capital. The core conclusion of this theory was that there would be a steady rate of growth of national income, with an endogenous rate of capital accumulation converging to a steady state, given an exogenous rate of population growth and technical progress. The theory of balanced growth was merely an attempt to explain what was assumed to be a stylized fact of the experience of the developed industrial countries in the long run. In addition, the empirical bases of these theories, being confined to the experience of a few countries in particular phases of their economic growth, were insufficient to explain all the causes of growth.

Although the causes of economic growth have been studied since the classical economists, the theories considered here derive mainly from the neoclassical interest in the subject in the first decades after the Second World War. Since then, interest in the subject moved on in the 1970s, when the economists shifted their attention to the short-term macroeconomic problems affecting most countries. Broadly speaking, the theory of growth developed in the 1950s and 1960s is found in almost every textbook on economic growth, and it has been the main diet for successive generations. It is a well-known fact that the theories and controversies on the subject of economic growth in the early postwar decades have improved the understanding of the nature of capital, both as a factor of production in the technical sense and as property in the capitalist sense.

The concentration on the steady state in 1950s was justified as a temporary device, and it was useful as a precise point of reference, but did not become a permanent method. The methods of economic growth discussed by neoclassical theorists did not clarify the very complex relationship between the short, medium, and long run. Most of the models relied on the assumption of the long run, which was not really related with the real features of economic growth. Moreover, despite substantial progress, the representations of technical progress that took place during this period still seemed inadequate, and the links with the microeconomics of invention and innovation were rather vague. Even though at the beginning of the 1960s entrepreneurial expectations started to gain an important role in the models of economic growth, it was still too early to see theorizing about the formation and role of expectations.

Our study of growth theory began with the fundamental notion of macroeconomic balance: savings equals investment. The increase in capital equipment creates more output. The savings rate and the capital-output ratio are the two most relevant parameters of the first models of growth. The capital-output ratio is the resulting increase in capital translated into output. These parameters allow us to derive an equation that relates the savings rate and the capital-output ratio to the rate of growth, which is the basic feature of the Harrod-Domar model. Both the savings rate and the rate of population growth vary with different levels of per capita income, which introduces the possibility that the rate of per capita growth may itself vary depending on the current level of per capita income. In addition, the level of per capita income may lead even for very long periods of time to low-income-level traps as a result of low rates of capital accumulation and high rates of population growth. A certain level of per capita income that not only satisfies basic needs but also helps increase the volume of economic activities may be considered as the threshold beyond which sustained growth occurs. The endogeneity of the capital-output ratio has led to the Solow model, in which the capital-output ratio adjusts with the relative availability of capital and labour. If capital grows faster than the labour force, then each unit of capital has less labour per capita, so the ratio of output to capital falls. If this ratio falls, then savings relative to capital stock falls, and this slows down the rate of growth of capital. The opposite happens if capital grows too slowly relative to labour.

The modern neoclassical theory of growth suggests that, in the long run, capital and working population grow at exactly the same rate. When capital and labour maintain a constant long-run balance, we have the *steady-state* capital stock. Solow in 1956 introduced his first neoclassical model of growth without technical progress, and then in 1957 he added technological change as a third factor to the aggregate production function. The neoclassical point of view was to think of technical change as a steady growth in knowledge that continually increases the productivity of labour. It becomes important to distinguish between the working population and the effective labour, which is the working population multiplied by the individual productivity. The effective labour grows as the result of population growth and technical change. This means that as the long-run capital stock (relative to effective labour) goes to a steady-state ratio, the capital stock per person keeps growing and does so at the rate of technical change. In the same way, per capita income keeps rising in the long run exactly at the rate of technical progress.

As we have seen in the previous chapters, a good part of the modern neoclassical theories of growth were dedicated to analyzing the properties of steady state and to finding out whether an economy not initially in a steady state will move later into a steady state if some conditions are satisfied. The most innovative finding of the modern neoclassical school is that an economy is said to be in a "steady state" if: (1) real output per man grows at a more or less constant rate over long periods of time; (2) the stock of capital grows at (around) a constant rate, exceeding the rate of growth of labour input; (3) the rate of growth of real output and the stock of capital goods tend to be about the same; and (4) the rate of profit of capital has generally a horizontal trend, with the exception of some changes associated with variations in effective demand. The third and the fourth conditions imply that the share of profits in total income will be constant over long periods of time.

The neoclassical concept of productivity growth is seen as labour-augmenting or equivalent to population growth in the simplest version of the neoclassical growth model. According to the studies of Solow (1957) and Kuznets (1971) if productivity growth prevails among the sources of economic growth, then most of the growth should be considered exogenous. One thing seems to be certain: the Solow residual factor does not explain the main part of productivity growth. So, there are limitations to the neoclassical framework. Long-run growth per capita may well be driven by technical progress alone, but this does not mean that technical progress is falling like manna from heaven. Through their actions, individuals determine the rate of technical progress, and if so, such actions should be part of an explanatory theory.

The perception that per capita growth settles down to equal the rate of technical progress leads to the notion of *convergence*. Based on this concept, it is supposed that income differences between countries must be eliminated in the long run. Another version, called *conditional convergence*, asserts that poor countries should grow faster than rich ones. Conditional convergence requires the existence of different rates of savings and population growth in developing countries; hence, there is the possibility for the poorest countries to catch up to the developed ones. Convergence is related to the idea of diminishing marginal productivity of capital. The idea is that a poor country has a higher marginal return to capital and thus shows a higher rate of per capita growth. The main problem with the neoclassical theory of growth was that it left the rate of growth almost unexplained. The steady growth rate of aggregate output illustrated as the sum of the growth rate of population and the rate of labour-augmenting technological progress was not explained by the theory. The neoclassical growth model was designed merely to explain the steady-state growth rate as the rate of output per person in terms of labour-augmenting technical progress and not to use other sophisticated tools such as the rate of learning; the rate of accumulation of knowledge, skills, and new ideas; the expanding variety of consumer goods; and so forth. This is why the neoclassical theory of growth was definitely exogenous. In Solow's words, "By arithmetic, then the growth rate of output per person or per worker was given by the rate of (labor-augmenting) technical progress. This was taken in the model to be a given number, certainly not explained within the model. In this sense, mainstream growth theory was indeed 'exogenous growth theory.' It could be said, and was said, that the theory left one key number, perhaps the key number, the rate of growth, unexplained" (Solow 2000, 98).

The neoclassical theory of growth reached its peak in the 1960s by concentrating on two main lines: the optimal rate of consumption and technical progress. The application of techniques of dynamic analysis to consumption and saving was the work of a young group of analytical guideline economists such as Cass (1965), Uzawa (1965), and Shell (1967), who in a few years were able to set up a whole revolution in macroeconomics and economic growth. A promising start on the empirical implementation of new growth models was made by Jorgenson and Griliches (1967). In their study, it appeared that 85 per cent of US economic growth was credited to endogenous determinants but might have been attributable as well to investments in new technology. However, in spite of exceptional progress on the analytical plan, even in the sophisticated growth models in which the trajectory of the consumption is obtained as optimal, the growth remains an exogenous fact, independent from the decisions taken on the demand side.

The endogeneity of technical progress, the real engine of economic growth, was developed along two lines of research, both stimulated from the contribution of Kaldor, although, significantly, it remained an incomplete plan.

The first line of research was based on the vintage approach, in which capital is the sum of vintage production for each year. Under this assumption, the relationship between growth and technical progress was found in the production of new capital goods. This type of model had constituted the main contribution of neoclassicals in the theory of growth, and despite numerous and ingenious attempts, the final result has been rather modest (Solow 1970b); technical progress still remains an exogenous variable, not making any difference if the productive improvement invests all the capital goods or only the new investments. Although succeeding in the attempt to render the Solovian model more realistic, these models have not been able to go beyond the exogenous vision of technical progress.

The second line of research has focused attention on an independent factor of production that not only is used in the production process but is also produced from the economic system. It has been a matter of exploration, in which technical progress comes to depend on the resources from the research sector. These intuitions have been developed mainly by Arrow, Uzawa, and Shell. Arrow advanced in 1962 his well-known model of growth in which the accumulation of knowledge comes through a process of social learning ("learning by doing"). Later Uzawa (1965) formalized a two-sector model, in which along with the sector producing consumer goods he also presents the sector producing technical changes. Another author who made a significant contribution in this tradition was Shell, who in a remarkable series of contributions (1966, 1967, and Shell and Heller 1974) developed the idea that economic growth depends on the accumulation of knowledge, which is considered like a public good. Despite the remarkable analytical intuitions, in particular the importance given to the role of knowledge, the first tradition of endogenous growth did not hold for very long, probably because of the difficulty in rendering the principle of increasing rate of return compatible with the theory of competitive equilibrium.

In the 1960s, in the middle of neoclassical development, the "controversy of two Cambridge schools" saw the MIT school of Solow and Samuelson and the post-Keynesian English school of Pasinetti, Garegnani, and Robinson on opposite sides on the evaluation of capital theory, on the role assigned to the application of mathematics in economics, on the implied ideological premises of the respective models, and, still more, on the way to indicate growth and the Harrodian instability.

The solution to the problem of *compatibility* in Harrod's equation could be reached through modifications of the capital-output ratio as proposed by Solow and Swan; through the modification of the rate of growth regarding population; or through the adjustment of the saving rate in the economy as a whole. In fact, all the representatives of the neoclassical school starting from Kaleckian formulations assumed that there exists a difference in the rate of saving on two different types of income – from labour and from capital – that could have, through mechanisms of redistribution, reached and maintained equilibrium.

Because equilibrium could effectively be reached and then maintained, there were different assumptions to add. Perhaps this was not the main point of contention: even though there were moments of disputation neither of the two "schools" became stiff on the fact that one of the two procedures was the only possible way toward the stability and equilibrium. The main dispute between the two schools was another, and conceptually it started earlier.

The neoclassical vision of aggregate capital, as the only homogenous good, allowed great expositive flexibility, but it was definitely unrealistic.

Furthermore, it seemed to be at a minimum theoretically inconsistent. There are two obvious questions from a neoclassical perspective. First, is it possible in a capitalistic economy to derive the marginal productivity of capital from a function of production in which different goods were added together in base of their value? Second, is it possible to measure the capital without first knowing its price?

According to Champernowne, Kahn, Kaldor, Pasinetti, Joan Robinson, Sraffa, and Garegnani, it was not. It was impossible in the light of the rate of interest to estimate capital because, according to Robinson, it was just what the theory of capital would have to determine. Moreover, the possibility of "reswitching techniques" in correspondence with different levels of interest rates (the cost of capital given in terms of the marginal product of capital) as demonstrated by Sraffa (1960), was sufficient to invalidate the neoclassical parable and the attempts to prove that the case of heterogeneous capital goods to the case of unique capital homogenous aggregate was general.

In fact, the "formal growth modelling failed to dominate the field of growth analysis, or to illuminate significantly the political economy of growth in either the advanced industrial or developing countries" (Rostow 1990, 351). The final word of Garegnani (1970a) made apparently official the victory of the English school in a controversy that to many of the participants, and to others, seemed ideological (Solow 1988, 15). The neoclassical school, however, even admitted "that the possibility of reswitching does seriously weaken the attraction of theorizing in terms of parable but do not concede that the new results make any serious difference to the neoclassical edifice *in its full generality*" (italics in original) (H.G. Jones 1975, 145).

But there was another point about which the two Cambridge schools differed: the assumption that the rationality of the individual was limitless. The type of flexibility proposed from the neoclassical parable through the capital-labour rate variable implied capital as malleable, not specific (whichever combination with labour) and not heterogeneous (a single type). This implicitly means that entrepreneurs are supposed not to make mistakes in expectations, markets are fully perfect, and prices perfectly transmit the right information about relative scarcity.

At the beginning of the 1970s, despite its achievements, the neoclassical theory of growth faced a period of decline, and it was found to face increasing difficulties on all fronts. First, it was not in a position to defend itself from the accusations of logical incoherence raised in spite of some fundamental theoretical ideas, such as the production function or the capital as an independent factor of production. Second, even its empirical analysis appeared modest and not in a position to explain economic development in its multiple economic, social, and cultural aspects. Third, the crisis of the neoclassical theory of growth became greater because of macroeconomic research was moving quickly from the phenomena of long period to that of short period, from the theory of growth to the theory of economic fluctuations, of stagflation, and finally of impact on rational expectations.

It is interesting to outline the different views of applied economics assumed by growth theorists. Their views were predominantly related to the use of growth models and to different approaches of argumentation. In the first three or four decades after the Second World War, some growth theorists disregarded the applied sides of other theories. The most argumentative theorist of the United Kingdom's Cambridge School, Joan Robinson (1980) heavily criticized the neoclassical theory of accumulation as being unable to create models that could be applied to the analysis of modern problems of growth. The neoclassical theorist, Solow (1997), vehemently argued that the Kaldor-Kalecki-Robinson-Pasinetti line was not able to assemble a serious theory of applied economics to resolve the problems of developed and developing economies.

Decades later, the supporters of endogenous growth theory, such as Barro (1991), Scott (1991) and Mankiw, Romer, and Weil (1992), have criticized Solow's (1956) model for not assuming externalities, for assuming diminishing returns to reproducible capital, and, thus, for not producing good applied results. In turn, Solow (2000) argued with those theorists who believe that empirical economics begins and ends with time-series analysis. He, in fact, stated,

> First of all, it is a mistake to dichotomise growth theory into an "exogenous" and an "endogenous" branch. *Every* area of economic theory will have to stop somewhere; it will rest on some exogenous elements. Some of those elements will be sociological in character, and some will even be economic. It is always a good thing to extend the scope of growth theory. One does that by finding a valid way to make some element that was previously exogenous into an endogenous or partially endogenous part of the extended theory. It is important to keep in mind that "exogenous" does not mean either "unchanging" or "mysterious" and certainly not "unchanging and

mysterious." It is a temporary designation, meaning that we try to work out in detail how the rest of the model adjusts to the exogenous elements, but not the other way round. (italics in original) (Solow 2000, 180–1)

The neoclassical growth models consisted mostly of macroeconomic models, which do not use microeconomic mechanisms. It is generally assumed that investment can raise productivity in the future through increasing per capita capital. These models do not explain why and how the increased capital per person may augment productivity. However, "growth theory flourished in the Fifties and Sixties, died and has now been resurrected" (Hahn and Solow 1996, 185).

A new wave of the neoclassical model occurred in the 1980s. Something new happened to the theory of growth, and the credit for rediscovering the problems of growth go without a doubt to Paul Romer (1986), with his pioneering article in the *Journal of Political Economy*, "Increasing Returns and Long-Run Growth." The problems of endogenous explanation of the technical progress and growth remained open, despite the revolutionary contributions during the 1960s. Karl Shell, in the opening argument in a conference of the International Economic Association in 1973, stated, "In order to explain economic development satisfactorily, an endogenous theory of technical change is required" (Rostow 1990, 342). Romer brought this problem back to the centre of the argument. In a few months, during which time Romer's second contribution (1987) appeared, and the contribution of other economists such as Prescott and Boyd (1987) and the fundamental work of Lucas (1988) came into sight, the whole field of economic growth returned all of a sudden to its old fashion, in particular the neoclassical production of growth theory. A plethora of complementary and alternative approaches appeared in the most important international economic journals related to the common origins and the neoclassic models of the 1960s, with their aggregate production functions combined with the optimized utility functions. However, these also concentrated on endogenous forms of growth where the rate of growth does not depend anymore on exogenous variables – like the rate of growth of population or the exogenous technical progress – but rather on the parameters of state of the growth equations; and the post-neoclassical growth theory or the endogenous growth theory was born.

The new theory of growth was characterized by the vastness and variety of models and the approach proposals, in comparison to the most circumscribed neoclassical models in the 1960s. Although some traces of the new models were already found in articles published in the 1960s, there is, nonetheless, a remarkable conceptual difference in how the endogenous growth theory tries to explain the "residual" of Solow, replacing the concept of diminishing returns with the limited concept of capital and the constant rate of capital meant in a wider sense. According to the classification of Van der Ploeg and Tang (1992), there are at least four possible ways by which the endogenous growth theory can explain the residual growth: (1) learning by doing; (2) human capital; (3) research and development (accumulations of knowledge); and (4) under the form of public infrastructure (Van der Ploeg and Tang 1992, 18).

The endogenous growth theory constitutes the most current development in the neoclassical program of growth theory. Beyond the technicalities with which this literature abounds, the essential element of the new wave of contributions can be seen in the light of the new conception of technical progress. Although in the traditional model the notion of technical progress is much wider and consequently rambling as it identifies itself in all that could rise from factor productivity, in the new literature, the endogenous element consists in the accumulation of knowledge – hence considered as endogenous to the economic system. From the evolution of the endogenous growth theory started in the 1980s, there can be distinguished two essential aspects: the new analytical contribution and the different economic interpretation. The first one is common to all classes of these models, which instead differ, and in a remarkable way, under the second aspect. Under the latter aspect, the necessary analytical ingredient to obtain the results of endogenous growth is to abandon the law of diminishing returns.

The fundamental technical condition to obtain the endogenous growth is that the productivity of investment should be independent, productive, and not diminishing in the course of the accumulation. The crucial element of the problem, in the intertemporal context in which the rational agent maximizes his or her intertemporal production function, is that the technology must be defined in such a way as to eliminate the effects of diminishing returns. For instance, Solow declares, "If the enemy of sustained growth is diminishing returns, the basic need is to eliminate or overcome the effect of diminishing returns to capital on the growth of output per person" (Solow 2000, 144).

If this is the common feature of the new class of endogenous growth models, it remains to make clear the second aspect – not less important –

of the reasons (and of the interpretations) that can justify the rejection of such an important principle as the law of diminishing returns. As the neoclassical theory focuses on the capital accumulation decision, the new theory of growth suggests studying the decisions that determine the rate of production of ideas.

In fact, there is a change of emphasis from the accumulation of physical capital to the accumulation of human capital, which aims for decisions that affect the rate of learning and the rate of accumulation of skills and ideas.

For Lucas, the way to get through this is to get back to the original research traced in the 1960s, placing at the centre of growth theory the accumulation of intangible capital rather than physical capital. As Kaldor had already revealed, knowledge is not a productive factor subject to the principle of scarcity involving the production function, and as a consequence, it cannot be considered as linear-homogenous of the first degree but rather of a higher degree. This shift of attention from physical capital to human capital is, in Lucas's view, the element that can explain the mechanisms of economic development. However, this is not sufficient if it is not accompanied by some appropriate analytical tools: in order to obtain a model of endogenous growth, the production function of human capital needs to have a linear form that, at every increment of capital, corresponds to a proportional increment of output.

In the perspective of P. M. Romer (1987 and 1990), the growth is endogenous under at least two aspects: first under the macroeconomic aspect because it depends on the proportions of resources assigned to the production of new ideas; second, under the microeconomic aspect because it is conditioned by investment decisions of the enterprises and, therefore, by the optimizing behaviour of individuals. The model of Romer might be seen as an original combination of the ideas formulated in the 1960s by Arrow and Shell, in which the elasticity of capital was assumed to be equal to unity. According to Lucas, the endogenous growth lies essentially on the hypothesis that the production function of knowledge is homogenous of the first degree. It is not the case that Solow has criticized the first wave of endogenous growth models for the fact that they assume in an implicit way the analytic assumptions that they had actually to explain.

The Solovian vision in the 1960s became the dominant approach mainly because it was introduced as an extension of the categories of traditional microeconomics to the dynamic case. All the doubts that could have put into discussion the Solovian approach have been put apart in order to choose a methodological decision to help better understand the process of growth – in the first place the idea of increasing rate of knowledge, which has been adapted to the model by the Marshallian expedient of an external effect. The new theory of endogenous growth has been developed two decades after the boom of neoclassical growth theories, when it was clear that the increasing anomalies could not be repaired within the traditional theoretical outline. The issue of convergence in the theory of growth, which was famous in the 1960s, was also marked by Kaldor in his stylized facts. It became an interesting problem as it became available in a new conceptual panorama compatible with a new explanation.

The theory of endogenous growth has constituted a remarkable case of scientific progress because it has overcome the existing differences between the principles of microeconomic research and those of macroeconomic research.

PART THREE

Endogenous Growth Theory

8

Toward the New Theory of Growth: Endogenous Growth and Technological Transformation

Modern endogenous growth theory embraces a broad structure of theoretical and empirical work that emerged in the 1980s. This research program distinguishes itself from neoclassical growth theory by underlining that economic growth is an endogenous process that is part of an economic system, not the result of forces coming from outside, like manna from heaven. Differently from neoclassical growth theory, the endogenous method does not focus on exogenous technological change to explain the increase of income per capita, but focuses instead on research and knowledge at the level of industry or firm, which also affects the behaviour of the economy as a whole.

The first appearance of *knowledge* – under the form of learning by doing – was made in the pages of Solovian models through the contribution of Arrow (1962) and his non-vintage version in Sheshinski (1967). From the first studies on the economy of information, led by scholars like Hayek (1945), Stigler (1961), and Machlup (1962), the importance of the flow of information in technology, in the market, and among competitors; the ways to obtain and diffuse it and its effectiveness in the competition between firms and corporations became more and more fundamental to macroeconomists and theorists of enterprise,[1] who assumed a dominant role in various research programs. Its role in growth theory, however, had not been deepened and its explicative power remained bound to the well-known neoclassical exogenous progress. The same learning by doing of Arrow is used to explore only one of the numerous ways in which knowledge is created and affects the productive activity within a company and the rate of growth within an economy. Romer, in his doctoral dissertation in 1983 – which is considered to be the basis of his article of 1986 – did not have to do more than to apply the same method introduced by Arrow, through learning by doing, to cross a limit that Arrow had not intended to pass: non-decreasing marginal productivity.

The introduction of endogenous growth theory was identified with the pioneering work of Paul Romer (1986) and Lucas (1988) during the 1980s and with the work of Rebelo (1991), Grossman and Helpman (1991a and 1991b) and Aghion and Howitt (1992) during the 1990s.

The mechanism, in order to remain a neoclassical Solovian model, was simple and effective: consider a constant economy of scale at the enterprise level (therefore conserving a competitive market structure) for which, through a positive and external effect of *knowledge*, there is an increasing productivity of scale at the level of the economy. The decreasing marginal productivity of capital is in some way eliminated without losing the competitive framework. The knowledge considered by Romer is a non-rival good: it is born like a sub-product from the production of other assets, but it is a sort of technological knowledge that tends to spread over the whole market, and all can use it without interfering with others. This is an important property that will be found in more complex models, which assume the intermediate goods as specific property of monopolistic innovators.

Endogenous growth theory does not embrace most of the neoclassical assumptions in order to incorporate market imperfections. The key innovation in this theory is that it involves a change in the theory of production. It assumes non-diminishing marginal returns to accumulate factors of production, which include not only physical capital but also human capital accumulated through education, know-how, and technical knowledge. It is, hence, not possible to wear out the growth potential latent in the accumulation of these factors. However, as in the neoclassical models, long-run economic growth is driven by the accumulation of knowledge based on production factors such as human capital, learning by doing, research and development (R&D), and innovation. In the long run, differently from most of the neoclassical models, it is the combination of these factors that causes factor productivity to increase and avoids the marginal return to physical capital from falling below profitable levels.

Endogenous growth theory assumes that technological progress is the result of R&D undertaken by profit-maximizing firms. R&D enters the production process as a factor of production and is used in combination with other inputs to produce output. The decision, to invest in R&D is undertaken only if there is an opportunity for profit.

The assumption that the determinants of long-run growth are endogenous to the decision-making process of the firm is a major different approach from the neoclassical growth theory and has important policy implications. Certainly, if long-run growth is determined by knowledge-based factors of production that are part of managing cost of the firm, then by changing the cost of those factors through, for example, trade policies, direct subsidies, or tax incentives, governments can influence directly and indirectly long-run growth.

Part three of this book, which includes chapters 8, 9, and 10, will give a detailed treatment of the new endogenous growth theory.

In chapter 8, some of the revolutionary models of endogenous growth in the late 1980s and early 1990s will be analyzed. But before starting with endogenous models, a short presentation of economic transformation and enterprise evolution in the last two decades of the twentieth century would be very useful and practical, in order to have a better idea of the environment in which the new endogenous growth theories were born.

ECONOMIC TRANSFORMATION AND THE BIRTH OF THE NEW ECONOMY

The development of information technology and the fusion of information technology with telecommunications was one of the main aspects of economic transformation in the 1980s and 1990s. Two main developments that started on early 1980s had deep consequences for the Western economy and the global economy at large. One was the introduction of personal computers and the other was the development of a new era of telecommunications. During this extraordinary age of huge technological transformation, personal computers entered the market and the Internet laid the groundwork worldwide for new business and entrepreneurial activities as never seen before. Personal computers, in the first 5 to 10 years, were adopted quickly by businesses and government organizations. In the early 1990s, PCs started being part of every home in most Western countries, and the microprocessor, the base of electronic revolution, was embedded in many tools and products in a variety of industries. The new era of telecommunications can easily be seen in the United States, where the breakup of the giant telephone company monopolies in 1982 triggered the creation of new companies like MCI and Sprint, which started a fierce race to build fiber-optic networks across the United States. And by the early 1990s, these companies transformed the telecommunication industry as they shifted from moving voice signals to moving data; this new phenomenon was finalized by the creation of a new data-communication-network, the network of networks called the Internet. On 8 February 1996, the American Congress passed the Telecommunication Act of 1996, which instituted the deregulation of the telecommunication industry and was the first major revision of telecommunications law in 62 years (the first Communication Act was passed in 1934 and was intended to regulate the rapid expansion of the communications industry in the United States). This act ended the monopolies for providers of local telephone service and opened the door to a variety of operators offering more competitive rates. Computers and data communications become inextricably linked, in this way helping the growth of digital infrastructure and increasing the connectivity of people and businesses around the globe. By the late 1990s wireless technology started dominating communications. Mobile telephone and data communications systems offered by vast antenna networks on the ground at first were dominated by big satellite projects and at a later stage allowed faultless connection to the information infrastructure anywhere on the planet. Hardware, software, and telecommunications companies experienced tremendous growth of a kind that had not been seen in decades, and creating the new information network happened to be one of the biggest business opportunities around the turn of the new millennium.

The growing digital infrastructure reduced significantly the cost of starting and running a small business, and opened new markets and new perspectives to new industries and small businesses.

This process brought the extinction of space through time and the birth of real time over clock time. The development of real-time economic activities and transactions with the help of new information technology like Internet business, intranet, and electronic money transfer, in the 1990s, is based on price signals and other incentives transmitted to economic participants simultaneously around the globe, apart from the time differences determined by spatial distances. The evolving globalization process in the last 20 years of the twentieth century has brought the unification of social space by creating a global network society and a new type of economy based on the space flow of information and on timeless time. The new economy has created so-called nodes and hubs, which are specific places of invention and innovation with defined social, cultural, and functional characteristics (think of Silicon Valley in California, the M4 Corridor in the UK, the Bangalore "Valley" in India, and the Technological Park of the city of São José dos Campos in San Paulo, Brazil). Between the nodes and hubs pass a huge flow of capital, knowledge and information, technological designs and controls, new ideas and applications. The technological nodes and hubs are hierarchically organized, depending on the weight of their relative functions in the network. Hubs play an important role in the coordination of the interaction of all of the elements present in the network; meanwhile nodes are locations that have the capability to build activities and organizations around a key function in the network. Therefore, by having a better look at the network of the global economy, we find that only sections of economies, industries, countries, and regions are linked up in proportion to their position in the international division of labour; meanwhile other sectors, agents, and players in the local economy are marginalized and disconnected. The global economy is highly dynamic, highly exclusionary, and highly unstable as it adjusts continuously to its competitive, information-driven environment, with the result that segments of economic structures are constantly upgraded, incorporated, or even created. National governments in developing countries, in order to succeed in placing segments of business and economic structures on the fast track by having access to the global market, have put in place a range of actions and policies consisting of developing and improving information infrastructure, and education and training for new and digital technology, which are the basis for a "real-time" economy. Furthermore, positive externalities have become more important; the accumulation of human capital through education plays a much greater role in the economy; government's share in GDP has increased significantly, as has the corporate share; and R&D has changed character and become far more important.

The R&D sector in the past three to four decades has increased rapidly in most industrialized countries, especially in the United States of America. For example, R&D in the United States financed by the federal government has increased from $60 billion in 1976 to over $110 billion in 2003, almost 5 per cent of the total federal budget of $2.1 trillion. The combined public and private sector R&D exceeds $250 billion a year, making the United States the largest investor in R&D, counting for more than 40 per cent of global R&D spending. In most developed countries

R&D is funded primarily by a single science agency that covers the goals of advancing science. The US federal R&D funding budget, however, is mission oriented; all programs are funded based on their contributions to national targets and foreign missions, each of which corresponds to a different department or national agency, such as NASA, the Department of Defense, the Department of Energy, the National Institutes of Health, the National Science Foundation, and so on. US federal research and development programs provide support for specific government goals, such as exploring space, improving the nation's health, and providing national security, but industry R&D is more closely oriented toward company-specific products and technological problems (RAND 2002, 15). Industry funds in R&D are focused in areas where basic research can be turned quickly into breakthrough products, such as chemistry and biotechnology, or in areas where large corporations can afford to spend on development for future possibilities in new products in information technology. Many governments invest large amounts to support education and research in universities and colleges. In the United States in 2000, the federal government supported almost 60 per cent of R&D carried out at US universities and colleges. In the 1990s about 35 per cent of bachelor's degrees, 30 per cent of master's degrees, and around 60 per cent of the doctorates awarded in the United States were in science and engineering fields (RAND 2002, 35). As another example, the science and engineering workforce in the United States has grown at a higher rate than the civilian labour force as a whole. According to National Science Board statistics (NSB 2002, Table 4–1), in 1999, 10.5 million employees held some level of science and engineering (S&E) related degrees, out of a total workforce of about 140 million. Of the 10.5 million, at least 8 million scientists and engineers held their highest degree in an S&E field. Of the 8 million who held their highest degree in an S&E field, 3 million were employed in science and engineering related jobs and the other portion of approximately 5 million individuals, despite having their highest degree in S&E, were employed in fields that were less related to science and engineering, such as management, executive positions, administrative jobs, sales and marketing positions, or non-S&E related teaching positions.

Furthermore, the number of patents issued in the United States increased more than 2.5 times between 1990 and 1999, reaching a peak in 1999 with 153,478 patents, of which 55 per cent were issued to US inventors and 45 per cent to foreign inventors, mostly from Germany,

Japan, France, and the United Kingdom (NSB, 2002). Just as an example, the IBM Corporation in the year 2001 received 3,454 patents, almost 10 per day (RAND 2002, 46).

The Networked Economy

The new technologies in information infrastructure at the end of twentieth century and at the beginning of the new millennium created the so-called Networked Economy, the New Economy, or the Real-Time Economy. Many companies and corporations in most of the industrialized countries – taking advantages of new information technologies to create a smaller and more adaptable economic unit – went through a process of deep reorganization described quite often as downsizing, outsourcing, and creating the virtual corporation. Business and various organizations around the globe begin shifting from vertical and hierarchical processes to networked ones, leading to remarkable improvements in efficiency and productivity. The Networked Economy is based on businesses that invest in new technology to increase productivity by adding value to the economy, and this is the key to sustained economic growth. Some economists and theorists, like Stanford University Professor Paul Romer in the 1980s, propose that the new technologies do not become very productive before at least one generation passes after their introduction, the time people need to master these new technologies and use them for their benefit. This is certainly true in the case of the introduction of personal computers in the workplace, where the work processes and the structure of organization begin mutating quickly to take full advantage of the new technology. Later, other economists did extensive research how to precisely measure the gains in productivity from such new technology and, most important, how to take into account the concept of quality improvement, which has for a long time been a vague concept.

In the 1990s the changes took place at a faster rate than in the previous decades because of new factors, such as the increased competition in a global and diversified economy, expanding markets, new ways of doing business (such as e-commerce), and staying up-to-date with the latest technology.

Broadly speaking, there are at least four signals of major workplace change; a change in the organizational structure, a new product or service, new management, and new technology. The organizational structure primarily changes through structural downsizing, outsourcing, acquisitions and mergers as a result of competition, improving sales and profit, or simply company growth and expansion. The second indicator of workplace change is the introduction of a new product or service, which has repercussions for changes in production, sales, profits, and customer service. This may bring growth, new markets, and new customers but at the same time new competitors. The third signal is new management. A major change in the board of directors, a change in chief executive officer, and eventually a change of president, may bring a period of transition during which high-level managers are likely to convey new policies and procedures and redesign the company strategies. Finally, the fourth indicator is a change in technology. Technological change can bring large transformations to the organization. It can easily change the production process, the working conditions (e.g., the introduction of PC, the Internet, and intranet), the work environment, and may very much influence the skills that employees use at work.

As a consequence of these new technologies, companies and other organizations, to keep up with the changes, had to revise corporate missions and goals, management practices, and day-to-day business functions. Corporations quickly began redesigning their short-term and long-term business strategies, and replacing traditional hierarchical organization charts with thinner structures concentrated around empowered teams able to embrace new changes and new technologies.

There are three additional relevant areas of the Networked Economy that need some special attention. These areas are: digital markets, the network enterprise organization, and the global division of labour.

The first area of the Networked Economy is the digital or real-time markets, which are the most evolved part of the digital revolution that affected the market places. The development of information technology through the introduction of personal computers, the Internet, intranet, and satellite television on a large scale has transformed the markets, from physical ones to digital. In the traditional market place the market price, which is the outcome of the interplay between demand and supply, needs agents to meet in a convenient physical place, and after hours of discussion, eye contact, and eventually complicated cost/profit calculations they decide on the best offer to close the agreement. In the digital market the deals are conducted over the Internet. There are online auction markets in which agents, dealers, and consumers post online what they are willing to offer and to pay. On an industrial scale, producers and manufacturing companies such as General Motors, Ford, Chrysler, General Electric, Siemens, Boeing, etc., have Web-based links to their qualified suppliers that allow the suppliers to make bids for production component and parts contracts. Online auction bidding can drive the costs to the buyer down by about 10–40 per cent. The digital market is also called e-commerce conducted over the Internet, which applies to purchases made through the Web by customers paying with a credit card or to business-to-business activities such as inventory transfers, where the transaction information is transmitted to banks for payment clearance and to vendors for filling the orders. The e-commerce and digital trade was further developed with the introduction of the Federal Electronic Signatures Act (2000) in the United States, which launched uniform national standards for determining the conditions under which contracts in electronic form are legally valid. This law was followed by similar regulations in other Western countries, which set the standards and bases for an unprecedented growth of digital trade. The cost-reducing prospect of e-commerce and digital markets constitutes the core of development, growth, and prosperity in a global market.

The second relevant area of the New Economy is the network enterprise organization, which has evolved in a modern flexible connectivity between operating units. The Real-Time Economy has reorganized economic activities in such a way that it is not so easy to classify them into the three traditional categories: primary (agriculture), secondary (industry), and tertiary (services). The revolution of information technology at the end of the twentieth century created the premises to group economic activities in a different order: "real-time" activities and "material" activities. For "real-time" activities, distance and location are no longer important choices when building facilities for economic operations. For the "material" activities group the choice of location for companies operating in such sectors as producing raw materials and other industrial components is still important, as it has to match the specific requirements for economic operations. As a result of the evolution of information technology the cost of shipping goods and of communication of information has dropped so significantly that plants, factories, and machinery for the final assembly of products and subassemblies can be located and installed anywhere in the world. The application of hardware, software, and modern technologies to the production process has made it possible to view production capacity in many sectors and industries as a commodity easily exportable worldwide. In fact, the precise reproducibility of the modern product has reduced the need to relocate engineering and design teams with manufacturing. Therefore, multinational corporations have at least three main characteristics. First, plants and facilities can be located globally in any country, if under certain conditions (such as the size of the market, political stability, tax incentives, etc.) there is a possibility for profit. Second, products and services, like standard commodities, can be shifted back and forth between countries. Third, products, components, spare parts, and services can be outsourced on a global basis, thanks to the use of global product design and advanced process technology. It means that moulded products, for example, can be manufactured cheaper and faster, following international standards, by remote control over the Internet. Outsourcing different processes and activities of a big company can indeed increase competition. The result is that the multinational company has moved from the traditional centralized corporate organization to a decentralized network enterprise organization where production activities and services are not produced internally but outsourced externally to competitive qualified suppliers and independent businesses dispersed over many different countries, who are providers of flexible capacity. The combination of information technology and advanced telecommunications enabled the modern technical structure of a company to move toward a flexible connectivity between operating units or suppliers, where the actual operating unit is transformed to a business project supported by the network and is not seen as an individual company. In addition, the creation of network enterprise of scattered manufacturing and flexible connectivity has lowered entry barriers for non-traditional participants. In developed countries, this has been resolved by creating a regulatory system managed by authorities issuing quality assurance certifications for manufacturing, such as ISO 9000, which is designed to award best supplier status to businesses and companies, allowing even small companies to compete and be part of this networked economy and flexible connectivity.

The third area of the Networked Economy requiring attention is a new global division of labour, extended from industrial countries to those on the periphery. The blend of information technology and telecommunications has facilitated the opportunity for companies to relocate operations and functions to places and countries where there is a cost-competitive skilled labour force available and good infrastructure. Corporations like General Electric, General Motors, Ford, Chrysler, Toyota, Honda, Siemens, Bombardier, Dell, Apple, and Nike have dispersed their operations in different parts of the globe looking for a competitive and skilled labour force, for assets, infrastructure, investment incentives and tax breaks available. The standardization of production processes and activities, thanks to new technologies, have enabled them to turn to real-time activities. For example, US corporations and firms like airlines, banks, and insurance companies outsource most of their standard duties and data-processing, like processing airline tickets, credit card transactions, bank transactions, insurance claims, and other raw data operations to countries in the Caribbean, Mexico, and India. The traditional division of labour (the value-added chain) into lower value-added and higher value-added activities based, respectively, in the peripheral and developed countries has dramatically changed with the introduction of real-time activities. In fact, many information or data-intensive activities previously labeled as high value-added activities have changed to real-time activities that can be located anywhere in the world. The classical case is the exportation of such high value-added activities as programming and development work by large software companies in industrialized countries like the United States, Canada, and those in Europe to developing countries like India, Singapore, and Thailand to take advantage of lower wages and benefits. At this stage of economic development the capital embodied in tools, equipment, and software has become very mobile, moving quickly and without obstacles from centre-core to periphery countries, while migration of labour has been much slower than the massive migration at the turn of the twentieth century. Labour migration has been affected mostly by political intervention aimed at keeping the cheap and qualified work force in Third World countries in order to produce all kind of commodities and services for the global market.

Emerging markets in Asia and Latin America are the leading global economic growth players today. And by the middle of the twenty-first century these countries, given their high rates of growth, most probably will be home to 50–60 per cent of the world's wealth and 70 per cent of its trade. The industrialized countries are trying to seize the sizeable growth opportunity presented by emerging markets. This means that the developed countries have to be more aggressive in controlling the comparative advantages, because they are no longer competing against global companies, but entire global value chains. Global value chains offer an extraordinary platform to participate and compete in local economies worldwide, as they allow some industrialized countries to take full advantage of benefits deriving from operating in other regions while optimizing their advantage and profit at home. In a new economic policy environment at the beginning of the twenty-first century, we observe the rise of a new state capitalism, where both developed and developing countries are engaged in assertive industrial policies to support their domestic flagship industries as they invest to see their companies achieve international success.

This has changed the concept of centre-periphery countries. Before, the core industrialized countries were geographically and socially distant from the periphery of Third World countries because of their high value-added activities, good infrastructure, and high standards of living. Nowadays, real-time activities have gradually transformed the centre-periphery geographical relationship into a social one, as some segments of less-developed countries perform high value-added activities in real time at lower wages than those in industrialized countries.

Although the term New Economy has often replaced the term Real-Time Economy or given that both terms have been used interchangeably to point to the same phenomena, there are differences that need to be addressed. The New Economy is a global phenomenon that points to the macroeconomic effects of the international economy in which, differently from the traditional economy, real-time transactions are of great importance. In contrast, the Real-Time Economy indicates the instantaneity of economic processes based on instant transactions. Comparing the traditional economy with the new economy, we see that in the traditional economy land, labour, and capital are the main three factors of production that run the economy. In the new economy the most important factors are know-how, the accumulation of human capital, creativity, and innovation. Knowledge and know-how embodied in software and technology in a wide range of products have become more important than capital, labour, and materials. Therefore, the production of knowledge and information has turned out to be the leading sector in the developed economies. For example, in the United States software companies alone employed more than 1,000,000 professionals in 2000, and employment in the industry was growing by 13–15 per cent each year, compared with just a 2.5 per cent increase in all other industries. The IT sector, which accounts for less than 10 per cent of US GDP contributes more than 35–40 per cent of the country's economic growth. The knowledge/information economy, differently from the traditional/neoclassical economy that observes the general rules of diminishing returns, obeys the rules of increasing returns, thanks to the excellent performance of the new information technology. The new based-knowledge economy, after decades of effort and investment in new technologies, has reached the capability to operate as a single unit in real time in the global market.

INCREASING RETURNS AND GROWTH: THE ROMER MODEL

Paul M. Romer[2] was one of the first economists in the 1980s to perceive that the new technologies can become very productive when they are used by trained people, and that therefore there is a need to introduce new growth theories reflecting increasing returns to scale. His pioneering work on the theory of growth, published in 1986, offers a model that is an alternative view of long-run prospects for growth. Romer's model differs from neoclassical theory in stating that the rate of investment and the rate of return on capital may increase rather than decrease with increases in the accumulation of capital stock. Therefore, the level of capital output for less-developed countries in the long run is not required to converge to catch up with the advanced countries. Furthermore, long-run growth is based on endogenous technical change and is determined for the most part by a progressive accumulation of knowledge and by the profit maximizing of agents. In a dissimilar way from the models that exhibit decreasing returns to scale, Romer (1986) supposes that knowledge grows without limit because there is continuous demand for it. Thus, the objective of Romer's model is to show increasing returns to scale and growth in the production function of consumption goods.

Romer's model, differently from neoclassical ones, depends on three central assumptions: increasing returns in the production of consumption goods, decreasing returns in the production of knowledge, and externalities. The diminishing returns to scale in the production of knowledge are required to ensure that both consumption and utility do not grow too quickly. The two-period model he created analyzes equilibrium with externalities and increasing returns.

Romer (1986) assumed that identical consumers have a twice differentiable, strictly concave utility function $U(c1, c2)$ and defined overconsumption of a single output good in two periods (1 and 2). It is also assumed that production of consumption goods in period 2 is an augmented function of the state of knowledge, given by k. The production of knowledge in period 2 comes from foregone consumption in period 1. The basic idea of this model is that there is a trade-off between consumption today and knowledge that can be used to produce more consumption tomorrow. The technology of the firm *i* depends on the firm's specific inputs *ki* and *xi* and on the aggregate level of knowledge

$$K = \sum_{i=1}^{N} ki$$

where *N* is the number of firms. It is supposed that on the production function of the form *F* (*ki*, *K*, *xi*), homogenous of degree one, and for any value of *K*, *F* is concave as a function of *ki* and *xi*. From the definition of the production function *F*, and assuming that *F* is increasing in the aggregate stock of knowledge *K*, we see that the function (Romer 1986, 1015),

$$F(\theta ki, \theta K, \theta xi) > F(\theta ki, K, \theta xi) = \theta F(ki, K, xi) \quad (8.1)$$

shows increasing returns to scale for any $\theta > 1$.[3] The two-period model is a competitive equilibrium with externalities, where each firm maximizes profits by taking the aggregate level of knowledge *K* as given. In period 1, consumers supply part of their bequest of output goods and all the factors *x* to firms. Conversely, in period 2, they purchase output goods with the proceeds from period 1. In this competitive model, consumers and firms maximize profits as much as they can by taking prices as given. It is considered that the number of firms, *N*, equals the number of consumers, *S*, so the per firm and per capita levels of values coincide. Denoting with $x\hat{}$ the per capita endowment of the non-increasing factors and with $e\hat{}$ the per capita endowment of the output good in period 1, the competitive equilibrium is given as a maximization problem:

$$\begin{aligned} &P(K)\text{: max} \quad U(c1, c2) \qquad (8.2)\\ &k \in (0, e\hat{}) \text{ subject to } c1 \le e\hat{} - k\\ &c2 \le F(k, K, x)\\ &x \le x\hat{} \end{aligned}$$

where *U* is strictly concave and *F* (*k*, *K*, *x*) is concave in *k* and *x* for each value of *K*. Function *P* (*K*) has a unique solution *k* for each value of *K*. In equilibrium, the aggregate level of knowledge in the economy is consistent with the level that is assumed when firms make production decisions. Let us define the function Ð: R → R that sends *K* into *S* (times the value of *k* that attains the maximum for *P* (*K*)). We now see the fixed points of

Đ that determine the competitive equilibrium. From (8.2), we have that $P(K^*)$ is a concave maximization problem with solution $k^* = K^*/S$, $c1^* \leq e\hat{} - k^*$, and $c2^* \leq F(k^*, SK^*, x\hat{})$. To find the maximization problem for the firm, we use the Lagrangian form for $P(K^*)$ with multiplier $p1$, $p2$, and w (Romer 1986, 1017):

$$Ł = U(c1, c2) + p1(e\hat{} - k^* - c1) + p2\,[F(k, K, x) - c2] + w\,(x\hat{} - x) \tag{8.3}$$

where the solution for $p1$, $p2$, and w are, respectively, $p1 = p2\,D1F(k^*, SK^*, x\hat{})$ and $w = p2\,D3F(k^*, SK^*, x\hat{})$. Considering the maximization problem of the firm,

$$\max p2\,F(k^*, SK^*, x) - p1k - wx \tag{8.4}$$

the sufficient conditions for a concave maximization problem imply that k^* and $x\hat{}$ are optimal choices for the firm.

In the same way for the consumer, we have that the income to the consumer is given by the following value:

$$I = p1e\hat{} + w\,x\hat{} = p2F(k^*, SK^*, x\hat{}) + p1(e\hat{} - k^*) \tag{8.5}$$

where the second part of the equation comes from the homogeneity of F in k and x. Using the necessary conditions $pi = Di\,Ui\,(c1^*, c2^*)$, where the problem $P(K^*)$ is used, we have that $c1^*$and $c2^*$ are solutions to the problem max $U(c1, c2)$ subject to the standard budget constraint, $p1\,c1 + p2\,c2 \leq I$. In addition, we know that the marginal rate of substitution for consumers is equal to the private marginal rate of transformation made out by firms $D1F(k^*, SK^*, x\hat{}) = D1U(c1^*, c2^*)/D2U(c1^*, c2^*)$, and this differs from the true marginal rate of transformation for the economy given as $D1F(k^*, SK^*, x\hat{}) + SD2F(k^*, SK^*, x\hat{})$ as the consequence of externalities. Broadly speaking, a fixed point of function Đ defined by a family of concave problems $P(K)$ is supported as a competitive equilibrium with externalities, which satisfies the restricted optimality conditions given by the optimality equation (8.2). The general equilibrium of the model is found at the fixed points of the function Đ. In fact, by substituting the constraints from $P(K)$, we can define a new function:

$$V(k, K) = U(e\hat{} - k^*, F(k, K, x\hat{})) \tag{8.6}$$

Function V is not concave as a result of increasing marginal productivity of knowledge, but rather for any fixed value K, it is concave in k, and the optimal choice of k for the optimization problem $P(K)$ is determined by $D_1V(k, K) = 0$. Hence, in the model originated by Romer (1983 and 1986)[4], the solution of the equilibrium quantities is characterized by the concave maximization problem.

THE NEOCLASSICAL PRODUCTION FUNCTION IN ROMER'S MODEL

Barro and Sala-i-Martin (1995) demonstrate Romer's (1986) model by using a neoclassical production function. We will follow them, not in order to show all the derivations of the model, but rather to understand the main characteristics and results of such a model. The neoclassical production function is written as

$$Y_i = F(K_i, A_iL_i) \qquad (8.a)$$

where Y denotes output, K denotes capital, L denotes labour, and A denotes the level of technology. This satisfies the neoclassical properties, such as positive and diminishing marginal products of each input, constant returns to scale, and Inada conditions. Combining the assumptions of learning by doing (Arrow 1962) and knowledge spillovers (the second key assumption is that knowledge is a public good and all the firms can access it at zero cost), A_i can be replaced by K, and so we can rewrite the production function for firm i as

$$Y_i = F(K_i, K\,L_i) \qquad (8.b)$$

If K and L_i are constant, then K shows diminishing returns to scale. Using the fact that each firm's capital usage is included in the production function, we have that the productivity of all firms is rising. As the production function is homogenous of degree one in K and K_i for given L_i, there are constant returns to capital at the social level, when K_i and K are supposed to expand together for a fixed amount of labour. This constant rate of social return yields nothing more than the endogenous growth process. According to this demonstration, a firm's profit can be written as follows:

$$\Pi = Li\ [f(ki, K) - (r + \delta)ki - w] \qquad (8.c)$$

where $f(\cdot)$ indicates the intensive form of the production function, $(r + \delta)$ represents the rental price of capital, and w denotes the wage rate. It is assumed that each competitive firm takes the factor price as given, so the profit maximization and the zero profit conditions are given as

$$\delta yi/\delta ki = fi(ki, K) = r + \delta \qquad (8.d)$$

$$\delta Yi/\delta Li = fi(ki, K) - kifi(ki, K) = w \qquad (8.e)$$

where $f(\cdot)$ is the partial derivative of $fi(ki, K)$ with respect to its first argument, and ki is the private marginal product of capital. In equilibrium, all firms make the same choices, so that $ki = k$ and $K = kL$ are valid. Given that $fi(ki, K)$ is homogenous of degree one in k and K, the average product of capital can be written as

$$fi(ki, K)/ki = f\ i(K/ki) = f(L) \qquad (8.f)$$

where $f(L)$ is the function for the average product of capital and satisfies $f'(L) > 0$ and $f''(L) < 0$. The average product is increasing in the size of the labour force, L. The marginal product of capital can be derived from equation (8.f) as

$$f1(ki, K) = f(L) - L\ f'(L) \qquad (8.g)$$

Thus, the private marginal product of capital is less than the average product and is invariant with k. Equation (8.g) also implies that the private marginal product of capital is increasing in L because $f''(L) < 0$. Then, after some manipulation, we obtain the accumulation of knowledge equation for k as follows:

$$\dot{k} = f(L)k - c - \delta k \qquad (8.h)$$

The equation above shows that the model has no transitional dynamics; the variables k and y always grow at the rate equal to the growth rate of consumption (Barro and Sala-i-Martin 1995, 145–50).

The difference between Arrow and Romer is that Arrow pictures the decreasing returns of learning by doing and therefore returns to an exogenous rate of growth. The heart of Romer's model is based on the accumulation of knowledge from agents who maximize profit. This knowledge, produced from a technology of decreasing returns, according to Romer, exhibits a positive externality: the technology produced by a firm cannot perfectly be kept secret or patented for a long time, and therefore, it helps other firms obtain the technology created by the pioneering firm. However, knowledge can be accumulated without any limit, and with other increasing factors, it shows increasing returns in the production of final goods. Romer knew the characteristics of increasing returns in the previous models, but he preferred to resolve in an altered way the problem of consumers' optimal choice, with respect to Arrow and his successors. He proposed that knowledge itself has increasing returns in the production function, but the search technology that produces it is based on the scale of decreasing returns, and this assures the existence of an optimal rate of growth for the knowledge. As a result, growth is endogenous because the externalities compensate for the decreasing marginal productivity in research. From the demand side, consumers have utility functions twice continuously differentiable and strictly concave; from the supply side, firms produce final goods through a production function twice continuously differentiable using a set of factors x and the present state of knowledge k. The production function $F(k_i, K, x_i)$, concave in k and x and homogenous of the first degree, shows an increasing rate of returns. In an infinite-horizon time, Romer pictures the increase of knowledge made by the foregone consumption in the first period (present period). By investing a sum I, we have that the function of knowledge accumulation is written as

$$k = G(I, k) \tag{8.7}$$

where the function G is concave and homogenous of the first degree. Knowledge is interpreted as a sub-product of investment, a phenomenon of learning by doing incorporated in capital goods, exactly the opposite case to that in which the production function is based solely on physical capital in the absence of knowledge.

ENDOGENOUS TECHNOLOGICAL TRANSFORMATION IN ROMER'S VIEW

The core of endogenous growth theory is that it attempts an unambiguous formulation of the process of technological progress. The basic idea of endogenous growth was to remove the rate of diminishing returns on the level of the per capita capital stock.

If technological progress dictates economic growth, what kind of economics governs technological advance? Romer's 1990 article tried to make technology "endogenous" and to explain it within the terms of his theory. He was able to create for the first time an unequivocal growth model with technical progress that takes into consideration the actions of private agents who react to market incentives.

To escape from the neoclassical theory of growth, three assumptions are required: first, Romer (1990) assumed that ideas were goods of a particular kind, which, differently from things, are "non-rival"; every person can make use of a formula, design, particular method, recipe, or blueprint at the same time. The second assumption is that the fabrication or the creation of ideas enjoys increasing returns to scale. A good is excludable if the title-holder, using technological change like a database or the legal system like a copyright, can prevent others from using it. So, technical progress takes place when the improvements in the technology give to firms or individuals benefits and rights that are partially excludable. Although these goods are expensive to produce, they are cheap, almost costless, to reproduce. Thus, regardless of whether it is used by one person or by more than one, the total cost of a design does not change much. However, if the business costs nothing to enter, then it is not worth doing so because competition pares the price of a design down to the negligible cost of reproducing it. The third assumption in Romer's endogenous technical change is that companies, in order to cover the fixed cost of inventing new ideas, need to enjoy some measure of monopoly over their designs by patenting or copyrighting them.

Technological progress and capital accumulation are the two main elements that drive economic growth. The actions of private agents have also a determinant role in responding to market incentives. In Romer's view (1990), there is only one type of labour, which is further distinguished as unskilled and skilled (considered as human capital). Nevertheless, this distinction is not essential for the results of his model. The

Romer model (1990) considers three sectors: a final output sector, an intermediate goods sector, and a research sector. The final output Y is expressed as a function of physical labour L, human capital allocated to final output $H\gamma$, and physical capital. Firms are assumed to produce a homogenous final output good that can be used for consumption or as an input for capital goods.

The technology for producing final output has the extension of the Cobb-Douglas production function.

$$Y(H_\gamma, L, x) = H_\gamma^\alpha L^\beta \sum_{i=1}^{\infty} x_j^{1-\alpha-\beta} \tag{8.8}$$

where $x = \{x_j\}_{i-1}^{\infty}$

is the number of potential inputs used by a firm that produces final output, L is the physical labour, and $H\gamma$ is the human capital dedicated to final output. These inputs are completely used up in the production function, as they are considered to be intermediate goods to produce final goods. This production function implies that all capital goods are perfect substitutes for each other. The total capital K is defined as being proportional to the sum of all different types of capital; therefore, all capital goods are perfect substitutes. From equation (8.8) we have that H and L are fixed, and K grows by the amount of foregone consumption. According to Romer (1990), research output depends on the amount of human capital dedicated to research. Therefore, if research (new designs) is treated as a discrete indivisible entity that is not produced by a certain production process, the technology for research (or new designs) would have to consider the numerous limitations and uncertainty. Instead of supposing that there are N discrete varieties of capital goods, it is supposed that there is a continuum of capital goods running from 0 to ∞. Using i as a continuous variable for different types of goods, we have that the sum in equation (8.8) is replaced by the following integral (1990, S83–4):

$$Y(H_\gamma, L, x) = H_\gamma^\alpha L^\beta \int_0^\infty x(i)^{1-\alpha-\beta}\, di \tag{8.9}$$

So, the output of new designs (new products) created by the researchers is written as a continuous function (flow of new products) of the inputs applied. If a researcher j possesses an amount of human capital

H_j and at the same time has access to a portion A_j of the total stock of knowledge, the rate of production of new products is $\delta H_j A_j$, where δ is a productivity parameter. Romer's assumption is that the rate of growth of A is proportional to the amount of human capital allocated to research in discovering new varieties of goods. Putting together all people engaged in research, the aggregate stock of new varieties of goods evolves according to the following equation:

$$\dot{A} = \delta H_A A \tag{8.10}$$

where H_A stands for the total human capital employed in research and A the stock of knowledge. The endogenous growth consists of that rate of growth of output that is proportional to the amount of human capital allocated to research in new designs. The two essential assumptions of the endogenous growth according to Romer (1990) are: first, allocating more human capital to research leads to a higher rate of creation of varieties of goods; and second, the stock of knowledge of the research sector in the economy is proportional to the human capital input in the research sector. Hence, the new assortments of capital goods are proportional to both the human capital input to research and the past inventions already incorporated in capital goods. In fact, H_A and A in the above equation are both linear.[5]

Knowledge enters into production in two different ways. First, a new program of research (or project) enables the production of a new good (capital good) to produce output. Second, a new research program (or design) increases the total stock of knowledge and, in so doing, increases the productivity of human capital in the research sector. At the aggregate level, the human capital devoted to final output H_Y and the total human capital employed in research H_A are related as follows:

$$H_Y + H_A = H \tag{8.11}$$

According to this relation, any person can dedicate human capital to either the final-output sector or the research sector.

The capital goods sector is assumed to produce differential capital goods. In Romer's model there is a technical prerequisite for production: the industrialist or the capital goods producer must first purchase the required license. The requirement for production function is that the market for capital goods must be monopolistically competitive. Capital goods are assumed to be produced from the final output on a one by one base. Hence, it follows that aggregate capital is given as

$$K = \dot{A}x + A\dot{x} = Y - C \tag{8.12}$$

where x is the stock, and along the balanced growth path, $\dot{x} = 0$. In this equation (8.12), capital goods are differential capital goods (considered as stock and not flow) and not intermediate goods, which are put together to make up the final output.

In the research sector, firms conduct research and development using new and economically valuable ideas that have a high price in the market. They develop new projects for the production of new types of capital goods. It is assumed that the market for designs is perfectly competitive, so the growth rate of A in research technology now is given as

$$\dot{A} = \eta_A(1 - \Phi)\, L \qquad \text{with } \eta_A > 0 \tag{8.13}$$

where A is the stock of knowledge and η_A is the productivity parameter of the growth rate that indicates an increase in the productivity of the private input L (physical labour) – which is equivalent to a reduction in the research (R&D) costs – stimulates growth. For the households sector, the only argument in the utility function is consumption. Households supply one unit of labour during each period of time. According to the Ramsey optimization rule the standard rule of optimal consumption in the households sector comes as the result of intertemporal optimization of the present value of the stream of instantaneous utility (taking into consideration the income restriction). Therefore, the optimal consumption is given as:

$$\dot{C} = C\,(r - p)/\sigma \qquad \text{with } \sigma, p > 0 \tag{8.14}$$

where r is the interest rate and σ and p are parameters of the present value of the stream of instantaneous utility. For the balanced growth solution, we must consider the relation between the growth rate of output and rate of return on investment. In the long run, both K and A are accumulated, so the wage paid for human capital in the final-output sector is proportional to A, and, from equation (8.10), we have the result that the productivity of human capital is proportional to A. Given that the productivity of human capital grows at the same rate in both sectors, the human capital dedicated to final output, $H\gamma$, and the total human capital employed in research, H_A, will remain constant if the price, P_A, for new designs is constant. Because the present discounted value of the stream of profit must equal the price P_A of the design, it follows that the price P_A is given as (Romer 1990, S91–3)

$$P_A = \frac{1}{r}\pi = \frac{\alpha+\beta}{r}\bar{x}\bar{p} = \frac{\alpha+\beta}{r}(1-\alpha-\beta)H_\gamma^\alpha L_\gamma^\beta \bar{x}^{(1-\alpha-B)} \tag{8.15}$$

In Romer's view, the necessary condition of determining the allocation of human capital between the final-output and the research sectors is that wages paid to human capital in each sector must be the same. The human capital receives almost all of the income from the research sector, the wage of which is $P_A\delta A$. The human capital wage implies

$$w_H = P_A\delta A = \alpha H_\gamma^{\alpha-1}L^\beta \int_0^\infty \bar{x}^{(1-\alpha-\beta)}\,di = \alpha H_\gamma^{\alpha-1}L^\beta A\bar{x}^{(1-\alpha-\beta)} \tag{8.16}$$

From equation (8.15), we substitute P_A into equation (8.16), and we get the equation of the human capital dedicated to final output $H\gamma$:

$$H_\gamma = \frac{1}{\delta}\frac{\alpha}{(1-\alpha-\beta)(\alpha+\beta)}r \tag{8.17}$$

The final output following neoclassical growth models is given as

$$Y(H_\gamma, L, x) - H_\gamma^\alpha L^\beta \int_0^\infty \bar{x}^{(1-\alpha-\beta)}\,di = H_\gamma^\alpha L^\beta A\bar{x}^{(1-\alpha-\beta)} \tag{8.18}$$

where the last part of the equation behaves just like the neoclassical model with labour and human capital augmenting technological change. Output grows at the same rate as A if L, $H\gamma$, and $\bar{x}$ are fixed. The accumulation of capital is given as $K = \eta A\,\bar{x}$, where A is the range of capital goods (durables) and η the units of capital required per unit of durable goods. Indicating by g the growth rate of A, Y, and K, and because K/Y[6] is constant, we have that the ratio for all variables involved in the production function is written as

$$g = \frac{\dot{C}}{C} = \frac{\dot{Y}}{Y} = \frac{\dot{K}}{K} = \frac{\dot{A}}{A} = \delta H_A \tag{8.19}$$

From (8.17), the relation between growth rate g and interest rate r (considering also [8.11]) implies (Romer 1990, S92),

$$g = \delta H_A = \delta H - \frac{\alpha}{(1-\alpha-\beta)(\alpha+\beta)} r \quad (8.20)$$

Equation (8.20) can be written in a more simplified form as

$$g = \delta H_A = \delta H - \varepsilon r \quad (8.21)$$

where ε is a constant that depends on the technology parameters α and β as in equation (8.17).

$$\varepsilon = \frac{\alpha}{(1-\alpha-\beta)(\alpha+\beta)} \quad (8.22)$$

Taking into account that the consumer's preference is given by $g = C^{\cdot}/C = (r - \rho)/\sigma$, where ρ is the discount rate,[7] we have the fundamental equation of the rate of growth, given as

$$g = \frac{\delta H - \varepsilon\rho}{\sigma\varepsilon + 1} \quad (8.23)$$

The fundamental equation implies that the long-run growth rate is completely determined by technology and preference parameters.

THE RATE OF GROWTH AND THE PRODUCTION FUNCTION

Another way to solve the balanced growth rate is by considering the production side of the economy:

$$Y = \eta_A (A, \varphi, L)^{\alpha L} K^{\alpha K} \quad (8.1)$$

The output technology given by equation (8.1) states that, along the balanced growth path, the Romer model is equivalent to a simpler neoclassical growth model of the Harrod-neutral technical progress type. Thus, the following relations hold along the balanced growth path: g: $Y^{\cdot}/Y = A^{\cdot}/A = K^{\cdot}/K = C^{\cdot}/C$

Because research technology (R&D) is linear in A, the growth rate of A as we have seen in 8.13 is given as:

$$\dot{A} = \eta A(1 - \Phi) L \qquad (8.m)$$

This equation shows that the parameter Φ must be a constant. The fundamental solution for the balanced growth rate is given by

$$g_M = \frac{\alpha_K \eta_A L - \rho}{\alpha_k + \sigma} \qquad (8.n)$$

where the productivity parameter ηA in the growth rate states that an increase in the productivity of the private input labour L, which is equivalent to a reduction in research and development costs, stimulates the rate of growth.

Growth is endogenous at least in two senses. First, it results from the optimizing decisions of private agents (households and entrepreneurs). Second, the productivity parameter ε (in the growth rate) indicates that an increase in the productivity of inputs as a consequence of more human capital that is dedicated to final output and research stimulates growth. Therefore, a subsidy to the research sector can affect the long-run growth rate. In this case, public policy is effective. The long-run growth rate implies a scale effect. The larger the economy, measured by human capital H dedicated to final output $H\gamma$ and the total human capital employed in research H_A, the higher the amount of labour L and human capital allocated to R&D and the higher the long-run growth rate. Last, the growth condition is $\delta H - \varepsilon\rho > 0$, which measures the size of the economy. That a measure of the size of the economy enters the growth condition implies that an economy must be sufficiently large in order to display sustained growth. This is the reason why large, developed Western economies with high rates of growth usually have huge research sectors compared to those in less-developed countries.

THE ROMER MODEL IN PERSPECTIVE

In his 1928 article about increasing returns, recalling Adam Smith's theme of the division of labour, Allyn Young assumes,

> In recapitulation of these variations on a theme from Adam Smith there are three points to be stressed. First, the mechanism of increasing returns is not to be discerned adequately by observing the effects of variations in the size of an individual firm or of a particular industry, for the progressive division and specialization of industries is an essential part of the process by which increasing returns are realised. What is required is that industrial operations be seen as an interrelated whole. Second, the securing of increasing returns depends upon the progressive division of labour, and the principal economies of the division of labour, in its modern forms, are the economies which are to be had by using labour in roundabout or indirect ways. Third, the division of labour depends upon the extent of the market, but the extent of the market also depends upon the division of labour. (Allyn A. Young 1928, 539)

More than sixty years later, Romer (1986 and 1990) found that the increasing return is determined mainly by technology and preference parameters and is the result of optimizing decisions of private agents (households and entrepreneurs). Hence, the rate of growth is stimulated by an increase in the productivity of inputs as a consequence of more human capital being dedicated to final output and research.

The interest of Romer's first article (1986), however, more than to describe the characteristics of the factors involved on the balanced path of growth, turned to demonstrating the existence of a solution of the competitive equilibrium for a general version of the model and, therefore, to demonstrating the compatibility of increasing returns to scale in the production function and the decreasing marginal productivity in research and externalities – in a framework still Solovian and with no need of external intervention.

In addition, Romer considers specific cases – for example, the Cobb-Douglas production function such as $f(k,K) = k^{v}K^{\gamma}$: with $0 < v \leq 1$ and $1 < \gamma + v$ and other linear functions – but prefers to assume capital and labour as fixed two factors, and then proceeds according to the ordinary techniques of dynamic optimization. In doing so, he demonstrates – like a social planner who maximizes the utility function of a representative consumer subject to production constraints, reaching the optimal when the production function is totally convex in k – that an equilibrium for the competitive case can exist, in absence of external interventions, but that this equilibrium is suboptimal.

Lucas developed some techniques that are not Pareto-optimal in order to analyze paths of equilibrium growth that is not steady state (Dixit 1990). In a competitive equilibrium, the positive externalities of the production of knowledge do not get "repaid" at the enterprise level, and therefore, the stimulus toward the production of knowledge turns out to be smaller than what is necessary to catch up to the optimal level from the society: "the social marginal product of knowledge is greater than the private marginal product in the non-intervention competitive equilibrium" (Romer 1986, 1026). This is a concept already present in Arrow, which was also suggested by Romer in order to correct the discrepancy.

Romer's model is one of those in which increasing returns to scale are necessary to reach endogenous growth; as demonstrated by Rebelo, this is a necessary condition for a "core" of capital goods. In fact, "First, the models discussed here make clear that increasing returns and externalities are not necessary to generate endogenous growth. As long as there is a 'core' of capital goods whose production does not involve nonreproducible factors, endogenous growth is compatible with production technologies that exhibit constant returns to scale" (Rebelo 1991, 519).

In the case of Romer, however, the situation is different, although the results are similar when the specification of the research sector is taken into account. Here the marginal productivity shows a decreasing rate of returns.

Another point of discussion is the ability of the model to generate increasing rates of growth. Romer cites some empirical studies of Angus Maddison (1979 and 1982) on the possibility, in the long run, that the rates of growth of productivity might be effectively increasing (Romer 1986, part III). As a matter of fact, "One revealing way to consider the long-run evidence is to distinguish at any point in time between the country that is the 'leader,' that is, that has the highest level of productivity, and all other countries. Growth for a country that is not the leader will reflect at least in part the process of imitation and transmission of existing knowledge, whereas the growth rate of the leader gives some indication of growth at the frontier of knowledge" (Romer 1986, 1008).

Moreover, Romer seems to be drawn toward the idea that the rate of growth is not negatively correlated with the level of capital or per capita output, and therefore there is no convergence between countries. As a matter of fact, there is no ground to exclude the possibility that the aggregate production function is best described as exhibiting increasing returns, whose importance, moreover, is confirmed from the studies of

Denison (1961). The fact remains that when there is no increase in population there will be no infinite increase in the rate of growth for the period taken into consideration.

Another aspect of Romer's model is that the production of knowledge is not intentional; it is a byproduct of investment, certainly not formulated through a specific field of research and development, like the learning by doing of Arrow or learning by watching of King and Robson (1993). Among many possible evolutions of the model that followed, only two are conceptually useful, because of their conceptual closeness to the original version, in order to show how the concept of knowledge from Romer (1986) is then developed until it becomes useful in explaining several traditions of neoclassical growth.

Learning by doing is present in Alwyn Young (1991), who proposed a model in which there exists an infinite number of goods, classified according to the sophistication of technical processes used in their production. Labour is the only factor of production, and the learning by doing that increases the productivity is limited for each good but exhibits spillovers among different goods. This is what guides the endogenous growth, given that the learning by doing is nourished from new inventions. In fact, Young (1991) envisaged that only when the rate of technical progress has become historically nearly continuous have steady rates of economic growth have taken place. In his model, learning by doing is non-appropriable by enterprises and the production takes place under the condition of perfect competition; but the "distribution" of knowledge in a range of an infinite number of goods under the condition of imperfect competition will be included in the new kind of endogenous growth models.

Conversely, there is another model where knowledge is in some way appropriable. Freeman and Polasky (1992) introduced an economy of overlapping generations where young agents can use their time to study, work, or have leisure; when they study, they learn production processes that will have a return in the second period to produce consumer goods. Knowledge guides growth because the agent's knowledge stock does not decrease from the transmission made to others; neither can the transmission of knowledge between two parties be observed or controlled by a third party. Indeed, the baggage of knowledge of this economy is divided into true knowledge, decomposed knowledge, and commercialized knowledge, and a second intangible good is incorporated into the agent through study: human capital, which is one of the most important factors of endogenous growth and will be discussed in the next section.

HUMAN CAPITAL AND ECONOMIC DEVELOPMENT: THE LUCAS MODEL

"I will begin by considering an alternative, or at least, a complementary, engine of growth to the 'technological change' that serves this purpose in the Solow model" (Lucas 1988, 17). The alternative considered by Lucas is in what

> Schultz (1963) and Becker (1964) call "human capital" to the model, doing so in a way that is very close technically to similarly motivated models of Arrow (1962), Uzawa (1965) and Romer (1986). By an individual's "human capital" I will mean ... simply his general skill level, so that a worker with human capital h(t) is the productive equivalent of two workers with ½ h(t) each, or a half time worker with 2h(t). The theory of human capital focuses on the fact that the way an individual allocates his time over various activities in the current period affects his productivity, or his h(t) level, in the future periods. (Lucas 1988, 17)

Lucas,[8] by assuming that learning and spillovers involve human capital, focuses on the average level of human capital available in the economy, rather than on the aggregate function of human capital. Therefore, instead of thinking of the accumulated knowledge or the experience of producers, we think about the benefits deriving from the average person who possesses a normal level of skills and knowledge.

In Lucas's model, individual workers make their decisions on how to allocate their time between acquiring education and working in a manufacturing or production sector on the basis of the intertemporal utility maximization.

Knowledge, a public good in Romer (1986), becomes a private and non-excludable good in Lucas, one that is incorporated into the physical body of a person who studies and is cumulative mainly through this process. However, more than the *knowledge* in Romer, in Lucas, the *human capital* is an intentional accumulation of knowledge. As the model of Romer (1986) has its precedents in those of Arrow and Sheshinski, the model of Lucas derives from the works of Uzawa (1965) and Shell (1967), where technical progress comes from a specific sector that allocates a certain level of resources. The practical problem of these models is the difficulty in reality in identifying a field that produces knowledge in the sense indicated by the theory: many endogenous economists support the idea that only the act of investment generates new ideas; human capital alone is not enough (Stern 1991). However, Lucas recognized that

> human capital is simply an unobservable magnitude or force, with certain assumed properties, that I have postulated in order to account for some observed features of aggregative behaviour. If these features of behavior were *all* of the observable consequences of the idea of human capital, then I think it would make little difference if we simply re-named this force, say, the Protestant Ethic or the Spirit of History or just "Factor X." After all, we can no more directly measure the amount of human capital a society has, or the rate at which it is growing, than we can measure the degree to which a society is imbued with the Protestant ethic.
>
> But this is *not* all we know about human capital. This same force, admittedly unobservable, has also been used to account for a vast number of phenomena involving the way people allocate their time, the way individuals' earnings evolve over their lifetimes, aspects of the information, maintenance and dissolution of relationships within families, firms and other organizations and so on. (Italics in original) (Lucas 1988, 35)

It has been already observed that the theory of endogenous growth leads back to a wide vision of capital. In this context, it becomes also very much necessary to have a vision of human labour not only as a numerical sum of the physical amount of the workforce but also something more complicated.

The main objective of the theory of human capital is to prove that the level of ability of an individual depends on how much the individual "invests" his time in improvement and learning and also on how much he invests in normal productive activity or leisure. Lucas formalizes just this important aspect: an individual can increase his human capital in a way conceptually similar to the process of physical accumulation by allocating resources temporally.

The original version of Lucas's model (1988) is very simple and is based on a series of assumptions: workers $N(t)$, who are part of an economic system, are identical; their skill level is defined as $h(t)$, with a value that goes from zero to infinite; and they devote a fraction $u(t)$ of their non-leisure time to current production and the remaining $1 - u(h)$ to human capital accumulation. The effective workforce in production is given by the sum of non-leisure time of skilled-average man-hours devoted to current production:

$$N^e = \int_0^\infty u(h)N(h)hdh \tag{8.24}$$

The equation for the technology of goods production is written as (Lucas 1988, 8):

$$N(t)c(t) + \dot{K}(t) = AK(t)^\beta \left[u(t)h(t)N(t)\right]^{1-\beta} h_a(t)^\gamma \tag{8.25}$$

where h_a is the average skill level, meant to capture the external effects of human capital, and A is the technology level, assumed as constant.

We remember that Uzawa (1965) had delineated an almost identical model of endogenous growth based on the allocation of labour to the educational sector. Relating technology to the growth of human capital $h(t)$, we obtain a general function of human capital accumulation:

$$\dot{h}(t) = h(t)^\xi G(1 - u(t)) \tag{8.26}$$

where the human capital accumulation function G is increasing. The Uzawa linearity assumptions will not help much, because he considers the diminishing returns. Mathematically, the relation must (a necessary condition) not be smaller than 1 in order for the push toward growth to continue interrupted. This means that there is constant proportionality in the learning abilities, which is difficult to demonstrate. In support of this strong solution, Lucas relies not only on Uzawa's work but also on the empirical studies of Rosen (1976). The fact is that, in a certain way, the function (8.26) already assumes the endogenous growth rather than explaining it, choosing the allocation of time between study and work. Lucas was aware of the "short cut" of his model and prevents the objections: essentially, the proportionality of the human capital is accepted only if it is considered to be akin to a social activity that regards groups of persons as those who practically would pass the whole body of knowledge from generation to generation without having to start every time from the beginning. As Lucas stated, "Human capital accumulation is a *social* activity, involving *groups* of people in a way that has no counterpart in the accumulation of physical capital" (Italics in original) (Lucas 1988, 19).

The optimal solution again consists of finding the optimal growth path of $K(t)$, $h(t)$, (t), $c(t)$, and $u(t)$ that maximizes the utility function of the representative agent, subject to two equations, (8.25) and (8.26). Considering the optimality problem with "prices" $\Phi(t)1$ and $\Phi(t)2$ that Lucas used to value the increments of physical and human capital respectively, the current value of Hamiltonian type takes the form

$$H(K,h,\varphi_1,\varphi_2,c,u,t) = \frac{N}{1-\sigma}(c^{1-\sigma)} - 1) + \varphi_1\left[AK^\beta (uNh)^{1-\beta} h^\gamma - N_c\right] + \varphi_2\left[\delta h(1-u)\right] \tag{8.27}$$

Considering also the consumption $c(t)$ and the time allocated to production $u(t)$, the first optimal conditions for the optimal problem are given by

$$C^{-\sigma} = \varphi_1 \tag{8.28}$$

$$\text{and } \varphi_1(1-\beta)AK^\beta (uNh)^{-\beta} Nh^{1+\gamma} = \varphi_2 \delta h \tag{8.29}$$

where, according to equation (8.28) on the margin, goods must be equally valuable in both uses – consumption and capital accumulation. We can say the same for equation (8.29); time must be equally valuable in both uses – production and capital accumulation. The rate of change of prices $\Phi(t)1$ and $\Phi(t)2$, consumption $c(t)$, and time devoted to production $u(t)$ are given as

$$\dot{\varphi}_1 = \rho\varphi_1 - \varphi_1 \beta AK^{\beta-1}(uNh)^{1-\beta} h^\gamma \tag{8.30}$$

$$\dot{\varphi}_2 = \rho\varphi_2 - \varphi_1(1-\beta+\gamma)AK^\beta (uN)^{1-\beta} h^{-\beta+\gamma} - \varphi_2\delta(1-u) \tag{8.31}$$

Equations (8.28) and (8.30) imply that the marginal productivity of capital condition has the form

$$\beta AK(t)^{\beta-1}(u(t)h(t)N(t))^{1-\beta} h(t)^\gamma = \rho + \sigma\frac{\dot{c}(t)}{c(t)} \tag{8.32}$$

where $c(t)^{\cdot}/c(t)$ is the per capita consumption. From equation (8.32), we have capital, $K(t)$, growing at the rate $c(t)^{\cdot}/c(t) + \lambda$, which is constant on a balanced growth path. The rate of growth of capital and consumption per head are equal to

$$\frac{\dot{c}}{c} = \frac{\dot{k}}{k} = \left(\frac{1-\beta+\gamma}{1-\beta}\right)\frac{\dot{h}(t)}{h(t)}g \tag{8.33}$$

In the case of a social planner, the efficient growth rate equilibrium of human capital along a balanced path is given by

$$\frac{\dot{h}(t)}{h(t)} = \frac{1}{\vartheta}\left[\delta - \frac{1-\beta}{1-\beta+\gamma}(\rho-\lambda)\right] \tag{8.34}$$

where γ is the exogenous population growth rate. This equation provides that the stock of human capital grows more slowly than the stock of physical capital when there is an externality γ. If there are no externalities, the stock of human capital would grow at exactly the same rate as the stock of physical capital. In the case of a capitalist economy (where ha is given), the balanced growth rate of human capital, denominated by $h(t)^{\cdot}/h(t)$, is written as

$$\frac{\dot{h}(t)}{h(t)} = \left[\vartheta(1-\beta+\gamma)-\gamma\right]^{-1}\left[(1-\beta)(\delta-(\rho-\lambda))\right] \tag{8.35}$$

where the rate of growth increases with the effectiveness δ of investment in human capital and diminishes with increased discount rate ρ; the presence of an exogenous component in the human capital sector does not influence the rate of steady growth but only the velocity of growth. In fact, equations (8.34) and (8.35), which describe the rate of growth of human capital in both contexts, are identical except for the presence of the external component.

BALANCED GROWTH RATE OF THE HUMAN CAPITAL

A different way to get to the balanced growth rate of the human capital following Lucas's analysis is as follows:

denoting $v = \dfrac{\dot{h}(t)}{h(t)}$ from (8.26)

implies that $v = \delta(1 - u)$, and from differentiating equation (8.32), the growth rate of consumption per capita is given as

$$\frac{\dot{C}}{C} = \left(\frac{1-\beta+\gamma}{1-\beta}\right) \qquad (8.o)$$

From differentiating both (8.28) and (8.29) and substituting for $\Phi^{\cdot}2/\Phi2$, we get

$$\frac{\dot{\varphi}_2}{\varphi_2} = (\beta - \sigma)\frac{\dot{c}}{c} - (\beta - \gamma)v + \lambda \qquad (8.p)$$

To find the equilibrium of the efficient path, we use equations (8.29) and (8.31), so we find

$$\frac{\dot{\varphi}_2}{\varphi_2} = \rho - \delta - \frac{\gamma}{1-\beta}\delta u \qquad (8.q)$$

Substituting u, eliminating $\Phi^{\cdot}2/\Phi2$ between (8.p) and (8.q), and solving for v in terms of c'/c, we get the solution for the efficient equilibrium growth rate of human capital:

$$v^{*} = \sigma^{-1}\left[\delta - \frac{1-\beta}{1-\beta-\gamma}(\rho - \lambda)\right] \qquad (8.r)$$

The equilibrium balanced path in place of (8.q) can be rewritten as

$$\Phi^{\cdot}2/\Phi2 = \rho - \delta \qquad (8.s)$$

In the same way as (8.r), substituting u, eliminating $\Phi^{\cdot}2/\Phi2$ between (8.p) and (8.s), and solving for v in terms of $c^{\cdot}/c$, we get the solution for the rate of growth of human capital along a steady-state path:

$$v = [\sigma(1-\beta+\gamma)-\gamma]^{-1}\left[(1-\beta)(\delta-(\rho-\lambda))\right] \qquad (8.t)$$

the same as (8.35). The model predicts that there is a sustained rate of growth independently from the external effects of γ, which could be positive or negative (Lucas 1988, 20–5).

Lucas's model (1988) may also be analyzed by using a Cobb-Douglas form (Barro and Sala-i-Martin 1995). By defining first the level of technology as $A_i = K/L$, the Cobb-Douglas equation is given by

$$Y_i = F(K_i, K/L, L_i) \tag{8.36}$$

Modifying the Cobb-Douglas production function by inserting Lucas's human capital, the production function with output Y for the firm i is simply written as

$$Y_i = A(K_i)^{\alpha}\left(\frac{K}{L}L_i\right)^{1-\alpha} \tag{8.37}$$

where $0 < \alpha < 1$. Substituting $y_i = Y_i/L_i$, $k_i = K_i/L_i$, and $k = K/L$ and then setting $y_i = y$ and $k_i = k$ (because, in equilibrium, all firms make the same choices), we get the average product of capital:

$$\frac{y}{k} = \dot{f}(L) = A^{1-\alpha} \tag{8.38}$$

which satisfies the general properties that y/k is invariant and increasing in L. The private marginal product of capital can be determined by differentiating equation (8.37) with respect to K_i while holding K and L fixed. In so doing, the result is

$$\frac{\partial Y_i}{\partial K_i} = A\alpha L^{1-\alpha} \tag{8.39}$$

The Cobb-Douglas production function makes it easier for us to compare the growth rate of a decentralized solution with that of a social planner. The decentralized growth rate is given as

$$\gamma_c = \left(\frac{1}{\varphi}\right)\left(A\alpha L^{1-\alpha} - \delta - \rho\right) \tag{8.40}$$

where γ_c is the growth rate of consumption that is equal to the growth rate of two variables, k and y. And the social planner's growth rate is specified as

$$\gamma_c = \left(\frac{1}{\varphi}\right)(AL^{1-\alpha} - \delta - \rho) \tag{8.41}$$

It is easy now to compare these two rates by using the human capital model of Lucas (1988). The only difference between the decentralized growth rate equation (8.40) and the social planner's growth rate equation (8.41) is the coefficient α. Given that $\alpha < 1$, the decentralized growth rate is lower than the social planner's growth rate, as seen in the learning-by-doing model of Romer (1986). The main reason for a higher social planner's growth rate is that the social planner internalizes the spillover of knowledge,[9] whereas the decentralized solution does not. In order to internalize the spillover of knowledge and to achieve the social optimum in a decentralized economy, there are two options. The first is to subsidize the purchases of capital goods by investment tax credits, and the other is that the government can generate the optimum by subsidizing production.

In Lucas's model, the scale effect disappeared: differently than for other models of R&D, the spillover acts through the average level of human capital, and this avoids the Romer effect. Instead, the rate of growth depends on the relative allocation of labour between R&D and production. What does this model really say? An example is when "the US economy 'ought' to devote nearly three times as much effort to human capital accumulation as it does, and "ought" to enjoy growth in per-capita consumption about two full percentage points higher than it has had in the past" (Lucas 1988, 26).

Lucas shows the combination of human capital and physical capital along the path of the steady state, but admits "the dynamics of this system are not as well understood as those of the one-good model" (1988, 25). It is possible to conjecture that, for the formation of two kinds of capital, the solution path will converge at some points. However, the final position will depend. Where an economy begins with a low level of human and physical capital it will remain permanently below another economy that is well equipped with human and physical capital. In a steady-state path, the capital/labour ratio is constant, and because physical and human capital are endogenous, countries that begin with a minor level of both factors will catch up to the industrialized nations' rate of growth but not their levels of development.

Lucas simply obtains a constant return of scale in all the inputs, imagining that all inputs are cumulative: instead of considering the human population and the labour force not to be reproducible (in an economic sense), he proposes an alternative, that human capital can be increased (or improved) through direct and specific investment. This is sufficient to generate endogenous growth in case the incentive to invest in human capital does not diminish with increases in human capital. Therefore, the function of production that includes human capital must at least have constant returns to scale with respect to that human capital. The externalities are not the cause of the endogenous growth. Despite this, they turn out to be important during the movements of population and regarding the consideration of welfare: the production function in fact exhibits constant returns to scale regarding capital in general and "private" human capital in particular. However, the rate of return is supposed to be increasing when the externalities of human capital are taken into account, in a situation very similar to the one already studied by Romer.

THE REBELO[10] AK GROWTH MODEL

There is a class of models that assumes all inputs in production to be accumulable. One group of models of this class is the so-called linear AK models, which basically assumed a linear relationship between output, Y, and a single factor of capital, K (of the same commodity).

The Rebelo (1991) model is one of the best-known AK growth models. Here, the economy is basically composed of two sectors: the capital sector and the consumption sector. The two factors of production and the main assumptions of the model are: the reproducible factor, which is assumed to be accumulated over time and is summarized by capital good K, and the non-reproducible factor, denoted by a composite good T. The capital stock has a technology that is linear in the capital stock, written as

$$I_t = AK_t\,(1 - \theta_t) \tag{8.42}$$

where $(1 - \theta_t)$ is a fraction of capital stock used to produce investment goods (I_t), A is a fixed technology parameter, and K is the total capital stock. The consumption sector combines the non-reproducible factor to produce consumption goods (C_t). The production function of the consumption sector is assumed to have a Cobb-Douglas function of the type

$$C_i = B(\theta_t K_i)^{\alpha}\, T^{1-\alpha} \tag{8.43}$$

where B is a parameter of the Cobb-Douglas function and T is the land service available in each period. It is assumed that population is constant. The households own the labour and capital and rent them to firms at competitive prices. A representative, infinitely lived consumer maximizes lifetime utility defined as (Rebelo 1991, 503)

$$U = \int_0^\infty e^{-\rho t} \frac{C_t^{1-\sigma}}{\sigma} \tag{8.44}$$

subject to the capital accumulation constraint:

$$k_t = Ak_t^\alpha - C_t \tag{8.45}$$

where C_t is per-capita consumption, ρ is the rate of time preference, σ is the inverse of the intertemporal elasticity of substitution, and $k = dk/dt$ (in this case, the rate of capital depreciation is assumed to be zero). Because the real interest rate is constant (in the steady state), it make certain that when it is possible for consumption to grow at a constant rate, it is also optimal to do so.

The maximization of representative households' overall utility in equation (8.44) implies that the growth rate of consumption per labour unit at each point is given as

$$g = \frac{\dot{C}_t}{C_t} = \sigma^{-1}\left[f'(t) - \rho\right] \tag{8.46}$$

Per labour unit, the production function can be written as

$$y_t = Ak_t^\alpha \tag{8.47}$$

where $y_t = Y_t/N_t$ and $k_t = K_t/N_t$. Taking into consideration the Cobb-Douglas production function (8.47), it implies that the equation (8.46) equals

$$\frac{\dot{c}_t}{c_t} = \rho^{-1}\left[A\alpha k_t^{(\alpha-1)} - \rho\right] \tag{8.48}$$

The growth rate of consumption per capita depends positively on the difference between the returns to capital and the discount factor and negatively on the inverse of the intertemporal elasticity of substitution.

Net income measured in terms of consumption goods is given by $Y_t = C_t + p_t I_t - \delta_t Z_t$ and grows at the following rate (Rebelo 1991, 504):

$$g_y = \alpha g_z = \alpha \frac{A - \delta_Z - \rho}{1 - \alpha(1 - \sigma)} \tag{4.49}$$

where $(A - \delta_Z)$ is the path of pure accumulation and ρ is the time preference ($-\delta$ is the path along which all production is consumed). According to Rebelo (1991, 504), there are three properties of competitive equilibrium. First, the economy expands always at rate g (no transitional dynamics). Second, the parameter B (equation [8.43]) and the amount of land services available in each period T do not determine the growth rate but only the level of consumption. Third, the shares of investment and consumption with respect to output ($p_t I_t / Y_t$ and C_t / Y_t) are constant despite that C_t and I_t grow at different rates. The rate of savings s, as in the neoclassical growth model, is given by the relationship of a composite capital good $Z^{\cdot} = s\ (Y_t / p_t)$, which, as above (8.49), implies the steady-state growth rate, given as

$$g_y = \alpha g_z = \alpha \frac{(A - \delta_Z)s}{1 - \alpha(1 - \sigma)s} \tag{8.50}$$

The idea of saving in the above equation has a broader meaning than in the usual neoclassical growth models. In fact, Z represents a combination of physical and human capital, and s is the portion of total resources dedicated to the accumulation of activities.

The assumption that the individual does not have free time is strong. Rebelo (1991) extends the model of Lucas (1988) by considering the physical capital used in the production of human capital (with no externalities in the final sector). The production function of the Cobb-Douglas form takes place as

$$A_1 = (\varphi_t K_t)^{1-\gamma} (N_t H_t)^{\gamma} = C_t + I_t \tag{8.51}$$

where Φ is the fraction of physical capital, N_t stands for units of labour, and H_t stands for units of human capital. The accumulation of human capital implies

$$\dot{H}_t = A_2 [K_t(1 - \varphi_t)]^{1-\beta} [(1 - L - N_t) H_t]^{\beta} - \delta H \tag{8.52}$$

where physical capital depreciates at rate δ; $K_t = I_t - \delta K_t$, L are hours dedicated to leisure; and $1 - L - N_t$ are the hours dedicated to the accumulation of human capital capable of generating $(1 - L - N_t)H_t$ units of labour (it is assumed that consumption and investment goods are produced in the same sector, and it also introduces a separate consumption sector, which does not make any change in the properties of the model). There are two conditions regarding the efficiency in production. The first condition observes the optimal allocation of physical capital stock. The competitive equilibrium requires the allocation of efficient resources in both sectors. In fact, the marginal productivity of physical and human capital, measured in terms of units of physical capital, has to be equal in both sectors by equating equations (8.51) and (8.52), for capital and consumption sectors (Rebelo 1991, 509–10):

$$(1-\gamma)A_1(\varphi_t K_t)^{-\gamma}(N_t H_t)^{\gamma} = q_t(1-\beta_t)A_2\left[(1-\varphi_t)K_t\right]^{-\beta}\left[(1-L-N_t)H_t\right]^{\beta} \tag{8.53}$$

and

$$\gamma A_1(\varphi_t K_t)^{1-\gamma}(N_t H_t)^{\gamma-1} = q_t\beta_t A_2\left[(1-\varphi_t)K_t\right]^{1-\beta}\left[(1-L-N_t)H_t\right]^{\beta-1} \tag{8.54}$$

where q_t is supposed to be the relative value of human capital in terms of physical capital. If we eliminate q_t from both equations (8.53) and (8.54), then the marginal rate of transformation must be identical (in these two equations), which implies

$$\frac{\gamma}{1-\gamma}\left(\frac{\varphi_t K_t}{N_t H_t}\right) = \frac{\beta}{1-\beta}\left[\frac{(1-\varphi_t)K_t}{(1-L-N_t)H_t}\right] \tag{8.55}$$

The second condition is the decision to invest in physical capital. The rate of investment, r, equals

$$r_t = (1-\gamma)A_1(\varphi_t K_t)^{-\gamma}(N_t H_t)^{\gamma} - \partial \tag{8.56}$$

whereas the rate of investment in human capital is articulated in terms of physical capital stock, given as

$$r_t^* = \beta A_2\left[(1-\varphi_t)K_t\right]^{1-\beta}\left[(1-L-N_t)H_t\right]^{\beta-1}(1-L) - \partial + \frac{\dot{q}_t}{q_t} \tag{8.57}$$

The equilibrium condition requires that the rate of returns from both activities be the same, so $r_t = r^*_t$. Thus, from equations (8.53), (8.54), (8.56), and (8.57), we will be able to generate a simple form of the steady state:

$$(1-\gamma)A_1\left(\frac{\theta_t K_t}{N_t H_t}\right)^{-\gamma} = \beta A_2 = \left[\frac{(1-\varphi_t)K_t}{(1-L-N_t)H_t}\right]^{1-\beta}(1-L) \tag{8.58}$$

which can be solved for capital-labour intensities in both sectors. Along the steady-state path, I_t, K_t, and H_t grow at the same rate as consumption, so the growth rate of net income, defined as $Y_t = C_t + L_t - \delta K_t$, is written as

$$\frac{\dot{Y}}{Y} = \max\left[\frac{\psi A_1^v A_2^{1-v}(1-L)^{1-v} - \delta - \rho}{\sigma}, -\delta\right] \tag{8.59}$$

where the optimal rate of consumption is given as $gc = (r - \rho)/\sigma$ and the steady-state real interest rate depends on the geometric average of two parameters in the production function

$$r = \psi A_1^v A_2^{1-v}(1-L)^{1-v} - \delta \tag{8.60}$$

where $v = (1 - \beta)/(1 - \beta + \gamma)$ and ψ are strictly positive functions of β and γ respectively. Equation (8.60) has a corner solution with zero investment and is analogous to equation (8.59). In this model, the rate of profit is determined by technology alone, and the saving-investment mechanism determines the growth rate.

An interesting fact is that the rate of growth correlated positively with the hours worked (in either the educational or productive sector), so the model predicts that economies with hardworking agents will grow faster compared to other underdeveloped economies (Rebelo 1991, 510–11). The model introduces dynamics of transition, which means that although the variables do not grow at the same rate, there is a trend toward equilibrium. The model, after all, is endogenous. In effect, the insertion of free time is only a facade in that it deducts resources from educational and productive activities without giving advantages to consumers, who do not find free time in their utility function and, therefore, do not choose leisure. Rebelo introduces the possibility of the endogenous choice of free time. However, in order to render this possibility consistent with the steady growth equilibrium, preferences have to be such that each person chooses a portion of consumption and a constant allocation of time between work, N_t, and leisure, L_t, when placed before constant real wages and a constant rate of real interest. There are two forms of instantaneous utility functions that allow this: the first function is concave, twice continuously differentiable, and homogenous of degree b (taken by the work of Becker [1965] and Heckman [1976]):

$$u\,(C_t, L_t H_t) \tag{8.61}$$

Given the steady real rate of interest $r = \psi A_1^v A_2^{1-v} - \delta$ where $(1 - L)^{1-v}$ is absent in the interest rate expression because of the dependence of utility on leisure (in efficiency units), the steady-state growth rate is given as

$$g_y = \max\left(\frac{\psi A_1^v A_2^{1-v} - \delta - \rho}{1-b}, -\delta\right) \tag{8.62}$$

where the optimal growth rate consumption is related to the real interest rate by $g_{ct} = (r_t - \rho)/(1 - b)$.

From equation (8.62), we have that the real interest rate is independent of preferences and the growth rate of marginal utility of consumption is independent of the consumption-leisure mix because the utility function is homogeneous.

In the second case, the utility function has a steady-state growth of the form (derived from King, Plosser, and Rebelo [1988])

$$\begin{aligned} u(C_t, L_t) &= \log(C_t) + v_t(L_t) \quad \text{if } \sigma = 1 \\ &\frac{C_t^{1-\sigma}}{1-\sigma} v_2(L_t) \quad \text{if } 0 < \sigma < 1 \text{ or } \sigma > \end{aligned} \tag{8.63}$$

The utility function in the second case, which is different from the first one, depends on preference parameters. As a matter of fact, from equation (8.57), we have that the parameter measuring the hours dedicated to leisure, L_t, depends on preferences between consumption and leisure, and the real interest rate, r, depends on technical change and on the parameters of the utility function. Therefore, the allocation of time between education, work, and leisure does not change the basic properties of the model. Rebelo, as opposed to Romer, does not consider the increasing returns and the externalities in the generation of endogenous growth; instead, he believes that endogenous growth is generated by production technologies that exhibit constant returns to scale.

The Rebelo AK model is often seen as a way of interpreting the foresight infinite-horizon consumption problems in economic growth. Usually in an infinite-horizon model, the agent has both labour and capital income. However, Rebelo uses only labour income by assumption.

PUBLIC POLICY AND ECONOMIC GROWTH

The greater attention paid to the role of government in the processes of development is a characteristic of endogenous growth models in contrast to neoclassical basic models, in which it is not possible for either the government or other institutions to influence permanently the rate of growth. A related phenomenon is therefore the outbreak of studies (cross-section studies) born with the objective of giving practical indications to policy makers. Three occurrences were related to these studies. First, the sign of difference between the rate of growth of market and optimality is not unique because the economy can go even faster than it might (when it goes through oversaving and/or undersaving, as in Solow's model). Second, should the direction toward which the role of government operates be clear and effective (and not misleading) – as in the static theory of welfare – the conclusions would have insufficient practical value because it would sometimes remain uncertain whether to give sufficient capacity and dimension to government intervention for it to be effective, which in most cases depends on the assumptions considered in the models. Third, most of the models implicitly assume the Ricardian neutrality of the public debt, whereas on the contrary (non-neutrality), the action of the government could be highly misleading and the rates of growth may slow. It turns out that the economic estimations based on endogenous growth models are viewed mainly as suggestive empirical regularities, not as behavioural relationships on which to measure responses to policy changes (Lucas 1988).

According to King and Rebelo (1990), public policy can influence the long-run growth rate. Both authors established a simple model with two sectors, the goods sector and the human capital sector; two kinds of capital – real capital and human capital – both of which are accumulable; and two lines of production, one for the social product and the real capital, which consist of quantities of the same commodity, and the other for the human capital. The production function related to two kinds of capital is assumed to be homogenous of degree one and strictly concave. In the goods sector, there is a constant returns-to-scale production technology with physical and human capital as inputs, and it is given as:[11]

$$C_t + I_t = Y_t = F_1(K_{1t}, N_{1t}H_t) \tag{8.64}$$

where physical capital and labour (composed by human capital) inputs are denoted as K_{1t} and $N_{1t}H_t$, respectively. In the second sector (the human capital sector), the human capital investment good is produced with constant returns to scale using two inputs (human and physical capital):[12]

$$I_{ht} = Y_{2t} = F_2(K_{2t}, N_{2t}H_t) \tag{8.65}$$

The physical capital is assumed to go under a neoclassical accumulation equation of the type

$$K_{j,t+1} - K_{j,t} = I_{jt} - \delta kjK_{jt} \tag{8.66}$$

where δkj is the depreciation rate in sector *j*. The evolution of human capital stock is given as (Rosen 1976 and King and Rebelo 1990):

$$H_{t+1} - H_t = \Theta\ (I_{ht}/H_{ht})H_t - \delta_h H_t \tag{8.67}$$

where Θ is the initial parameter or the benchmark parameter (the first and the second derivate of $D(\Theta)$ is respectively greater and less than zero). Human capital is embodied in workers' time, and it determines the allocation of human capital. In equation (8.67), there is an adjustment cost that permits steady growth to happen if I_{ht} and H_t grow at the same time. The utility function and the preference over consumption take the form

$$U = \sum_{t=0}^{\infty} \beta^t \frac{1}{1-\sigma}(C_t^{1-\sigma} - 1) \qquad \text{for } 0 < \sigma < \infty \tag{8.68}$$

In the above utility function, constant growth in consumption is optimal if the interest rate is constant over time. According to King and Rebelo

(1990, S137), the parameterization of human capital accumulation technology implies that human capital declines at a depreciation rate if there is no investment expenditure ($\Theta = 0$), and there are no "adjustment costs" at zero gross investment, and as a result, the derivate is equal to 1, $D\Theta\ (I_h/H) = 1$ at $I_{ht} = 0$. The general form of parameter function Θ is given as

$$\theta\left(\frac{I_H}{H}\right) = \left[\frac{I_H}{H} + \theta^{\frac{1}{1-\theta}}\right]^{\theta} - \theta^{\frac{\theta}{1-\theta}} \tag{8.69}$$

The individual human capital accumulation is part of the individual's decision problem, and the wage rate, the price of investing in human capital, and the interest rate are assumed as given. The individual's maximization lifetime utility is subject to an intertemporal budget constraint and involves both consumption, C_t, and human capital investment, I_{ht}. It is given as

$$U = \sum_{t=0}^{\infty} [R(\tau)]^{-t} C_t \leq B_0 + \sum_{t}^{\infty} [R(\tau)]^{-t} (wNH_t - pI_{Ht}) \tag{8.70}$$

where $R(\tau)$ is the market discount factor, Bo is the level of initial financial assets, and wNH_t is the labour rate or the individual income (composed of human capital inputs). Consumption does not influence the rate of human capital formation. The determination of optimal growth rate requires involving the inverse of the adjustment technology, which allows inputs to yield a flow of human capital outputs. This function, called ψ, is included in the function of human capital equation:

$$\frac{I_{Ht}}{H_t} = \psi\left\{\left[\frac{H_{t+1} - (1-\delta_H)H_t}{H_t}\right]\right\} \tag{8.71}$$

Afterward, we substitute this equation into the lifetime budget constraint and we maximize it with respect to human capital stock. As a result, we get the efficiency condition:

$$wN = [R(\tau) - \gamma_h]\, pD\psi\ (\gamma_h - 1 + \delta_h) + p\psi\ (\gamma_h - 1 + \delta_h) \tag{8.72}$$

Implicitly, equation (8.72) determines the expression for the optimal growth rate of human capital in the presence of adjustment costs (King and Rebelo 1990, S139):

$$\gamma_h = \gamma\ [w/p, R(\tau), \delta_h] \tag{8.73}$$

The expression (8.73) states that the growth rate depends positively on the wage rate w and negatively on the price of investing in human capital p. It depends also positively on the interest rate $R(\tau)$ and on the depreciation rate of the capital goods δ_h (like investment in human capital). Indirectly, it depends on the parameter Θ of the adjustment cost. The price of investment in human capital is determined by domestic technology and taxes along the world interest rate. Given the wage rate w in the goods sector, determined as $w = (1 - \tau_1)D_2F_1(k_1,1)$, we finally have the price of investment good written as

$$p = \frac{[R(\tau) - 1 + \delta_{k2}]\upsilon_k + w\upsilon_n}{1 - \tau_2} \tag{8.74}$$

where τ_2 is the tax rate at sector 2 and υ_k and υ_n are functions of the relative factor price for sector 2.[13]

If the labour income is subject to the tax rate τw, then the after-tax income becomes $(1 - \tau w)w$, which makes the human capital growth and the individual income growth (wNH_t) slow. But if labour is the only input into human capital investment (no direct taxation), then human capital p is proportional to $(1 - \tau w)w$, so it does not affect the growth rate.[14]

Unlike basic neoclassical growth models, there are no transitional dynamics, and an increase in the income tax rate has effects on short- and long-run growth rates. The empirical research of King and Rebelo (1990) showed that a 10 per cent increase in the income tax rate, from 20 to 30 per cent, reduces the growth rate of the economy from 2 to 0.37 per cent. The effects of taxation in general depend largely on aspects of the production technology, and this reflects the fact that the human capital sector is a basket of many different activities and complex relationships. Hence, the estimation of several parameters of individual technologies for investment in human capital is an intricate process that may not always provide satisfactory conclusions. But what we can draw from the King and Rebelo model (1990) is that in both open and closed economies, small changes in tax rates can lead to stagnation for long periods if public policies do not guarantee incentives for growth.

SOME CONCLUSIONS ABOUT THE NEW THEORY OF GROWTH

Paul Romer was the first economist to study the fact that spillovers could be related with the accumulation of knowledge.[15] His groundbreaking study in the mid-1980s began the modern literature on endogenous growth theory. In fact, Romer demonstrated that spillovers could reach a level that can overcome even the decreasing returns to capital and sustain a steady state of growth in per capita output. In other studies Romer was able to improve his original model by explaining that companies will invest in research and development (R&D) even knowing that any ideas will ultimately benefit their competitors in the long term. One reason for this was that companies will take advantage of continuous innovation in the short term and overall it will help per capita output grow indefinitely. Romer's model does not completely displace the neoclassical model, but fills an important gap in the neoclassical theory by providing the source of technological progress.

Lucas, unlike Romer, chose the accumulation of human capital as the main feature of his endogenous model. In fact, by assuming that learning and spillovers involve human capital, he focused on deliberate accumulation of human capital through direct investments rather than the aggregate of knowledge. We may think about the advantages obtained from the average person who possesses the level of skills and knowledge accumulated over time. For Lucas, knowledge is a private and non-excludable good (not public, as for Romer), which is incorporated into the physical body of a person, mainly through studies and knowledge accumulation (even through experiences). Human capital affects individual firms' outputs but is not considered in the profit-maximizing decisions.

Later Rebelo, in contrast to Romer, did not take into account the increasing returns and externalities needed to generate endogenous growth, but only considered production technologies that exhibit constant returns to scale.

The role of government in the processes of growth is part of a significant contribution brought to economic literature by King and Rebelo in the early 1990s. Their view was that differences in the rate of growth among several countries were caused by government policies and in particular by the use of incentives affecting the accumulation of physical and human capital. Public policy is a powerful tool that influences small, open economies with freely mobile capital, with effects ranging from the stagnation to "growth miracles." Government also has the option to slow down growth through fiscal policy that can help disincentivize the accumulation of capital. An additional effect of public policy, resulting in increasing returns in the private sector comes as a consequence of investments made by government in both tangible (roads, railroads) and intangible (education, protection of copyrights, etc.) infrastructures; the basic concept is that public capital, included in the production function of enterprises, leads to increasing returns. Then again, the financing of these investments might happen through taxation, which could decrease the rate of growth.

During the 1990s many thinkers about growth economics developed a variety of models that expanded the idea of endogenous growth, having in common a fundamental characteristic: the effects of increasing returns to capital. Some growth models deal with the importance of accumulating human capital and increasing skills through formal education or on-the-job training. Others have focused on international trade, particularly on how the international pattern of comparative advantage influences trade and growth. Still others take into consideration the relationship between convergence and endogenous growth theory or examine any possible link between fiscal policy and endogenous growth. In the next chapter, a new typology of growth models will focus on devoting resources to innovated consumer goods for the market.

9

Endogenous Growth: Innovation and New Consumer Goods

This chapter presents a discussion of some alternative models of intentional industrial innovation. Unlike Romer, for whom growth is mainly obtained through the production of a variety of intermediate goods, Grossman and Helpman (1991a and 1991b) deal with innovation that serves to expand the range and the quality of finished goods available on the market. Firms devote resources to research and development in order to invent new goods that substitute imperfectly for the existing ones, and producers earn monopoly rents, which serve as the reward for their prior R&D investment and efforts. Growth then comes as a result of the combination of two mechanisms: the production of an expanding variety of consumer goods and the accumulation of knowledge (Solow 2000). Economic growth also is based on intentional industrial innovation. Innovation helps raise the quality of fixed assets. Commercial research is driven by profit opportunities, as the producers of high-quality (new brand) goods earn positive profits in their competition with manufacturers of lesser quality goods. Industrial research is focused on increasing the variety of products. Returns from R&D result in monopoly rents in imperfectly competitive product markets. Labour as a factor of production is employed in both R&D and the manufacturing sector. The innovative products may be either consumer goods or intermediate products. The intermediate goods contribute to total factor productivity in manufacturing final goods.

According to Grossman and Helpman (1991a) there are two opposing forces that help the process of growth. The first force is when intertemporal knowledge spillovers lead to a decrease in the cost of innovation. This effect increases the incentives for innovation and so encourages growth. The second one is when the value of innovations decreases as the number of available competitive goods increases, which reduces the incentives to innovate and hence reduces the rate of growth. The achievement of the steady-state growth is attained through the strength of intertemporal knowledge spillovers. After introducing alternative methods of innovation, such as expanding product variety and raising product quality, as a primary factor of production, Grossman and Helpman extended the range of endogenous models by introducing other factors of accumulation, like physical and human capital. Human capital accumulation in almost all endogenous growth models is considered an important factor in determining the rate of growth. In fact, any changes in the steady-state stock of human capital (unskilled and qualified labour) affect the long-run rates of innovation and growth.

This chapter considers models in which innovation and technological progress reveal an expanding number of product varieties and quality improvements. Even changes in product assortments are considered to be basic innovation, which may lead to the creation of new industries.

TECHNOLOGY AND EXPANSIONS IN THE VARIETY OF PRODUCTS: THE GROSSMAN-HELPMAN MODEL

Commonly speaking, industrial research is usually aimed at reaching two goals: minimizing the cost of production of existing commodities by discovering new processes and inventing entirely new products or commodities (product innovation) that substitute for the old ones. In most industries, the new products perform similar functions to those performed by existing goods, save for providing greater quality and new functions. So, new products expand variety in consumption and specialization in production. Grossman and Helpman in the early 1990s (1991b, 43–67), Spence (1976), and Dixit and Stiglitz (1977) in the mid-1970s introduced models with a variety of consumer products, which have been used to study technological change and economic growth in industrialized countries.

The best-known model of endogenous growth theory about the expansion of product variety is that of Grossman[1] and Helpman[2] (1991b). In their work there is a combination of trade elements and models with invented goods and patents, or models with quality improvements in existing goods.

They acknowledge that the growth theory of the 1990s is an extension, not a rejection, of the growth theory in the 1960s. The objective of

Grossman-Helpman model is to prove that there is endogenous growth in new products with expanded variety as a result of innovations, inventions, and intensive research.

The Grossman-Helpman (1991b) model starts off with a description of consumer's behaviour. The main assumption is that the representative household tends to maximize the current value of utility over an infinite horizon (overall utility) (Grossman and Helpman 1991b, 45–74). Intertemporal preferences are of the form

$$U_0 = \int_0^\infty \log(D) e^{-\rho t} dt \tag{9.1}$$

where $(D)e^{-\rho t}$ represents an index of consumption at time t, and ρ is the discount rate. The index D characterizes households' tastes for diversity in consumption. The instantaneous logarithmic utility in (9.1) implies that the intertemporal elasticity of substitution is constant and equal to one. The index of consumption, D, is a specification of the constant-elasticity-of-substitution function between every pair of goods. It is given as

$$D = [\int_0^N x(j)^\beta \, dj]^{\frac{1}{\beta}} \tag{9.2}$$

where the number of currently invented goods is denoted by n and the amount of goods j by $x(j)$. The instantaneous utility function implies a constant intratemporal elasticity of substitution among differentiated consumer goods, given as $\varepsilon = 1/(1-\beta) > 1$. The parameter β reflects the perceived differentiation in a set of products. The utility function given by (9.2), which is the result of the work of Dixit and Stiglitz (1977) conveys the basic idea of product variety or "taste for variety," and it is characterized as follows: the consumption goods enter the utility function symmetrically and substitute imperfectly with other consumption goods (consumption goods are assumed heterogeneous). A household that spends an amount, E, maximizes instantaneous utility by buying x units of brand j at price $p(j)$. The number of units is written as

$$x(j) = \frac{Ep(j)^{-\varepsilon}}{\int_0^n p(j')^{1-\varepsilon} dj'} \tag{9.3a}$$

where ε gives the constant price elasticity. To better fit the model to their purposes, Grossman and Helpman (1991b) used the Dixit-Stiglitz preferences, which have the following properties: first, because the perceived differentiation parameter β belongs to the set of products (0,1), the constant elasticity of substitution (CES) is constrained by $1 < \varepsilon < \infty$. This means that new goods are imperfect substitutes for old goods. Second, the CES equals the price elasticity of demand if all other prices are held constant (large group case). This implies the aggregate demand to have a particular simple form. It is simply assumed that innovative products are not superior to older varieties, despite the fact that they have been invented later in time. Because there is a complete symmetry between old and new products, there is no possibility for product obsolescence in the model. From equation (9.2), at any moment we have a constant return to scale. So, in the situation of competition, the equilibrium price, p_D, equals the unit cost of manufacturing (Grossman and Helpman 1991b, 47):

$$p_D = [\int_0^N p(j)^{1-\varepsilon}\, dj]^{\frac{1}{1-\varepsilon}} \tag{9.4}$$

In a different way, the optimal supply price can be considered as a constant markup over marginal cost: $p(j) = mc\ (j)/\beta$ with $0 < \beta < 1$, where β indicates the extent of market power. Following Either (1982), equation (9.2) may alternatively be interpreted as a production function. In this case, $x(j)$ denotes differential producer goods or services. The production function then describes the idea of an increase in productivity as a result of an increasing degree of product specialization (or the classic Smithian idea of the extended division of labour). From equation (9.2), it implies that

$$D = n^{\frac{1}{\beta}} x$$

It can also be shown that total factor productivity increases with the number of differentiated inputs and is given by

$$N^{\frac{(1-\beta)}{\beta}}$$

This effect is called the Smith-Either effect. Under this interpretation, D denotes a homogenous consumer good. The aggregate demand under the Smith-Either effect is given as

$$Y = (\int_0^N [x(i)]^\beta\, di)^{1/\beta} = (Nx^\beta)^{1/\beta} = XN^{(1-\beta)/\beta} \qquad \text{with } X = Nx \tag{9.5}$$

The household's maximization problem can be resolved in two stages: first (static optimization), the allocation of a given amount of expenditures is chosen to maximize instantaneous utility. Second (dynamic optimization), the time path of expenditures is determined in such a way that intertemporal utility reaches a maximum. In the static optimization, the maximization of the instantaneous utility function (9.2), subject to

$$E = \int_0^N x(j)p(j)dj$$

yields the demand for good j (the same as 9.3a):

$$x(j) = \frac{Ep(j)^{-\varepsilon}}{\int_0^N p(j')^{1-\varepsilon}\, dj'} \qquad (9.3b)$$

Because the specified preferences reflect a taste for diversity, the optimal allocation involves equal production of all known varieties. To achieve the dynamic optimization, the static allocation must be efficient at all times. By noting that $D = E/p$D and by substituting for D in (9.1), the intertemporal utility function can be reformulated as a dynamic allocation problem. So we have

$$U_o = \int_0^\infty e^{-\rho t}[\log(E) - \log(p_D)]dt \qquad (9.6)$$

where p_D represents a price CES index, given by

$$p_D = [\int_0^N p(j)^{1-\varepsilon} dj]^{\frac{1}{1-\varepsilon}}$$

and E is the amount spent by households. The maximization utility function (9.6) is subject to the intertemporal budget constraint $E'/E = r - p$ (Grossman-Helpman 1991b, 28). Prices also are normalized so that nominal spending equals unity at every point in time and, therefore, $r = p$.

Now it is time to consider the technology for product development. Here, producers are engaged in two distinct main activities. First, they manufacture products that have been invented in the past. Second, they are involved in a constant research process to develop new varieties of products for the market.

Because of the patent protection, each differentiated product is assumed to be manufactured by a single company. The production technology is assumed simple and reads $x(j) = L(j)$, where L is the supply of units of labour services at every moment in time. The specified technology used by the unique supplier of variety j maximizes the operating profits:

$$\Pi(j) = p(j)\, x(j) - wx(j) \tag{9.7}$$

by charging a price $p(j) = w/\beta$, where w is the wage-rate. In equilibrium, all varieties are priced equally, and hence, we can drop the index j and write $p = w/\beta$. By noting further that $E = Nxp = 1$ and having the symmetric demands and $E = 1$, operating profits may be expressed as

$$\Pi = 1 - \beta/N \tag{9.8}$$

At this stage, the competition effect becomes clear: the profits of manufacture decrease with the number of consumer goods. It is assumed that the stock market value of a firm, at a given period, equals the present discounted value of its profit stream. Thus, the value of a typical firm manufacturing intermediate goods is given by (Solow 2000, 160),

$$v_t = \int_0^\infty e^{-[R(\tau)-R(t)]}\pi(t)dt \tag{9.9}$$

where $R(t)$ represents the cumulative discount factor at time t.[3] The arbitrage in capital markets ensures equality between the normal yield and riskless loans. It is written as

$$\pi + v' = rv \tag{9.10}$$

where rv is the later return for an investment of size v.

Innovation, by considering technology (R&D), is produced by using two inputs: labour, L_A, and capital, $k(A)$. Labour is the private input, whereas capital is a public input. The technology for product innovation implies

$$\dot{A} = a^{-1}\, k(A)\, L_A \tag{9.11}$$

According to Grossman and Helpman, knowledge is assumed to depend on the number of goods invented up to the present and is expressed by the knowledge capital function $k(A)$. The R&D technology implies that costs of a research project yield a function of the form $\dot{A} = a^{-1} k(A)\, l_A$, where designs amount to wl_A, (where w is the cost of the wage and l is labour invested in the design), whereas cost research value is given by $v\dot{A} = a^{-1} k(A) l_A$. Another assumption of Grossman and Helpman (1991b) is that firms are free to enter into R&D. Free entry into R&D implies that an active research sector ($\dot{A} > 0$) requires the equality between costs and the value of research. However, if costs exceed the value of R&D, no research takes place. The value of the monopoly profits for an innovation must be the same as the cost of innovation:

$$v = wa/K(A) \text{ for } \dot{A} > 0 \text{ and } v = wa/K(A), \text{ for } \dot{A} = 0 \tag{9.12}$$

where a is a parameter, and K is the stock of knowledge available. K depends on the past innovations and, hence, is an externality of a single enterprise that benefits all the others. The combination of free entry and constant returns to scale in the research prevents entrepreneurs from earning excess returns. The equilibrium in the labour market requires that

$$L = L_A + L_M = a\dot{A}/K(A) + 1/p \tag{9.13}$$

where the demand resulting from the R&D sector is given by $L_A = a\dot{A}/K(A)$ and the demand stemming from manufacturing is $L_M = Ax = 1/p$ (normalization $E = xAp = 1$). Furthermore, because employment must be non-negative, equilibrium prices must satisfy

$$p > 1/L \tag{9.14}$$

In equilibrium, all varieties are priced equally at p, so the pricing equation is written as

$$p = w/\alpha \tag{9.15}$$

Combining the free entry condition (9.12), the pricing equation (9.15), and the employment constraint, we arrive at the conclusion that R&D is profitable only when the reward for successful research is pretty high. This value is given as

$$\bar{v} = \alpha a/L \tag{9.16}$$

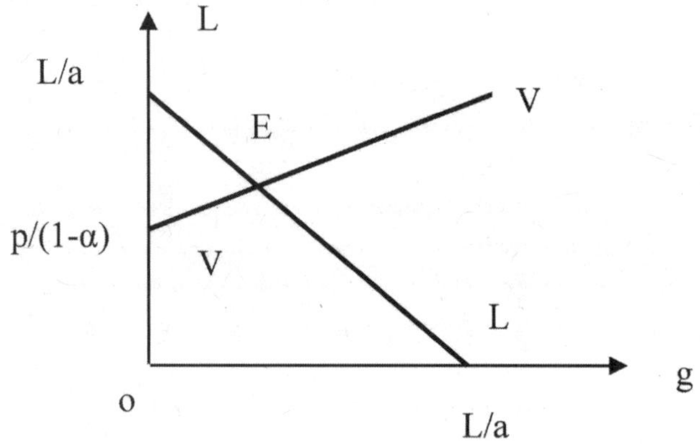

Figure 9.1 Steady-state growth equilibrium in the Grossman-Helpman model

R&D takes place if the rate of new goods' brands introduced per unit of time equals employment in research. Representing with $v = 1/nv$ the inverse of the economy's aggregate equality value and with $g = n^{\cdot}/n$ the instantaneous rate of innovation, the equilibrium growth path implies

$$g = L/a - \alpha V \text{ for } V < L/\alpha a' \text{ and } g = 0 \text{ for } V \geq L/\alpha a' \qquad (9.17)$$

From the definition of V and g ($V^{\cdot}/V = -g - v^{\cdot}/v$) we have a differential equation of the type

$$\frac{\dot{V}}{V} = V(1-\alpha) - g - p \qquad (9.18)$$

where p is the equilibrium price for all product varieties. The steady-rate of innovation is given as

$$g = (1-\alpha)\frac{L}{a} - \alpha p \qquad (9.19)$$

In the steady-rate equilibrium, represented at point E in figure 9.1, product development is always continuous at a constant rate g.

The line VV in figure 9.1 is upward sloping and shows the combination of V and g that implies $V^{\cdot} = 0$. From the Fisher arbitrage equation, $v^{\cdot} = pv - (1 - \alpha)/n$, we see that a smaller aggregate value of the stock market is related with a faster decline in firm value. Above the VV line, the number of varieties grows less rapidly than the firm's value falls, whereas the opposite is true below the line. The reason for this is that with a faster rate of innovation, the more quickly an innovation becomes obsolete and, thus, the faster profits fall. The more innovation activity takes place, the faster the initial monopoly profits vanish (the Schumpeterian point). The other curve, the LL, is downward sloping. Normally, a fixed supply of labour has to be allocated between research and production. Along this relationship, the more production takes place, the fewer resources are devoted to innovation. Grossman and Helpman see innovation and production as competing activities, and this is the reason that line LL is downward sloping. The intersection point E is where the dynamic forces in the economy have no effects on changes in the value of the stock market and on the rate of innovation over time. The economy stands at this stage only if the expectations of profit are fulfilled. On the contrary, if the initial expectations are not fulfilled, the dynamic system would drive the rate of innovation to zero and increase the value of the stock market.

According to the Grossman-Helpman model (1991b), entrepreneurs seek technological gains in response to profit opportunities. When they appropriate all the benefits from research and development, the process of investment technology runs into diminishing returns. Inventions serve to expand the range of available products.

In this model, the progress is not uniform among sectors: contrary to the Aghion and Howitt (1992) model (see next chapter), the innovations do not have effects on all industrial products but rather only on some specific sectors; and differently from the model of Segerstrom, Anant, and Dinopoulos (1990), the innovation happens at the same time in various sectors. In the Segerstrom-Anant-Dinopoulos model, which belongs to the same family, the inventions that occur in different sectors require time and are inversely related to the amount of labour allotted for this scope in a decreasing rate. The entrepreneurs are involved in innovations because of the profit opportunities. Speaking about economics, the process of growth through the expansion of product varieties shows large similarities to microstudies in industrial organization.

IMPROVEMENTS IN THE QUALITY OF PRODUCTS

In the early 1990s, Grossman and Helpman (1991a and 1991b), moving along the lines of Romer, spoke about quality ladders like a succession of new qualities and improvements of the same product. They assume that

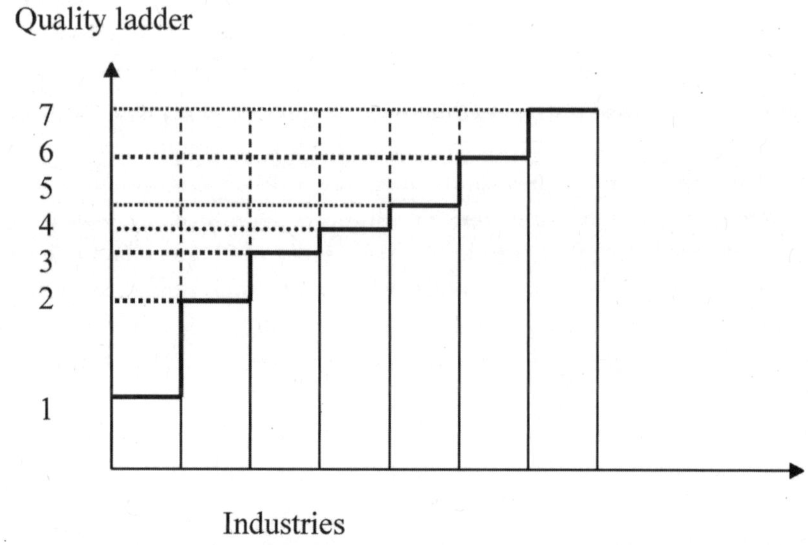

Figure 9.2 Quality ladders and product varieties

every product can be improved an unlimited number of times and that each improvement provokes a big jump in the quality of services that goods provide. According to them, "The economics of quality improvement have been studied by industrial organization economists in their work on patent races. Beginning with Loury (1979), Dasgupta and Stiglitz (1980), and Lee and Wilde (1980), much effort has been devoted to understanding the incentive that firms have to bring out new and improved products. This literature typically views R&D competition as a once-and-for-all race for technological supremacy" (Grossman and Helpman 1991a, 43).

Competition in industrial organization is all about technological supremacy. Entrepreneurs race with each other to bring out new products in order to replace the old ones. After a while, individual products become obsolete, so firms engage in research in order to obtain profits before their rivals. What's more, innovators may sometimes be able to benefit from observing and analyzing the research successes of their rivals. In an increasing number of industries, success occurs with a probability per unit of time that is proportional to the total R&D resources engaged in improving the quality of products. In Grossman and Helpman (1991b, Ch. 4), each product j is produced in an indefinite number of vertically differential varieties. The researcher who is in charge of quality improvement of product *j* maintains a monopoly right to manufacture the *j*th intermediate good at the quality level.

The quality-ladder process is illustrated in figure 9.2. The horizontal axis shows the number of products in different industries, and the vertical axis shows the quality obtained in each sector. Over time, the quality-ladder position in a single sector either stays constant or jumps directly to the next step. In every industry, the producers and researchers compete to introduce the next generation of products. When some successful researchers achieve a technological breakthrough in the line *j*, the quality product of that industry jumps by one generation to the next stair, as indicated in figure 9.2.

Turning to the formal specification of the model, we have that consumers share a common intertemporal utility function, given as (Grossman-Helpman 1991b, 87–9),

$$U_t = \int_t^{\infty} \log(D) e^{-\rho(\tau - t)} d\tau \tag{9.20}$$

where $(D)e^{-\rho(\tau-t)}$ represents an index of consumption at time t and ρ is the discount rate (the same as in equation [9.1]). Log $D(\tau)$ represents the flow of utility at time t. The household's instantaneous utility is given by

$$\log D(t) = \int_0^1 \log\left[\sum_m q_m(j) x_{mt}(j)\right] dj \tag{9.21}$$

where $xmt(j)$ denotes the consumption of quality m of product j at time t and qm is the quality product. The consumers maximize utility by spreading their consumption across the product lines and by purchasing the single quality brand $mt(j)$ that carries the lowest price per unit of quality. So, the static demand function is given as

$$xm(j) = E(t)/pm(j) \text{ for } m = mt(j), \text{ and } xm(j) = 0 \text{ otherwise} \tag{9.22}$$

where $E(t)$ is the consumption at time t and $pm(j)$ represents the price of quality m of product j at time t. The solution for the intertemporal maximization problem for households that satisfy the intertemporal budget constraint is characterized by

$$E^{\cdot}/E = r - \rho \tag{9.23}$$

It is assumed that in an oligopolistic competition, there are two competitors: the leader and the follower. According to Bertrand's competition law, if firms in the same industry are able to produce goods of the same quality, each sets a price equal to unit cost and each earns zero profit. It is also assumed that industry leaders undertake no research in the general equilibrium, and the followers carry on innovations, finding themselves a step ahead of the former leaders that they have displaced. Then all the products bear the same limit price:

$$p = \lambda w \tag{9.24}$$

where w is the unit cost to manufacture a production unit and λ is the parameter of the unit manufacturing cost of innovative products. The price yields the demand for product per unit of time, $E / \lambda w$, and the flow of profits is given as

$$\Pi = \frac{(\lambda - 1)wE}{\lambda w} = \left(1 - \frac{1}{\lambda}\right)E \tag{9.25}$$

where E is also known as the flow of spending (Grossman and Helpman 1991a, 46). An entrepreneur, to improve his continuum state-of-the-product, invests resources at intensity i for a time interval of length dt. He has the probability idt to do very well in taking the next step up the quality ladder for the targeted product. To achieve an R&D intensity of i, the entrepreneur must invest ai units of labour for a time interval dt at cost wa_tidt. The new firm (the follower) should choose its research intensity so as to maximize $(vidt - wa_tidt)$, which requires that either the optimal scale of operation is zero or the (finite) investment in R&D must have the market value $v = wa_t$. Turning now to the stock market value of the company, the ownership of the shares pays dividends πdt at a time interval dt. The owners of the leader company enjoy capital gains $(\dot{v}dt)$ if no entrepreneur succeeds in displacing them. However, if the leader's product has been improved, then the shareholders of the follower company will suffer a total capital loss of amount v. This is supposed to happen with probability idt. All shares bear an expected rate of return $(\pi + \dot{v})/v - i$ per unit time. Using the value market $v = wa_t$, we have the no-arbitrage condition as

$$\frac{\pi}{wa_t} + \frac{\dot{w}}{w} = \dot{R} + i \tag{9.26}$$

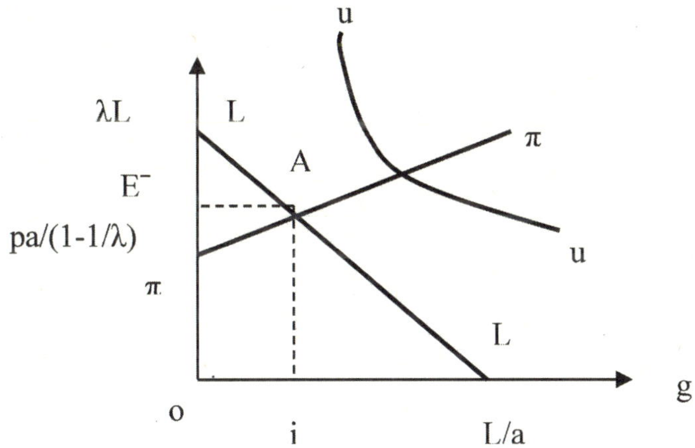

Figure 9.3 Equilibrium in the quality-ladder model

This condition equates the cost of R&D to the expected present discounted value of profits. Recalling the flow of profit, $\Pi = (1 - 1/\lambda)E$ and (9.26), we have a differential equation for spending:

$$\frac{\dot{E}}{E} = \frac{(1-\frac{1}{\lambda})E}{a_t} - \rho - i \tag{9.27}$$

This equation shows that the rate of growth increases with the level of spending and decreases with aggregate R&D intensity. The R&D sector employs *ati* workers, so the equilibrium in the labour market requires that (Grossman and Helpman 1991a, 49),

$$ati + E/\lambda = L \tag{9.28}$$

The dynamics and the equilibrium of the quality-ladders model are represented in figure 9.3.

The line LL represents the resources constraint, and line ππ describes a combination of *E* (flow of spending) and *i*, such that $E^{\cdot} = 0$. According to the model, the economy must always lie along line LL, with spending rising above ππ and falling below line uu. For the initial values of *E* above E^{-}, the intensity rate *i* approaches zero at a point where the level of spending implies expected profits in excess of R&D costs. The economy, in equilibrium, jumps to the steady state at point A. In the dynamic equilibrium, each product is improved with probability *idt* in the interval length time *dt*. The innovation in several sectors is tied to the resources of R&D allotted to that specific product, but although the progress is not uniform between sectors, for the law of large numbers, a constant fraction *i* of the products are continually being improved. Every new design increases the quality of each final consumer good along its quality ladder; it is produced from a monopolist (which obtains the control of it through a license), sold to the producers of the final goods, and then used until a new design is discovered (contrary to the models with horizontal differentiation); therefore, the innovations replace the old products and there is obsolescence (Grossman and Helpman 1991a, 48–9). This brings a constant and endogenous rate of growth, measured in terms of the utility *u*, interpretable as the rate of growth of final output or as the consumption index adjusted to the quality. The constant growth rate *g* is supposed to be the rate of increase of *u* or the rate of consumption index *D* adjusted to quality. The rate of growth of *g* is given as

$$\log D(t) = \int_0^1 \log q_t(j)dj - \log w - \log \lambda \tag{9.29}$$

where the wage-rate (and unit cost) w is constant (along the equilibrium equation $w = (1/a)V$), so growth in the consumption index stems solely from quality upgrading. The innovations, given by the integral on the right-hand side, improve over time. Denoting by $f(m,t)$ the probability of exactly m improvements in a time interval of length t, and summing up the possible values of m, it implies

$$\int_0^1 \log q_t(j)dj = \sum_{m=0}^{\infty} f(m,t)\log \lambda^m \tag{9.30}$$

The right-hand side equals the product of $\log\lambda$ and the expected number of improvements in the interval of length t. The expected number of improvements is denoted as it. As a result, the rate of consumtion index D takes the form as

$$\text{Log } D(t) = it\log\lambda - \log w - \log\lambda \tag{9.31}$$

and the growth rate is

$$g = i \log \lambda \tag{9.32}$$

The intensity i of R&D is given as

$$i = \frac{(1 - 1/\lambda)L}{a_t} - \frac{\rho}{\lambda} \tag{9.33}$$

From equations (9.32) and (9.33), we have the result that the speed of innovation and the rate of growth are faster the larger is the labour force, L, and the greater is the productivity of labour in R&D. The steps of the quality ladder are larger if the output growth is faster. R&D efforts expand for two reasons: the resources effect and the incentive effect. In fact, an increase in λ not only raises i but also stimulates growth directly as the technology improvements become larger and faster. Generally speaking, research and development responds to profitability incentives and the economy as a whole shows increasing returns to scale.

From equation (9.32), the effect of scale of labour L and the effect of technological parameter a (inversely related to labour productivity) are obviously similar to results which are obtained in models that consider the accumulation of physical and human capital where the agent can allocate his time to three possible activities: to work as a non-professional worker, to work as a professional worker, or to accumulate human capital. Differently from other models, there are also possible negative externalities here. Apart from the positive effects, an innovation diminishes the costs of future innovations and there are distortions, brought from monopolies, which render innovation possible but also diminish the consumer's surplus. In fact, from a welfare point of view, it is possible to invest more than is necessary in R&D because of the "business stealing effect."[4] The negative externalities are seen in those firms that, using new innovations, render obsolete the previous investments in R&D: the result is that the economy will grow at a slower rate than that optimal social one; which effect prevails depends on the level of monopolistic power and the dimensions of the innovation. The effect based on the rate of innovation has created two distinguished groups of growth models: the *variety-based* and *quality-based* models. In the case of variety-based models, the equilibrium rate of innovation is always too slow; on the contrary, in the quality-based models, the rate of innovation is usually high and stable.

IPHONE, A CONTINUED METAMORPHOSIS

In 2004 Apple Inc. started working on a new-generation phone with unprecedented features. Apple gathered a large team of about 1,000 talented and high skilled employees – engineers, programmers, and software developers – to work on the very secret program called "Project Purple." After almost three years and an estimated cost of over US$ 150 million, Apple CEO Steve Jobs finally uncovered to the public the first generation of the iPhone on 9 January 2007 in a convention centre in San Francisco. The new iPhone OS (renamed iOS in 2010), different from all mobile operating systems at the time, was designed not only with basic communication functions but also with unmatched new capacities such as multitasking, graphics, and touch screen functions in order to meet growing consumer demands. The development of this unprecedented communication device, which had personal computer functions and features, made the iPhone an instant global success among young people, and led other mobile phone competitors such as Blackberry, Samsung, Nokia, and LG to emulate it.

Because of the great achievement in customer satisfaction of the iPhone OS in the first year of its life, Apple released in 2008 a new improved iPhone version named 3G, and in June 2009, another version called 3GS. The iPhone quickly attracted users of all ages and it began also to be used for business. Improved versions of the iPhone 3GS were introduced in 2010 and 2011, named, respectively the iPhone 4 and iPhone 4S, with even better features and functions than the previous models in an attempt to win customer's loyalty. In fact, the iPhone 4 had a faster processor with a higher-resolution camera (960 × 640), a VGA front-facing camera for video calling, and a 5-megapixel rear-facing camera with 720p video capture. In September 2012, Apple went further by releasing a totally improved product, called the iPhone 5, with exceptional features, such as the high-resolution 4-inch "Retina display," an all-digital Lightning connector, and a new A6 processor, to make clients very pleased by its performance.

The innovation and product development of the iPhone from its first generation to the latest one is seen as a classic example of how product development and improvements lead to increased quality of each final consumer good along its quality ladder, which can bring new consumer demand, new profit opportunities, and growth even in the peak of a recession such as that of the 2008–09 crisis in North America.

THE ACCUMULATION OF HUMAN CAPITAL THROUGH EDUCATION

Expenditures for education, training, and medical care could all be considered to be investments in human capital. Grossman and Helpman (1991b, 112–40) allowed for accumulation of skills through education. They utilized the work of Findlay and Kierzkowski (1983), where there is an education sector that requires no skilled labour. Grossman and Helpman attempted to integrate factor accumulation into the theory of growth based on endogenous innovation. Several opportunities are introduced for technical training, whereas the stock of human capital and unskilled labour are considered as endogenous. In fact, as individuals spend more time in school, they increase their human capital value.

The object of this model, which considers the accumulation of human capital through education, is an economy of overlapping generations where each agent lives a finite period of time T.

For simplicity, Grossman and Helpman (1991b, Ch. 5) assume that each agent lives for two periods. Each individual must decide whether to work as an unskilled worker, to work as a skilled worker, or to invest in education and spend the time accumulating human capital. Individuals who do not invest in education work as unskilled workers in both periods of their lives, whereas individuals who invest in education work as skilled workers in the second period of their lives. Only individuals who plan to work as skilled workers invest in education. The lifetime utility of an individual born at time t is given as

$$U_t = \int_t^{t+T} e^{-\rho(\tau - t)} \log D(\tau) d\tau \tag{9.34}$$

where $D(\tau)$ represents the index of consumption at time τ and $\rho(\tau - t)$ is the discount factor. Let w_H and w_L denote the wage of one unit of skilled labour and the wage of one unit of unskilled labour, respectively. The unit manufacturing cost of innovative goods is given as $c_x(w_L, w_H)$, and the price for them is set as

$$px = 1/\delta cx(wL, wh) \qquad (9.35)$$

The demands for unskilled labour and human capital in the research and development activity are $a_{L\gamma}(w_L, w_h)\gamma$ and $a_{H\gamma}(w_L, w_h)\gamma$, correspondingly, where γ is the rate of innovation. In the same way, the quantities of unskilled labour and human capital employed in the manufacturing sector are $a_{L\gamma}(w_L, w_h)\gamma$ and $a_{H\gamma}(w_L, w_h)\gamma$, where γ represents the aggregate quality of manufactured output. The factor market clearing requires that the quantity of skilled and unskilled labour and the demand of skilled and unskilled labour in the manufacturing sector equals the aggregate supplies of unskilled labour L and the aggregate of human capital H. They are written as

$$a_{L\gamma}(w_L, w_h)\gamma + a_{L\gamma}(w_L, w_h)\gamma = \mathrm{L} \qquad (9.36)$$

$$\text{and } a_{H\gamma}(w_L, w_h)\,\gamma + a_{H\gamma}(w_L, w_h)\gamma = \mathrm{H} \qquad (9.37)$$

Individuals who invest in education relinquish their earnings as unskilled workers in the first period of their lives and provide skilled labour input in the second period of their lives. The present value of lifetime earnings as an unskilled worker is given by (Grossman-Helpman 1991b, 125–7),

$$\int_{t}^{t+T} e^{-\rho(\tau-t)} w_L \, d\tau = \frac{1}{\rho}(1-e^{-\rho T})w_L \qquad (9.38)$$

Individuals spend the first S years in school, and then in the second period of their lives, they receive a flow salary of $w_h\, h(S)$ (as skilled workers). The present value of this income stream equals

$$\int_{t+S}^{t+T} e^{-\rho(\tau-t)} w_H h(S) d\tau = \frac{1}{\rho}(e^{-\rho S} - e^{-\rho T})w_H h(S) \qquad S \le T \qquad (9.39)$$

The individuals choose the optimal duration of training when they decide to spend time on education. So, the first-order condition of optimal alternative training implies

$$1 - e^{-\rho(T-S)} = \frac{ph(S)}{h'(S)} \qquad (9.40)$$

where $-\rho(T - S)$ is the discount rate of the difference between the time T (finite interval time) and time S of years spent in school. The optimal alternative of investment in education for those who decide to become skilled workers is independent of the wage-rates (as in equation [9.40]). Another assumption by Grossman and Helpman (1991b, Ch. 5) is that individuals are identical and each type of labour input is essential for production. In equilibrium, individuals must be indifferent between investing in education and working as unskilled workers in both periods. The present value of lifetime from the two paths must be equal to

$$\frac{w_H}{w_L} = \frac{1 - e^{-\rho T}}{(e^{-\rho S} - e^{-\rho T})h(S)} \tag{9.41}$$

This is the fundamental equation of the Grossman-Helpman human capital accumulation model, which states that the long-run relative factor prices depend on the discount factor and technology used for human capital accumulation. Human capital and technological change here are both endogenized. Because persons who invest in education during their first period of life give up earnings as unskilled workers, then during the second period – thanks to skills acquired during education – their salary as skilled workers, $w_h h(S)$, in equilibrium, must exceed the salary of unskilled workers. Denoting by ξ the fraction of population N that decides to spend time in education, we have that the remaining individuals working as unskilled workers are represented as

$$L = (1 - \xi_s)N \tag{9.42}$$

A fraction of the population, denoted by $(T - S)\xi_s N/T$, takes jobs that require skills and qualification. Each worker has acquired the measure $h(S)$ of human capital. As such, the human capital for skilled workers is expressed as

$$H = \frac{T - S}{T}\xi_S N h(S) \tag{9.43}$$

The above equation shows the relationship between the fraction of the population that has opted to acquire education and the level of educational achievement of the representative trained worker. Individuals will choose to go for education and be skilled, given that the productivity and the wage are much higher, rather than working as unskilled workers. But if for some reason the relative wage of unskilled labour increases, closing the gap with skilled workers, individuals will remain indifferent between looking for education and working as unskilled workers. For the system to be in equilibrium, the relative wage of skilled workers must fall. In this way, as the relative supply of skilled workers increases, the relative wage of skilled labour declines, raising the wage of unskilled workers until the system is back in equilibrium.

Grossman and Helpman have revealed that extra human capital engaged in skilled work reduces research costs and increases the long-run growth rate. The education sector in this model requires no skilled labour, so the incentives to invest in human capital depend only on exogenous education technology and time preference. The wage-rate is fixed exogenously as a result of education and time spent for schooling. Furthermore, an exogenous increase in the productivity of the schooling technology in turn results in higher rates of technological change and lower relative wages.

HUMAN CAPITAL AND TECHNOLOGICAL CHANGE: THE EICHER MODEL

Eicher (1996) considered an overlapping generation model with individuals who live for two periods. Private incentives encourage individuals to invest in education, and non-rival inventions are the result of the educational process. According to Eicher,[5] in the first period, young individuals will be able to decide whether to enter the education sector as students by paying tuition fees or to start working in production. Individuals who enter production work as unskilled labour in the first period can retire as such in the second period. Individuals who enter the education sector in the first period can become skilled workers in the second period and can work either in production as engineers or in education as teachers. Investment in human capital is not an easy process. It requires borrowing against future income to finance education fees and consumption during time spent in school. The objective of the Eicher model is to prove that the rate of economic growth depends on the effectiveness of labour in research, on the demand for skilled labour, on the accumulation of human capital, and on the absorption of new technology.

In Eicher's model (1996), the education sector at time t uses teachers, students, and the newest technology to produce a new non-rival technological vintage, vt+1:

$$v_{t+1} - v_t = \mu v_t \min [\gamma P_t, S_t], \qquad \gamma > 1 \text{ and } \mu > 0 \tag{9.44}$$

where S_t is the number of students who invest in education, P_t is the number of skilled workers or teachers who work in education, γ is an exogenously specified student-teacher ratio, and v_t is the level of technology in period t. Based on this model, the students who want to be skilled enter the education sector and pay the salary of teachers and education staff; therefore the tuition bill per student depends on the student-teacher ratio and the wage of teachers.

In Eicher's model (1996), the new technological vintages that are invented in the education sector are assumed to be non-rival. Output is produced in two sectors: high-tech and low-tech. The high-tech sector employs the newest technology as well as skilled and unskilled labour inputs, who then adapt the new technology to the production process. This relationship is given by a linear homogeneous production function:

$$H_t = v_t F[U_t, E_t] \tag{9.45}$$

where U_t is unskilled labour input and E_t is skilled labour or engineers' input. Conversely, the low-tech sector employs old technology and only unskilled workers and has a function of the type

$$L_t = v_{t+1} \delta U_t \tag{9.46}$$

where U_t is the unskilled labour, v_{t+1} is the old technology, and δ is the productivity parameter of unskilled workers in the low-tech sector. The low-tech sector serves as a "reserve army" for unskilled labour and absorbs the surplus labour force that may come from the skilled sector if this sector goes down. Production of the consumption goods takes place in entirely competitive sectors; thus, profit-maximizing firms take as given the wage of skilled workers w_E, the wage of unskilled workers in the high-tech sector w_{uh}, and the wage of unskilled workers in the low-tech sector w_{uL}. Profit maximization yields the standard first-order conditions as follows: [6]

$$w_t^E = v[f(\frac{U_t^H}{E_t}) - f'(\frac{U_t^H}{E_t})(\frac{U_t^H}{E_t})] \tag{9.47}$$

$$w_t^{UH} = v_t f'(\frac{U_t^H}{E_t}) \tag{9.48}$$

$$w_t^{UL} = \delta v_{t-1} \tag{9.49}$$

Factor market clearing requires that

$$w_t^{P} = w_t^{E} \tag{9.50}$$

$$w_t^{UL} = w_t^{UH} \tag{9.51}$$

Equation (9.50) states that the wage of engineers in the high-tech sector equals the marginal product in the high-tech sector. In the same way, equation (9.51) states that the marginal product of unskilled workers equals its marginal product in both sectors. From the combination of equations (9.47) to (9.51), we get the relative wage of skilled workers to unskilled workers, written as

$$\frac{w_t^{E}}{w_t^{UH}} = g[\frac{\delta}{1+\mu S_{t-1}}] \qquad g'(.) < 0 \tag{9.52}$$

where g is a composite of two functions, ξ and λ, and the factor demand is given as $U_h/E_t = \lambda\ [v_t/v_{t\text{-}1}]$. The relative wage in the high-tech sector depends only on the relative factor prices $w_{E(t)}\ /w_{UH(t)} = \xi\ U_h/E_t$.. The relative wage of educated compared to uneducated workers in period t depends on investment in education in period $t - 1$, on the productivity of education μ, and on the productivity of unskilled workers δ. Investing in education in period $t - 1$ will help augment the demand for skilled workers in period t and put a pressure to increase the wages for educated workers.

Therefore, there is a positive relationship between the human capital investment at period t and the relative wage at period $t + 1$. Individuals maximize the utility:

$$W_j = \ln C_t + \beta \ln C_{t+1} \qquad \beta > 0, \tag{9.53}$$

where β represents the discount factor, j indexes the worker type (skilled or unskilled), and C_t represents the per capita consumption in period t. Individuals who invest in education borrow in the first period to pay tuition and then work in the second period to pay the first-period loan (they also purchase the first-period consumption). Individuals who choose to work in the first period receive income in the first period and can then save for the second-period consumption. An increase in β depresses individuals' (or students') demand for funds because more consumption is postponed into the future. In equilibrium, total borrowing must be equal to total savings, and because individuals are initially identical, they must be indifferent between either career path (skilled or unskilled), so

$$Wu = Ws \tag{5.54}$$

where Wu and Ws are, respectively, the unskilled and skilled wage. Career arbitrage, bond market clearing, and the utility maximization all yield investment in education St and the stock of human capital allocated to the education sector Pt. Both St and Pt are given as (Eicher 1996, 134),

$$S_t = \frac{\theta}{\dfrac{w_t^E}{\gamma w_t^U} + 1} \tag{9.55}$$

$$P_t = \frac{\theta}{\dfrac{w_t^E}{w_t^U} + \gamma} \tag{9.56}$$

The stock of human capital, from equation (9.55), depends positively on the marginal propensity to save, θ; negatively on the cost of tuition w_E/γ; and on an index of cost of funds $1/w_U$. By considering the marginal cost of human capital investment we see that it has a decreasing value in S_t and the higher the wage of skilled labour in period t, the higher the cost of schooling and, thus, the lower the S_t. The higher the wage of unskilled labour, the higher the supply of funds; likewise, the lower the cost of schooling, the higher the number of students. The marginal benefit of human capital investment is increasing in $S_{t\text{-}1}$. The higher the human capital investment is in period $t - 1$, the greater the technological progress, and the higher the demand is for skilled labour, the higher the wage of skilled workers. A high wage of skilled labour at time t represents a high cost of human capital accumulation to students in that period. The equilibrium interest rate is given as

$$(1 + r_t) = \frac{w_{t+1}^E}{w_t^U + w_t^E / \gamma} \tag{9.57}$$

The interest rate is the benefit/cost ratio of investing in human capital. Equation (9.57) says that as students expect the relative wage to rise in the future, they increase the demand for borrowing, which increases the interest rate. Here, students who decide to borrow money and invest in human capital in the first period not only carry a higher income in the next period but also help increase skilled labour in the education sector to create technological progress, which in turn increases production and relative wages. Eicher (1996) shows that although an increase in the effectiveness of labour in research increases the relative demand for skilled labour, the relative wage, the rate of technological change, and long-run growth, it also decreases the relative supply of unskilled labour. There is a difference between this model and that of Grossman and Helpman (1991b, 122–30): whereas in the second model the incentives to accumulate human capital are independent of the cost of absorbing technology, in the Eicher model the rate of economic growth and movements in the relative wages are sensitive to the interaction between accumulation of human capital and absorption of new technology. So, the "missing link" in the previous endogenous model among technological changes, relative wages, and skilled labour is the absorption effect, which allows positive relationships between technological change, relative wages, long-term fluctuations of relative supply, and the wage of skilled labour.

PRODUCT DEVELOPMENT AND INTERNATIONAL TRADE

Grossman and Helpman tried to capture some of the complexities in product development and international trade between countries. In doing so, they demonstrated the flaws in some of the often-advocated simpler solutions to technology diffusion; for example, they proved how free trade could sometimes exacerbate existing gaps in institutions, skills, and technology. Grossman and Helpman made a series of studies and wrote a number of articles that examined the effects of trade on technology in an open economy. This issue is also discussed in detail in their outstanding work *Trade and Growth* (1991b, 237–55) where they argued that there are some mechanisms by which a country's international trade might affect the rate of growth. The first is that international trade opens channels of communication that facilitate the diffusion of technology between countries. The second is that international trade and international integration enlarge the size of the market in which firms operate. Finally, the third mechanism is that international competition encourages entrepreneurs in different countries to reach for and pursue new ideas and technologies.

The main model for trade and growth developed by Grossman and Helpman is a three-goods (intermediate goods, final goods, and R&D) and a two-country economy, with skilled and unskilled labour as the two inputs. There is a trade-off between the production of final goods and R&D, both of which are human-capital intensive. It is assumed that if demand is high for final goods, there may be a reallocation of resources from R&D to final goods production. This will have the effect of increasing current output at the cost of tomorrow's output. The increased demand for final goods increases the incentives and rewards for R&D goods.

Grossman and Helpman (1991b, Ch. 9) started by considering the trade model where two countries operate in autarky with no channels of communications. Aggregate spending in each country is normalized at $E(\tau)i = 1$ for all τ (interest rate). The variety of differentiated products in both countries bears a price

$$p_i = \frac{w_i}{\alpha} \qquad i = A,B \tag{9.58}$$

where wi is the wage rate in country i as well as the marginal and the average cost of a unit of output, α is a given parameter that characterizes different tastes for variety, and $i = A,B$ is the index of two countries that share the flow of knowledge. Furthermore, they also share common preferences and a common discount rate, ρ. The nominal interest rate $(\tau)i$ is equal to the discount rate ρ. The market value of the representative firm and the cost of developing a new product in country i is equal to

$$v_i = \frac{w_i \alpha}{n_i} \qquad i = A,B \tag{9.59}$$

where ni is the local stock of knowledge capital and the measure of products developed in country i. The nominal interest rate $E(\tau)i$ is equal to the discount rate ρ. Arbitrage condition equates the total return on equity claims to the interest rate (or discount rate ρ):

$$\frac{(1-\alpha)}{n_i v_i} + \frac{\dot{v}_i}{v_i} = \rho \qquad i = A,B \tag{9.60}$$

Equilibrium in the labour market requires equality between the sum of the demands by R&D for labour and the exogenous factor supply. Therefore, the equilibrium labour market is given as

$$\left(\frac{\alpha}{n_i}\right)\dot{n}_i + \left(\frac{1}{p_i}\right) = L_i \qquad i = A,B \tag{9.61}$$

In the steady state, the no-arbitrage condition requires that

$$(1-\alpha)V_i = \rho + g_i \qquad i = A,B \tag{9.62}$$

where Vi denotes the inverse of the aggregate stock market value in each country i. Combining equations (9.58) and (9.59), we have that equilibrium in the labour market (in the steady state) becomes

$$g_i + \alpha V_i = \frac{L_i}{a} \qquad i = A,B \tag{9.63}$$

From equations (9.62) and (9.63), we can get the long-run rate of innovation (Grossman and Helpman 1991b, 240):

$$g_i = (1-\alpha)\frac{L_i}{a} - \alpha p \qquad i = A,B \tag{9.64}$$

where the manufactured output grows at the rate $g_i(1 - \alpha)/\alpha$.

Now it is assumed that communication channels for technical information – but not commodity trade – are opened between two countries, so the knowledge stock in country i is given as

$$K_{ni} = n_i + \mu_i n_j \qquad j \neq i \tag{9.65}$$

where μ_i is the fraction of products available in country j that are not available in country i. The knowledge stock in each country is given by $K_n = n_A + \mu n_B$, where $0 < \mu < 1$. As in the autarky, the cost of developing a new product in country i and the free entries ensure that

$$v_i = w_{iA}\frac{\alpha}{(n_A + \mu n_B)} \qquad i = A,B \tag{9.66}$$

The international diffusion of knowledge normally reduces the input requirements for R&D in each country, so the labour-market-clearing condition takes the form

$$\frac{\alpha}{(n_A + \mu n_B)n_i} + \frac{1}{\rho_i} = L_i \qquad i = A,B \tag{9.67}$$

which gives the equality between the sum of the demands for labour by R&D and the factor supply required by enterprises. The equilibrium in the labour market, in the steady state, in both countries, including the μ fraction, becomes

$$L_A + \mu L_B = a(g + \alpha V_i) \quad i = A,B \tag{9.68}$$

The solution for the long-run rate of innovation in the world economy with international knowledge spillovers but without commodity trade (as assumed) is written as

$$g = (1-\alpha)\left[\frac{L_A + \mu L_B}{a}\right] - \alpha\rho \tag{9.69}$$

Equation (9.69), differently from equation (9.64), contains the fraction μ, which is the overlap of the research projects in two countries. In the Grossman-Helpman trade model the opening of international channels of communication accelerates innovation and growth between countries. Research undertaken in both countries accumulates more quickly than would the local research of knowledge in isolated countries and thus contributes to a global stock of knowledge (Grossman and Helpman 1991b, 243–6). This also implies a rapid reduction in the cost of product development in both countries, which in turn helps entrepreneurs introduce new varieties at a faster rate.

A broader conclusion about diffusion of technology and international trade is that a factor price equalization will eventually ensure that both trading countries enjoy identical growth rates of output and consumption irrespective of their factor donation. In addition, an equiproportionate increase in the active labour force has the effect of accelerating the long-run growth process. This is based on an assumption made by Romer, that policies intended to increase human capital should be unequivocally positive for long-run growth. If the increase in technology in two different countries has a different rate, then even the spending shares on final goods must change, creating some problems and limitations to the Grossman-Helpman trade model as in the case of the technology gap between developed countries (DC) and less-developed countries (LDC).

A static analysis of such a gap in the context of trade was carried out by Alwyn Young (1991), who considered economies without knowledge spillovers but in which differences in the potential for learning by doing (which is determined by the stock of technology) enable the LDC to outgrow the DC. However, in recent history, the technology gap seems to have increased rather than decreased.

Sometimes, according to Grossman and Helpman, if a country well gifted in technology is bigger than its trading partner, trade may not be advantageous to growth in the long run, and given that knowledge spillovers in factor technology are imperfect it will lead to long-run growth disparities between countries. It has been shown in several studies since the early nineteenth century that trade is beneficial to growth for all countries, but still nowadays it is difficult to measure technology variables in terms of growth and openness, because the convergence between countries could occur as a result of many factors, such as capital accumulation, knowledge spillovers, factor price equalization, or technology transfers.

Some empirical evidence from East Asian countries led to the conclusion that investment in R&D helped develop them as import-substituting economies and later benefited trade-developing high-tech industries that served both the domestic market and the large markets of advanced countries.

INNOVATION AND IMITATION: THE SEGERSTROM MODEL

Generally speaking, economic growth in developed countries is characterized by innovation and imitation. Firms invest considerable resources in R&D to improve products and capture related profits, and when they are successful, other firms, attracted by these profits, try to imitate them. The works of Krugman (1979), Grossman and Helpman (1991a and 1991b, 281–324), and Segerstrom (1991) include theoretical research on technological diffusion, innovation, and imitation. Krugman (1979) studied the innovation and imitation process on the assumption that innovation occurs in one country called "North" but is carried out in a different country called "South" that is technologically behind North. Each new product is first produced in the North before the technology eventually spreads to the South. In Krugman's model, the rates of innovation and imitation are taken as exogenous parameters, whereas in the later models (in the 1980s and 1990s), they are taken as endogenous. In effect, in the Segerstrom[7] model (1991) as well as in the Grossman and Helpman model (1991a), innovation and imitation occur in the same economy with no differences in the level of technology; innovator and imitator share positive industry profits as a result of their ability to engage in a no-collision game. Although firms engage in costly innovative and imitative activities, they do not do so in the same industry and at the same time. For firms engaged in the imitation process, the imitation is profitable only if, first, the imitators are able to earn positive profits in competition with the original inventor, and second, the rules regarding patents, licenses, and copyright are not so strict as to make imitation too expensive.

The objective of Segerstrom's model is to show that there is a lot of dynamism and growth in those industries where firms are engaged in this innovative and imitative process. The Segerstrom model (1991) analyzes an economy where all households are aggregated into a representative single household, which maximizes its intertemporal utility:

$$U = \int_{0}^{\infty} e^{-\rho t} u(t) dt \qquad (9.70)$$

where ρ is the discount rate and $u(t)$ is the consumer's instantaneous utility at time t. The assumed utility function gives a positive value to the increased variety of available goods. Essentially, for a given income, a consumer will become better off if he is offered a wider selection of goods (Krugman 1979). Every household (or consumer) maximizes the discounted utility subject to an intertemporal budget constraint:

$$\int_{0}^{\infty} e^{-R(t)} E(t) dt = A(0) \qquad (9.71)$$

where $R(t)$ is the cumulative interest factor up to time t, $A(0)$ is the asset at time 0, and $E(t)$ is the household's expenditure at time t, which is given as

$$E(t) = \int_{0}^{1} \sum_{j=o}^{\infty} p_{jt}(w) d_{jt}(w) dw \qquad (9.72)$$

where $p_{jt}(w)$ is the price of a product of quality j produced by industry w at time t, and $d_{tj}(w)$ is the quantity consumed at time t. The representative consumer allocates expenditure $E(t)$ to maximize his utility function at a time t. The Euler condition for this consumer using condition (9.72) is given as

$$\sum_{j=J(w)} \gamma^J d_{jt}(w) = \frac{E(t)\gamma^h}{p_{ht}(w)} \tag{9.73}$$

where $\gamma > 1$ is the extent to which higher-quality products improve on lower-quality products, $Jt(w)$ is the set of variable quality levels with the lowest quality-adjusted prices $p_{jt}(w)/\gamma$, and $h_t(w)$ is the highest quality level. From (9.73), it is implied that the aggregate demand function is written as

$$d_{jt}(w) = E(t)/p_{jt}(w) \tag{9.74}$$

The consumer's level of expenditure, E, is determined by his steady-state assets, A. The equation for this yield is (Segerstom 1991, 814),

$$\frac{\left[\frac{dE(t)}{dt}\right]}{E(t)} = r(t) - \rho \tag{9.75}$$

which implies that the consumer's expenditure is equal to the market interest rate $r(t)$ minus the consumer's discount rate over time. Each leader innovates to capture the entire market. When all the firms are charging a price of 1, a single firm that is the quality leader earns a profit, which is given as

$$\pi(p) = [(p - 1)E]/p \quad p \leq \gamma \tag{9.76}$$

where p is the leader's price. The profit for the leader is maximized if $p = \gamma$, where γ is the high-quality product. Choosing $p = \gamma > 1$, the industry leader earns a positive profit flow that is given as

$$\pi^L = (1 - \frac{1}{\gamma})E \tag{9.77}$$

In industries with only one quality leader, the leading firm earns dominant profit flows. It is possible that this quality leader might charge a price higher than γ and collude with firms producing lower-quality products, although normally this does not happen. However, in industries with two quality leaders Segerstrom (1991) shows that no firm has the incentive to engage in imitative R&D. The proportion of industries with a single quality leader is denoted by α (α industries), and the proportion of industries with two quality leaders is denoted by β (β industries). Aggregate demand for manufacturing workers in α industries is $c = E/p = 1/p/(\gamma w)$ and in β industries it is $c = E/p = 1/p = 1/w$. Regarding the aggregate demand for R&D workers, we have that in one-leader industries, it is αC, and it is βI in two-leader industries, where C is the probability that the leader innovates (or the intensity of imitation) and I is the probability of having two leaders in industry innovation. Hence, the equilibrium condition of the labour market is

$$T = (\alpha/\gamma w) + (\beta/w) + \beta a I + \alpha a C \tag{9.78}$$

where L is the fixed supply of skilled labour. As soon as innovation occurs in an industry, this industry switches from the group of β industries to that of α industries, and when imitation happens in an industry, this industry switches from α industries to β industries ($\beta = 1 - \alpha$). According to the Segerstrom model, in a steady-state equilibrium, every time a new high-quality product is discovered in some industries, imitation must occur in some other industries. Hence, the rate at which industries leave the group of two-leader industries, βI, is equal to the rate at which industries leave the group of one-leader industries, αC. So, the steady-state values of the proportions α and β are given as

$$\alpha = [I/(C + I)] \text{ and } \beta = [C/(C + I)] \tag{9.79}$$

There are two major cases for incentive firms (firms that have incentives to engage in imitative R&D activities) involved in innovation and imitation activities. The first case is when incentive firms are engaged in imitative activities. Denoting v_c as the expected discounted reward for succeeding in the imitative R&D race and τ as the random time duration of an imitative R&D race, the expected benefit of engagement in imitative R&D for an industry is

$$\int_0^\infty Ben(\tau = s) v_c e^{-\rho s} ds = \int_0^\infty (Ce^{-cs}) v_c e^{-\rho s} ds = \frac{v_c C}{\rho + C} \tag{9.80}$$

where ρ is the discount rate, τ is the random time duration assumed to be exponentially distributed, and C is the imitative investment. In the same way, the expected cost of engaging in imitative R&D in an industry is

$$\int_0^\infty (\int_0^t a_c C e^{-ps} ds) C e^{ct} dt = \frac{a_c C}{\rho + C} \tag{9.81}$$

where a_c is the unit of labour per unit of time (c stands for copying) for each firm involved in the imitative R&D process. Thus, combining (9.80) and (9.81), the expected profit from engaging in imitative R&D is

$$\pi_C = \frac{C(v_c - a_c)}{\rho + C} \tag{9.82}$$

Then, from equations (9.80), (9.81), and (9.82), we obtain the equation of steady-state equilibrium into the labour market:

$$C = C_L(I) = \frac{I(L - \frac{2a_c\rho}{\gamma - 1}) - I^2(\frac{2a_c}{\gamma - 1})}{(\frac{2a_c}{\gamma - 1} - L) + I(a_I + a_C + \frac{2a_C}{\gamma - 1})} \tag{9.83}$$

where L is the labour force. The function $C_L(I)$ denotes how much investment in imitative R&D within an industry or sector is consistent with full employment of labour in the economy and zero discounted profits in each level of innovative investment, I (Segerstrom 1991, 819).

Now we consider the second case, where incentive firms are engaged in innovative activities. Denoting v_i as the expected discounted reward for succeeding in the innovative R&D race and τ as the random time duration of an innovative R&D race, the expected benefit of engaging in an innovative R&D race for an industry is

$$\int_0^\infty Ben(\tau = s) v_c e^{-ps} ds = \int_0^\infty (Ie^{-Is}) v_c e^{-ps} ds = \frac{v_I I}{\rho + I} \tag{9.84}$$

where ρ again is the discount rate and I is the innovative investment. Hence, the expected cost of engaging in innovative R&D for an industry is written as

$$\int_0^\infty (\int_0^t a_c I e^{-ps} ds) I e^{It} dt = \frac{a_I I}{\rho + I} \tag{9.85}$$

Combining equations (9.84) and (9.85), we see that the expected profit from engaging in innovative R&D is

$$\pi_I = \frac{I(v_I - a_I)}{\rho + I} \tag{9.86}$$

The free entry into innovative in R&D races implies that *vi* = *ai* (the expected discounted reward equals the unit of labour per unit of time) in all innovative R&D races. The firm that succeeds in innovation in an industry earns a large share of profit flow until another firm succeeds in imitating, and then the innovating firm has to share the profits with the follower or the imitator. The time duration of the imitative R&D race is

$$v_I = \int_0^\infty \left(\int_0^s \pi e^{-\rho t} dt + e^{-\rho t} v_c\right) ds = \frac{\pi + C v_c}{\rho + C} = a_I \tag{9.87}$$

where π is the profit flow. From this, the steady-state equilibrium zero profit in each R&D race thus yields

$$C = C_I(I) = \frac{(2a_c - a_I)\rho + 2a_c I}{(a_I - a_C)} \tag{9.88}$$

The function $C_I(I)$ denotes how much imitative investment in R&D is consistent with zero discounted profits in both innovative and imitative R&D races. If C increases, firms enjoy profits for a shorter period. Higher profits also imply higher collusive effects with imitators, and thus to maintain zero discounted profits in both innovative and imitative R&D races, innovative R&D must also increase. Conversely, the consumption growth rate in the steady state is given as

$$g = \frac{\dot{C}}{C} = \frac{\dot{A}}{A} = (\log \gamma)\beta I = \frac{IC}{I + C} \tag{9.89}$$

where A is an index of technology, which represents the geometric average of the level of productivity throughout all product lines. The steady-state growth rate g is an increasing function of both innovative (I) and imitative efforts (C). Innovation increases competition and decreases profits. In such a case, the leaders increase their innovative activity in order to get rid of their competitors. Segerstrom (1991) proved that an increase in the government subsidy to innovative R&D increases the steady-state intensity of imitative R&D (C), decreases the steady-state intensity of innovative R&D (I), and increases the steady-state rate of economic growth (g). In fact, government subsidy reduces the cost of engaging in innovative R&D because leader firms earn enough profits to allow the innovative R&D race to slow, thus allowing followers to augment the rate of imitation. In Grossman and Helpman (1991a), imitative and innovative R&D is driven by factor price differences across countries. New products developed in the North are copied by imitation efforts engaged in the South. Conversely, in the Segerstrom model, factor price differences are not as important, but what is essential is that firms are assumed to take advantage of opportunities whenever they find themselves in a position to collude. Therefore, they draw benefits from collusion.

OPTIMAL TAXATION AND ENDOGENOUS GROWTH

The analysis of the influence of taxation on economic growth has been of great interest for many economists since the mid-1980s. A good part of the research that has appeared since then has focused its attention on differences in government policies and the relationship between public policies and growth. Some examples of the work in optimal taxation include Judd (1987, 1990), Auerbach and Kotlikoff (1987), King and Rebelo (1990), Lucas (1990b), Jones, Manuelli, and Rossi (1993), and Turnovsky (1995, 1996, 2000). These models differ in the situations they analyze and the type of fiscal contexts they take into consideration. Judd (1987) treated the effects of marginal changes in taxes on exogenous growth. Auerbach and Kotlikoff (1987) included in their analysis overall modifications in taxes with overlapping generations by using exogenous growth tools. King and Rebelo (1990) treated tax policies that affect individuals who try to accumulate physical and human capital. Lucas (1990b) studied the effects of optimal taxation in an endogenous growth model using human capital as an externality. Finally, Turnovsky (1995, 1996, and 2000) analyzed the optimal choice between capital and consumption taxes in a model in which government spending is introduced as an imperfect substitute in the utility function.

In the Jones-Manuelli-Rossi (1993) model, government expenditure is a productive input in capital formation. In this economic model, it is assumed that labour supply is elastic and the production function for human capital has human capital and market goods as inputs. Human capital that is engaged directly in the sector producing human capital is not taxed, but all other factors utilized in producing the market goods used by that sector are taxed. The simple case of the Jones-Manuelli-Rossi (1993) model consists on a one-sector economy with human and physical capital and inelastically supplied labour. The utility function of representative household implies

$$\max \Sigma_t B_t u_t(c_t) \quad (9.90)$$

which is subject to constraint conditions:

1 $k_{t+1} \leq (1 - \zeta_k)k_t + x_{ht}$
2 $h_{t+1} \leq (1 - \zeta_k)h_t + x_{ht}$
3 $\Sigma_t p_t (c_t + x_{kt} + x_{ht}) \leq \Sigma_t p_t[(1 - \tau_{kt}) r_t k_t + (1 - \tau_{ht}) w_t h_t + T_t]$

where k_t and h_t are the physical and human capital, respectively. The term T_t is the transfer from the government to consumer sector, treated as a lump sum. Terms τ_{kt} and τ_{ht} are the tax rates of two factors, physical and human capital, r_t and w_t are the rental prices of capital and labour in terms of consumption, and p_t is the price of time consumption. The consumer's budget constraint is given as

$$\Sigma_t p_t(c_t - T_t) \leq W_o = k_o [(1 - \tau_{ko})r_o + 1 - \zeta_h] + h_o[(1 - \tau_{ho})w_o + 1 - \zeta] \quad (9.91)$$

The planner's problem is expressed as choosing among the variables $c_t, k_t, h_t, x_{kt}, x_{ht}, \tau_{kt}, \tau_{ht}, r_t, w_t$, and p_t in order to maximize the representative consumer's welfare. After some simplification using the conditions defining competitive equilibrium, the planner's problem becomes (Jones, Manuelli, and Rossi 1993, 489),

$$\max \Sigma_t B_t u_t(c_t) \quad (9.92)$$

subject to:

1 $\Sigma_t p_t(c_t - T_t)u'(t) = W_o$
2 $c_t + x_{kt} + x_{ht} + g_t = F(k_t, h_t)$
3 $k_{t+1} \leq (1 - \zeta_k)k_t + x_{ht}$
4 $h_{t+1} \leq (1 - \zeta_k)h_t + x_{ht}$

The maximization of the representative agent's welfare subject is given as

$$Wo = [(1 - \tau ko)Fk(0) + 1 - \zeta k)]ko + [(1 - \tau Ho)\, Fh(0) + 1 - \zeta k]ho \qquad (9.93)$$

The solution for the planner is to set taxes τko and τHo at high levels in order to finance the government expenditures and then set them back to zero. If the tax rate is high, then investment at time o will be close to zero. Given this, capital taxation in the next period takes the character of a lump-sum tax. Consumption growth rates would also be at low levels. Thus, to avoid this ongoing problem, bounds on the tax rate should be low enough to guarantee a positive flow of investment in all periods. Jones, Manuelli, and Rossi (1993) conclude that eliminating all distorting taxes (especially those on capital) could have an astonishing effect on the US growth rate – as much as 8 percentage points per year.

A few years later, Turnovsky (2000) elaborated a model in which, differently from other growth models, the agent, because of taxes and government spending, is persuaded to substitute consumption with labour, therefore leading to more work and more earnings and less leisure.

In this model, the economy consists of N individuals who have an infinite planning horizon and possess perfect foresight, and the labour supply is assumed to be elastic and is determined by the consumption-leisure-trade-off agents. It is assumed that the representative agent (the consumer) is endowed with a unit of time that can be allocated either to leisure, l, or to work $1 - l$. The output of an individual firm is determined by a Cobb-Douglas production function:

$$y = \alpha' G_p^{\beta}(1-l)^{\varepsilon} k^{1-\beta} = \alpha'(G_p / k)^{\beta}(1-l)^{\varepsilon} k \qquad (9.94)$$

where k indicates the individual's capital stock and Gp is a public good given as government spending on the economy. The production function is linearly homogenous in factors that are being accumulated (capital and government expenditure). The public good is given as

$$Gp = gp\, Y \text{ and } Gc = gc\, Y \qquad (9.95)$$

where gp and gc are the fractions of aggregate output Y and consumption output Y, respectively. Combining equations (9.94) and (9.95), we have that the aggregate output for the whole economy in equilibrium (of AK technology) is given as

$$Y = (\alpha g_p^{\beta})^{1/(1-\beta)}(1-l)^{\varepsilon/(1-\beta)} \tag{9.96}$$

where α = α'Nβ. According to Turnovsky, the productivity of capital depends positively on the fraction of time devoted to work and the share of productive government expenditure. In a decentralized market economy, the representative agent's welfare is given by the utility function

$$U = \int_0^{\infty} \frac{1}{\gamma}(cl^{\theta}G_c^{\eta})^{\gamma} e^{-\rho t} dt \tag{9.97}$$

where c is the consumption of after-tax income generated by labour and holdings of capital. This agent's welfare is subject to the consumer accumulation equation:

$$k^{\cdot} = (1 - \tau w)w(1 - l) + (1 - \tau k)rkk - (1 + \tau c)c - T/N \tag{9.98}$$

where rk is the return of capital, w is the real wage rate, τw is the tax on wage income, τk is the tax on capital income, τc is the consumption tax, and T/N is the agent's share of lump-sum taxes [$w = dy/d(1 - l) = \phi y/(1 - l)$, and $rk = dy/dk = (1 - \beta)y/k$ (Turnovsky 2000)]. In an absence of debt, government expenditures are financed by taxes and satisfy the balanced budget:

$$Y(gc + gp) = \tau wNw(1 - l) + \tau krkK + \tau cC + T \tag{9.99}$$

In the decentralized economy, individuals respond to tax incentives.[8] A higher tax on consumption reduces the consumption-income ratio, and in a similar way, a higher tax on labour income (given leisure l) reduces the consumption-output ratio. Any increases in the tax rates, τw, τk, and τc, decreases the fraction of time devoted to work, diminishes the rate of return on capital to that of consumption, and reduces the equilibrium growth rate:

$$d\psi/d\tau i < 0 \quad \text{and} \quad dl/d\tau i > 0 \quad i = k, w, c \tag{9.100}$$

An increase in government consumption expenditure or government production expenditure, financed by lump-sum taxation, will raise the growth rate and employment as

$$d\psi/dgp > d\psi/dgc > 0 \quad \text{and} \quad dl/d\tau p < dl/dgc < 0 \tag{9.101}$$

Plainly speaking, an increase in government consumption expenditure, differently from an increase in tax rates, leads to an immediate decrease in the growth rate of capital, which reduces the rate of return on consumption and persuades the agent to alternate consumption with labour, thus leading to less leisure and more earnings. It induces workers to devote a larger portion of their time to work, which in turn increases the long-run rate of growth.

In the Turnovsky model (2000), the endogeneity of labour supply causes both consumption and labour income tax to have some adverse affects on the growth rate, which is due to the adverse wealth effect (increasing the marginal utility of wealth) and leads to the substitution of leisure and consumption with work. The optimal fiscal policy induces tax rates that meet two simple conditions: τw, τk, and τc

$$\tau w = -\tau c \quad \text{and} \quad k = 0 \tag{9.102}$$

which means that the tax on labour income must equal the tax consumption with the opposite sign, whereas capital income should remain untaxed. The optimal tax structure in Turnovsky analysis requires that consumption and leisure be taxed uniformly.

THRESHOLD EFFECTS AND POVERTY TRAPS: THE AZARIADIS-DRAZEN MODEL

Azariadis and Drazen (1990) extended the spillover models of Romer (1986) and Lucas (1988) to demonstrate that if non-convexities in the production function were sufficiently strong, countries that are similar in all aspects except for initial conditions may have steady states each corresponding to different levels of long-run per capita income. Azariades[9] and Drazen,[10] in their model, take into consideration an intergenerational education externality, in which during the current generation a substantial amount of human capital is accumulated and the human capital accumulated in the previous generation influences positively the productivity of current human capital. As a consequence, a country may find itself in a low-development trap (or poverty trap) if the human capital investment of the last generation was too low.

The objective of the Azariadis-Drazen model is to prove that there is a low-development trap in those countries where an insufficient investment in education in the last generation discourages education and training of skilled labour in the current generation, which delays growth and prosperity.

The assumption in this model is that there is a continuum of overlapping generations in which each individual lives two periods and all individuals have access to a common training technology. The average quality of labour supplied by the younger generation at time $t+1$ is given as

$$Xt+1 = Xth\ (\tau t, Xt) \tag{9.103}$$

where τt is the fraction of time being invested in labour quality and formal education and training and h is the human capital accumulated by the previous generation. During training, individuals are assumed not to have any financial benefits, so the discontinued lifetime income is written as (Azariades and Drazen 1990, 510)

$$X_{t+1} = (1-\tau_t)w_t x_t + w_{t+1} x_t h \frac{(\tau_t, x_t)}{R_t} \tag{9.104}$$

where wt is the earned wage (income) from workers and Rt is the gross yield on loans. Maximizing the τt leads to a first-order condition for individual choice of labour quality by homogeneous individuals:

$$R_t = \frac{w_{t+1}}{w_t} h_t(\tau_t, x_t) \tag{9.105}$$

Given that, by assuming that all individuals have equal ability and equal access to credit, they choose the same rate of investments. The evolution of average skills implied by individual decisions is given as

$$Xt+1 = xt\ h\ (\tau t, xt) \tag{9.106}$$

The equation that balances investment with saving is defined as (Azariades and Drazen 1990, 511),[11]

$$Nt+1\ Kt+1 = s[Rt, wt, xt\ (1 - \tau t), wt+1\ xt+1] \tag{9.107}$$

where $Nt = (1 - \tau t)xt + xt$ is the labour supply in effective units (by young and old individuals) and the function $s[Rt, wt, xt\ (1 - \tau t), wt+1\ xt+1]$ expresses savings by a representative household with a relative income wt, xt. If the utility function is homothetic, then there is a unique balanced growth path where the scale factor A is constant. The steady states are balanced growth paths, described as

$$h(\tau,x)=\frac{s[f'(k),(1-\tau)w(k)x,h(\tau)w(k)x]}{kx(2-\tau)} \quad (9.108)$$

$$R=h'(\tau,x)=f'(k) \quad (9.109)$$

$$\text{and } x_t=[h(\tau,x)]^{t-1} \quad (9.110)$$

where wage-rate $w(k) = f(k) - kf'(k)$ is given as a function of capital intensity. The saving function s is linearly homogenous with respect to households' income. Thus, equations (9.108), (9.109), and (9.110) are reduced to a more simple form of steady-growth path at the following rate:

$$g=\frac{k}{w(k)}=s[f'(k),\frac{1-\tau}{(2-\tau)H(\tau)},\frac{1}{2-\tau}] \quad (9.111)$$

where $H(\tau) = h(\tau, x)$ and the saving function s is increasing in its first and second arguments and decreasing in the third argument. Equation (9.111) possesses a unique solution, which is a balanced growth path supported by labour-augmenting technical progress in the accumulation of human capital.

The Azariades-Drazen model focuses on two locally stable balanced growth paths: one path consists of an underdeveloped trap with minimal labour quality and zero growth in per capita income, and another path consists of a higher labour quality and a positive growth. To formalize this, it takes into consideration training technology h, as

$$h(\tau,x) = 1 + \lambda(x)\,\tau \quad (9.112)$$

where λ is the private yield on human capital, an increasing function of x, which means that the labour quality is higher if the training quality is higher. Assuming that technical progress is labour augmenting (so scale factor A is constant), we have non-convexities in training technology, which displays positive threshold externalities. In particular, from equations (9.105) and (9.106), we have that

$$Rt\geq (wt{+}1/wt)\,\lambda,\ \text{if } \tau t> 0 \quad (9.113)$$

$$X_{t+1}/X_t = 1 + \lambda(x_t)\tau_t \tag{9.114}$$

Equation (9.114) describes the human capital accumulation, and equation (9.113) states that positive human investments are taking place if the yield on physical capital is greater than the yield on human capital. If the previous generations invest less in education, then, in turn, education tends to become unappealing for the current generation. Given $k/w(k)$ as an increasing function of k, we get two expressions that demonstrate the underdevelopment traps:

$$\frac{f'(k_{t+1})w(k_t)}{w(k_{t+1})} \geq \lambda \tag{9.115}$$

$$k_{t+1} = \frac{s}{2}[f'(k_{t+1}), \frac{w(k_t)}{w(k_{t+1})}, 1]w(k_{t+1}) \tag{9.116}$$

There exists a unique stationary solution k^- to equation (9.116), which is locally stable. Further, for $\lambda = \lambda^- = f'(k)$, there exists a family of underdevelopment-trap equilibriums corresponding to no investment in training and education. There is an equilibrium position with positive investment in training and education along the steady-state path. This equilibrium is a sequence that satisfies equation (9.114), and it is written as

$$\lambda(x_t)w(k_{t+1}) = f'(k_{t+1})w(k_t) \tag{9.117}$$

The above equation[12] admits at least one steady-state solution. Thus, there is a steady state (τ^*, k^*) with $f'(k^{*}) = \lambda^\wedge$, which has a local saddle-path stability and corresponds to a high-growth path (Azariades and Drazen 1990, 515). As mentioned earlier, the two locally balanced growth paths or the two equilibriums will coexist if individuals invest in human capital, which in return compensates individuals with high-quality labour for a longer preparation time. Azariades and Drazen proved with empirical evidence that threshold externalities are associated with human capital accumulation. Technically speaking, the threshold externalities are sufficient to produce multiple, locally stable balanced growth paths very analogous to the variant of the neoclassical model of growth. The necessary condition for a steady growth path is a high ratio of human investment to per capita income (keeping other variables constant).

Rapid growth cannot occur without qualified labour, which means there must be a high level of human investment relative to per capita income. Low-development traps occur when insufficient investment in education from past generations discourages training and skilled labour for the current generation, which, therefore, also hinders further growth. This is why countries with unequal initial human capital endowments may keep growing at different rates forever; it is an issue that relates to public policy. Azariades and Drazen proposed government intervention in the education sector, human capital, basic research, and credit rationing. Subsidies to these sectors will lead to Pareto improvements.

Bernard and Durlauf (1996) later proved that the multiple regimes of the Azariades-Drazen model were theoretically consistent with the finding of conditional convergence in the data. Galor (1997) further supported the Azariades-Drazen model by arguing that the data-generated process follows a multiple-regimes model rather than a single steady-state model of the Solow type.

Another author, Redding (1996), considered multiple development paths that were developed in the Azariadis-Drazen model, although he did so under different assumptions about human capital accumulation. Redding analyzed an economy in which households decide on their investment in human capital taking total factor productivity as given, whereas firms invest in total factor productivity growth, taking the human capital stock as given. This process constitutes a strategic complementary where the multiple expectational equilibriums must be coordinated.

Because of the strategic complementary between R&D and education, there is no need for threshold externalities in the accumulation of human capital to generate multiple equilibriums. There are two equilibriums: one in which workers invest in human capital in order to cover the fixed cost of R&D (thus, R&D is profitable) and another in which they do not invest and, as a consequence, R&D remains unprofitable. These two equilibriums are interpreted as "high skills" and "low skills." The "high-skills" equilibrium dominates its "low-skills" counterpart, which has a lower rate of growth (Redding 1996). As suggested by Redding, the economy will most probably find itself in a fast-growth path if households expect firms to invest in R&D and if firms expect households to invest in human capital accumulation. However, if both agents have negative expectations, the growth rate of the economy is low and probably tends to zero. Education policies and R&D subsidies appear as powerful mechanisms to move the economy from a low-development trap to a high-development stage.

GROWTH WITHOUT SCALE EFFECTS: THE YOUNG MODEL

The scale effect is one of the dilemmas in the theory and practice of endogenous growth models. In fact, in the growth literature, a great deal of attention has been devoted to the problem of the scale effect.[13] In most of the endogenous models, growth is driven by the accumulation of non-rival knowledge. The non-rivalrous nature of knowledge is considered when one person's use of certain knowledge does not diminish another person's use of the same knowledge. This important property of knowledge is used in several early models of R&D-based growth, such as those of Romer (1990), Grossman and Helpman (1991b), and Aghion and Howitt (1992). These endogenous growth models, which formalize the idea that innovation is the primary source of economic growth, are often characterized by the scale effect. They imply that the rate of economic growth increases with the amount of resources devoted to the research sector.

A few years later, however, Jones (1995a) pointed out that growth with scale effects is inconsistent with empirical facts. Over the past four decades, the Organization for Economic Co-operation and Development (OECD) is an international organization, mostly European, which helps governments engaged in the economic, social, and governance challenges of a globalized economy) countries have experienced a tremendous increase in the number of people involved in R&D activities, while the growth rates of per capita income have shown no equivalent increase. In fact, if the number of R&D scientists, researchers, and engineers in developed countries has risen several times over the past years, the total factor productivity growth rates of these economies have remained largely constant or, in some cases, have declined. This observation has led to new models of R&D-based growth that did not incorporate scale effects, such as Jones (1995b), Smulders and Van de Klundert (1995), Alwyn Young (1998), Li (2000), and Peretto and Smulders (2002). Most of these models have two main assumptions. The first is that the scale of the economy affects the firms that accumulate their own knowledge. The second is that R&D productivity depends on the accumulated public knowledge, which is independent of the scale of the economy.

The Alwyn Young[14] (1998) variant of endogenous growth theory with scale effects, which will be analyzed here, shows that any increase in the reward to innovation in a large economy will disappear in the long run because of the large number of products in the market. In order to maintain a constant rate of productivity, an advanced economy has to allocate a large number of R&D scientists and engineers to innovate and improve the quality of a large number of products.

Alwyn Young (1998, 47–61) used Dixit and Stiglitz (1977, 297–308) preferences to prove how product variety can eliminate the increased rents associated with an expansion in market size, thus making the development of new quality products and the growth of economy independent of the scale effect. The Young model has both a vertical and a horizontal dimension, which are two forms of innovative activities. The vertical dimension (or innovation), which is called also vertical quality improvement, can lead to sustained growth. Conversely, the horizontal one, called horizontal product introduction, does not lead to growth. Starting with the vertical dimension, using a Dixit-Stiglitz production function, we assume that output is a constant-elasticity-of-substitution composite of a variety of goods:

$$Y(t) = \left(\int_0^\infty [q_i(t)x_i(t)]^\sigma \, di \right)^{1/\sigma} \tag{9.118}$$

where $q_i(t)$ and $x_i(t)$ denote the quantity and the quality, respectively, of intermediate input i used at time t. The economy, populated by L consumers, each of whom supplies one unit of labour all the time, maximizes the present discounted value of the logarithm of consumption given by

$$\max U = \sum_{t=0}^{\infty} B^t \ln[C(t)]$$

The maximization of the final-output producers, for a certain level of consumer expenditure, yields the constant-elasticity-of-substitution demand for each intermediate input (Alwyn Young 1998, 48):

$$x_i^D(t) = \frac{E(t)p_i(t)^{-\tau} q_i(t)^{\tau-1}}{\int_0^{N(t)} p_i(t)^{1-\tau} q_i(t)^{\tau-1} \, di} \tag{9.119}$$

where $\tau = 1/(1 - \Sigma)$; $E(t)$ is the aggregate consumer expenditure, evolving according to $E(t + 1)/E(t) = [1 + r(t)]C$; $p_i(t)$ is the price of product i, and $N(t)$ is the number of products at time t. The firms will face the same costs whether they improve an existing product or introduce a new one. The initial dilemma for each firm is to maximize the net discounted competitive profits:

$$\max_{p_i(t),q_i(t)} \frac{[p_i(t) - c]x_i^D(t)}{1 + r(t-1)} - F[(q_i(t), q(t-1)] \tag{9.120}$$

where the product quality $q(t - 1)$ is the same for each sector (Alwyn Young 1998, 48–51). Differentiating with respect to $p_i(t)$ and $q_i(t)$, we get the first- and the second-order conditions, respectively:

$$\frac{[p_i(t) - c]x_i^D(t)}{1 + r(t-1)} - F[(q_i(t), q(t-1)] \tag{9.121}$$

$$\text{and} \left[\frac{p_i(t) - c}{1 + r(t)}\right]\frac{\partial x_i(t)}{\partial q_i(t)} - \frac{\partial F[q_i(t), q(t-1)]}{\partial q_i(t)} = 0 \tag{9.122}$$

Further, the free entry for firms using the technological opportunity (which represents the intertemporal spillover of knowledge) implies that net profit will be zero:

$$F[q_i(t), q'(t-1)] = \frac{[p_i(t) - c]x_i^D(t)}{1 + r(t-1)} \tag{9.123}$$

Following Alwyn Young's model (1998, 49), we divide equation (9.123) by (9.122) and, rearranging (9.122) and (9.121), we get the equilibrium relation:

$$\frac{p - c}{c} = \frac{1}{E_{p_i}^{x_i}} \tag{9.124}$$

where E_j^i denotes the elasticity of i with respect to j. Equation (9.124) gives the relationship between the firm price and the elasticity of demand. The price set by firms in the relation (9.124) equates the unit profit margin to the inverse of the elasticity of demand. Another equilibrium relation occurs when the elasticity of the research cost with respect to quality is equal to the elasticity of demand:

$$E_{q_i}^C = E_{q_i}^D \tag{9.125}$$

Equations (9.124) and (9.125) can be written in a different functional form using the parameters of research and production:

$$\frac{p-c}{c} = \frac{1}{\tau} = 1-\sigma \tag{9.126}$$

$$\text{and } \phi \frac{q(t)}{q(t-1)} = \tau - 1 = \frac{\sigma}{1-\sigma} \tag{9.127}$$

Based on these two functions, we see that the elasticity of demand with respect to price and the elasticity of demand with respect to quality are independent of the size of the market and the number of entrants. As such, the equilibrium markup and rate of product improvement[15] are determined by research and production parameters. In the case of the labour market, we hold that the total labour used in manufacturing and research is equal to the available supply, L. The equilibrium relation for the labour used in manufacturing is given as

$$L_M(t) = \frac{E(t)}{p} c = \sigma E(t) \tag{9.128}$$

where $L_M(t)$ is the labour used in the manufacturing sector, $E(t)$ is the elasticity of the consumer's expenditure, p is the price per unit, and c is the unit marginal cost. In the same way, the labour used in research is given as

$$L_R(t) = N(t-1) f e^{\frac{\phi q(t+1)}{q(t)}} \tag{9.129}$$

where N is the number of entrants and $fe^{\frac{\phi q(t+1)}{q(t)}}$ is the research investment per firm. Accordingly, the labour market-clearing condition is

$$L(t) = \sigma E(t) + N(t+1) f e^{\frac{\phi q(t+1)}{q(t)}} \tag{9.130}$$

Alwyn Young (1998, 50) determined the number of products by using a free-entry relation using equation (9.123):

$$fe^{\frac{\phi q(t)}{q(t-1)}} = \frac{(1-\sigma)E(t)}{N(t)[1+r(t-1)]} \tag{9.131}$$

Switching equation (9.131) by moving one period forward, substituting that into equation (9.130), and then using the first-order condition for the growth of consumer expenditure, given by [$E(t+1)/E(t) = [1 + r(t)]$ C)], allow us to solve the value of consumer expenditure as a function of different parameters:

$$L = \sigma E(t) + \frac{(1-\sigma)E(t+1)}{1+r(t)} = E(t)[\sigma + (1-\sigma)B] \tag{9.132}$$

Now we must find the number of entrants N (N in this case refers to the number of new firms) that invest in R&D to improve the current generation of products. Substituting (9.132) into (9.131) and rearranging for the total number of entrants as a function of aggregate market size (given by L) and other parameters, we have

$$N = \frac{(1-\sigma)E(t)}{[1+r(t-1)]fe^{\frac{\phi q(t)}{q(t-1)}}} = \frac{(1-\sigma)BL}{[\sigma+(1-\sigma)B]fe^{(\tau-1)}} \tag{9.133}$$

where N firms invest in R&D and product improvements by a factor of $(\tau - 1)/\phi$. Following Alwyn Young (1998, 50–2), we need to examine the impact of scale effect on growth and the level of income. From the expression of output given in equation (9.118), the total output of the economy is given by

$$Y(t) = q(t)x'(t)N(t)^{\frac{1}{\sigma}} \tag{9.134}$$

where $x'(t)$ is the demand for each intermediate input, which equals

$$x'(t) = \frac{E(t)}{p(t)N(t)} = \frac{\sigma L}{c[\sigma+(1-\sigma)B]N(t)} \tag{9.135}$$

Therefore, the output per capita, $y(t)$, is given as

$$y(t)=\frac{\sigma q(t)N(t)^{\frac{(1-\sigma)}{\sigma}}}{c[\sigma+(1-\sigma)B]} \tag{9.136}$$

In equilibrium, the number of product varieties N (N in this relation refers to the number of product varieties) is constant. Hence, growth in this economy is driven by the growth of product quality. Given that the elasticity of demand with respect to product quality is independent of L, changes in the scale of economy have no implications on the long-run growth of output per capita, which is given as $q(t)/q(t-1) = (\varepsilon - 1)/\phi$. Therefore, according to Alwyn Young (1998, 51–3), the level of utility is related to the level of scale. From expression (9.136), the logarithmic growth of output per capita between two periods can be decomposed by long-run components:

$$\ln\left[\frac{y(t)}{y(t-1)}\right]=\ln\left[\frac{q(t)}{q(t-1)}\right]+\left(\frac{1-\sigma}{\sigma}\right)\ln\left[\frac{N(t)}{N(t-1)}\right] \tag{9.137}$$

This equation shows that any increase in product quality is independent of the scale of the economy. In the absence of the scale effect, all the policy actions to increase or decrease the rents offered to creative entrepreneurs will only influence the level of income and not the long-run growth rate. In fact, the subsidies to R&D will change the total pool of rents offered to entrepreneurs and the level of income without putting pressure to the elasticity of demand with respect to quality. Up to this point, we have discussed the vertical dimension, which has an intertemporal knowledge spillover. Alternatively, in the horizontal dimension (or innovation), the knowledge spillover is incorporated by specifying the costs of innovation, given by

$$F[q_i(t),q'(t-1),N(t-1)]=\frac{fe^{\frac{\phi q(t)}{q(t-1)}}}{N(t-1)} \tag{9.138}$$

where the research cost of the innovation (the left side of [9.138]) of a new product is inversely related to the degree of product variety $[N(t-1)]$. Most of the equilibrium relations on the horizontal innovation remain the same as before (in vertical innovation); however, the free-entry condition is now given as (Alwyn Young 1998, 53)

$$\frac{fe^{\frac{\phi q(t)}{q(t-1)}}}{N(t-1)} = \frac{\left[p_i(t)-c\right]x_i^D(t)}{1+r(t-1)} = \frac{(1-\sigma)E(t)}{N(t)\left[1+r(t-1)\right]} = \frac{(1-\sigma)BL}{N(t)\left[\sigma+(1-\sigma)B\right]} \tag{9.139}$$

By rearranging $N(t)$ and $N(t-1)$, we have again the free-entry condition in a simpler form:

$$\frac{N(t)}{N(t-1)} = \frac{(1-\sigma)BL}{fe^{\tau-1}\left[\sigma+(1-\sigma)B\right]} \tag{9.140}$$

Despite the fact that the growth rate of product quality $q(t)/q(t-1)$ remains equal to $(\tau-1)/\phi$, the growth rate of product variety is now an increasing function of the scale of the economy. There is no need for scale to be positively related with growth, because the level effects of the innovative dimension can completely disperse the increased pool of rents brought about by a rise in market size, and they can do so without allowing any increase in innovation activity. In effect, if there are several dimensions (not only two) where intensive research and innovation activity can lead to sustained growth, but there is one additional dimension whose spillovers are not sufficient to lead to growth, then increases in the pool of rents will dissipate, thereby generating changes in income only and without having any scale effects on the long-run rate of growth.

When the marginal product of the horizontal dimension in R&D diminishes more rapidly than that of the vertical dimension (in R&D), there is no scale effect; regardless, growth will be achieved in the long run by changes in institutional, technological, and policy parameters that will influence the incentive to perform R&D (Howitt 1999, 728). One year after Alwyn Young's contributions, Howitt (1999), in his model of endogenous growth, predicted that during a period of steady growth, the portion of GDP allocated to R&D should remain constant. Studying the case of the United States since the mid-1950s, Howitt observed that the total expenditure on R&D has remained pretty much stable – between 2.2 per cent and 2.9 per cent of GDP every year between 1957 and 1996.

These data on trends in US R&D mostly confirms the validity of the endogenous innovation growth theory.

INNOVATION AND NEW CONSUMER GOODS: SOME CONCLUSIONS

Technological change and expansions in the variety of products describe basic innovations, whereas quality improvements represent the sophistication of products and techniques. Discoveries and expansions in the new products are not direct substitutes for the old products but rather just innovation. In the quality-improvement process, goods of higher quality are close substitutes for those of lower quality.

Generally speaking, quality improvements tend to make the old goods outdated in a short time, whereas a new variety of products does not put the old varieties out of the market. In developed countries, higher R&D efforts are focused on quality improvements rather than basic innovations, because the incentive to seek monopoly rents is higher for quality improvements compared to simple innovations. In this chapter, we have seen that extra human capital engaged in skilled work reduces research costs and increases long-run growth rate. As the productivity of education increases, individuals who initially were indifferent between seeking education and working as unskilled workers then prefer to become skilled. In the Eicher overlapping generation model, students expect the relative wage to rise in the future, so they decide to borrow money and invest in human capital in the first period in order to carry a higher income in the next period. An increase in the productivity of labour increases the relative demand for skilled labour, which, in turn, increases the rate of technological change and the long-run growth.

We have also seen that the opening of international channels of communication accelerates innovation and growth in different countries. Research undertaken by multiple countries working together builds knowledge more quickly than local research conducted in isolated countries. This level and type of communication also contributes to a global increase of knowledge and a rapid reduction in the cost of product development.

Coe and Helpman (1993) focused on the effects of R&D among trading partners for a variety of developed, open-economy countries. This empirical study follows the theoretical literature of Grossman and Helpman (1991a and 1991b), which focuses on R&D as the primary source of innovation in the economy. The transmission mechanism can occur directly by one partner learning about "new technologies and materials, production processes, or organizational methods" or indirectly through access to imports that facilitate innovation.

By discussing the issue of trade and technological progress, it may appear that the ones who have the most to gain from trade liberalization are the high-tech countries, such as the United States and other Western countries that have significant comparative advantages in terms of R&D and human capital relative to countries with transitioning or developing economies.

Nonetheless, the relationship between the residual of endogenous growth models and trade is important in view of certain recent trends, which have affected developed economies in particular. By term "residual," we mean any factor that affects output other than labour or capital, which in the modern literature has been replaced by technological progress. The importance of human capital in developed economies shows how important it is to categorize and study the other complicated inputs of production, such as knowledge and technical progress, rather than to study only labour and capital, which may count for a good portion of the "residual" in the growth models.

10

Endogenous Growth and the New Schumpeterian Approach of "Creative Destruction"

"Creative destruction" refers to the constant process of the innovation mechanism by which new production units replace obsolete ones. This idea was invented by Joseph Schumpeter (1942), who considered it "the essential fact about capitalism." The process of creative destruction infuses major aspects of macroeconomic activities – not only long-run growth but also short-run economic fluctuations, structural adjustment, and the functioning of factor markets. At the microeconomic level, several decisions in different organizations are chacterized by restructuring and reorganizing the production arrangements. These decisions involve multiple parties as well as strategic and technological considerations. The efficiency of these decisions not only depends on their managerial aspects but also on the existence of good institutions and favourable market conditions that provide a suitable transactional framework and long-term macroeconomic stability.

The Schumpeterian theory represents a different approach from the AK version of endogenous growth theory, as it is based on presenting technological progress as a form of capital accumulation. In AK theories, the main reason for growth was the private process of thrift, an essentially classified process involving no interpersonal conflict. Conversely, Schumpeterian theory identifies that technological change is a social process, and that since the start of the Industrial Revolution, workers' skills, capital equipment, and technological knowledge have been totally transformed and in most cases rendered obsolete, destroyed by the same inventions that have created fortunes for others. As a consequence, the rents from successful innovation are temporary, and this possibility is regularly taken into account by entrepreneurs in their decisions about spending on research and development. Most of the investments in R&D are motivated by the expectation that monopoly rents can be created as the result of reaching a technological leadership in the industry. Furthermore, investing in innovation is a costly and long process, and there is a trade-off for industries between investing a large portion of their productive resources in innovative processes or instead devoting them to current production.

There is a widespread newer idea that technical progress is constituted from advanced equipment created through an extended process of innovation, through learning by doing, and through accumulation of knowledge – rather than the usual older representation of technology as "manna from heaven" that falls on all production processes in identical measure independently of their vintage. What's more, this new conception of technical progress is more original and achievable. To suppose that it is impossible for enterprises to replace old machines with new ones in order to increase productivity is unrealistic. Hence, the question posed is: which implications permit enterprises to employ new technologies in order to interrupt the fall of profits?

Introducing these new hypotheses, the relationship between technical progress and unemployment becomes more complex. Enterprises, pushed from the search for unearned income from a monopoly (or dominant) position, make extensive efforts to introduce new products and new production processes: the entrepreneur is intrinsically an innovator. The competitive process of the capitalist system is not represented as a static situation in equilibrium, where enterprises maximize profits and where technological progress is usually taken for granted; instead, inasmuch as the innovative activity is incessant and the entrepreneurial profit gushes from the innovation, the breach of the stationary equilibrium is contained within the nature of capitalism. The competition is what really counts and, in a dialectic antagonism, is the essence of capitalist development. In fact, the competition is a continuous crash between innovators yesterday, who have acquired an extra profit, and imitators today – until new innovators put out on the market concurrent enterprises. This process of "creative destruction" is considered to be the "essential fact" of capitalism, on which the foundation of the capitalist system is based and evolves. The original contribution of Aghion and Howitt (1992) was based on Schumpeter's concept of "creative destruction." It describes a free market economy that is constantly distressed by technological innovations from which some entrepreneurs succeed by creating and adopting new technologies while others lose. The 1992 model was later generalized and applied to a variety of different questions, all included in their well-known textbook *Endogenous Growth Theory*, published in 1998. This work provides an integrated approach to the analysis of growth, with the objective of bringing Schumpeter's theory of development back into the mainstream of macroeconomic theory.

In this chapter, several endogenous growth models that treat the Schumpeterian approach of creative destruction will be analyzed in a historical context.

EMBODIED TECHNOLOGICAL PROGRESS AND THE PROCESS OF CREATIVE DESTRUCTION

In this section, we will see in what way and within which limits an embodied technical progress inserted in a context of balanced growth connects the model using costs of search to the Schumpeterian theory. The question that may arise is: in what way does the concept of "creative destruction" enter the search models?

We begin by saying that, based on the assumption made about an embodied technical progress,[1] the increase in productivity benefits only those who possess new machinery; in fact, it is assumed that technical progress is uniform and approximately exponential in time. The capital goods at the moment of their construction incorporate the recent knowledge but do not have use of every successive technological improvement. Therefore, the product obtained at time t with capital of vintage τ is equal to

$$Y_\tau(t) = F(K_\tau(t), p(\tau)L_\tau(t)) \qquad (10.1)$$

where $K\tau(t)$ is the capital constructed in the period τ at time t, $L\tau(t)$ is the total job used at time t, and $p(\tau)$ is the parameter of the productivity for a single enterprise remaining fixed and is determined in base of the age τ of capital goods, whereas for new capital goods it increases to an equal exogenous rate g:

$$p(t) = p_0 e^{gt} \qquad (10.2)$$

If the entire economic system is being developed along a path of balanced growth growing at the same exogenous rate as the technical progress, the costs of enterprises are also increasing at a rate g. In addition, it is assumed that enterprises cannot use new capital goods to replace old ones, so productivity is fixed: there will be, therefore, a time in which the activity of the enterprises that possess obsolete machinery will stop being profitable, thereby determining the "destruction" of these enterprises and putting them out of business. However, the destruction is "creative" because it provokes an ongoing procreation in the entrepreneurial world, where the old enterprises are replaced with new ones. It is clear that the mechanism described here generates unemployment if we consider a labour market in which imperfections prevent the fired worker from being immediately hired by other enterprises.

Before proceeding with other sections, a formal demonstration of what we have just asserted is necessary in order to understand how the destruction of old enterprises as a result of embodied technical progress presents irreducible aspects of the process of creative destruction, as described in detail in the Schumpeterian theory.

In the first place, the fact that the growth of technical progress occurs at an exogenous rate is less adapted to the reality of the innovative activity, which is instead – according to Schumpeter – fruit of the entrepreneurs' initiative. However, it is opportune and interesting to briefly expose a model of endogenous growth of Schumpeterian formulation that was originated by Aghion and Howitt (1992). The main assumption here is that there is no capital accumulation and the final good is produced according to the function

$$Y = p_j f(m_j) \tag{10.3}$$

where p_j is the productivity related to m_j, which is the intermediate good used in production. In addition, the innovation produced in the research sector consists of a new intermediate good that, being associated with a greater productivity p_j, renders the previous one obsolete:

$$\frac{p_{j+1}}{p_j} = \gamma > 1 \tag{10.4}$$

Moreover, the innovation is produced according to the Poisson process[2] with a certain arrival rate equal to Φz, with z representing the number of enterprises dedicated to research and Φ being a constant greater than zero that indicates the productivity of research. Based on some assumptions, it can be demonstrated that the expected rate of growth of output is equal to

$$gy = \Phi z ln\ y \tag{10.5}$$

The growth is, therefore, a function of Φ, z, and y that is the amplitude of the innovation: it is endogenous with respect to z, given that any form of subsidy that increases the number of enterprises engaged in the research sector also raises the expected rate of growth.

In the second place, the assumption that a steady-growth state is far from the idea of economic development found in Schumpeter, according to whom growth does not take place on a regular basis.[3] This happens because the innovations are not uniformly distributed over the course of time but rather appear in blocks. The appearance, at some point, of a large number of entrepreneurs, which begins the expansion process, disturbs in a certain way the course of the economic system. Depressions are a necessary consequence of the expansion period, representing a phase of reflection and a necessary adjustment of the entire economic system to the new situation that the big wave of innovations has initiated. Schumpeter connected the depression phase with the emergence of unemployment, having stated that what is being caused by the technical transformations is "technological unemployment."

In the third place, the representation of technological progress as being akin to productive capacity as a result of the introduction of new machinery, does not completely render "justice" to the complexity of the Schumpeterian notion of innovation. The innovative activity might consist of a new production process that reduces costs, the production of new goods that better satisfy actual needs, the opening of a new market, or the creation of new forms of job organization.

In the modern Schumpeterian idea (Aghion and Howitt 1992 and 1998), the rate of creative destruction provides a standard interpretation for product market instability: each innovation creates a temporary monopoly rent while also destroying the current incumbent's market power. Successful innovation is often seen as a source of temporary market power, eroding the profits and position of old firms yet ultimately giving up ground to the pressure of new inventions commercialized by the rise of new competitors. Many of the dynamics of industrial change, such as the transition from a competitive to a monopolistic market and vice versa or the introduction of new products can be explained through the pioneering concept of creative destruction.

ENDOGENOUS GROWTH AND CREATIVE DESTRUCTION: THE AGHION-HOWITT MODEL

The model of Aghion[4] and Howitt[5] (1992) incorporates the Schumpeterian idea of "creative destruction." It emphasizes the role of industrial innovations in the improvement of quality products and capital goods. The research activity develops designs for new products, which are intrinsically more productive than the pre-existing ones. As a result, better products render the previous ones obsolete. According to the Schumpeterian theory, technical progress creates loss through the destruction of rents as well as gains. The amount of research conducted today depends on the expected duration of the rent generated by innovation. If there is expectation, then a great deal of research activity will be carried on in the future; however, if the expected benefit from today's innovation is low, then little research activity will be financed today.

Overall, the Aghion-Howitt model has as its objective to prove that there is endogenous growth based on the Schumpeterian theory of creative destruction, where new innovations and improvements in the quality of products render previous innovations and products obsolete.

In the model (Aghion and Howitt 1992), three categories of labour are assumed: unskilled labour, used only in the production of consumption goods; skilled labour, used in both the intermediate and the research sectors; and specialized labour, used only in the research sector. There are also assumed three sectors: research, intermediate, and the final goods sector, which produces consumption goods. The production function for the final (consumption) goods sector, which uses only unskilled labour, is given as

$$Y(i)_t = A(i)x(i)_t^{\alpha} L^{\beta} = A(i)x(i)_t^{\alpha} \qquad (10.6)$$

where i indexes inventions by the order of introduction, $x(i)_t$ is the flow of the intermediate good produced by the monopolist during interval t, and $A(i)$ is a parameter indicating the productivity of the last intermediate input invented before time t. The intermediate goods sector uses skilled labour alone, given in linear form as

$$x(i)_t = N_{1t} \tag{10.7}$$

where N is the flow of skilled labour used in the intermediate sector and $x(i)$ is the flow of intermediate input. When a new invention arrives, the productivity parameter $A(i)$ associated with the input used in final production bounds to a higher level. Thus, new intermediate goods increase the productivity parameter A by the factor $\gamma > 1$. Therefore, in the research sector, the law of productivity motion is written as

$$A(i) = A_0\gamma^i \text{ or equivalently } A(i) = \gamma a(i-1) \tag{10.8}$$

Focusing on the relations between time intervals, which are characterized by different technological innovations (given by i), we have that the sector of final goods is competitive, so firms try to maximize profits as much as they can. The profit expression for a firm is given as

$$\pi_F(i) = A(i)x(i)^\alpha - p(i)x(i) - w_L(i) \tag{10.9}$$

where $p(i)$ is a constant elasticity demand function for the intermediate input $x(i)$, written as $p(i) = \alpha A(i)x(i)^{\alpha-1}$, as in P.M. Romer (1990). In the intermediate goods sector, given the demand constraint, the monopolist chooses production so as to maximize profit:

$$\begin{aligned} &\pi_I(i) = p(i)x(i) - w_t(i)x(i) = \alpha A(i)x(i)^\alpha - w_t(i)x(i) \\ &p(i) = \alpha A(i)x(i)^{\alpha-1} \end{aligned} \tag{10.10}$$

where w_t is the wage of skilled labour used in this sector, and is defined as a function of index i. The Cobb-Douglas solution for equation (10.10) implies

$$\begin{aligned} &x(i) = \left(\frac{w_t(i)}{A(i)\alpha^2}\right)^{\frac{1}{\alpha-1}} \\ &p(i) = w_t(i)/\alpha \text{ and } \pi(i) = [(1-\alpha)/\alpha]w_t(i)x(). \end{aligned} \tag{10.11}$$

In the research sector, a firm employing the research factors z and s (or i index) experiences innovation with a Poisson arrival rate of $\lambda\Phi(z,s)$. The intention of the firm is to maximize the expected profit from research choosing Φ:

$$\Pi r = \lambda\Phi\ (z,s)\ V_{(t+1)} - w_t(z) - w_t(s) = \\ \lambda\Phi\ (i)\ V_{(i+1)} - w_s(i)\ \Phi(i) \tag{10.12}$$

where $V_{(i+1)}$ is the value of i + first innovation, w_s is the wage-rate of a specialized worker, and $\lambda\Phi$ is the probability of discovering a new design by employing Φ workers. Given that Φ has constant return and from the Kuhn-Tucker condition for maximization, it follows that

$$\Phi(i) > 0 \qquad w_s(i) = \lambda V_{(i+1)} \tag{10.13}$$

$$\text{and } \Phi(i) = 0 \qquad w_s(i) > \lambda V_{(i+1)} \tag{10.14}$$

We now need to determine the value of $V_{(i+1)}$, which is the solution for the advanced research sector. The value $V_{(i+1)}$ to an outside research firm is the expected present discounted value of the flow of monopoly profits Πi generated by the t + 1st innovation over an interval whose length is random and is distributed with parameter $\lambda\Phi(i + 1)$ (the expected duration of the monopoly is $1/\lambda\Phi(i + 1)$). Hence, the value to an outside firm is given as

$$V(i+1) = \frac{\pi(i+1)}{r + \lambda\varphi(i+1)} \tag{10.15}$$

The value to a monopolist who is looking to create the next innovation is $V_{(t+1)}$ -V_t, which is less than the value $V_{(t+1)}$ to an outside firm; as a result, he chooses not to do research. Despite this, innovation raises productivity because the producer of an innovation captures the rents from the productivity gain during at least one interval. After that, rents are captured by other innovators based on the present innovation.

The problem arising now is how to allocate the fixed flow N of skilled labour between manufacturing and research. Combining (10.12), (10.13), (10.14) and (10.15), we have the stationary equilibrium condition:

$$\frac{w(N - n_t)}{\lambda\varphi n_t} \geq \frac{\gamma\pi(w(N - n_{t+1}))}{r + \lambda\varphi n_{t+1}} \tag{10.16a}$$

or, using the index form,

$$\frac{w_t(i)}{\lambda} = \frac{\pi_I(i+1)}{r+\lambda\varphi(i+1)} \qquad (10.16b)$$

where $N = n_t + x_t$ and $\lambda\Phi n_t$ and $\lambda\Phi n_{t+1}$ are the rates of creative destruction at time t and $t + 1$. In this case, growth is positive because innovations arrive at the Poisson rate $\lambda\Phi n_t > 0$. Equation (10.16a) determines research employment at t as a function of research employment at $t + 1$: $n_t = \xi\,(n_{t+1})$, where ξ is a strictly decreasing function when it has a positive value. The left-hand side of each equation (10.16a) and (10.16b) is the marginal cost of research (the cost of a worker in R&D divided by his or her marginal productivity), and the right-hand side is the marginal benefit of research, that is, the present discounted value of the rent (private discount rate), which is generated by an innovation, where discounting takes into account the obsolescence rate of innovation. Furthermore, the marginal cost of research is increasing with the current employment in research (using current technology). The marginal benefit of research is decreasing with future (or expected) employment in R&D.

There are two reasons why current research depends on future research: first, an increase in research in the next period discourages research in the current period by raising future wages, which reduce the flow of profit $\pi(i + 1)$ captured from the next innovator; second, it shortens the expected lifetime of the monopoly enjoyed by the innovator when the rate of creative destruction $\lambda\Phi(i + 1)$ is raised.

From equation (10.6) of consumption goods technology, we have the result that the marginal product, the flow of monopoly profits, and the flow of intermediate goods produced are defined as

$$p_t = w_t/\alpha, \qquad \pi_t = [(1-\alpha)/\alpha]w_t x_t, \text{ and } x_t = \left(\frac{w_t}{\alpha^2}\right)^{\frac{1}{\alpha-1}} \qquad (10.17)$$

Considering the Cobb-Douglas function from equation (10.17), the unique stationary equilibrium is given by the following expression (Aghion and Howitt 1992, 333):

$$1 = \frac{\lambda\gamma\left(\frac{1-\alpha}{\alpha}\right)(N-\varphi)}{r+\lambda\varphi} \qquad (10.18)$$

Hence, the research employment is given as

$$\varphi(n) = \frac{\gamma N \frac{1-\alpha}{\alpha} - \frac{r}{\lambda}}{1 + \gamma \frac{1-\alpha}{\alpha}} \tag{10.19}$$

where $\Phi(n) = n$ is the linear research technology. Expression (10.19) shows that the amount of research employment n in a stationary equilibrium decreases with the rate of interest r, increases with the size of each innovation γ, increases with arrival parameter λ (the efficiency of R&D), and increases with the endowment N of skilled labour. The condition for Φ to be positive is

$$r < \lambda \gamma \frac{1-\alpha}{\alpha} N \tag{10.20}$$

where the parameter α is a measure of the degree of market power and $(1 - \alpha)$ is the Lerner measure of monopoly power $[(p(i) - MC(i))/p(i)]$.

To reach the balanced growth expression, we introduce t indices. In the interval, during which the ith innovation is adopted, real output is

$$Y(i) = A(i)x(i)^{\alpha} = A(i)(N - \varphi(i))^{\alpha} \tag{10.21}$$

where $Y(i)$ remains constant through all periods in which technology i is adopted. Considering the above expression together with equation (10.8), and given that in balanced growth equilibrium, intermediate input $x(i)$ is constant, the real output implies

$$Y(i + 1) - \gamma Y(i) \leftrightarrow lnY(i + 1) = lnY(i) + ln(\gamma) \tag{10.22}$$

From the expression (10.22), we have that the time path of the log of real output will be a random step-function starting at $lnY(0)$, where the size of each step is equal to the constant $ln\lambda$; the time between each step $(\Delta 1, \Delta 2, \ldots)$ is a sequence of variables exponentially distributed with parameter $\gamma\Phi(n)$. In the Aghion-Howitt model, it is shown that real output is a non-stationary stochastic process, and exactly a random walk with constant positive drift given as

$$lnY_{t+1} = lnY_t + \varepsilon_t \tag{10.23}$$

$$\text{where } \varepsilon_t = ln\gamma \, N(t, t + 1) \tag{10.24}$$

What expression (10.24) states is that growth rate ε_t, between t and $t + 1$, is equal to the size of each innovation $ln\gamma$ times the stochastic number of innovations occurring between t and $t + 1$. The probability of N follows a Poison process with rate of arrival $\gamma\Phi(n)$. In particular, from the property of Poisson processes, we have that the economy's average growth rate (AGR) and the economy's variance growth rate (VGR) are given by (Aghion and Howitt 1992, 336),

$$\text{AGR} = E(\varepsilon_t) = ln\ \gamma\lambda\Phi(n) \text{ and VGR} = \text{Var}\ (\varepsilon_t) = (ln\gamma)^2\ \lambda\Phi(n). \tag{10.25}$$

The combination of average growth rates allows us to know the effects of parameter changes on the average growth rate. Both average growth rates and its variances are increasing functions of the size of innovation as well as the proportion of the skilled labour force employed in research. AGR is raised by increases in the arrival parameter, the size of innovations, the amount of skilled labour, and the degree of market power. Parameter changes have the same qualitative effects on VGR and AGR. Thus, it is easy to relate the fundamental parameters of the model to the predicted growth rate of the economy. Investigating the Aghion-Howitt model further, we have a comparison between different laissez-faire solutions with a choice of social planner who maximizes the representative consumer's utility. Because agents are risk-neutral and there is no physical capital, the planner will simply choose the sequence $\Phi(n)$, which maximizes

$$U(0) = \int_0^\infty e^{-t}\, E(Y_t \,|t_0 = 0)$$

Restricting the analysis to the stationary solutions, we denote the probability $E(t)$ which will be exactly i innovations up to time t as $\pi(i,t)$:

$$E(Y_t \Big| t_0 = 0) = \sum_0^\infty \pi(i,t) A_0 \gamma^i (N - \varphi(n))^\alpha\, dt\lambda \tag{10.26}$$

where the innovation process given as a Poisson process with parameter $\lambda\phi$ is given as

$$\pi(i,t) = \frac{\lambda\varphi(n)t^i e^{-\lambda\varphi(n)t}}{i!} \tag{10.27}$$

By combining equations (10.26) and (10.27), we have the following maximization problem:

$$\max U(0) = \frac{A_0(N-\varphi(n))^{\alpha}}{r-\lambda\varphi(n)(\gamma-1)} \tag{10.28}$$

that identifies $U(0)$ as the initial flow of output $A_0\Phi^a$ discounted at the rate $r - \lambda\Phi(n)(\gamma - 1)$, which is less than the rate of interest r because the stream of output will be growing over time. The stationary socially optimal level of research n that maximizes U is given only when it is interior (or fulfil the first-order condition). So we get

$$\frac{\alpha(N-n)^{\alpha-1}}{\lambda\varphi(n)} = \frac{(\gamma-1)(N-n)^{\alpha}}{r-\lambda\varphi(n)(\gamma-1)} \tag{10.29}$$

Here, different from the equation of stationary condition (10.16a), we have a social discount rate $r - \lambda\Phi(n)$ instead of the private discount rate, which is less than the rate of interest. For the social planner, the intertemporal spillover (or the benefit of the next innovation) will continue without end. For the private research firm, there is no benefit beyond the successful innovation. The expression for the total output $F(N - n)^a$ replaces the flow of profit that appears in (10.16a). This is called the "appropriability effect," which means that the monopolist cares only about his surplus and not about the total welfare effect of innovation. The multiplicative term $(\gamma - 1)$ in (10.29) corresponds to a business-stealing effect; that is, the planner realizes that innovation causes destruction together with the creation of welfare. The marginal product of skilled labour $\alpha(N - n)$ appears instead of the wage in (10.16a). This is the monopoly distortion effect.

In the creative destruction model, there is a unique steady-state equilibrium in which the division of labour between research and manufacturing remains unchanged over time. The rate of growth in equilibrium is without doubt an increasing function of the propensity to save, the productivity of research technology, and the degree of market power enjoyed by a successful innovator. From the social planner analysis, we have the result that the positive externalities, the intertemporal spillovers, and the appropriability effects have the propensity to make the average growth rate not quite optimal, whereas the negative externalities and the business-stealing effects tend to make it greater. Because of these externalities, the laissez-faire average growth rate may be either more or less than optimal.

GROWTH AND UNEMPLOYMENT: THE CONTRIBUTION OF SEARCH THEORY

In the first part of this work, we have seen how Solow, choosing to study steady-state growth with a level of constant unemployment, had set aside the aspects of the Harrod model regarding the relationship between growth and unemployment. Solow's choice is justified if the economy is structured in a historical perspective: as it happened, during the 1950s and 1960s, the economy was able to grow in a regular way and nearly without unemployment. Since then and for a long time, economic growth and the labour economy have been considered by neoclassical theory as two distinguished fields of research. It may appear bizarre that, until the 1990s, no neoclassical economist had raised the problem of reconciling the stylized facts of growth explained by Solow with other stylized facts equally important but not considered, such as the presence of unemployment. However, inasmuch as the interaction between growth and unemployment was non-existent, the problem did not appear interesting: from the beginning of the twentieth century at least until the 1970s, the unemployment rate has not shown any trend, but the economy and, with it, the intensity of capital and productivity have constantly increased. For a long time, the core theorists of unemployment have paid attention to the fluctuations of unemployment and income mainly in the short run rather than in the long run. As a result, the interaction between the long-run unemployment rate and the steady path of growth has not been part of any intensive research.

By the end of the 1960s, the neoclassical theory turned a corner, asserting with Phelps and Friedman that the unemployment rate is compatible with the inflation rate, and this would be the natural rate of unemployment toward which the economy tends in the long run. The microeconomic foundations of the respective models that were formulated by these two economists are different. Phelps bases his theory of natural equilibrium on the imperfections in information that characterize the labour market; whereas Friedman builds his theory on the working class's misperception of the price of labour. Despite these differences, the conclusion drawn from the contributions of Phelps and Friedman is the same: the trade-off between inflation and unemployment is a phenomenon of the short run. In the long run, once the agents' expectations have been realized, the economy tends to reach an independent rate of unemployment because of the dynamics of prices. Moreover, in both Phelps and Friedman, the relative problems related to growth are ignored, or, better, it is assumed that the economy grows at an exogenous and constant rate, as demonstrated by Solow. Friedman tried to connect steady-state growth to the theory of unemployment with a particularly significant step: With that level (the natural rate) of unemployment reached, real salaries tend on average to grow at a "normal" secular rate that can be maintained indefinitely if the accumulation of capital, technological improvements, and so on maintain their long-run tendencies.

In steady-state growth, there is a capital and productivity increase according to the trend of the long period, which influences the level of unemployment, thereby allowing wages to augment at a normal rate. But is the concept of natural unemployment, as usually presented, really extendable to a growing economy such as that described by Solow? The concept of the natural rate of unemployment, as defined by Friedman and Phelps in the 1960s, is somewhat inadequate because it was, in part, "developed" to explain the relation between inflation and unemployment in the context of a static economy. Alternatively, the model of Solow, completed with the introduction of technological progress, is incapable of giving an account of the existence of a small, constant, and positive unemployment rate.

The neoclassical theory of growth, which is able to explain the stylized facts of growth, is in jeopardy if it faces another stylized fact, such as the presence of unemployment. If, in fact, the model of Solow wants to represent faithfully the modern economic systems, then it is unacceptable if it fails to adapt itself so as to be able to describe what actually happens in the labour market in the long run.

In addition, Solow (1994 and 2000) recently admitted that separating the fields of search theory from those of unemployment and growth has constituted an error. According to him, the level of employment, which is generally considered equal or proportional to the level of population, grows in time, and with this, all the problems of coordination disappear because it is assumed that the level of employment is always equal or proportional to the level of labour force. A large part of macroeconomics tries to explain why and when the employment (L) is different from the labour force (N). The tradition in economics, however, was to separate the study of such a problem from the study of growth. Few contributions have come out of this tradition (Solow 1994, 19).

The first contribution outside the habitual stream was that of Pissarides, who turned his attention to what effects technical progress has on employment in the long run in a search model (Pissarides 1990, *x*). The innovation of his model is the redefinition of the natural rate of unemployment as a rate at which the flow of the unemployed to employment is equal to that of the employed to unemployment. Moreover, thanks to the introduction of the rational expectation assumption, the economists' interest in the monetary aspects of the labour market (the trade-off between unemployment and inflation) that has characterized the past search models has vanished. According to Pissarides (1990), the theory of unemployment is, above all, a macroeconomic theory. It consists of two representative agents – the enterprises and the workers who move between two states, occupation and unemployment – and has as the main objective the determination of the equilibrium rate of unemployment for the economy as a whole. Pissarides' intention is to set up a model capable of moving through steady-state equilibrium in the presence of an equilibrium rate of unemployment. The model should be able to explain the existence of a constant rate of unemployment and a constant rate of vacant places in an economy characterized by the stylized facts of growth. Some core economists believe that if an unemployment model is consistent with the requirements of a balanced growth in the long run, then it constitutes the point of departure for the successive additions that will explain unemployment in a real economy, and this is why the neoclassical model is considered to be so important (Pissarides 1990, 11).

The search theory developed by Pissarides and later taken into consideration by Aghion and Howitt[6] is in a position to answer why, in the past three decades, the growth and productivity have lost their neutral character regarding unemployment. Since the 1970s, a slow rate of growth and productivity has occurred simultaneously with an increase in the rate of unemployment. The neoclassical interpretation of these phenomena appears to be uniform, although in actuality, we have on one side those who believe that the phenomena constitute the test verifying whether growth influences the labour market and on the other those who are more traditional and think that there is no interaction between labour and growth, at least in the long run. As an example, Layard, Nickell, and Jackman (1991) did not see substantial differences between labour and growth over the past decades and, thus, formulated a model in which the increase in the rate of productivity does not have any effect on the natural rate of unemployment.

Few economists, except the theorists of job search, have tried to delve deeper in order to determine the relationship between economic growth, technical progress, and unemployment. Before going into details (in the next section) of the model with search costs, we will say a few words about the contributions of Rothworn (1999) and Gordon (1995), which are analogous to those of Layard, Nickell, and Jackman, because they use the same approach.[7] Basically, in the work of Rothworn and Gordon, the demand for labour is replaced by a "price equation," which represents the possible combination of price and occupation that is consistent with the maximization of profit for monopolists and competitive enterprises. In this equation, the labour supply is replaced by a "salary equation" (wage-setting) or a dealing mechanism, which occurs between the enterprise and the union according to the Nash equilibrium.

Rothworn, without performing or conducting an in-depth analysis by creating economic models, reached the following conclusion: assuming the elasticity of substitution between capital and labour in a CES function of production is inferior to the unit (one),[8] technical progress (of Harrod-neutral type) provokes an increase of unemployment, whereas an increase in the rate of growth of productivity causes an acceleration of unemployment. However, the effect of technical progress can be balanced, according to Rothworn, over the course of time with the accumulation of capital, whose rate of growth is positively correlated with reduction in the rate of unemployment. Alternatively, Gordon (1995) asserted that the trade-off between unemployment and productivity is possible only in the short run and is generated from a structural shock (he made reference to "wage setting shock" and "energy price shock"). In the long run, however, a dynamic adjustment of capital is required in order to cancel the trade-off.

JOB CREATION AND JOB DESTRUCTION: THE MORTENSEN-PISSARIDES MODEL

The model of Mortensen[9] and Pissarides[10] (1994) corresponds to the matching models of unemployment with non-cooperative wage behaviour. In this model, labour market and frictions indicate that there is a costly encumbrance which delays the process of filling openings, and as a result the endogenous job destructions and the closing of jobs closely interact with job creations and the creation of new vacancies. Salaries and wages in the market are determined by a complex process of bargaining and a specific allocation rule of the rent generated by a job. Salaries are often interpreted as the result of bargaining between workers and employers. The fundamental hypothesis is constituted from a labour market of the atomistic type (in which there is a multitude of agents working in absence of an auctioneer who would render their choices compatible) and is characterized by the presence of frictions of various kinds. The term *friction* is used in a wide sense to indicate all that interferes with the instantaneous exchange of jobs.

In the labour market context, the key friction that potentially rationalizes the job search is the imperfect information regarding job opportunities and the fact that enterprises have not always succeeded in finding the necessary workers to cover the vacant positions. Thus, the job search characterizes workers and enterprises, inasmuch as both must support the costs that result from the imperfections of the market, and both are represented by the function of job matching. In the Mortensen-Pissarides model (1994), the labour market is populated by a fixed unit-measure continuum of workers. Each worker exogenously supplies a flow of one unit of efficient labour. A worker is either unemployed and looking for a job or employed and producing. There is no on-the-job research. Regarding the firms' side, it is assumed that a job is either vacant and looking for a worker or filled and producing. There is a continuum of jobs in the market, the measure of which is endogenously determined in equilibrium. A filled and operating job produces an output flow of px, where p is an index of aggregate productivity and x is a job-specific productivity shock. The labour market is then affected by search frictions. At any date t, the number of encounters between unemployed job seekers and vacant job slots is given as a function of the number of unemployed workers u_t and vacant jobs v_t by the matching function, $m(u_t,v_t)$. Here, $\Phi_t = v_t/u_t$ is referred to as labour market rigidity. On average, a vacant job opening meets $q(\Phi_t) = m(v_t,u_t)/v_t = (1/\Phi_t,1)$ unemployed workers per unit time. Similarly, an unemployed worker finds $m(v_t,u_t)/u_t = \Phi_t q(\Phi_t)$ job vacancies per unit of time. Because of search friction, the act of bringing a worker and a firm together in a match is associated with a surplus, which is somehow a share between the employer and the worker that depends positively on match productivity, px. The vacant and occupied job functions for the firm implies that the expected profit for a vacant job V and from an occupied job J are given as,

$$rV = -cp + q(\Phi)\,[J(1) - V] \tag{10.30a}$$

$$\text{and } rJ = p\text{-}w\text{-}\lambda J \tag{10.30b}$$

where cp is the cost flow of a vacant job, V and J are respectively the asset value of a vacancy and of a filled job, $q(\Phi) = (1/\Phi_t,1)$ is the rate at which the vacancy job is filled and λ is the Poisson rate at which the flow into unemployment occurs. The present value of income of an unemployed worker is defined by

$$rU = b + vq(\Phi)\,[J(1) - V] \tag{10.31}$$

where b is the exogenous value of leisure or employment income and v the vacancy rate. Filled jobs are destroyed when a productivity shock arrives and makes the asset value of a filled job negative, $J(x)$. So we have

$$rJ(x) = px - w + \delta(\int \max\,[J(z), V - T]\; dF(z) \tag{10.32}$$

The function of filled jobs for the firm is given as

$$rJ(x) = px - w + \delta(\int \max\,[J(z), V - T]\; dF(z) - J(x)) \tag{10.33}$$

where $F(z)$ is the distribution function of a fresh draw of x, δ is a shock occurring with a constant intensity following a Poisson process,[11] and $J(x)$ is the value of a filled job, which is a strictly increasing function of match productivity x. Therefore, there exists a unique cutoff value R of productivity, defined by

$$J(R) = V - T \tag{10.34}$$

which defines the job destruction. The job destruction rate is thus equal to $\delta F(R)$. From the combination of (10.30a), (10.33), and (10.34), we get

$$rJ(x) = px - w + \delta\int_R^1 [J(z) - J(x)]\,dF(z) + \delta F(R)[V - T - J(x)] \tag{10.35}$$

Considering that $J'(x) = p/(r + \delta)$, and then using integration by parts in the equation (10.35), we have the condition that implies

$$rJ(x) = px - w + \delta F(R)\left[V - T - J(x)\right] +$$
$$\frac{\delta p}{(r+\delta)}\int_R^1 [1 - F(z)]dz - \delta[1 - F(1)][J(1) - J(x)] + \delta[1 - F(r)][J(R) - J(x)] \qquad (10.36)$$

where $\delta[1 - F(1)] = 0$ and $J(R) = V - T$. Combining (10.35) and (10.36), we finally arrive at

$$(r+\delta)J(x) = px - w + \delta(V - T) + \frac{\delta p}{r+\delta}\int_R^1 [1 - F(z)]dz \qquad (10.37)$$

Equation (10.37) gives the productivity in terms of the ratio of vacancies to unemployment and the parameters of the model. Free entry in the search market implies that firms exhaust all profit opportunities from posting job vacancies. In other words, they post vacancies up to the point at which the marginal vacant job opening is worth zero. Because vacant jobs can be advertised or withdrawn at no cost and without delay, it must be the case that

$$V = 0 \qquad (10.38)$$

holds at all times. Combining the four equations (10.30a), (10.34), (10.37), and (10.38) implies

$$\frac{c}{q(\varphi)} = \frac{p(1-R)}{r+\delta} - T \qquad \text{(CC)} \qquad (10.39)$$

and $$R + \frac{\delta}{r+\delta}\int_R^1 [1 - F(z)]dz = \frac{w - rT}{p} \qquad \text{(DD)} \qquad (10.40)$$

where equation (10.39) is the job creation condition (CC) and (10.40) is the job destruction condition (DD). The joint determination of the job creation and job destruction conditions is illustrated in Figure 10.1.

The job destruction curve may slope up or be parallel to the abscissa Oθ because at higher R, the opportunity cost of employment is higher, and thus there is more job destruction. The job creation curve slopes down because at a higher θ, job destruction is more likely; as a result, there is less job creation. An increase in R shifts the job destruction curve up and the job creation curve down with an ambiguous effect on θ.R

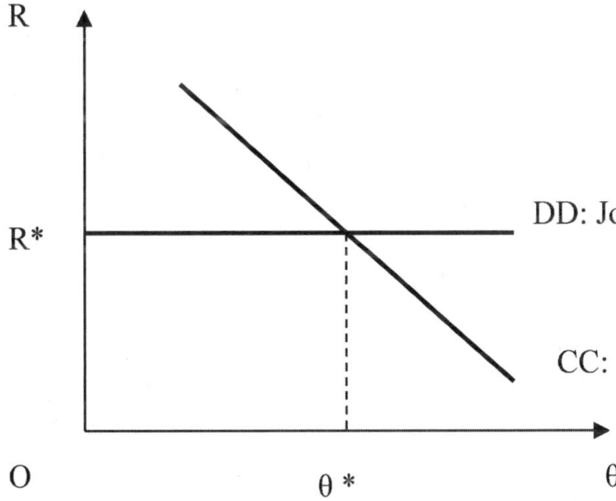

Figure 10.1 The joint determination of job destruction and job creation

and θ are "jump variables" that always assume their steady-state values, R^* and θ^*. Hence, it implies that

$$\dot{u}_t = -m(u_t, v_t) + \delta F(R^*)(1 - u_t) = -\theta^* q(\theta^*)u_t + \delta F(R^*)(1 - u_t) \quad (10.41)$$

The final equation of this model is the steady-state condition for unemployment, or the well-known Beveridge curve. The flow out of unemployment as a result of job creation equals the flow into unemployment as the result of job destruction at the points on the curve. The endogenous job separation rate is $\delta F(R^*)$, and the job matching rate per unemployed worker is $\theta^* q(\theta^*)$, so the first-order linear with a steady-state solution that gives the equation for the Beveridge curve is

$$u^* = \frac{\delta F(R*)}{\delta F(R^*) + \theta^* q(\theta^*)} \quad (10.42)$$

A graphic rendering of the steady-state equilibrium u and v is given by the Beveridge curve of the type $m(u,v) = \delta F(R^*)(1 - u)$, where $v = \theta^* u$ is the definition of θ. The job creation flow is given as $\theta^* u$, and the job destruction flow is written as $\delta F(R^*)(1 - u)$. The Beveridge curve and the job creation are depicted in Figure 10.2.

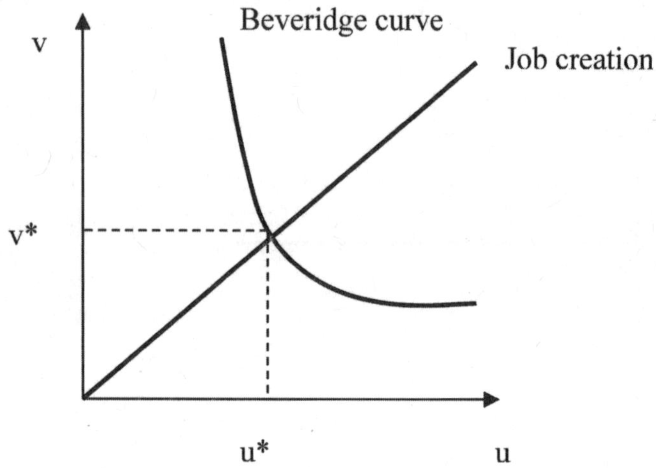

Figure 10.2 Beveridge curve and the job creation condition

The Beveridge curve is convex to the origin in vacancy unemployment space. Higher vacancies imply more job matchings. Thus, unemployment needs to be lower for a stationary matching rate; at the same time, higher vacancies also means more job destruction, so unemployment in this case needs to be higher in order to maintain the stationary job destruction rate. As a result, there is an uncertainty about the curve's precise shape. It is also assumed that the matching effect on the Beveridge curve dominates the job destruction effect, and as a consequence of this, the curve slopes down. The line from the origin to the Beveridge curve represents the equilibrium solution for *R* obtained from (10.38) and (10.39) and is referred to as the job creation condition. Knowing the reservation productivity, equilibrium vacancies and unemployment are presented at the intersection of the job creation condition with the Beveridge curve. In the case of a net positive productivity shock, job creation increases and job destruction decreases.

Moreover, the Mortensen-Pissarides model is extended further to the case when one of the aggregate variables changes probabilistically. Therefore, it is considered the case where the aggregate productivity "fluctuates" between a low and a high value (p_l, p_h), according to a Poisson process with rate μ. It is assumed that shifts from one regime to another are unanticipated and expected to be permanent.

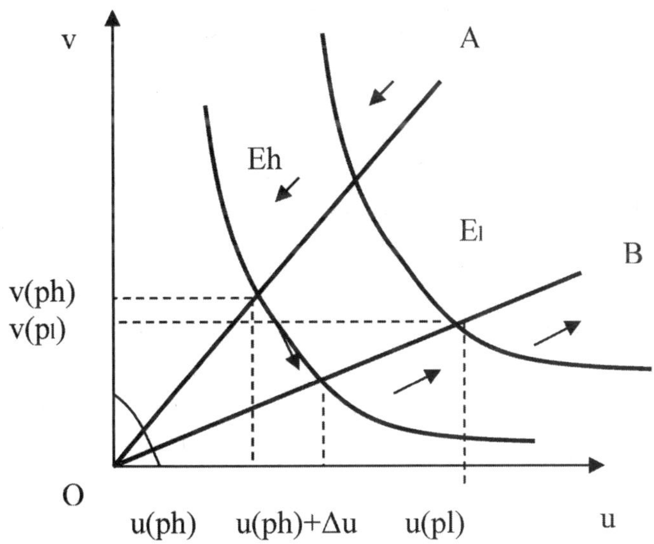

Figure 10.3 Aggregate productivity fluctuations

Figure 10.3 gives the aggregate productivity fluctuation between a low and a high value where the impression of counter-clockwise loops around the Beveridge curve. If cyclical shocks are anticipated, the existing gap between the reservation productivity at a high and low regular price is less than what would normally be in the steady-state analysis. Therefore, job destruction alters less as the price adjusts, than a simple comparison between two steady states would require. Furthermore, the gap continues to grow as the probability of a changing steady state, measured by the Poisson rate μ, continues to drop. The condition of job destruction eventually increases in intensity as the price changes are expected to augment the cycle of the job destruction rate, in the short run after the change in price. When labour productivity changes randomly, it becomes apparent that the anticipation of cyclical change reduces the cyclicality of job destruction, whereas the short-run response of job destruction to shocks increases the cyclicality of job destruction. Thus, the rate of job creation [$JC = \theta q(\theta)$] is procyclical, and the rate of job destruction [$JD = \delta F(R)$] is countercyclical; these two rates are negatively correlated over the cycle. So, job creation and job destruction behave in such a way as to move in opposite directions when the economy is hit by a cyclical shock. Therefore, the cyclical behaviour of unemployment is asymmetric:

- following a positive shock ($p_l \rightarrow p_h$): $\Delta u = 0$ and $u^{\cdot} = -\theta_h q(\theta_h)u_l + \delta F(R_h)(1 - u_l) < 0$
- following a negative shock ($p_l \rightarrow p_h$): $\Delta u = (1 - u_h)[F(R_l) - F(R_h)] > 0$ and $u^{\cdot} > 0$

Hence, in the short-run dynamics, there is an asymmetry in job destruction that is consistent with the conclusion that job destruction is more cyclical. Job destruction increases more rapidly and by more at the beginning of a recession than it decreases at the beginning of a boom, and the job creation process has even more unstable dynamics than the job destruction process.

Simulation of the Mortensen-Pissarides model has proven that when the United States is hit by a cyclical aggregate shock it demonstrates a reasonably good cyclical behaviour of job creation and job destruction. The conclusions of Mortensen and Pissarides are similar with those of Davis and Haltiwanger (1990), where the degree of dispersion presented in peculiar shocks comes as a result of change in aggregate events. In fact, when the dispersion of productivities is lower, the job destruction is lower, as productivity is higher and job creation is growing. But, if the dispersion of productivities is higher and lasts longer, the job destruction is higher and continues for a longer period, which may take months or even years, and the job creation slows down to a minimum and stays there as long as the job destruction has not converted to a lower rate. This effect must be one among many other reasons why the deep crisis and high rate of job destruction hitting the United States in the period 2008–12 was taking so long to turn to a higher rate of job creation.

In the case of constant aggregate productivity, job creation and job destruction move in opposite directions during the cycle; thus, there is no dominant force in the unemployment cycle.

GENERAL PURPOSE TECHNOLOGIES AND THE RATE OF GROWTH

Most economists have viewed technological progress as being incremental, but a few have focused on the role that drastic innovations play by introducing discontinuity into the process of growth. The type of drastic innovation studied by some economists has recently been called general-purpose technologies (GPTs). A GPT has the potential to affect the entire economic system and can lead to far-reaching changes in social factors, such as working hours and constraints on private life. GPTs, a term coined first by Bresnahan and Trajtenberg (1995), are technologies that have the potential to make important impacts on many sectors of an economy. Three main characteristics are recognized in GPTs: pervasiveness, technological dynamism, and innovational complementarities with other forms of advancement. Pervasiveness, occurrence, or frequency is seen when a GPT is used in a number of different sectors, where it makes available a basic generic function, such as rotary motion that can be used in several technologies. Technological dynamism supports constant innovation, which allows for large increases in productivity. And last, innovational complementaries occur when the productivity of R&D increases as a result of innovation in the GPT (Helpman 1998, 16). Examples of GPTs are the steam engine, electricity, and the computer. By definition, a GPT is a technology that has four necessary conditions: scope for improvement, a wide variety of uses, Hicksian complementary (output change as a response of change in input price),[12] and technological complementaries (Helpman 1998, 16–43).

In "A Time to Sow and a Time to Reap," Helpman and Trajtenberg (1998, 55–83) insert GPTs in an endogenous growth model with one sector. A GPT arrives exogenously at fixed time intervals, each requiring its own intermediate inputs. This simple model generates long cycles, alternating between productivity slowdown and acceleration. Each cycle normally contains two separate phases. During the first phase, both productivity and output have negative growth, and the economy stagnates. In the second phase, an advanced GPT is applied, which results in growth with rising productivity, real wages, and profits. The production function of a final good that has been produced with a GPT is given as (Helpman and Trajtenberg 1998, Ch. 4),

$$Q_i = \lambda_i D_i \qquad \lambda > i \tag{10.43}$$

where i is the general purpose technology (GPT) and λ_i is the productivity level of $GPTi$: meanwhile D_i is written as

$$D_i = \left[\int_0^{ni} x_i(j)^\alpha \, dj \right]^{1/\alpha} \tag{10.44}$$

where $x_i(j)$ is an assembly of a continuum of components, n_i is the number of available components, and $1/(1 - \alpha) > 1$ is the elasticity between two components. All components are assumed to be manufactured, independently of the GPTs, with one unit of labour per unit of output, so the marginal cost equals the wage-rate w. Next, the constant elasticity demand function for component $x_i(j)$ is

$$x_i(j) = \frac{p_i(j)^{\frac{-1}{(1-\alpha)}} D_i}{\left[\int_0^{ni} p_i(j)^{\frac{\alpha}{(1-\alpha)}} dj\right]^{\frac{1}{\alpha}}} \tag{10.45}$$

where $p_i(j)$ is the price of component j, which equates marginal revenue to marginal cost (w):

$$p_i(j) = p = (1/\alpha)w \tag{10.46}$$

All components of the GPT are employed in equal quantities x_i, and the equilibrium is given as

$$D_i = n_i^{\frac{(1-\alpha)}{\alpha}} X_i \tag{10.47}$$

where $X_i = n_i x_i$, is the aggregate employment of components by users of the GPT. Final output is produced with those GPTs whose productivity level λ_i, in combination with other components, minimizes the costs. It is assumed that, at the beginning, there is one GPT with $m = 1$ (Helpman 1998, 59). Then, a second generation of GPT ($i + 1$) appears when appropriate complementary inputs have been developed. So, we have

$$0 < \mu = \frac{1}{\lambda^{\frac{\alpha}{(1-\alpha)}}} < 1 \tag{10.48}$$

where μ is a parameter. The profit stream for each component is

$$\pi_i = \frac{(1-\alpha)wb_iQ_i}{\alpha n_i} \tag{10.49}$$

where each user x_i employs b_iQ_i/n_i units of the n_i components with cost Q_i. The present value of the firm, which equals its profits based on the Helpman–Trajtenberg model, is given as

$$v_i(t) = \int_t^{\infty} e^{-R(T,\tau)} \pi_i(\tau) d\tau \tag{10.50}$$

where $R(t,\tau) = \int_t^\tau r(z)dz$

stands for the discount factor from time τ to *t*, and *r* is the discount factor. Furthermore, by differentiating equation (10.50 with respect to *t*, the arbitrage condition yields

$$\pi_i/v_i + v_i^{\cdot}/v_i = r \qquad (10.51)$$

with a free-entry condition into R&D, $v_i \le wa$. The resource constraint of an economy with *m* GPT units and *L* units of labour implies (Helpman and Trajtenberg 1998, 60)

$$a\sum_{i=1}^{m} n_i + \sum_{i=1}^{m} b_i Q_i = L \qquad (10.52)$$

where an_i and b_iQ_i are the units of labour and manufacturing components used in production and *L* is the economy labour demand. Normalizing the consumer spending to a constant value *E* = 1 with the differential equation for consumption, we have the result that nominal interest rate *r* equals the discount rate:

$$p_Q(t)\sum_{i=1}^{m} Q_i(t) = 1 \text{ and } r(t) = \rho \qquad (10.53)$$

Helpman and Trajtenberg (1998, Ch. 3) assumed that during the first phase, a new GPT arrives at predetermined time intervals of length (T_i, $T_{i+}\Delta_1$) in which the ($i-1$)th general purpose technology is employed in the final output. In this phase, the number of GPT components remains the same, and the no-arbitrage condition with free-entry condition implies

$$w^{\cdot}/w = \rho \text{ for } t \in (T_i, T_{i+}\Delta_1) \qquad (10.54)$$

where the differential in wage-rate is equal to the discount rate ρ. During the first phase, there is no profit because the innovators expect the profit to be realized in the future. Thus, the differential equations in this phase yield two solutions: the first solution is for the wage-rate and the second one for the number of products (Helpman and Trajtenberg 1998, 63):

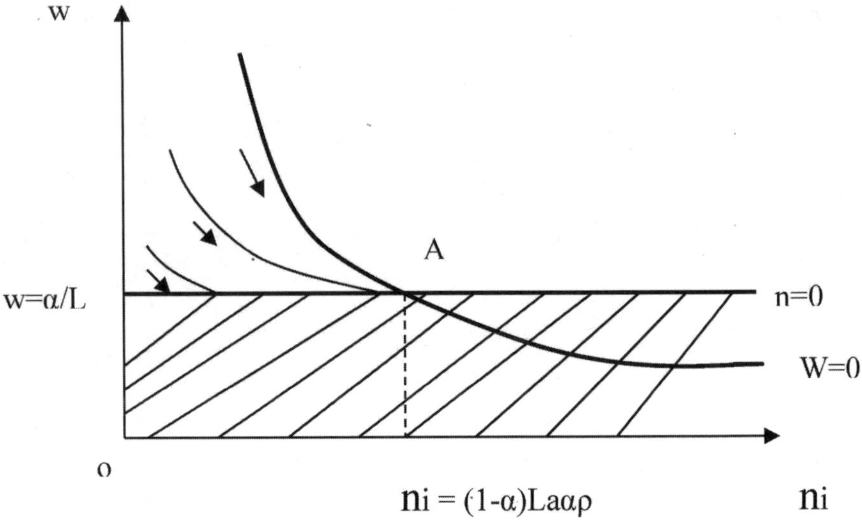

Figure 10.4 Wage dynamics in the second phase

$$w(t) = w(T_I)e^{\rho(t-T_i)} \text{ for } t \,\varepsilon\, (T_i, T_{i+}\Delta_1) \tag{10.55}$$

$$n_i(t) = \frac{L}{a}(t - T_i) - \frac{\alpha}{paw(T_i)}[1 - e^{-\rho(t-T_i)}] \text{ for } t \,\varepsilon\, (T_i, T_{i+}\Delta_1) \tag{10.56}$$

where both wage-rate and the number of products rise over time.

During the second phase, the GPT has the lowest unit labour requirement, and this technology is employed by all manufacturers, which results in profitability. The differential equation for the wage-rate and the number of products in the second phase implies

$$w = \rho w - \frac{1-\alpha}{\alpha n_i} \text{ for } t \,\varepsilon\, (T_{i+}\Delta_1, T_{i+}\Delta_e) \tag{10.57}$$

$$\text{and for } w \geq \alpha/L,\ t \,\varepsilon\, (T_{i+}\Delta_1, T_{i+}\Delta_e) \tag{10.58}$$

The motion of these two equations in the second phase is depicted as a hyperbola. In figure 10.4, the intermediate trajectory w = o is a saddle path that converges at the stationary point A. Three curves describe dynamic trajectories that converge at the saddle point. The equilibrium depends on the length of the cycle and how the new GPTs are expected to become available. However, if there is no new GPT available, then the saddle path (point A) is the unique equilibrium trajectory that satisfies both the present value equation (10.50) and the resource constraint equation (10.52).

As with all new technological change, there is also a relationship between GPTs and the rate of growth. The measurement of a GDP is done by using the input side (instead of the output side) as the total of wages and profits. Using the price of final output as $[p_q = (1/\alpha)\ wb]$ (where wb/α is the unit cost), the profit stream from equation (10.49), and the normalization equation (10.53), we have that the nominal GDP equals $wL + 1 - \alpha$. Dividing the nominal GDP by the price of final output p_q, we get the value of real GDP (Helpman and Trajtenberg 1998, 70):

$$G(t) = \left[L + \frac{1-\alpha}{w(t)} \right] \alpha \lambda^k n_k(t)^{\frac{(1-\alpha)}{\alpha}} \tag{10.59}$$

where λ and α are parameter values, n_k is the number of products (which is continuous in time), and k is the index of general purpose technologies used in the production of final output. From the second term (outside the square brackets in [10.59]), we can see that the real GDP is continuous as far as the wage-rate is also continuous. During the first phase of the cycle, the real GDP (or the real output) keeps declining as the wage rises, whereas the number of components available for production of the final goods remains constant. The real GDP growth begins only during the second phase, when the economy has developed components that are more than sufficient for the new GPT and when the production of new goods is performed by using new technologies. In this phase, the wage-rate declines. Consequently, although the economy suffers productivity losses during the first phase, it nonetheless recovers during the second phase of the cycle.

The main aspect of the Helpman-Trajtenberg model (1998, 55–83) is that it reallocates the resources between current production and R&D in order to develop new elements that are complementary with the new GPT technology. GPTs arrive exogenously at fixed time intervals, each requiring its own intermediate inputs. This simple model generates long cycles, alternating between productivity slowdown and acceleration. In the fourth chapter of their book, Helpman and Trajtenberg extended the model by considering a continuum of sectors with varying productivity gains from the GPT; however, each sector nonetheless requires its own intermediate input, which leads to multiple equilibrium trajectories (Helpman and Trajtenberg 1998, 85–144). This basic model is further developed by Aghion and Howitt (1998, 151–64). Here, the model has two sectors, plus a third one that contains a set of confined resources. These resources produce "outlines" that are needed before a new GPT can appear. Furthermore, there is a second stage involving new components to the innovation process that endogenizes the arrival times of successive GPTs.

Aghion and Howitt (1998) also developed a new concept of technology diffusion in the form of technology spillover between the users (firms), which require a specific GPT that can help achieve further progress. In the Aghion-Howitt model, technologies arrive at a rate determined by a Poisson arrival process, which is influenced by the flow of labour units. The productivity and the arrival rate of new technologies are endogenously determined; therefore, they are constant in their stationary equilibrium.

THE THEORY OF TRANSFORMATIONAL GROWTH IN NELL

The theory of transformational growth, in broader terms, describes the changes in institutions and working markets as innovation take place and help to explain and analyze the causes and effects of these changes. The work of Edward J. Nell[13] in the 1990s helped in the development of the theory of transformational growth; his book was published as *The General Theory of Transformational Growth* (1998). The year 1998 seemed to be a fruitful year for theory on economic growth; Helpman (and Trajtenberg 1998, 55–83) published *General Purpose Technologies and Economic Growth* and Aghion and Howitt published the renowned volume *Endogenous Growth Theory* based on the Schumpeterian idea of "creative destruction." Nell's *Theory of Transformational Growth* reconsiders the development of capitalist society in a succession of stages, in each of which markets adjust differently, and in doing so, give rise to market forces leading to continuous improvements and innovations, which move the system toward the next stage. The method which triggers the *Theory of Transformational Growth* is based primarily on doing fieldwork and later building models that have a firm relationship with institutions. The meaning of fieldwork is to understand people's actions as a result of their thinking and behaviour and how these actions, taken as a whole, bring changes in the society. Fieldwork has first to understand the society or industry being studied and then translate the figures observed in economic terms that can be read. Nell's study (1998) shows that there are two types of fieldwork. The first consists of drawing a scenario of institutions and practices that applies to all activities of a certain kind of particular society or social setting and is independent of the state of mind of particular agents. The second type regards the economy from a different perspective that can give a different picture of the behaviour of economic agents such as their preferences, values, expectations, and motivations. The analysis of the fieldwork can put together the prototype of behaviour, motivation, and ways of working, creating, and making activities for economic agents. It can offer the basic guidance and training to understand the structure of behaviour in a society, from which it can set the guidelines to construct theory and build models able to characterize the real world satisfactorily. The fieldwork analysis needs to develop stylized facts by interpreting the empirical studies and statistics from the fieldwork on different sectors of a society and put up the essential assumptions in which economic models should be built .

The General Theory of Transformational Growth starts with a critique of equilibrium. For growth to start the economy must become unbalanced or unstable. From the state of imbalance, the economy will produce forces that will set up a mechanism adjusting the original imbalance and at the same time creating a new imbalance. The departure of part of the labour force from agriculture in the eighteenth and nineteenth centuries set out the Industrial Revolution. Excess labour from agriculture that entered in the cities became the product of the revolution itself, which set the premises for large-scale innovation in developed urban areas. In return, new methods and machines created as a result of innovation were used in agriculture, raising productivity and thus forcing other people to abandon agriculture. The imbalance generates a response which, consecutively, produces forces to adjust the initial imbalance and recreate a new state of imbalance and so on until it becomes a trend. Therefore, in the Transformational Growth theory, a structural imbalance is regularly reproduced as the economy runs and grows (Nell 1998, 19).

Nell's analysis distinguishes two systems of growth based on historical facts. The first one is a "craft" economy based on small-scale production carried out by small groups of skilled workers assisted by animals, water, or primitive mechanical power with very low productivity. The second system is an "industrial" economy that is based on mass production carried out by specialized workers operating in factories, plants, and assembly lines. The "craft" condition describes the primary sector of production or the first stage toward a more developed economy, and the "industrial" condition portrays the manufacturing sector as a more advanced stage of development (Nell 1998, 30). The craft economy can easily function in a stationary system where there is no or very little growth. But also it can grow and eventually expand through a simple system of lending of household savings to shops, stores, and new firms. The price of commodities in the craft society is stable, as there is no pressure for improvement and growth unless the economy is hit by a food shortage or an epidemic disease. As in every economy, the craft economy has the capability to create successful artisan shops, businesses, and trades where skilled workers and tradesmen can deliver better products and have more reliable delivery times using the same tools and equipment without investing in new shops and factories. The labour force, given the low productivity of simple tools, basic equipment, and low levels of organization, is used in a massive way in all sectors from mining to agriculture, transport, and manufacturing. In almost every commodity there is a consistent amount of fixed labour and hands used to produce it.

In the "industrial" economy things look different. First of all, an industrial society cannot settle into a stationary condition for a long time. It must expand to avoid recession, and the commodity prices are the reflection of growth. The technology improvement and capital investment are the foundation of an industrial society. Competition depends on cost-cutting and improved product design built into the production process through investments in new equipment and technology. Renovating the existing plants or building new ones will help expand production of new tools and equipment to produce mass production commodities for the increasing population living in urban areas. Thanks to advanced equipment, machines, and sophisticated organization, the labour force used to produce commodities is much smaller and more specialized than in a craft economy (Nell 1998, 32).

The craft-based economy is often described as the primary sector of the industrial economy. The cost and prices differ in both economies. In a craft-based economy labour cost is a larger portion of the overall costs to produce commodities. Large amounts of labour are used in almost every process of production. As a result, large variations in demand cannot be matched by adjusting the operation costs. They can be adjusted only by adjusting productivity. A fall in demand will bring a fall in profits, as productivity will take time to adjust. Therefore, firms have to sell excessive inventories at any price offered by the market, forcing prices down. Market prices will reflect the price of excessive inventory and not the real price based on the cost of production.

In the industrial economy, in contrast, the variable costs including labour are a large portion of the cost to produce commodities, so the operating costs and output can be adjusted to variations in demand, keeping the production at low levels if required. Once demand goes up the production will rise, keeping the price at a more stable level than in a craft-based economy. In the industrial and mass production era, any variation on demand will lead to changes in output and employment but the general prices will not be affected, because they are independent of the level of activity. The operations and production activities are planned together with investment based on expectations of market growth, in contrast with the unstable prices of the craft economy (Nell 1998, 36).

Growth, according to Nell (1998), is a market-driven process, and the price mechanism has an important role in attracting investments and igniting growth. In a mass-production economy, unit costs are in large part constant, but what changes is the employment and output within a normal wide range. Hence, prices can be maintained at their long-term levels, but will be allowed to oscillate temporarily around the equilibrium price levels. Based on the price level at the market, the production process can be adjusted at varying levels of intensity in response to market demand, and the employment force can be attuned to requirements by laying off and recalling workers to accommodate production levels. The mass-production economy in Nell (2010, 15–17) is represented by a straight line of output rising from the origin, $Y = aN$, with a slope equal to the average productivity of labour and showing constant marginal returns as depicted in figure 10.5. The wage bill is assumed equal to consumption and is characterized by a straight slopped curve, $W = C$, rising from the origin. Meanwhile, the aggregate demand, given by line $C + I$, rises to the right of the investment point in the vertical axis.

For simplicity, government spending is excluded and is taken into account only in the expenditure characterized by the line $C + I$. It is assumed that investment is taken as exogenous and determines the

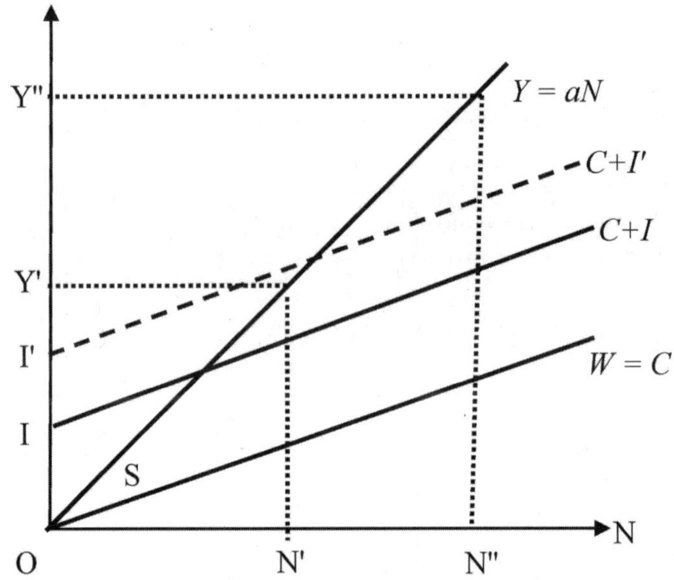

Figure 10.5 Adjustment in the mass production economy

realized profit. In fact, if households save a certain portion of wages the consumption line, C, will sway below (or stay at the same level as) the wage line and profits will be reduced. But if part of householders get wealthier and consume more in spending than others based on the level of activity, the $C + I$ line will shift upwards, increasing the margin of profit. A rise in investments will increase consumption and employment in defined proportion. In effect, the $C + I$ line will move to the new $C + I'$ line, adjusting consumption in the same direction as the investment line. As suggested by Nell (1998) many empirical studies in the postwar period found that real wages, employment, and output are positively correlated. Therefore, by simply drawing a steeper wage line, the $C + I$ line will also be steeper, and it will intersect the output line at a higher level of output and employment. Money has its own effect on the real economy. With high interest rates, businesses will cut or at least postpone their investments; meanwhile households will increase their rate of savings, as it is more profitable for them to save money in the bank and cut back on buying durable goods. Low interest rates and stable pricing will increase investment and household spending on consumable and durable goods, boosting the level of employment.

In the short run, demand adjustment for goods and services depends on investment spending and household consumption. The level of investment in the short run will create enough cash flow and income needed to keep the existing production capacity, and in the long run will create a new capacity, expanding the labour force. Therefore, in the long run it will be necessary to take into consideration the effects of the capacity creation brought about by the investment spending. The price mechanism will be the adjusting force of the relationship between saving and investment, consumption and labour force. This system works pretty well for a fixed price economy based on Harrod-Domar model. But in a mass-production economy, investment spending should be considered together with planning for growth. Investment plans along with the choice of technology, product design, and long-term prices tend to be determined together. Firms and corporations will build new capacities in response to the expectation of growth in demand stimulated by new products, competitive prices, and lower costs. The growth of the market based on the accelerator will be combined with the pricing system. Therefore, growth and price are determined together. The formalization of this process is given by three equations (Nell 2010, 19).

$$g = (w/p, y),\ g'(w/p) < 0\ ;\ g'(y) > 0 \quad (10.60)$$
$$w/p = w(g,y),\ w'(g)>0\ ;\ w'(y)>0 \quad (10.61)$$
$$y = y(g,w/p),\ y'(g)>0\ ;\ y''(g)<0 \quad (10.62)$$

where *g* is the rate of growth, *w* is money wages, *y* is output, and *p* is the price level. The first equation is the wage-accumulation curve, assumed to be linear and negatively sloped, and determines growth and productivity. Based on this equation, higher prices mean a lower rate of growth of demand, and vice-versa with lower prices. The second equation is the wage-rate-growth of demand relationship and has the S (sigmoid) shape. Here, higher prices will create the ground for further funds that will be invested for a higher rate of growth. The S-shape curve of the second equation shows that a rise in the level of the real wage will increase the rate of growth of demand, as higher incomes will create additional consumption, and generate supplementary investment. Lower levels of the real wage will bring no increase in the rate of growth of demand at least in the short run (Nell 1998, Chs. 10 and 11). The third equation gives the relationship between productivity growth, output growth, and the real wage. These equations, differently from the

Solow and Harrod-Domar models, which approach only the growth-consumption side, connect the wage-price-profit side of the system with the growth-consumption side (Nell 2010, 19). Theoretically, under certain assumptions and conditions, these equations have a unique positive solution, which constitutes the stable growth equilibrium. Practically, the system is not stable but in a continuous transformation as households change their patterns of spending. The system puts excessive pressure on profits, which leaves the firms no choices other than to reduce costs using a structural and organizational transformation. In addition, businesses try to meet the consumer changes and become more innovative. The innovation and improvement will lead to a new production function with a different structural cost, giving rise to changes and adjustments in the system. This is not a steady growth economy but a continuously changing and adjusting economy – as Nell calls it a 'transformational economy' (1998, Ch. 11). Any plans for growth through new investment in equipment and facilities or through the reorganization and reconstruction of present facilities has to come in combination with plans for prices, as the expected growth will depend on and benefit from the anticipated prices. The equilibrium in a transformational economy is very difficult to define and measure, because improvement, innovation, and productivity increase all the time. The only possible thing to look to is to determine the direction, speed, and expansion of economic change.

The transformational growth theory of Nell offers an alternative approach on economic growth. In a different way from many theories, where most of the economic analysis is prescriptive rather descriptive, Nell's theory is based primarily on rational choice. And the particular feature on this theory is that the methodology is based on doing fieldwork and then building relationships between economic institutions and technologies evolving in a single productive dynamic system in combination with an adequate price level. This particular methodology has implications for deeper econometric studies to test all the economic relations involved in the process of growth. Some of these relationships are reliable and can be consistently established; others are unreliable; and more volatile relationships may be ascertained. This brings the conclusion that transformational growth theory should be divided in two main components – the reliable and tested economic relationships and the unstable ones.

LIMITS OF GROWTH: THE STOKEY MODEL

Recent contributions have analyzed pollution and environmental concerns within the setting of endogenous growth models. Many new growth models deal with pollution rather than with non-renewable natural resources. For the most part, such models simply extend standard neoclassical growth models by including the environment and pollution generation. Generally speaking, pollution leads to a decline in optimal growth as a result of the environmental cost to production. There is a trade-off between consumption and pollution that is vital for the performance of the economy as a whole. If the environmental costs rise to a certain point during the process of growth, then decreasing activities induce a decline in the long-run rate of return, which, finally, can limit growth.

Gradus and Smulder (1993) and Nancy Stokey[14] (1998) in their studies considered ecological preferences and an assortment of technologies with constant returns on accumulated inputs to allow for a steady growth. The work of Gradus and Smulder (1993) showed a negative relation between optimal growth and the level of pollution in the case of constant returns to capital with endogenous abatement activities, which determine the level of pollution. Alternatively, Stokey (1998) analyzed a model of pollution with linear production technology and an endogenous environmental emission standard that produces an inverted U-shaped relationship between per capita income and ecological quality. According to Stokey as the economy grows and becomes wealthier, a path with steady growth depends on how the trade-off between consumption and the level of pollution evolves. In fact, if the environmental costs of continued growth become sufficiently high, society will not be willing to pay and, as a result, growth will cease. However, growth may continue without bound if enhanced productive capacity allows for consumption and also if growth improves the quality of environment and maintains pollution within certain limits.

The objective of the Stokey model is to prove how the standard emission and pollution level develops over time as well as how the presence of pollution influences the long-run growth rate.

The main assumption of this model is that the final output is produced by a variety of technologies that differ in their levels of cleanliness, and the pollution and technology are embedded in a one-sector endogenous growth model with a linear technology (*AK*). So, let $z \in [0,1]$ be the measure of "dirtiness" of an index of technology used to produce output *Y*. The actual output is determined as $c = yz$, measured on a per capita basis. The aggregate production function is $Y = AKz$, which means that by using a cleaner technique, less output per unit of input is produced. The social planner thus chooses the path for consumption and for technology in use so as to maximize the utility function of households. Therefore, in order to do this, the planner's problem is to select between maximizing output, given as $c(t)$, and and eventually minimizing the pollution, given as $z(t)$:

$$\max \int_0^{\infty} e^{\rho t} \left[\frac{c^{1-\sigma} - 1}{1-\sigma} - \frac{B}{\gamma}(Akz^{\beta})^{\gamma} \right] dt \tag{10.63}$$

where $k^{\cdot} = Akz - c$. According to Stokey (1998, 10), total pollution declines and output, given by the aggregate production function, *Akz*, grows if

$$0 < 1k^{\cdot}/\beta k < -z^{\cdot}/z < k^{\cdot}/k \tag{10.64}$$

Although sustained growth is possible, it is not optimal. The system normally converges to a steady state. Assuming that $A/\beta < A - \rho$, where parameter ρ is low (households are patient), the pollution technology β is convex, and the technology *A* is high, we have the result that during the switch to the steady state, both consumption and the emission standard satisfy

$$\omega \geq k^{(\omega-1)} / m \tag{10.65}$$

$$z = 1 \text{ if } \omega \geq k^{(\omega-1)} / m$$

$$z = \left(\omega m k^{(1-\omega)}\right)^{\psi} \text{ if } \omega \geq k^{(\omega-1)} / m \tag{10.66}$$

where *m* and ω are functions of the technology and preference parameters, and ψ is the shadow value of capital. When the capital stock reaches the critical level defined by $wm = k^{w-1}$, the pollution controls are instituted. According to this model, the dirtiest technology is used before capital stock reaches the critical level, and after it passes this level, a cleaner technology is used. Thus, the total pollution during the transition in our Ak model is given as

$$x = Akz^{\beta} = Ak \text{ if } z = 1 \tag{10.67}$$

$$x = Akz^{\beta} = A((m\omega)^{\beta} k^{\beta-1})^{\psi} \text{ if } z< 1 \tag{10.68}$$

The pollution grows while $z = 1$ and $z< 1$ decline. The condition for the pollution to decline is given as

$$\beta\frac{\dot{\omega}}{\omega}+(\beta-1)\frac{\dot{k}}{k}<0 \tag{10.69}$$

The system is in the steady state only if $\rho > (\beta - 1)/\beta$, where $\rho > 1$ ensures that total pollution grows in the early stages of development and declines as the economy approaches the steady state, indicated by taking an inverted U-shape pattern over time. To analyze the rate of growth with pollution, it is important to study the rate of return on capital. The production function includes the capital stock and the pollution level, x:

$$Y=(AK)^{1-1/\beta}x^{1/\beta} \tag{10.70}$$

The marginal product of capital is written as

$$r=\left(\frac{\beta-1}{\beta}\right)A^{1-1/\beta}k^{-1/\beta}x^{1/\beta} \tag{10.71}$$

From equation (10.71), we see that the real return on capital declines for any fixed level of pollution. However, if the pollution grows in proportion to capital, then the real rate of return is maintained. Consumption and pollution grow at the same rate, so the real interest rate is given as

$$r=\left(\frac{\beta-1}{\beta}\right)Az \tag{10.72}$$

The rate of return on capital is reduced when the optimal emission standard becomes stricter. The relation between the rate of return and the emission standard in the steady state is written as

$$r_{ss}=\left(\frac{\beta-1}{\beta}\right)Az_{ss}=\rho \tag{10.73}$$

The stricter emission standards that accompany the growth cause a reduction of the rate of return on capital, thus pushing it below the level required to persuade further capital accumulation; as a result, the growth will, in time, cease. In the case of exogenous technical change, sustained growth in capital and the continued reduction of the pollution are well matched with a constant rate of return.

When exogenous technical change is embedded in the Stokey model that uses pollution technology and preferences, we have that the growth rate of capital, g_k, in a balanced growth path is written as

$$g_k = \frac{\gamma(\beta-1)g}{(1-\alpha)\gamma(\beta-1)+(\sigma+\gamma-1)} \tag{10.74}$$

In the presence of technical change and in the absence of environmental concerns, output, consumption, and the capital stock would grow at the rate $g/(1-\alpha)$, but in the presence of pollution, the rate of growth gets slower. The total pollution, including the rate of growth (with technical progress), implies (Stokey 1998, 14)

$$\begin{aligned} x &= Ae^{gt}k^{\alpha}z^{\beta} = Ae^{gt}k^{\alpha} \text{ if } z = 1 \\ x &= Ae^{gt}k^{\alpha}z^{\beta} = \left(Ae^{gt}k^{\alpha}\right)^{1-\beta} y^{\beta} \text{ if z} < 1 \end{aligned} \tag{10.75}$$

Along with the balanced growth path, the pollution rate of growth yields

$$g_x = \beta g_k - (\beta-1)(g+\alpha g_k) = \frac{1-\sigma}{\gamma} g_k \tag{10.76}$$

The output in terms of capital stock, technical change, and pollution level is written as

$$Y = (Ae^{gt}k^{\alpha})^{1-1/\beta} x^{1/\beta} \tag{10.77}$$

which is compatible with a constant interest rate. The marginal rate of capital is now

$$r = \frac{\alpha(\beta-1)}{\beta}\frac{y}{k} \tag{10.78}$$

Given that, in the steady state, the ratio y/k is constant, the interest rate also is constant. The interest rate declines during the transition period but is constant along the balanced growth path (Stokey 1998, 15–18).

The economy converges to a balanced growth in the long run at a slower velocity than it would enjoy in the absence of environmental effects. Thus, during transition, pollution is a simetric function of income, as empirically found by Grossman and Krueger (1995). Consequently, in the Stokey model, the pollution and the emission standards affect growth in the long run and the rate of return on capital.

Governmental policies implemented so as to regulate pollution consist mostly of three instruments: direct regulation of emission standards, a voucher system, and a pollution tax. Under direct regulation, the rate of return on capital is higher than in the case of voucher or tax schemes; pollution vouchers are attached to capital and the rental price of capital is the sum of the values of capital itself and the pollution rights that come with it. Hence, the ownership of capital brings the right to emit a specified level of pollution; so the government, under direct regulation, must know the cost function for each company involved in pollution. Conversely, under a tax or voucher system, the government needs to know only the aggregate cost function from which the appropriate price is chosen and the government then allows the market to allocate efficient emissions across firms. Here, emissions have a market price that is entirely separate from the return to capital.[15] The market return to capital determines the incremental value of investment and provides the correct incentive to save.

SOME CONCLUSIONS ABOUT ENDOGENOUS GROWTH AND CREATIVE DESTRUCTION

Endogenous growth theory attempts to understand the relation between knowledge and the structural characteristics of an economy as well as how such interaction results in growth. The intention of the Aghion-Howitt *Endogenous Growth Theory* textbook (1998) has been to establish some continuity with older traditions and also to provide an incorporated approach to the analysis of growth. Their approach is based on Schumpeter's notion of creative destruction, in which the destruction is "creative" because it provokes continued procreation in the entrepreneurial world, resulting in the replacement of old enterprises with new ones. By focusing on innovation, creative destruction allows us to understand how organizations are affected by long-run growth by analyzing their effects on economic agents' incentives for innovative activities. Aghion and Howitt provided the instruments to handle endogenous technical change within a dynamic general equilibrium setting. The combination of these tools with institutions, organizations, market structures, and government policies creates the premises to understand the rate of endogenous growth. The notion of sustainable development leads to the proposition that constant positive growth rates of output are sustainable if the quality of the environment does not fall below a critical ecological threshold (Aghion and Howitt 1998, Ch. 5). Generally speaking, the AK-type and Schumpeterian models are used to determine conditions under which economic growth is sustainable.

Aghion and Howitt, among others, demonstrated that where the pollution to output ratio is invariable (the AK model), long-run positive growth cannot be reconciled with a non-decreasing quality of the environment. Alternatively, in the Schumpeterian situation, technological progress allows the pollution to output ratio to fall sufficiently, so the long-run positive growth can be achieved. Therefore, output growth is sustainable only if new technologies improve, thereby diminishing the pollution-output ratio. Aghion and Howitt[16] also discussed frictional unemployment and the rate of growth, basing their analysis on the Mortenson-Pissarides matching model. The Mortenson-Pissarides (1994) model is extended to an endogenous separation rate, which is attained by assuming overhead costs, decreasing returns to scale, and a fixed factor productivity in perfect competitive firms that normally employ few workers and human capital to produce output, jointly with an exogenously growing total factor productivity.[17] When total factor productivity has grown sufficiently, then a firm has to shut down, the workers eventually to be dismissed, and a search for new jobs has to be started. In this situation, faster growth has two effects. First, the job creation effect, mostly known from Pissarides (1990), increases the equilibrium level of vacancies and thus reduces the rate of unemployment. Second, the duration of workers employed in a firm plunges (due to the direct creative destruction effect), the value of a new technology drops faster, and, therefore, profits fall faster during the firm's life span (because of indirect creative destruction effect).

Overall, as the growth rate rises, at first unemployment rises but, after some threshold level, falls again. So when growth is endogenous, the unemployment rate does not change as the growth rate increases when higher growth is caused by a higher frequency of innovations, but it does rise if the growth rate is caused by a change in the size of innovations.

In this chapter, we also analyzed a relatively new economic concept called general purpose technologies (GPTs), which have the potential to affect the entire economic system. GPTs are new ideas and new techniques that have an impact on many sectors. The scope of a GPT is the improvement on technologies utilized for a wide variety of uses, such as steam, electricity, the internal combustion engine, motor vehicles, and so forth. Some authors in Helpman (1998)[18] have argued that technological learning occurs under conditions of uncertainty and unpredictability about the future. According to them, the impact of GPTs does not derive exclusively from intrinsic technological characteristics but rather from interactions with the "facilitating structure" of the economy, such as physical and organizational capital, infrastructure, public policy, trade, location, and existing technologies. In other words, the study of GPTs should take careful account of the historical and social context surrounding any GPT.

The General Theory of Transformational Growth is another new perception of growth developed brilliantly by Edward Nell in the 1990s that starts with a critique of general equilibrium supporting creative destruction and economic instability giving rise to continued transformation of economy as consumers change their patterns of spending. This theory has a form of pragmatism based on doing fieldwork and its mechanism has to do with the methodological and philosophical questions about the role of contracts and obligations when considering the function of institutional organizations, and with the circulation of money and monetary policies in order to understand productivity and structure of production. Particularly interesting in this theory is the connection between the wage bill of capital goods and the capital needs in consumer goods, then going on to dynamics of passing from a craft economy to a mass production economy which requires new development policies and strategies. And what is more innovative in this theory is that differently from standard macroeconomic models there is no single "investment function," but an investment entity composed of two parts, investment planning and investment spending. Investment planning consists of planned investments for innovation, new products, and the industrial expansion, and it requires careful planning for prices and costs. Investment spending instead includes all other investments that depend on earnings and finance.

In this chapter, we also investigated the limits of growth. The publication of the Club of Rome's report, *Limits to Growth* in 1972,[19] sparked an intense and polarized debate that remains alive to this day. In fact, the task of understanding the existence of any limits to economic growth has become a primary goal for many economists. It is a well-known fact that the innovation process is a necessary but not sufficient ingredient in making unlimited growth sustainable according to the optimal theory of growth. Environmental policy plays an important role in sustainable growth and environmental improvement. By simply imposing environmental regulations on an economy, a Pareto-optimal situation is reached and social welfare is maximized (Ariga 2002). In many countries, a well-constructed environmental policy has been shown to be favorable to economic growth rather than limiting it. In the long run, tax instruments are able to move the market equilibrium steady growth path to a socially optimal one. Moreover, it is increasingly likely that, theoretical arguments describing the potential of technology and human creativity, real-world complications, uncertainty, and basic human aspirations will also have a major role in shaping the future pattern of environmental degradation and human welfare.

GROWTH FROM MANUFACTURING: A LESSON FROM CHIEF EXECUTIVES

After widely considering theoretical growth tools in this book it is interesting to know what the manufacturing sector in different countries "has to say" about growth. The World Economic Forum published in May 2013 a report named "Manufacturing for Growth," in collaboration with Deloitte Touche Tohmatsu Limited. This was the result of a one-year project that involved interviewing more than 70 chief executive officers (CEOs) of multinational manufacturing companies and industry leaders around the world between August 2012 and January 2013. The recommendations made by the CEOs varied, based on the industry sector and regional circumstances, but there were at least five particular public policy areas where common ideas converged: (1) Executives suggested that tax policy should be competitive and based on a simplified tax system. Countries could be more competitive if they lowered the overall effective corporate tax rate, in this way freeing resources companies could use for growth. (2) Executives called for governments and policy makers of different countries to increase the number of free trade agreements and reduce non-tariff trade barriers and simplify procedures for border crossings. (3) Executives indicated that countries promoting clean and sustainable sources of energy at a competitive cost would have a noteworthy advantage over other nations. The development of efficient infrastructures and national energy policies through alternative sources of clean energy would be an estimable asset for current and future generations. (4) Executives expressed that the ability of their organization to attract a well educated workforce, creative and talented workers would make them feel more than satisfied. An educated workforce develops superior talent and creativity, which brings innovation and growth. Industry leaders would like to see an increasing number of graduates in STEM fields (science, technology, engineering, and mathematics). (5) Executives believe that research and development, science and technology would promote advanced manufacturing, growth, and competitiveness. The countries and policy makers that sustain R&D in technology and innovation in different industries of the manufacturing sector will have a net advantage over other nations.

Business leaders expressed the necessity for the public and private sectors to collaborate with each other and in partnership with national research centres, universities and research foundations. The best practices of the public-private partnerships are demand-driven and have objectives focused on specific market requirements.

Manufacturing gives particular emphasis to global value chains. The ability of a country to be competitive today depends on its participation in international trade and in the global supply chains. In the past decades the global supply chains have grown quickly, covering different categories of production such as components, subassemblies, and finished goods. The exports of intermediate goods in the last few years have exceeded the export values of final and capital goods, shifting the international trade from "trade in goods" to "trade in value-added." The import-export flows of intermediate goods have increased substantially in the past decade. For example, a dynamic region like South Asia imported more intermediate goods than it exported, showing a high level of integration with global supply chains. It is also true that a vibrant super power like China does not capture the value generated through its value chain exports. There is a trend of a growing gap between where goods are produced and exported and where the added value is created and captured. For example, China captures the added value of about half of its manufacturing exports. There is a shifting end of the regional and inter-regional markets. The growth in the industrial global North seems to be slower than the rapid growth in the global South. In the five-year period 2005–10, the commodities imported by the European Union and in the United States increased by 27% and 14%, respectively. Meanwhile, over the same period the developing economies of the global South expanded aggressively the volume of goods they imported: China by 111%, Brazil by 147%, India by 129%, and South Africa by 51%. This trend can easily be noticed on Table 10.1 regarding the manufacturing sector. Emerging countries such as China, Brazil, India, and South Korea increased manufacturing exports tremendously over an 11-year period compared with global North countries such as Canada, Japan, and the United States.

Concluding, the CEOs of world-class manufacturing multinational organizations recommend competitive tax policy, policies promoting free-trade partnerships, effective public-private partnerships with emphasis on R&D and innovation attracting the most skilled and talented workers, and developing new perspectives on the complicated global value chains. These key elements of growth in manufacturing as suggested by top executives are neither more nor less than the recommendations deriving from endogenous growth theories and models that we have seen in chapters 8, 9, and 10.

Table 10.1 Manufacturing exports, selected countries, 2000 and 2011

Country	*Manufacturing exports, 2000 ($ billions)*	*Manufacturing exports, 2011 ($ billions)*
China	219.3	1,768.5
Germany	459.2	1,226.3
United States	644.6	952
Japan	449.4	724.8
South Korea	154.9	473.5
Singapore	117.5	279
Taiwan	141.0	270.7
Canada	175.4	202.3
India	26.0	151.7
Brazil	31.6	84.2

Source: Deloitte Touche Tohmatsu Limited, 2013 Global Manufacturing Competitiveness Index. World Economic Forum 2013.

Overall Conclusions about the Survey on Growth Economists and Capital Theorists

The debate about growth and development that began after the Second World War has become the most challenging and frequently discussed one in economic forums, conferences, and literature. Growth modeling has attracted an astonishing concentration of research talent and effort, yielding results of great interest and value. Growth is a phenomenon that involves the whole economy and intersects with many important issues, such as capital, labour, technological change, unemployment, environmental constraints, institutional arrangements, and organizations. As such, examinations of the relationships between these factors have raised many still-unresolved questions that have challenged growth theorists and policy makers to develop new ideas about the dynamic forces of growth.

The early growth models developed in the 1940s and 1950s, based on Harrod and Domar's and Solow's work, have the rather unpleasant property that growth naturally comes to an end. In these models, the growth process is seen as self-limiting and can only be maintained by exogenous factors, such as technological change and population growth. Only the growth rate of physical capital is explained by these models, and other sources of growth – such as technological progress – are assumed to be exogenous (and therefore unexplained by the models). Dissatisfaction with this approach has led to more recent interest in endogenous growth theory, which has tried to explain the growth of output per capita in endogenous terms. Only in the past three decades has it become natural to ask whether an economy could endogenously generate continuing growth.

The neoclassical phase of growth modeling was inspired by the relatively steady and unexpected growth in advanced industrial countries after the Second World War. None of the growth models developed during and after the postwar recovery were capable of illustrating the causes of the great boom of the 1950s and 1960s. These causes, which included technological phenomena, favorable terms of trade and flourishing international commerce, monetary stability, and excellent macroeconomic performance, were not sufficiently represented in the structure of growth models elaborated by many economists. It was assumed that technological progress was not simply absorbed or adopted by a country but rather was embodied in capital stock as part of investment in new capital, mostly in advanced countries. The absorptive process required political, social, cultural, and economic analysis to understand the high rate of growth in industrial countries during the boom period and, at the same time, to explain the status of underdevelopment in many countries in Latin America, Africa, the Middle East, and Asia. When mainstream economists sought to relate analysis of the growth rate to the historical facts of economic growth, many questionable propositions were raised. It is widely understood that the evolution of single national economies and the world economy in the 1970s and 1980s violated most of the stylized facts that mainstream growth economists had assumed, including the ideas of a warranted path of growth and the steady-state rate of growth.

In 1956, Solow examined whether the interest rate and the related savings might be driven down by a steady rise in the capital-labour ratio so as to reach the stationary state. His view was that population growth would bring down the capital-labour ratio if net investment were to cease for a period of time. Therefore, a jump in the investment rate might increase the capital-labour ratio, thereby slowing the rate of population increase and subsequently yielding a sustained increase in output per capita. This type of model, which considers technical progress to be an exogenous variable, had long been the main contribution of the neoclassical theory of growth. In Solow's view, decisions producing technical progress are not specified. The model analyzes the effects represented by the production function of the Cobb-Douglas type. However, technical progress is the result of many decisions: those made by consumers, by firms, by school systems, by research activities, and so forth.

Lucas (1988) argues that technical progress is the result of decisions made by consumers who devote some of their time to improving their professional skills, which they will offer to firms in the form of qualified labour to be used for production. Labour is measured not in physical units but rather in efficiency units, the product of the physical unit multiplied by a variable that expresses the effect of qualification. Lucas also argues that investment in human capital drives the growth process. Highly skilled workers are able to use more sophisticated capital equipment, are more flexible in their approach to problems, and are more likely to think of ways in which production can be organized more efficiently. The elegancy of Lucas's model is built on the simple assumption of identical agents (in their ability, measured by human capital) who are able to divide their time between production and study. The assumption that the individual does not have free time is strong. Rebelo (1991) later extended the model of Lucas (1988) by considering the physical capital involved in the production of human capital in the final sector, even in the absence of externalities.

The work that especially reawakened the examination of growth theory was that of Paul M. Romer (1986), who argued that a byproduct of the investment process is an increase of knowledge about production, which means that a firm investing in new equipment learns how to produce more efficiently. This process is called "learning by doing," a term introduced by Arrow in his model published in 1962. The knowledge that firms acquire through investment is able to spill over into the economy via the movement of ideas and workers. As a result, that knowledge benefits other firms and industries. Technical progress in this model is basically the result of firms attempting to increase the variety of intermediate goods. The accumulation of capital is thus an increasing aggregate of intermediate commodities that enters into a production function together with labour. Therefore, an increase in the variety of commodities that comprise capital spurs the growth of general production.

Endogenous growth theory has moved from the simplest $Y = AK$ model to a more complicated range of models. The first step in this process was to develop models with two sectors of production. For example, one sector might produce goods or services, while the other sector produces innovations in technology or knowledge, which are then freely used in both sectors. The next step was to introduce the assumption that microeconomic decisions are behind the research process, in order to better explain the accumulation of knowledge. Research is a critical tool to help explain the process of accumulation and even the rate of growth.

In several endogenous models there are some facts regarding research that have become relevant. First, new technical knowledge and research discoveries that benefit companies, organizations, and the general public are made by a number of firms spending enough resources on R&D to make profits. Second, research is lucrative because it gives firms temporary monopolies through the patent system. Third, other firms are able to "copy" prior innovations in order to build the next generation of innovations. Thus, the theory of monopolistic competition is integrated into the modern theory of growth. These new theories have endeavoured to connect the microeconomic facts with the macroeconomic events.

Some complex models have been developed in order to analyze the effects of trade on technology and on long-term economic growth. The most important contribution is Romer's 1990 model, in which the great value of human capital as a vehicle of R&D encourages the residual of the endogenous growth process. The payback of R&D consists of new innovations, which guarantee monopolistic rents for entrepreneurs through licensing and patenting. In addition, since new innovations are added to the stock of non-excludable knowledge, they increase productivity by reducing the marginal cost of new innovations. Romer suggests that trade would be beneficial to technological innovation; this is the case superficially because technological innovation provides access to new markets, as well as fundamentally because it integrates the market for human capital. He cites the example of the US counties that had access to navigable waterways in the nineteenth century; as a result, in comparison to more disconnected countries, the United States had higher rates of patenting during that time.

Grossman and Helpman (1991a and 1991b) later assumed that technical progress consists essentially of enlarging the set of consumer goods and of the accumulation of knowledge. The decisive factor for endogenous growth seems to be simply the accumulation of knowledge.

An interesting approach to cyclical growth was later developed based on the notion of general purpose technologies (Bresnahan and Trajtenberg 1995, and Helpman and Trajtenberg 1998). In this approach, new GPTs require the discovery of new intermediate goods, and as a result, the economy must wait until some intermediate components are mounted up before it is profitable for firms to switch from the previous GPT. Eventually, however, these new GPTs do come to affect the entire economic system. Although each new GPT raises output and productivity in the long run, it can also cause cyclical fluctuations while the economy adjusts. As the spread of a new GPT occurs over a long period of time, most of the costly experimentation that facilitates the GPT's spread is generally concentrated in relatively short periods. The most illustrative example of a GPT is the electrification of the manufacturing system in the twentieth century, which was not realized in the United States until the 1920s, a full generation after the technical fundamentals had been put in place (Paul 1991). Diffusion was delayed in part by the need to refine the core of technology, but even more so because of the need for organizational and managerial adjustments by both suppliers and users of electricity. Once underway, however, electrification had a dramatic impact on total factor productivity growth in the United States, which jumped from less than 1 per cent per year before the First World War (1914) to more than 5 per cent per year during the 1920s.

Another phenomenon of endogenous growth is social learning: the way most firms learn to use a new technology is not to discover everything on their own but rather to learn from the experience of other firms in similar situations. Normally, firms that face similar problems use the procedures of successful firms as a "template" from which to adopt new procedures. Initially, however, only a negligible improvement in knowledge can take place, because successful achievement in any given sector requires firms to make independent discoveries with modest direction from the successful experience of others. Once the discoveries continue for a sufficient amount of time, there will come a point when new firms will start using new technologies.

A wide range of government-provided services, such as transport networks and utilities, is also thought to have an impact on the efficiency of production. Barro (1990 and 1991) argued that these services could be seen as inputs to the production process and that there are externalities to their provision. Further, government assurance of property rights through investment in police services, courts, and defence may also raise the incentive to accumulate private capital. Firms in the industrialized world devote a significant proportion of their profits to the development of new products and processes. Endogenous growth theory has made significant efforts to model the R&D process as one in which firms make purposeful investments in R&D, which may produce new varieties of goods or simply raise the quality of existing goods (Aghion and Howitt 1992). An important feature of these models is the concept of creative destruction: the discovery of new goods makes old products obsolete, so firms go bankrupt and their capital equipment is made obsolete. Cross-section evidence suggests that countries with high rates of economic growth tend to have high levels of human capital as well as high levels of physical investment. It is possible, then, that causality is reversed, and that a high level of growth causes high investment. Another interpretation is that innovative countries invest more in physical capital because the returns for doing so are higher and the physical capital is more advanced in innovative countries than elsewhere; hence, it is more productive. Many empirical studies on human capital have recommended that highly qualified workers with good experience can be up to twice as productive as those with no qualifications. Further evidence on human capital also suggests that there are significant remuneration and benefits to R&D spending and that these benefits spill over to other firms and industries. There are also significant relationships between public sector capital formation, such as infrastructure investment and private sector productivity.

Economic theory and empirical evidence indicate that technological progress, through its impact on factors of production, is a key determinant of long-run economic growth; indeed, for some countries, it is the most important determinant. However, this does not in itself provide an economic justification for government intervention to reallocate resources in favour of R&D. In a market economy, government intervention is usually justified by the market's failure to provide an efficient or socially desirable allocation of resources. Market failure is also evidenced in the case of R&D investment, where the effects of externalities and market imperfections are extended not only beyond individual firms but also beyond a country's borders.

Endogenous growth theory relaxes many of the neoclassical assumptions in order to incorporate market imperfections, such as those mentioned above. However, as in the neoclassical models, long-run economic growth in endogenous growth theory is driven by the accumulation of knowledge-based factors of production, such as human capital, learning by doing, R&D, and innovation. In the long run, it is the accumulation of these factors that causes factor productivity to increase and prevents the marginal return to physical capital from falling below profitable levels.

Endogenous growth theory presumes that technological progress is the result of R&D that has been carried out by profit-maximizing firms. Based on this theory R&D enters the production process as a factor of production and is used in combination with other inputs. As with any investment decision, R&D is not undertaken unless there is an opportunity for profit.

The different range of assumptions determining long-run growth, which are endogenous to the decision-making process of the firm, is a major departure from the neoclassical growth theory and has important policy implications.

The first generation of endogenous growth models (Romer 1986, Lucas 1988, Rebelo 1991) were less concerned with how spillovers take place than with treating the process as exogenous. These models considered the effects of knowledge spillovers on growth, but they did not specify *how* knowledge spills over, even though the significant issue in modeling knowledge-based growth rests on the spillover of knowledge. This was to some extent remedied, however, in the second generation of endogenous growth models (Schmitz 1989, Segerstrom, Anant, and Dinopoulos 1990; Segerstrom 1991; Aghion and Howitt 1992; and Cheng and Dinopoulos 1992). The models featuring a neo-Schumpeterian structure design market entry as an R&D race in which a portion of R&D will eventually be transformed into successful innovations.

The crucial characteristic of the neo-Schumpeterian models is that they generate growth of per capita output endogenously, without assuming that technological change takes place outside the model's structure. Hence, they are known as pure endogenous growth models. Although all these models share the same basic idea, each relies on different mechanisms to put long-run growth in motion. Some models explain the forces that lead to technological change, whereas others modify the construction of the model so that investment in physical or human capital sustains growth.

The endogenous growth models are highly theoretical by nature, so they do not give explicit policy recommendations. However, they do consider certain kinds of policies that influence growth in the long run, such as lowering barriers to trade, reducing taxes on capital income, focusing government spending on services that improve the quality of life of the community, and emphasizing public spending on infrastructure to increase productivity in the private sector. Several endogenous growth models underline innovation as the key point of long-run growth and look principally to high levels of training and a well-educated labour force as the key inputs to R&D. Although these models are currently too crude to support the argument that governments should subsidize training or education, they nonetheless demonstrate that governments should avoid discouraging investment in human capital.

The early endogenous growth models based on theoretical assumptions have given way to more realistic ones that have better experimental support. Recent studies in growth economics have proved that it is becoming difficult to make a clear distinction between the neoclassical and endogenous growth models, because the differences between the two are steadily dwindling. In this interpretation, many of the most recent models are better viewed as an expansion of neoclassical models rather than substitutes for them. The growth models that include comprehensive details of the economics of innovation development offer an important bridge to a complete description of the process of technological transformation.

To conclude this long survey, we would like to propose some lessons and suggestions that emerge from reviewing the modern theory of growth.

First of all, the neoclassical model of growth is still the most powerful and useful theory of growth we have. It is the first growth model in all textbooks in economic growth around the globe. The strength of the neoclassical model is that it expresses the complicated real world in key economic relationships that can be understood by most people, including students, teachers, researchers, economists, policy analysts, and policy makers. What has changed, however, is the interpretation. The role and the meaning of capital in economic growth have come to be viewed more broadly. Capital accumulation, in a way different from the traditional vision, conveys a high stock of human knowledge, investments in education, training, innovation, R&D, improvements in quality and variety of products, and investment in physical capital (such as infrastructures, transport network, utilities, and public services). All of these factors transmit positive externalities and, in turn, have a positive impact on modern and developed economies.

Second, given the multitude of models in economic growth, it has become increasingly difficult to dichotomize growth theory into exogenous and endogenous branches. Recent work in endogenous growth has demonstrated how to model technological progress, which is exogenous in the neoclassical growth theory. This has led to a new research study based on so-called semi-endogenous models. However, endogenous models are not presented only as alternatives to the neoclassical model, but can also be seen as complements. The combination of knowledge in endogenous growth models with technological progress in exogenous growth models has given powerful tools to economists, analysts, and policy makers.

Third, there is a natural predisposition for growth theory to focus on steady states. The basic neoclassical model normally has an equilibrium path that converges at the steady state. Even for a standard endogenous growth model, it is much easier and more communicable to frame one's responses in terms of steady-state consequences than to determine how the entire path of growth changes (in case of parameter changes). And when we talk about steady state, we mean the long-term growth that is a primary concern for all growth theorists, analysts, and policy makers. Over the long run, most economies seek to reach high outputs and focus on the supply-side factors, such as the accumulation of physical and human capital, the progression of technology, the competition of national industries with international markets, the improvement of the standard of living, and so forth. However, the demand side presents paths that are disturbed by recessions, booms, and different types of macroeconomic fluctuations that affect the steady state. So, the work of growth theorists should focus on how both the short-run fluctuations (on the supply and the demand side), and a large number of factors that are treated as endogenous, respond to long-run growth rates.

Fourth, the latest works on economic growth have focused their attention on innovations on the production side, thereby contributing standard theories of household behaviour in order to help explain saving and consumption decisions. However, future studies of consumption and saving theory, as well as further progress in microeconomics, may improve our understanding of the unknown sides of economic growth.

Fifth, government-provided services and political stability have made an impact by raising the growth rate and encouraging investment from both domestic residents and those abroad. Recent work on economic growth suggests that a more active government could be beneficial by helping certain kinds of domestic and foreign capital yield positive externalities. At this point, growth economists should concentrate their efforts on measuring the magnitude of these externalities in order to offer clearer policy prescriptions to policy makers.

Sixth, most growth and capital theory has assumed for a long time that inputs and key resources are abundant, or at least that inputs and resources are substitutable in case they cannot meet the demand. At the dawn of the twenty-first century, nothing is taken for granted, and if the key global resources, such as petroleum and energy supply, experience a sudden drop, then some of the modern growth models might also run out of options.

At the close of this long survey, I hope the reader finds the mainstream growth economists and their theories in the postwar period to be clearer and more comprehensible. When I first began studying this field of economics, I was very confused, perplexed, and puzzled about the vast number and complexity of theories and their relations to the real economic world; maybe I still am. However, after reading hundreds of articles, papers, notes, models, comments, essays, books, book reviews, and textbooks on growth economics and capital theory, I have been able to extract a thread that has helped me write this survey of the major theorists in the modern theory of growth. I hope it will give the reader a revealing glimpse of the quantity – and quality – of the literature on economic growth out there in the field, where economists and theorists struggle every day to provide a fuller understanding of this phenomenon we call the global economy.

Notes

INTRODUCTION

1 Modern industrial countries are those that have reached a high level of economic achievement through utilization of natural and human resources to increase production, per capita income, and consumption.

2 The Marginalist Revolution followed the birth of marginal utility theory in the 1870s and explains the economic behaviour of consumers in terms of marginal utility.

3 We are not even quite sure that using mathematics in economic models to represent real world facts is the right thing to do. In fact, Nell, paraphrasing Bonnafous's investigation of econometrics, suggests:

> Contemporary currents in scientific thought allow us to abandon the (essentially metaphysical) idea of a necessary and pre-established adequacy between mathematics and reality. To paraphrase Bonnafous (1972, 11), "the world of inexact science, in particular, does not appear to be organized according to mathematical laws. Furthermore, it is interesting to observe that, in the nineteenth century, at the same time that the idea of a universal truth provided by mathematics was discredited by the emergence of alternative axiomatic systems, because of Walras, a narrow view of rationality rapidly gained dominance in economic science, subscribing to a Platonic and Cartesian approach to science ... such work in pure economics continues to be widely pursued today." (Nell and Errouaki 2013, xxiii)

4 From a chronological viewpoint, the starting point for modern growth theory is Ramsey's classic article (1928). Ramsey was the first to treat the problem of household optimization, which goes beyond the application of a standard growth theory (for more, see Barro and Sala-i-Martin 1995).

5 For the definition of vintage framework models, see chapter 5, "Technical Progress and Growth in Neoclassical Perception."

6 Reviewing this literature after more than a decade of its development, Sen concluded that "growth economics is guided much more by logical curiosity than by a taste for relevance" (1970, 36).

CHAPTER ONE

1 Adam Smith was born in 1723 in Kirkcaldy, a small town near Edinburgh, Scotland. His father was a lawyer and civil servant who died shortly after Adam was born, so Smith was raised by his mother and guardians appointed in his father's will. At age fourteen, Smith was sent to the University of Glasgow to study moral philosophy, mathematics, and political economy. In 1774, he won a scholarship to Oxford University and studied at Balliol College for six years. In 1751, Smith was hired to fill the Chair of Logic at the University of Glasgow. A year later, he was appointed to the Chair of Moral Philosophy. His lectures on ethics, *The Theory of Moral Sentiments* (1759), became his first literary success. Charles Townshend hired Smith to teach his stepson, the young Duke of Buccleuch. Smith resigned from the professorship at Glasgow to accompany the young duke to France. During this time, around 1764, he started writing a book called *The Wealth of Nations*, which was finally published in 1776. This work brought Smith both fame and fortune in the United Kingdom and around the world. Adam Smith died in 1790.

2 David Ricardo was born in London in 1772 to a prosperous Jewish family. His father was a broker. His first two years of schooling were in Holland (his father's country of origin, where his family maintained close ties). He then had a common school education in England, and at the age of fourteen, Ricardo entered his father's brokerage firm. Later he married Priscilla Wilkinson, the daughter of a Quaker surgeon, and converted to Christianity, which created a conflict with his father. Because of this, having to support his own family without his father's help, he began his own brokerage firm. By the age of twenty-six, he had made a great fortune in the stock exchange, which allowed him the leisure to then pursue his intellectual interests. In 1819 Ricardo bought a seat in the House of Commons and quickly became a recognized expert on financial matters in Parliament. David Ricardo died in 1823.

3 Karl Marx was born into a middle-class Jewish family in Trier, Germany, in 1818. He was first educated at home by his parents and Baron

von Westphalen, a close friend of his father. After attending high school in Trier, he went to the University of Bonn to study law. Afterward, he dropped his studies in law and went to the University of Berlin to pursue his interests in philosophy. In 1841 Marx received a PHD in philosophy. Two years later, he married the daughter of Baron von Westphalen. He first worked as editor of the liberal left newspaper *Rheinische Zeitung* until the paper was closed by Prussian authorities. He then moved to Paris, where he began to associate with socialists and communists. There he met Frederick Engels, the son of a wealthy textile manufacturer and a well-known economist. Engels and Marx became very close friends. Engels later became the long-life collaborator of Marx and provided financial support during the rest of his life. Because of his radical ideas, after a short period Marx was expelled from Paris and moved to Brussels. Soon he was expelled from Brussels as well and finally moved to London, where he was accepted by British authorities. Marx lived in London for the rest of his life, spending most of his time at the British Museum reading and writing about economics. He died in 1883.

CHAPTER TWO

1 In economics, the multiplier coefficient is the ratio between the total increase in income resulting from the stimulating effect of an initial expenditure or investment and the initial expenditure itself.

2 Joseph Schumpeter (1883–1950) was born to middle-class parents in Triesch, Moravia (then part of the Austro-Hungarian Empire and now part of the Czech Republic). His father, who owned a textile factory, died when he was very young. His mother soon remarried and moved to Vienna, where Schumpeter attended high school with the aristocratic elite. He received an excellent education in the humanities but inadequate grounding in mathematics and science. As a law student at the University of Vienna, Schumpeter took several courses in economics. After receiving a doctorate in law in 1906, he went to Cairo to practice law and to manage the finances of an Egyptian princess. In 1909, he accepted a teaching job at the University of Czernowitz and, two years later, was appointed to a chair in political economy at the University of Graz. Schumpeter then became interested in politics. In 1918, he became a member of the German Socialization Commission, and in 1919, he became finance minister of Austria but resigned after seven months in office. His political career was both short and unsuccessful. In 1925, Schumpeter accepted an

appointment as Professor of Economics at the University of Bonn. Seven years later, he had a position at Harvard University, where he remained until his death in 1950.

3 For more about the concept of "creative destruction," see the Aghion-Howit model in Chapter 10. The original contribution of Aghion and Howitt (1992) was based on Schumpeter's concept of "creative destruction."

4 For further research see Tylecote and Day 1991.

5 Roy Harrod (1900–1978) was born in Norfolk, England, in 1900, the only child of a highly educated family. The boy won a scholarship that enabled him to go to Westminster School. He lost his father when he was eighteen, but he remained closely attached to his mother to the end of her long life. From Westminster, Harrod went to New College, Oxford. After graduating in philosophy and history, he began as a lecturer in the modern history of economics. Soon after, he was made a fellow of Christ Church College, where he remained until 1967. Spending a term in Cambridge during the 1930s, he became a close friend of Keynes, then already a celebrity, who stimulated his interest in economics. Harrod returned to Oxford to administer and teach at Christ Church College. To his disappointment, Oxford never offered him a professorship; he remained a reader until his retirement in 1967. Harrod was never awarded with the Nobel Prize in economics. In fact, Assar Lindbeck, the chairman of the Nobel Prize Committee, wrote that Harrod would have been awarded a Nobel Prize for his contributions in economics if he had lived longer. Harrod died on March 1978.

6 The acceleration principle is a theory of investment in modern macroeconomics. It states that the level of investment is accelerated through the rate of increase in output (gross domestic product). Each level of output needs a certain amount of capital. So if output is expected to rise, the amount of capital within the system also will increase.

7 Multiplier focuses on the relationship between spending and consumption. In this case, it refers to an expenditure multiplier. The principle of multiplier holds when spending made by the government, corporations, or households moves up national income. This is called the multiplier effect.

8 Harrod, in his original paper (1939), used the symbol C instead of v, which is preferred in the most recent literature and indicates the capital-output ratio. Here the symbols of his original paper are used; hence C and not v is used.

9 Technological progress is defined as neutral when it leaves unchanged the balance between labour and capital. For more, see in chapter 5 "The Neutrality of Technical Progress in Hicks and Harrod."

10 The difference between $e = (C_1 - C_0)/C_1$ and $e = u(C_1)-[u(C_0)/u(C_1)]$ disappears when it is expressed in terms of differential equations.

11 Evsey Domar was born in Łodź, Poland, in 1914. He was raised in Manchuria and immigrated to the United States in 1936. He received his bachelor of arts from UCLA in 1939, a master of science from the University of Michigan in 1940, another master of science from Harvard University in 1943, and his doctorate from Harvard University in 1947. Domar came to the Massachusetts Institute of Technology (MIT) in 1957 as a visiting professor from Johns Hopkins University; he received tenure a year later. Before coming to MIT, Domar taught at the Carnegie Institute of Technology, at the University of Chicago, and Johns Hopkins. He retired in 1984. Among Domar's pupils in macroeconomics was Robert William Fogel, winner of the 1993 Nobel Memorial Prize in Economic Sciences. Domar was an expert in the Soviet economy during the Cold War and an early proponent of Keynesian economic theory. Domar, apart from being a professor, also served as a consultant for the RAND Corporation, the Ford Foundation, the Brookings Institution, the National Science Foundation, the Battelle Memorial Institute, and the Institute for Defense Analysis. Domar was a fellow of the American Academy of Arts and Sciences, of the Econometric Society, and of the Center for Advanced Study in the Behavioral Sciences. He was on the executive committee of the American Economic Association from 1962 and became the organization's vice president in 1970, when he was also president of the Association for Comparative Economic Studies. He died on 1 April 1997.

12 In the original model, the propensity to save is indicated as α and the ratio of output to capital as s. Normally, in standard growth models, the marginal propensity to save is indicated as s and the ratio of output to capital as k. Here we will stick to the common use of s and k (respectively, the marginal propensity to save and ratio of output to capital) (Domar 1948, 781).

13 A comparison of these magnitudes with statistical data depends on the method of estimate and period chosen. For example, during 1869 to 1929, the American D/G, in real terms ranged between 50% and 70%, and during 1929 to 1950, it was 64%. From Kuznets, we find that, between 1869 and 1908, the American D/G in real terms was only 45%,

and in 1909–1928, the D/G averaged over 60%. For more details see Domar 1953.

14 The corresponding function formulas are

$$\frac{R}{G} = e^{-rm}; \text{ and } \frac{R}{D} = \frac{m}{e^{m} - 1}$$

(Domar 1953, 9).

15 "It is to be observed that the increase in capital per unit of capacity (in so far as it occurs) due to a given once-and-for-all in rate of interest requires a once-and-for-all bout of capital accumulation ... when the appropriate 'deepening of capital' has taken place there is no further need for accumulation. Thus to maintain a given rate of accumulation, under this influence, a continually falling rate of interest is necessary" (Robinson 1949, 75).

CHAPTER THREE

1 Nicholas Kaldor (1908–1986) was born in Budapest, Hungary, into a Jewish family. His father was a legal consultant, and his mother came from a well-known family of bankers and businessmen. Kaldor grew up in fairly affluent surroundings and received a good education. He attended a model high school in Budapest that was famous for using the Socratic method of teaching. In 1925, Kaldor enrolled at the University of Berlin. Two years later, he went to the London School of Economics (LSE), where he graduated in 1930. Two years later, he was appointed as an assistant lector at the LSE, and in 1934, he became a lector. Later, in 1942, he was just a reader. He left the LSE in 1947 to become Director of the Research and Planning Division of the Economic Commission for Europe. He returned to the academic life as a fellow of King's College Cambridge in 1949, becoming a reader in 1952 and a professor of economics in 1966. In 1951, Kaldor was appointed to the Royal Commission on the Taxation of Profits and Income. Throughout the 1950s and the 1960s, he served as an adviser to both British and foreign governments. He was also a special adviser to the Chancellor of the Exchequer from 1964 to 1968 and again from 1974 to 1976. Kaldor retired from academic life in 1975.

2 Kaldor's principal contributions to the construction of the post-Keynesian theory of growth and distribution are found in the following articles: "Alternative Theories of Distribution" (*Review of Economic Studies*, 1956), "A Model of Economic Growth" (*Economic Journal*, 1957), "Capital Accumulation and Economic Growth" (in the *Theory of Capital*,

1961) and "A New Model of Economic Growth" (with J. A. Mirrlees in *Review of Economic Studies*, 1962).

3 As a matter of fact, it does not make any difference whether these new investment opportunities reflect the scrapping of the old equipment, the population growth, or technological progress (Kaldor 1954, 63).

4 In fact, the productivity of labour in American industry from 1870 to 1945 rose at about twice the annual rate of that in European industry. This could be explained, according to Kaldor, by the fact that the higher expansion of American business created prolonged periods of acute labour shortage in the economy, which stimulated both the high rate of immigration prior to 1914 and also the invention of labour-saving devices, such as the belt-line assembly and the single-purpose machine tool, as well as the methods of mass production and standardization. Conversely, the sudden decreasing rate of the population growth in the 1920s by reducing the rate of growth must have been a major cause of the Depression in the 1930s (Kaldor 1954, 68).

5 Kaldor, among others, argued that the measurement of capital stock in terms of money values corrected for price changes raises peculiar problems of its own on account of two facts: first, the capital goods produced in any period are technically and physically different from the capital goods produced in previous periods and, therefore, cannot simply be added to the latter; second, the value of the existing capital stock at any moment is not the sum of the values of the capital goods produced in the past but rather simply the existing value of capital less accrued depreciation (Kaldor 1957, 598–9).

6 In earlier articles (1940 and 1951) Kaldor criticized the use of the acceleration principle in connection with trade cycle models, because it assumes a constant relationship between output and capital, whereas the recognition of a changing relationship between these two variables is essential for understanding the cyclical mechanism. For the purpose of a long-run growth model, it is legitimate to divide time into "periods" long enough for capital stock to fully adjust to the expected output, which means the "acceleration principle" is appropriate to characterize investment behavior for such periods (Kaldor 1960).

7 In this version (1957), Kaldor has assumed that productivity depends on net investment, but in the later version (Kaldor and Mirrless 1962) he has assumed that growth of productivity in the economy is entirely due to the infusion of new "machines" into the system through gross investment.

8 For more see Hahn and Matthews 1964.

9 For more see also Kaldor 1978.

10 This interest seems to have been influenced by his teacher Allyn Young at the London School of Economics in the late 1920s.

11 Luigi Pasinetti was born in September 1930 at Zanica, near Bergamo in Northern Italy. He completed his primary and secondary education in Bergamo and received his BA degree (laurea) from the Catholic University of Milan in 1954. He obtained a PHD in economics at the University of Cambridge in 1962 with a well-known dissertation entitled "Multi-sector Model of Economic Growth." At Cambridge, he came into close contact with well-known thinkers such as Richard Kahn, Nicholas Kaldor, Joan Robinson, and Piero Sraffa. His first appointment (to a research fellowship) was at Nuffield College, Oxford (1959–61). In 1961, he became a fellow of King's College in Cambridge. In 1973, he was appointed as a reader in economics at the University of Cambridge. Pasinetti remained there until 1976, at which time he returned to Italy at the University of Milan, where he became the chairman of the Faculty of Economics (1980–83) and director of the Department of Economics. Pasinetti is the heir of the "post-Keynesian" school. He was a leading economist of the controversies on capital theory, income distribution, and the theory of value that were disputed between Cambridge in the United Kingdom, and Cambridge, Massachusetts, in the United States during the 1960s and 1970s.

12 In his model, Pasinetti (1962) has substituted Kaldor's original equation (1957) of distribution between wages and profits with equation (3.31), which stands for the distribution of income between workers and capitalists, and with equation (3.33), which stands for the distribution of income, wages, and profits.

13 Pasinetti placed some restrictions on s_w in order to limit the validity of the mathematical formulations to the range in which it has an economic meaning $s_w < I/Y$ and $s_w > I/Y$, where I/Y is the equilibrium in the investment-income ratio (Pasinetti 1962, 270).

CHAPTER FOUR

1 These economists are Marshall, Jevons, Walras, Wicksell, Pareto, Clark, Edgeworth, and Fisher.

2 Solow was born in Brooklyn, New York, in 1924. Having graduated from Harvard in 1947, he obtained his PHD, also from Harvard, in 1951. The dissertation addressed random processes as a cause of the inequality of incomes, and income distribution remained one of his lifelong interests. In

1950 Solow joined the faculty of the Massachusetts Institute of Technology as an assistant professor of statistics. Four years later he was made an associate professor, and in 1957 he became a professor of economics. Solow developed a close fellowship and collaboration with Paul Samuelson. Under the Kennedy administration, he worked as a senior economist on the staff of the Council of Economic Advisers, and under President Johnson, he served on the Commission on Income Maintenance Programs. For five years in the late 1970s, he was a director of the Federal Reserve Bank of Boston. Over the years, he received many honours, including the John Bates Clark Medal of the American Economists Association, a number of honorary degrees, and, finally, in 1987, the Nobel Prize. Solow's field has been macroeconomics. In 1999 President Bill Clinton awarded Solow the National Medal of Science. Like other eminent economists of his generation, he published no big works; most of his publishing appears as papers and articles. After early work on linear models, Solow became attracted to problems of economic growth. Together with Samuelson (1953), he showed that a closed von Neumann system with substitute factors has a unique structure and a stable growth rate. Later he dedicated himself primarily to the creation of models in the theory of growth and macroeconomics.

3 Until the divergence between the natural rate of growth and steady rate of growth disappears, it is sufficient, according to Solow, to assume that prices are flexible and to introduce a production function that allows the substitution between two factors: capital and labor. He attracted no attention, as the paper was published in German in a German journal during the war. Despite this, Tinbergen was involved in developing a new methodology, through the use of the mathematical taxonomy (mathematical classification), which was not easy to understand for many economists. Moreover, his main subject was not balanced growth but rather various types of unbalanced growth.

4 Named for the Japanese economist K.I. Inada, who introduced them into growth theory in his masterpiece paper (Inada 1963).

5 Notice that at any k, we can derive investment per person, i, output per person, y, and, residually, consumption per person ($c = C/L = y - i$).

6 The analysis proposed here is taken from Solow's article in 1956 (69–74). A similar analysis is found in the well-known textbook of growth theory by Barro and Sala-i-Martin (1995), 46–9.

7 James Tobin (1971, Vol 1. Ch. 8) was one of the first economists to generalize the Harrod-Domar model by allowing for factor substitution. At

the same time, he also added the demand for real cash balances, which is satisfied either by money paid out as transfer payments or by deflation. The path of economic growth thus became dependent partly on monetary factors.

8 The definition of "neutrality" is not univocal. Given the production function (4.6), we can say that: a) Technological progress is Hicks-neutral if the ratio of marginal productivities remains invariable for a given capital-labor ratio. The Hicks-neutral progress can be written as $Y = F(K, L, t) = T(t)\, F(K, L)$, where T is an index of the state of technology and $T(t) \geq 0$; this type of technological progress is defined as product augmenting. b) The technological progress is neutral in the sense of Solow if the relative quota of input shares LFL/KFK remain unchanged for a given labor-capital ratio. This definition implies a production function of the type $Y = F(B(t)\, K, L)$.The index of the technology in this case is $B(t)$, and $B(t) \geq 0$. This type of technological progress is called capital augmenting because an improvement in technological progress increases output in the same way as an increase in the stock of capital. The concept of Solow neutrality is relevant with regard to vintage capital models. For more about technological progress, see chapter 5 in this book.

9 A proof of this affirmation is found in Solow (1999a). In effect, Solow simplifies a demonstration given by Uzawa 1961a.

10 For a formal treatment of the production function, see Burmestier and Dobell 1973, 67–75.

11 The phrase "*two* knife-edges" means that there is a balance between the actual and the warranted rate of growth ("macroeconomic stability") as well as a balance between the warranted and the natural rate of growth ("employment stability").

12 Sen 1965, 279–280, and Sen 1970, 230. This paper was presented by Sen for the first time at the International Economic Association Roundtable Conference on the Theory of Interest Rates at Royaumont, France, in 1962.

13 In order to simplify the reading of this work for non-mathematical readers, other alternative production functions, such as the neoclassical growth with a Cobb-Douglas production function (including logarithmic differentiation), will not be treated here.

14 Leif Johansen was born in Eidsvoll, Norway, in May 1930. From 1958 to 1959, he spent some time at the University of Cambridge in the United Kingdom, and he received his PHD from the University of Oslo in 1961. His earlier work on a doctoral dissertation was published as *A Multi-*

sectoral Study of Economic Growth (Amsterdam: North-Holland, 1960; 2nd. ed., New York: American Elsevier, 1974). For the whole of his academic life, he was Professor of Economics at the University of Oslo (1965–82), where he succeeded Ragnar Frisch on the latter's retirement in 1965. From 1960 to 1964, he served as an adviser to the Norwegian Ministry of Finance on economic planning and between 1980 and 1981 on the Royal Commission on Money and Credit. He was co-editor of the *Journal of Public Economics* and, for various periods, associate editor of the editorial board of other scientific journals. He was awarded the Fridtjof Nansen Award for outstanding contributions to economics in 1979 by the Norwegian Academy of Sciences and Letters. Johansen died unexpectedly in 1982 at the early age of fifty-two.

15 For more details, see James and Belz 1938.

16 Wassily Leontief was born into an educated family in St Petersburg, Russia on 5 August 1906. His father was a professor of labour economics at the University of St Petersburg and his mother was an art historian. In 1921 Leontief entered the university at the age of 15. There he studied sociology, philosophy, and classics of political economics. During his studies at the university he had the courage to criticize the new communist regime, and for this he was jailed a few times. Despite his troubles he was able to graduate from the University of Leningrad (Petersburg) in 1925. After six months he left the Soviet Union and went to the University of Berlin, where he studied economics and in 1928 received his PHD. Immediately afterwards he joined the Institute for World Economics at the University of Kiel. In 1929 he spent one year in China as an economic consultant to the Ministry of Railways. In 1931 Leontief accepted an offer of employment from the National Bureau of Economic Research in New York. A few months later he was offered another job at Harvard. There he started developing the input-output models. He stayed at Harvard University 44 years. He served also as the president of the American Economic Association. In 1973 he was awarded the Nobel Prize in economics. In 1975 he moved to New York University as a director of the Institute for Economic Analysis, where he continued his relentless research on input-output techniques. Leontief died in 1999.

17 The first edition of *Tableau Économique* was published in 1758.

18 A categorization of the inverse-positive matrices consists on that each element of inverse of the leading (n –1) x (n –1) principal submatrix is less than or equal to the corresponding element in the inverse of the original matrix.

19 Edmund Phelps was born in 1933 near Chicago, but he grew up and spent his school years in Hastings-on-Hudson, New York, where his family moved when he was six years old. In 1951 he went to Amherst College as an undergraduate, receiving his BA 1955. Phelps then went to Yale University for graduate studies in economics, receiving his PHD in 1959. His dissertation showed that demand shocks have a higher influence than cost shocks on the correlation between changes in prices and in output. From there, Phelps went to work as an economist for the RAND Corporation in 1959. In 1960, while also teaching at Yale, he took a research position at the Cowles Foundation, where he had the chance to interact with other top economists working on growth theory, such as David Cass or fellow Nobelist Tjalling Koopmans. In 1966 Phelps left Yale and moved to the University of Pennsylvania, where he was offered a tenured position as Professor of Economics. Phelps spent the academic year 1969–70 at the Center for Advanced Study in Behavioral Science at Stanford University. In 1971 Phelps then moved to the economics department at Columbia University. In 1982 he was appointed the McVickar Professor of Political Economy at Columbia. In 2006 he was awarded the Nobel Memorial Prize in Economic Science for his contribution to a sophisticated explanation of how wages, unemployment, and inflation interact with one another.

20 In the second essay on the golden rule of accumulation in 1965 (the first essay was published in 1961), Phelps formulates a more complete demonstration of the neoclassical optimal growth. For this reason, here we will take into consideration the second contribution of Phelps. To simplify the study of Phelps's model, mathematical demonstrations are omitted.

21 The neoclassical production function has the following properties: it is twice differentiable (smooth marginal products), it is strictly concave (diminishing marginal products), and it has everywhere positive first derivative (marginal products). For the Harrod-Domar case, see Phelps 1965, 800–4.

22 For more on dynamic inefficiencies see R.J. Barro and X. Sala-i-Martin 1995 and D. Romer 2001.

23 For more see Samuelson's turnpike theorem (1965a).

24 For clarification Von Neumann's article was first published in German (1937) and then translated and published in English in 1945.

25 Frank Plumpton Ramsey was born on 22 February 1903, in Cambridge, United Kingdom, where his father, also a mathematician, was master of Magdalene College. He entered Winchester College in 1915 and

later returned to Cambridge to study mathematics at Trinity College. In 1924, with Keynes's support, Ramsey became a fellow of King's College, Cambridge. In 1926 he became a university lecturer in mathematics and, later, director of studies in mathematics at King's College. In 1927 Ramsey published the influential article "Facts and Propositions," in which he proposed what is sometimes described as a redundancy theory of truth. Keynes, however, encouraged Ramsey to work on economics, and Ramsey responded by writing three papers in economic theory, all of which were of fundamental importance, though only many years later did they receive their proper recognition by the community of economists. Ramsey's three papers in economics were on subjective probability and utility (1926), optimal taxation (1927), and optimal one-sector economic growth (1928). Suffering from chronic liver problems, Ramsey contracted jaundice after an abdominal operation and died in January 1930 at Guy's Hospital in London at the age of twenty-six

26 Tjalling C. Koopmans was born in 1910 in Graveland, the Netherlands, the third son of Sjoerd Koopmans and Wijtske van der Zee, who were both schoolteachers; his father was principal of a Protestant school. At seventeen, Koopmans went to the University of Utrecht, where, in the first three years, his principal emphasis was on mathematics, in particular analysis and geometry, which were taught in a precise but traditional style. In mid-1933 Koopmans moved to Amsterdam and met Tinbergen, from whom he received some lectures in mathematical economics. In 1936 he received a PHD in physical sciences from the University of Leiden. Between 1936 and 1938, Tinbergen was called to the financial section of the League of Nations for what became his pioneering work on a model of business cycles in the United States. In 1940, when the war spread to Western Europe, Koopmans, along with his wife and newborn daughter, moved to the United States, where he joined the staff of the Cowles Commission for Research in Economics, affiliated with the University of Chicago. In 1948 he succeeded Jacob Marschak as director of research, a position he held for a six-year period. In 1955 he accepted an appointment at Yale University, and in 1975 Koopmans was awarded the Nobel Prize for his contribution in activity analysis and optimal economic growth. He died on 26 February 1985.

27 David Cass was born in 1937 in Honululu, Hawaii. He earned an BA in economics from the University of Oregon in 1958. Because he thought of becoming a lawyer to follow family tradition, he entered the Harvard Law School. However, he soon discovered that he hated studying law,

and he left the program after one year to serve in the army from 1959 to 1960. Cass then entered the economics PHD program at Stanford University where, in 1965 he graduated in economics and statistics with a dissertation on optimal growth; parts of the dissertation were later published under the title "Optimum Growth in an Aggregative Model of Capital Accumulation" (1966).After graduation, Cass worked from 1965 to 1970 as an assistant professor in the economics department of Yale University and as a research associate at the Cowles Commission for Research in Economics in New Haven, Connecticut. In 1970 he left New Haven for Carnegie Mellon University in Pittsburgh, where he was a Professor of Economics until 1974. During his time there, he began to collaborate with Karl Shell, who, at this time, was a professor at the University of Pennsylvania. In 1974 Cass left for the University of Pennsylvania, where he was a Professor of Economics until his death in 2008 in Philadelphia after a long illness.

28 The production function has positive marginal productivity for each factor and diminishing marginal substitution between factors, expressed by the conditions $f(k) > 0, f'(k) > 0, f''(k)$for $k> 0$,and the aggregate production function is presented by the limit conditions $\underset{k\to 0}{f'}(k) = \infty$ and $\lim_{k\to\infty} f'(k) = 0$ (Cass 1966, 834).

29 For more details regarding the solutions of these differential expressions see Cass 1965.

30 Koopmans (1960, 1964, 1965), in his theory of optimal economic growth used a discrete concept of time for utility function and consumer preferences. In fact, he used two alternative notions. The first one is the utility function of consumption path xt, $t = 1, 2,\ldots$, in terms of a one-period utility function $u(x)$ and an aggregate function $V(u, U)$, which can be defined by the recursive relation $U(x1, x2,\ldots) = V(u(x1), U(x2, x3,\ldots))$. The second alternative is an attempt to express formally the present preference for flexibility in future preferences between different commodities of the same timing.

31 The modern literature in economic growth often used to call this model the Ramsey-Cass-Koopmans model, as it was developed by three authors in different times: Ramsey (1928), Cass (1965), and Koopmans (1965). Here for simplicity, is called the Cass-Koopmans model.

32 Uzawa Hirofumi was born in 1928 in the provincial town of Yonago in Tottori Prefecture in western Japan. His family moved to Tokyo when he was four years old. He majored in mathematics at Tokyo University and went on to its graduate school, obtaining a doctorate in mathematics.

Uzawa initiated the field of mathematical economics in post–Second World War days and was one of the founders of the multisector growth theory of neoclassical economics. In the 1970s and 1980s he criticized modern neoclassical economists – especially Chicago scholars like Milton Friedman, Robert E. Lucas, and Gary S. Becker – for their theories based on REH (the rational expectation hypothesis). His opinion on modern economics tends toward a political critique of the neoliberal policies that spread all over the world in the 1980s, which favoured notions such as free market, privatization, and small government. Professor Uzawa has also served for more than thirty years as senior advisor in the Research Institute of Capital Formation at the Development Bank of Japan. He has been one of the leading economic theorists for the past four decades. In recent decades, he has become particularly well known for applied research in the areas of the economics of pollution, environmental disruption, and global warming as well as the theory of social common capital. Uzawa is Director of the Research Center of Social Common Capital at Doshisha University and Emeritus Professor of Economics at the University of Tokyo. He is a fellow and former president of the Econometric Society and a former president of the Japan Association for Economics and Econometrics.

33 The Inada conditions are: $fi(0) = 0$, $fi(\infty) = \infty$, and $fi'(0) = \infty$, $fi'(\infty) = 0$ (Inada 1963).

34 We can also define $yc = \lambda c fc(kc)$ as consumer sector intensive production function and $yi = \lambda i fi(ki)$ as investment-sector-intensive production function. In the same way, labor market and capital market prices can also be expressed as $w = fc - kcfc' = p \cdot (fi - kifi')$ and $r = fc' = p \cdot fi'$.

35 Which corresponds to equation 23 in Uzawa's original model (1961a)

36 James Tobin was born in 1918 in Champaign, Illinois. His parents were Louis Michael Tobin, a journalist working at the University of Illinois at Urbana-Champaign, and Margaret Edgerton Tobin, a social worker. Tobin attended primary school at the University Laboratory High School of Urbana, Illinois. In 1935, he was admitted with a national scholarship at Harvard University. He graduated in 1939 with a thesis giving critical analysis of Keynes's mechanism for introducing equilibrium involuntary unemployment. Tobin immediately started graduate studies, also at Harvard, earning his MA in 1940. In 1941 he interrupted graduate studies to work for the Office of Price Administration and Civilian Supply and the War Production Board in Washington, DC. At the end of the war, after serving as an officer in the US Navy, he returned to Harvard and resumed

studies, receiving his PHD in 1947 with a dissertation on the consumption function. In 1950 Tobin moved to Yale University, where, in 1957 he was appointed Sterling Professor. He remained at Yale for the rest of his academic career. He served as president of the Cowles Foundation between 1955 and 1961 as well as 1964 and 1965. His main research interest was to provide microfoundations to Keynesian economics, with a special focus on monetary economics. Tobin was awarded the John Bates Clark Medal in 1955 and the Nobel Memorial Prize in Economics in 1981. He held the position of president of the American Economic Association in 1971. In 1988 Tobin retired from Yale. He died on 11 March 2002, in New Haven, Connecticut.

37 The rate of return per unit of time on a unit of real money balance is given by a corresponding increase in the individual's health per unit of time generated by a price change:

$$\frac{\dfrac{d\dfrac{M}{p}}{dt}}{\dfrac{M}{dp}} = -\pi$$

38 To get to equation (4.139) we consider the steady-state growth path where the effective labor supply and the nominal quantity of money, grow at the constant rates n and ψ, respectively. The steady-state path is given as

$$\frac{\dot{k}}{k} = \frac{\dot{K}}{K} - \frac{\dot{L}}{L} = \frac{\dot{K}}{K} - n = 0 \qquad (4.f)$$

where per capita physical capital and per capita real money balances are constant. In the same way using the constancy of m=M/pL we have another equation that defines the convergence to the steady-state path, given as

$$\frac{\dot{m}}{m} = \frac{\dot{M}}{M} - \frac{\dot{p}}{p} - \frac{\dot{L}}{L} = \psi - \pi - n = 0 \qquad (4.g)$$

where the rate of increase of the price level is equal to the rate of increase of the quantity of money. Therefore, both the physical capital and the total real money expand at the constant rate n along the steady path. The $\pi = p'/p$, which is the rate of change of the price level and is constant along the path. The real rate of interest given as $r=f'(k)$ is constant. Substituting (4.136) into (4.137) and dividing by K, and using (4.f) and (4.g) we have a new form of steady-state.

$$\frac{F(K,L)}{K} = \{\lambda n - s[1 + \lambda(n + \pi + r]\} + n = 0 \qquad (4.h)$$

Dividing numerator and denominator of the first term by L and re-arranging the terms in (4.h) we get the steady-state condition that satisfies the steady-state value of k.

$$\left\{s\left[1+\lambda(n+\pi+r\right]-\lambda n\right\}f(k)=nk \tag{4.i}$$

where π and r are constant along the path (Levhari and Patinkin 1968, 720–1).

39 See also H.G. Johnson 1966.

40 Miguel Sidrauski was born in 1939 in Buenos Aires, Argentina, where he completed his early and undergraduate studies. Sidrauski entered graduate studies at the University of Chicago in 1963 and in 1966 completed his PHD with a dissertation on rational choice and monetary growth under the supervision of Hirofumi Uzawa and Milton Friedman. After completing his PHD, he was appointed as an assistant professor at MIT. Tragically, Sidrauski died of cancer in 1968 at the end of his second year at MIT. He was only twenty-eight years old. He was survived by his wife and two-month-old daughter.

41 Private saving = disposable income minus consumption; public saving = excess of taxes over government expenditure, and national saving = private savings plus public savings.

CHAPTER FIVE

1 The elasticity of substitution between factors is given as $Es = (dk/k)/d(w/r)/(w/r)$, where k is capital per labour ratio and w/r is the wage-rental ratio. If $Es > 1$, it implies that $P/Y \uparrow$ (increases) and $w/y \downarrow$ (decreases), so we have labor saving. If $Es < 1$, it implies that $P/Y \downarrow$ and $w/y \uparrow$, so we have capital saving. The ratios P/Y and w/y are the shares of profits and wages in national income.

2 Uzawa, in his article on neutral inventions, analyzes Harrod's neutrality using Robinson's invention classification. In fact, he called Harrod neutrality the Robinson theorem, which basically states that the technical invention represented by $F(K, L, t)$ is Harrod neutral if and only if the production function $F(K, L, t)$ is of the form $F(K, L, t) = G(k, A(t)L)$ with a positive function $A(t)$ (Uzawa 1961b, 119).

3 If K/Y is constant and $\pi > 0$, then technical progress is Harrod labour saving. If K/Y is constant and $\pi < 0$, then technical progress is Harrod capital saving, and $\pi = 0$ when K/Y is constant (H.G. Jones 1975, 168).

4 According to Black, "if a production function exists, and can be differentiated with respect to capital, this shows the effects of the rate of invest-

ment on the rate of increase of possible output, and thus generates a technical progress function. If a technical progress function exists, the relation between investment and the rate of growth of possible output may take a form which allows us to integrate it with respect to the rate of investment. In this case we can obtain a function relating the cumulative total investment, i.e., the capital stock, to the possible production, so that the process of integration yields a production function" (Black 1962, 166).

5 Phelps considers a very similar form of "general" production function in terms of aggregate output, $Q_t = B_0 e^{\mu t} J_t^{\alpha} N_t^{1-\alpha}$, where $e^{\mu t}$ is the vintage for the contemporary machines (Phelps 1962, 554).

6 The effective capital $J(t)$ can be expressed as the adding up of each vintage, v, using the integration form minus infinity (the past distant time) to time t, $J(t) = \int_{-\infty}^{t} e^{zv} I(v) dv$, where $z = [(\lambda/\alpha) + \delta]$, λ is the constant rate of technical progress and δ is the depreciation rate, respectively, as time proceeds. In the same way, the total output produced at time t, $Q(t)$, is equal to the sum of the outputs produced by machines of each different vintage and is given by the integration form $Q(t) = \int_{-\infty} Q_v(t) dv$. At every point t in time, there exist machines of every age, from those constructed in the far distant past to those constructed at the present moment (Solow 1962a and 1962b; Phelps 1962 and 1963).

7 Vintage models incorporate a specific transmission mechanism, which is the new investment, and play a strategic role in generating economic growth. Leif Johansen (1972) used production models with vintage framework by specifying ex-ante frontier technology for new units and short-run production possibilities for the sector as a whole, which defines the distinction between short-run efficiency and changes in technology when investing in new capacity. Technical change manifests itself by the change in the capacity distribution caused by the addition of new capacity and the scrapping of old. Productivity change is studied through change in capacity distribution over time. Johansen considers a "growth equation" (1972, 171–5) that captures the essence of change by allowing the identification of the effects of new capacity, scrapping of old capacity, and an increase in the technology of existing capacity.

8 "The elasticity of the limiting exponential growth path with respect to the investment ratio depends only on the capital elasticity of output, which is independent of the type of technical progress[;] … thus … the limiting long-run growth rate depends on the rate of technical progress and not on the type of progress" (Phelps 1962, 567).

9 The measurement of capital services is complicated and not as straightforward as the measurement of labour services because the consumer of a capital service is usually also the supplier of the service (Jorgenson and Griliches 1967).

10 The long form of the bias in the rate of growth of factor productivity is given using exponential parameters by substituting (5.46), (5.47), and

$$\frac{\Delta P^*}{P^*}-\frac{\Delta P}{P}=-w_I\frac{\Delta Q^*}{Q^*}-v_K\left[\frac{I}{\int_{-\infty}^{t}e^{-\delta(t-s)}\frac{Q^*(t)}{Q^*(s)}I(s)ds}-\frac{I}{\int_{-\infty}^{t}e^{-\delta(t-s)}I(s)ds}\right] \tag{5.49}$$

(Jorgenson and Griliches 1967, 258)

11 David Levhari is a professor emeritus of economics at the Hebrew University of Jerusalem, Israel, and a frequent member of public commissions on economic issues.

12 Eytan Sheshinski is a Sir Isaac Wolfson Professor of Public Finance at the Hebrew University of Jerusalem, Israel, and has been a visiting professor in the Department of Economics and Woodrow Wilson School at Princeton University since 1997. He was born in 1937 in Israel. He graduated with a BA in economics in 1961 and with an MA in economics and statistics from the Hebrew University of Jerusalem in 1963. He received his PHD from the Massachusetts Institute of Technology in 1966. In the past, Sheshinski has been an assistant professor at Harvard University and the Massachusetts Institute of Technology and a visiting professor at Stanford University, UC Berkeley, and Columbia University.

13 Professor Christian von Weizsäcker presented his research during a 1962–63 sojourn at MIT. This paper was later published as Kennedy 1964.

14 Think of *V1* as "labour" and *V2* as "capital."

15 In fact, the dual relations *(dF/dVi)/(dF/dVi)* = –*Wi/WJ* and *(dM/dWi)/(dM/dWi)* = –*Vi/VJ* hold (Samuelson 1965).

16 Amartya Sen was born in the village of Santinikeran in Bengal, East India, in 1933. His family is from Dhaka, which is now the capital of Bangladesh. His father was a professor of chemistry at Dhaka University. Sen received a BA in economics from the Presidency College in 1953 and then a BA, MA, and PHD in economics from Cambridge University. In Cambridge, he studied economics with both Piero Sraffa and Joan Robinson. After graduating from Trinity College, Cambridge, in 1959, he remained at Jadaupur University and Cambridge University. In 1963 he decided to leave Cambridge altogether and went to Delhi as professor of economics

at the Delhi School of Economics and at the University of Delhi. He taught in Delhi until 1971. In 1971 he returned to England, accepting a teaching position at the London School of Economics. Then, in 1977 he moved to Nuffield College, Oxford. Three years later, Sen became Drummond Professor of Political Economy, a position previously held by Edgeworth and Hicks. In 1987 Sen moved to the United States, becoming a professor of economics at Harvard University. In the late 1980s and early 1990s, he lectured in different famous American universities, including Stanford, Berkeley, Yale, Princeton, Harvard, UCLA, and the University of Texas at Austin. In 1998 Sen returned to England, where he became master of Trinity College in Cambridge. In 1998 he received the Nobel Prize in Economic Science.

17 Sen 1960 was reviewed by Hicks (1962).

18 Kenneth Arrow was born in New York City in 1921 to a middle-class family of Romanian-Jewish origin. His undergraduate education at City College in New York was made possible only by the existence of that excellent free institution and the financial sacrifices of his parents. His father, whose business was highly successful in the 1920s, had lost everything during the Depression of the 1930s. Kenneth graduated in 1940 with a BS in social science and a major in mathematics. Arrow intended to be a high school teacher, but with no employment prospects, he enrolled at Columbia University to study mathematical statistics with Harold Hotelling. In 1941 Arrow received an MA in mathematics and then went off to serve in the Second World War (during 1942–46, he served as a weather officer in the US Army Air Corps, rising to the rank of captain). He spent 1946–49 partly as a graduate student at Columbia University and partly as a research associate of the Cowles Commission for Research in Economics at the University of Chicago, where he had the rank of assistant professor of economics in 1948–49. In 1949 he was appointed assistant professor of economics and statistics at Stanford University and remained there until 1968. In 1968 he accepted a position at Harvard University but returned to Stanford in 1979. He received the John Bates Clark Medal of the American Economic Association in 1957. He was president of the Econometric Society in 1956 and the Institute of Management Sciences in 1963 and president-elect of the American Economic Association in 1972. In 1972 Arrow, jointly with John Hicks, won the Nobel Prize in Economic Science. It was awarded for "pioneering contributions to general equilibrium theory and welfare theory."

19 For further details, see Levhari 1966.

20 These conditions and the expression "social capability" were introduced for the first time by Ohkawa and Rosovsky (1973).

CHAPTER SIX

1 Joan Robinson was born Joan Maurice in Surrey, England, in 1903. Her father was a military general and, later in life, head of one of the colleges making up the University of London. Her mother was the daughter of a Cambridge University professor. Robinson attended St Paul's, a famous girls' school in London, where she studied history. Later she went to Girton College, Cambridge, where she studied economics. She spent a few years in India with her husband, economist Austin Robinson. From 1925, she spent more than half a century teaching and lecturing in Cambridge. Because Robinson was a woman, she did not become a full-time member of Cambridge University until 1948. In the 1930s, Robinson was an active participant in the "Cambridge Circus," a small group of economists helping Keynes to develop his ideas in his *General Theory*. She died in 1983.

2 Because the price of equipment is rising relative to wage rates. So for capitalists, using capital saving technologies is likely to be more convenient despite that they have in use labour-saving machines (J. Robinson 1952, 108–9).

3 Piero Sraffa was born in Turin, Italy, in 1898 into a wealthy and distinguished Jewish family. His father, Angelo Sraffa, was a well-known lawyer who both practiced his profession and taught commercial law in various Italian universities. Piero studied in his town and graduated at the University of Turin with a work on inflation in Italy during and after the First World War. His tutor was Luigi Einaudi, one of the most important Italian economists, a well-known specialist in public finance, and later a president of the Italian Republic. After graduation, Sraffa worked at an Italian bank, but he left this job in order to spend some time in England studying British monetary problems. From 1921 to 1922, he studied in London at the London School of Economics. In 1922 he was appointed director of the provincial labour department in Milan, then as professor of political economy in Perugia and later in Cagliari, Sardinia. As the Fascist government became gradually more repressive, Sraffa sought employment outside of Italy, and Keynes helped arrange a lectureship for him at Cambridge University. After a few years, Keynes created ex novo for him the charge of Marshall Librarian. Keynes also arranged for Sraffa

to edit the works of David Ricardo for the Royal Economic Society. Sraffa's collecting and editing of Ricardo's works, begun in 1931, turned out to be a twenty-year task, and the publication in ten volumes finally began in 1953. For this work, he received the Söderström Gold Medal of the Swedish Royal Academy of Sciences (a precursor to the Nobel Prize in Economic Science). In 1972, he was awarded an honorary doctorate by the Sorbonne in Paris, and in 1976 he received another one from Madrid's Complutense University. He died in 1983.

4 Inflation normally occurs when there is a fall in the market value or purchasing power of money, which is equivalent to a rise in the general level of prices. Deflation is the opposite phenomenon to inflation.

5 A financial instrument is called a contract based on the combination of capital assets, which serves as a medium of exchange or as a unit of measurement for goods. Based on this definition, money is nothing more or less than an agreement (either explicit or implicit) among a community to use something like a medium of exchange that serves as an intermediary market good. The money or the agreement can be easily added up. Here comes the difference with the aggregate value of capital.

6 For further details, see Sraffa 1926.

7 The most standard definition of the paradox of thrift, which was proposed by John Maynard Keynes, states that if everyone saves more money during a deep recession, aggregate demand will drop, which will lower total savings in the population. It emphasizes that the attempts by households to save a greater proportion of their income may not lead to an increase in the overall level of savings. The paradox is simply explained by analyzing increased savings in an economy. If a population, during a given period of time, saves more money than the average savings (the marginal propensity to save increases), then total for companies will decline. This decrease in economic growth means fewer raises or even recession, which translates to the population's total savings remaining the same or even declining because of lower incomes and a weaker economy.

8 See also J. Robinson 1955.

9 See also Harcourt 1976 and Harcourt 1969.

10 David Gawen Champernowne was born in 1912 into an Oxford academic family. He went to school at Winchester College, and from there, he began as a scholar at King's College, Cambridge. While still an undergraduate, he published his first paper (on "normal numbers"). His academic career was spread between the London School of Economics

(1936–38), Oxford (1945–59), and Cambridge (1938–40 and 1959–78). After academic work at Cambridge and the London School of Economics, during the war (1940–41), he worked in the prime minister's statistical department to supply quantitative information to help the government make decisions. Later he worked with John Jewkes at the Ministry of Aircraft Production's Department of Statistics and Programming. During his academic career, he proved to be a genuine pioneer in both economic theory and statistics. Champernowne died in Budleigh Salterton, Devon, in August 2000.

11 A different way to formulate the chain index method of measuring capital is by denoting the cost per unit of capital of equipment type *Ts* as C(s, R, W), where *R* is the interest rate and *W* the wage rate. For all *s*, the cost C is given as

$$C(s, R, W) = C(s+I, Rs, W) \qquad (6.a)$$

where *Rs* indicates the rate of interest at which the equipment of type *Ts* and *Ts+I* are competitive. The same definition can be adopted with a continuous range of equipment *Tz*, with *z* a continuous variable. The unit of capital in a discrete series of selected basic equipment is such that for all *z* and *W*

$$\left\{\frac{\partial}{\partial_Z} C(z, R, W)\right\} R = R_Z \qquad (6.b)$$

where, *Rz* is the interest rate at which *Tz* is competitive (Champernowne 1953, 125).

12 "Wicksell process" or "Wicksell effect" involves changes in the value of the capital stock associated with different interest rates arising from either inventory revaluation of the same physical stock resulting from new capital prices or differences in the physical stock goods. Wicksell effect has the interest rate depending on exogenous technical properties of capital in the models with heterogeneous capital goods.

13 The curve of production function depicted in appendix iii by Champernowne was based on Robinson's theory of capital (J. Robinson 1953; Champernowne 1958, 242).

14 Wicksell 1934 [English version], (1911, Original version published in Sweden).

15 *Malleable* means that one kind of machine can be instantaneously and costlessly transformed into another kind or that capital goods can be substituted for labour and other inputs in the production of homogenous output. The "malleability of capital" in the neoclassical context was necessary in order to calculate the marginal productivity of capital.

16 To calculate the rate of return in perpetuity, a stock of machines at the new level $V + 1/v$ is required, with annual production of machines rising by d/v and a permanent addition of d men to the machine-building sector. The machine sector requires n/v men to operate permanently on the new machines. They produce a flow of consumable goods nc/v higher than the depreciation rate of $b(d + n/v)$. The society as a whole, sacrificing b units of consumption, realizes a perpetual flow of $nc/v - b(d+n/v)$ units of consumable goods. The rate of return in the second period is given as $r = (nc/vb - n/v - d)$ (Solow 1963, 33–4).

17 $(Yb - Ya)$ is supposed to be a vector whose components are all zero except for the first one, which is positive.

18 Paul Samuelson was born in 1915 in Gary, Indiana, but his parents soon moved to Chicago, where he was educated in the Chicago public school system. He received a BA from the University of Chicago in 1935 and an MA in 1936 and a DPhil in 1941 from Harvard University. He came to MIT in 1940 as an assistant professor of economics and was appointed associate professor in 1944. He served as a staff member of the radiation laboratory from 1944 to 1945 and was a professor of international economic relations (part-time) at the Fletcher School of Law and Diplomacy in 1945. Samuelson was appointed a full professor at MIT in 1947 at the age of thirty-two. He was a Guggenheim Fellow from 1948 to 1949. In 1947 Samuelson received the first John Bates Clark Medal from the American Economic Association, awarded annually to the most promising economist under the age of forty. He was a Social Science Research Council predoctoral fellow from 1935 to 1937, a member of the Society of Fellows, Harvard University, 1937–40, and a Ford Foundation Research Fellow from 1958 to 1959. He received honorary doctor of law degree from the University of Chicago and Oberlin College in 1961 and from Indiana University and East Anglia University in 1966. His *Economics: An Introductory Analysis*, first published in 1948, has become the bestselling economics textbook of all time; it has sold more than a million copies and has been translated into many languages around the world. Paul Samuelson's many contributions to neoclassical economic theory were recognized with a Nobel Memorial Prize in 1970.

19 The difference between a jelly world and heterogeneous capital goods consists mostly in the following facts: in a jelly world or in a one-capital-good world, there is a marginal process of substitution of capital for labour, whereas in a world with heterogeneous capital goods, there are

different equilibrium stationary states, each with its own past and future expectation. In other words, the process consists in passing from one state to another and not on substituting capital for labour in historical time (Harcourt 1976).

20 It is also assumed that the alpha good is homogeneous independently of age. This means that physical depreciation is always directly proportional to the physical stock of alpha, $K\alpha$. If the new gross alpha capital goods is denoted by $G\alpha$, the net capital formation is given as $K\alpha = G\alpha - \delta K\alpha$, where δ is the rate of capital depreciation.

21 In the neoclassical parable or the Austrian simple model, labour occurs consistently before production of final output. So when the structure of production is extended, as going from a short period of production denoted *Ia* to a longer period *Ib* and to a still longer period *Ic*, each unit of consumption good is produced with successively less total labour – from, say, ten units of labour, down to nine, down to eight units of labour. In going from *Ia* to *Ic*, the average period of production rises and reduces the total labour needed per unit of output. By going from *Ia* to *Ib*,the society accumulates more goods to fill the long period, *Ib*, and the society consumes more with a lower interest rate. At *Ic*, the lowering of the interest rate leads directly to the extension of the period of production and to the conventional characteristics of the neoclassical capital theory parables founded by the Austrian school. The Austrian school maintained the position that the capital intensity of any industry is due to the roundaboutness of the particular industry and consumer demand.

CHAPTER SEVEN

1 Simon Kuznets was born into a Jewish family in Pinsk, Russia (now in Belarus), and was educated in Kharkiv, Ukraine. He moved to the United States in 1922 to join his father, who had left Russia for the United States before the First World War. He was educated at Columbia University, receiving his BSC in 1923, MA in 1924, and PHD in 1926. Between 1925 and 1926, he spent a year and a half as research fellow of the Social Science Research Council. It was this work that led to his book *Secular Movements in Production and Prices*, published in 1930. As professor of economics and statistics, he taught at the University of Pennsylvania, part-time, from 1931 to 1936 and full-time from 1936 to 1954. Between 1927 and 1960, he worked as a member of the staff of the National Bureau of Economic Research. He investigated and worked mainly on

national income and capital formation in the United States. As chairman of the Social Science Research Council Committee on Economic Growth (1949–68), he worked primarily on a comparative quantitative analysis of economic growth of nations. In 1954 Kuznets moved to Johns Hopkins University, where he was professor of political economy until 1960. From 1960 until his retirement in 1971, Kuznets taught at Harvard University. He was also associate director of the Bureau of Planning and Statistics and director of research. After the war, he held different positions, such as chairman of the Falk Project for Economic Research in Israel during 1953 to 1963; member of the Board of Trustees and honorary chairman, Maurice Falk Institute for Economic Research in Israel, since 1963; and chairman, Social Science Research Council Committee on the Economy of China, 1961–70. Kuznets won the 1971 Nobel Prize in Economics for his empirically founded interpretation of economic growth which has led to new and deepened insight into the economic and social structure and process of development.Simon Kuznets died on 8 July 1985, at the age of eighty-four.

2 Kuznets 1965, 97–141. The six characteristics of modern economic growth are summarized in an article published in 1973 in *The American Economic Review*, which contains the lecture Kuznets delivered in Stockholm in December 1971 when he received the Nobel Prize in Economic Science. The first characteristic is the high rates of growth of per capita product and of population that developed countries have experienced in the first decades after the Second World War. Second, the rate of rise in productivity (i.e., of output per unit of all inputs) is high even when there are included inputs of other factors in addition to labour. Third, the rate of structural transformation of economy is high as a result of the shift from agriculture to non-agricultural pursuits and from industry to the service sector. In fact, the share of the labor force in the agricultural sector in the United States declined from 53.5% in 1870 to 7% in 1960.. Fourth, the important structures of society and its ideology have changed rapidly. Urbanization and secularization are part of the modern society. Fifth, the developed countries, thanks to the increased power of technology in transport and communication, have the propensity to reach out to the rest of the world. Sixth, the spread of modern economic growth is mainly limited in the industrialized countries, and the economic performance in countries counting for three-quarters of the world population still falls short of the minimum levels feasible with the potential of modern technology. (Kuznets 1973, 248–9).

3 An important finding of Kuznets (1955) is the decline in the share of net capital formation and the related movements of capital-output ratio (rising from 1869 to 1888 and 1909 to 1928 and declining thereafter). In common sense, the decline in net capital formation can be explained in terms of deficient investment demand and the declining of capita-output ratio can be treated as determined by technological changes. Kuznets rejects this position, however, pointing out that capital-output ratio is determined, in part, by industrial structure of the economy and that the industrial structure is capable of change to accommodate factor supplies. Moreover, a variety of techniques is available to produce any given good, and the technique selected will reflect the factor supplies. Kuznets tends to escape from this position, considering new technology on the capital-output as independent of factor supplies. In fact, he treats the capital-output ratio as a variable responsive to phenomena other than technical change.

4 Later Deininger and Squire (1996) found that the coefficients *b* and *c* in that regression are now the wrong signs for an inverted U, and, indeed, the coefficients are not significant.

5 Arthur Lewis was born in 1915 in St Lucia, a small island in the Caribbean archipelago, then still a British territory. Lewis completed his secondary education at the age of fourteen. He spent the intervening four years as a junior clerk in public service. At age eighteen, he enrolled at the London School of Economics (LSE) to obtain a bachelor of commerce degree. Lewis obtained his BSc in 1937 and PHD in 1940 at the London School of Economics. An outstanding scholar, Lewis was appointed assistant lecturer during his tenure at LSE, the first appointment of a black person made by the prestigious institution. He lectured the first-year course on economic analysis. He was appointed full professor at Manchester University in 1948 at the age of thirty-five. In 1959 he was appointed vice chancellor of the University of the West Indies. In 1963 he was appointed a full professor in the department of economics at Princeton University (a position in which he would remain until his retirement in 1983). In 1970 he became director of the Caribbean Development Bank. In 1979 he won the Nobel Prize in Economic Sciences, becoming the first black person to win a Nobel Prize in a category other than peace. He died on 15 June 1991 in Bridgetown, Barbados.

6 Gunnar Myrdal was born in Gustaf, Dalarna, Sweden, on 6 December 1898. He graduated from the Law School of Stockholm University in 1923 and began practicing law while continuing his studies at the university. He married Alva Reimer in 1924 and received his JD in economics in

1927. From 1925 to 1929, he studied for periods in Germany and Britain, followed by his first trip to the United States in 1929–30 as a Rockefeller Fellow. Myrdal became an associate professor at the Institute of International Studies in Geneva (1930–31). In 1933 he was appointed to the Lars Hierta Chair of Political Economy and Public Finance at the University of Stockholm as the successor of Gustav Cassel. In addition to his teaching activities, Professor Myrdal was active in Swedish politics and was elected to the Senate in 1934 as member of the Social Democratic Party. In 1938 the Carnegie Corporation of New York commissioned him to direct a study of the African American community. The material that he collected and interpreted was published in 1944 as *An American Dilemma: The Negro Problem and Modern Democracy*. Returning back to Sweden in 1942, he was reelected to the Swedish Senate, served as member of the Board of the Bank of Sweden, and was chairman of the Post-War Planning Commission. From 1945 to 1947, he was Sweden's minister of commerce. Then, from 1947 to 1957, Myrdal was executive secretary of the United Nations Economic Commission for Europe. In 1974 Myrdal, together with Friedrich Hayek, was awarded the Nobel Prize in Economics "for their pioneering work in the theory of money and economic fluctuations and for their penetrating analysis of the interdependence of economic, social, and institutional phenomena." Myrdal died on 17 May 1987, in Stockholm.

7 Myrdal was confronted with the problems of development when he was working (1947–57) as executive secretary of the United Nations Economic Commission for Europe (ECE) and United Nations regional economic commission for the Far East (ECAFE) and Latin America (ECLA). His first major works in development were published in 1956, *An International Economy: Problems and Prospects*, stemming from a lecture at Columbia University in May 1954, and *Economic Theory and Underdeveloped Regions*, derived from lectures at the Central Bank of Egypt in 1956 and published separately one year later.

8 Myrdal (1957a, 55) in his original work, *Economic Theory and Under-Developed Regions*, uses the term "backwash effects," but here the term will be used as "backward effects."

9 Walt Rostow was born in New York City to a Russian Jewish immigrant family on 7 October, 1916. He attended Yale University, graduating at age nineteen and completing his PHD dissertation in 1940. He also won a Rhodes Scholarship to study at Balliol College, Oxford. After completing his education, he started teaching economics at Columbia University.

During the Second World War, Rostow served as a major in the Office of Strategic Services (OSS) under William Donovan. In 1945 Rostow joined the State Department in Washington as assistant chief of the German-Austrian division. Later he was involved in the development of the Marshall Plan. From 1946 to 1947, he returned to Oxford to teach as the Harmsworth Professor of American History. In 1958 Rostow became a speech writer for President Dwight Eisenhower. When Kennedy became president in 1961, he appointed Rostow as deputy to his national security assistant, McGeorge Bundy. Later that year, he became chairman of the State Department's policy planning council. In early 1966 he was named special assistant for National Security Affairs, where he was a main figure in developing the government's policy in the Vietnam War and where he remained until February 1969. After his government service, he accepted a teaching position in political economy at the University of Texas, where he continued to teach and to write books on history, economics, and international affairs. He continued to teach history and economics until his death in 2003 at the age of eighty-six.

10 According to Rosovsky, "Rostow is without a doubt the most famous economic historian of our age. His works have been translated into many languages; practically all books on economic development and history cite him extensively; he has been lavishly praised by Cambridge economists and the London *Economist*; and finally, the term 'take-off' has become a standard part of our mid-century vocabulary. No other living economic historian occupies a similar position" (Rosovsky 1965).

11 In 1960, shortly after the publication of *Stages,*the International Economic Association (IEA) invited eighteen distinguished economists to a conference at Konstanz to discuss Rostow's work. Three years later, a book edited by Rostow, *Economics of Take-off into Sustained Growth,* was published (at one time, it was referred to simply as the "Green Book"). For details, see Rostow 1963, 471–2.

12 Hollis B. Chenery was born in 1919, in Richmond, Virginia, and grew up in Virginia and Pelham Manor, New York. Hollis's father was an oil and gas magnate, and it was clear Hollis would never have to work a day in his life. Instead, he chose to study and earned his bachelor's degree from the Universities of Arizona. He was an Army Air Corps officer in the Second World War and received master's degrees from the California Institute of Technology and the University of Virginia. He was awarded a PHD by Harvard in 1950. Chenery joined the US Agency for International Development in 1961 and rose to become an assistant administrator. He

left in 1965. He was a professor of economics at Stanford from 1952 to 1961, a Guggenheim fellow in 1961, and a professor of economics at Harvard from 1965 to 1970 and again after leaving the World Bank. Chenery was the World Bank's vice president for development policy from 1972 to 1982. In 1977 the bank, which then administered $40 billion in loans, made a fundamental change in its development strategy by trying to focus more on projects meeting the needs of the very poorest people in underdeveloped countries. Chenery made several other career stops along his life: petroleum engineer, meteorologist, real estate investor, banker, and horse breeder. Chenery died in 1996 in Santa Fe, New Mexico, at the age of seventy-seven.

13 The twenty-seven structural variables are saving; investment; capital inflow; government revenue; tax revenue; education expenditure; school enrollment ratio; private consumption and government consumption; food consumption; primary, industry, utilities, and services share in production; total exports; primary exports; manufacturing exports; services exports; imports; labour allocation between primary, industry, and services; urbanization; birth and death rates; and the share of the highest 20% and lowest 40% in personal distribution of income (Chenery and Taylor 1968 and Chenery and Syrquin 1975).

14 $P = p(Xm/Xa), p' > 0$ is a function of the relative outputs of agricultural and manufactured goods when the latter serves as a numeraire. A sufficient, but not necessary, condition for this assumption is that all individuals in the society have the same homothetic preference map (Harris and Todaro 1970, 128–9).

15 An illustration of the Harris-Todaro model is the following: Supposing the urban wage is twice the rural wage ($W_m = 2W_a$), then migration will continue as long as the expected urban wage is greater than the rural wage ($M_t > 0$ if $pW_m > W_a$); as long as the probability of finding a job in the urban sector is greater than 0.5 ($p > 0.5$), the expected urban wage is greater than the rural wage ($pW_m > W_a$), and migration continues ($M_t > 0$).

16 Albert Otto Hirschman was born in Berlin, Germany, in April 1915. He studied at the University of Berlin from 1932 to 1933, when he moved to France, where he studied at the École des Hautes Etudes Commerciales and Institut de Statistique, Sorbonne, in Paris from 1933 to 1935. He then studied at the London School of Economics from 1935 to 1936 as an International Student Service Fellow. He attended the University of Trieste (Italy) from 1936 to 1938, where he earned his doctorate in

economics in 1938. While completing his education, Hirschman became involved in the Second World War in Europe. He fought in the French Army in 1940, and in 1941 he immigrated to the United States, where he became a naturalized citizen. Hirschman was a Rockefeller Fellow in international economics at the University of California, Berkeley, from 1941 to 1943 before joining the US Army. He served in the army from 1943 to 1945 and then served as economist for the Federal Reserve Board from 1946 to 1952. Hirschman moved to Colombia to serve as financial advisor to the National Planning Board of Colombia from 1952 to 1954. It was in Colombia that Hirschman began to formulate his better-known theories of development. He then returned to the United States in 1956, accepting a position at Yale University from 1956 to 1957 and continuing as a visiting research professor of economics until 1958. He moved to Columbia University in 1958, where he was professor of international economic relations until 1964. During this time, he was also director of the Latin America Project of the Twentieth Century Fund from 1960 to 1963. Hirschman spent the next ten years of his academic career at Harvard University, where he was professor of political economy from 1964 to 1974. In 1974 he accepted a position as a professor in the School of Social Science at the Institute for Advanced Study in Princeton, New Jersey. In 1985 he became an emeritus professor. In honour of his achievements, the Institute for Advanced Study in Princeton established the Albert O. Hirschman Chair in Economics in May 2000.

17 The term "late latecomers" includes countries of Latin America and Asia in the twentieth century to differentiate them from the other "late" European industrialized countries of the nineteenth century like Germany, Italy, and Russia.

18 For more about the Singer-Prebisch thesis see the work of Prebisch (1950 and 1959) and Singer (1949 and 1950).

19 For more about the development of structuralist models see Dutt and Ros 2003.

CHAPTER EIGHT

1 In early 1960s none of the theorists of the enterprise were interested in applying the "flow of information technology" or "industrial knowledge" in economics. Only in the late 1980s did the "industrial knowledge" became ground of economists' theories in explaining growth and the ambiguities of a competitive market.

2 Paul Michael Romer was born in 1955 and is the son of former Colorado governor Roy Romer. Romer earned a BS in physics in 1977 and a PHD in economics in 1983, both from the University of Chicago. Paul is a professor of economics in the Graduate School of Business at Stanford University and a Senior Fellow of the Hoover Institution. Before joining Stanford's faculty in 1996, he taught at a number of schools, including the University of Chicago, the University of Rochester, and the University of California at Berkeley. In 2002 Paul was awarded the Horst Claus Recktenwald Prize in Economics for outstanding achievement and contributions to the field. He also was awarded the Distinguished Teaching Award at Stanford University's Graduate School of Business in 1999 and elected a fellow of the American Academy of Arts and Sciences in 2000. He is a fellow of the Econometric Society and a research associate with the National Bureau of Economic Research, and he was a member of the National Research Council Panel on Criteria for Federal Support of Research and Development, a member of the Executive Council of the American Economics Association, and a fellow of the Center for Advanced Study in the Behavioral Sciences.

3 The standard definition of a concave function is that a function $f(x) = f(x1,...xn)$ defined on a convex set S is concave in S if $f((1 - \lambda)\, x^\circ + \lambda x) \geq (1 - \lambda)\, f(x^\circ) + \lambda f(x)$ for all $x^\circ, x \varepsilon S$, and all $\lambda \varepsilon (0.1)$.

4 As mentioned earlier in this section, Romer's 1983 doctoral dissertation was never published, but the idea was taken from here and is believed to be the basis of his article of 1986.

5 Considering the growth rate of research technology A, evolving as

$$A = \delta H_A A^\phi \quad (8.i)$$

where $\Phi = 1$ makes equation (8.10) valid. In fact, for $\Phi < 1$, the rate of growth is given as:

$$A = \delta H_A A^{\phi-1} \quad (8.j)$$

so that Y in this case will be

$$(\alpha - \beta)\, A = (\alpha + \beta)\delta H_A A^{\phi-1} \quad (8.k)$$

As time goes on, $Y^\cdot$ falls to zero because δ is constant and $(\Phi - 1)$ is negative. Asymptotically, as A tends to zero, the rate of growth Y also goes to zero. In short, if $\Phi < 1$, there is no endogenous growth. If $\Phi > 1$, A goes to infinity (by integrating the differential equation [8.10]). For time series T, A tends to infinity as $t \to T$, and then output $Y^\cdot$ goes to infinity (at the same time T). Therefore, equation (8.10) is valid only in the case of $\Phi = 1$ (Solow 2000, 150–4).

6 The ratio of consumption/output is given as $C/Y = 1 - K^{\cdot}/Y = 1 - K^{\cdot}/K(K/Y)$.

7 In the consumer's preference, the rate of growth of current utility $(1 - \sigma)g$ must be less than the discount rate ρ.

8 Robert Lucas was born in 1937 in Yakima, Washington, the oldest child of Robert Emerson Lucas and Jane Templeton Lucas. The family restaurant (the Lucas Ice Creamery) went bankrupt, and during the Second World War, the family moved to Seattle. Lucas attended Seattle Public Schools, graduating from Roosevelt High School in 1955. He obtained a scholarship from the University of Chicago, where he majored in history. He then obtained a Woodrow Wilson Doctoral Fellowship and entered the graduate program in history at the University of California. Recognizing that economic factors were the key forces moving history, Lucas shifted his focus to economic history. He returned to Chicago, where he started studying economics. In the fall of 1960 he began to study Milton Friedman's price theory sequence. His PHD dissertation, awarded in 1964, used data from US manufacturing to estimate elasticities of substitution between capital and labour. In 1963 Richard Cyert, the new dean of the Graduate School of Industrial Administration at Carnegie Institute of Technology (now Carnegie-Mellon University), offered Lucas a faculty position, where he stayed until 1974. In 1974 he returned to Chicago as a faculty member, and in 1980 he became the John Dewey Distinguished Service Professor. Since 1982 (after a separation), he has lived with Nancy Stokey (his colleague at Chicago), and both have collaborated in papers on growth theory, public finance, and monetary theory. In 1995 Lucas received the Nobel Prize in Economic Science, primarily for his contribution to rational expectations and money neutrality.

9 Internal knowledge spillover is positive learning or knowledge externalities between programs or plants within a production organization.

10 Sérgio Rebelo was born in Viseu, Portugal, in October 1959. He received a "Licenciatura" in economics from the Portuguese Catholic University in 1985, a Master in Operations Research from Instituto Superior Técnico in 1987, and a PHD in economics from the University of Rochester in the United States in 1989. His first job was at Northwestern University. After two years at Northwestern, he decided to return to Portugal, to the Portuguese Catholic University and the Bank of Portugal. Two years later, Rebelo received the Olin Fellowship at the National Bureau of Economic Research (NBER), which allowed him to spend a full year doing

research at the NBER in Boston. While he was in Boston, the University of Rochester offered him a tenured position. He is currently the Tokai Bank Distinguished Professor of International Finance at the Kellogg School of Management, Northwestern University. He is also a fellow of two important research networks in economics, the National Bureau of Economic Research in the United States and the Center for Economic Policy Research in Europe. Professor Rebelo has served as a consultant to the World Bank, the International Monetary Fund, the Board of Governors of the Federal Reserve System, the European Central Bank, the McKinsey Global Institute, and other organizations.

11 Using the Cobb-Douglas function, the consumption/physical investment could be written as $F_1 = A_1 K_1^{(1-\alpha 1)} (N_1 H)^{\alpha 1}$.

12 In the same way, using the Cobb-Douglas function, the human capital investment is given as $F_2 = A_2 K_2^{(1-\alpha 2)} (N_2 H)^{\alpha 2}$.

13 $w/[R(\tau) - 1 + \delta k2]$

14 In a neoclassical growth model, the burden of an unanticipated income tax or an increase in the income tax rate lowers the rate of return on capital and produces a shift in the level of the steady-state path but does not affect the steady-state growth rate. During the transition period to the steady-state path, an increase in the income tax τ causes the growth rate to slow down. In fact, from the production function and the growth rate of consumption per labour unit, we have that an inclusion of the income tax rate,

$$\frac{\dot{c}(t)}{c(t)} = \sigma^{-1}\left[(1-\tau)A\alpha k(t)^{\alpha-1} - \rho\right] \quad (8.u)$$

causes a decrease in the rate of growth immediately, but, in terms of per labour units, it eventually goes to zero (during the steady state).

15 Per definition a spillover is an action taken by one person or firm that affects another person or firm.

CHAPTER NINE

1 Gene Grossman was born in New York on December 1955. He received his BA in economics from Yale University in 1976 and his PHD from the Massachusetts Institute of Technology in 1980. Professor Grossman joined the faculty of Princeton University in 1980 and holds a joint appointment in the Department of Economics and the Woodrow Wilson School of Public and International Affairs. He was an assistant professor of economics and international affairs at Princeton University from

1980 to 1985. Then from 1985 to 1988, he became an associate professor of economics and international affairs at the same university. Since 1992 Grossman has served as the Jacob Viner Professor of International Economics at Princeton University and was also was chair of the Department of Economics from 2002 to 2005. Professor Grossman has received numerous professional honours and awards, including the Harry G. Johnson Award from the Canadian Economics Association and fellowships from the Alfred P. Sloan Foundation and the John Simon Guggenheim Memorial Foundation. He was elected a fellow of the Econometric Society in 1992 and a fellow of the American Academy of Arts and Sciences in 1997. He is a research associate of the National Bureau of Economic Research and of the Center for Economic Policy Research.

2 Elhanan Helpman was born in March 1946 into a Jewish family in Jalal-Abad in the Fergana Valley, in the former Soviet Union. His family moved to Poland, where he attended a Jewish school. Later his family emigrated to Israel, where he completed elementary and high school. Initially he wanted to study engineering, but during his military service (1963–66), he changed his mind and decided to study economics. He graduated with a BA in economics and statistics from Tel Aviv University in 1969. He continued his education at Tel Aviv University and graduated with an MA in economics in 1971. He enrolled at Harvard University in 1971 and graduated with a PHD in economics in 1974. He then returned to Israel, where he was a lecturer and later a university professor from 1974 to 2004 at Tel Aviv University. Since 1997 he has been a professor of economics at Harvard University. Professor Helpman has received numerous honours and awards, including the Mahalanobis Memorial Medal from the Indian Econometric Society in 1990 and the Israel Prize in 1991. Helpman has been a member of the advisory board of the Bank of Israel, the Council for National Planning, and the National Council for Research and Development.

3 In equilibrium, arbitrage opportunities between the equity and the bond market cannot exist by definition. The no-arbitrage condition accordingly reads $\pi + v' = rv$. It equates the returns on equities to the returns on bonds of the same size. It should be noticed that the no-arbitrage condition results if one differentiates both sides of the firm value with respect to time. The no-arbitrage condition accordingly implies that firms are valued according to their fundamentals (it can be readily shown that the derivation of v with respect to time requires the Leibnitz rule twice). The dynamic evolution of v can be readily derived from the no-arbitrage

condition, from the expression for operating profits $\pi = (1 - \beta)/N$, and from the relation $r = p$ (Solow 2000, 155–71).

4 The business stealing effect is when a given firm raises its own profits by taking away some of the profits of rival firms.

5 Theo S. Eicher received his BA in Chinese studies and economics from Grinnell College in 1988 and his MA in economics from Columbia University in New York in 1991. His PHD dissertation in 1994 from Columbia University was about endogenous human capital and technological change. Eicher has been at the University of Washington in Seattle since 1994, as assistant professor of economics (1994–2000), associate professor (2000–06), and currently as professor and Robert R. Richards Distinguished Scholar. He is also the director of the UW Center for Economic Policy Research and a research professor at the IFO Institute of Economic Research at the University of Munich in Germany. In the past, Eicher has held visiting positions as German Science Foundation Mercator Research Professor at the University of Munich and as a visiting professor at Barcelona University, Zurich University (ETH), GREQAM (Universite de la Mediterranee Marseille), Tuebingen University, and University of Oxford (Nuffield College).

6 Human capital H is written as an intensive form, $F[Ut, Et] = f[Ut, Et]\, Et$. From here, we can get the first-order conditions (Eicher 1996, 132).

7 Paul S. Segerstrom received his BA in economics and mathematics magna cum laude from Brandeis University in 1979 and his MA in economics from Brown University in 1981. He obtained a PHD in 1985 from the University of Rochester with a dissertation in creative destruction and stochastic games. Segerstrom is currently a Tore Browaldh Professor of International Economics at Stockholm School of Economics.

8 Under certain conditions involving tax rates, the system lies on its balanced growth path, which is represented by four equations:

a) intertemporal optimality $\frac{(1-\beta)}{\kappa(l)}(\frac{C}{Y}) = \frac{1-\tau_w}{1-\tau_c}$;

b) Euler equation $\psi = \frac{1}{1-\gamma(1+\eta)}\left\{(1-\tau_k)(1-\beta)(\frac{Y}{K}) - \rho\right\}$

c) resource constraint $\psi = [(1-g_p-g_c)-(\frac{C}{Y})](\frac{Y}{K}) - \rho]$

d) and production function $(\frac{Y}{K}) = (\alpha g_p^{\beta})^{1/(1-\beta)}(1-l)^{\varphi/(2-\beta)}$ (Turnovsky 2000).

9 Costas Azariadis was born in Athens, Greece, in 1943. He attended the National Technical University in Athens and received a degree in chemical engineering in 1969. He then attended Carnegie Mellon University, receiving an MBA in 1971 and his PHD in 1975. Azariadis's first academic appointment was as an assistant professor at Brown University between 1973 and 1977, where he was tenured in 1977 and promoted to full professor in 1983, after which he moved to the University of Pennsylvania. In 1992 he moved to UCLA. There he served as the director of UCLA's Program for Dynamic Economics from 1993 to 1997 and again from 2000 to 2006. In addition, Azariadis has held brief visiting positions all over the world.

10 Allan Drazen received his PHD from MIT in 1976. His primary fields of interest are political economy and international economics. His research includes political budget cycles, models of democratization, and political economy of development. He is currently a professor of economics at the University of Maryland as well as Hebrew University of Jerusalem and also a member of NBER.

11 Scale factor is described as $At = A\ (ktxt,xt)$.

12 There is also another sequence that satisfies equation (9.114) and yields $(kt + 1) = s[f'(kt), (1 - \tau t)\ w(kt)/(1 + \lambda(xt)\ \tau t,w(kt + 1)]\ (2 - \tau t)$ (Azariades and Drazen, 1990, 515).

13 As said by Howitt, when the population rises, so does the rate of technological progress and the growth rate of output per person. A larger population stimulates not only the supply of R&D workers but also the demand for their services by increasing the size of the market that can be captured by a successful innovator. The combined effect of these two forces on growth is referred to as the "scale effect" (Howitt 1999, 715).

14 Alwyn Young was educated at Cornell, Tufts University, and Columbia. He holds two PHDs, one in economics and another in law and diplomacy. From 1990 to 1995, Young was assistant professor at MIT's Sloan School of Management, and then from 1995 to 1997, he was a professor of economics at Boston University. In 1997 Young was appointed the Joseph Sondheimer Professor of International Economics and Finance at the University of Chicago. Later he was a professor of economics and the Leili and Johannes Huth Fellow at the London School of Economics in the United Kingdom. Young's research interests include productivity growth and international trade, and he is well known for his pioneering work on growth in the East Asian economies and, more recently, on the economics of AIDS in Africa.

15 For $(\theta - 1)/\phi > 1$, the products are improved in equilibrium.

CHAPTER TEN

1 According to the neoclassical theory of growth, a new technology is embodied in capital equipment when it allows an increase in output from the same quantity of input but requires the construction of new capital goods before the knowledge can be made effective (see chapter 5 in this book).

2 A random event X is assumed to be governed by a Poissen process with a certain arrival rate z, which mathematically means that time T is what we have to wait for in order for X to occur. T is a random variable whose distribution is exponential with parameter z: $F(T) = \text{Pr}ob\ (T) = 1 - e^{-zt}$, so the probability density of T is $f(T) = F'\ (T) = ze^{-zt}$, which is the probability that the event will occur some time within the short interval between T and $T + dt$ and is approximately equal to $ze^{-zt}\, dt$. Thus, z is the probability per unit of time that the event will occur now or the "flow probability" of events (for more details, see Lambert 1985).

3 A description of the business cycle is found in Schumpeter (1942). According to Aghion and Howitt, "However, the emergence in the 1980s of real business cycle literature, emphasizing productivity shocks as a main driving force behind cyclical fluctuations, called into question the traditional division of macroeconomic theory between trend and cycles and suggested a return to the Schumpeterian view of growth and cycles as a unified phenomenon" (Aghion and Howitt 1998, 233).

4 Philippe Aghion was born in Paris, France, in August 1956. He received his BA in mathematics from the École Normale Supérieure in Paris. In 1981 he received a Diplome d'Études Approfondies d'Économie Mathématique from the University of Paris I. In 1983 he was studying for a doctoral program (third cycle) in economic mathematics at the University of Paris I, Pantheon-Sorbonne. Finally, in 1987 he received his PHD in economics from Harvard University. From 1987 to 1989, Aghion was an assistant professor at Massachusetts Institute of Technology. From 1990 to 1991, he was deputy chief economist at EBRD in London, and from 1992 to 1996, he was an official fellow at Nuffield College in Oxford. From 1996 to 2000, Aghion was a professor of economics at the University College London (UCL), and in 2000 he moved to the United States to teach economics at Harvard University.

5 Peter Wilkinson Howitt was born in 1946 in Canada. He received his BA from McGill University in 1968 and his MA in economics from the University of Western Ontario in 1969. Howitt received his PHD from Northwestern University (Illinois) in 1973. His dissertation was about the theory of monetary dynamics. He started his academic career as assistant professor at the University of Western Ontario in 1972. From 1977 to 1981, he was an associate professor of economics at the same university, and in 1981 he became a full professor, a position he held until 1996. From 1996 to 2000, Howitt was a professor of economics at Ohio State University, and from 2000 to the present, he has been a professor of economics and the Lyn Crost Professor of Social Sciences at Brown University. Howitt and Aghion are the creators of the modern Schumpeterian approach to the theory of economic growth.

6 Even the conclusions are, at least apparently, divergent: the model of Aghion and Howitt (1998, Ch. 4) accepts all the fundamental premises in the work of Pissarides except the technical progress that is assumed to be incorporated in machines. Moreover, Aghion and Howitt extend the model of Pissarides in an economy where growth is endogenous.

7 The contributions of both Rothworn (1999) and Gordon (1995) use the same tools as Layard, Nickell, and Jackman (1991). Furthermore, Daveri and Tabellini (1997) use the same instruments in their study about the relation between growth, unemployment, and taxation: the idea is that taxing the income generated from labor provokes a salary increase and, therefore, a substitution of labour with capital for enterprises. In a decentralized economy, there is a reduction in investments if the marginal productivity of capital diminishes, and as a consequence, the rate of growth then slows.

8 The constant elasticity of substitution (CES) is a property of some production functions and utility functions which combines two or more types of productive inputs into an aggregate quantity. The CES production function, in economics, is a category of production function that presents constant elasticity of substitution. As a matter of fact, the production technology has a constant percentage change in factor (e.g., labour and capital) proportions due to a percentage change in marginal rate of technical substitution.

9 Dale Thomas Mortensen was born in February 1939. He received his BA in economics from Willamette University in 1961 and his PHD in economics from Carnegie Mellon University in 1967. He started his

academic career in 1965 as assistant professor of economics at Northwestern University in Evanston, Illinois, where he then became associate professor in 1971, and in 1975 was named the Ida C. Cook Professor of Economics, a position he holds to this day. Although he has been on the faculty of Northwestern University since 1965, he has also held visiting appointments at the University of Essex, Hebrew University, New York University, California Institute of Technology, and Cornell University. Mortensen and Pissarides pioneered the theory of job search and search unemployment and extended it to study labor turnover, R&D, personal relationships, and labour reallocation. Dale Mortensen was awarded the Nobel prize in Economics for 2010 along with two other distinguished economists.

10 Christopher Antoniou Pissarides was born in Nicosia, Cyprus, but he has been a resident of the United Kingdom since 1974. He attended the University of Essex, where he received his BA in economics in 1970 and his MA in economics in 1971. In 1973 he received his PHD from the London School of Economics (LSE) with a dissertation titled "Individual Behaviour in Markets with Imperfect Information." His first appointment was as an economist at the Central Bank of Cyprus in 1974 and lecturer in economics at the University of Southampton until 1976. From 1976 until 1982, he was a lecturer in economics at LSE, and from 1982 to 1986, he was appointed as a reader in economics. Then, in 1986 he finally became a professor of economics at LSE, where in 2006 he also received the title of Norman Sosnow Professor of Economics. He has held visiting appointments in several universities in Europe and North America. He has also written extensively on unemployment and labour market policy issues. Christopher Pissarides shared the Nobel Prize in Economics for 2010 with Dale Mortensen and Peter Diamond for their job search theory.

11 The most common definition of a Poisson process (named for the French mathematician Siméon-Denis Poisson) is when events, denoted by random variables (like $Z(t)$ where $t \geq 0$), occur incessantly and separately from one another.

12 The Hicksian concept of complementary and substitutability in production theory refers to the signs of quantity responses to a change in price input. Output effect is combined with the substitution effect.

13 Edward J. Nell was born in Riverside, Illinois, a suburb of Chicago, on 16 July 1935. He was the only son of Marcella and Edward Nell. His father was a journalist and taught at Northwestern University, while his mother was a public school administrator and later became a professor

of education at Roosevelt University. Nell attended Princeton University, where he studied mathematics, physics and philosophy. He received his bachelor's degree magna cum laude in 1957 (in the Woodrow Wilson School). In 1957 he went to Oxford University thanks to a Rhodes Scholarship. He attained a First in PPE in 1959 at Magdalen College. From 1959 until 1962 he continued to study economic analysis at Nuffield College (Oxford University) where he finally completed his doctoral thesis. He returned to the United States to teach at Wesleyan University, but later went back to the United Kingdom to lecture at the University of East Anglia, and afterwards doing research at Cambridge University. During his career he taught economics and gave sets of lectures and seminars on over 20 universities in Europe, North America, and Australia. Nell's contributions are mostly in macroeconomic theory and growth economics, monetary analysis, economic methodology, and philosophy.

14 Nancy Laura Stokey was born in 1950. She received her BA in economics from the University of Pennsylvania in 1972 and her PHD from Harvard University in 1978, her thesis advisor being Kenneth Arrow, a Nobel Prize laureate in Economics. She began her career as an assistant professor of economics at Northwestern University in 1978, and was promoted to associate professor in 1982 and then professor of economics in 1983. From 1988 to 1990, she was the Harold Stuart Professor of Managerial Sciences at the Kellogg Graduate School of Management at Northwestern University. In 1990 she moved to Chicago to teach economics until 1997. In 1997 she became Frederic Henry Prince Professor of Economics at the University of Chicago, where in 2004 she obtained the title of Distinguished Service Professor of Economics. Stokey has published significant research in the areas of economic growth, development, and econometrics. She is a member of the National Academy of Sciences and was a vice president of the American Economic Association in 1996 and 1997. She lives with Nobel Prize in Economics laureate Robert Lucas.

15 Baumol and Oates 1979, Chs. 16 and 17; Baumol and Oates 1988, Chs. 11 and 12.

16 Aghion and Howitt 1998, 123–143, is an extended version of Aghion and Howitt 1994.

17 Indicating the overhead costs with *a*, decreasing returns to scale with $\beta < 1$, the fixed factor productivity with *At*, and the human capital with *x*, the function for output is given as (Mortenson and Pissarides 1994).

18 Richard G. Lipsey, Cliff Bekar, and Kenneth Carlaw (Helpman 1998, Ch. 8), 194–218.

19 The Club of Rome was founded in April 1968 by Aurelio Peccei, an Italian industrialist, and Alexander King, a British scientist. Part of the initial group were also Hugo Thiemann, director of the Battelle Memorial Institute in Geneva, Max Kohnstamm (Netherlands), former Secretary General of the ECSC, Jean Saint-Geours, Ministry of Finance in Paris, and Erich Jantsch, author of *Technological Forecasting*. The small international group of six met at a villa in Rome, Italy, where it got the name. The Club of Rome raised considerable public attention in 1972 with its commissioned report *The Limits to Growth*. The book considered the positive and negative effects of a rapidly growing world population and finite resource supplies. The authors of this work were Donella H. Meadows, Dennis L. Meadows, Jørgen Randers, and William W. Behrens III. The book sold 12 million copies, translated in many languages around the world.

Bibliography

Abramovitz, M. 1956. Resource and Output Trends in the United States since 1870. *American Economic Review* 46: 5–23.

– 1962. Economic Growth in the United States. *American Economic Review* 52: 762–82.

– 1986. Catching Up, Forging Ahead and Falling Behind. *Journal of Economic History* 46: 385–406.

Aghion, P., and P. Howitt. 1992. A Model of Growth through Creative Destruction. *Econometrica* 60 (2): 323–51.

– 1994. Growth and Unemployment. *Review of Economic Studies* 61: 477–94.

– 1998. *Endogenous Growth Theory*. Cambridge, MA: MIT Press.

Ahluwalia, M.S. 1976. Inequality, Poverty and Development. *Journal of Development Economics* 3: 307–42.

Allais, M. 1962. The Influence of the Capital-Output Ratio on Real National Income. *Econometrica* 59(5): 124–32.

Ariga, J.M. 2002. Internalizing Environmental Quality in a Simple Endogenous Growth Model. University of Maryland, Department of Agricultural and Resource Economics.

Arndt, H.W. 1978. *The Rise and the Fall of Economic Growth: A Study in Contemporary Thought*. Melbourne, Australia: Longman Cheshire.

Arrow, K.J. 1962. The Economic Implications of Learning by Doing. *Review of Economic Studies* 29: 155–73.

– 1983. *Collected Papers of Kenneth J. Arrow, Vol. 1: Social Choice and Justice*. Cambridge, MA: The Belknap Press of Harvard University Press.

Arrow, K.J., H.B. Chenery, B.S. Minhas, and R.M. Solow. 1961. Capital-Labor Substitution and Economic Efficiency. *Review of Economics and Statistics* 43: 225–50.

Asimakopulos, A. 1969. A Robinsonian Growth Model in One-Sector Notation. *Australian Economic Papers* 8: 41–58.

– 1970. A Robinsonian Growth Model in One-Sector Notation – An Amendment. *Australian Economic Papers* 9: 171–6.

Asimakopulos, A., and J.B. Burbidge. 1974. The Short-Period Incidence of Taxation. *Economic Journal* 84: 267–88.

Asimakopulos, A., and G.C. Harcourt. 1974. Proportionality and the Neoclassical Parables. *Southern Economic Journal* 60: 481–843.

Atkinson, A.B. 1969. The Time Scale of Economic Models: How Long Is the Long Run? *Review of Economic Studies* 34(2): 137–52.

Auerbach, A., and L. Kotlikoff. 1987. *Dynamic Fiscal Policy*. New York: Cambridge University Press.

Azariadis C., and A. Drazen. 1990. Threshold Externalities in Economic Development. *Quarterly Journal of Economics* 105(2): 501–26.

Balassa, B. 1981. *The Newly Industrializing Economies in the World Economy*. New York: Pergamon Press.

Barro, R.J. 1986. Reputation in a Model of Monetary Policy with Incomplete Information. *Journal of Monetary Economics* 17: 3–20. Reprinted in T. Person and G. Tabellini.

– 1994. Is Inequality Harmful for Growth? Theory and Evidence. *American Economic Review* 84(3): 600–21.

– 1990. Government Spending in a Simple Model of Endogenous Growth. *Journal of Political Economy* 98: S103–25.

–1991. Economic Growth in Cross Section Countries. *Quarterly Journal of Economics* 106(2): 407–43.

Barro R.J., and X. Sala-i-Martin. 1995. *Economic Growth*. New York: McGraw-Hill.

Baumol, W.J., and W.E. Oates. 1979. *Economics, Environmental Policy, and the Quality of Life*. Englewood Cliffs, NJ: Prentice-Hall.

– 1988. *The Theory of Environmental Policy*. Cambridge: Cambridge University Press.

Becker, G.S. 1964. *Human Capital*. New York: Columbia University Press for the National Bureau of Economic Research.

– 1965. A Theory of the Allocation of Time. *Economic Journal* 75: 493–517.

Bernard, A., and S. Durlauf. 1996. Interpreting Tests of the Convergence Hypothesis. *Journal of Econometrics* 71: 161–73.

Besomi D. 1995. From the Trade Cycle to the "Essay in Dynamic Theory." The Harrod-Keynes Correspondence, 1937–1938. *History of Political Economy* 27(2): 309–43.

– 1997. Statics and Dynamics in Harrod's *Trade Cycle*. *Review of Political Economy* 9 (2): 181–209.

– 1998. Harrod and the "Time-Lag Theories of the Cycle." In G. Rampa, L. Stella, and A.P. Thirlwall, eds., *Economic Dynamics, Trade and Growth: Essays on Harrodian Themes*, New York: Macmillan, 107–48.

– 1999. *The Making of Harrod's Dynamics*. London, New York: Macmillan.

Bhagwati, J., and T.N. Srinivasan. 1974. On Reanalyzing the Harris-Todaro model: Policy Rankings in the Case of Sector-specific Sticky Wages. *American Economic Review* 64: 502–8.

Black, J. 1962. The Technical Progress Function and the Production Function. *Economica* (New Series) 29(114): 166–70

Blaug, M. 1968. *Economic Theory in Retrospect*. Homewood, IL: Richard D. Irwin.

– 1974. *The Cambridge Revolution: Success or Failure? A Critical Analysis of Cambridge Theories of Value and Distribution*. London: Institute of Economic Affairs.

– 1985. *Great Economists since Keynes: An Introduction to the Lives and Works of One Hundred Modern Economists*. Brighton, Sussex: Wheatsheaf Books.

Bliss, C.J. 1968. Rates of Return in a Linear Model. Cambridge, mimeographed, 9.

– 1970. Comment on Garegnani. *Review of Economic Studies* 37(3): 437–8.

– 1974. *Capital Theory in the Short Run*. Buffalo, NY, mimeographed.

– 1975. *Capital Theory and the Distribution of Income*. Amsterdam: North-Holland; New York: American Elsevier .

Bolland, A.L. 2003. *The Foundations of Economic Method: A Popperian Perspective*, London: Routledge.

Boggio, L., and G. Seravalli. 1999. *Sviluppo e crescita economica*. Milan: McGraw-Hill.

Brems, H. 1957. Constancy of the Proportionate Equilibrium Rate of Growth: Result or Assumption? *Review of Economic Studies* 24: 131–8.

Bresnahan, T.F., and M. Trajtenberg. 1995. General Purpose Technologies: Engines of Growth? *Journal of Econometrics* 65: 83–108.

Buchanan, N.S. 1945. *International Investment and Domestic Welfare*. New York: Pergamon Press.

Burmeister, E., and R.A. Dobell. 1973. *Mathematical Theories of Economic Growth*. New York: Macmillan.

Burmeister E., and S.J. Turnovsky. 1972. Capital Deepening Response in an Economy with Heterogeneous Capital Goods. *American Economic Review* 62: 842–53.

Carabelli, A. 1988. *On Keynes's Method*. London: Macmillan.

Casarosa, C. 1998, *Manuale di Macroeconomia*, Rome: Carocci.

Cass, D. 1965. Optimum Growth in an Aggregative Model of Capital Accumulation. *Review of Economic Studies* 32: 233–40.

– 1966. Optimum Growth in an Aggregative Model of Capital Accumulation: A Turnpike Theorem. *Econometrica* 34: 833–50.

Cassel, G. 1918. *The Theory of Social Economy*. London: Unwin.

– 1921. *The World's Monetary Problems*. London: Constable and Company.

Cate, T., ed. 1997. *An Encyclopedia of Keynesian Economics*. Cheltenham, UK: Edward Elgar.

Champernowne, D.G. 1953–54. The Production Function and the Theory of Capital: A Comment. *Review of Economic Studies* 21(2): 112–35.

– 1958. Capital Accumulation and the Maintenance of Full Employment. *Economic Journal* 67(270): 211–44.

– 1962. Some Implications of Golden Age Conditions When Saving Equal Profits. *The Review of Economic Studies* 29(3): 235–7.

Chaudhuri, P. (1989), *Economic Theory of Growth*. New York and London: Harvester Wheatsheaf.

Chenery, H.B. 1953. The Application of Investment Criteria. *Quarterly Journal of Economics* 67: 76–96.

– 1960a. Interindustry Research in Economic Development. *American Economic Review* 50(2): 649–53.

– 1960b. Patterns of Industrial Growth. *American Economic Review* 50(4): 624–54.

– 1986. *Industrialisation and Growth*. Oxford: Oxford University Press.

Chenery, H., and M. Syrquin. 1975. *Patterns of Development, 1950–1970*. Oxford: Oxford University Press for the World Bank.

Chenery, H., and L. Taylor. 1968. Development Patterns: Among Countries and Over Time. *Review of Economics and Statistics* 1(4): 391–416.

Cheng, L.K., and Dinopoulos, E. 1992. Schumpeterian Growth and Stochastic Economic Fluctuations. University of Florida, mimeographed.

Chichilnisky, G. and Heal, G. 1986. *The Evolving International Economy*. Cambridge: Cambridge University Press.

Clark, C. 1937. *National Income and Outlay*. London: Macmillan.

– 1940. *Conditions of Economic Progress*. London: Macmillan.

Clark, J.B. 1889. The Possibility of a Scientific Law of Wages. *Publication of the American Economic Association* 4: 39–63.

– 1891. Distribution as Determined by a Law of Rent. *Quarterly Journal of Economics* 5(3): 289–318.

– 1907. *Essentials of Economic Theory As Applied to Modern Problems of Industry and Public Policy*. New York: Macmillan.

Clarke, P. 1988. *The Keynesian Revolution in the Making, 1924–36*. Oxford: Clarendon Press.

Clower, R.W. 1965. The Keynesian Counter-Revolution: A Theoretical Appraisal. In F.H. Hahn and F.P.R. Brechling, eds., *The Theory of Interest Rates*. London: Macmillan. Reprinted in R.W.

– 1984, *Money and Markets: Essays by Robert Clower*, ed. A.D. Walker. Cambridge: Cambridge University Press, 34–58.

Coates, J. 1996. *The Claims of Common Sense: Moore, Wittgenstein, Keynes and the Social Sciences*. Cambridge: Cambridge University Press.

Coe, D., and E. Helpman. 1993. International R&D spillovers. Working Paper No. 5-93. The Foerder Institute for Economic Research, Tel Aviv University.

Cohen A.J., 2010. Capital Controversy from Böhem-Bawerk to Bliss: Badly Posed or Very Deep Questions? Or What Can "We" Learn from Capital Controversy Even If You Don't Care Who Won. *Journal of the History of Economic Thought* 32(1): 1–21.

Cohen A.J. and Harcourt G.C., 2003. Whatever Happened to the Cambridge Capital Theory Controversies? *Journal of Economic Pespectives* 17(1): 199–214.

Corden, W., and R. Findlay. 1975. Urban Unemployment, Intersectoral Capital Mobility, and Development Policy. *Economica* 92: 59–78.

Costa, G. 1970. Considerazioni su alcuni concetti e problemi di Harrod. *Rivista Internazionale di Scienze Sociali*, mimeographed.

– 1972. Lo sviluppo ciclico nella teoria di Harrod: Una interpretazione, formalizzazione critica. *Rivista Internazionale di Scienze Sociali*, mimeographed.

Cozzi, T. 1972. *Teoria dello sviluppo economico. Le grandi teorie e i modelli di crescita aggregati*. Bologna: Il Mulino.

Dasgupta, P., and I. Serageldin, eds. 1999. *Social Capital: A Multifaceted Perspective*. Washington, DC: World Bank.

Dasgupta, P. and J.E. Stiglitz. 1980. Uncertainty, Industrial Structure, and the Speed of R&D. *Bell Journal of Economics* 11: 1–28.

Daveri, F., and G. Tabellini. 1997. Unemployment, Growth and Taxation in Industrial Countries. Mimeographed.

David, P.A. 1991. Computer and Dynamo: The Modern Productivity Paradox in a Not-Too-Distant Mirror. In *Technology and Productivity: The Challenge for Economic Policy*, 315–48. Paris: OECD.

Davidson, P. 1972. *Money and the Real World*. London: Macmillan, 2nd ed., 1978.

Davis, H.S. 1955. *Productivity Accounting, Research Studies 37*. Philadelphia: University of Pennsylvania Press.

Davis, J.B. 1994. *Keynes's Philosophical Development*. Cambridge: Cambridge University Press.

Davis, S.J., and J. Haltiwanger. 1990. Gross Job Creation and Destruction: Microeconomic Evidence and Macroeconomic Implications. (Bureau of Census, CES Paper 90–100). Washington, DC: Author.

Debraj, R. 1998. *Development Economics*. Princeton, NJ: Princeton University Press.

Debreu, G. 1959. *Theory of Value: An Axiomatic Analysis of Economic Equilibrium* (Cowles Foundation Monograph No. 17). New York: Wiley.

Del Punta, V. 1970. Sterility of the "Cambridge School": Criticism of the Marginal Productivity Theory. Selected Paper (No. 5, 1971) from *Rivista di Politica Economica*: 1–42.

Deininger K.W. 1995. *Technical Change, Human Capital and Spillovers in United States Agriculture, 1949–1985*. New York: Garland Publishing.

Deininger, K.W., and L. Squire. 1996. A New Data Set Measuring Income Inequality. *World Bank Economic Review* 10(3): 565–91.

Denison, E.F. 1957. Theoretical Aspects of Quality Change, Capital Consumption, and Net Capital Formation. In Franco Modigliani, ed., *Problems of Capital Formation: Concepts, Measurement, and Controlling Factors: Studies in Income and Health*, Vol. 19, 215–61. National Bureau of Economic Research, Conference on Research in Income and Health. Princeton N.J.: Princeton University Press.

– 1961. *The Sources of Economic Growth in the United States*. New York: Committee for Economic Development.

– 1979. *Accounting for Slower Economic Growth: The United States in the 1970s*. Washington, DC: Brookings Institution.

Desrousseaux, J. 1961. Expansion stable et taux d'intèrèt optimal. *Annales des Mines* November 31–46.

Dixit, A.K. 1976. *The Theory of Economic Growth*. Oxford: Oxford University Press.

– 1990. *Optimization in Economic Theory*. Cambridge, MA: MIT Press.

Dixit, A.K., and J. Stiglitz. 1977. Monopolistic Competition and Optimum Product Diversity. *American Economic Review* 67(3): 297–308.

Dobb, M.H. 1951. *Some Aspects of Economic Development: Three Lectures*, Delhi: Ranjit Publishers, for the Delhi School of Economics

– 1960. *An Essay on Economic Growth and Planning*. London: Routledge and Kegan Paul.

– 1973. *Theories of Value and Distribution since Adam Smith: Ideology and Economic Theory*. Cambridge: Cambridge University Press.

Domar, E.D. 1946. Capital Expansion, Rate of Growth and Employment. *Econometrica* 14: 137–47.

– 1947. Expansion and Employment. *American Economic Review* 37: 34–55.

– 1948. The Problem of Capital Accumulation. *American Economic Review* 38: 777–94.

– 1952. Economic Growth: An Econometric Approach. *American Economic Review* 42: 479–95.

– 1953. Depreciation, Replacement and Growth. *Economic Journal* 63: 1–32.

–1957. *Essays in the Theory of Economic Growth*. Oxford: Oxford University Press.

– 1961. On the Measurement of Technological Change. *Economic Journal* 71: 709–29.

Dougherty, C.R.S. 1972. On the Rate of Return and the Rate of Profit. *Economic Journal* 88: 1324–50.

Drandakis, E.M. 1963. Factor Substitution in the Two-Sector Growth Model. *Review of Economic Studies* 30: 217–28.

Dutt, A.K. 1990. *Growth, Distribution and Uneven Development*, Cambridge: Cambridge University Press.

Dutt, A.K., and Ros, J., eds. 2003. *Development Economics and Structuralist Macroeconomics: Essays in Honor of Lance Taylor*, Northampton, MA: Edward Elgar.

Eatwell, J.L. 1974. Controversies in the Theory of Surplus Value: Old and New. *Science and Society* 82: 281–303.

Edwards, C. 1959. Resource Fixity and Farm Organization. *Farm Economics* 41: 747–90.

Eicher, T.S. 1996. The Interaction between Endogenous Human Capital and Technological Change. *Review of Economic Studies* 63 (1): 127–44.

Eisner, R. 1952. Underemployment Equilibrium Rates of Growth. *American Economic Review* 92: 820–931.

– 1958. On Growth Models and the Neo-Classical Resurgence. *Economic Journal* 98: 707–21.

Either, W.J. 1982. National and International Returns to Scale in the Modern Theory of International Trade. *American Economic Review* 72 (3): 389–405.

Fellner, W. 1960. Emergence and Content of Modern Economic Analysis. New York: McGraw-Hill.

– 1961. Two Propositions in the Theory of Induced Innovations. *Economic Journal*. 71: 234–42.

Fei, J., and G. Ranis. 1964. *Development of the Labor Surplus Economy: Theory and Policy*. Homewood, IL: Richard D. Irwin.

– 1966. Agrarianism, Dualism and Economic Development. In I. Adelman and E. Thorbecke, eds., *The Theory and Design of Economic Development*. Baltimore: The Johns Hopkins Press.

Ferguson, C.E. 1969. *The Neoclassical Theory of Production and Distribution*. Cambridge: Cambridge University Press.

– 1972. The Current State of Capital Theory: A Tale of Two Paradigms. *Southern Economic Journal* 39: 160–76.

Fields, G. 1975. Rural-Urban Migration, Urban Unemployment and Under-Development, and Job-Search Security in LDCs. *Journal of Development Economics* 2: 165–87.

Findlay, R., and H. Kierzkowski. 1983. International Trade and Human Capital. *Journal of Political Economy* 91: 957–78.

Fisher, F.M. 1970. Aggregate Production Functions and the Explanation of Wages: A Simulation Experiment. (Working Paper 61). Department of Economics, MIT.

– 1971. The Existence of Aggregate Production Functions: Reply. *Econometrica* 39 (2): 405.

Fisher, I. 1907. *The Rate of Interest*. New York: Macmillan.
– 1930. *The Theory of Interest*. New York: Macmillan.
Freeman, C., J. Clark, and L. Soete. 1982. *Unemployment and Technical Innovation: A Study of Long Waves and Economic Development*. London: Pinter.
Freeman, C., and L. Soete. 1994. *Work for All or Mass Unemployment?* London: Pinter.
Freeman, S., and S. Polasky. 1992. Knowledge-Based Growth. *Journal of Monetary Economics* 30(1): 3–24.
Friedman, M. 1960. *A Program for Monetary Stability*. New York: Fordham University Press.
– 1968. The Role of Monetary Policy. *American Economic Review* 58: 1–17.
– 1969. *The Optimum Quantity of Money and Other Essays*. Chicago: Aldine Publishing.
Galenson, W., and H. Leibenstein. 1955. Investment Criteria, Productivity, and Economic Development. *Quarterly Journal of Economics* 69: 343–70.
Galor, O. 1997. Convergence? Inferences from Theoretical Models. *Economic Journal* 106: 1056–69.
Garegnani, P. 1960. *Il capitale nelle teorie della distribuzione*. Edited by A. Giuffre. Milan: Pubblicazioni della Facoltà di Economia e Commercio dell'Università di Roma, xii.
– 1970a. Heterogeneous Capital, the Production Function and the Theory of Distribution. *Review of Economic Studies* 37(3): 407–36.
– 1970b. A Reply. *Review of Economic Studies* 37(3): 439.
– 1973. Summary of the Final Discussion. In James A. Mirrlees and N. H. Stern, eds., *Models of Economic Growth*, 365. London: Macmillan.
Gerschenkron, A. 1953. Social Attitudes, Entrepreneurship and Economic Development. *Explorations in Entrepreneurial History* 6: 1–19.
– 1962. *Economic Backwardness in Historical Perspective*. Cambridge, MA: Belknap Press of Harvard University Press.
– 1969. History of Economic Doctrines and Economic History. *American Economic Review* 59: 1–17.
Gerschenkron, A and Nancy Nimitz. 1953. *A Dollar Index of Soviet Iron and Steel Output 1927/28–1937*. Santa Monica, CA: Rand Corporation.
Godfrey, M. 1979. Rural-Urban Migration in a "Lewis-model" Context. *The Manchester School* 47(3): 230–47.
Gomulka, S. 1971. *Inventive Activity, Diffusion and the Stages of Economic Growth*. Institute of Economics, University of Aarhus, Aarhus, Denmark, Monograph, 82.
Goodwin, R. 1951a. The Nonlinear Accelerator and the Persistence of Business Cycles. *Econometrica* 19: 1–17.
– 1951b. Econometrics in Business Cycle Analysis. In A.H. Hansen, ed., *Business Cycles and National Income*, ch. 22. New York: Norton.

Gordon, R.J. 1995. Is There a Trade-off between Unemployment and Productivity Growth? (Discussion Paper no. 1159) London: Centre for Economic Policy Research, mimeographed.

Gradus, R., and S. Smulders. 1993. The Trade-Off between Environmental Care and Long-Term Growth: Pollution in Three Prototype Growth Models. *Journal of Economics* 58: 25–51.

Griliches, Z. 1963. The Sources of Measured Productivity Growth: United States Agriculture, 1940–60. *Journal of Political Economy* 71: 331–46.

– 1973. Research Expenditures and Growth Accounting. In B. R. Williams, ed., *Science and Technology in Economic Growth*. New York: Wiley.

– 1988. Productivity Puzzles and R&D: Another Explanation. *Journal of Economic Perspectives* 2 (4): 9–21.

Grossman, G. M., and E. Helpman. 1989a. Endogenous Product Cycles. (Working Paper No. 2913) National Bureau of Economic Research.

– 1989b. Growth and Welfare in a Small Open Economy. (Working Paper No. 2970) National Bureau of Economic Research.

– 1989c. Product Development and International Trade. *Journal of Political Economy* 97: 1261–83.

– 1990. Comparative Advantages and Long-Run Growth. *American Economic Review* 80: 796–815.

– 1991a. Quality Ladders in the Theory of Growth. *The Review of Economic Studies* 58(1)(January): 43–61.

– 1991b. *Innovation and Growth in the Global Economy*. Cambridge, MA: MIT Press.

Grossman, G.M., and A. Krueger. 1995. Economic Growth and the Environment. *Quarterly Journal of Economics* 110: 353–77.

Haavelmo, T. 1954. *A Study in the Theory of Economic Evolution: Contributions to Economic Analysis*. Amsterdam: North-Holland.

Haberler, G. 1936. *Prosperity and Depression*. Geneva: League of Nations.

– 1937. Review of Harrod's *The Trade Cycle*. *Journal of Political Economy* 45: 690–7.

Hagemann, H. 1995. Technological Unemployment. In *The Political Economy of Full Employment*, chapter 2, edited by Philip Arestis and Mike Marshall. Aldershot: Edward Elgar.

– 1997. The Rate of Return Debate. In *Capital Controversy, Post-Keynesian Economics and the History of Economic Thought*, Philip Arestis, Gabriel Palma, and Malcolm Sawyer, eds., Vol.1, 148–60. London: Routledge.

Hahn, F. H. 1960. The Stability of Growth Equilibrium. *Quarterly Journal of Economics* 74: 206–26.

– 1965. On Two-Sector Growth Models. *Review of Economic Studies* 32: 339–46.

– 1972a. *The Share of Wages in the National Income: An Enquiry into the Theory of Distribution*. London: Weindenfeld And Nicolson.
– 1972b. *Notes on Vulgar Economy*. Cambridge, mimeographed.
– 1973. *On the Notion of Equilibrium in Economics: An Inaugural Lecture*. Cambridge: Cambridge University Press.
– 1984. *Equilibrium and Macroeconomics*, Oxford: Basil Blackwell.
– 1987a. On Involuntary Unemployment. *Economic Journal* 97: 1–16.
– 1987b. Information, Dynamics and Equilibrium. *Scottish Journal of Political Economy, Scottish Economic Society* 34(4): 321–34.
Hahn, F.H., and F.P.R. Brechling, eds. 1965. *The Theory of Interest Rates*. London: Macmillan.
Hahn, F.H., and R.C.O. Matthews. 1964. The Theory of Economic Growth: A Survey. *Economic Journal* 74:825–32.
Hahn, F.H., and R.M. Solow. 1996. *A Critical Essay on Modern Macroeconomic Theory*. Oxford: Blackwell.
Harcourt, G.C. 1965. A Two-Sector Model of Distribution of Income and the Level of Employment in the Short Run. *Economic Record* 91: 103–7.
– 1969. Some Cambridge Controversies in the Theory of Capital. *Journal of Economic Literature* 7(2): 369–405.
– 1972. *Some Cambridge Controversies in the Theory of Capital*. Cambridge: Cambridge University Press.
– 1973. The Rate of Profits in Equilibrium Growth Models: A Review Article. *Journal of Political Economy* 81: 1261–77.
– 1976. The Cambridge Controversies: Old Ways and New Horizons – or a Dead End? *Oxford Economic Papers* 28(1): 25–65.
Harcourt, G.C and Kerr P., eds. 1982. *The Social Science Imperialists: Selected Essays*. London: Routledge & Kegan Paul.
Harcourt, G. C., and P. A. Riach, eds. 1997. *A "Second Edition" of the General Theory*. Vol. 2. London: Routledge.
Harris, D.J. 1973. Capital Distribution and the Aggregate Production Function. *American Economic Review* 81: 100–13.
Harris, J.R. and M.P. Todaro. 1970. Migration, Unemployment and Development: A Two Sector Analysis. *American Economic Review* 60(1): 126–42.
Harrod, R.F. 1933. *International Economics*. Cambridge: Cambridge University Press.
– 1936. *The Trade Cycle: An Essay*. Oxford: Clarendon Press.
– 1937a. Mr Keynes and traditional theory. *Econometrica* 5: 74–146.
– 1937 b. Review of *Essays in the Theory of Employment* by Joan Robinson, *The Economic Journal* 47 (186): 326–30.
– 1938. Scope and Method of Economics. *The Economic Journal* 48(191): 383–412.
– 1939. An Essay in Dynamic Theory. *The Economic Journal* 49: 14–33.

– 1948. *Towards a Dynamic Economics*. London: Macmillan.
– 1951. *The Life of John Maynard Keynes*. London: Macmillan (2nd edition 1963).
– 1952. *Economic Essays*. London: Macmillan.
– 1953. Full Capacity vs. Full Employment Growth: Comment. *Quarterly Journal of Economics* 67(4): 553–9.
– 1956. *Foundations of Inductive Logic*. London: Macmillan.
– 1960. Second Essay in Dynamics Theory. *Economic Journal* 70: 273–93.
– 1973. *Economic Dynamics*. Aldershot, England: Macmillan.
Hawkins, D. and Simon, H.A., 1949. Note: Some Conditions of Macroeconomic Stability. *Econometrica* 17: 245–8
Hayek, F. 1945. The Use of Knowledge in Society. *American Economic Review* 35: 519–30.
Heckman, J. J. 1976. A Life-Cycle Model of Economics, Learning and Consumption. *Journal of Political Economy* 84(4): S11–S44.
Helpman, E., ed. 1998. *General Purpose Technologies and Economic Growth*. London: MIT Press.
Helpman, E. and Trajtenberg, M. 1998. A Time to Sow and a Time to Reap: Growth Based on General Purpose Technologies. In E. Helpman, ed., *General Purpose Technologies and Economic Growth*. London: MIT Press.
Hicks, J.R. 1932. *The Theory of Wages*. London: Macmillan.
– 1937. Mr Keynes and the "Classics": A Suggested Interpretation. *Econometrica* 5: 147–59.
– 1949. Mr Harrod's Dynamic Theory. *Economica* (New Series) 16: 106–21.
– 1950. *A Contribution to the Theory of the Trade Cycles*. Oxford: Clarendon Press.
– 1962. Review of Sen's book, *Choice of Techniques: An Aspect of the Theory of Planned Economic Development. The Economic Journal* 72 (286): 379–81.
– 1965. *Capital and Growth*. Oxford: Oxford University Press.
– 1973. *The Capital and Time: A Neo-Austrian Theory*. Oxford: Clarendon Press.
Hiram, D.S. 1955. *Productivity Accounting*. Philadelphia: University of Pennsylvania Press.
Hirschman, A.O. 1958. *The Strategy of Economic Development*. New Haven, CT: Yale University Press.
– 1968. The Political Economy of Import-Substituting Industrialization in Latin America. *Quarterly Journal of Economics* 82(1): 1–32.
Hirshleifer, L. 1958. On the Theory of Optimal Investment Decision. *Journal of Political Economy* 66: 329–52.
Howitt, P. 1999. Steady Endogenous Growth with Population and R&D Inputs Growing. *Journal of Political Economy* 107(4): 715–30.

Inada, K.I. 1963. On a Two-Sector Model Economic Growth: Comments and a Generalization. *Review of Economic Studies* 30(2): 119–27.

James, R.W., and M.H. Belz. 1938. The Significance of the Characteristic Solutions of Mixed Difference and Differential Equations. *Econometrica* 6: 326–43.

Jevons, W.S. [1871] 1957. *The Theory of Political Economy*. 5th ed. New York: Kelley and Millman.

Johansen, L. 1959. Substitution versus Fixed Production Coefficients in the Theory of Economic Growth: A Synthesis. *Econometrica* 27: 157–76.

– 1972. *Production Functions: An Integration of Micro and Macro, Short-Run and Long-Run Aspects*. Amsterdam: North-Holland.

Johnson, George. E. 1971. The Structure of Rural-Urban Migration Models. *East African Economic Review* 60: 126–42.

Johnson, Glen L. 1960. The State of Agricultural Supply Analysis. *Farm Economics* 42: 435–52.

Johnson, H.G. 1966. The Neoclassical One-Sector Growth Model: A Geometric Exposition and Extension to a Monetary Economy. *Economica* (New Series). 33(131): 265–87.

– 1967. *Essays in Monetary Economics*. London: Allen and Unwin.

– 1971. *The Two-Sector Model of General Equilibrium*. (The Yrjö Jahnsson Lectures, 1970) London: Allen and Unwin.

– 1973. *The Theory of Income Distribution*. London: Gray-Mills Publishing Ltd.

– 1974. The Current and Prospective State of Economics. *Australian Economic Papers* 13: 1–27.

Jones, C.I. 1995a. Time Series Tests of Endogenous Growth Models. *Quarterly Journal of Economics* 110(2): 495–525.

– 1995b. R&D-Based Models of Economic Growth. *Journal of Political Economy* 103(4): 759–84.

Jones, H.G. 1975. *An Introduction to Modern Theories of Economic Growth*. London: Thomas Nelson and Sons.

Jones, L., R. Manuelli, and P.E. Rossi. 1993. Optimal Taxation in Models of Endogenous Growth. *Journal of Political Economy* 101(3): 485–517.

Jorgenson, D.W., and Z. Griliches. 1966. Sources of Measured Productivity Change: Capital Input. *American Economic Review* 56: 50–61.

– 1967. The Explanation of Productivity Change. *Review of Economic Studies* 34: 249–83.

Jossa, B. 1993. *Macroeconomia*. Torino: Cedam.

Judd, K.L. 1987. The Welfare Cost of Factor Taxation in a Perfect-Foresight Model. *Journal of Political Economy* 95: 695–709.

– 1990. Optimal Taxation in Dynamic Stochastic Economies: Theory and Evidence. (manuscript) Stanford, CA: Hoover Institution.

Junankar, P.N. 2000. *The Economics of Unemployment*, Vols. I and II. Cheltenham, UK: Edward Elgar.

Kahn, A.E. 1951. Investment Criteria in Development Programs. *Quarterly Journal of Economics* 65: 38–61.

Kahn, R.F. 1959. Exercises in the Analysis of Growth. *Oxford Economic Papers* 11: 143–56.

Kaldor, N. 1940. A Model of the Trade Cycle. *The Economic Journal* 50(197): 78–92.

– 1951 Hicks on the Trade Cycle. *The Economic Journal* 61(244): 833–47.

– 1954. The Relation of Economic Growth and Cyclical Fluctuations. *The Economic Journal* 64(253)(March): 53–71. (A lecture delivered to the Institut de Science Économique Appliquée in Paris on 23 May 1953.)

– 1956. Alternative Theories of Distribution. *Review of Economic Studies* 23: 94–100.

– 1957. A Model of Economic Growth. *Economic Journal* 67(268): 591–624.

– 1960. *Essays on Economic Stability and Growth*. London: Duckworth.

– 1961. Capital Accumulation and Economic Growth. In F.A. Lutz and D.C. Hague, eds., *The Theory of Capital*, 177–220. London: Macmillan.

– 1964. *Essays on Economic Policy*. 2 vols. London: Duckworth.

– 1972. The Irrelevance of Equilibrium Economics. *Economic Journal* 82: 1237–55.

– 1978. *Further Essays on Economic Theory*. London, Duckworth.

– 1989. The Case for Regional Policies. In F. Targetti and A.P. Thirlwall, eds., *The Essential Kaldor*. New York: Holmes and Meier.

Kaldor, N., and J.A. Mirrlees. 1962. A New Model of Economic Growth. *Review of Economic Studies* 29: 174–90.

Kalecki, M. 1962. Observation on the Theory of Growth. *Economic Journal* 72: 132–53.

– 1965. *Theory of Economic Dynamics*, 2nd ed. London: George Allen and Unwin.

Kendrick, J.W. 1961. Some Theoretical Aspects of Capital Measurements. *American Economic Review* 51: 102–11.

Kennedy, C. 1961. Technical Progress and Investment. *Economic Journal* 71(282): 292–9.

– 1964. Induced Bias in Innovation and Theory of Distribution. *Economic Journal* 74: 541–7.

Keynes, J.M. 1919. *The Economic Consequences of the Peace*, Vol 2. London: C.W. Macmillan.

– 1921. *A Treatise on Probability*. London: C.W. Macmillan.

– 1936. *The General Theory of Employment, Interest and Money*. London: C.W. Macmillan.

– 1937. The General Theory of Employment. *Quarterly Journal of Economics* 51: 209–23.

Khan, M.A. 1980. The Harris-Todaro Hypothesis and the Heckscher-Ohlin-Samuelson Trade Model: A Synthesis. *Journal of International Economics* 10: 527–47.

King, J.E. (ed). 1994. *Economic Growth in Theory and Practice: A Kaldorian Perspective.* Aldershot: Elgar.

King, M.A., and M.H. Robson.1993. A Dynamic Model of Investment and Endogenous Growth. *Scandinavian Journal of Economics* 95: 445–66.

King, R.G., C.I. Plosser, and S. Rebelo. 1988. Production, Growth and Business Cycles: The Basic Neoclassical Model. *Journal of Monetary Economics* 21: 195–232.

King, R.G., and S. Rebelo. 1990. Public Policy and Economic Growth: Developing Neoclassical Implications. *Journal of Political Economy* 98(5): S126–50.

Koopmans, T.C. 1957. *Three Essays on the State of Economic Science.* New York: McGraw Hill.

– 1960. Stationary Ordinal Utility and Impatiance, *Econometrica*, 28(2): 287–309.

– 1964. Economic Growth at a Maximal Rate, *Quartely Journal of Economics*, 78: 335–94.

– 1965. On the Concept of Optimal Economic Growth. *Semaine D'Étude sur le Rôle d'Analyse Économétrique de Plans de Développement* 28: 225–300.

Kregel, J.A. 1971. *Rate of Profit, Distribution and Growth: Two Views.* London: Macmillan.

– 1973. *The Reconstruction of Political Economy: An Introduction to Post-Keynesian Economics.* London: Macmillan.

Kristensen, T. 1974. *Development in Rich and Poor Countries.* New York: Praeger, Kugler.

Krugman, P. 1979. A model of Innovation, Technology Transfer, and the World Distribution of Income. *Journal of Political Economy* 87(2): 253–66.

Kuznets, S. 1930. *Secular Movements in Production and Prices.* Boston: Houghton Mifflin.

– 1949. Social Science Research Council, Committee on Problems and Policy, Minutes of the Meeting of January 8, 1949, Appendix, "Memorandum on Setting up of a Social Science Research Council Committee on a Study of Economic Growth," prepared by Simon Kuznets, 8 December 1948.

– 1955. Economic Growth and Income Inequality. *American Economic Review* 45(1): 1–28.

– 1957a. Quantitative Aspects of the Economic Growth of Nations II: Industrial Distribution of National Product and Labour Force. *Economic Development and Cultural Change* 5 (supplement).

– 1957b. Comment on Edward F. Denison, "Theoretical Aspects of Quality Change, Capital Consumption, and Net Capital Formation," *Problems of Capital Formation. Studies in Income and Health* 19: 272
– 1964. *Postwar Economic Growth: Four Lectures*. Cambridge, MA: The Belknap Press of Harvard University Press.
– 1965. *Economic Growth and Structure: Selected Essays*. New York: Norton.
– 1966. *Modern Economics of Growth Rate, Structure And Spread*. New Haven, CT: Yale University Press.
– 1971. *Economic Growth of Nations*. Cambridge, MA: Harvard University Press.
– 1973. Modern Economic Growth: Findings and Reflections. *The American Economic Review* 63(3): 247–58.
– 1979. *Growth, Population, and Income Distribution: Selected Essays*. New York: Norton.
Laibman, D., and E.J. Nell. 1975. Reswitching, Wicksell Effects and the Neoclassical Production Function. New York, mimeographed.
Lambert, P.J. 1985. *Advanced Mathematics for Economists: Static and Dynamic Optimization*. Oxford: Blackwell.
Lange, O. 1957. Some Observations on Input-Output Analysis. *Sankhya (Indian Economic Journal)* 17: 305–36.
Layard, R., S. Nickell, and R. Jackman. 1991. *Unemployment, Macroeconomic Performance and the Labour Market*. Oxford: Oxford University Press.
Lee, T. and L.L. Wilde. 1980. Market Structure and Innovation: A Reformulation. *Quarterly Journal of Economics* 94: 429–36.
Leibeinstein, H. 1954. *Theory of Economic-Demographic Development*. Princeton, NJ: Princeton University Press.
– 1957. *Economic Backwardness and Economic Growth*. New York: Wiley.
Leijonhufvud, A. 1968. *On Keynesian Economics and the Economics of Keynes: A Study in Monetary Theory*. London: Oxford University Press.
Lekachman, R. 1964. *Keynes' General Theory: Reports of Three Decades*. London: Macmillan.
Leontief, W. 1936. Quantitative Input and Output Relations in the Economic System of the United States. *Review of Economic Statistics* 18: 105–25.
– 1941. *The Structure of the American Economy, 1919–1929*, Cambridge, MA: Harvard University Press.
– 1949a. Recent Developments in the Study of Interindustrial Relationships. *The American Economic Review* 39(3): 211–25.
– 1949b. Structural Matrices of National Economics. *Econometrica* 17: 273–82.
– 1951. Input-Output Economics. *Scientific American* 185(4): 15–21.
– 1953. *Studies in the Structure of the American Economy: Theoretical and Empirical Explorations in Input-Output Analysis*. New York: Oxford University Press.

– 1971. Theoretical Assumptions and Nonobserved Facts. *American Economic Review* 61: 1–7.
– 1986. *Input-Output Economics*, 2nd Ed. New York: Oxford University Press.
Leontief, W., A.P. Carter, and P. Petri. 1977. *The Future of the World Economy.* New York: Oxford University Press.
Levhari, D. 1965. A Non-substitution Theorem and Switching of Techniques. *Quarterly Journal of Economics* 79: 98–105.
–1966. Extensions of Arrow's "Learning by Doing." *Review of Economic Studies* 33: 117–31.
Levhari, D., and D. Patinkin.1968. The Role of Money in a Simple Growth Model. *American Economic Review* 58 (4): 713–53.
Levhari, D., and E. Sheshinski. 1969. The Relation between the Rate of Return and the Rate of Technical Progress. *Review of Economic Studies* 36: 363–79.
Lewis, W.A. 1954. Economic Development with Unlimited Supplies of Labour. *The Manchester School, Economic Social Studies* 22(2): 139–91.
– 1955. *The Theory of Economic Growth*. Homewood, IL: Richard D. Irwin.
– 1972. Reflections and Unlimited Labor. In L. DiMarco, ed., *International Economics and Development: Essays in Honor of Raul Prebisch*, 75–96. New York: Academic Press.
– 1978a. *The Evolution of the International Economic Order*. Princeton, NJ: Princeton University Press.
– 1978b. *Growth and Fluctuations 1870–1913*. London: Allen and Unwin.
Li, C-W. 2000. Endogenous vs. Semi-Endogenous Growth in a Two-R&D-Sector Model. *Economic Journal* 110(462): 109–22.
Loury, G. 1979. Market Structure and Innovation. *Quarterly Journal of Economics* 93: 395–410.
Lucas, R.E. 1987. *Models of Business Cycles*. Oxford: Basil Blackwell.
– 1988. On the Mechanics of Economic Development. *Journal of Monetary Economics* 22: 3–42.
– 1990a. Why Doesn't Capital Flow from Rich to Poor Countries? *American Economic Review* 80: 92–6.
– 1990b. Supply-Side Economics: An Analytical Review. *Oxford Economic Papers* 42(2): 293–317.
– 2000. Some Macroeconomics for the 21st Century. *Journal of Economic Perspectives, American Economic Association* 141: 159–68.
– 2005. Reflections on Economic Growth. (Meeting Papers192.) Society for Economic Dynamics.
Lucas, R.E., and A. Atkeson. 1995. Efficiency and Equality in a Simple Model of Efficient Unemployment Insurance. *Journal of Economic Theory* 66(1): 64–88.

Lucas, R.E., and A.F. Haug. 1997. Long-run Neutrality and Superneutrality in an Arima Framework: Comment. *American Economic Association* 87(4): 756–9.

Lundberg, E. 1937. (Review of) *Studies in the Theory of Economic Expansion. Zeitschrift für Nationalökonomie* 8(5): 494–8.

– 1961. *Produktivitet och räntabilitet*, Stockholm: P.A. Norstedt and Söner.

Machlup, F. 1962. *The Production and Distribution of Knowledge in the United States*. Princeton, NJ: Princeton University Press.

Maddison, A. 1979. Per Capita Output in the Long Run. *Kyklos* 32(1, 2): 412–19.

– 1982. *Phases of Capitalist Development*. Oxford and New York: Oxford University Press.

Malinvaud, E. 1953. Capital Accumulation and Efficient Allocation of Resources. *Econometrica* 21: 233–68.

Malthus, T.R. 1960 [1798]. *An Essay on the Principle of Population*. Oxford World's Classics reprint (reprint of 1798 and 1892 edition), New York: Modern Library.

Mankiw, N.G., D. Romer, and D.N. Weil. 1992. A Contribution to the Empirics of Economic Growth. *Quarterly Journal of Economics* 107: 407–37.

Mansfield, E., and E. Mansfield, eds. 1993. *The Economics of Technical Change*. Cheltenham: Edward Elgar.

Mantoux, E. 1999 (1st ed. 1946). *The Carthaginian Peace or the Economic Consequences of Maynard Keynes*. London and New York: Oxford University Press.

Marshall, A. 1890. *Principles of Economics*. London: Macmillan.

– 1919. *Industry and Trade*. London: Macmillan.

– 1920. *Principles of Economics*, 8th ed. London: Macmillan.

– 1923. *Money, Credit and Commerce*. London: Macmillan.

– 1930. *The Pure Theory of Foreign Trade*. London: London School of Economics and Political Science.

Marx, K. 1967 [1867]. *Capital, A Critique of Political Economy [Das Kapital]*, Vols. I–III. New York: International Publishers.

– 1997. *Il capitale*. Rome: Editori Riuniti.

Matthews, R.C.O. 1964. The New View of Investment: Comment. *Quarterly Journal of Economics* 78(1): 164–72.

– 1980. *Economic Growth and Resources, Vol. 2: Trends and Factors*. New York: St Martin's Press.

– 1982. Comments on M. Feldstein: Inflation, Tax Rules and the Accumulation of Residential and Nonresidential Capital. *Scandinavian Journal of Economics* 84: 313–15.

McCool, T. 1982. Wages Subsidies and Distortionary Taxes in a Mobile Capital Harris-Todaro Model. *Economica* 99: 219–34.

Meade, J.E. 1936. *An Introduction to Economic Analysis and Policy*. London: Oxford University Press.

– 1937. A Simplified Model of Mr Keynes' system. *Review of Economic Studies* 4: 98–107.

– 1961. *A Neoclassical Theory of Economic Growth*. London: Allen and Unwin.

– 1962a. *A Neoclassical Theory of Economic Growth*. London: Oxford University Press.

– 1962b. The Effect of Saving on Consumption in a State of Steady Growth. *Review of Economic Studies*. 29(3): 227–34.

– 1975. The Keynesian Revolution. In M. Keynes, ed., *Essays on John Maynard Keynes*, 82–88. Cambridge: Cambridge University Press.

Meadows, Donella H., Dennis L.Meadows, J. Randers, and William W. Behrens III. 1972. *The Limits to Growth*. New York: Universe Books.

Meek, R. L. 1967. *Economics and Ideology and Other Essays: Studies in the Development of Economic Thought*. London: Chapman and Hall.

Menger, C. 1985 (1st ed. 1871). *Principles of Economics*. Trans. by J. Dingwall and B.F. Hoselitz. New York: New York University Press.

Metzler, R.A. 1951. The Rate of Interest and the Marginal Product of Capital: A Correction. *Journal of Political Economy* 59: 67–8.

Millikan, M.F., and W.W. Rostow. 1957. *A Proposal: Key to an Effective Foreign Policy*. New York: Harper and Brothers.

Minami, R. 1973. *The Turning Point in Economic Development: Japan's Experience*. Tokyo: Kinokuniya.

Mirrlees, J.A. 1973. Introduction. In J.A. Mirrlees and N.H. Stern, eds., *Models of Economic Growth*. London: Macmillan.

Mirrlees, J.A., and N.H. Stern, eds. 1973. *Models of Economic Growth*. London: Macmillan.

Moggridge, D.M. 1992. *Maynard Keynes: An Economist's Biography*. London: Routledge.

Morishima, M. 1969. *Theory of Economic Growth*. Oxford: Clarendon Press.

– 1973. *Marx's Economics: A Dual Theory of Value and Growth*. Cambridge: Cambridge University Press.

Mortensen, D.T., and C.A. Pissarides. 1994. Job Creation and Job Destruction in the Theory of Unemployment. *Review of Economic Studies* 61(3): 397–415.

Myrdal, G. 1957a. *Economic Theory and Under-Developed Regions*. London: Gerald Duckworth and Company.

– 1957b. *Rich Lands and Poor: The Road to World Prosperity*. New York: Harper and Brothers (U.S. ed.).

National Science Board (NSB). 2002. Science and Engineering Indicators – 2002. (NSB-02-1), Arlington, VA: National Science Foundation.

Neary, P.J. 1981. On the Harris-Todaro Model with Intersectoral Capital Mobility. *Economica* 48: 219–34.

Nell, E.J. 1967. Theories of Growth and Theories of Value. *Economic Development and Cultural Change* 16: 15–26.

– 1998. *The General Theory of Transformational Growth*. New York: Cambridge University Press.

– 2010. Transformational Growth: From a Marshallian Neo-classical System to Keynesian Growth. Paper presented at the Sraffa Conference at the University di Roma 3 (Uniroma 3), Rome.

Nell, E.J., and K. Errouaki. 2013. *Rational Econometric Man: Transforming Structural Econometrics*. Cheltenham, UK and Northampton, MA: Edward Elgar.

Nelson, R.R. 1956. A Theory of the Low-Level Equilibrium Trap. *American Economic Review* 46: 894–908.

– 1994. What Has Been the Matter with Neoclassical Growth Theory? In G. Silverberg and L. Soete eds., *The Economics of Growth and Technical Change: Technologies, Nations, Agents*, 290–324. Aldershot: Edward Elgar.

Ng, Y.K. 1974a. Harcourt's Survey of Capital Theory (review article). *Economic Record* 50(129): 119–29.

– 1974b. The Neoclassical and the Neo-Marxist-Keynesian Theories of Income Distribution: A Non-Cambridge Contribution to the Cambridge Controversy in Capital Theory. *Australian Economic Papers* 13: 124–32.

Nurske, R. 1953. *Problems of Capital-Formation in Underdeveloped Countries*. New York: Oxford University Press.

Nuti, D.M. 1974. On the Rates of Return on Investment. *Kyklos* 27: 345–69.

O'Donnell, R. 1982. *Keynes, Philosophy and Economics: The Philosophical Foundations of Keynes's Thought and Their Influence on His Economics and Policy*. London: Macmillan.

Ohkawa, K. 1972. *Differential Structure and Agriculture: Essays on Dualistic Growth*. Tokyo: Kinokuniya.

Ohkawa, K., and H. Rosovsky. 1973. *Japanese Economic Growth: Trend Acceleration in the Twentieth Century, Studies of Economic Growth in Industrialized Countries*. Stanford, CA: Stanford University Press.

Panico, C. 1998. Old and New Growth Theories: What Role for Aggregate Demand? Mimeographed. Reprinted in N. Salvadori, ed., 2003, *Old and New Growth Theories: An Assessment*, 53–66. Aldershot: Elgar.

Pasinetti, L.L. 1962. Rate of Profit and Income Distribution in Relation to the Rate of Economic Growth. *Review of Economic Studies* 29: 267–79.

– 1965. A New Theoretical Approach to the Problems Of Economic Growth. *Pontificae Academiae Scientiarum Scripta-Varia* 28.

– 1966. Paradoxes in Capital Theory: A Symposium: Changes in the Rate of Profit and Switches of Techniques. *Quarterly Journal of Economics* 80(4): 503–17.

– 1969. Switches of Techniques and the "Rate of Return" in Capital Theory. *Economic Journal* 79(315): 508–31.

– 1970. Again on Capital Theory and Solow's "Rate of Return." *Economic Journal* 80(318): 428–31.

– 1972. Reply to Mr Dougherty. *Economic Journal* 82: 1351–2.

– 1974. *Growth and Income Distribution: Essays in Economic Theory*. Cambridge: Cambridge University Press.

Patinkin, D. 1956. *Money, Interest and Prices: An integration of Monetary and Value Theory*. Evanston, IL: Row-Peterson.

– 1965. *Money, Interest and Prices*, 2nd ed. New York: Harper and Row-Peterson.

– 1976. *Keynes's Monetary Thought: A Study of Its Development*. Durham, NC: Duke University Press.

Peretto, P. 1998. Technological Change and Population Growth. *Journal of Economic Growth* 3: 283–11.

Peretto, P., and S. Smulders. 2002. Technological Distance, Growth and Scale Effects. *Economic Journal* 112(481): 603–24.

Phelps, E.S. 1961. The Golden Rule of Accumulation: A Fable for Growthmen. *American Economic Review* 51: 683–743.

– 1962. The New View of Investment: A Neoclassical Analysis. *Quarterly Journal of Economics* 76(4): 548–67.

– 1963. Substitution, Fixed Proportions, Growth and Distribution. *International Economic Review* 4(3): 265–88.

– 1965. Second Essay on the Golden Rule of Accumulation. *American Economic Review* 55: 793–814.

– 1968. Money-Wage Dynamics and Labor Market Equilibrium. *Journal of Political Economy* 76(July/August Part 2): 678–711.

– 1973. Inflation in the Theory of Public Finance. *Swedish Journal of Economics* 75: 67–82.

Piaget, J. 1971. *Structuralism*. New York: Harper and Row.

Pilvin, H. 1953. Full Capacity versus Full Employment Growth. *Quarterly Journal of Economics* 67(4): 545–52.

Pissarides, C.A. 1990. *Equilibrium Unemployment Theory*. Oxford: Blackwell.

– 1993. Unemployment and Vacancies in Britain. *Economic Policy* 3:499–559.

– 2000a. *Equilibrium Unemployment Theory*, 2nd ed. Oxford: Blackwell.

– 2000b. The Economics of Search. Mimeographed, London School of Economics.

Pissarides, C.A., and G. Vallanti. 2002. Productivity Growth and Employment: Theory and Panel Estimates. London: Center for Economic Performances, LSE, mimeographed.

Prebisch, R. 1950 *The Economic Development of Latin America and Its Principal Problems* New York: United Nations.

– 1959. Commercial Policy in the Underdeveloped Countries. *American Economic Review* 49: 251–73.

Prescott, E.C. and J.H. Boyd. 1987. Dynamic Coalitions, Growth and the Firm. *American Economic Review, Papers and Proceedings* 77: 63–7.

Pressman, S. 1999. *Fifty Major Economists*. London: Routledge.

Polak, J.J. 1943. Balance of Payments Problems of Countries Reconstructing with the Help of Foreign Loans. *Quarterly Journal of Economics* 57: 208–40.

Postel-Vinay, F. 2000. The Dynamics of Technological Unemployment. Paris: INRA-LEA, and Vancouver: University of British Columbia, mimeographed.

Pugno, M. 1992. *Roy F. Harrod*. Bologna: Il Mulino.

Quesnay, F., 1968 (1758). *The Economical Table (Tableau économique)*. New York: Bergman.

Ramsey, F.P. 1928. A Mathematical Theory of Saving. *Economic Journal* 38: 543–59.

Rebelo, S. 1991. Long-Run Policy Analysis and Long-Run Growth. *Journal of Political Economy* 99(3): 500–21.

Reddaway, W.B. 1936. The General Theory of Employment, Interest and Money [review]. *Economic Record* 12: 28–36.

Redding, S. 1996. Low-Skill, Low-Quality Trap: Strategic Complementarities between Human Capital and R&D. *Economic Journal* 106(435): 458–70.

Ricardo, D. 1821. *On the Principles of Political Economy and Taxation*, 3rd ed. London: John Murray.

– 1951. *The Works and Correspondence of David Ricardo*, 11 volumes, ed. P. Sraffa. Cambridge: Cambridge University Press.

Robinson, A. 1947. John Maynard Keynes 1883–1946. *Economic Journal* 57: 1–68.

Robinson, J. 1937. *Introduction to the Theory of Employment*. London: Macmillan,

– 1938. The Classification of Inventions. *Review of Economic Studies* 5:139–42.

– 1949. Mr Harrod's Dynamics. *Economic Journal* 64: 68–85.

– 1952. *The Rate of Interest and Other Essays*. London: Macmillan.

– 1953 The Production Function and the Theory of Capital. *Review of Economic Studies* 21(2): 81–106.

– 1955. The Production Function. *Economic Journal* 65 (257):67–71.

– 1956. *The Accumulation of Capital*. London: Macmillan.
– 1962a. *Essays in the Theory of Economic Growth*. London: Macmillan.
– 1962b. A Neo-Classical Theorem. *The Review of Economic Studies* 29(3): 219–26.
– 1964a. Solow on the Rate of Return. *Economic Journal* 74: 410–17.
– 1964b. Pre-Keynesian Theory after Keynes. *Australian Economic Papers* 3: 25–35.
– 1970. Capital Theory Up to Date. *Canadian Journal of Economics* 3:309–17.
– 1971a. The Existence of Aggregate Production Functions: Comment. *Econometrica* 39: 405.
– 1971b. *Economic Heresies: Some Old-Fashioned Questions in Economic Theory*. New York: Basic Books.
– 1973. *Collected Economic Papers*, vol. 4. Oxford: Basil Blackwell.
– 1974. *History versus Equilibrium*. London: Thames Polytechnic.
– 1975a. Introduction, 1974. Comments and Explanations. In *Collected Economic Papers*, 2nd ed.,Vol. 3, 3–14, Oxford: Basil Blackwell.
– 1975b. Letter to Editor. *Cambridge Review* xcvi: 91–2.
– 1975c. Review of L.L. Pasinetti, *Growth and Income Distribution: Essays in Economic Theory*, 1974. *Economic Journal* 85: 397–9.
– 1975d. The Unimportance of Reswitching. *Quarterly Journal of Economics* 89: v32–9.
– 1980. *What Are the Questions? and Other Essays: Further Contributions to Economics*. Armonk, NY: M E Sharpe.
Romer, D. 2001. *Advanced Macroeconomics*, 2nd ed. New York: McGraw-Hill.
Romer, P.M. 1986. Increasing Returns and Long-Run Growth. *Journal of Political Economy* 94(5): 1002–37.
– 1987. Growth Based on Increasing Returns Due to Specialization. *American Economic Review* 77(2): 56–62.
– 1990. Endogenous Technical Change. *Journal of Political Economy* 98(5, part II): S71–S102.
Rosen, S. 1976. A Theory of Life Earning. *Journal of Political Economy* 84(4): S45–S67.
Rosenstein-Rodan, P.N. 1943. Problems of Industrialization of Eastern and South-Eastern Europe. *Economic Journal* 53: 202–11.
– 1961. Notes on the Theory of the Big Push. In H.S. Ellis and H.C. Wallich, eds., *Economic Development in Latin America*. New York: Macmillan.
Rosovsky, H. 1965. The Take-Off into Sustained Growth Controversy. *Journal of Economic History* 25(2): 271–75.
Rostow, W.W. (1959). The Stages of Economic Growth. *The Economic History Review* 2(1): 1–16.

– 1960. *The Stages of Economic Growth: A Non-Communist Manifesto*. New York: Cambridge University Press.
– ed. 1963. *Economics of Take-Off into Sustained Growth*. (Proceedings of a conference held by the International Economic Association.) London: Macmillan.
– 1975. *How It All Began: Origins of the Modern Economy*. New York: McGraw-Hill.
– 1978. *The World Economy: History and Prospect*. Austin: University of Texas Press.
– 1980. *Why the Poor Get Richer and the Rich Slow Down: Essays in the Marshallian Long Period*. Austin: University of Texas Press.
– 1990. *Theorists of Economic Growth: From David Hume to the Present*. Oxford: Oxford University Press.
Rowthorn, R.E. 1972. *Vulgar Economy*. Cambridge, mimeographed.
– 1974. Neo-classicism, neo-Ricardianism and Marxism. *New Left Review* 86:63–87.
– 19xx. Unemployment, Capital-Labor Substitution, and Economic Growth. (IMF) *International Monetary Fund Working Papers, 99/43*, mimeographed, 1–38 .
Salter, W.E.G. 1960. *Productivity and Technical Change*, 1st ed. Cambridge: Cambridge University Press.
– 1966. *Productivity and Technical Change*, 2nd ed. with an addendum by W.B. Reddaway. Cambridge: Cambridge University Press.
Samuelson, Paul. A. 1947. *Foundations of Economic Analysis*. Cambridge, MA: Harvard University Press.
– 1962. Parable and Realism in Capital Theory: The Surrogate Production Function. *Review of Economic Studies* 29(3): 193–206.
– 1965a. *A Catenary Turnpike Theorem Involving Consumption and the Golden Rule. American Economic Review* 16: 486–96.
– 1965b. A Theory of Induced Innovation along Kennedy-Weisacker Lines. *Review of Economics and Statistics* 47(4): 343–56.
– 1966. A Summing Up. *Quarterly Journal of Economics* 80(4): 568–83.
– 1971. Understanding the Marxian Notion of Exploitation: A Summary of the So-Called Transformation Problem between Marxian Values and Competitive Prices. *Journal of Economic Literature* 9: 399–431.
–1972. The Economics of Marx: An Ecumenical Reply. *Journal of Economic Literature* 10: 51–7.
– 1973. Samuelson's "Reply on Marxian Matters." *Journal of Economic Literature* 11: 64–8.
– 1974. Interest Rate Determinations and Oversimplifying Parables: A Summing Up. Buffalo, mimeographed.

Sato, K. 1974. The Neoclassical Postulate and the Technology Frontier in Capital Theory. *Quarterly Journal of Economics* 88(3): 353–84.

Sato, R. 1963. Fiscal policy in A Neo-Classical Growth Model: An Analysis of Time Required for Equilibrating Adjustment. *Review of Economic Studies* 30(1): 16–23.

Saving, J. 2000. The Effect of Welfare Reform and Technological Change on Unemployment. Federal Reserve Bank of Dallas, Economic and Financial Review, mimeographed.

Schmitz, J.A., Jr. 1989. Imitation, Entrepreneurship, and Long-Run Growth. *The Journal of Political Economy* 97(3 June): 721–39.

Schmookler, J. 1966. *Invention and Economic Growth*. Cambridge, MA: Harvard University Press.

Schultz, T.W. 1963. *The Economic Value of Education*. New York: Columbia University Press.

– 1964. *Transforming Traditional Agriculture*. New Haven, CT: Yale University Press.

Schumpeter, J.A. 1934 [1911]. *The Theory of Economic Development: An Inquiry into Profits, Capital, Credit, Interest and the Business Cycle*. Cambridge, MA: Harvard University Press. (1934 translation of 1911 German edition, *Theorie der wirtschaftlichen Entwicklung*.)

– 1939. *Business Cycles: A Theoretical, Historical and Statistical Analysis of the Capitalist Process*. New York: McGraw-Hill.

– 1942. *Capitalism, Socialism and Democracy*. New York: Harper.

– 1946. John Maynard Keynes, 1883–1946. *American Economic Review* 36: 495–518.

– 1954. *History of Economic Analysis*. London: Allen and Unwin.

Science and Technology Policy Institute (RAND). 2002. Federal Investment in R&D. Arlington, VA: National Science Foundation.

Scott, M.F. 1991. *A New View of Economic Growth*. Oxford University Press, Oxford.

Segerstrom, P.S. 1991. Innovation, imitation, and economic growth. *Journal of Political Economy* 99 (4): 807–27.

Segerstrom, P.S., T.C. Anant, and E. Dinopoulos. 1990. A Schumpeterian Model of the Product Life Cycle. *The American Economic Review* 80(5): 1077–91.

Sen, A.K. 1957. Some Notes on the Choice of Capital-Intensity in Development Planning. *Quarterly Journal of Economics* 71(4): 568–71.

– 1960. *Choice of Techniques: An Aspect of the Theory of Planned Economic Development*. Oxford: Basil Blackwell.

– 1965. The Money Rate of Interest in the Pure Theory of Growth. In F.H. Hahn and F.P.R. Brechling, eds., *The Theory of Interest Rates*, 268–80. London: Macmillan.

– 1967. Isolation, Assurance and the Social Rate of Discount. *Quarterly Journal of Economics* 81(1): 112–14.
– 1970. *Growth Economics: Selecting Readings*. Harmondsworth: Penguin.
– 1974. On Some Debates in Capital Theory. *Economica* 91: 328–35.
Shell, K. 1966. Toward a Theory of Inventive Activity and Capital Accumulation. *American Economic Review* 56: 62–8.
– 1967. A Model of Inventive Activity and Capital Accumulation. In K. Shell, ed., *Essays on the Theory of Optimal Economic Growth*, 67–85. Cambridge, MA: MIT Press.
Shell, K., and D. Cass. 1976. The Structure and Stability of Competitive Dynamical Systems. *Journal of Economic Theory* 12: 31–70.
Shell, K., and W.P. Heller. 1974. On Optimal Taxation with Costly Administration. *American Economic Review* 64(2): 338–45.
Sheshinski, E. 1967. Tests of the Learning by Doing Hypothesis. *Review of Economics and Statistics* 60: 1002–37.
Shinkai, Y. 1960. On Equilibrium Growth of Capital and Labor. *International Economic Review* 1(2): 107–11.
Sidrauski, M. 1969. Rational Choice and Patterns of Growth. *The Journal of Political Economy* 77(4): 575–85.
Singer, H. 1949. *Relative Prices of Exports and Imports of Under-developed Countries*. New York: United Nations.
– 1950. The Distribution of Gains between Investing and Borrowing Countries. *American Economic Review* 40: 473–85.
Skidelsky, R. 1983. *John Maynard Keynes, Vol. I: Hopes Betrayed, 1883–1920*. London: Macmillan.
Smith A. 1937 [1776]. *An Inquiry into Nature and the Causes of the Wealth of Nations*. New York: Modern Library.
– 1970. *Wealth of Nations*, edited by A.S. Skinner. Harmondsworth: Penguin.
Smulders, S., and T. Van de Klundert. 1995. Imperfect Competition, Concentration and Growth with Firm-Specific R&D. *European Economic Review* 39(1): 139–60.
Solow, R.M. 1956. A Contribution to the Theory of Economic Growth. *Quarterly Journal of Economics* 70: 65–94.
– 1957. Technical Change and the Aggregate Production Function. *Review of Economics and Statistics* 39(3): 312–20.
– 1961. Note on Uzawa's Two-Sector Model of Economic Growth. *Review of Economic Studies* 29(1): 48–50.
– 1962a. Technical Progress, Capital Formation, and Economic Growth. *American Economic Review* 52: 78–86.
– 1962b. Substitution and Fixed Proportions in the Theory of Capital. *American Economic Review* 29: 207–18.

– 1963. *Capital Theory and the Rate of Return* (Professor Dr F. De Vries Lectures, 1963). Amsterdam: North-Holland.
– 1967. The Interest Rate and Transition between Techniques. In C.H. Feinstein, ed., *Socialism, Capitalism and Economic Growth: Essays Presented to Maurice Dobb*, 30–9. Cambridge: Cambridge University Press.
– 1970a. On the Rate of Return: Reply to Pasinetti. *Economic Journal* 80: 423–8.
– 1970b. *Growth Theory: An Exposition.* (The Radcliffe Lectures delivered at the University of Warwick, 1969). Oxford: Clarendon Press.
– 1987. Prize Lecture, *Growth Theory and After*, Lecture to the memory of Alfred Nobel, 8 December 1987.
– 1988. Growth Theory and After. *American Economic Review* 78 (3): 307–17.
– 1993. An Almost Practical Step toward Sustainability. *Resources Policy* 19(3): 62–172.
– 1994. *Lezioni sulla Teoria Endogena*. Rome: La Nuova Italia Scientifica.
– 1997. *Learning from "Learning by Doing": Lessons for Economic Growth*. Stanford, CA: Stanford University Press.
– 1999a. Notes on Social Capital and Economic Performance. In P. Dasgupta and I. Serageldin, eds., *Social Capital: A Multifaceted Perspective* (based on discussions at World Bank's workshop held in Spring of 1997), 6. Washington, DC: The World Bank.
– 1999b. Neoclassical Growth Theory. In J.B. Taylor and M. Woodford, eds., *Handbook of Macroeconomics*, Vol. 1, (1st ed.), 637–67. Amsterdam: Elsevier.
– 2000. *Growth Theory: An Exposition*, 2nd ed. Oxford: Oxford University Press.
Solow, R.M., and J.E. Stiglitz. 1968. Output, Employment, and Wages in the Short Run. *Quarterly Journal of Economics* 88: 537–60.
Spaventa, L. 1973. Notes on Problems of Transition between Techniques. In J.A. Mirrlees and N.H. Stern, eds., *Models of Economic Growth*, 168–87. London: Macmillan.
Spence, M. 1976. Product Selection, Fixed Costs, and Monopolistic Competition. *Review of Economic Studies* 43 (2): 217–35.
Sraffa, P. 1926. The Laws of Return under Competitive Conditions. *Economic Journal* 36: 535–50.
– 1960. *Production of Commodities by Means of Commodities: Prelude to a Critique of Economic Theory*. Cambridge: Cambridge University Press.
Sraffa, P., and M. H. Dobb, eds. 1952. *The Works and Correspondence of David Ricardo*. Vol. 7. Cambridge: Cambridge University Press.
Srinivasan, T.N. 1964. Optimal Savings in a Two-Sector Model of Growth. *Econometrica* 32: 358–73.

Stern, N. 1991. The Determinants of Growth. *The Economic Journal* 101: 122–39.
Stigler, G. 1961. The Economics of Information. *Journal of Political Economy* 69: 213–25.
Stiglitz, J.E. 1967. Distribution of Income and Wealth among Individuals. (Cowles Foundation Discussion Papers 238.) New Haven, CT: Cowles Foundation, Yale University.
– 1973a. The Badly Behaved Economy with the Well-Behaved Production Function. In James A. Mirrlees and N.H. Stern, eds., *Models of Economic Growth*, 117–37. London: Macmillan.
– 1973b. Recurrence of Techniques in a Dynamic Economy. In James A. Mirrlees and N.H. Stern, eds., *Models of Economic Growth*, 138–67. London: Macmillan.
– 1974a. The Cambridge-Cambridge Controversy in *The Theory of Capital*: A View from New Haven: A Review Article. *Journal of Political Economy* 82: 893–903.
– 1974b. Alternative Theories of Wage Determination and Unemployment in LDCs: The Labor Turnover Model. *Quarterly Journal of Economics* 88(2): 194–227.
– 1976. The Efficiency Wage Hypothesis, Surplus Labour, and the Distribution of Income in L.D.C.s. *Oxford Economic Papers* 28: 185–207.
Stokey, N. 1998. Are There Limits to Growth? *International Economic Review* 39(1): 1–31.
Stoneman, P. 1983. *The Economic Analysis of Technological Change*. Oxford: Oxford University Press.
– ed. 1995. *Handbook of the Economics of Innovation and Technological Change*. Amsterdam: North Holland.
Svennilson, L. 1963. Economic Growth and Technical Progress. In *Residual Factor and Economic Growth*. Paris: OECD.
Swan, T. W. 1956. Economic Growth and Capital Accumulation. *Economic Record* 32: 334–61.
Taylor, L. 1967. Aggregate Structural Change: Recent Time Series and Cross-Section Evidence. PHD dissertation, Harvard University.
– 1983. *Structuralist Macroeconomics*. New York: Basic Books.
– 1990. *Socially Relevant Policy Analysis: Structuralist Computable General Equilibrium Models for the Developing World.* Cambridge, MA: MIT Press.
– 1991. *Growth, Income Distribution and Inflation: Lectures on Structuralist Macroeconomic Theory.* Cambridge, MA: MIT Press.
– 2004. *Reconstructing Macroeconomics: Structuralist Proposals and Critiques of the Mainstream*. Cambridge, MA: Harvard University Press.

Thirlwall, A.P., and C. Kennedy. 1972. Surveys in Applied Economics: Technical Progress. *The Economic Journal* 82: 11–72.

Tinbergen, J. 1935. Annual Survey: Suggestion on Quantitative Business Cycle Theory. *Econometrica* 3: 241–308.

– 1960. Optimum Savings and Utility Maximization Over Time. *Econometrica* 28: 481–9.

Tinbergen J. and Polak J.J. 1950. *The Dynamics of Business Cycles*. Chicago: University of Chicago Press.

Tobin, J. 1955. A Dynamic Aggregate Model. *Journal of Political Economy* 63(2): 103–15.

– 1956. The Interest-Elasticity of Transaction Demand for Cash. *Review of Economics and Statistics* 38: 241–7.

– 1965. Money and Economic Growth. *Econometrica* 33: 671–84.

– 1968. Notes on Optimal Monetary Growth. *Journal of Political Economy* 76 (4): 833–59.

– 1971. *Essays in Economics*, Vol.1, *Macroeconomics*, Chicago: Markham; Amsterdam and London: North Holland.

–1973. Cambridge (U.K.) v. Cambridge (Mass.). *The Public Interest* 31: 102–9.

–1975. *Essays in Economics*, Vol. 2, *Consumption and Econometrics*. Chicago: North Holland.

Todaro, M.P. 1969. A Model of Labor Migration and Urban Unemployment in Less Developed Countries. *American Economic Review* 59 (1):138–48.

– 1986. Internal Migration and Urban Employment: Comment. *American Economic Review* 76 (3): 566–9.

Turnovsky, S. 1995. Methods of Macroeconomic Dynamics, 1st ed. Cambridge, MA: MIT Press.

– 1996. Optimal Tax, Debt, and Expenditure Policies in a Growing Economy. *Journal of Public Economics* 60: 21–44.

– 2000. Fiscal Policy, Elastic Labor Supply, and Endogenous Growth. *Journal of Monetary Economics* 45: 185–210 (This paper was presented originally in 1998 as a Discussion Paper in Economics at the University of Washington)

Tylecote, R.F., and J. Day. 1991. *The Industrial Revolution in Metals*. London: The Institute of Materials.

Uzawa, H. 1961a. On a Two-Sector Model of Economic Growth. *Review of Economic Studies* 29 (1): 40–7.

– 1961b. Neutral Inventions and the Stability of Growth Equilibrium. *Review of Economic Studies* 28: 117–224.

– 1963a. Production Functions with Constant Elasticities of Substitution. *Review of Economic Studies* 29: 291–9.

– 1963b. On a Two-Sector Model of Economic Growth II. *Review of Economic Studies* 30(2): 105–18.

– 1964. Optimal Growth in a Two-Sector Model of Capital Accumulation. *Review of Economic Studies* 31(1): 1–24.
– 1965. Optimal Technical Change in an Aggregate Model of Economic Growth. *International Economic Review* 6: 18–31.
Valavanis-Vail, S. 1955. An Econometric Model of Growth: U.S.A., 1869–1953. *American Econometric Review* 95: 208–21.
Van der Ploeg, F., and J. G. P. Tang. 1992. *The Macroeconomics of Growth: An International Perspective*. Oxford: Oxford University Press.
Van Zanden, J.L. 1995. Tracing the Beginning of the Kuznets Curve: Western Europe during the Early Modern Period. *Economic History Review* 48(4): 643–64.
Vivarelli, M. 1995. *The Economics of Technology and Employment: Theory and Empirical Evidence*. Cheltenham: Edward Elgar.
Von Neumann, J. 1945. A Model of General Equilibrium. *Review of Economic Studies* 13: 1–9. (English translation of 1937 German article "Über ein ökonomisches Gleichungssystem und eine Verallgemeinerung des Brouwerschen Fixpunktsatzes," *Ergebnisse eines mathematischen Kolloquiums* 8: 73–83).
Walras, L. 1954 [1874]. *Elements of Pure Economics*. Homewood, IL: Irwin.
Weizsäcker (von), C.C. 1962. *Wachstum, zins und optimale investifionsquote*. Basel: Kyklos-Verlag.
– 1965. Existence of Optimal Programs of Accumulation for an Infinite Time Horizon. *Review of Economic Studies* 32: 85–104.
Wicksell, K. 1911. *Föreläsningar i Nationalekonomi*, 2nd ed., vol. 1.
– 1934 [1911]. *Lectures on Political Economy*, Vol.1. London: George Routledge and Sons.
World Economic Forum. 2013. Manufacturing for Growth: Strategies for Driving Growth and Employment. Geneva: Author.
Wright, J.F. 1975. The Dynamics of Reswitching. *Oxford Economic Papers* 27: 21–46.
Yoichi, F. 1965. The Period of Production in Two-Sector Models of Economic Growth. *International Economic Review* 6: 240–4.
Young, Allyn A. 1928. Increasing Returns and Economic Progress. *Economic Journal* 38(152): 527–42.
Young, Alwyn. 1991. Learning by Doing and the Dynamic Effects of International Trade. *Quarterly Journal of Economics* 106(2): 369–405.
– 1993. Invention and Bounded Learning by Doing. *Journal of Political Economy* 101: 442–73.
– 1998. Growth without Scale Effects. *Journal of Political Economy* 106(1): 41–63.
Young, W. 1987. *Interpreting Mr Keynes: The IS-LM enigma*. Oxford: Polity Press.

– 1989. *Harrod and His Trade Cycle Group: The Origins and Development of the Growth Research Programme*. London: Macmillan.

Young, W., and F. Lee. 1993. *Oxford Economics and Oxford Economists*. Basingstoke and London: Macmillan.

Index